DISCARDED

D1591478

Unknown Island

A University of Arizona Southwest Center Book
Joseph C. Wilder, Editor

Unknown Island

SERI INDIANS, EUROPEANS, AND

SAN ESTEBAN ISLAND IN THE GULF OF CALIFORNIA

Thomas Bowen

Published in cooperation with
the University of Arizona Southwest Center

ALBUQUERQUE • UNIVERSITY OF NEW MEXICO PRESS

© 2000 by Thomas Bowen
All rights reserved.
FIRST EDITION

Library of Congress Cataloging-in-Publication Data

Bowen, Thomas.
    Unknown island : Seri Indians, Europeans, and San Esteban Island in
the Gulf of California / Thomas Bowen. — 1st ed.
        p.   cm.
    Includes bibliographical references and index.
    ISBN 0-8263-2083-X (cloth) — ISBN 0-8263-2084-8 (pbk.)
    1. Seri Indians — History. 2. San Esteban Island (Mexico) — History.
    I. Title.

F1221.S43 B69 2000
972´.dc21   99-006981

For Ed,
for Roberto, Jesús, and Porfirio,
and of course,
for Julian

Contents

CONTENTS

List of Maps

List of Figures

A Guide to Pronouncing Seri Words

Seri Orthographic Symbol	International Phonetic Association Symbol	English Approximation
a	a	*fa*ther
c	k	*c*ut
cö	kʷ	(labialized *c*)
e	æ	c*a*t
f	ɸ	*f*ish
h	ʔ	o*h* oh! (glottal stop)
i	i	mach*i*ne
j	x	voiceless velar fricative (as in Scottish "lo*ch*")
jö	jʷ	labialized, lightly articulated *j*
l	ɬ	voiceless fricative *l* (as in Welsh *ll*)
m (see Notes)	m	*m*at
n	ɳ	*n*et
o	o	n*o*
p	p	*p*en
qu	k	*c*ut
r	ɾ	(as in Spanish "pe*r*o")
s	s	*s*ing
t	t̪	*t*op
x	x	voiceless uvular fricative (as in French "lett*r*e")
xö	xʷ	labialized *x*
y	j	*y*es
z	ʃ	*sh*ip

Notes

1. *m* in unstressed syllables assimilates to the point of articulation of the following consonant. Thus the *m* in *comcáac* 'people' is pronounced as the *ng* in the English "sing."

2. *m* following *c* or *cö* is pronounced as a nasalized *w*.

3. Double consonants and vowels (such as the *ee* in *heeme* 'agave') represent long sounds.

4. Stress is usually on the first syllable of the root. It is written orthographically only if it is not on the first syllable of the word (as in *comcáac* 'people').

5. A special thanks goes out to Mary Beck Moser for providing this pronunciation guide.

A Note on Quotations

Quoting extensively from both manuscripts and published works, in English and Spanish, and spanning several centuries, raises problems of how to handle various kinds of errors, unwieldy grammatical constructions, and loss of intelligibility created by excerpting passages from their context. On the one hand, it is essential to remain faithful to the original text, but on the other, it is important that quoted passages make sense to the modern reader. Although it has proved impossible to be absolutely consistent, the following conventions have been adopted here:

1. Following standard practices, quoted passages translated from Spanish have been recast into modern literate English. Anomalous spellings of proper nouns have not been altered, though in cases where the identity is not obvious, the modern spelling follows in brackets.

2. Many passages from both Spanish and English sources need some clarification, and additions to the text are enclosed in brackets. These include explanatory remarks, supplemental punctuation, and corrections of errors of fact.

3. For works in English, typographical errors and similar minor printing errors that are clearly inadvertent (such as misprinting "of" as "or") have been silently corrected to avoid the odious notation "[sic]." Otherwise, all passages originally written in English have been quoted verbatim, allowing unconventional spelling and grammar to convey information about the writer, the times, and the circumstances above and beyond the message of the words themselves. Passages originally written in Spanish, of course, have been unavoidably sanitized by the translation process.

4. Diacritical marks on non-English words generally follow the usage of the original text. They have been silently added in a few instances where omission was clearly inadvertent.

Acknowledgments

Many people and agencies have contributed to every stage in the development of this book. It is a pleasure to acknowledge the generous assistance and encouragement of José Luis Acevedo, Daniel Anderson, Conrad Bahre, Durwood Ball, Dan Bench, Walter Birkby, Beatriz Braniff C., Elfego Briseño, Anne Bullard, Peter Butz, Bruce Coblentz, Del Cover, Harry Crosby, Dana Desonie, Janet Fireman, Caroline Fisher, Bernard Fontana, Nancy Ford, Gordon Gastil, Vincent Halter, Julian Hayden, William Hendricks, Ernest Hildner III, James Hills, Thomas Jones, Roger LaJeunesse, Howard Lawler, Severiano León, Charles Lowe, Jr., Alberto Lucero, Ronald Mahoney, Stephen Marlett, John McGuire, Reid Moran, Keith Muscutt, Barbara Oakleaf, Arturo Oliveros, Walt Peterson, Eric Ritter, Rebeca Rivas de López, Alexander Russell, Scott Ryerson, Thomas Sheridan, Charles Spurlock, Jr., Raymond Turner, Enriqueta Velarde G., Dirk van der Elst, Enrique Villalpando C., Gwinn Vivian, Ann Wagner, Sara Watson, Terri Watson, Michele Wellck, and Joseph C. Wilder. I am especially grateful to Richard Felger and Elisa Villalpando C. for sharing their insights about the Seris and San Esteban Island in many discussions that have spanned nearly two decades. I am also deeply indebted to Roberto Herrera M. for his help in piecing together the island's history and for his thoughtful interpretations of the archaeological remains.

It is hard to overstate the extent to which Edward Moser and Mary Beck Moser have contributed to this project, for it would never have materialized without them. Edward Moser recorded and transcribed the Seri accounts of the San Esteban people in the first place, and he generously passed this material on to me to organize into publishable form. After his death, Mary Beck Moser kindly gave me permission to continue working with his notes. Since then, she has patiently answered seemingly endless questions and painstakingly checked many facets of the oral accounts with Seris who still have knowledge of the San

Esteban folk. In addition, I am deeply indebted to her for contributing unpublished information which has done much to enhance and enrich the text.

Several members of the Club Deportivo de Bahía Kino cheerfully provided boat transportation to San Esteban, often in very rough weather: Alan Ferraris, Eldon Heaston, Robert Jarratt, George Weary, and William Zuliger. And I offer very special thanks to Eldon Heaston and Joan Heaston Jarratt for their extensive help and gracious hospitality during the many years of fieldwork.

The archaeological fieldwork was authorized under a series of permits issued by the Instituto Nacional de Antropología e Historia and the Programa Forestal y de la Fauna Silvestre. The project has been supported in part by generous grants from California State University, Fresno, the Agnese N. Lindley Foundation, and by the Arizona State Museum through the University of Arizona Visiting Scholar Program. I am especially grateful to the University of Arizona Southwest Center and the Amerind Foundation for underwriting part of the cost of publication.

Drafts of the manuscript were read in whole or in part by Martha Brace, Patricia Brace, Richard Felger, William Hendricks, Reid Moran, Mary Beck Moser, and Gary Nabhan, and I thank them all for their perceptive comments and suggestions. I am indebted to Thomas Sheridan for graciously allowing me to quote extensively from the page proofs of his then-unpublished *Empire of Sand*. I am deeply grateful to Cathy Moser Marlett and Anne Austin for their expertise and care in creating the drawings and maps, and to Kevin Horstman for his computer wizardry in compiling the aerial photo mosaic of San Esteban and for restoring the 1875 photo of Seris on board the U.S.S. *Narragansett*. And I acknowledge with great pleasure the staff of the University of New Mexico Press for its superb work and singular good cheer in making this book a reality.

I would like to extend a warm and heartfelt thanks to my three friends and colleagues who shared in the archaeological fieldwork on San Esteban: Dan Bench, Dana Desonie, and Elisa Villalpando. Their tireless efforts, superb observations, and unparalleled companionship made the many weeks we spent together on that extraordinary island the experience of a lifetime. And finally, my deepest thanks goes out to Marty Brace for her unwavering good cheer and encouragement in bringing this project to completion.

Figure I.1   San Esteban Island. View of lower Arroyo Limantour from the beach area near El Monumento, looking northwest. April 1987.

Figure I.2   San Esteban Island. View of upper Arroyo Limantour from the western sea cliffs, looking east-southeast across the island nearly to the eastern shore. Most of San Esteban's flat terrain, comprising less than 20 percent of the island's surface, is visible in this and the photograph above. January 1984.

Introduction

A Seri Boy and an Ethnohistorical Puzzle

Sometime in the latter part of the nineteenth century, a Seri boy and his family left their traditional home on Tiburón Island and went to live on the neighboring island of San Esteban. Why they decided to leave Tiburón is not certain, but it may have been to escape an outbreak of snail fever, which had killed several of their relatives. The boy's father was already acquainted with San Esteban, for this was still a time when people moved around a lot, and he had lived there previously. But for the boy, it was an entirely new experience. The island was a rugged and mountainous place, with unfamiliar plants and animals and not much water (Figures I.1 and I.2). Even more startling, San Esteban was inhabited by a strange people. Like the boy, these people were Seris, but they were very different from the relatives and friends he had known on Tiburón Island. They spoke in a peculiar sing-song manner, and they did things in odd ways. They were a wild and reckless bunch, constantly fighting and gambling, and sometimes they staked their own lives on a contest. Compared to other Seris, they were so backward that they did not even use bows and arrows, preferring to throw rocks as weapons. And they knew almost nothing of the Mexican world. They did not know what firearms were, and most of them had never even seen a horse. Living among these strange people was to leave a deep impression on the boy, one that stayed with him for the rest of his life.

How long the boy and his family remained on San Esteban Island is not known. From time to time they would leave and paddle their raft-like balsas across the treacherous eight-mile channel to the southwest coast of Tiburón Island. Here, they would stay for a while at a camp called *Cyaxoj* before returning to San Esteban. On the last of their trips to *Cyaxoj*, the boy's father fell ill and died. Because of this, his mother said that she and the children would not go back to San Esteban. This proved to be a fortunate decision, because not long afterward a gunboat with government soldiers on board came and rounded up the San Esteban Islanders. Few, if any, were ever seen again.

During the time the boy lived on San Esteban, his family grew to include nine people. His father was Quicilio (or José Antonio) and his mother was María Juana Necia. He had a (probably) older sister named Angelita (1867–1936), an older brother called Ilario Covilla, and a twin sister Margarita. His younger siblings were Refugio, an unnamed boy who died, and Chona (d. 1955). As the boy grew up, he became known among the Seris as *Hast Ano Ctam* 'mountain from man,' a name that connotes "man from San Esteban Island" because the island's terrain is so rugged (Felger and Moser 1985:412). But for use with outsiders, he was given the name of the turn-of-the-century President of Mexico, and thus was called Porfirio Díaz (Figures I.3 and I.4).

Figure I.3   Porfirio Díaz (probably) with ethnologist WJ McGee at Rancho San Francisco de la Costa Rica. Photograph by William Dinwiddie, November 1894. (Courtesy National Anthropological Archives, Smithsonian Institution, Washington, D.C. [No. 4264].)

Figure I.4   Porfirio Díaz (18??–1959) with linguist Edward Moser (1924–1976) at El Desemboque. Photograph by Mary Beck Moser, 1957.

Porfirio Díaz died as an elderly man, long blind from cataracts, on July 29, 1959. Less than a year and a half before his death, he spoke on tape to linguists Edward and Mary Beck Moser about his youth on San Esteban Island and the strange Seris who lived there. Because of his advanced age, he spoke only with difficulty and sometimes so slowly that his words were hard to understand. But he was still able to recall quite a bit about these peculiar people whom he had known so many years before, and who soon afterward had been wiped out by government troops.

At the time of Díaz's death, it was common knowledge among the Seris that a culturally and dialectically distinct band of their kinsmen had once lived on San Esteban Island. However, they had been gone so long that most people recalled little about them. Díaz himself had outlived his parents and siblings—those who had been on the island with him—and nobody else still alive had ever had any direct contact with the San Esteban folk. For these reasons, many Seris thought of Díaz in later life as "the last San Esteban man," though he was never a member of that group.

Although Porfirio Díaz's recollections, recorded on tape, are the only direct testimony that exists today about the San Esteban people, two other Seris (now deceased) knew a fair amount about them. These were Roberto Herrera Marcos (Figure I.5) and Jesús Morales (Figure I.6). Both were relatives of Díaz, and as young men, they had many opportunities to hear about the San Esteban people

*Figure I.5
Roberto Herrera
(1916–1988) at
El Desemboque,
January 1981.*

from Díaz, his siblings, and other elderly Seris who had known them. Most importantly, Morales and Herrera shared a lifelong interest in traditional Seri culture and history. Both men made a special effort to remember what the old people told them about these strange folk, and much of their knowledge has been preserved on tape and on paper. With their deaths, the last direct link between the modern Seris and the San Esteban people was severed. What the Seris today say about these folk falls completely within the realm of oral tradition, for it is based almost entirely on what they recall hearing from Porfirio Díaz, Roberto Herrera, and Jesús Morales. The wellspring of Seri information has run dry.

Europeans have known of San Esteban Island, more or less, since 1539, when Francisco de Ulloa made the first European circumnavigation of the Gulf (Maps I.1 and I.2). Ulloa sailed through the channel between San Esteban and Tiburón Islands, and both he and his pilot, Francisco de Preciado, made passing mention of the island in their journals. During the seventeenth century, pearl hunters explored the region, and some noted what they saw in the general vicinity of San Esteban, if not the island itself. In the following century, the Jesuits who built the Baja California chain of missions launched a number of expeditions to explore the peninsula and the Gulf, and two of the padres sailed directly past San Esteban Island. The first clearly recorded European circumnavigation of the island took place in 1750, in the aftermath of a military campaign against hostile Seris on Tiburón Island. In 1826, former Royal Navy Lieut. R. W. H. Hardy became the first known European

Figure I.6 Jesús Morales (1904?–1975) at El Desemboque, January 1967.

to set foot on San Esteban, though he did so just long enough to club some sea lions on the beach.

Soon after the middle of the nineteenth century, ships were sailing and steaming past San Esteban Island in considerable numbers. For a while, guano mining on Gulf islands brought a steady stream of cargo ships into the region. U.S. transport vessels carrying supplies to Ft. Yuma plied a regular shipping lane past San Esteban, while Mexican coasting vessels increasingly ferried goods through this region on their way from Guaymas and Mulegé to the new ports opening on the upper Gulf. In 1875, the crew of a U.S. Navy hydrographic survey vessel charted the waters surrounding the island. Two years later, entrepreneurs from Guaymas actually set up a short-lived distilling operation on San Esteban. In 1882, a powerful Mexican promoter obtained a government concession to colonize and develop cottage industries on the island, though nothing ever came of the scheme. Several times during the nineteenth century, the Mexican government tried to punish Seris who raided Sonoran settlements by sending military expeditions to nearby Tiburón Island, where the culprits often sought refuge.

Although these and other European dramas played out in the vicinity of San Esteban, not a shred of unambiguous evidence has come to light to suggest that Europeans were ever aware of Seris living on San Esteban Island. Thus we are faced with an interesting ethnohistorical question. Is it possible—or credible—that a small band of Indians could have lived on this remote island, as the Seris maintain, and that Europeans never knew about them?

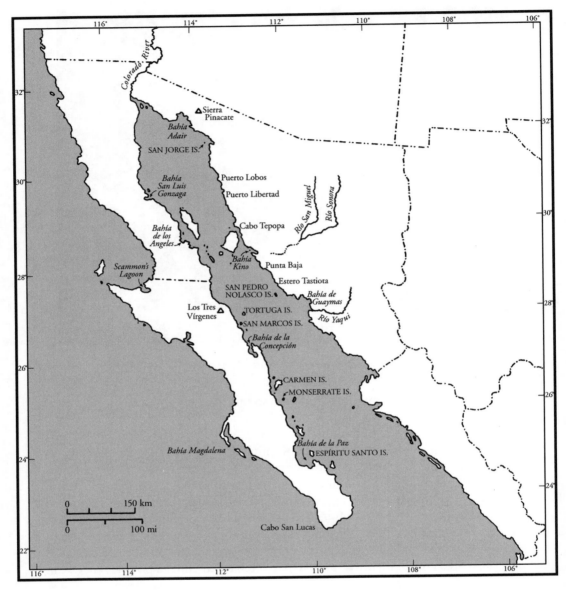

MAP I.1   The Gulf of California: Geographic features.
Map by Cathy Moser Marlett and Anne Austin.

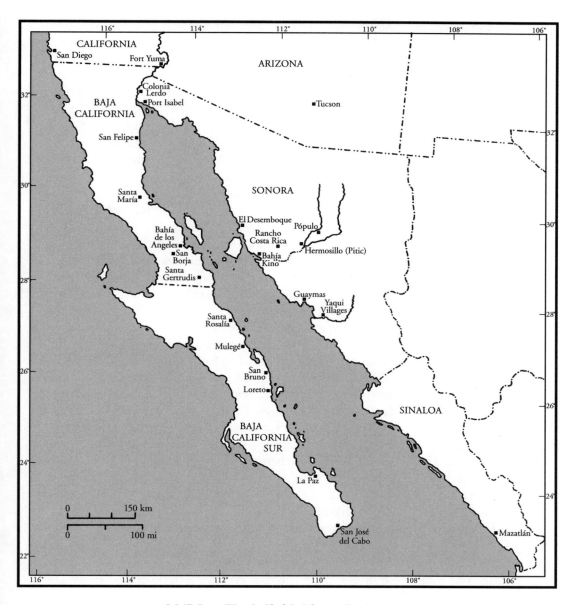

MAP I.2   The Gulf of California: Settlements.
Map by Cathy Moser Marlett and Anne Austin.

In fact, there are many reasons for thinking that this is a realistic possibility. Although there was much European activity in the Gulf as a whole, and at times even on nearby islands, the record suggests that few people sailed to San Esteban, and fewer still went ashore. During the Colonial period, activity was concentrated mainly in the southern Gulf. Many early sailors who did venture into the "Midriff region" between about 28° and 30° north latitude, where San Esteban is located (Map I.3), found their frail ships trapped helplessly in the grip of ferocious currents and winds or battered by terrifying storms. Before long San Esteban and its two neighbors, Tiburón and San Lorenzo, became known as the "Salsipuedes" (Get-Out-If-You-Can) Islands—treacherous places wisely avoided. Nineteenth century steamships were largely immune to the fierce winds and currents, but they simply bypassed the island on their way to some-where else. Most vessels traveling through the Midriff had no reason to steer close enough to the island to detect human activity on shore, and the high sea cliffs that surround much of the island would have hidden the interior from view anyway. For Europeans, San Esteban seems to have offered few useful resources, and until late in the nineteenth century, was apparently never a destination.

Nineteenth century officials and intellectuals certainly knew San Esteban was there, for it was routinely depicted on maps of the period. But the intelligentsia knew little else about it, for it is the one island that is consistently missing from many contemporary written descriptions of the Gulf. The Europeans most likely to have been familiar with San Esteban were the ordinary folk who plied the Gulf but held no stature in official record-keeping circles. People such as itinerant prospectors, sea lion hunters, and the *vagabundos* who made a precarious living off the sea had little need, or perhaps interest, in keeping formal records of what they saw and who they encountered. Others, such as smugglers, pirates, and the many illegal pearl hunters, would have actively concealed their pursuits and whereabouts. And until the twentieth century, those who sailed the Gulf were mostly illiterate. Thus the Europeans most likely to have seen Seris living on San Esteban were probably those least likely to have recorded what they saw.

The one independent means of assessing the existence of the San Esteban people is archaeology. People worldwide turn natural materials into artifacts and modify the landscape by building structures. They are also slovenly. They dump garbage out their front doors, litter the countryside with discarded tools, and fail to dismantle their constructions when they leave. Past peoples may occasion-ally elude the written word, but they cannot easily escape the archaeological record, for their presence will be betrayed by their trash. The archaeology of San Esteban testifies to considerable human activity, and many of those who left their mark there were clearly Seris. The important question is whether these remains were left by a resident population, as the Seris today claim, or merely by Seris who made periodic visits from Tiburón Island.

In sum, the archaeological record, the known documents, and the shadowy side of the historic record all leave open the possibility that the Seri accounts of the San Esteban people could be based on historic fact, as judged by the canons of the European historical tradition. Exploring this possibility is the

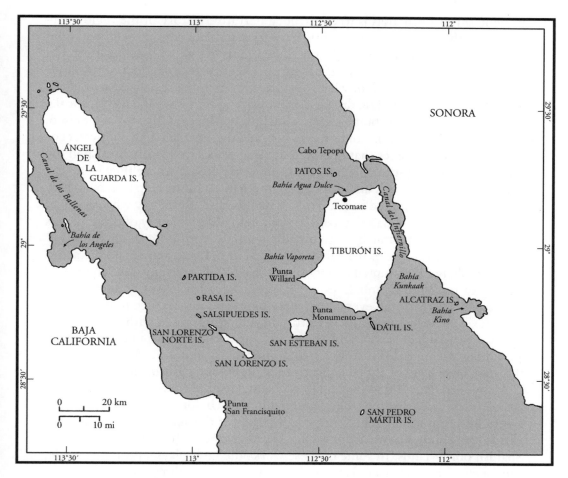

MAP I.3   The Midriff Islands. Map by Cathy Moser Marlett and Anne Austin.

underlying theme of this book. To begin, Part I relates what the modern Seris say about the San Esteban people. Parts II–IV look at the documentary record of Europeans in the Gulf, especially those who ventured into the vicinity of San Esteban Island. Part V provides an overview of the island's archaeological remains. The objective of Part VI is to evaluate whether these sources of information enable us to determine whether the San Esteban people really existed.

The chapters that relate the Seri oral accounts and describe the archaeology focus specifically on San Esteban Island. But most of the historical chapters are broader in scope, encompassing the other Midriff islands and even the Gulf as a whole. There are two principal reasons for this expanded perspective. First of all, to understand why so few Europeans seem to have visited San Esteban, it is essential to know what kinds of people were drawn to the Gulf, why they went there, and where they did go if not to San Esteban. And the simplest way to provide this information is to construct a narrative history of the region surrounding the island. Secondly, it is hard to genuinely comprehend what did happen in the region without placing these events in a wider social context. On one level, it is true that the Gulf has its own history, independent of the lands that encircle it. Yet much of what took place, even in the restricted area of the Midriff, was determined on dry land, most often in Sonora and Baja California, but also in far more distant locations, including Mexico City, San Francisco, New York, Washington, London, Madrid, and the Vatican. The political, economic, and social forces that operated in these places frequently furnished the motives that brought people into the Gulf, determining where they went and what they did. Thus, machinations on an international scale help to explain how and why events unfolded in the Midriff islands, and ultimately why so few of these events involved San Esteban. To be intelligible, a history of these islands must draw on events much more broadly than just within the Midriff itself.

But while this book draws on a wider field of political and economic activity, it should not be assumed that it offers a "balanced" or in any way "complete" history of the Midriff, much less a comprehensive history of Sonora or Baja California. Many of the events that were of crucial importance to northwestern Mexico's turbulent political history have nothing to do with San Esteban or the other Midriff islands and, therefore, are not mentioned in these pages at all. Others are included mainly for what they reveal about the Midriff, though this may have been of trivial concern to contemporary Europeans.

Many readers will find that some of the incidents recounted here are familiar historical tales that have been told many times before (though usually with a very different slant). This is especially true for the activities of the Jesuits, which are widely known from a long list of classic and recent works on the Spanish borderlands. In some of these works the Gulf plays a prominent role, and much of the background material used here has been drawn from these well-known sources. But other events of the Colonial period are not so familiar, and wherever feasible, the early European encounters with the Midriff islands are related in the words (translated where necessary) of the original observers.

Historians have written much less about the nineteenth century Gulf. At the time, many commentators expressed strong opinions, often misguided, about Tiburón Island and its Seri inhabitants, though they said far less about the other Midriff islands. Many of the relevant printed sources for this period are scattered and not easily accessible. And much important material has neither appeared in print nor in English. For the two chapters on the twentieth century, which focus exclusively on San Esteban Island, it has been possible to draw on a variety of sources ranging from the oral history of Mexican fishermen and modern Seris to the publications of scientists, who have been among the most important of San Esteban's recent visitors.

Thus, while this book revolves around a specific ethnohistorical problem, the Midriff islands themselves have a rich and colorful history, and it is a story that is worth telling for its own sake. It begins with the events that lead up to the discovery of San Esteban and its neighboring islands in 1539 and extends to the present, which for practical reasons is defined in most cases as the 1980s. And it is very much a multicultural story, for it involves Spaniards, Mexicans, North Americans, French, British, and of course the Seri Indians, both "ordinary" Seris and the putative San Esteban people. But it should be understood that the history related in these pages is nothing more than a narrative account, accompanied by a minimum of interpretation. Those looking for deep insights into social process or advances in theory will not find them here. Yet there may be a niche for even a simple narrative, for with exception of an excellent but necessarily brief summary paper (Bahre 1983), there has never been any general account of the human use of San Esteban and the other Midriff islands.

So why write about San Esteban and the Midriff islands? Certainly because there is an ethnohistorical puzzle to be solved. Certainly because the modern Seri oral accounts seem to provide an extraordinary native ethnography of an unknown people who lived in one of the world's most marginal habitats. Perhaps, too, in order to illuminate the value of oral tradition and the limits of conventional documentary history as sources of information about non-Western peoples. And certainly because there is a unique historical tale to be told of how humans have made use of a little-known part of the world, as seen from the perspectives of the modern Seri Indians, the early Europeans who passed through the region, recent Mexicans and North Americans, and the archaeological remains of all those who failed to pick up their trash.

UNKNOWN ISLAND

I.

The Seri Indians of San Esteban Island

Originally, the Seri Indians (or Comcáac, *as they call themselves) were not the single group they are today. Soon after they were first encountered by Europeans, early in the seventeenth century, it was realized that the Seris were divided into several territorially distinct bands. These groups were politically independent of each other, and not all responded to the presence of European settlers in the same way. For many Seris, relations with these newcomers took a hostile turn which quickly evolved into a vicious cycle of deadly raids and reprisals. As warfare and disease decimated these groups, eventually too few people were left to sustain the separate bands as viable units. By sometime in the nineteenth century, the band structure collapsed, and the remaining Seris coalesced into the single group that has persisted to the present. At least, that is what happened to most Seris.*

The Seris today say that one of the original bands managed to maintain its integrity for some time after the others had merged and lost their identities. It was possible, they say, because this small group, which came to live in isolation on a remote island, had little contact with Europeans. When contact finally came, it was catastrophic, for the members of this band were summarily rounded up and exterminated. Few if any survived.

These Seris who were wiped out were the San Esteban people. Europeans, though eventually responsible for their demise, were apparently never aware of a separate band of Seris living on San Esteban Island, for no mention of these people in the historic record has yet been found. As a result, what we know of the culture and history of the San Esteban people comes entirely from the Seris themselves. Chapter 1 relates what the modern Seris know about these strange folk.

· 3 ·

ONE

Recounting the Past:
Modern Seri Oral Accounts
of the San Esteban People

Origins

The Seri name for themselves is *Comcáac* 'People.' They call San Esteban Island *Coftécöl* 'Chuckwallas-large.' This word is a combination of *coof*, the name of the large chuckwalla that lives there, and *caacöl* 'large (plural)' (Felger and Moser 1985:132). The people who lived there are known today simply as *Coftécöl Comcáac* "The People of San Esteban Island" or sometimes as *Xica Hast Ano Coii* 'Things Mountain In-who-are' or "They Who Live in the Mountains" (Moser 1963:16; Felger and Moser 1985:98), so named because the island is so rugged (Figure 1.1 and Map 1.1).

There are at least five different accounts of how the San Esteban people came to live on their island (see Appendix A). Porfirio Díaz gave the simplest account, saying that the people were created on San Esteban Island as a separate group at the beginning of time and that they continued to live there until their extinction.

Most versions say that the people lived first on Tiburón Island before they migrated to San Esteban. One states that they initially lived both on the southwest coast of Tiburón Island and on San Esteban, and later came to live on San Esteban more or less exclusively.

According to another account, the San Esteban people originally lived near Tecomate, a place with abundant water on the north end of Tiburón Island. Fighting among themselves somehow resulted in their drifting toward the southwest coast of Tiburón, and from there eventually out to San Esteban Island.

Chico Romero said that all the Seris originated on Tiburón, beginning with a first man and woman. As the tribe grew, they began to disperse. While some took off for the mainland, others went to San Esteban Island.

The most detailed account was given by Roberto Herrera. He said that the San Esteban people were the first people to live on Tiburón Island. Nobody knows where they came from, how they arrived there, or when. But for a time

Figure 1.1   Aerial view of San Esteban Island. This image is an uncontrolled mosaic of four aerial photographs, digitally compiled by Kevin C. Horstman.

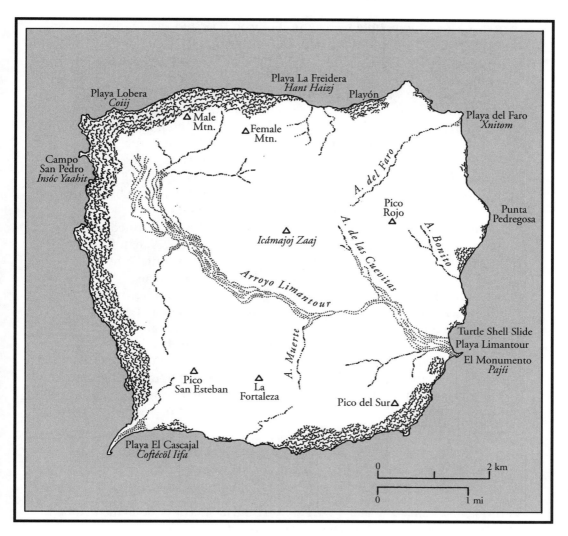

MAP 1.1   San Esteban Island and its major features. Textured areas represent sea cliffs.
Additional geographical information can be found in the gazetteer in Appendix D.
Map by Cathy Moser Marlett and Anne Austin.

they were the only people to live on Tiburón. He said that fighting among themselves may have split the group, and one faction left the island and moved south along the mainland. Those who remained were the ancestors of the San Esteban people.

The people who stayed on Tiburón did not make full use of the island. They lived mainly along the shores of the southwest and west coasts, where the sea was deep, and in the nearby mountains. They did not often utilize the shallow waters along the north or east coasts. Nor did they spend much time in the interior of the island. They did not have the bow and arrow, and so they did not hunt deer. ["Strange," observed Herrera, "but said to be true."] They simply preferred living off the deep ocean and were specialists with the balsa raft and spear which they used for fishing and hunting sea turtles.

Meanwhile, continued Herrera, other Seri groups had established themselves on the mainland coast across the channel from Tiburón. A man from one of these groups got the idea of moving to Tiburón, and eventually he interested some others in going there to live. So these people went over to Tiburón on balsas and began to confront the San Esteban people. The invaders were equipped with bows and arrows, and the San Esteban people felt pretty much defenseless against them. Although they never actually fought each other, the mainland Seris began to take over the island. The San Esteban people were gradually pushed southward to the southwest coast of Tiburón, and finally onto San Esteban Island itself.[1] Sometimes they would return to the southwest coast of Tiburón,[2] which continued to be regarded as part of their territory (Map 1.2), but mostly they just lived on San Esteban. They lived there until they were rounded up and taken away by government soldiers.

The People

Porfirio Díaz estimated that the San Esteban band included 100 adult men. Roberto Herrera believed the total population was around 250 people (see Note 10).

It is said that the San Esteban people were large and well built. But this was not uniformly so. A man called *Siip Lams Quiho* 'Young-man Jewfish He-who-finds' was especially large and was famous as the champion balsa paddler, but his brother *Cöimáxp* 'White' was a very small man.[3] As a young boy, *Cöimáxp* was proud to be a San Esteban person and claimed that he could do anything better than other Seris. Another San Esteban man, apparently, was a dwarf.

The San Esteban folk had darker skin than other Seris. But their faces were pale, especially those of the women, because of all the agave they ate.[4] They also had raised lines on one or two fingernails of the left hand. Díaz said that this was true of the entire population and that it was a trait they were born with, not something they did to themselves.[5]

They did not wear much clothing. Children and old men wore nothing at all. The adult men wore a simple breechclout made of pelican skin. Díaz recalled that the women wore a short skirt of sea lion skin, but others said that they wore

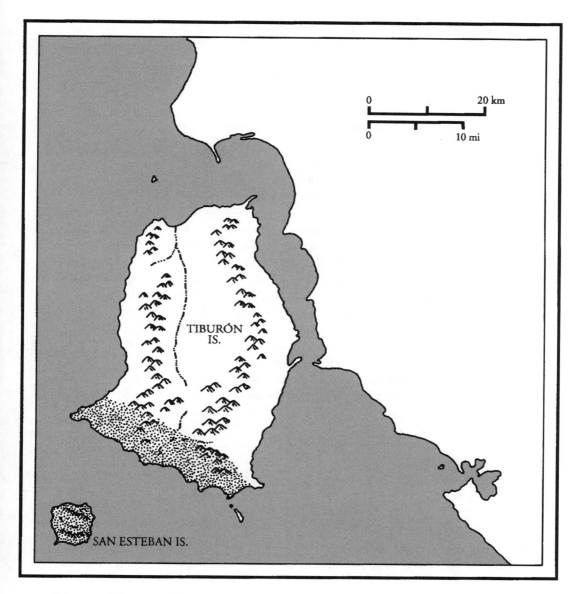

Map 1.2   Territory of the San Esteban people. Their territory may have extended part way up the western coast of Tiburón Island. (After Felger and Moser 1985:Map 6.2.) Map by Cathy Moser Marlett and Anne Austin.

a breechclout like the men. Sometimes people protected their feet with sandals made from animal skins. At night they slept without any kind of blanket. They all wore their hair long.

These people were famous for their great strength and agility. They were so adept at climbing the steep terrain of their island that they were likened to mountain sheep. The men would carry the meat of a whole sea lion wrapped up in its own skin up the sea cliffs and over the mountains to camp.[6] When they were not carrying a burden, they would run through the mountains.[7] They could throw rocks from the shore so powerfully that they could kill sea lions out in the water. When they threw rocks at their enemies, they would often break their bones or kill them outright.[8] They were strong swimmers, and it was said that they would sometimes swim out to where the sharks were, just to prove their bravery. And especially, they were powerful and expert at paddling their balsas.

But above all, the San Esteban people were a wild and reckless bunch. They were so crazy and unpredictable that the other Seris were scared of them. Although they were friendly towards other Seris, they were constantly getting into vicious fights among themselves. When a person was wronged, he would not ignore or forget the injustice. He would hold a grudge until he could catch the culprit and beat him up. Sometimes he would wait in ambush and then attack him. When a quarrel broke out within a camp, people at other camps would sometimes hear about it and would sneak over at night and hide. The next morning when the troublemaker left camp, they would attack him and beat him up. Even women fought savagely among themselves, often with rocks and clubs, and sometimes their husbands would join in. It was said that these people loved to fight and would even fight for no reason at all.

The San Esteban people were also great gamblers, and in this pursuit they were even more reckless and crazy. The men would often stake their own lives on a bet or contest. The game most vividly recalled was a form of "chicken," played on a steep slope of volcanic ash above the sea cliffs just north of Playa Limantour (Figure 1.2). Taking a running start at the top, each man would jump into an inverted sea turtle shell and career down the slope. The last man to scramble out of his shell and cling to the edge of the cliff was the winner. Anyone who failed to eject in time went sailing over the cliff to his death on the rocks a hundred feet below.[9] When a married man went over the edge, his widow could be claimed by the first man to shout *Ohohooo acom quih hatyáahi* 'Hey look—his wife-is-mine!'[10]

Although they were afraid of these wild and dangerous people, the other Seris looked upon them condescendingly as backward and primitive folk.[11] They spoke a different dialect of the language, which other Seris understood only with some difficulty. Once when a San Esteban boy came to Tiburón Island, the other Seris found that they could understand him, but not well. They had to ask him to repeat himself when he talked. Another time, a San Esteban man asked the people on Tiburón for a skin to make sandals, and these people did not understand him. Instead of asking for *ziix ináil* "skin" he asked for *zah ináil*, and the other Seris thought at first that *zah* must be some unfamiliar kind of animal.

*Figure 1.2   Turtle-shell slide from Playa Limantour, looking north.
The slide is the bare slope in the center of the photograph.
January 1987.*

It was said that their speech was musical, and it is often referred to today as "singing talk." When a San Esteban person said *ohoh* it came out as *ohohooo* (as in the first word of the sentence quoted above), with the intonation rising very high on the last syllable. Once when a San Esteban person was visiting Tecomate, the Tecomate people called other Seris over from nearby camps just to come hear him talk.[12]

The San Esteban people knew almost nothing of the Mexican world because they almost never traveled to the mainland of Sonora. Once a group of San Esteban people went to visit some Seris on Tiburón who had brought some stolen horses to their camp. They were amazed at the animals, and they gave the people there small gifts to let them watch the horses eat, which was a great thrill to them.[13] They also knew nothing about firearms. When one man saw a rifle for the first time, he picked it up and sighted down it backwards, complaining that it was crooked.[14] They had no idea why guns made noise. Once when they were being shot at, they blew up some sea turtle bladders, tied them to their waists, and popped them in reply.

Porfirio Díaz thought of the San Esteban people as almost a separate tribe. He said they pretty much lived apart from the other Seris. When they did visit other Seris, relations were peaceable.[15] Sometimes they invited the Seris on Tiburón to come visit them. A few people would go, but they were pretty scared because the San Esteban people were so wild and unpredictable. When a man from Tiburón came to visit, it was the custom for a San Esteban woman to send her daughter into the hills with the man, where they might have intercourse. Thus the grandfather of a woman still living, on his first visit to San Esteban, decided to stay out all night with a girl. No one thought anything about it the next morning.

Most people say that the San Esteban folk did not intermarry with other Seris. However, Jesús Morales said that the famous San Esteban man, Coyote Iguana, married a woman from the Tastiota area on the mainland, and that his mother was also a Tastiota woman (Lowell 1970:148). Chico Romero recalled that a boy from Tiburón once married a San Esteban girl. At first they stayed on Tiburón, but later they went to live with her relatives on San Esteban. No other cases of marriage with San Esteban people are remembered.

Making a Living

Despite the small size of their island, the San Esteban people had access to a rich food supply between the resources of the land and the surrounding sea (Felger and Moser 1976:19). The modern Seris simply assume that the San Esteban people ate most of the foods that were available to them, many of which were eaten by all Seris.[16] Consequently, only a few foods and food-getting techniques are singled out as peculiar to the San Esteban people.

The Seris say that by far the most important food plant for the San Esteban people was the agave (maguey). Only one kind of agave occurs there (Figure 1.3), and it is found nowhere else.[17] It is known as *heeme* today, but the San Esteban people called it *xica istj caitic* 'things its-leaves soft' (i.e., "soft-leafed thing"). Because it grows in profusion all over the island and because edible plants can be found all year long, it was eaten in great quantity. After the plants were dug up out of the ground, the leaves were removed, and the hearts were baked.[18] The cooked hearts, often mixed with sea turtle fat, are said to taste like coconut (Felger and Moser 1985:222).

There are two kinds of large columnar cactus on the island that produce a great quantity of fruit. These are the cardon and *pitahaya agria* (Figure 1.4).[19] The San Esteban people did eat some cactus fruit, but they did not like it too much. Instead, they preferred to make wine from the juice.

Much more is known about their use of animal foods. The largest terrestrial animals on the island are two species of two-foot-long lizards: the piebald chuckwalla (Figure 1.5) and the spiny-tailed iguana (Figure 1.6). The San Esteban people ate large numbers of both.[20] When a person went after chuckwallas, he would cut one of the slender branches from the white-stem milkweed[21] and bring it to the rocky places where chuckwallas live. Then he would whip the branch through the air so the sound would frighten the animal, which would try to find another hiding place. When the hunter heard the chuckwalla move, he would dig it out.[22] People say that there are piles of rocks where chuckwallas have been dug out in this way (Felger and Moser 1985:230–31).[23]

*Figure 1.3   Agave above the
sea cliffs at the northwestern
corner of San Esteban. The summit
of Male Mountain (Hast Ctam)
lies behind. January 1984.*

*Figure 1.4   Pitahaya agria (foreground) and cardon cacti (background)
in lower Arroyo Limantour. January 1981.*

Figure 1.5   Piebald chuckwalla. April 1987.

Figure 1.6   Spiny-tailed iguana. This one is 27 inches from nose to tip of tail. January 1984.

The sea provided much of the animal food for the San Esteban people. Even when they lived on Tiburón Island, it is said that they did not make much use of land animals, preferring sea foods. From the intertidal zone on San Esteban, they caught large numbers of octopuses and sea snails.[24] Sea birds were hunted along the shore. Fish of many kinds were eaten in great quantity. The small horn shark was an important fish.[25] Once a San Esteban boy, who was visiting other Seris, was asked if they had much food over there. He said, sure they did, because his father brought home many horn sharks.

People fished both from shore and on the open sea in their balsas. In both cases, the sole method of taking fish was to spear them. The fish spear was a simple wood shaft that had a row of barbs carved on one edge of the tip. The men were so expert with it that when they speared a fish the thrust would usually kill it outright.[26]

Fish were sometimes lured to shore. A man would stand along a rocky stretch of beach. From there, he would toss strips of white cortex from the giant rainbow cactus[27] into the water as bait, and then bang on a rock with his spear shaft. As the fish came in to feed, he would spear them (Felger and Moser 1985:130, 261).

One of the most important foods was the California sea lion, which inhabited many of San Esteban's small cobble beaches.[28] The men would often hunt them from above by sneaking down the steep mountain slopes above the shoreline. While they were sleeping, the animals were attacked using rocks that were thrown with deadly force and accuracy (Felger and Moser 1985:53). Sometimes, even swimming sea lions were killed by the powerful throw of a rock from shore. Once the animal was killed, it was skinned, cleaned, and butchered right there on the shore.[29] The hunter wrapped the meat of the entire animal in its own skin, slung it over his shoulders and around his neck, climbed back up the treacherous slopes, and carried the meat back to camp.

The San Esteban men were known as expert sea turtle hunters. Yet strangely, they did not like turtle meat and ate it only when other foods ran low.

Food was relatively abundant, but water was not.[30] It is said that the San Esteban people expected water to be shared during dry times, and one could count on a fight by refusing water to others who were without. The Seris today vaguely recall five sources of fresh water on the island. Four of these are said to be temporary sources, consisting of bedrock pools where water would collect after a big rain. The most important of these was located in the northwestern part of the island, somewhere near the base of Male or Female Mountain. The Seris say that this pool would hold water for a long time. It is known as *Seenel Iitxo* 'Many Butterflies,' named for all the butterflies that would come there to drink. Little is known of the other three pools. One is thought to be high in an arroyo in the southwestern corner of the island. Another is near the northeastern corner. The third is south of the big camp called *Icámajoj Zaaj* (described below).[31]

The other water source, called *Haxáacoj* 'Water-large,' is the only one said to have been more or less permanent. It is near the southwestern corner of the island. The Seris say that here one can lift up the rocks in the arroyo just behind the beach, dig down in the sand, and always find water. According to

Roberto Herrera, this one water hole produced enough water for the entire population, even in the summer. Others say that it failed from time to time, or even regularly, forcing the people to leave San Esteban and retreat to the southwest coast of Tiburón (Felger and Moser 1976:19).[32]

Around Camp

The San Esteban people, like some of the other Seri bands, recognized the *ihízitim* as an important division of society and territory (Map 1.3). The word designates both the geographical region and the group of related families traditionally identified with that region. Each *ihízitim* was named. It is said that San Esteban Island and its people were divided into four of these units (Moser 1963:20). Their names are:

1. *Pajíi* 'Flint'
2. *Xnitom* [gloss unknown]
3. *Coiij* 'Tubular'
4. *Coftécöl Iifa* 'Chuckwalla-large Peninsula'

The Seris say that the San Esteban people would normally live in the territory of their own *ihízitim*. But they were not restricted to it nor did they prevent others from using its resources. People would go live with another *ihízitim* if food became scarce in their own area. At times, even three of the groups might live together in the territory of the fourth, but when food was plentiful again, the people would always return to their own *ihízitim* territory.[33] There were no chiefs, either of the *ihízitim* or of the San Esteban people as a whole.

Each *ihízitim* had a main camp, and the name for both came from a prominent landmark near the camp.[34] Little is remembered of these camps beyond their names and locations. The best known of the four camps was the one on the eastern side of the island, next to the huge rock monolith called *Pajíi* 'Flint' (El Monumento), named for the mottled red jasper that outcrops there (Figure 1.7). The camp offered good protection from storms during the winter months. In extreme conditions, the people could retreat into a small cave known as *Pajíi Zaaj* 'Flint Cave' in the base of El Monumento itself.[35] The camp called *Xnitom* [gloss unknown] was at the northeastern corner of the island. The name of the camp known as *Coiij* 'Tubular' is said to come from the spiral appearance of a mountain near the northwestern corner of the island. It is said that the fourth camp *Coftécöl Iifa* 'Chuckwalla-large Peninsula' (Playa El Cascajal) was located in a protected area just east of the shingle spit at the southwestern corner of the island (Figure 1.8).

Three additional camps along the coast are recalled. One of these, *Insóc Yaahit* "Where Black Skipjack[36] Is Fished," was on the western side of the island.[37] It offered protection from summer storms. A huge rock here protrudes from the beach, much like *Pajíi*, with a cave in its base called *Zaaj An Cheel* 'Cave [gloss unknown].' Nearby is a sea cave named *Hascam Caacoj Quih An Iházquim* 'Balsa Large the Put-inside' (Figure 1.9). It is large enough for a boat to enter and

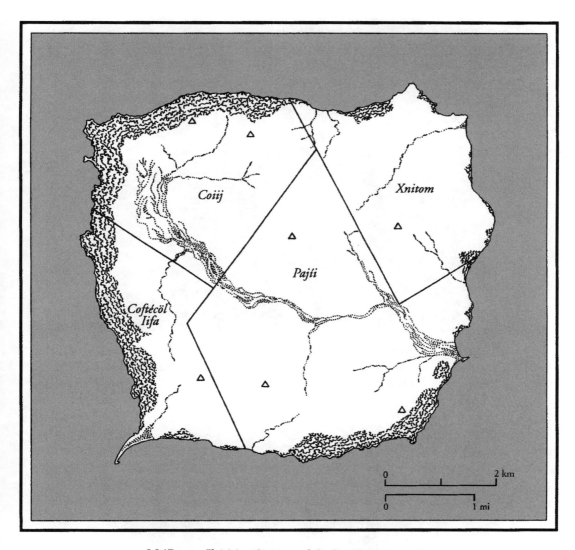

MAP 1.3 Ihízitim *divisions of the San Esteban people.*
Textured areas represent sea cliffs. (After Moser 1963:Fig. 5.)
Map by Cathy Moser Marlett and Anne Austin.

Figure 1.7 Pajíi *(El Monumento) looking south-southeast. The traditional camping place is near the base of the monolith. San Pedro Mártir Island is visible on the horizon just to the right. April 1987.*

Figure 1.8 Coftécöl Iifa *(El Cascajal), the shingle spit at the southwestern corner of San Esteban. Photograph looks northeast from the tip of the spit. April 1980.*

*Figure 1.9   One of several sea caves on the western coast of San Esteban Island,
near Campo San Pedro. April 1993.*

remain partly hidden. It acquired its name because a San Esteban man once
paddled his large balsa into the cave and hid during a time of danger.[38]

The other two camps are on the north coast. One (Figure 1.10) is called *Hant
Haizj* 'Land Mashed' [i.e., "Mud"] for reasons no longer remembered.[39] The
other was a cave known as *Zaaj An Cooxp* 'Cave Inside White.' It was probably
located somewhere along the eastern half of the north coast, where a conspicuous white volcanic tuff is exposed.

The most famous camp of the San Esteban people is the only inland camp
still remembered.[40] It is said to be a large cave about a mile and a half from the
beach (Figure 1.11). Today it is called *Icámajoj Zaaj* 'Cook-agaves Cave,' because
of the agave baking pits nearby.[41] But the name the San Esteban people used for
it was *Iip Hant Itox Zaaj* "Cave Where the Tails Drag," because there is coarse
sand outside the cave where the tails of scurrying chuckwallas leave their mark.
The Seris say that the cave has a huge entrance. Although it is not very deep, it
is big enough that twenty families were able to live in it. People lived there for
so long that the ceiling was blackened by smoke from their fires. Some Seris say
that the walls of the cave have paintings on them in red and blue.[42]

The San Esteban people preferred to live in caves. They would sometimes
camp in the open, but they did not like to live on dunes.[43] When they camped
in the open they would build huts. These had a framework of driftwood or agave
stalks and were covered with branches. Porfirio Díaz said that no trace of these
huts is left. Outside the caves, he said, there may be some animal bones, but

Figure 1.10   Playa La Freidera, location of the Seri camp Hant Haizj, *with
Female Mountain* (Hast Cmaam) *behind. Photograph looks west-northwest. April 1980.*

Figure 1.11   The caves (G4) and the mountain known as
Icámajoj Zaaj, *looking northwest. January 1987.*

there are no mounds of trash.[44] Some men had as many as five wives, and the whole family would live in the same hut or cave.[45]

Agave hearts had to be baked to be edible, but otherwise the San Esteban people did not do much cooking. In fact, some Seris today think they did not even use fire very much. Almost any food was eaten raw when people were hungry or were traveling in a balsa. They ate sea turtle meat raw, and they would drink the blood right out of the turtle's carapace. When they went to Tiburón Island, they would sometimes eat rabbit raw. Fish were almost never cooked, even in camp. Since no preparation was needed for fish, young children would play along the beach for days at a time, sleeping there, and subsisting on small fish they could catch. When food was cooked, it was usually boiled in pottery vessels.[46]

There is some question about who made this pottery. Most Seris simply assume that the San Esteban people made their own pottery. Eugenio Morales believes that they made pottery, but only when they went to Tiburón Island. He says they would bring the pots back with them when they returned to San Esteban. Another Seri thinks that they did not make pottery at all and that the little they used was obtained from other Seris (Mary Beck Moser 1981:pers. comm.).

Sea turtle bladders were also used as containers to store water, cactus fruit, and many other things. When people were traveling, they carried water in sea lion stomachs. These were softened by soaking them in water and could be rolled up when they were not being used.[47]

Porfirio Díaz said that the San Esteban people had very few possessions.[48] They had no metal tools at all. They did make knives of several materials. Some were made from stones carefully split to produce a sharp blade. Others were made from long sticks split carefully to make a sharp end and a cutting edge. Sea shells were also used as knives.[49] Roberto Herrera said that agave was cut either with stone knives or knives made from the sharpened rib of a deer, cow, or horse, obtained from the people on Tiburón Island. He said they did not make them from sea lion bones. No other tools were made from bone.

Only a few other implements are attributed to the San Esteban people. Pounding rocks were any natural rocks of suitable size. Carrying nets were woven of mesquite root fiber, but this material had to be gathered on Tiburón because there are so few mesquite trees on San Esteban. It is said that the people used agave roots to make their hair brushes because the grasses that other Seris used did not grow on their island (Felger and Moser 1985:159). Similarly, the San Esteban people had to go to the waterhole called *Xapij* "Reedgrass" on the southwest coast of Tiburón to gather reedgrass (carrizo cane[50]) to make their most important item, the balsa raft (Felger and Moser 1985:309).

Getting Around

The reedgrass balsa was crucial to the existence of the San Esteban Islanders. It provided them with an important means of obtaining food, gave them contact with other Seris, and enabled them to escape to Tiburón when the water

Figure 1.12   A one-person balsa with its owner, Ramón Blanco, using a turtle harpoon as a paddle. (Normally, balsas were paddled in a kneeling position.) This was probably the last balsa in use. Photograph taken in Bahía Kino by Edward H. Davis, May 1922. (Courtesy National Museum of the American Indian, Smithsonian Institution, New York [formerly Heye Foundation] [No. 24086].)

on their island ran out. Unlike other Seris, the San Esteban people depended on the balsa as an item of daily necessity, and each man owned one (Figure 1.12).

Most balsas were identical to the one-person craft commonly used by the other Seris.[51] The San Esteban people also had larger two-person balsas capable of carrying several large sea turtles. The largest of all were huge craft that could carry as many as three families—six adults and nine or ten children—and required more than one person to paddle. Shade for the passengers was provided by three parallel hoops, attached to the gunwales, which were covered with sea lion skins.[52]

The San Esteban people were the undisputed masters of the balsa. They would set out in any kind of weather, and when it was cold, they would sometimes paddle at night to keep warm. People in their balsas were protected by power obtained from the spirits of sea creatures. There is no recollection of any man being lost at sea in a storm. Drownings did occur, but it is said that they were caused by sharks that would attack and overturn balsas, not by poor seamanship. Shamans were able to make their own currents to carry them wherever they wished to go, even against a strong wind.

Although people fished from shore, a great deal of fishing was done at sea from balsas. Sea turtles could not be hunted at all without them. The San Esteban men were considered the best turtle hunters, even though it is said that they did not often eat turtle meat.

The San Esteban people were great travelers. They frequently paddled over to the southwest coast of Tiburón Island. Although they seldom if ever traveled beyond Tiburón to the Sonoran mainland, they often went west to San Lorenzo Island and sometimes to the peninsula of Baja California.[53]

Many trips were made to San Lorenzo to gather wild tobacco, which the San Esteban people called *poora*.[54] The leaves were brought back and dried. Smoking the dried leaves, which the San Esteban people did a lot, is said to have made them "crazy."

The Seris say that the San Esteban people sometimes went to live on San Lorenzo Island for long periods of time when food on their own island ran low. Once a group of people lived there a whole year.[55] When they were finally returning to San Esteban, the short man known as *Cöimáxp* 'White' was killed and eaten by a great white shark. Jesús Morales tells the story:[56]

Cöimáxp was one of the San Esteban Island people. He was a grown person, but he was small. When there was a water jug sitting there, when he sat behind it, only the top of his hat was visible.

A group of these people were first on San Esteban Island, but they left there and went to San Lorenzo Island to look for food. They ate sea lion but had eaten all of them [and] so [they] went to the other island. On the north of that island is another small island[57] which has an area that resembles an estuary. The people called it an estuary, although it wasn't one (Figure 1.13).[58] The people stayed there and ate. They ate sea lion.[59] They ate fish they caught there, and the meat of the big black iguana.[60]

After a year, one of them said, "Perhaps we should return to San Esteban. The new year has arrived. Perhaps we should return."

So seven balsas returned. They crossed the sea. Their balsas were loaded with sea lion meat. Each balsa had a family also.

When they were coming near the small island, the sea roared and one of the people said, "Here comes a huge animal! Paddle! Paddle!"

The balsa in front was that of a man called Blue Shirt Man. A huge white shark came up to the balsas, grabbed some of the people, and ate them. *Cöimáxp* being with them, he died.

Then Blue Shirt Man went along real fast in his balsa. When the shark reached his balsa, the balsa went faster than ever and seemed to jump the fast current magically. It was his power that did it.[61]

Then the balsa landed on the peninsula on San Esteban Island. On the south side of the peninsula,[62] they landed the balsa and built a fire. The shark smelled the fire and stayed right there in the water. It stayed there for two days. The next morning, from the direction of the islands called *Hastojícöla* 'mountains-tall'[63] a roaring was heard. The animal came from that direction. He would come out of the water and roar. He was coming toward them.

*Figure 1.13   Aerial view of San Lorenzo Island, looking northwest.
The dark feature on the second peninsula is a salt water lagoon. April 1967.*

It came straight after the great white shark. On its coming it came straight for it. When it came to it, when they came together, they rose up out of the water and churning the water, it rushed up onto the shore.

Then it threw the balsa high up onto the shore where the people were watching while that animal that came killed the large white shark. The large animal was like a chuckwalla.[64] Coming there, it killed the shark. After it killed the shark, the animal left in the same manner that it had come.

Then the people launched the balsa and tied their belongings to it. The Seri were near the camp called *Pajíi*. There is a big arroyo that goes along there.[65] The others were there.

Going there, when they arrived there they told them: "The balsas and the people have disappeared." In that way *Cöimáxp*, the little one, died.

That is the end of the story about *Cöimáxp*'s death.

San Esteban people also traveled to Baja California, mostly to explore and sometimes to raid.[66] They seldom if ever went there to live. *Cöimáxp* was one of those who sometimes went there.[67] Often a man would go alone on his balsa, even as far as Mulegé.[68] Roberto Herrera said that when they went to the peninsula, they would paint each other on their backs, but he did not know why that was done.

One story relates the experiences of a group of San Esteban men who set out for Baja California to explore and raid. They paddled southward along the coast of the peninsula, going ashore occasionally to look around. Eventually they arrived at a large bay. Here a river flowed into the sea at an estuary that was overgrown with trees.[69] The men paddled up the estuary, cutting their way through the heavy branches and overgrowth as they did so. They arrived on land and walked inland, but saw nothing. So they paddled farther south until they saw smoke. They walked toward the smoke and came to a small village. The men there wore trousers, and the women were dressed in long skirts and long blouses, but they spoke a language the San Esteban men could not understand. The Seris began killing the villagers with arrows, but some got away.[70] Then they saw a ghostly form down by the water. They ran down to it and saw that it was lying down, sleeping, with its chest heaving like a person. It jumped up, yanked arrows out, and ran away. Then it stopped and began throwing whale bones at the Seris. After that it ran to the sea, waded in, and disappeared under the water.[71] The men returned to the houses, stole what they wanted, took the loot to their balsas, and hurriedly paddled back to San Esteban. Their power helped by giving them a swift and favorable current for the return trip.

Another expedition to Baja California occurred long ago, when the San Esteban people were being pushed off Tiburón Island by mainland Seris. Because of all the trouble and fighting at that time, a group of San Esteban people left the island in eight large balsas. They never returned. However the Seris say that today there are some very dark-skinned people who live in Mulegé and are called "Cachanillas." They say that the Cachanillas are the best sea turtle hunters in Baja California, and that they can exist for a long time just eating turtle meat. From time to time, they have come to the Sonoran coast, sometimes in a sailboat, once in a boat with a motor. They are very friendly toward the Seris, but they seem to keep to themselves when they are around Mexicans, as do the Seris. Shortly before 1940, they came over to El Desemboque and stayed for several months, living and working with the Seris. It is said that the two groups addressed each other by the Spanish term *pariente* (relative). The Seris believe they are the descendants of the San Esteban people who went to Baja California and disappeared (Bowen 1976:96).[72]

One of the greatest travelers, as well as the most famous San Esteban person of all, was Jesús Ávila, better known as Coyote Iguana. Unlike the other San Esteban people, he spent a great deal of time on the Sonoran mainland and became thoroughly familiar with the outside world. He was known as a great shaman and for his wide-ranging exploits. But he is most famous (or notorious) among both Seris and Mexicans as the man who abducted the Mexican girl Dolores (Lola) Casanova in 1850. Jesús Morales and Roberto Herrera have described his life and exploits at length (Lowell 1970).[73]

The Supernatural

Very little is known about the way the San Esteban people viewed their relationship with the supernatural world. Their belief system seems to have centered on a group of figures known collectively as *Hast Cocyáat* 'Mountain [or Rock]

Be-bosses.' These beings were people at first but transformed into spirits. It is said that two of these people-spirits, a male and a female, are responsible for the location of San Esteban Island.[74] This happened because they got into an argument. The male spirit said that San Esteban should be close to Tiburón and facing it so that it would be easy to go back and forth. The female spirit said no, that San Esteban should be far away so it would not be so easy to go back and forth. The female spirit won out and that explains why the island got placed farther away. It also explains why women since then have been the stingy ones.[75]

The chief spirit, called *Hast Cmique* 'Mountain Person,' apparently had a role in defining the moral code of the people. A female shaman of San Esteban told the others that *Hast Cmique* said it is wrong to kill animals without a reason, such as wounding them and leaving them to die. A person who mistreats a chuckwalla, for instance, by throwing it into the sea,[76] will be punished when he is at sea, perhaps by being subjected to a strong wind.

Both men and women could become shamans. To do so required direct contact with the spirits by means of a vision quest. Today, people are not sure whether the San Esteban people ever sought visions in caves and in the mountains as did the other Seris.[77] For the most part, they sought visions at sea. A man would set out alone in his balsa for four days, paddling into the channel between San Esteban and Tiburón Island.[78] He took with him only a bull roarer, two whistles, and a small pottery jar. The current would carry him away in one direction, and then it would reverse and bring him back. The vision seeker would fill the jar with sea water and ironwood bark and drink the mixture. It made him slightly drunk and sea animals would appear and come to him.[79]

San Esteban shamans had special powers. A shaman in his balsa could make his own current to carry him wherever he wanted to go, even against a strong wind. One person was able to calm a strong wind by taking a seaweed-covered rock from the sea, laying firewood on it, and burning it. Roberto Herrera said that *Cmaacoj Ofícj Coil* "Old Blue Shirt Man" was a powerful shaman. One time he saw an enemy coming toward San Esteban Island in a boat. He quickly made a fetish of plants and dipped it in the sea. Then he walked along the shore, holding the fetish, and sang a song:

> Blue wind that I make
> Coming from my body.
> Wind that roars
> That blows and blows
> That is put on the sea.
> The roaring wind comes.
> It comes from my body.

This made the wind come from the north and south, and then from above as a whirlwind. The enemy's boat could not move in any direction but was tossed around and wrecked (Mary Beck Moser 1981:pers. comm.).

It is thought that the San Esteban people held the same fiestas as the other Seris, during which they danced and ate agave and shellfish. It is also thought that they probably viewed death in much the same way as other Seris, and that the San Esteban people shared a belief in the same afterlife. When a child died, it is said that the father would tell its mother that it was not necessary to die.[80] Roberto Herrera speculated that the San Esteban people may have buried their dead by putting the body in a cave or crevice, along with pottery and other possessions, and then sealing it up.[81]

Extinction

The Seris say that for most of the time the San Esteban people lived on their island, they had only fleeting contact with outsiders. They say that there were a few times when armed men came ashore and tried to kidnap some of the people. Once these intruders managed to capture a few adults. Mostly they tried to take children but without much success. The people would retreat into the mountains and then throw rocks at the intruders.[82] The San Esteban people could throw rocks with such force and accuracy that they were able to chase off the intruders, breaking bones, and even killing some (see Note 8).

One time, however, a ship came and succeeded in capturing everyone. Almost all the San Esteban people died.[83]

According to Roberto Herrera, before the extinction took place, wars and epidemics had already decimated the other Seri bands. Many of these Seris had been guilty of raiding, and the government sought to exterminate the remaining people wherever they could be found.[84] Because of this, all the Seri groups on the mainland had to unify for protection, and everybody sought refuge on Tiburón Island. The Seris today suspect that these people who fled to Tiburón tried to escape government punishment by blaming their own killings and robberies on the San Esteban people. The San Esteban people were innocent, but they paid with their lives for the killings of other Seris.

One account of the massacre was probably told either by Porfirio Díaz or Jesús Morales. A group of Seris were camped at *Xnit*, on the east coast of Tiburón Island, when a Mexican ship sailed up to the lower end of the Canal del Infiernillo (about 10 miles north of *Xnit*). Some soldiers with their colonel came ashore and promised the people gifts if they would go to *Pazj Hax*, a waterhole about two miles inland. These Seris told the San Esteban people, who were camped at *Cyaxoj* on the southwest coast of Tiburón, to come over to where the soldiers were. The San Esteban people, who had never seen soldiers before, left their balsas at *Cyaxoj* and walked over the mountains to *Xnit*. From there, they walked all together up the beach to the ship, and then to the waterhole (Map 1.4).[85]

At the waterhole, the soldiers made a corral of stone (Figures 1.14 and 1.15). When the people arrived there, the adults put down their children in order to receive gifts. None of the San Esteban people spoke Spanish. The soldiers put

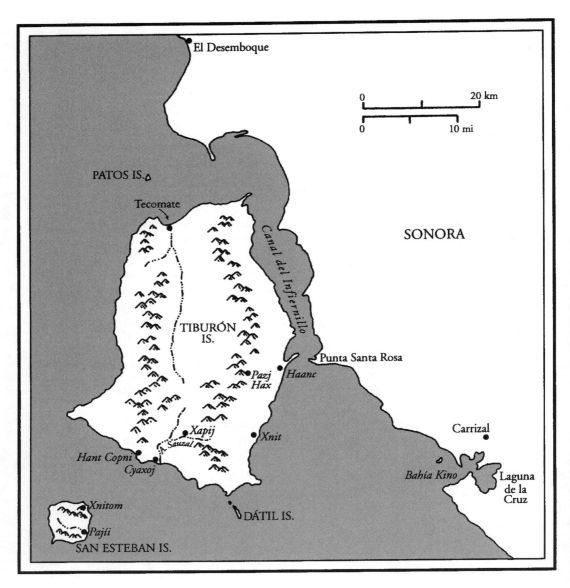

MAP 1.4   *Tiburón Island and its vicinity.*
Map by Cathy Moser Marlett and Anne Austin.

Figure 1.14   The stone corral at Pazj Hax *on Tiburón Island. Photographed by Governor Izábal's men in December 1904. (From García y Alva [1905–1907].)*

the adults in the stone corral and killed many of them with rifles.[86] They took the children away to the ship. They took a few of the men and women to the ship, too. The ship headed for Guaymas, and other Seris later heard that the men had been thrown overboard.[87] Some of the people were not killed. These people were taken to Pueblo de Seris, outside Hermosillo.[88] Here they worked for bits of food, but they all died of disease.[89] Thus although the San Esteban people did not kill or rob, they received the punishment for the other Seris who killed and robbed on the mainland.

A second version was told by Roberto Herrera. He said it was the Governor himself who sent the boat that killed the San Esteban people, thinking they were the guilty Seris.[90] The boat first went to San Esteban. Some of the people went on board, and the boat took them to Tiburón, to the waterhole at *Pazj Hax*. Others followed on their balsas. At *Pazj Hax* the soldiers made a corral of stone (Figures 1.14 and 1.15), and they put the people inside as they arrived. The corral was huge! The soldiers began to give them small gifts, but only things like handfuls of sugar, and they began taking the children. The San Esteban people did not know Spanish, and some thought they were being forced to sell their children. One woman offered her little boy for two handfuls of flour—a high price because he was such a good boy.

Then the soldiers took everyone over to Punta Santa Rosa, on the mainland. Here they gathered firewood and burned many of the men. They strung the other men together through their hands with wire and took them away, never to be seen again.[91] The women were taken to Guaymas, and from there they were sent south in another boat.[92] The Seris learned this from some other Seri

Figure 1.15   The stone corral at Pazj Hax *on Tiburón Island in December 1980, looking south-southwest. This photograph was taken from just outside the north wall (foreground) and looks down the east wall (at left). The cliff on the right forms the corral's west wall.*

women who had been sent to Guaymas with the San Esteban women, and who were later allowed to return to Tiburón Island. The few San Esteban people that survived simply mixed in with the Seris who were living on Tiburón Island. A few even lived for a time at Pueblo de Seris.

According to a third account, the entire San Esteban band had been congregated at one camp when they were rounded up, and there was only a single survivor. This was Old Blue Shirt Man, who by then was an old man. He went to live with the other Seris on Tiburón and married a woman from there. He even visited some Mexican ranches. It was from him that the other Seris learned much of what is known about the San Esteban people and their history.[93]

II.

Europeans and the Gulf of California from 1532 to 1800

The initial European discovery of San Esteban Island took place as early as 1539, but for a long time afterward, sightings of the island were few and far between. The Spaniards had begun to explore the Gulf of California a mere 13 years after Hernán Cortés marched into the great Aztec city of Tenochtitlán. The wealth of the Aztecs had convinced the conquistadores *that there must be other fabulous empires waiting to be discovered, and in 1532 and 1533, Cortés himself sent ships to explore northward from the Pacific coast of New Spain. Both expeditions met with disaster, but the second expedition returned from the southern Gulf with reports of natives wearing pearl ornaments. This set the stage for voyages over the next 150 years, for during that period nearly all of the European expeditions to the Gulf set out in search of pearls.*

Though the early ventures were driven by visions of wealth, Spanish monarchs expressed concern for the souls of the native peoples, and priests began to accompany the early pearl hunting expeditions. But saving souls was incompatible with pearling. In the late seventeenth century, the Crown granted the Jesuit Order exclusive rights to minister to the spiritual needs of the Indians on the peninsula of Baja California, and a tiny band of bold padres soon began to construct a spiritual empire there. Thus by the early eighteenth century, pearlers found themselves sharing the Gulf with the Jesuits, who were now making regular shipping runs across the Gulf to supply their expanding chain of missions.

Pearl hunters and Jesuits alike operated mostly in the southern half of the Gulf, but both groups undertook occasional exploratory voyages north-

ward. In 1539, Francisco de Ulloa, the first European to sight San Esteban, sailed all the way to the head of the Gulf on behalf of Cortés. In 1615, a pearl fishing expedition led by Juan de Iturbe landed on Tiburón Island and became the first known Europeans to make contact with the Seris. A few pearlers scouted the upper Gulf later in the seventeenth century, and pearls were actively hunted there during a few brief periods in the following century.

The Jesuits explored the upper Gulf for different reasons. One was to search for other routes by which their peninsular missions might be supplied. On behalf of the Crown, they also sought to determine whether Baja California was a peninsula or an island. If a strait connected the north end of the Gulf with the Pacific Ocean, the precious Manila galleons could seek safety from storms and pirates in the excellent harbors of the eastern shore of Baja California. Meanwhile, on the mainland side of the Gulf, Spanish soldiers pursuing marauding Seris were becoming increasingly familiar with the Sonoran coast. In 1750, the Spaniards in Sonora took their military might into the Gulf itself by invading Tiburón Island, by now a refuge for Seri raiders.

But for these early forays, the Gulf was a difficult and dangerous sea. Shipwreck, with loss of property and life, was commonplace. And the Midriff islands of Tiburón, San Esteban, and San Lorenzo, the gateway to the upper Gulf, became notorious as the worst section. Most of the time, Europeans had little reason to venture into the region, and as a result, places like San Esteban Island were seldom observed and rarely, if ever, visited.

TWO

Power, Pearls, and Pirates:
Early European Exploration of the Gulf of California

The European Discovery of the Gulf of California

When Hernán Cortés and his small army of adventurers entered the Aztec capital of Tenochtitlán in November of 1519, they were dazzled by what they beheld. The city was an urban wonder, the architectural and commercial equal of any in Europe. This metropolis was also the residence of the emperor Moctezuma, an urbane and sophisticated man who ruled a vast empire that stretched far from the capital in all directions. And this empire, the Spaniards were quick to note, was fabulously wealthy. Moctezuma received his strange visitors with punctilious courtesy and hospitality, totally misjudging their intentions and capabilities. By August 1521, through a combination of daring military moves and incredible good luck, the Spaniards had managed to assassinate Moctezuma, paralyze his army, and capture his city. The Aztec empire had been conquered in the name of the Spanish Crown. Its conqueror, Hernán Cortés, was rewarded with fame and fortune, and was granted the governorship of New Spain by a delighted King.

The fall of the Aztec empire did not end the conquest of New Spain but rather fueled the flames of the Spanish quest for empire and riches. As word of Cortés's success spread, adventurers intent on grabbing a piece of the new-found wealth or duplicating Cortés's feat elsewhere began to pour into the region, creating a dangerous climate of greed and intrigue. With the belief that great fortunes were at stake, this was not a time of unswerving loyalties and honorable motives, and Cortés realized that his hold on power was exceedingly tenuous. If he did not move decisively to secure and extend his realm, he risked losing his position and prestige to political rivals who were all too eager to replace him.

The fundamental assumption that motivated every aspiring *conquistador* in New Spain was, of course, that the Aztec empire was only the first of many empires ripe for conquest. Rumors abounded of rich lands with golden mountains, vast rivers, and great cities, and these rumors were reinforced by long-standing legends and by romantic novels of the period that were widely misconstrued as history. One legend told of the Seven Cities of Cíbola (or Antilia), which many believed were places of great wealth located somewhere in the Americas. Another influential work was a tale of adventure entitled *Las Sergas de Esplandián* (The Exploits of Esplandián), which described a great island of gold and pearls inhabited only by women known as "Amazons." This island, called "California," was situated somewhere "on the right hand of the Indies," which many readers interpreted as lying just west of the North American continent. And of special importance was the Strait of Anián, the anticipated passage through or above the North American continent that would provide a short route from Europe to the riches of the East Indies (Leighly 1972:7–9; Miller 1974:6; Weber 1992:23–25, 40–41; Crosby 1994:4).

Like most of his contemporaries, Cortés bought into these fables, and he quickly laid plans for an exploratory voyage northwest up the Pacific coast, where he believed the Amazon Isles and the Strait of Anián would be found. By 1522, he had shipwrights constructing a fleet of vessels for the expedition. But the venture was delayed by a succession of political crises and disasters at the shipyard, and it was a full 10 years before he was able to mount an expedition northward (Miller 1974:5–7; Weber 1992:38–40).

Finally, in the late spring of 1532, Cortés had two ships ready to set sail from Acapulco. Their voyage did not last long. After barely surviving a seven-day storm, the vessels reached Sinaloa where one was wrecked and the other ran aground. Both crews were attacked by hostile Indians, and of the entire company, there were only three survivors.

Cortés launched a second expedition, also consisting of two vessels, at the end of October 1533. On the second night at sea, they separated from each other and never met up again. One sailed some distance up the mainland coast before returning to Acapulco. The crew of the other vessel, after murdering their despotic captain, continued to explore northwestward and became the first Europeans to reach the peninsula of Baja California. They put in at Bahía La Paz, and as a landing party of about 20 men went ashore to formally take possession of the land for the Crown, they were attacked by Indians. Only one Spaniard escaped back to the ship, which quickly returned to the mainland. But the lone survivor of the shore party reported that the Indians wore ornaments of pearls, thereby establishing the myth of great wealth in the land that came to be known as California.

Despite these two debacles, the report of pearls, coupled with the intelligence that a powerful political rival was preparing his own voyage to the peninsula, persuaded Cortés to try again. This time he would personally lead a large expedition and establish a colony on the peninsula. Setting out from the Mexican coast with three ships and a large company of settlers, on May 3, 1535 he arrived at Bahía La Paz, which he named Santa Cruz. Here the Spaniards established a small settlement. The colonists, however, were completely dependent on food from the mainland. As the small stock they had brought with them dwindled and two of the ships failed to return from a resupply mission, a desperate Cortés set out for the mainland in the remaining vessel. By the time he returned with food, a number of settlers had died of starvation, and half of the remainder, it was said, now died of overeating. Cortés again departed, leaving 30 colonists under the command of Francisco de Ulloa and supplies for 10 months. But the colony could not sustain itself, and late in 1536, Ulloa and the remaining settlers abandoned Santa Cruz and returned to New Spain. For all the suffering, only a small number of inferior pearls had been obtained (Chapman 1939:51; Miller 1974:7, 13–14).

The Discovery of San Esteban Island

The final, and in certain respects the most successful voyage of exploration sent out by Cortés was the result of unanticipated events that began in 1536. First of all, in that year the King appointed Antonio de Mendoza to the newly created post of Viceroy of New Spain. It was a position to which Cortés had aspired, and the appointment created a bitter rivalry between the two men. Secondly, in the same year Álvar Núñez Cabeza de Vaca and three companions wandered into the northern fringes of New Spain after an eight-year trek across the continent from Florida. As they related the details of their incredible odyssey, they told of great cities to the north, which they had not personally seen but had been described to them by Indians along the way. These tales played into the legends of the fabulous Seven Cities and fired the imaginations of Spaniards eager to duplicate Cortés's achievement.

Viceroy Mendoza entered the arena of conquest by dispatching a small reconnaissance party to ascertain the truth of Cabeza de Vaca's tale. It was led by Fray Marcos de Niza and guided by a Moor named Estevanico, who had accompanied Cabeza de Vaca on his epic journey. On March 7, 1539, the small expedition headed north. As they neared their destination, Estevanico and part of their Indian entourage went on ahead. Several days later, the Indians returned without Estevanico, whom they said had entered a town and been killed. Fray Marcos proceeded to a vantage point on a hill where he could observe the town, but went no farther. The party retreated and arrived back in Mexico City late that summer.

The "city" that Niza had seen from a distance was one of the Zuni pueblos of New Mexico. In his report, however, Niza enthusiastically portrayed it as larger than Mexico City and told of Indians wearing turquoise and pearl oyster shells. His tale was excitedly received by Spaniards who were prepared to interpret the "city" as one of the fabulous Seven Cities of legendary fame. Largely on the strength of Niza's report, Mendoza began to organize a full-scale expedition of conquest into the very region that Cortés believed he had exclusive license to explore and exploit (Weber 1992:42–47; Radding 1997:30–31).

Cortés acted quickly to preempt Mendoza's move. With the ships currently at his disposal, Cortés decided to launch another expedition by sea to the northwest. Rather than lead it himself, he placed the expedition under the command

of Francisco de Ulloa, the man who had taken charge of the final days of the
Santa Cruz colony. In terms of Cortés's objectives, the expedition was a failure,
for nothing of monetary value was discovered. However, it became the first
voyage to explore the entire length of the Gulf of California. And in the process, Ulloa and his crew became the first Europeans to sight San Esteban Island.

The itinerary of the voyage was carefully recorded in two journals very different
in character. One was written by Ulloa himself (Wagner 1924). The other was
penned independently by one of his pilots, Francisco de Preciado ([1540] 1904).

Ulloa set sail from Acapulco on July 8, 1539 with a fleet of three ships. The
largest was the *Santa Agueda*, from which he led the expedition. The two smaller
vessels were the *Trinidad*, piloted by Preciado, and the *Santo Tomás*. The voyage did not begin well. Within three weeks of leaving port, stormy winds had
broken the main mast of the *Santa Agueda*, and the expedition had to put in on
the Colima coast for repairs. After a delay of nearly four weeks, the three vessels again set sail northwestward, but a few days later they were hit by a ferocious squall off the coast of Sinaloa. The *Santo Tomás* signaled that she was
shipping water, and her hull was beginning to leak. It was agreed that if the
vessels separated in the storm, they should run for Santa Cruz (Bahía La Paz),
the one known safe harbor where damage could be repaired.

The two larger vessels soon lost sight of the *Santo Tomás* and headed for the
safety of Santa Cruz. They never saw the stricken vessel again. After waiting in
vain for 2½ weeks, Ulloa decided to continue without her. About September 12,
the two remaining vessels set sail across the Gulf to the mainland, reaching the
Río Sinaloa about two days later.

The expedition continued to explore up the Sinaloan coast and on to Sonora. On
September 17 or 18, the two vessels anchored in the superb sanctuary of Guaymas
harbor, which they named the "Puerto de los Puertos" (Port of Ports) (Ulloa [1540]
1924:321), and Ulloa sent Preciado up a nearby hill to plant a cross and take possession of the land in the name of Cortés. They spent two days exploring the bay.
On the beaches they saw several recently-deserted Indian camps containing "divers
pieces of earthen pots as finely made as those in Spaine" (Preciado [1540] 1904:212).
But no live Indians were to be seen, having retreated, perhaps, at the sight of these
strange-looking intruders in their large ships.

On September 19, the Spaniards left Guaymas and headed northwest, following the contours of the coastline. The following day they passed by San Pedro
Nolasco Island, which Ulloa believed (correctly) was uninhabited. By now, the
ships were entering the constricted region of the Midriff and the crew began to
catch glimpses of the peninsula on the opposite side of the Gulf. Some 35 miles
farther, they arrived at a cape which they named "Cabo de las Playas" (Cape of
the Beaches), probably Punta Baja, where they apparently anchored for the
night (Preciado [1540] 1904:212). The next day's sailing took them about 50
miles up a coast that Preciado described as "full of little hilles without grasse or
trees" (Preciado [1540] 1904:213). That evening, they dropped anchor very
close to Tiburón Island, or possibly off the east coast of the island itself. They
were under the impression that Tiburón Island was a peninsula jutting out from

the mainland, not having explored far enough into Bahía Kunkaak to discover that the island is separated from the mainland by the narrow Canal del Infiernillo (McGee 1898:52).

On September 22, they sailed past San Esteban Island:

> Following the said course, thirty leagues beyond this little island [San Pedro Nolasco], we entered into a strait[,] formed by the mainland and an uninhabited island[,] which was four leagues wide and twelve long. There is very deep water between it and the mainland. It lies in latitude 31°. At its entrance there are two little islets. We named it San Miguel strait, for we passed through it on Saint Michael's day. (Ulloa [1540] 1924:322–23)

Ulloa, of course, was nowhere near 31° latitude, and the "mainland" was actually Tiburón Island. Otherwise, his narrative provides a reasonable description of the channel between the southwest coast of Tiburón Island and San Esteban, the "uninhabited island." The channel is in fact approximately 30 leagues (78 miles)[94] northwest of San Pedro Nolasco Island, and two small islets, Dátil (Turners) and Cholludo, lie at its entrance. Ulloa overestimated the channel's length by about 50 percent, but his figure of four leagues (10 miles) for its width is only about two miles greater than its actual width at the narrowest point.

Preciado, who was on the other ship, interpreted the strait quite differently but with equal accuracy:

> The next day we followed our voyage beginning to saile before breake of day Northwestward, and we came into the midst of a Streight or mouth which was 12 leagues broad from one land to the other, which Streight had two Ilands in the midst thereof being 4. leagues distant the one from the other: and here we discerned the countrey to be plaine, and certaine mountaines, & it seemed that a certaine gut [narrow passage] of water like a brooke ran through the plaine. This streight (as far as we could perceive) was very deep, for we could finde no botome: and here we saw the land stretching afarre off from the one shore to the other, and on the Westerne shore of the haven of S. Cruz, the land was more high with very bare mountaines. The day following we passed on our way toward the North, and sailed some 15. leagues, and in the midst of our way we found a circuit or bay of 6. leagues into the land with many cooves or creeks, and the next day following continuing our course we sailed some 10. leagues, and the coast in this dayes journey was all of high mountains naked and bare without any tree. (Preciado [1540] 1904:213)

What Preciado designated as the "Streight" is not the relatively narrow channel separating Tiburón Island from San Esteban as described by Ulloa, but the entire constriction that forms the Midriff section of the Gulf between Tiburón Island, mistaken as the mainland, and Baja California. Interpreted this way, the distance from the closest point on the southwest coast of Tiburón to the peninsula is about 35 miles, very close to Preciado's estimate of 12 leagues. The two islands "in the midst" of the strait would be San Esteban and San Lorenzo, which are in fact separated by about 4 leagues (10 miles). And the observation by both Preciado and Ulloa of the strait's deep water eliminates any possibility that the expedition might have sailed up the shallow and shoal-ridden Canal del Infiernillo, between Tiburón Island and the true mainland. In fact, the Infiernillo is almost certainly the feature Preciado referred to as the "gut [narrow passage] of water like a brooke," for had they experienced strong tidal currents rushing southward out of the Infiernillo, they might well have mistaken it for a river flowing from a great plain (McGee 1898:52).

Preciado's narrative suggests that it took a full day to get through the channel between San Esteban and Tiburón. The following day they headed due north rather than northwest, following the west coast of Tiburón Island. Midway through the day's sail, the feature they took to be a bay intruding six leagues (16 miles) into the coast must have been the north entrance to the Infiernillo, which separates the north coast of Tiburón Island from Cabo Tepopa on the mainland (McGee 1898:52).

From Tiburón Island, Ulloa and Preciado continued on to the head of the Gulf, where they discovered the Colorado River and established that Baja California was a peninsula firmly connected to the mainland. But Ulloa was anything but inspired by the coastline they had seen in the:

> 104 leagues from El Puerto de los Puertos [Guaymas]. The character of the land—of that land which comes down to the sea—is poor, very poor.... In all these 104 leagues we did not see a person, or sign of any. I do not believe that such land can be inhabited. (Ulloa [1540] 1924:325)

They found the landscape equally bleak as they descended down the peninsular side of the Gulf, and they saw no trace of Indians until they reached Bahía San Luis Gonzaga. Nor did they see any indication that the two Midriff islands of Ángel de la Guarda and San Lorenzo were inhabited as they sailed past them a few days later (Ulloa [1540] 1924:329–30).

In November, the two vessels rounded the southern tip of Baja California. Faithful to Cortés's instructions, Ulloa again turned northwestward to explore up the Pacific coast of the peninsula. By the time the expedition reached Cedros Island, sickness, severe weather, and structural damage to the *Santa Agueda* finally forced the two vessels to part company. On April 5, 1540, Preciado turned south toward New Spain, arriving in port two weeks later. Ulloa pushed on northward in the *Trinidad*, but little is known of this voyage, and there has even been some question as to whether he ever returned (Preciado [1540] 1904:275–78; Bancroft 1884:80–81; Wagner 1924:311–14, 1937:20).

As far as San Esteban is concerned, the members of Ulloa's expedition must be credited with being the first Europeans to sight the island, but there is no indication that anyone went ashore there. All we know from the accounts is that Ulloa thought San Esteban to be "uninhabited" and Preciado found the entire region desolate.

While Ulloa and Preciado were exploring the Gulf by sea, Viceroy Mendoza continued to organize his land expedition to the north, and Cortés had been unable to block him. The man Mendoza had selected to lead the expedition was a young provincial governor named Francisco Vázquez de Coronado. When Preciado arrived back in New Spain in April 1540, Coronado and his men were already gearing up for their long march northward. But news of Ulloa's discoveries in the Gulf must have leaked almost immediately upon Preciado's return, for Mendoza's final plan called for a simultaneous expedition by sea to resupply Coronado's army. Ships were to sail to the head of the Gulf and ascend an undetermined distance up the Colorado River, rendezvous with the land forces, and deliver supplies. The man chosen to lead the naval expedition was Hernando de Alarcón, who would thus become the second European to traverse the length of the Gulf.

Perhaps because his duties lay at the head of the Gulf, Alarcón left a detailed account of his activities there but revealed little of the voyage up and back. He departed with two ships from New Spain on May 9, 1540. Like Ulloa, he was hit almost immediately by a tremendous storm, forcing his vessels to put in for repairs on the Colima coast. Soon the expedition was joined by a third ship which had been stocked with food for Coronado's army. From its crew, Alarcón learned that Coronado had already begun his march northward some 17 days earlier. As they entered the Gulf, the three vessels steered close to the mainland, hoping to find some sign of the land forces.

When Alarcón reached the head of the Gulf, he ascended the Colorado River some 35 or 40 miles but found no trace of Coronado's army. After waiting three weeks or more, he buried some letters for Coronado, erected a cross, descended the river, and sailed back down the Gulf, again staying close to shore in the vain hope of spotting the troops. Alarcón arrived back in Colima without ever making contact with the land force, although his letters were found by Melchior Díaz, one of Coronado's captains, who had been dispatched to search for the ships (Alarchon [1540] 1904:279–318; Bancroft 1884:82–88).

Of the trip up the Gulf, all Alarcón records is that:

> I followed my course along the [mainland] coast without departing from the same, to see if I could find any token or any Indian which could give me knowledge of him [Coronado]: and in sailing so neere the shore I discovered other very good havens [harbors], for the ships whereof Captaine Francis de Ullua was Generall for the Marquesse de Valle [Cortés] neither sawe nor found them. (Alarchon [1540] 1904:280)

Which "very good havens" he discovered is not known, nor is his precise route up the Gulf. Although Alarcón hugged the coastline, like Ulloa he apparently assumed Tiburón Island to be a peninsula and passed through the Midriff region by way of the channel between Tiburón and San Esteban Islands (Bolton 1964:154, inside front cover). Indeed, a map of the Gulf, drawn the following year by one of his pilots, Domingo del Castillo, shows Tiburón as a cape (see Figure 3.1). Since Alarcón himself wrote nothing at all about the Midriff region, we can only conjecture as to what he might have seen.

In the spring of 1541, Mendoza again directed Alarcón to prepare for a voyage to the Colorado River in support of Coronado's troops, but troubles developed elsewhere and the expedition never put to sea (Riley 1997:6–7). A year later, the tattered remains of Coronado's army returned empty-handed to New Spain after wandering for two years through the American Southwest and the western plains.

Other Gulf expeditions were vaguely contemplated around this time, but none materialized. The experiences of Ulloa and Alarcón had put a damper on voyages of conquest by establishing that there were no fabulous kingdoms accessible from the Gulf. If fortunes were to be made in the region, they would have to come from other, less glamorous, kinds of enterprises.

The Quest for Pearls

These enterprises were pearl fishing expeditions. Nobody had forgotten that pearls had been seen during Cortés's voyages to the peninsula, nor was there any shortage of adventurers and entrepreneurs willing to risk huge sums for an opportunity to seek a fortune in pearls. For the next century and a half, nearly every voyage into the Gulf would be a pearling expedition. And for another two centuries after that, the quest for pearls would continue to provide one of the main motives that lured people into the Gulf.

During the first 50 years after Ulloa's voyage, at least a few pearl hunters ventured forth. But nearly all of these were small clandestine operations, undertaken without official sanction, and consequently there is little record of them (Mosk 1931:62, 1934:50; Gerhard 1956:240, 1982:290–92). Real returns required large-scale expeditions, and most importantly, all expeditions required government authorization. The first such authorization was issued by Viceroy Velasco about 1552 to a group headed by Juan Yáñez, who went to considerable expense to outfit a Gulf expedition. His men seem to have set out on at least one voyage, though what became of the venture is not known (Gerhard 1982:290–91).

In 1573, the Spanish monarch Felipe II issued a decree that specified the regulations that would henceforth govern all Gulf pearl fishing ventures. This, and supplemental decrees, required first and foremost that all expeditions be licensed by the government, on pain of death to violators. Licensed explorers were encouraged to record new geographical knowledge and information about any natives encountered. Natives were to be treated well, and special emphasis was to be placed on bringing them into the Christian fold. Those intent on exploiting the pearl beds were specifically prohibited from engaging natives as divers, for which Negroes were to be used. And most importantly, one-fifth of the proceeds (the Royal Fifth) was to be set aside as the Crown's share of the profits (Wagner 1930:191; Mosk 1931:64–65, 92).

These were costly conditions, but a license granted the successful petitioner an absolute monopoly on pearl fishing rights for a specified number of years. With vast potential fortunes at stake, the competition for a license was often fierce. Over the next century, litigation among competitors over the validity of licenses was so common that many aspiring pearl hunters found themselves embroiled in extended court battles, and relatively few officially sanctioned pearl fishing expeditions actually reached the Gulf.

The first license to incorporate the full spectrum of the royal decrees was issued in 1585 to a partnership headed by Hernando de Sanctotis, and it granted the members a 10 year monopoly on pearling rights. One of the partners managed a number of sorties into the Gulf in small boats and seems to have had considerable success finding pearls, but the group was ultimately unable to fulfill its contract (Wagner 1930:192–94; Gerhard 1956:240; Mathes 1966:11–12). In 1593, the license was transferred to a syndicate led by Sebastián Vizcaíno, who promised not only to explore the coast while fishing for pearls, but also to establish a colony on the peninsula. Though not a requirement for a license, colonization was a prospect which the Crown viewed with great favor. Thus Vizcaíno prepared to launch the first large-scale pearling expedition to operate under the terms of the royal decrees. In the course of his voyage, he may have become the first licensed pearler to reach the Midriff islands.

On June 15, 1596, Vizcaíno departed from Acapulco with three ships, a large company of settlers, soldiers, Franciscan missionaries, horses, artillery, and other supplies. Three months later, after several tentative landings, the company disembarked at the site of Cortés's old colony of Santa Cruz, renaming it La Paz for the peaceful reception they received from the Indians. While the colonists set about constructing a small settlement, Vizcaíno with 80 men in his two smaller vessels headed north up the peninsular coast to explore and hunt pearls. This exploratory voyage ended abruptly at about 27° N. latitude. Here a shore party was attacked for forcibly seizing a large pearl from an Indian woman, and 19 of the Spaniards drowned as they tried to retreat back to the ship. When the survivors reached La Paz, they began to agitate to abandon the enterprise altogether and return to New Spain. Three days later a fire broke out and quickly spread throughout the settlement, destroying more than half the buildings along with much of the food and ammunition. With the settlement in shambles and supplies now running precariously low, Vizcaíno reluctantly agreed to abandon the colony (Vizcaíno [1596] 1930:204–14).

But Vizcaíno was not yet ready to abandon his search for pearls. On October 28, as the colonists set sail for home, he and 36 men, with food for two months, set out on one more attempt to explore northward. The results were nearly disastrous:

> Proceeding on my voyage, on the second day a north wind began to blow, so contrary and so violent that we rode out the storm in great risk for six days almost without hope of saving our lives, as the coast is dangerous, the sea narrow, the land unknown, and islands everywhere. It was a miracle that we could lay the ship to and save our lives. When the storm was over we found

ourselves in 27°, which was where the nineteen soldiers had been drowned.... There we took water, which we found to be good, and remained two days, as we did not have the wind to pass onward.

On November 9, I made sail with the land wind, and went along the coast up to 29°, where with a northwest wind no less violent than the first I fell back to the Isla de Lobos, which is in 26°. Here the ship began to make [take in] much water, which alarmed us considering the danger in which we were, as the winds were contrary and the sea was narrow to run before them. The islands were very close together, and full of warlike Indians, the ship was alone and very battered, and, if any disaster should occur, we could get no help from any quarter. . . .

From this island [Lobos] I made sail and with a little southwest wind again attempted the enterprise, this time reaching the Cabo de San Antonio in 29½°. We had a view of the country at 30°, which was all bare mountain, rough and desert country like the first. From there we could not pass on because it truly seemed that there came upon us all the fury of hell. Night caught us near the land and was so dark and so charged with thunder, lightning, and rain squalls that we were at the point of death. The wind was east-northeast blowing directly on the coast which we were following, and the sea reached the sky. We wished to lay the ship to, fearing that we would strike the land which was very near, but we did not dare to do so on account of its weakness. We went to tacking, and so we passed almost two days with greater hardship and misery than could be imagined. November 14 dawned with the sea somewhat calm, and we found ourselves between five small islands. While making all sail to get out from among them all the gudgeons of the rudder broke, leaving the ship without anything to steer with and in greater danger than ever. Seeing this misfortune and the danger in which we were, and that the currents were carrying us on the coast, the chief pilot made some braces to the rudder with the ends of cables with which the rudder went back into its place, and thus we passed the time until the sea all calmed down and we escaped from between the islands. (Vizcaíno [1596] 1930:214–16)

And so with a makeshift rudder, a badly leaking vessel, and wet and rotten food, Vizcaíno turned his crippled vessel toward New Spain. How far up the Gulf he actually got is difficult to determine, for his report does not give much geographical detail. Some commentators, perhaps not clearly distinguishing this second attempt from the first foray north, have doubted that Vizcaíno got much above 27° (Wagner 1930:216n54, 217n56; Gerhard 1956:241). Though he may not have reached the 29½° he claimed, which would have put him at the upper end of the Midriff, he may have come close. It is hard to imagine what the "five small islands" could have been if not members of the San Lorenzo chain, lying a little south of 29°. In any case, Vizcaíno and his disgruntled colonists were all back in New Spain by early December. Though the expedition overall had been a failure, Vizcaíno did return with a few pearls and a favorable report on the pearling potential of the region, thereby setting the stage for nearly all voyages into the Gulf during the following century.

Over the next several years, the undaunted Vizcaíno, along with others, sought authorization to explore the Gulf for pearls, but their requests were denied. When a license was finally granted in 1611, it went to a company in Seville, organized by Tomás de Cardona. Armed with a 10-year license, the company's fleet set sail for New Spain in July 1613, with Cardona's nephew, Nicolás de Cardona, in charge of the field operations. After purchasing 28 Negroes in the West Indies to use as divers, the company reached Mexico and established headquarters in Acapulco. Here they proceeded to construct three frigates, which were ready to sail in January 1615. Before the fleet could set out, however, rumors reached Acapulco that Dutch pirates had rounded the horn, plundered Peru, and were headed northward. Fearing the worst, government officials commandeered the company's vessels to help secure Acapulco from possible attack. Two months later, with the danger past, the Cardona expedition put to sea with its three vessels, a large contingent of soldiers and sailors, the Negro divers, and two Franciscan friars (Mosk 1934:50–54). Although Cardona was to affix his signature to the subsequent first-person account of the expedition, the fleet sailed under the command of Juan de Iturbe, while Cardona himself remained safely behind in New Spain (Clavigero [1789] 1971:134; Mosk 1931:93–94, 1934:53; Wagner 1937:145; Chapman 1939:159–62; Mathes 1974:17–18; Portillo 1982:245–46).

The expedition sailed up the coast as far as Mazatlán, and from there made an easy crossing to the peninsula. They set out immediately to explore north-ward for pearl beds. Iturbe put in at Bahía La Paz and found the Indians there still well disposed toward Spaniards. But this was not the case farther north:

> I left this place [La Paz] and reached a nice beach in twenty-seven degrees[,] for I was in need of water. I disembarked with thirty harquebusiers and two mastiff dogs. Suddenly over six hundred Indians with bows and arrows appeared firing their first volley. I was wounded and I released the two dogs at them, and since they had never seen anything like them, they retreated. With this we brought them to peace and the next day many of them came to hear Mass. At this place General Sebastián Vizcaíno came to take on water, and because he had not gotten along well with the Indians or due to some mistreatment of them by his soldiers, at the time of disembarkation, they killed thirty of his men. They [the Indians] kept the ship's boat, pieces of which I have seen on the beach, and I had five Christian heads, which the Indians keep as a memento of their victory, in my hands. (Cardona [1627–1632] 1974:101–102)

From here, Iturbe continued on to the Midriff and crossed the Gulf to the Sonoran side. Though he and his crew did not stop at San Esteban, they went ashore on Tiburón Island, and in so doing, probably became the first Europeans to make contact with the Seris:

> I sailed onward to thirty degrees north latitude and from there we saw the opposite shore, which is the opposite coast of Florida [i.e., Sonora], at a dis-

tance of eight or ten leagues to the east. I crossed to reconnoiter it and anchored there. I found that it was a large island inhabited by Indian fishermen who were naked[,] and whose women wear buckskin aprons made from deer skins and [wear] glass beads on their throats and ears. Desirous of knowing with whom they communicated, Christians or enemy, we asked them questions but we could not find out anything definite[,] although we conjectured that they came from New Mexico. This island was one league from the mainland and Indians from there came out to it, for after being there for three days taking on water and firewood[,] many people had gathered there. (Cardona [1627–1632] 1974:102)

From Tiburón, they made a side trip to Patos Island:

Three days I was on the island[,] and in the afternoon I set sail. Having sailed for four leagues[,] and since it was night and the area was unknown, we anchored. Throughout the night strange noises, like dogs tending livestock, were heard from the shore. At sunrise we saw a small white island [Patos Island][,] and I took the ship's boat with some of the personnel and went to it. We found a great number of sea lions, so many that we almost could not reach shore without passing over them. We killed many of them to remove [their] oil with which to tar the ship, for which it is marvelous, and to burn in the lanterns. (Cardona [1627–1632] 1974:102)

Later the same day, Iturbe and six soldiers took the ship's boat and visited a Seri beach camp on the mainland, where a Seri was sending smoke signals:

about two o'clock in the afternoon we saw many smoke fires on a beach on the mainland[,] and they were so thick and fast burning that I felt obligated to go and see what it could be.... It was four long leagues from the ships to the smoke[,] and having arrived and disembarked[,] I found two small boats made from cane. The ground was swept and watered[,] and there were many bird feathers of various colors hung about, [but] nothing else. It seemed to me to be some fishermen's villages. An Indian was there, naked, although he did wear shoes like soles of folded deer hide. He did not stop dancing just a short distance from us. The sun was bright and hot[,] and I tried to attract the Indian peacefully with gifts. He came peacefully and[,] asking him where his companions were, he made it understood that they would come in the morning when the sun was over the hills, for they have no other clock than estimating the rising and setting of the sun. It should be considered that the smoke fires which we saw were many[,] and one Indian alone could not have made them, especially making fire with such labor as rubbing one stick against another. (Cardona [1627–1632] 1974:103)

The shore party did not have an easy time trying to return to their ship in the skiff:

To avoid problems we embarked again at the hour of nightfall, and in our passage we were caught in a great storm of hail, wind, thunder, and rain, which was the first storm we encountered after seven months of sailing. We were about to sink and drown, for the sea had flooded the boat, and it was necessary to bail the water with hats and two broken earthen jugs. We reached the aforesaid large island [Tiburón] but being unable to double it, we spent the night in complete silence and hard labor [trying to keep the skiff afloat]. At sunrise we went inland and saw many deer, pigeons, hares, partridges [California quail], doves, and many varieties of birds, and then we embarked for the ships. (Cardona [1627–1632] 1974:103–4)

The expedition continued up the Sonoran coast, apparently reaching the head of the Gulf (at an impossible 34° latitude, by their estimation). There they convinced themselves that they saw a strait separating the peninsula from the mainland, thereby adding fuel to the emerging belief that Baja California was an enormous island. Finally, food shortages and bad weather forced them back, and a while later they arrived in Sinaloa (Mosk 1931:101–5).

After this exploratory voyage, Iturbe apparently made several more forays into the Gulf for pearls, returning periodically to the mainland to resupply. The venture ended in November 1616 when Captain Iturbe finally sailed into Acapulco. In a year and a half, he had lost only one vessel and part of its crew, not to shipwreck, but to the notorious Dutch pirate Joris van Spilbergen, whom he had unfortunately encountered along the west coast of Mexico (Mosk 1934:54–55; Mathes 1974:16–17; Portillo 1982:258–64). The pearls the expedition had gathered were sent to Mexico City for official appraisal. Their total weight was 14½ ounces, with the largest weighing ¼ ounce. Their value was placed at 672 pesos, out of which was taken the Royal Fifth. There is considerable evidence, as one might expect, that not all the pearls found were declared to the authorities and that the actual profits for the Cardona Company were considerably greater. Hence the effect of the expedition was to convince potential fortune seekers that the Gulf was rich in pearls, insuring that the quest for wealth would continue there (Venegas [1759] 1966a:182; Mosk 1934:59–61; Gerhard 1956:241–42; Mathes 1974:17).

In 1619, Nicolás de Cardona began preparations for a new expedition, but a series of shipwrecks and obligatory service elsewhere prevented the scheme from ever materializing. Not until 1632 was there another officially sanctioned voyage into the Gulf. This time it was led by Francisco de Ortega, a wily man who turned out to be highly skillful at manipulating the wheels of government for his own ends (León-Portilla 1973).

Ortega made three voyages, in 1632, 1633, and 1636. On the first voyage, he did not get much higher than La Paz and the pearls he acquired were mostly flawed (Carbonel de Valenzuela [1632] 1992; Nava [1632] 1992; Mosk 1931:128). It was a voyage of some historical significance because he brought along the first known diving bell, a device made of wood and lead that supposedly would enable one or two people to stay below for 10 to 12 days at a time (Mosk 1931:121). Whether the contraption was actually used is not reported.

The following year Ortega set out again. This time he promised the government that he would establish a colony on the peninsula. The expedition sailed to La Paz, and there the colonists began to build a settlement. Meanwhile, Ortega and his divers worked their way up the coast as far as about 27°, charting pearl-oyster beds along the way and bestowing on many of the peninsular islands their modern names (León-Portilla 1973:69). When winter winds put a halt to pearl diving, the colony, which of course had never been the real purpose of the venture, was abandoned, and the expedition returned to the mainland (Ortega [1634] 1992; Mosk 1931:130–43).

Ortega embarked on his final expedition in 1636. This time he reached the Midriff islands, where he discovered an enormous placer of pearl oysters and a group of unknown Indians who had never seen Europeans. But it was a decidedly irregular expedition.

Although Ortega had entered the pearling business in 1632 with a government license, he launched his final voyage more with deceit than official sanction. Shortly after returning from his second voyage, he had become entangled in a complicated legal struggle involving rival claims of pearling authorizations. To further complicate the situation, in 1635 the viceroyship in Mexico City changed hands before he was able to straighten the matter out. To retain legal status, Ortega would have had to revalidate his license with the new viceroy. Not only would this have been a time-consuming process, but under the challenge of competing claims, he would have risked losing his license altogether.

Ortega, who had been in Sinaloa preparing for a new expedition as these problems unfolded, saw a golden opportunity in his remoteness and moved swiftly. By intimating that he had actually set sail from elsewhere before the change in government, he was able to persuade the local authorities that his license from the former viceroy was still valid. With this clever ploy, he wangled an official inspection of his vessel from the Captain of the Garrison in Sinaloa, effectively preempting any future accusation that he was making an illegal or clandestine voyage. On January 11, the very day the inspection papers were signed, he slipped out of port in his lone frigate to begin his "authorized" voyage of "discovery" undertaken "in the name of His Majesty" (León-Portilla 1973:59–61).

Sailing with fair winds, Ortega and his crew quickly crossed the Gulf and sighted La Paz two days later. But before they were able to disembark, a furious winter storm broke, and the vessel was blown south and wrecked. As Ortega's clerk describes it:

> that night a north wind arose, and since we were unable to round either point of the aforementioned cove, we cast anchor in twelve *brazas* [5½ fathoms] of water. We rode out the storm for two nights and a day. [But] at dawn on the eve of Saint Sebastián [Day] a cable broke, [we began] to drag anchor, [and] the wind and the sea rose so [high] that we were driven into shore, where the frigate broke up. All the people made it to shore on one of the pieces, with no one injured. We gave thanks to God for the great mercy He had bestowed

upon us, for with such a heavy sea and wind, the pieces of the frigate were cast up on shore, [coming to rest] higher than it looked like the sea had ever before reached.... This storm which wrecked us lasted for eleven days, without the wind letting up [either] at night or during the day. Had we been at sea, it would have been impossible to avoid sinking. (Ortega [1636] 1944:105)

But Ortega, who was an accomplished shipwright, was not about to give up the expedition:

then Captain Francisco de Ortega set to work [building] a topmast boat, making use of the planks from the frigate and some native [Baja] California lumber. He finished making the boat in forty-six days.... On the 27th of February ... we launched it, and the entire company embarked in it [along with] the stores from the frigate, which had showed up on shore. [Thus] we left the place where the frigate had been wrecked. (Ortega [1636] 1944:105)

With his new patchwork boat, Ortega returned to La Paz and spent a week gathering supplies. He then set sail up the Gulf, zigzagging between the peninsula and the various islands, discovering and naming rich oyster beds, and finding a number of fine pearls. On March 20, the expedition arrived at their previous high point. They continued on up the coast to San Marcos Island (at the time called Las Tortugas), where the local Indians steered clear of them, and put in at a large bay on the peninsula. On April 4, they reached a low-lying peninsula jutting out to a point which they named "Punta la Caiman" (possibly Punta San Francisquito). From this location (which they placed at an impossible 34¾° N. latitude), they could see across the Gulf clearly and correctly estimated the distance to be about 25 leagues (65 miles) (Ortega [1636] 1944:108). From "Punta la Caiman," Ortega set sail for the Midriff islands, putting in at one he named "San Sebastián." Despite the garbled geography of his report, perhaps intended to conceal his destination[95], the island he visited may well have been Tiburón, the large harbor or bay on the western side Bahía Agua Dulce (Figure 2.1), and the Indians he encountered none other than the Seris:

We left this point on the twelfth of April, steering west-northwest under a northeast wind. We arrived on the fourteenth of April at an island which was five leagues from the mainland. When we dropped anchor on this island, fully fifty Indians without any weapons came to the beach. From the harbor on the island's western side, we brought the boat into shore. The Indians came up to us with great fear, throwing dirt into the air, which is a sign of peace among them. [They are] a different nation from [the] others we have seen up till now. We gave them some knives, and they were very demonstrative with them, as if they had never seen such things, and they gave us some grains of burned and abraded pearls. It is a very cold land, and because it was the end of April, we could not tolerate it. The Indian women of this island, all of those we saw, were dressed in the skins of deer and lions, and they gave some of them to us.

Figure 2.1   Bahía Agua Dulce and Tecomate, near the northwestern corner of Tiburón Island, looking east. Tecomate, the location of the most famous Seri camp, water source, and shellmound (probably the one Ortega named "San Roque"), is situated in the deepest part of the bay on the right. January 1977.

They eat maize and do not like other food, and they indicated by signs that there is maize inland. (Ortega [1636] 1944:108–9)

Of course, Ortega was most interested in the pearls:

In this bay, which is on the western shore, we discovered a shellmound of pearls. When we asked the natives of this island by signs where they obtained the pearls [they had given us], they indicated it [the shellmound]. It is very full of shells [and] this placer is very large, extending more than a league. The Indians refused to dive, saying by signs that it was too cold. A diver whom we had brought explored it [the placer] and found it to be a good one.

The Indians of this island are a good-looking [people], very robust and well-featured. We gave the name San Roque to this shellmound and [the name] San Sebastián to the island. It has a circumference of forty leagues, [and] it runs from northwest to southeast. At its head, which we saw to the southeast, we found another placer of pearl shells, which we explored and found to be very rich. It was named the San Francisco shellmound. Here, Pilot Cosme Lorenzo measured the sun; this island is located at a latitude of thirty-six degrees.

There are wells of brackish water on [this island], which is what the Indians drink. In a ravine on the eastern shore, we found water in some pools, which collects there when it rains. There are many pitahayas and *ciruelos* [plum trees] and much mescal [agave]. The Indians sustain themselves on these. (Ortega [1636] 1944:109)

Ortega and his party apparently spent nearly three weeks on San Sebastián Island. Finally, about May 3, they bid farewell to the Indians and continued their voyage up the coast. For three days, they sailed northwest, reaching 36½° by their reckoning. But supplies were running low, so when a strong northwest wind arose, Ortega decided to call it quits and head for home. After nine days, on May 15, the expedition reached port in Sinaloa, and Ortega submitted a report of his trip to the authorities the following day.

If Tiburón was indeed Ortega's "San Sebastián Island," his would have been the second known European encounter with the Seris there. Crossing from the peninsular side, he must have passed close to San Esteban Island en route. If so, it would be one of the only islands he failed to mention in his report, though it would be a logical omission if he were bent on concealing a trip to Tiburón.

While Ortega was deftly manipulating the authorities to legitimate his third voyage, an accomplished and energetic navigator named Pedro Porter y Casanate was petitioning for a pearl fishing license through proper viceregal channels. However, Porter's road to the Gulf would be a long one fraught with adventure, narrow escapes, and catastrophe. In both 1635 and 1636, he was awarded licenses, outfitted a ship at his personal expense, and was on the verge of setting sail, only to have his licenses canceled in the administrative confusion that accompanied the change in viceroys. To expedite the matter, Porter set off for Spain in order to plead his case directly before the King, but his ship was captured off Cuba by Dutch pirates. Six months later, he was rescued by a band of Spanish pirates, and eventually made his way to Spain. While waiting for a response from the Crown, Porter joined the Spanish fleet in a battle against the French, in which he lost his son and barely escaped with his own life. With still no word, he took over command of a Spanish naval vessel and set sail on a relatively uneventful voyage to the West Indies (Mosk 1931:163–67; Mathes 1992a:245–46).

Royal authorization for Porter's pearling expedition was finally granted in 1640, on the condition that he first serve more naval duty against the French. In 1643, he departed for New Spain and Sinaloa, where he built a shipyard and began constructing two vessels. But a saboteur's fire in 1644 destroyed the shipyard and one of the vessels, throwing Porter into bankruptcy. He was bailed out by government loans and an appointment to the governorship of Sinaloa, which enabled him to rebuild his ships. Official duties consumed Porter's attention during 1646–1647, but the following year he and his vessels were finally ready to set sail. On October 23, 1648, Porter sailed northward from Sinaloa on a voyage of some 76 days. And in the summer of 1649, he again sailed up the Gulf on a cruise that lasted three months (Porter y Casanate [1645] 1992, [1651]

1970b:889; Mosk 1931:175–86; Chapman 1939:165–66;; Mathes 1970:xlvi–
xlvii; Portillo 1982:320–30).

After his return from these voyages, Porter reported to the King that he had
thoroughly explored and charted the entire Gulf, corrected the egregious errors of earlier navigators, and named and determined the correct position of its
features, including some 24 islands. How far Porter sailed on his first trip is not
certain, but it seems likely that he turned back well short of the Midriff islands
(Portillo 1982:321–24). On the second trip, he most certainly reached them.
Though he claimed to have kept detailed diaries and charts of his observations,
only two general summaries of the expeditions seem to have survived (Porter
y Casanate [1649] 1970a; [1651] 1970b). But one of the few places specifically
described in these summaries is the Midriff region, including the Seris'
("Caeras") island of Tiburón, along with San Esteban and San Lorenzo:

> on the New Spain side I found a very spacious port, which I named Santiago
> [Bahía Kino]. In front of it, there is a very large inhabited island which is called
> Caeras. Next to this [island], going across the Gulf, [there are] two small
> barren islands which close off [the Gulf], leaving some very narrow channels.
> (Porter y Casanate [1651] 1970b:889)

This and other comments imply that Porter interpreted the Midriff islands
as the land barrier that defined the actual head of the Gulf, with the narrow
channels between the islands providing the passage to the sea he believed lay
beyond. Not wishing to quit without exploring beyond this point, he attempted
to sail through one of these channels, with results so violent and frightening that
he described the experience at length:

> after entering [the channel] I could not follow it, because I was violently
> pushed away by a current that carried me to the shoreline of [Baja] Califor-
> nia, which is very high and precipitous next to the Straits. Seeing that I was
> in great danger, I tried again to enter a very narrow channel that is formed by
> reefs of an island. When I entered [it] I saw from the bow a slab of rock, con-
> cealed in the middle of the channel, that was covered by scarcely two *palmos*
> [about 16 inches] of water. While carefully trying to steer away from this
> hazard, I was caught in a current which carried me violently into another
> channel and then up close to the precipitous rocky shore. Finding myself
> [trapped] inside this channel, carried along by the current, I thought that all
> was lost, because a shoal [seemed to] stretch in front of the bow from the coast
> of [Baja] California to that of New Spain. The choppy appearance of the sea
> and the churning of the water made it look as though it were a field of rocks.
> [But] because I was forced to pass through there, I discovered that it was a
> strong current that flowed with great noise from one coast to the other. I
> passed through this twisting current with much travail. This channel is exceed-
> ingly deep and is about six to seven leagues wide. The Shores are very high
> mountains, without any beaches where one can anchor. I spent several days

sailing up this channel, and encountered extraordinary and exceedingly fierce twisting currents that crossed in various places like [the] courses of deep-water rivers. They churned the sea with much noise and with whirlpools, chop, and great swells that overcame the ships and pushed against the sail and oars sending us backwards. With all of these setbacks, Nature prevented my passage through this channel. I realized from this delay the likelihood of shipwreck, [which would] preclude any hope of returning to New Spain. For several days, I searched laboriously [for a way out] without much hope, until the eve of San Lorenzo, Patron of our [voyage of] discovery, when a favorable wind arose. We were swept away in the channels of the islands by a current that carried each ship separately, and my flagship ended up spinning around furiously and violently. Finally free of these great dangers, we regrouped the following day and resumed the survey of the coasts of New Spain and [Baja] California. (Porter y Casanate [1651] 1970b:889–90)

Porter may have managed to sail northward as far as Ángel de la Guarda Island (Portillo 1982:321). But he concluded that the passage through the Midriff was far too difficult and dangerous to be a practical route to the presumed sea that lay beyond, for he had been almost helplessly entrapped there:

unable to enter or exit through the channel which I tried [to sail through]. Within the channel, I believed many times that all was lost. I was unable to follow my heading, nor able to tack. I was in continual danger from the swift currents which sent me [running] first toward [Baja] California and then toward New Spain, [causing me to] drift from my course and separating one ship from the other.... If we had not had oars, it would have been impossible to bear away from the coasts and islands, or to make an exit from this new channel. For this reason it is called *Salsipuedes*. (Porter y Casanate [1651] 1970b:891)

Though of course Porter eventually managed to free himself, the dark humor of the term "Salsipuedes" (Get-Out-If-You-Can) so graphically expressed his experience, and those of other navigators who entered the Midriff region, that the name stuck. Over the next 150 years, the islands that created these turbulent waters—Tiburón, San Esteban, and San Lorenzo—were commonly referred to collectively by this cynical but appropriate name.

Porter's difficulties navigating his way through the Midriff apparently prevented him from going ashore on any of the islands there or making any significant contact with the Seris, for the native peoples he describes are exclusively peninsular Indians. He may have followed the 1649 trip with brief forays into the Gulf in 1650 and 1651, but by 1652 ill health forced him to turn his frigates over to the Crown and resign his post as Governor of Sinaloa. Three years later, with health restored, Porter departed for Chile, where he served with distinction until his death in 1662 (Mosk 1931:187–88; Mathes 1970:xlvii–xlviii; 1992a:251–52).

In the 30 years after Porter's voyages, several more licenses were granted to other pearlers, but none of them sailed as far as the Midriff. By this time pearling had become an established part of the commercial scene in New Spain.[96] Entrepreneurs setting out for the Gulf were no longer entering totally uncharted waters, and expeditions were now comparatively routine if still sometimes perilous undertakings.

In all likelihood, unauthorized pearlers played a much larger role than those with official sanction in acquiring a working knowledge of the Gulf and in their impact on native populations. These shadowy figures seem to have roamed the Gulf in considerable numbers from the mid-1500s onward, crossing over in small boats from the coasts of Sinaloa and Sonora. But because their activities were completely illegal, they were not inclined to leave a record of their experiences, and their presence is known largely from the many off-hand remarks of more reputable observers of the period (Venegas [1759] 1966a:195–96; Clavigero [1789] 1971:195; Bancroft 1884:170, 185, 195; Mosk 1934:50; Gerhard 1956:240, 242; Mathes 1966:13–14).

Whether these illicit pearl hunters acquired any greater familiarity than the licensed pearlers with the Midriff islands, particularly San Esteban, can only be a matter of speculation. But it is clear that the conventional wisdom by the late seventeenth century was that the best prospects for pearling were in the southern Gulf, far south of the Midriff.

Pirates in the Gulf

Throughout the seventeenth century, the Crown became increasingly convinced of the need to establish permanent settlements on Baja California and bring the virtues of Christianity to the natives. For many years, the government believed that pearl hunters might be the people to carry out these endeavors. While colonization and missionizing never became official conditions on which pearling licenses were granted, it became clear to entrepreneurs that those who promised, at their own expense, to combine these royal objectives with their own pearl hunting activities were more likely to be rewarded with a license. In effect the Crown, whose treasury was chronically depleted by foreign wars, tried to finance the colonization of the peninsula with a portion of the profits that a licensed pearl hunter might accrue. But the pearl hunters showed little concern for the King's interests once they entered the Gulf, and it is no wonder that little was accomplished toward either of the royal goals (Chapman 1939:168).

The government's concern with settling the peninsula evolved in part out of growing fears about its security from foreign interests and more immediately to provide protection from the threat of pirates. When Spain first carved out its New World empire, the Pacific coast of the Americas was so remote from Europe that for a time it remained firmly under Spanish control. Foreigners could not get there without either making the perilous voyage around the horn of South America or crossing the immense and little-known span of the Pacific.

Thus, for a while, fabulously wealthy cargoes could be shipped along the west coast between Peru and New Spain with little concern for piracy.

In 1564, the security of the west coast of New Spain acquired even greater importance. In that year, a fleet of four Spanish ships sailing from Acapulco succeeded in crossing the Pacific and taking possession of the Philippines, giving Spain direct access to the wealth of the East Indies. The return trip to Mexico the following year marked the first of some 250 nearly annual voyages of the famed riches-laden Manila galleons. The return voyage, however, was a grueling five-and-a-half month ordeal as the vessels rode the great northward arc of the Japan Current toward New Spain (Chapman 1939:84–96; Gerhard 1960:37–40). By the time they were swept southward and land was first sighted along the Baja California coast, some of the crew and passengers had inevitably died, and others were desperately ill with scurvy. It was essential to put in to land as soon as possible to heal the sick, resupply, and make repairs to the ships. Baja California thus acquired importance to the Crown not only for its supposed wealth in pearls, but also for its strategic value to the Philippine trade (Dunne 1968:28; Burrus 1984:47; Crosby 1994:5).

But with such riches flowing in and out of the west coast of the Americas, the halcyon days of secure shipping did not last long. In 1578, the English freebooter Francis Drake rounded the horn and sailed up the west coast of South America, plundering Spanish ships and towns as he went. With his vessel laden with treasure, Drake cruised northward and explored some of the Alta California coast before heading westward across the Pacific to England. Though he did not touch on the peninsula nor attack the Manila galleons, he had effectively opened the way for others. Thus in October 1587, Drake's countryman, Thomas Cavendish, rounded the horn and sailed to the southern tip of Baja California. After lying in wait for a month, Cavendish finally sighted the galleon *Santa Ana* off Cabo San Lucas. Unable to withstand cannon barrages, the overladen and poorly defended Spanish ship surrendered. Its crew was put ashore, the vessel burned, and Cavendish set sail for England with its fabulously rich cargo (Gerhard 1960:81–94; Mathes 1969). For the Spaniards, the era of safe shipping on the west coast had come to an abrupt end, and it was feared that Baja California would become as much a hideout for Spain's enemies as a potential haven for ailing galleons.

For the next two centuries, pirates and privateers periodically wreaked havoc along the Pacific coast, attacking Spanish shipping and coastal towns from South America to New Spain. Some of these were Dutch pirates, who became known as "Pichilingues," while others were English and French. In the wake of their attacks in the south, rumors frequently circulated that the freebooters were headed for Baja California intent on intercepting the Manila galleons. After the devastating and humiliating capture of the *Santa Ana*, the Spaniards took some measures to protect their vulnerable ships. Cannon and small arms were issued to the vessels, and the galleons were ordered to stay well out to sea to avoid being sighted by pirates lurking about the peninsula. This, however, would deprive the scurvy-ridden crews of the early landfall they so desperately needed. When rumors of impending pirate attacks were particularly rife, pearling ships or any other available vessels would be commandeered and sent out to warn the galleons and escort them to port (Gerhard 1963:2–3). And, of course, throughout the seventeenth century, the government favored pearlers who promised to establish colonies on the peninsula, under the assumption that a settled peninsula would be less attractive as a hideout for pirates.

Ironically, despite Spanish fears and persistent rumors, the galleons were rarely in peril. In their 250 years of service, fewer than half a dozen vessels were ever threatened, and apart from the *Santa Ana*, only one other galleon was ever captured off the coast of New Spain. Moreover, pirates were never more than sporadic visitors to the Gulf of California. For almost a century after Cavendish's success, not a single pirate is known to have actually entered the Gulf or touched on Baja California (Gerhard 1963:1–4). The basic reason for this is that, except for the galleons and occasional pearling vessels, there was nothing to raid. During that period, there were no European settlements on either shore of the peninsula nor on the Sonoran side of the Gulf, and without towns, there was no shipping. The galleons were a fabulous quarry, but intercepting them was a long shot at best. Even getting to the Gulf during the winter, when the galleons were due, was a tedious and uncertain ordeal of endless tacking against contrary winds. Thus for most pirates, the Gulf had little to offer compared to the rich towns and shipping along the coasts of New Spain and Peru.

The ill-founded reputation of the Gulf as a haven for pirates and privateers rests largely on the exploits of a very few groups in the late seventeenth and early eighteenth centuries. One of these was a motley collection of mostly French buccaneers. Some of them had come into the Pacific with Captain François Grogniet and deserted, striking out on their own late in 1686 in a "rotten little bark" and two sailing canoes (Gerhard 1963:4). After a few months and several raids along the coast of New Spain, this group joined forces with another band of pirates who had both a seaworthy ship and an anonymous journalist who kept a record of their exploits. Over the next few years, they plundered and murdered their way through New Spain and South America, wreaking havoc and terror. Although they made the Tres Marías Islands their principal port of refuge, they also made use of Baja California (Gerhard 1958; 1963:4–7).

In the summer of 1688, this band of pirates discovered a wonderfully protected and well-watered cove inside Bahía La Paz. Here they spent two months repairing their ship, fishing, and hunting turtles. On September 11, they set out on an exploring venture to the north. They crossed the Gulf to the mainland side and began working their way up the coast. Though they found the country empty and bleak, they continued on to about 28°, where the Gulf seemed to narrow to a channel only a league in width. Probably they had entered the Canal del Infiernillo, which separates Tiburón Island from the Sonoran mainland. Here they turned back and began the arduous trip southward. After several weeks of tacking against the strong southerly winds of late summer, they finally dropped anchor in Bahía La Paz on October 20. They spent almost another two months recuperating there, and on December 10 set sail southward for another season of pillaging along the coast of New Spain (Gerhard 1963:5–6).

Two years later, on August 12, 1690, the same pirates returned to their hide-out in Bahía La Paz to careen their ship and sit out the hurricane season, stay-ing until November 7. In January 1691, they made a final trip back to the peninsula, this time putting in at Cabo San Lucas. After a week there taking on water, they departed for good and made their way to South America (Gerhard 1963:7). The legacy of this ruthless band of pirates is the name of the snug cove where they had spent so much time. Though they were not Dutch, their cove has been known ever since as Bahía Pichilingue.

In November of 1709, the most famous privateer of the period, Woodes Rogers, arrived at the southern tip of Baja California intent on capturing a Manila galleon. On New Years Day 1710, the galleon *El Encarnación* appeared off Cabo San Lucas. After an all night chase and a battle of several hours, Rogers finally succeeded in capturing the vessel and its prize cargo. A second galleon was sighted a few days later and was also attacked, but this time the English sustained heavy damage and were driven off. Nevertheless, Rogers sailed from Baja California with a treasure valued at two million pesos (Rogers 1712; Gerhard 1960:214).

Cabo San Lucas was again visited in 1721 by George Shelvocke, a privateer-turned-pirate. Shelvocke was on his way back to England after a raiding spree along the coast to the south and had come to the peninsula to take on water and wood before setting out into the Pacific. He stayed only a few days (Shelvocke [1726] 1928:216–20).

The French buccaneers who explored from Bahía Pichilingue northward to Tiburón Island are the only pirates known to have sailed up the Gulf beyond the southern tip of Baja California. The main value of the region, for the few pirates who went there, lay in its remoteness. With no towns and little sea traffic, the Gulf was a place they could go to find a safe harbor, careen their vessel, make repairs, and take on wood and water without interference from outsiders. Af-ter 1697, however, this began to change as the Jesuits arrived on the peninsula and gradually established a chain of mission settlements. The earliest missions were too far north to have much effect on pirates. But as the numbers of people, including soldiers, slowly began to increase, the peninsula became less attrac-tive as a hideout. When settlements were finally established at La Paz in 1720 and San José del Cabo in 1730, pirates lost their two most useful haunts (Gerhard 1963:8–10). Though there were a few ominous appearances of foreign vessels in later years, by 1730 the threat of pirate attacks on the galleons was, for all practical purposes, over.

Pirates or not, Baja California was still crucial as a landfall for the galleons and their suffering crews who needed a protected harbor on the west coast with water, fresh food, and a settlement. The Jesuits, who began arriving on the peninsula in 1697, were well aware of this, and on orders from the Crown, expended a great deal of effort over the next 70 years exploring in vain for a suitable port. The mission of San José del Cabo became the only settlement close to the Pacific coast that could serve in this capacity, and a galleon grate-fully put in there in January of 1734. The following October, however, the

Indians revolted and killed the resident missionary. Thus by a terrible twist of fate, when the crew of the 1735 galleon landed at San José expecting aid, they were instead ambushed by hostile natives who killed 13 of the Spaniards (Venegas [1759] 1966b:123–54; Clavigero [1789] 1971:285–87, 300–301; Dunne 1968:276–77; Crosby 1994:116–17).

Though San José del Cabo later became a regular stop, it was not the ideal port because it was so far south of the first landfall on the peninsula. With crew and passengers dying on board, a more northerly port was badly needed. As late as 1766, fewer than two years before the Jesuits were expelled from New Spain, Father Wenceslaus Linck, responding to royal orders, spent two fruitless months exploring the northern peninsula for a port where galleon crews could recover from their ordeals (Burrus 1967:65–66).

THREE

Spreading the Word:
Jesuit Missions and Exploration of the Upper Gulf

By the late 1670s, it had become clear that the practice of granting pearl fishing monopolies to entrepreneurs who promised to colonize the peninsula and convert the natives had not worked. In most cases, the expeditions had devoted most of their efforts to finding pearls and little to settling the land (Chapman 1939:168). In 1679, royal approval was granted for still another pearl fishing expedition, but this time the accompanying colonization and missionary effort was to be a well-planned and carefully prepared undertaking that would be financed by the royal treasury. Although the actual results were no more successful than earlier expeditions, this was a pivotal venture because it set the stage for the first successful settlement of the peninsula a decade later. The recipient of the license was Don Isidro Atondo y Antillón, the Governor of Sinaloa and an experienced navigator and soldier. The task of ministering to the natives was assigned to the Jesuit Order, and the three missionaries who accompanied the expedition were Fathers Matías Goñi, Juan Bautista Copart and, most importantly, Eusebio Francisco Kino. Kino was only the first in the long succession of literate, highly educated, and prolific Jesuit missionaries who kept detailed records of their activities on and around the peninsula. And many of their reports describe the Gulf, for throughout the Jesuit period the only way to or from Baja California was by sea.

On January 17, 1683, after three years of preparation, Atondo and his fleet of three vessels set sail with the three missionaries, about 100 carefully selected soldiers and colonists, and supplies. Contrary winds kept the expedition at sea for several weeks, but the vessels finally anchored in Bahía La Paz on April 1, and construction of a settlement began. However, the infant colony did not last long. By early July, food was almost exhausted, and the expedition's supply ship, battered by storms, had been unable to cross the Gulf with fresh stores. Then in a rash move, Atondo had three Indians executed in retaliation for minor pilfering. Short of food and fearing a massive reprisal for these murders, the Europeans abandoned the settlement on July 14.

The expedition regrouped on the mainland and set out again on September 29. After a stormy crossing, the colonists landed on October 6 at a new site north of La Paz, where they again began to build a settlement. The new colony was given the name of San Bruno.

For a while, life in the colony went smoothly. However, the settlers increasingly realized their lack of self-sufficiency. After 18 months, they had seen only one light rain. Drinking water was scarce, crops were failing, and food supplies were dwindling. The supply ship, on which they were completely dependent, was frequently beaten back to the mainland for weeks at a time by storms and adverse winds as it tried to cross the Gulf. By May of 1685, scurvy had broken out, and on mustering the soldiers, Atondo found only 15 men well enough to respond (Bolton 1936:199). The handwriting was on the wall. A conference was held, and despite Kino's ever-optimistic protests, it was decided once again to abandon the peninsula (Bolton 1936:87–202; Dunne 1968:26–37; Hammond 1967:11–13).

On May 8, 1685, the colony split up. Atondo and Father Goñi headed south to fish for pearls while Kino and the seasoned captain of the supply ship, Blas de Guzmán, ferried the sick to the Yaqui missions on the Sonoran mainland. Once this mercy mission had been accomplished, Kino and Guzmán set out to explore the Gulf northward in search of better sites for settlement. As it turned out, this trip would acquaint Kino with the Seris and give Guzmán a brief view of San Esteban Island.

Guzmán and Kino sailed from the Río Yaqui on June 13, 1685, quickly crossing to Baja California near the Tres Vírgenes volcanoes (north of present Mulegé). For six days, they tacked up the coast against the wind, making only slow headway. The country as they neared the Midriff was not promising, so rather than try to pass northward through the notorious channels between the three Salsipuedes islands (which Guzmán termed "Los Dragones" [Guzmán 1685]), they turned eastward and crossed over to the Sonora coast. On June 19, they anchored in a bay they named "San Juan Bautista," known today as Bahía Kino.

Thinking, as did Ulloa and Alarcón, that Tiburón Island was a peninsula and that passage northward would have to run through the channel on its southwestern side, Guzmán left Father Kino with the ship, and taking 10 sailors, set out in the ship's launch to reconnoiter. From Bahía Kino, they took the launch some 12 miles west to the southern tip of Tiburón Island, where they made camp for the night. The next day, they continued up the southwest coast of the island another five miles. Here they landed at a beach where they must have seen either Seri watercraft or pools of water, for they named it "Playa de Balsas." Guzmán climbed a high hill and surveyed the strait between Tiburón and San Esteban Island, concluding that it was not safe for his ship. This decision effectively ended any thoughts of further exploration to the north, and the next day Guzmán's party returned to the ship.

For the next 45 days, the expedition was stranded in Bahía Kino. Southwesterly winds had sprung up and blew with such force that the ship dragged anchor despite its protected location. But there were camps of Seris on the shores of the bay, and Kino devoted his time to establishing rapport with them. Though the Indians entreated him to stay, on August 9 the winds shifted, and the Europeans set sail for the Yaqui villages, arriving three days later (Bolton 1936:202–5).

The Atondo expedition had not met with success. The missionaries had done well, but the colony had folded from starvation and sickness, Atondo's pearling sojourn had produced little of value, and the royal treasury was out more than 200,000 pesos (Bolton 1936:213; Dunne 1968:39; Burrus 1971:32). Within a year, English pirates were again seen off the coast of New Spain, and for a while, it appeared that the Crown would sponsor another colonizing attempt in an effort to secure the peninsula. But official interest waned as events elsewhere drained the royal treasury, and the government unequivocally withdrew its support for the reoccupation of the peninsula.

In 1687, with government plans for the peninsula in limbo, Kino was transferred to the frontier of the Pimería Alta in Sonora. But the experience at San Bruno had inspired him deeply, and he believed that the vision of a Christianized peninsula must not be abandoned. Where government sponsored colonies had failed, might not Jesuit administered missions succeed? True to character, Kino began to envision a Spartan missionary effort, unencumbered by civil concerns, led by a dedicated band of Jesuit fathers, and supplied from the Jesuit missions in Sonora with smaller, less costly boats (Bolton 1936:215–17, 223–26; Burrus 1984:20).

The man who took up the cause and saw it through to fruition was Father Juan María de Salvatierra. In December of 1690, Salvatierra paid an official visit to Kino to evaluate the mission situation in the Pimería Alta. The two men proved to be kindred spirits. During the next month as they rode together through the region, they talked extensively of the prospects of Baja California. By the time he departed, Salvatierra shared completely Kino's unswerving idealism for a revitalized mission program on the peninsula (Venegas [1754] 1929:134–36; Bolton 1936:263–66; Dunne 1968:38–39; Burrus 1971:27–28; Crosby 1994:10–14).

Over the next several years Salvatierra, with Kino's support, worked incessantly toward obtaining authorization to renew missionary work in Baja California. With the government unwilling to invest in any more peninsular expeditions, Salvatierra turned to private contributions to underwrite the entire venture. The "Pious Fund for the Californias" was created with Father Juan de Ugarte as its treasurer, and the two padres began soliciting donations from wealthy benefactors. Perseverance paid off, and authorization to begin missionary work was finally granted by the Viceroy in early February 1697. The agreement gave the Jesuits unprecedented freedom in administering the missions, and for all practical purposes, the peninsula itself. There was no provision for settlement apart from the missions themselves, which would exclude meddlesome civil authorities and colonists who seemed to thrive on abusing the Indians. The missionaries were empowered to select and dismiss the military officers and soldiers who would safeguard the missions, and to place strict controls on their activities. In particular, this would enable the Jesuits to prohibit mission personnel from engaging in pearl fishing, which would minimize further exploitation and alienation of the natives. But, the authorization reiterated, under no circumstances would the Crown assume any financial obligation for the venture (Dunne 1968:41, 320; Burrus 1971:31–32; 1984:22–26, 56–59; Weber 1992:241; Crosby 1994:15–20).

Salvatierra began preparations immediately and with nine men set sail from the mouth of the Río Yaqui on October 11. To his great consternation, Kino, who had intended from the first to accompany him, was suddenly detained by troubles in the Pimería and, as it turned out, never again set foot on the peninsula. Salvatierra's party crossed the Gulf, and on October 19, 1697, after trying several sites, landed at a well-watered place they named Nuestra Señora de Loreto Conchó. On November 23, a second missionary, Francisco María Piccolo, arrived. The permanent European occupation of Baja California had begun (Dunne 1968:43–47; Crosby 1994:3, 22–26).

Life at the Loreto mission was no easier or any less precarious than it had been for previous settlers. Within a year, the little band had weathered two serious Indian attacks and had faced such a food shortage that they were reduced to eating their livestock feed (Burrus 1971:34–36). However, a settlement had been built, and the two fathers soon began the first of many exploratory expeditions. In 1699, they founded a second mission, San Francisco Javier de Biaundó, and on March 19, 1701, they were joined by Juan de Ugarte, who had surrendered his role as treasurer of the Pious Fund for what was to become a distinguished career in the field. When later that year, the new king, Felipe V, was persuaded to authorize a modest contribution to the financial support of the now destitute Baja California enterprise, there was reason for guarded optimism that the missions would survive (Clavigero [1789] 1971:191; Dunne 1968:80, 103; Burrus 1984:48, 57).

And the Baja California enterprise did survive. Over the next 65 years, the Jesuits established a network of 18 missions spanning most of the length of the peninsula. But the success of this shoestring venture came only in the face of enormous difficulties and many disasters. Probably the weakest link in the entire operation, especially in its early years, was the utter dependence on provisions from the mainland, for the peninsula was found to be largely unfarmable (Crosby 1994:150–54, 211–12). When Loreto was founded, Salvatierra had only three small boats with which to ferry supplies, leaving the colony vulnerable to the changeable and often treacherous conditions of the Gulf. As the settlers quickly learned, a crossing that took only a day under favorable conditions could be delayed weeks or even months when conditions soured. Contrary winds which sometimes blew for weeks on end could prevent a boat from even leaving port, while ships caught by violent storms could be blown uncontrollably from one side of the Gulf to the other. Most of the Jesuit vessels were poorly constructed, frail, and often dilapidated from continual service. During Salvatierra's time, the Jesuits lost to shipwreck about one vessel a year (Clavigero [1789] 1971:170, 195, 219, 225, 232; Chapman 1939:178; Crosby 1994:77, 145–48).

If a supply ship failed to arrive, starvation was a very real specter. Because of this insecurity, in 1701 Salvatierra joined Kino in Sonora to reconnoiter the head of the Gulf to try to determine if a land route could be found from Sonora that could supply the peninsular missions more reliably (Venegas [1754] 1929:42–43, 194–95; Bolton 1936:450–62; Dunne 1968:83–93). Although this landmark exploration produced high hopes, a feasible passage was never developed. For the remainder of the Jesuit tenure on the peninsula, the only route for supplies and communication was across the turbulent Gulf.

It was the shipwreck of one of the mission supply vessels that led to the next Jesuit exploration of the Midriff islands. In August 1709, one of the original and most reliable vessels, the *San Javier*, left Loreto with 3,000 *scudi* on a routine supply run to the Yaqui missions to purchase provisions. As the vessel was crossing the Gulf, it was caught in a violent summer storm. By the time the storm subsided three days later, the *San Javier* had been blown far up the Sonoran coast into Seri country. It had finally run aground on a shoal some 40 miles north of Guaymas, in the vicinity of Estero Tastiota. Though several of its crew drowned, others managed to escape to shore. The survivors buried the money on the beach for safekeeping and made their way southward in a canoe to the Yaqui villages. From here, a pearling vessel was dispatched to relay news of the disaster to Salvatierra at Loreto.

Salvatierra decided to personally take charge of the salvage operation. On October 6, he departed from Loreto in the only ship available, a dilapidated bark named *El Rosario*, arriving at Guaymas two days later. While the *Rosario* ferried a small company of carpenters up the coast to the stranded *San Javier*, Salvatierra resolved to make the trip overland in the hope of pacifying and converting Seris along the way. The journey proved to be a terrible ordeal for lack of water, and Salvatierra arrived at the *San Javier* only to find the repair crew out of food and starving. Fortunately, the few stores Salvatierra had brought with him helped alleviate the immediate food shortage.

Rebuilding the *San Javier* proved to be a major undertaking. After the vessel had been abandoned, it had been discovered by Seris who ransacked it and partly dismantled its hull to obtain its metal nails. During the two months it took to make the vessel seaworthy, the repair crew periodically suffered more food shortages, for even though provisions were sent in, it had been a bad year throughout the region. For Salvatierra, the time needed to refit the boat provided an unexpected opportunity to work among the nearby Seris. Though they were initially hostile, he visited their rancherías, and like his old friend Kino many years before, gradually won their friendship and trust. He brought together factions that had been traditional enemies and succeeded in establishing peaceful relations. Many Seris were baptized, and they asked that a missionary be sent to them (Venegas [1759] 1966a:404–9; Clavigero [1789] 1971:216–18; Burrus 1971:54–59).

By the time the *San Javier* was ready for service, Salvatierra was convinced that the Seris were ready to become receptive and willing converts. To follow through would require establishing a mission for them on their own coast. But the Jesuits were short handed and ill-funded, and Salvatierra himself was needed in Loreto. Nevertheless, the distance from the peninsula to the Seri coast was not very great, for the peninsula was plainly visible from the Sonoran side. Moreover, Salvatierra could see the three Salsipuedes islands spanning the Gulf between the two shores. Might not Baja California serve as a base from which to carry out the conversion of the Seris, with the stepping-stone position of the islands facilitating the crossing (Venegas [1754] 1929:211–12; 1966a:411; Burrus 1971:59)?

On December 7, with both the *San Javier* and the *Rosario* in Bahía Kino, Salvatierra prepared to depart for Loreto, but by way of the islands so that he could reconnoiter this potential route:

> I took leave of them [the Seris], and on the night of the Vigil of the Immaculate Conception, we left port with a light land breeze. At daybreak, we arrived at the first large island [Tiburón], two or three leagues [5 to 8 miles] out from the mainland, and in places less. But the wind blew to the southeast over the island such that we were not able to regain our wind for Loreto Conchó until the afternoon.... We named the first island, which we called Santa María, and sailed to the mouth of the strait which lies between the first island of Santa María and the next one which follows it. [Illegible] of all the seafaring people do not consider [the width of] the strait between the [first] island and [second] island [to be] more than three and a half leagues [9 miles]. We headed west across this strait and then, with a very gentle wind and calm sea, ran for the second island [San Esteban], more in the middle [of the Gulf]. [It is a] high and very mountainous island, without foothills, a few leagues in extent. There are signs of metal-bearing earth and indications of anchorages on the island. Although the Retis [Seris] Indians had denied to us that this second island lacks water, still, because of the rough and steep hills, we are doubtful of the truth [of this]. We named this second island El Niño Perdido, or El Salvador. We departed from it [and] worked [our way] close to the strait between the second island and the third. [The strait] is only two leagues [5 miles] wide, and very shortly we reached the third island [San Lorenzo], which we called San Joseph. This third island [illegible] close to the mainland of [Baja] California. (Salvatierra 1710:402)

From there, the expedition sailed down the coast of the peninsula toward the missions. Despite their evil reputation, Salvatierra's voyage among the Salsipuedes islands had gone smoothly. From this benign experience, he concluded that the passage would be navigable by small boats and even canoes and that these islands would provide a feasible link between the peninsular missions and the Seri coast.

Salvatierra's remarks about his route show that he sailed toward the southeastern corner of San Esteban and then skirted the island along its south coast. This is consistent with his description of the island, because from that perspective it would indeed appear to be quite long, and as he sailed past the south coast, he would have been presented with a vista of some of the island's highest peaks rising directly out of the sea. It is understandable that he would have misinter-preted the vivid colors of the volcanic rocks and ash fall deposits as indicators of metallic ore, and with such tranquil seas, he could not have known that the seemingly fine anchorage of the southwestern shingle spit provides only mar-ginal protection when the weather turns. But his convoluted remark indicating that the Seris knew of water on San Esteban establishes the earliest known documentary evidence that Seris were at least familiar with the island. Whether they also told him of people living there is not known, but if so, he probably dismissed it. If he did not believe that the island had water, he certainly could not have believed that people lived there. Had he thought otherwise, a man with Salvatierra's zeal for saving souls would surely have made a banner note of it.

Despite Salvatierra's placid voyage past the three islands, nothing ever came of this proposed route to link the two coasts, and the next missionary to visit the Salsipuedes islands had a very different experience. This man was Father Juan de Ugarte.

After the founding of Loreto in 1697, the mission chain had gradually ex-panded outward. Twenty years later, four more missions had been founded, though none more than about 100 miles from Loreto. By this time, Jesuit ship-ping had made the peninsular coast south of Loreto relatively familiar, but little was known of the northern Gulf. Pearlers, both licensed and unlicensed, had probably scrutinized the region for more than a century, but their observations were not a matter of public record. Indeed, despite the explorations of Ulloa, Alarcón, and Kino, there remained widespread conviction and hope that Baja California was an island. For the government, this was not merely an academic issue, for a strait connecting the Pacific with the Gulf would enable the Manila galleons to sail directly into the Gulf soon after their first landfall, giving their sick and exhausted crews sheltered harbors and protection from pirates. For two decades, the Jesuits had resisted even this slight potential civil intrusion into their exclusive domain. But by 1719, under heavy Viceregal pressure, the mis-sionaries intensified their explorations for a potential port. Though their effort was largely directed southward and toward the Pacific coast, Ugarte was deter-mined to head north up the Gulf to find out if Baja California really was an island (Dunne 1968:156–57; Crosby 1994:89–95; 100–101).

Salvatierra himself had always wanted to explore northward, but lack of per-sonnel and adequate ships had kept such a project beyond reach (Venegas [1759] 1966a:447; 1966b:25). Ugarte, an explorer of the same caliber as Kino and Salvatierra, enthusiastically took up the challenge. But this time, it would be done properly, starting with a ship that was equal to the task. As Hubert Howe Bancroft put it:

> to make these perilous voyages a good staunch ship was indispensable, such
> a one as the missions had never had, and were not likely to have if they went
> on buying and begging worn-out rotten old hulks only fit to drown Jesuits in.
> So thought Padre Juan, and with characteristic energy he determined to have
> a ship built in [Baja] California under his own eyes and according to his own

ideas. He hired some shipwrights from the other side [of the Gulf], where he intended at first to get also his timber; but he heard of some large trees some thirty leagues above Mulegé, and went thither in September 1718. He found the trees, but in such inaccessible ravines that the builder declared it impossible to use them. But Ugarte, disregarding this opinion ... returned to the timber country with three mechanics and all the Indians he could induce to follow him. Even the gentiles of the mountains afforded some aid; and after four months of hard work he had not only felled and prepared the timber, but had opened a road for thirty leagues over the sierra, and with oxen and mules had hauled his material to the coast at Mulegé. The 16th of July the craft was blessed and christened the *Triunfo de la Cruz*, and the 14th of September she was launched amidst great rejoicings. (Bancroft 1884:439)

The actual construction of the *Triunfo de la Cruz* and a smaller sister ship, a 30-foot deckless sloop christened the *Santa Bárbara*, had been supervised by a master English shipwright named William (or Guillermo) Stratford (also rendered Strafford and Estrafort). By the following spring, Ugarte was ready to set sail with his two new vessels and a canoe, along with the versatile and accomplished Stratford, who would now be serving as pilot. Though it would prove to be as harrowing a voyage as any that preceded it (Venegas [1759] 1966b:46–65; Clavigero [1789] 1971:246–54; Dunne 1968:208–16), the expedition began smoothly enough:

We then left Loreto on May 15 [1721]. Passing by Mulegé, we dropped anchor without going ashore, [and] Rector Sebastián de Sistiaga came on board. [After] saying good-by to His Reverence we set sail, hoping to cross over to the other shore to the port of the Seris [Bahía Kino], which we reached after five days of sailing.... There appeared on the beaches an Indian with a cross, who withdrew after planting it in the sand. We landed there, seized the cross, [and] called to the Indian with signs of friendship. He gave a shout [which] made all the Indians who had been hiding come out. (Ugarte [1722] 1958:21)

Twelve years earlier, Salvatierra had told the Seris at Bahía Kino that Europeans who so honored the cross were men of peace, and his message was alive and well. Once it was clear that these visitors were missionaries and not pearlers or soldiers, they were received enthusiastically. The Seris resupplied the ships with drinking water and requested that Ugarte visit their kinsmen at Tecomate on Tiburón Island. Ugarte agreed, and the following day the tiny fleet set sail into the treacherous Canal del Infiernillo, accompanied by a Seri who would help guide them with hand signals through the channel's shoals. Meanwhile, Stratford went ahead in the canoe to take soundings, tediously waving a flag to signal the ships whether to sail on or drop anchor to avoid running aground. The next morning Stratford set out ahead on a day trip in the canoe to investigate the north end of the channel. Soon afterwards, the *Triunfo de la Cruz* sailed past the last of Stratford's soundings and immediately ran aground. Ugarte concluded that:

had the ship not been new and very strong, the wind blowing past the stern would have destroyed us there. [We] threw out an anchor from the stern, hauling it [the ship backwards] by the rope. At the same time, we pushed against the sand bank with six large oars which we carried for emergencies, and with great effort refloated the ship.... At this time, the little sloop [*Santa Bárbara*] arrived. Because it required little depth, it passed easily over the shallows, [and] the command was given to go on ahead to reconnoiter. By four in the afternoon the canoe had not returned, and we had also lost sight of the little sloop. I feared that something bad had happened to the canoe, such as being capsized by the currents or falling into the hands of the Indians, whom they say were cruel. A sailor was posted at the masthead, and seeing that the water had a bluish cast which indicated where it was deep, we decided to set sail. The sailor remained at the masthead so that he could continually warn another [sailor] with the sounding lead, by which we maintained about two fathoms, and on one occasion we passed over a fathom and a half. The Indian who came with us saw that we sometimes headed toward the mainland, as the meandering channel [seemed to] require, [and] he strenuously signaled us to tack [instead] toward the island. With this effort and care, we reached [a spot] where the Indian told us by signs that the bottom had run out of shoals, that the sea was deep, and [that we had arrived at] the mouth of the channel. (Ugarte [1722] 1958:23–24)

Here they found the canoe and the *Santa Bárbara* unscathed, and the vessels anchored for the night. The next morning, the tiny fleet sailed along the north end of Tiburón Island to Bahía Agua Dulce (see Figure 2.1). After three anxious days, the expedition had completed the first known European traverse of the Canal del Infiernillo.

As the expedition approached the bay, the Seris who first saw them coming put on an immediate display of armed hostility. Some of these people were refugees from the Sonoran mission of Nuestra Señora del Pópulo, where they had suffered severe mistreatment by Spanish soldiers. However, the Indians who had greeted Ugarte at Bahía Kino interceded, assuring their kinsmen that these Europeans were missionaries, not soldiers, and the initial hostility gave way to a friendly reception. The Indians guided the Europeans into Bahía Agua Dulce, where they found safe anchorage, good water, and the Seri camp of Tecomate. Ugarte, who was still on board ship, had developed a severe case of rheumatism and was now in such pain that he could hardly stand, sit, or even lie down. But the Seris clamored for him to come ashore, and he was received there by the Indians with great reverence. Ugarte in turn blessed each of them and in the next few days baptized 40 Seri children. As Dunne remarks (1968:210), this was the first and likely the last time a sacrament was ever administered on Tiburón Island.

As the Europeans headed northwestward, the smooth sailing that had favored them as far as Tecomate deteriorated, and they soon began to face one crisis after another. As they worked their way up the Sonoran coast, a shore party from the *Santa Bárbara* nearly died of thirst when their boat, badly damaged by outrushing tides, left them stranded on shore. Rough seas began to plague the expedition and inflict damage on all the vessels. Yet despite mounting problems, the expedition succeeded in reaching the mouth of the Colorado River. Because the weather was deteriorating, the anchorage poor, and the vessels already battered, they did not try to ascend the river. But Ugarte and Stratford were able to amass a great deal of evidence to indicate that there was no strait leading to a sea beyond. On July 16, they weighed anchor and headed down the peninsular side of the Gulf (Venegas [1759] 1966b:51–62; Dunne 1968:210–14).

The voyage south began poorly and quickly worsened. Another shore party from the *Santa Bárbara* returned to their vessel only to discover that sudden tides had broken it in half. Their makeshift repairs barely got them back to the *Triunfo de la Cruz*, which by now had suffered considerable damage. Food and water shortages had become chronic for everyone, and scurvy began to break out. And Ugarte's rheumatism still left him barely able to move.

With the weather turning ominous, Ugarte suggested that the crew of the vulnerable *Santa Bárbara* abandon ship and come aboard the *Triunfo de la Cruz*. But the captain believed that they could reach Loreto if they hugged the relatively safe peninsular coast, though this later forced the expedition to split up. As Ugarte and Stratford approached the Midriff region, they began:

> to encounter small islands that are not depicted on any of the ancient or modern maps. We put in to the mouth of a port [Bahía San Luis Gonzaga] which, as the pilot said, "the King could not have a better one in all his realm." The little sloop entered and investigated it. Thus protected from all the winds, we pressed onward, and when we arrived at the island of Santa Inez [Ángel de la Guarda], the little sloop entered [the strait] between the mainland of [Baja] California and the island. This [island] forms a channel [Canal del las Ballenas], along with many other islands that follow [Partida, Rasa, Salsipuedes, and San Lorenzo] … which continue on to the outlet of [the] Salsipuedes [region]…. We cast off from shore [and headed] away from these islands. Finding ourselves in front of an island [San Esteban] which is west of the island of Tiburón, we tried to make the port [Tecomate] that we had examined [previously] on that island in order to clean the ship of goose-barnacles, which, aside from the currents and contrary winds, greatly impeded our exit [from the Salsipuedes region] against the wind [i.e., to the southeast]. (Ugarte [1722] 1958:44–45)

Ugarte admitted that they had no alternative but to land, for the crew was in worse condition than the ship. By now most had been stricken with scurvy, and only five sailors were healthy enough to man the ship. Ugarte himself had developed such a severe upper-body rash that his clothes stuck to his skin and removing them drew blood. As they neared Tecomate:

> the Indians did not appear because they were under the bushes, hidden, and armed, until one of their lookouts discovered that the priest was in the canoe.

Crying "Padre, Padre," they all came out, and without waiting for the canoe to arrive on shore, they entered the water to greet the priest. Joyfully we went ashore. The Indians began to bring some pitahaya fruits, and after that refreshment and a fresh water bath, we began to revive. (Ugarte [1722] 1958:45)

The Seris brought the exhausted men firewood, drinking water, and fresh food, including some delicious little clams for the starving Ugarte, who had been unable to stomach their own rations of salted and dried meat. As some measure of health returned, the sailors set about cleaning and caulking the ship, and the expedition again prepared to leave Tecomate. Their intent was to tack southward down the west side of Tiburón and exit the Salsipuedes region through the channel between the southwest coast of Tiburón and San Esteban Island. But their experience turned out more like Porter y Casanate's ordeal some 70 years earlier:

[Having] finished cleaning the ship, we got ready to leave. Casting off into the first mouth [channel] of Salsipuedes, which is between the island [of Tiburón] and another island [San Esteban] of the three that form the entrance [to the Salsipuedes region], we had almost managed to round the [southwestern tip of the] island of Tiburón by dint of turning windward, when such powerful currents carried us away that in six hours we lost [all] the progress we had gained in eight days. These are not currents like one sees elsewhere in the Gulf, where one scarcely notices a choppiness or a little noise like that produced by a school of fish. These currents create foaming breakers and the noise is like a river that runs through a boulder field. They are not single flows, but are like half circles that collide with each other, [and] because there are many different islands, the currents come from many different places. The first time we passed through the current it had a strange effect on those on board; after several of these encounters our fear diminished. [Nevertheless], we strove to regain [the progress] that we had lost.

After prayers, a squall gathered in the east which greatly alarmed us. After furling the mainsail and taking in two reefs, we were waiting to meet the weather when everyone on board saw, above the cross painted on the pennant, a very bright light that afterwards, in the darkness of the squall, we saw more clearly without confusing it with flashes of lightning. The squall made the magnetic needle spin [and] the seas met the sky. Though it lasted four hours, on the ship we hardly felt any strong motion, like [being] in a castle. At daybreak, when the light was on the vane, we found ourselves almost in the same place [where we had been the previous night], despite where the ship had drifted. We would have been lost in the darkness of night and the violent weather had not the ship been surrounded by islands at a distance of one, two, and three leagues. (Ugarte [1722] 1958:46–47)

A storm hit them again the following night, and for three days and nights, the *Triunfo de la Cruz* was swept around the Salsipuedes islands, unable to break out of the currents. The crew took heart from the reappearance each night of the

St. Elmo's Fire over the cross painted on the pennant, which they considered a sign of divine protection. For these three days, the ship had been manned around the clock by the five least ill crew members, and now they too were falling sick from exhaustion and lack of sleep. By this time, the vessel had been trapped among the Midriff islands for more than three weeks, and Ugarte realized that they again urgently needed to put in to land. After consulting with Stratford, the explorers steered once again for Tecomate, dropping anchor in its protected harbor just before they were hit by another furious storm.

Ugarte was so gravely ill that he considered crossing to the mainland by canoe and trying to make his way overland to Guaymas, but he was talked out of it. Finally, after about four days holed up at Tecomate:

> the following [day] dawned calm [and] we rowed out from port to put ourselves in open water. About ten in the morning (sixteenth of August, Saturday), a fresh breeze came along. In fourteen hours, it had carried us past the third mouth of Salsipuedes [the channel between San Lorenzo Island and the peninsula], which follows the coast of [Baja] California, [thereby] achieving in these few hours what we had not been able to attain in [the past] twenty-four days. Everyone felt great joy at seeing us outside [the Salsipuedes region], and because of the following incident: Since it was morning and there were heat clouds over the coast of [Baja] California, as the sun came out three rainbows formed over this island [San Lorenzo] and the mainland [i.e., the peninsula]. These were the triumphs with which [Baja] California received the *Triunfo de la Cruz*, and that is why this island was named *La Isla de Triunfo*. (Ugarte [1722] 1958:48)

They had finally escaped from the Salsipuedes islands, but the adventure was not yet over. On the morning of August 29 or 30, as they were nearing Mulegé:

> a storm had developed in the north and northeast that showed such malice that we decided to furl the sails and take two reefs in the mainsail. As the storm approached, it was so overcast that even before noon it seemed as if it were time for evening prayers. But what caused [us] the most terror was a waterspout, which was no more than half a league away. During this entire voyage, I had never had such a terrifying day nor did we hold out much earthly hope, for as I have said, two masts were worn out. [It was a] good occasion to take heart in God to lift our spirits and ask Him [for deliverance].... [We] crossed [through] the entire storm to [the] mainland of [Baja] California, only a little water falling on us and sending us only a little fresh breeze. At four-thirty in the afternoon, we were inside the bay [Bahía del la Concepción, near the mission of Mulegé]. (Ugarte [1722] 1958:49)

After two weeks recuperating at Mulegé, the crew of the *Triunfo de la Cruz* set out on the short sail to Loreto. They arrived on September 15, just a few days after their sister ship the *Santa Bárbara*, and four months after their departure (Venegas [1759] 1966b:62–65; Dunne 1968:216).

And so ended one of the most remarkable voyages in the history of the Gulf. Although the expedition had spent a total of about a month among the Midriff islands, the only real landing Ugarte and his men made was at the Seri camp of Tecomate on Tiburón Island. They did not go ashore on San Lorenzo or San Esteban, nor did they see any signs of people on either island. Writing 25 years later, all that Stratford recalled of the three Salsipuedes islands was that:

> there are pearl shells on the beaches of this island [San Lorenzo], but it was not investigated. This island is named San Miguel. Its length is eight leagues [21 miles] and [it is] two [five miles] in width. To the east of this island, there is another named Salsipuedes [San Esteban] at a distance of eight leagues [21 miles]. It is square, mountainous, and is about seven leagues [18 miles] in circumference. It appears to have pearl shells on its beaches, but it was not examined on account of the aridity of the island and lack of water. There are many currents, and crossing the California strait from it [San Esteban] east to west [actually, west to east], at a distance of six leagues [16 miles], is the island of Tiburón, inhabited by gentile Indians and apostates of the Seri nation. [This island is] named, it might be mentioned, for [the] sharks that are in these regions. (Stratford [1746] 1958:59)

Ugarte and Stratford had been convinced that there was no strait at the head of the Gulf, and Ugarte relayed the evidence for their views to the Viceroy in his report of the voyage. Nonetheless, their observations did little to settle the question, and many serious academics, including Jesuit scholars Miguel Venegas and Andrés Burriel, continued to argue that Baja California was an island (Dunne 1968:207, 216). But the expedition had accomplished another objective that was not controversial. It had established that there were good harbors, water, and friendly Indians along the peninsular coast in the northern Gulf (in contrast with the sterile mainland side). This showed that the mission chain could be extended northward and, despite Ugarte's experiences, that it was feasible to supply these prospective missions up the Gulf by ship (Dunne 1968:217–18).

But the Jesuits became preoccupied with other matters, including a native revolt in the south, and it was 25 years before attention was again turned toward the north. In 1746, a new expedition was commissioned with virtually the same objectives as Ugarte's voyage. It was to scout northward up the Gulf for harbors to support projected missions in the north and to determine, yet again, whether Baja California was an island.

The new venture was led by another outstanding Jesuit explorer, Father Fernando Consag, who departed from Loreto in June 1746, with four small canoes. With such meager craft and a directive to look for harbors, Consag did not stray far from the peninsular coast. He traversed the Midriff region without incident, passing through the channel between the peninsula and San

Lorenzo Island. He reached the Colorado River by mid-July and determined to his satisfaction that there existed no strait to the sea. Despite the evidence of Consag's report, many more years passed before the myth of the California island finally faded completely (Venegas [1759] 1966b:308–53; Dunne 1968:319–24; Crosby 1994:126–27).

Consag reported on two excellent harbors that eventually enabled the Jesuits to establish and maintain their two most northerly missions. San Francisco de Borja, founded in 1762, was reached by way of Bahía de los Ángeles. Santa María de Ángeles, founded in 1767, the last year of the Jesuits' tenure in the Americas, could be supplied from Bahía San Luis Gonzaga. Supplying these missions required the first regular shipping from Loreto through the Midriff region, a passage that became routine if no less hazardous with time (Palóu [1783] 1966:205–9; Clavigero [1789] 1971:340; Sales [1794] 1956:93; Bancroft 1884:472). For the boats that made the trip, there was no reason to stray far from shore, and thus no reason to think that these supply vessels sailed anywhere near San Esteban Island.

The last Jesuit expedition to the Midriff islands was undertaken by Wenceslaus Linck, the founding missionary of San Borja, and its purpose was quite different from previous ventures. Some of the Indians who lived along the coast reported that they had seen large fires on Ángel de la Guarda Island. Assuming that these must have been built by natives, Father Linck determined to explore the island and provide for the spiritual needs of any Indians he found living there. In the spring of 1765, he set sail with a party of soldiers and Indians from Bahía de los Ángeles in the mission launch. Though Linck's original report has not survived, the trip was described both by fellow missionary Miguel del Barco (Burrus 1967) and their contemporary, Jesuit historian Francisco Javier Clavigero ([1789] 1971):

> On reaching the island they went ashore and reconnoitered a considerable part of it. They not only did not come across any natives, but did not detect as much as a footprint of man or animal; no, they did not find even a water hole. And from what they could see of the rest of the island, they logically concluded that it was all uninhabited. This reasonable deduction they could not prove to the point of evidence through personal exploration of the entire island for lack of water; and, consequently, they were forced to take to their boat and return to the bay from which they had set out. (Burrus 1967:27)

But once again the Salsipuedes region lived up to its reputation, and Linck and his companions found themselves trapped in the channel:

> as they neared the bay they encountered such a violent wind that they could make no headway, but were forced to return to the island they had just left.
>
> On later attempting to reach the bay, they met with a like or worse result. The land wind had become so fierce that it tore away the lower sail or the rope fastening it while the one opposite held. As a result the launch was hurled on its side to the consternation of all, as they realized how close they were to being drowned. . . .

They sailed back and forth to the mainland several times without encountering any opposing wind; but on attempting to return to the island, they again ran into a head-on wind similar to the one that had kept them from landing at the bay [Bahía de los Ángeles]. Inasmuch as they were close to the southern tip of the island, they had no difficulty in rounding it and in finding shelter; but because fierce thirst gave them no respite, they were forced to put all their trust in divine Providence to try their fortune by embarking again. They decided not to attempt to make for the bay itself, but rather to reach a point somewhat to the south of it, in the hope that the wind would prove favorable for their landing there. (Burrus 1967:27–28)

This time they succeeded in landing, and they were able to get water from the local Indians. At last, the winds shifted, and the expedition sailed into Bahía de los Ángeles. As to the fires on Ángel de la Guarda that had spawned the expedition in the first place:

Father Link [Linck] was persuaded that the island was uninhabited and that the fires seen by his neophytes had been lighted by some [Baja] Californians carried there on their rafts, or perhaps by some pearl fishermen who had come from Sinaloa. (Clavigero [1789] 1971:346)

In fact, archaeological remains on Ángel de la Guarda show that the island has been extensively utilized by Indians, but it is not clear whether it was still being used during Linck's time or only in the more distant past.

With Linck's expedition to Ángel de la Guarda, Jesuit exploration of the Gulf came to an end. For many years, hostility toward the Jesuit Order had been brewing both in Europe and the Americas. Some of this ill-feeling grew out of the generalized anti-clerical sentiments that accompanied the growing revolutionary movements that were soon to erupt throughout western Europe. Some of the antipathy was directed specifically at the Jesuits, who were widely considered to be a bastion of the old and corrupt order because of their long-standing influence in the royal courts, their educational system, their supposed wealth, and the success of their mission programs. But they were losing favor in the royal courts as well. Suspicions developed that Jesuit missionaries were circumventing the Crown by creating their own fiefdoms and becoming wealthy from the labors of their native charges. The Jesuit exclusionary policy in Baja California, by keeping out settlers and civil authorities and essentially administrating the peninsula as a preserve for the missionaries and their native converts, was particularly fertile ground for breeding rumors. For decades it had been said that the Jesuits there were carrying on contraband trade with the Manilla galleons and Dutch freebooters, gouging both Indians and soldiers for essential supplies, skimming profits from silver mines, extracting forced labor from the Indians, and amassing a fortune in pearls (Chapman 1939:181; Dunne 1968:408; Crosby 1994:63). Portugal had already expelled the Jesuits from its colonies in 1759, and France had followed suit in 1764. On June 25, 1767,

Viceroy Croix in Mexico City opened a double-sealed decree from King Carlos III ordering the immediate expulsion of the Jesuits from New Spain. It took several months for word to reach the missionaries in remote Baja California, but on February 5, 1768, the Jesuits departed from the peninsula (Weber 1992:242; Crosby 1994:371–86).

As the Jesuits were preparing to leave the peninsula, a company of Franciscan friars arrived to replace them. However, the Franciscans stayed only briefly until they were ordered north to establish a mission system in more promising Alta California. In 1772, they in turn were replaced on the peninsula by the Dominicans.

The Franciscans, and to a lesser extent the Dominicans, continued to travel by boat up the peninsular coast to the northern missions (Palóu [1783] 1966:205–9; Arrillaga [1796] 1969:23), but neither group was much interested in exploring the Gulf itself. Indeed, the Gulf had been no kinder to them than to the Jesuits. The main corpus of Franciscans who took over from the Jesuits spent 80 days trying to get across the Gulf. When the Dominicans took over, one group of the initial contingent was shipwrecked en route to the peninsula and four missionaries drowned. Leaving was equally hazardous. When Father Luis Sales was recalled to the mainland in 1790, he was one of the few to survive as his ship broke up in a furious storm off Mulegé (Sales [1794] 1956:183–84; Bancroft 1884:708; Dunne 1968:417).

The Dominicans remained on the peninsula until the mission system was turned over to the secular clergy in 1834 (Burrus 1984:57). By then the missions were already moribund, for essentially all of the Indian converts had long since died off in the waves of epidemic disease that had periodically swept through the peninsula since the early Jesuit years (Aschmann 1967:181–253; Gerhard 1982:295–96; Weber 1992:241; Crosby 1994:389).

Pearling in Jesuit Times

The beginning of the seventeenth century brought an important change in the pearling industry. The Jesuits had accepted the task of establishing missions throughout the peninsula which, in the government's estimation, would go a long way toward assuring the security of the peninsula from foreign intervention. Moreover, the Jesuits had assumed, initially, the full responsibility for financing the operation. Under these new conditions, the licensing requirement for pearl hunters lost most of its value to the Crown, for there was no longer any need to use the bait of a long-term monopoly on pearling rights as a means of colonizing the peninsula at the expense of the licensee, a policy which had met with little success anyway. However, the Crown was still interested in maintaining some control over pearling in order to insure that the treasury would continue to receive the Royal Fifth. Accordingly, in 1703 the policy of granting exclusive monopolies to large-scale entrepreneurs was replaced by one that enabled small enterprises to petition for government licenses. This effectively opened the way for almost anybody to get into the pearling business as a petty entrepreneur, or *armador*, if he could find a small boat, outfit it with supplies, and get divers to work for him for the season (Barco [ca. 1770s] 1980:251; Mosk 1931:206–9; Chapman 1939:177).

The Jesuits, who were just gaining a foothold with the Indians, viewed the new policy with some alarm because it had been the unlicensed small-scale pearlers who had committed some of the worst outrages against the Indians (Venegas [1759] 1966a:50, 182, 450; [1759] 1966b:30; Clavigero [1789] 1971:134, 138, 227). They maintained that the Indians who had been exploited and abused by pearlers often generalized their hatred to all Europeans, which made the task of Christianizing the Indians all the more difficult. During most of their tenure on the peninsula, the Jesuits tried to discourage most pearling activity and closely control the remainder, in part by requiring *armadores* to register at Loreto (Venegas [1759] 1966a:336–37, 450–55; Clavigero [1789] 1971:135, 194–95, 203, 376–78; Dunne 1968:141, 145–46; Crosby 1994:69–73, 296–97). Many, of course, did not, and illegal expeditions continued throughout the period (Mosk 1931:207–20; 1941:461).

Despite the Jesuits' concerns, the pearling industry as a whole was already sliding into a long decline by the time the missionaries arrived on the peninsula. One and a half centuries of nearly uninterrupted exploitation had seriously depleted the more accessible oyster beds (Barco [ca. 1770s] 1980:257–58). Up to 1740, pearl hunters had mostly confined their activities to the coast and islands south of Mulegé and especially the famous placers around La Paz (Mosk 1931:211; Gerhard 1956:246). The mollusk they sought was the "true" pearl oyster, called *concha de perla fina* or simply *madre perla* (*Pinctada margaritifera*), which was most common in the southern Gulf (Barco [ca. 1770s] 1980:255; Brusca 1980:280). However, this situation changed briefly during the 1740s, after a tremendous storm in the central Gulf uprooted great numbers of mollusks and threw them onto the peninsular beaches, probably not far south of the Midriff (Crosby 1994:321, 509). These northern mollusks, which became known as *concha nácar*, were a different species (*Pteria sterna*) than those customarily harvested in the south. But local Indians discovered that they too contained pearls, and they took some specimens to the nearby mission of San Ignacio. A soldier stationed there by the name of Manuel de Ocio seized the opportunity by resigning his post and outfitting a pearling expedition to the central Gulf to look for the *concha nácar*. In the two years of 1743–1744, he is reputed to have gathered some 400 pounds of pearls which, though of low quality, made him a very rich man (Barco [ca. 1770s] 1980:258–62; Clavigero [1789] 1971:74–75; Gerhard 1956:246; Crosby 1994:321–24).

Ocio, and others who immediately followed, were able to work the northern Gulf placers for only a few years before the beds were essentially exhausted. Many of these beds were located along the peninsula opposite the Midriff islands, and as Father Consag observed on his 1746 expedition, they occurred as far north as Bahía San Luis Gonzaga (Venegas [1759] 1966b:340). It is not known whether Ocio's crews or other *armadores* extended their search for pearls to the nearby Midriff islands, but it would have made obvious sense to at least take a look there. After all, it was certainly common knowledge that along the southern peninsula the off-shore islands had produced some of the finest placers.[97]

On the Sonoran side, sometime in the 1720s, pearl beds were discovered along the Sonoran coast extending northward from Cabo Tepopa, just north of Tiburón Island. These became known as the San Xavier or Tepoca placers (Stratford [1746] 1958:62). Not much is known about them, but they were evidently responsible for a short-lived pearling boom in the area. For a brief time, profits were high, and according to one contemporary and probably greatly exaggerated estimate, 1,000 pearlers were working these beds at the end of the decade (Sheridan 1979:320; 1999:122). Some of these men must have gone ashore on Tiburón Island itself, because it became known that water was available at Tecomate (Correa [1750] 1946:555). However, the Tepocas and other Seris in the vicinity did not take kindly to this massive invasion of their territory, and it was not long before Seris and pearlers clashed. In 1729, the Spaniards responded by sending a military expedition to the coast to round up the hostile Seris and relocate them at the Sonoran missions out of the way of the pearlers. Although 151 Indians from Tiburón Island were sent to Pópulo, these were probably not the Seris who had been harassing the pearlers, nor did they remain long at the mission before escaping back to the island (see p. 84). In 1730, some 40 pearling crews were back at work, but the next year Seris killed several crews and drove off others. By 1733, the Tepoca placers had been abandoned (Mosk 1931:212–13).

Over the next several years there were several attempts to rework the Tepoca beds, but with little success. Seris and pearlers clashed again in 1735, and several of the latter were killed (Anssa [1735] 1932:160–61). In 1741, a reconnaissance party on the mainland coast discovered pearl oyster beds along the Canal del Infiernillo, but Seri hostility prevented their exploitation (Stratford [1746] 1958:63; Mosk 1931:214). In 1774, the Governor of Sinaloa sponsored an expedition to try once again to work the Tepoca beds. Two small vessels, with divers and a detachment of soldiers, set out from Guaymas in June and began combing the area for pearl shells. After a month of intensive searching they had found almost none, and the expedition returned to Guaymas a failure (Mosk 1931:230–34).

By the end of Jesuit times, pearling in the Gulf had become a stagnant industry. The basic cause was that the major placers accessible to divers throughout the Gulf had long since been so thoroughly overexploited that very few pearlers were able to make much of a profit. Ironically, one of the Jesuits' chief concerns, the ruthless exploitation of peninsular Indians as divers, had ceased to be a problem. European diseases had so heavily decimated the native population that there were few Indians left outside the mission settlements who could be pressed into service. By the mid-eighteenth century, local divers had largely been replaced by Yaqui Indians brought over from Sonora, and to a lesser extent by "Negroes" and "Mulattos" (Mosk 1931:211). Father Johann Jakob Baegert, who weathered the Jesuits' final 17 years at a post in the southern peninsula, gives a dour account of the pearling scene during his time:

The whole [Baja] California pearl fishing amounts to this. Every year in the summertime, eight, six, or twelve poor Spaniards (who, the whole lot of them, own nothing but whatever they earn by hard labor), as for instance, discharged soldiers and a few others like them, come from Sonora, Sinaloa, and other places on the Mexican mainland opposite the shore of California. They come in little boats or skiffs, hoping to make a small fortune, and bring with them a supply of corn, several hundred pounds of stone-dry beef, some Mexican Indians who are willing to dive for pearls, for the [Baja] California natives have shown up to now no desire to risk their lives for a few yards of cloth.

The divers are tied to a rope and lowered into the ocean. They pick up the shells and mother-of-pearl, or pry them loose from the bottom or the rocks, throw them into a sack, and when they can no longer hold their breath, they emerge and dump the trash or treasure brought up from limbo. The shells are then counted, but not opened, and one out of five is for the king. Most of the shells are empty, in others are black pearls, in some white ones, but mostly small and poorly shaped. If a Spaniard, after six or eight weeks of fear and hope, sweat and misery, has a net profit of one hundred American pesos, he esteems this a rare fortune which does not come to all of them, [and] ... (which in America is a very small and insignificant amount.)... I have only heard it said of two men, whom I also know, that they had something worthwhile after more than twenty years of pearl fishing. The others were just as poor after their pearl fishing as they had been before. (Baegert [1772] 1952:45)

For the remainder of the eighteenth century (and well into the next), pearl hunting struggled along much as Baegert described it. Between 1775 and the end of the century, there was rarely a year with more than a half dozen pearlers known to be operating in the Gulf (Sales [1794] 1956:21; Mosk 1931:233–39; Gerhard 1956:248).

Cartography of the Midriff Islands

The Jesuits who labored in Baja California and Sonora not only described their lands in words but also represented them on maps. Unlike their academic brethren in Europe, who freely allowed their unfettered expectations and prevailing geographical theories to influence what they depicted, most of the field missionaries drew what they saw, or at least what they thought they saw. Consequently, their maps of the region, especially of the Midriff, were among the most accurate of the entire Colonial period.

Charting the Gulf of California, of course, long antedated the arrival of the Jesuits, and had begun with the first exploratory voyages into the region. From the first forays of Cortés, the value of compiling basic geographic information, whether through narrative descriptions or maps, was obvious to everyone. Pearl hunters had a pressing need for practical knowledge of the Gulf. In addition to determining the locations of productive placers, they needed to know the navigational hazards that threatened them, where there were sheltered anchorages, and where drinking water and firewood could be found. The Crown's interest was broader but every bit as keen. Fundamentally, it needed to establish the nature and extent of the empire it claimed. But there were important practical matters at stake as well. None was more critical than determining whether Baja California was an island, which would enable the precious Manila galleons to enter the Gulf from the northwest and make an early landfall in its protected harbors. Although the answer to this question had been determined by Ulloa in 1539, the issue was so important that hope, debate, and searches for the "missing" strait continued for more than two hundred years afterward before incontrovertible evidence finally settled the matter (Leighly 1972).

Despite the crucial importance of cartography, maps produced by the early explorers were rarely published or otherwise made widely available. This was regarded as a matter of national security by the government of New Spain, which believed that any map that fell into foreign hands was an open invitation to plunder the wealth of Spanish America. As a result, many of the maps published during the Colonial period were produced by foreigners who had never been to the Americas. For lack of data, these map-makers were forced to rely heavily on second-hand information, hearsay, and theory, and the results sometimes bore only limited resemblance to reality. For two hundred years, some cartographers continued to portray Baja California as an enormous island, and other smaller imaginary islands populated the Gulf until even later. But though fanciful representations persisted, fundamentally realistic representations of the Gulf, including the Midriff, began to appear around the beginning of the eighteenth century through the exploratory efforts of the Jesuits in Sonora and Baja California.

The first Gulf maps were drawn in the 1530s by members of Cortés's expeditions, and consequently these show only its southern reaches. However, a 1541 map by Domingo del Castillo not only portrays the full Gulf, but uses the name "San Estevan" for the first time (Figure 3.1). Castillo had sailed to the head of the Gulf with Alarcón in 1540, and he may also have accompanied Ulloa there the previous year (Barrera Bassols 1992:228) or else had access to information from that expedition (Wagner 1924:312, 380). Both expeditions must have sailed through the strait between Tiburón and San Esteban Islands, mistaking Tiburón Island for a peninsula. Hence Castillo seems to have depicted Tiburón as a great finger-like arc, projecting outward from the mainland, which he labeled "C. del Tiburón" (Cabo del Tiburón). A large amorphous island appears well south of this Tiburón "cape," but otherwise none of the Midriff islands are represented.

In Castillo's map, the name "San Esteban" does not appear in the Midriff, but it does occur in two other places. On the Pacific side of Baja California, it clearly refers to Cedros and Natividad Islands, which were indeed originally named "San Estevan" by Ulloa in 1539 (Wagner 1937:23–42). About two degrees north

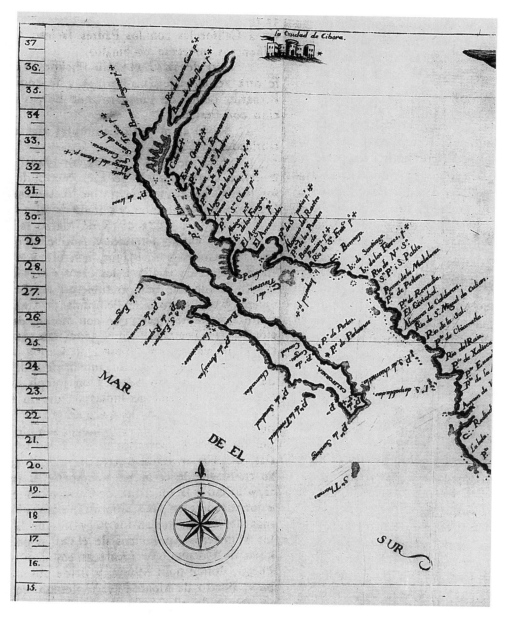

*Figure 3.1   Detail of Domingo del Castillo's 1541 map of the Gulf, from a 1770 copy.
(For the full map, see Sykes 1915:Fig. 1; Wagner 1937:Pl. 8; or Barrera Bassols 1992:220.)
(Courtesy Huntington Library, San Marino, California [No. 20678].)*

of the Tiburón "cape" the phrase "P^ta. de S^n. Estevan" (Punta de San Esteban) also appears inexplicably alongside a pair of long, narrow, and nonexistent islands. Unfortunately, Castillo's map is known only from much later and imperfect copies (Wagner 1937:32; Leighly 1972:12–13; Barrera Bassols 1992:220, 228), such as the 1770 version illustrated in Figure 3.1, and it is possible that the enigmatic juxtaposition of the name and the imaginary islands originally arose as a copying error. Errors of this kind were common in early manuscript maps and, once committed, were faithfully reproduced in subsequent copies (Wagner 1937:498). Whether the present San Esteban Island owes its name in some way to these two mythical islands is uncertain, though it could be that San Esteban was later recognized as a conveniently placed chunk of land to which an already entrenched name could be easily attached.

Although San Esteban Island is recognizable on a few other early maps (e.g., Wagner 1937:Pl. 26) it was not until the Jesuit period that the island became consistently represented and identified. One of the earliest Jesuit depictions accompanied an extraordinary description of the Seris, penned in 1692 as a letter to a superior by Adamo Gilg, missionary of Nuestra Señora del Pópulo. It was not a general map of the Gulf but a drawing specifically of the Seri coast, which Father Gilg had personally visited earlier in the year. Bahía Kino and the surrounding region are depicted clearly and accurately. Tiburón Island, given the Latin name "Insula Serorum" (Seris' Island), and San Esteban, unnamed, appear approximately correct in shape, relative size, and position. With admirable honesty, Gilg gave the sea beyond those two islands the simple Latin designation "*incognitum*" (unknown) (Gilg [1692] 1965:41).

Of the Jesuit cartographers, Father Kino was far and away the most influential. One of the great strengths of his maps, which came to be widely appreciated, was that they were based upon personal observation. Kino was an extraordinarily active explorer, and over the course of his life, his maps underwent considerable change as he accumulated wide-ranging direct experience with the region. One of his first maps of the Gulf, drawn in 1695–1696 and predating his land expeditions to the head of the Gulf, reflects contemporary belief by depicting Baja California as an island. On the other hand, it incorporates Kino's first-hand observations gained during his work both on the peninsula and in Sonora. For the Midriff region, which Kino had traversed with Captain Guzmán in 1685, the islands of Tiburón, San Esteban, and San Lorenzo (and apparently even San Pedro Mártir) are all placed in roughly their correct relative positions (Burrus 1965:Pl. 8).

Kino's best known map was compiled in 1701 after he had completed an overland trek around the head of the Gulf to the Colorado River. Based on this experience, in the new map Kino showed the Gulf unmistakably ending at the mouth of the river and depicted the land that joins the peninsula to the mainland (Burrus 1965:Pl. 10). For the Midriff, the three Salsipuedes islands retain their approximately correct positions, although the larger scale of this map makes it clear that Kino knew little of their sizes and shapes. As on most of his maps, Kino labeled Tiburón Island "San Agustín," but he did not separately name San Esteban and San Lorenzo. When the map was published in different languages, this created some interesting translation problems:

> Two amusing mistakes were made with the enigmatic "Get-out-if-you-can-islands" (Islas de Sal-si-puedes). Both the French and the German editors thought that "Sal" (the present imperative of the verb "salir") meant salt and translated the word accordingly "Sel" and "Saltz." Hundreds of subsequent maps will reproduce this same mistake. The German editor seeing the "I." (abbreviation for Isla in Spanish, and Isle in French) next to Tiburón, mistook it for the numeral and accordingly called the two Islas de Sal-si-puedes "2. Saltz-Insel." (Burrus 1965:49)

Kino's final map of 1710 again shows the three Salsipuedes islands in their approximate positions, this time labeling Tiburón Island "Seris" and leaving San Esteban and San Lorenzo unnamed. By now, Kino had glimpsed Ángel de la Guarda Island, which he mistook for two separate islands, and he included them on the map as "San Vincente" and "Santa Ynez" along with an extra unnamed island, which he placed near the Sonoran shore (Burrus 1965:Pl. 13, 52–53).

While some rather fanciful maps continued to be published, Kino's maps became the basis of much of the cartography of the Gulf during the eighteenth century. These subsequent maps differed in the precise way they corrected certain of Kino's errors while perpetuating others and introducing new ones. Most depicted, with varying degrees of accuracy, the three Salsipuedes islands and placed them more or less correctly relative to each other (McGee 1898:62–66; Burrus 1965:1, 50, 68–69). One secular map, produced by a cavalry officer named Gabriel de Prudhom and dated 1733, emphasizes the Seris' insular homeland with oversized and prominently-labeled Tiburón Island. San Esteban is clearly represented and accurately positioned, but the name "S. Esteban" is attached to an island in the location of San Pedro Mártir (Brown Villalba et al. 1982:560; Barrera Bassols 1992:233). Among later Jesuit maps, Father Consag's 1746 map not only labels the three Salsipuedes islands as such, but also names each individually (Figure 3.2). Consag applied Kino's old term "San Agustín" to Tiburón Island, but both San Esteban and San Lorenzo are labeled with their modern names. Even the north island of San Lorenzo is given its alternate modern name, Ánimas Island.

Not all Jesuits produced accurate depictions of the islands, particularly those who had never been in the Gulf (e.g., Nentvig [1764] 1980:frontis). But by the second half of the century, many maps, both Jesuit and secular, not only placed San Esteban Island more or less correctly but also named it explicitly (e.g., Venegas [1759] 1966a:between 12–13; Hernández Sánchez-Barba 1957:opposite 248; Brown Villalba et al. 1982:31). Now and then, alternate names were used, as in Nicolás de Lafora's map of 1771, which calls the island "Triunfo" (Kinnaird 1958:inside back cover), the name given it in 1750 by Manuel Correa (see p. 88). The name "San Esteban" was sometimes reworked in maps published in languages other than Spanish, as in two eighteenth century French

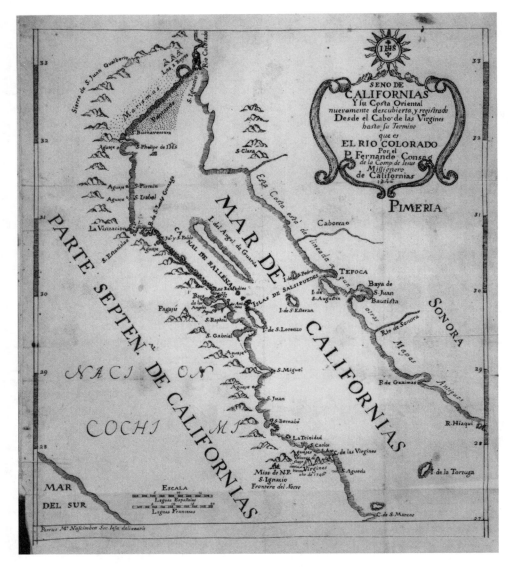

Figure 3.2   Fernando Consag's 1746 map titled Seno de Californias y su Costa Oriental.... *as redrawn by Pedro María Nascimben. (Courtesy Huntington Library, San Marino, California [HM 1293].)*

maps that rendered it "I. S. Ican" and "I. de S. Etienne" (Leighly 1972:Pls. 20, 24). And occasionally, recent scholars have mistaken other islands that appear on earlier maps for San Esteban. The vague island that Father Juan Nentvig labeled "S. Juan Bautista" on his 1762 map is almost certainly not San Esteban, as the annotators of the 1980 edition of Nentvig's book suggest, but tiny Alcatraz Island in Bahía Kino, which at the time was uniformly known as "Bahía de San Juan Bautista" (Nentvig [1764] 1980:endsheets, 78).

FOUR

Punishing the Seris (I):
Spanish Military Expeditions
to Tiburón Island

The Spaniards sent military expeditions to the Seri coast several times during the eighteenth century. On three of these occasions, soldiers actually landed on Tiburón Island, and on one of them, a support ship circumnavigated Tiburón and probably San Esteban Island as well. Because these expeditions were motivated by events on the mainland, they set out from the Sonoran coast rather than the peninsular side of the Gulf. They were the first in a long succession of military operations intended to round up and punish, relocate, or exterminate the Seris, that extended into the beginning of the twentieth century.

The Spanish colonization of Sonora had proceeded earlier and under different circumstances than the settling of Baja California, although in both places the Jesuits had been in the vanguard. These intrepid evangelists had reached the Mayo Indians of northern Sinaloa soon after 1600, and by 1617 were founding missions among the Yaquis in southern Sonora. From there, rather than continuing to the northwest along the arid coast into Seri country, the Jesuits pushed their mission chain directly northward up the well-watered river valleys of eastern Sonora, bringing their message to the agriculturally-based Pimas and Ópatas. Unlike Baja California, though, Sonora was never reserved as an exclusive domain for the Jesuits and their native charges. Soldiers, ranchers, miners, and civil authorities came with them, establishing a mosaic of secular communities alongside the missions. Thus by the middle of the seventeenth century, a variety of communities had sprung up around the periphery of Seri territory, but not in it. By then, Sonoran settlers and missionaries had heard of the Seris, but there had been few direct contacts and little was known about them (Spicer 1962:105; Sheridan 1999:17–18

Shortly after midcentury, the Seris became much more visible as some groups moved inland, began to steal livestock, and mounted small-scale raids on the settlers and mission Indians. Raiding among different Seri bands and between

Seri and Piman groups, who considered each other traditional enemies, had probably been going on since prehispanic times. But when the Seris began attacking Pimas who had settled into the mission communities, their depredations became a matter of Spanish concern. The first recorded armed Seri-European encounter erupted in 1662, when Spanish soldiers attacked a group of Seri families as a reprisal for raids on some mission Pimas. The Seris resisted, and nearly all the adults were wiped out. The children were taken by the soldiers and distributed among the Spanish villagers (Gilg [1692] 1965:41).

Having unleashed the sword on the Seris, the Spaniards turned to the other side of their native policy by attempting to reduce the Indians to mission life. In 1679, Father Juan Fernández established a mission called Nuestra Señora del Pópulo in the lower Río San Miguel valley, hoping that rations of food would begin to lure marauding Seris into a settled, well-regulated Christian existence. Though he won some initial converts, the mission was abandoned four years later, after many Seris died in an epidemic and Fernández was transferred elsewhere (Gilg [1692] 1965:42). Father Adamo Gilg revitalized the mission in 1688 and established two outlying *visitas*, also with some initial success, but his efforts ultimately foundered too. Crop failures and other immediate factors were only part of the problem. The nomadic Seris were not well suited to the sedentary regimen of mission life, especially at such a distance from their coastal homeland and kinsmen. Relatively few became genuine converts, and those who could not tolerate a settled existence escaped back to the coast. Still others drifted in and out of the mission settlements, living on rations when their traditional food supply ran low. Many Seris, unencumbered with European notions of private property, viewed Spanish livestock and crops as fortuitous additions to the natural food supply, and considered them there for the taking. Some Indians turned to thievery and raiding as a way of life, and even Seris attached to the mission succumbed occasionally to this irresistible temptation. The Spaniards began to respond to these depredations with force, and before long Seris and Spaniards were locked into a hopeless cycle of raids, reprisals, and all-out military campaigns that were to continue for the next 250 years (Spicer 1962:105–7; Sheridan 1999:13–14, 20).

It was persistent Seri raiding that triggered the first of the full-blown military expeditions to the coast, and eventually to Tiburón Island. Late in 1699, some Salinero Seris staged a series of raids on settlements in the Río San Miguel valley, and a call for help went out to the military. In January 1700, 15 soldiers under the command of Lieut. Juan Bautista de Escalante arrived and found that one of the raids had left some missionized Tepoca Seris dead. The soldiers pursued the raiders toward Pópulo and captured one of the guilty Salineros, whom they found hiding out in the mountains. He was promptly executed to set an example for other miscreants. Then on February 18, Escalante and his soldiers, joined by 100 Indian auxiliaries and Father Gilg of the Pópulo mission, marched to the Seri coast in pursuit of the Salinero raiders who were still at large. They reached the coast on February 23, but found that the Indians had already escaped by balsa to Tiburón Island. Escalante and his men spent several hours exploring the area around Bahía Kino and on the following day began their march back to the Río San Miguel valley.

Though Escalante had returned empty-handed, he was determined to put an end to Seri raiding, and on March 4, he again set off toward the Gulf. This time his intent was to offer the Salineros peace if they would leave the coast, relocate in the Río San Miguel valley, and submit to mission life. While the troops established a camp some distance behind the shore, Indian emissaries were sent ahead to inform the Salineros of the Spanish intentions. On the night of March 9, while the force was waiting for word from the envoys, a group of hostile Seris staged a hit-and-run raid on the Spanish camp. But others wanted peace, and an initial group of 40 Indians arrived four days later to accept the Spanish offer. On March 17, Escalante set out to round up those who had remained on the coast and bring them into the fold. Eight days later he had gathered together 115 Seris and was ready to deliver them to the missions. (Escalante [1700] 1999:50–53).

Though he had accomplished his main goal, Escalante was by no means done with the Seris, for he had been severely provoked by the attack on his camp and his own failure to find the attackers. On March 26, leaving the mission-bound Indians to begin their trek under the supervision of others, Escalante and his troops again turned toward the sea. This time it was to be a punitive expedition, and on the first of April, the troops arrived at Bahía Kino. What happened next has been the subject of some confusion. According to Escalante's contemporary, Lieut. Juan Mateo Mange, the Spaniards found some Seri balsas on the beach, and in an extraordinarily bold move, climbed on these craft and crossed the Canal del Infiernillo to Tiburón Island. In this account, the soldiers, once on Tiburón, spent several days searching the island for Seris. They saw few but attacked those they encountered. All told they killed nine Indians and took prisoner a few more, an action they believed would serve as a warning to the others. With this done, Escalante and his men left the island and returned to the Río San Miguel valley, where they turned the captives over to Father Gilg at Pópulo (Mange 1954:147–48).

According to this version of events, summarized in 1788 by Jesuit historian Francisco Alegre ([ca. 1780s] 1960:166–67) and later by McGee (1898:61), Hernández (1902:16–17), and Tweed (1973:38), the Escalante punitive campaign would have been the first Spanish military expedition to set foot on Tiburón Island. However, Escalante's own diary contains no record of a Spanish crossing to Tiburón. As he himself tells it, on April 2, the day after arriving at Bahía Kino, he and his men rode south along the beach to Laguna de la Cruz, where they encountered a Seri camp. As they approached the camp, it was the Indians who took to their balsas in an effort to escape. The Spaniards rode into the water in pursuit of the fleeing Seris and managed to intercept four Indians, whom they killed or took prisoner. The following day, Escalante captured some of the Salineros who had raided his camp a month earlier, and with that task accomplished began his march back to the Spanish frontier. Though Escalante had seen Tiburón Island lying just "two [or] three gunshots away" (Escalante [1700] 1999:55) and knew that hostile Seris had taken refuge there, his account makes no mention of any action there. Evidently, three more decades would pass before the Spaniards would launch their first military invasion of Tiburón Island.

Most of the Indians Escalante had sent to the mission eventually escaped and found their way back to the coast, but his expedition had been about as successful at rounding up Seris as any that followed over the next two centuries. Moreover, his decisive military response may have had an impact on potential raiders, for the next two decades were a time of relative tranquillity for Sonora.

During the 1720s, the fragile peace began to erode as pearl hunters and Seris clashed in the vicinity of the recently-discovered Tepoca pearl oyster beds located along the mainland coast several miles north of Tiburón Island. In 1729, after several pearling crews had been killed, provincial Governor Manuel Bernal de Huidobro organized a large military expedition to the Seri coast. His intent was to invade Tiburón Island using canoes supplied by the pearlers, round up all the Seris, and resettle them in the San Miguel missions where they could be Christianized and controlled (Sheridan 1979:320, 1999:126). Huidobro and his soldiers set out from Pópulo on August 16, accompanied by Father Nicolás de Perera, Gilg's successor at Pópulo. When they reached the strategic waterhole of Carrizal, near Bahía Kino, Huidobro sent two mission Seris as envoys to try to persuade the Tiburón people to come to the mainland, where he would provide them with a feast. Indians came from two rancherías, one located on the north end of the island (probably Tecomate) and the other "on the west side" (the southwest coast). In all, 151 Tiburones reluctantly agreed to go to Pópulo.

With the voluntary surrender of these Indians, Huidobro saw no further need to invade Tiburón. This was fortunate for the Spaniards, because storms had turned back the pearl fishing canoes that were supposed to transport them to the island (Perera [1729] 1999:129). So after eight days on the coast, the expedition ended peacefully and without any Spaniards setting foot on Tiburón Island.

The Spaniards were surprised that the Indians who came to the mainland displayed none of the hostility they had expected. This was because Huidobro had rounded up the wrong people. These Seris were peaceable and innocent residents of the island, not the mainland raiders the Spaniards had intended to capture. Father Perera naïvely concluded that Seri raiders did not use Tiburón Island as a refuge, but he clearly recognized that the Tiburones were a people of very different character:

> The inhabitants are a good people, without malice and free from the wickedness of those of this shore. Given the docility of their natural disposition, I hope to the Lord that they remain in the pueblo. (Perera [1729] 1999:130)

Once at Pópulo, however, even the gentle Tiburones quickly became disillusioned with the harsh reality of mission life. Their children had died, and they had not understood that their relocation was intended to be permanent. They soon began disappearing back to the coast, and with a newly acquired mistrust of the Spaniards, some may have allied themselves with the hostile Tepocas and Salineros (Vildósola [1735] 1932:151–52; Perera [1740] 1999:132).

As skirmishes with pearlers on the coast and raiding in the interior intensified, the Spaniards soon mounted another campaign against the Seris. This time it was led by Captain Juan Bautista de Anza, and for the first time, a Spanish military force actually landed on Tiburón Island. Unfortunately, few details of this campaign are known. The expedition included not only Spanish soldiers but Yaqui Indians, whose expertise with small boats was intended to facilitate getting the troops and supplies to the island. Even so, crossing the Canal del Infiernillo in canoes proved extremely difficult, and only a few soldiers, along with some horses and supplies, succeeded in landing (Vildósola [1735] 1932:152). Once on Tiburón, what specific action took place is unclear, for Anza reported only that he "was able to carry out some punishment [of the Seris] which caused them fear, which was not a small accomplishment" (Anssa [1735] 1932:160).

This first military expedition to Tiburón Island evidently did have an effect, for again there was a brief lull in the violence that plagued Sonora (Sheridan 1979:321, 1999:126).

But the peace was short-lived. During the next two decades, Sonora slid into a state of widespread civil unrest. The continuing influx of Europeans led to more frequent encounters with Indians, and since the interests of these two groups were seldom compatible, the encounters were often hostile. The Seris resumed their raiding on the western periphery while Apaches periodically harassed the frontier to the north. In 1740, a rebellion against Spanish oppression broke out among Yaquis and Mayos in the south. Meanwhile, disputes that had been gradually brewing between the Jesuits and the Sonoran civil authorities erupted into a major power struggle. By 1748, the problems had become so serious that the Viceroy removed the governor of the province and sent an Inspector General, José Rafael Rodríguez Gallardo, to investigate the situation.

Rodríguez Gallardo concluded that the hostility of the Indians was the underlying cause of Sonora's widespread unrest, and he branded the Seris as the worst offenders. Any solution, therefore, would have to deal decisively and unmercifully with the "Seri problem." He maintained that past attempts to subdue the Seris had failed because only the ringleaders had been punished. In order to succeed, all the Seris must be captured or exterminated. This would require that the Seris be attacked and eliminated from their primary place of refuge, Tiburón Island. And to be sure this solution would be a lasting one, captured Seris must be permanently deported to other parts of New Spain. Even the Jesuits, no friends of the civil authorities by this time, reluctantly concurred that there was probably no other realistic option for dealing with the recalcitrant Seris (Sheridan 1999:141-42, 169).

The person responsible for putting this policy into effect was the new Governor, Diego Ortíz Parrilla, who arrived in June of 1749. The Seri situation was already tense because of actions recently taken by Rodríguez Gallardo himself. Believing that Nuestra Señora del Pópulo was a haven for Seri marauders, he established a presidio of soldiers next to the mission. For its support, he expropriated agricultural fields that the mission Seris had been working for years and allowed the soldiers to use the Indians as forced labor. The infuriated Seris revolted at this abuse and for a while wreaked terror on the countryside. A few months after Ortíz Parrilla took office, the rebellion subsided, but it was an uneasy truce at best (Spicer 1962:107; Tweed 1973:58–71; Sheridan 1979:324–27, 1999:141).

Meanwhile, Ortíz Parrilla wasted little time implementing the new policy. In the spring of 1750, he launched the prelude to his campaign with the sudden arrest of the mission Seris, imprisoning the men and deporting the women to Guatemala. Those who escaped joined their hostile kinsmen in the desert. In this single move, Ortíz Parrilla destroyed the last vestiges of Seri tolerance and trust. From this point on, most Seris would be united in a deep and permanent hatred for the Spaniards.

Having dealt with the mission Indians, Ortíz Parrilla devoted the rest of the spring and summer to final preparations for a full-scale invasion of Tiburón Island. By August, he had assembled a force of around 700 men, consisting of some 600 ground troops, most of them Pima auxiliaries, plus a naval fleet of seven support ships manned mainly by Yaquis. Accompanying the expedition as chaplain was Father Francisco Antonio Pimentel, who kept a detailed, if highly romanticized, journal of the campaign. When the first summer rains came, an advance party set out to fortify a base camp at the Carrizal waterhole near Bahía Kino. On September 10, after all the troops were in place at Carrizal, Ortíz Parrilla arrived on cue and staged a grand entrance into the camp (Pimentel [1750] 1999:189)

Four days later, a reconnaissance party of about 150 men and 25 horses crossed the channel to the eastern shore of Tiburón to search for water and pasturage. The party included two friendly Seris who were sent on ahead to try to persuade their hostile kinsmen to surrender. The envoys returned with a message from the rebel leader, a Salinero known as "Canta La Flecha Que Mata" (The-Arrow-that-Kills Sings), who replied that if the Spaniards would return to the Río San Miguel valley, he would meet with them there later. He said that he and his people were very content on Tiburón. He had sent messages to those Seris still on the mainland to come back to the island, and he asked that those people not be harmed. He also said that his warriors were prepared to attack the Spaniards but that he did not wish to do that. Through the envoys, he sent the Governor both a cross and an arrow to show that his people were willing to give up their weapons for peace (Pimentel [1750] 1999:191; Sheridan 1979:329). But the Spaniards interpreted this eloquent symbol as signifying that the Indians did not care whether there was war or peace. Ortíz Parrilla had come to fight, and so on September 18, the army marched northward to Punta Santa Rosa, at the narrowest part of the Canal del Infiernillo. The next morning they crossed to Tiburón Island and established a camp. The following day, a patrol set out to engage the Seris.

This first sortie nearly resulted in mutiny as the Spanish soldiers began to comprehend the grim reality of their undertaking. They would be facing a well-prepared and determined enemy on their own terrain, in the enervating heat of summer with inadequate water. They had been ordered to search out the enemy in the island's highest mountains, and as they approached the base of the rugged range, the soldiers balked. Despite repeated coaxing, Ortíz Parrilla (who would remain safely below to command the operation) could not persuade them to proceed. Finally, the Pima auxiliaries, who said they had come a long way to kill the evil Seris, broke the stalemate, and the reluctant soldiers headed into the mountains. Two days later, they returned claiming victory, having killed three men and two women of a group of Seris who were trying to hide from them (Pimentel [1750] 1999:194–97).

Encouraged by this encounter, a large force was sent out on September 24 with food for six days. When a messenger reported back that the troops were heading for Tecomate, two ships were dispatched in support, but adverse winds and strong currents prevented them from rounding the northeast point of the island. The soldiers returned four days later, having spent the last 38 hours without water, but with further victorious claims. They had found some Seris who had fled to Tecomate and had attacked these Indians in caves where they were trying to hide. The Indians fought back, some with arrows and others by throwing stones so violently that they broke the legs of two of the Pimas. But when the battle ended, the soldiers had killed 10 Seri men and had taken 28 women and children as prisoners (Pimentel [1750] 1999:200–201).

After one more brief patrol that encountered no one, the campaign ended. The Spaniards concluded that the remaining Seris had scattered, and on the evening of October 2, the expedition returned to the mainland.

In their two weeks on Tiburón Island, the 600 Spanish and Pima ground troops had managed to kill about 15 Seris. According to the captives, perhaps an equal number had died of wounds. Among the dead was the rebel leader, The-Arrow-that-Kills Sings (Pimentel [1750] 1999:205). Although the Spaniards claimed they had dealt the Seris a crushing blow, they had made contact with only a small fraction of the Seri population, most of whom had completely evaded the soldiers. The Indians had neither been exterminated, nor captured, nor subdued. But to the Seris, the invasion of their homeland was one more outrage to be added to the recent injustices at Pópulo. The indiscriminate hunting down and killing of their people, some of whom were probably innocent Tiburones, left them more bitter than ever. Within a year, they would be locked in a devastating 20-year guerilla war with the Spaniards. In the meantime, Ortíz Parrilla portrayed the achievements of the expedition as a glorious victory, and the army's return to the Río San Miguel valley was accompanied by triumphal celebrations. For his part, Father Pimentel, the expedition chronicler, composed a romance in which he likened Ortíz Parrilla to Caesar and Alexander the Great (Pimentel [1750] 1946:558–71).

Though the expedition was not a very convincing military success, it did accomplish some basic exploration of the island. Much of the eastern and northern parts of Tiburón were traversed on foot, perhaps for the first time by Europeans. At the end of the campaign, Ortíz Parrilla and Manuel Correa, a pilot with experience in the Philippines, sailed one of the ships completely around

Tiburón Island. From this trip, Correa produced a careful description of the entire coastline that included landmarks that can be readily identified today. In the course of this voyage, the two Spaniards almost certainly made a side trip to San Esteban Island. According to Correa's report:

> To the west of this coast [the southwest coast of Tiburón Island] there are four islands, three lying in a northwest to southeast direction, closer to the coast of [Baja] California, and at a distance of eight or nine leagues [21 to 23 miles] from here. The last and smallest is almost due south of Punta de Alvarado [Punta Willard] and separated from the nearest land of this island [Tiburón] by about four leagues [10 miles]. It is approximately round in shape and must have a circumference of nearly five leagues [13 miles]. It is a mountainous land, dry and rough, with very few beaches on its shores. This island is called El Triunfo. (Correa [1750] 1946:557)

Though Correa and Ortíz Parrilla must have circumnavigated San Esteban in order to be able to describe the island so precisely, it is clear that they saw no people there, nor any evidence of inhabitants. Since they had just completed a campaign whose purpose was to track down Seris, Correa surely would have mentioned Indians had they seen any. On the voyage around Tiburón, Correa was careful to note the balsas they saw on the beaches, but he makes no mention of any watercraft on San Esteban. The Seris, however, have always had good communication among themselves. Considering what had just been happening on Tiburón, had there been any Seris on San Esteban when Correa and Ortíz Parrilla arrived, they probably would have kept well hidden. As to the name "El Triunfo," Correa presumably bestowed it to commemorate the expedition's ersatz victory, not knowing that Padre Ugarte had applied the name to neighboring San Lorenzo Island 29 years earlier.

Before the end of the century, Spanish soldiers were again on Tiburón Island, but this time on a brief mission of peace. The events that led to Ortíz Parrilla's 1750 invasion of Tiburón had touched off 20 years of sporadic but bitter warfare between Seris and Spaniards. Although there was no clear victor, by the early 1770s many exhausted Indians were ready to compromise in exchange for a truce. One group of Tiburón Island Seris declared themselves willing to submit to mission life, but on the condition that a missionary come to them and that they be allowed to continue living near their traditional homeland. The new Governor, Mateo Sastre, agreed, believing this an opportunity to finally subdue the Indians. Accordingly, in the summer of 1772, he dispatched a party of eight soldiers under Lieut. Manuel de la Azuela to assess the coastal landscape and select a mission site. Accompanying the military party was Juan Crisóstomo Gil de Bernabé, an intensely devout Franciscan friar known for wearing a hair shirt and scourging his flesh in penitence, who would become the Seris' short-lived missionary. Emissaries for the Tiburón people requested that the mission be situated at the waterhole of Carrizal, close to their island (where Ortíz Parrilla had based his invasionary force two decades earlier). To be assured that this site would be generally acceptable, the Spaniards crossed the strait to Tiburón Island, and in a brief and peaceful meeting with some of the Indians there, obtained their agreement. Some three months later, on November 26, the Carrizal mission was dedicated (Gil de Bernabé [1772] 1999:407; Kessell 1975:73–85).

But not all the Seris who were living on Tiburón Island at that time wanted a reconciliation with the Spaniards, and neither the mission nor its devout founder lasted long. On March 7, 1773, Fray Juan was murdered by hostile Indians and the fledgling mission was abandoned, barely three months after its establishment. The immediate capture of the assailants by friendly Seris did much to defuse this potentially explosive situation. The Spaniards refrained from launching another retaliatory campaign, and about 50 of the friendly Indians voluntarily resettled at Pitic (modern Hermosillo). But gradually these people slipped away to return to their homeland, and raids by hostile Seris resumed.

In 1782, José de Gálvez, who by now was Minister of the Indies, conferred with the Spanish King about the deteriorating Seri situation and reported that:

> His Majesty believes that to chastise the Seris and their relatives on Tiburón Island it would be advisable as soon as possible [i.e., when the war with Great Britain was over] to mount a vigorous and well-planned expedition against this island in an effort to annihilate all its perfidious inhabitants capable of bearing arms. (Gálvez, in Kessell 1975:89)

Although there was no immediate response to this regal advice, 11 years later a Franciscan administrator in Sonora, Francisco Antonio Barbastro, proposed a highly original solution that would, he believed, not only pacify the Seris but also solve many of Sonora's economic problems. Like many before him, he believed that the key to ending Seri raids was to deprive the hostile Indians of their Tiburón Island refuge. He also believed that the way to stimulate economic development in the province was to commit a supply ship to an annual voyage from southern Mexico to Guaymas. But what was most novel was that Barbastro proposed that the two endeavors be linked together. And if the King were unwilling to undertake these steps directly, he argued, it could be achieved privately. The first step would be to thoroughly assess the resources of the region:

> His majesty should then promise to bestow the title of Marquis or Count of Tiburón, and dominion over Tiburón Island, upon the subject who undertakes the pacification and conversion of the island's Indian inhabitants, its settlement, and the development of the island's resources. I am convinced that there is at least one [person], and perhaps many, who would be honored to undertake this endeavor and share in the fortune to be made there....
>
> Once Tiburón Island and its coasts are secured we will have achieved peace in the province. The Tepocas, Tiburones, and the Seris at Pitic will have no place left to hide. (Barbastro [1793] 1991:2)

But there was one hitch:

The island will not be self-sustaining so it will have to be provisioned by the province [i.e., from the Sonoran mainland]. The villa of Pitic is close by and very productive[,] and commerce with Tiburón Island will enrich its population. (Barbastro [1793] 1991:3)

Although Barbastro maintained that there was widespread agreement that the island did have sufficient water to support cattle:

Tiburón Island is said to be unsuitable for agriculture. If the king's frigate were berthed in Guaymas[,] it would be possible to sell commodities to and purchase grain from the province to maintain the island's settlers and soldiers. The frigate could remain in the Port of Guaymas—a good, secure port—and a smaller boat could be used to transport cattle to Tiburón and other smaller islands in the area. (Barbastro [1793] 1991:2)

Which "smaller islands" Barbastro had in mind, he failed to specify, but they probably would have included San Esteban. By this time, the existence of both San Esteban and its neighboring islands were generally known, if only as outlines on the maps consulted by officials such as Barbastro. As to his development plan, Barbastro was a visionary ahead of his time. It would require Mexican Independence and the very different set of political and economic circumstances of the nineteenth century for the idea of colonizing Tiburón and its neighboring islands to generate either government or private support (see Chapter 8).

III.

Europeans and the Midriff Islands in the Nineteenth Century

The final decades of the eighteenth century brought a long and steady decline in European activity in the Gulf. By 1800, there were fewer people navigating its waters than at any time in the previous century. The era of great exploratory voyages had come to an end with the unequivocal proof that Baja California was not an island, and that the long-sought strait connecting the upper Gulf with the Pacific Ocean did not exist. Exhaustion of the accessible pearl oyster beds had reduced the pearling industry to a few canoe loads of divers eking out a bare subsistence living. Pirates, who were never a major presence in the Gulf, had ceased to be a serious threat. The decline of the Baja California missions had put an end to the regular shipping runs across the Gulf. Epidemic diseases had decimated the peninsular Indians, leaving some 2,000 Europeans and mestizos as the only inhabitants of an isolated and greatly depopulated land. On the Sonoran side, the single port of Guaymas was still only tenuously linked with the settlements of the interior, and contact between these interior towns and the outside world was maintained more reliably by land routes.

The nineteenth century proved to be a time of profound change which transformed the Gulf region from a stagnant colonial backwater into a rapidly developing frontier of international importance. In 1821, the newly independent Republic of Mexico began to exchange Spanish isolationism for a foreign policy that opened the Gulf to the global maritime community, with its great diversity of trade goods, ideas, and people. By midcentury, a large volume of commercial activity had moved up the Gulf to Guaymas, which had grown from a mere landing to a major port of entry for Sonora. As its commercial importance swelled, Guaymas, along with other Gulf ports, was occasionally visited by foreign men-of-war on peacetime patrol, and it fell under attack when war broke out. By the mid-1850s, ships from San Francisco were traversing the entire length of the Gulf several times a year, bringing supplies to the mouth of the Colorado River to be ferried on to Arizona Territory.

The rapid pace of change during the latter half of the century was brought about in part by technological developments that were reshaping much of the nineteenth century world. Steam power was perhaps the most important innovation, for steamships finally liberated navigators from the mercy of the Gulf's notorious winds and currents. By adding a crucial measure of reliability and safety, steamers made possible the first regularly scheduled transportation throughout the Gulf.

New technology and the discovery of new resources, coupled with changes in national economic policy, also began to bring both Mexican and foreign entrepreneurs to the region. For a number of years, guano mining became an important Gulf enterprise. The introduction of the diving suit transformed pearl fishing from a petty entrepreneurial activity into an industry dominated by large corporations. A government concession system aimed at attracting foreign capital spurred a variety of land development and colonization schemes, including plans to establish permanent settlements on San Esteban and other Midriff islands.

Scientific study of the natural history of the Gulf also began in the nineteenth century. It was also during this time that the Gulf was first accurately and completely charted. This put an end to the confusion that had surrounded the geography of the upper Gulf, and finally established which of the Midriff islands that appeared on earlier maps actually existed and where they were located.

A few things, however, did not change. Large-scale military campaigns against the Seris continued periodically throughout the nineteenth century, including, apparently, the expedition that wiped out the San Esteban people. And, in keeping with the times, the prevalent attitude toward the Gulf was that its resources existed to be exploited and turned into quick profits. Even San Esteban Island, long bypassed by Europeans, was eventually determined to have modest resources and became, in a minor way, a field for economic exploitation.

FIVE

Pursuing the Peso (I):
The Harvest of the Sea

Pearling in the Nineteenth Century

The first decades of the nineteenth century produced little change in the pearling industry. Each year a few tiny boats set out for the placers, their rag-tag crews hoping against all odds to strike it rich. In 1811, an official decree freed pearling from government regulations and duties, but the catch was still so poor that the measure did little to stimulate the industry (Mosk 1931:246–47).

After 1821, when Mexico won independence from Spain, the new government relaxed the old colonial laws that had discouraged foreign interests in its resources. This prompted a newly-formed English company, the General Pearl and Coral Fishery Association of London, to launch an expedition to explore the pearling possibilities of the Gulf. The company's hopes for success lay with the use of an experimental diving bell and in exploitation of the rich pearling grounds that supposedly existed in the largely forgotten northern Gulf. The man sent to carry out the investigation was Lieut. R. W. H. Hardy, formerly of the Royal Navy, whose account of his adventure (Hardy [1829] 1977) is one of the classics of nineteenth century travel literature.

Hardy arrived in Mexico City in July of 1825 and spent the next several months securing a government concession for the venture. In early December, he departed for Guaymas, where he had arranged to meet the brig *Wolf* and the schooner *Bruja*, the expedition's two vessels. Faced with still more official business in Guaymas, he dispatched the two vessels on reconnaissance missions. The *Wolf* was instructed to determine the value of the well-known Loreto placers and test the diving bell, while the *Bruja* was to explore Tiburón Island, which was rumored to be the best prospect for new discoveries (Hardy [1829] 1977:97, 235–36, 145–46). Neither vessel had much success, and the *Bruja* returned in wretched condition. Finally on July 17, 1826, Hardy set sail with his two ships, their crews, and four Yaqui divers (Hardy [1829] 1977:226–30).

The two vessels crossed the Gulf to Loreto, and there they parted company. The *Wolf* with three of the divers was sent to work the pearl beds along the peninsula to the south. Hardy, with the shallow-draft *Bruja* and a single diver, began to explore northward, testing pearling grounds and exploring on shore. On the afternoon of August 3, the vessel entered the Midriff region and anchored in a small bay on the peninsular coast. The next morning Hardy set sail for the Midriff islands, and that afternoon, became the first known European to set foot on San Esteban Island:

> At six, A.M., we weighed anchor, and stood along-shore with a light breeze, which afterwards changed to the north-west, and carried us between the islands called "Sal si Puedes," (get back if you can). About five, P.M., the wind died away, and we remained drifting with the current, which here runs strong, sometimes to the south-east, and sometimes in the opposite direction; and, being immediately in front of one of the islands [San Esteban], I went on shore to examine it.
>
> I found it about seven miles in circumference, and very mountainous. The hills are chiefly composed of a red stone, which has very much the appearance of cinnabar. We landed on a small sandy bay, on which twenty or thirty seals were basking in the sun. We approached with caution, having clubs in our hands; and falling suddenly upon them, made an attack; but they were too active for us, and escaped with only a few parting blows. We therefore went in search of others, whose yet undisturbed slumbers might give us an opportunity of retrieving our credit. We were not kept long in suspense; and stealing upon these with more care and activity, we succeeded in killing twelve of them.… It was my object to get their skins, supposing them to be of the double fur, as well as to obtain oil from their fat. The latter object we accomplished; but as their skins were not of fur, we threw them away as useless. This island has no name attached to it in any of the maps; I therefore, thought myself *justified* in calling it *Seal Island*, in commemoration of our achievements. (Hardy [1829] 1977:279–80)

Hardy's own map suggests that his route past San Esteban lay on the west side of the island. If so, he may have gone ashore at the southwestern tip, which provides marginal anchorage, and is the only place on the west side where "hills of red stone" would have been clearly visible. From here, however, the way to the interior of the island is immediately blocked by high peaks, and indeed Hardy gives no indication that he strayed far from the beach. Though a prolonged calm apparently forced him to remain at San Esteban for four days, he seems not to have explored the island further. The fact that he says nothing about Indians on San Esteban is certain evidence that he saw none, for the Seris utterly captivated his attention at his next destination, Tiburón Island.

On August 9, the *Bruja* left San Esteban, sailed up the west side of Tiburón and dropped anchor at Tecomate, where they were immediately confronted by Seris. After an exchange of gifts and assurances that he had come with peaceful motives, Hardy was implored to minister to the headman's wife, who was desperately ill. With great trepidation Hardy, who admitted to a complete lack of medical skills, tended the woman as best he could and administered some medicine. Amazingly, she soon recovered, and the overjoyed Seris painted his face in gratitude.

With friendly relations firmly established, Hardy spent the next three days exploring Tiburón, including a hike across its north end. Despite the widespread Mexican belief, he found no evidence of gold there. The Seris seemed completely unfamiliar with the substance, though they knew a source of lodestone. Moreover, Hardy was unable to find any of the fabled placers in the vicinity of the island. He did see deposits of the inferior *concha nácar*, an oyster the Indians ate, but found not a single pearl among the shells his party examined (Hardy [1829] 1977:280–92).

On August 13, the *Bruja* left Tiburón and the Seris and headed north. After a long and eventful voyage around the head of the Gulf and into the treacherous Colorado River, Hardy descended the peninsular coast, passing with some anxiety through the Midriff region, and finally sailed into Guaymas harbor on September 21. He had returned with few pearls and no gold, but a first-hand knowledge of the geography of the northern Gulf and some perspective on the widespread tales of riches on Tiburón Island:

> At Pitic [Hermosillo], it is customary to say, that, when boys, they accompanied their fathers to examine some gold-place near the island of Tiburón, but that the ferocity of the Indians rendered a permanency there impracticable. With such persons, the desire of raising themselves into importance, by imposing upon the credulous, is a prevailing passion. We delight to dream of dangerous adventures, and sable tribes guarding with poisoned missiles, regions of inexhaustible wealth.... Independent of this, the narrators of marvelous stories in this country are aware, more especially with respect to the island of Tiburon, that there are none who could contradict the statement. But the most singular feature in the case is, that when I returned ... and represented the delusions into which I had been led by erroneous representations, the very individuals who had related to me these visions of a vivid imagination, expressed neither astonishment nor disappointment at what I told them; as if they had always treated as exaggerations, what they felt a singular pleasure in reporting as matters of fact! (Hardy [1829] 1977:98–99)

And as to pearls and the company that had sent him to the Gulf:

> I had almost forgotten to mention a very curious circumstance with respect to the pearl-oyster, namely, that on the coast of Sonora there are none at all, except at Guaymas; and that to the northward of 28°.30'., I could not discover any trace whatever of that shell on either side of the gulf. Moreover, I remarked that pearl-oysters, in shallow situations, are almost totally unproductive. These circumstances I mention to prevent future speculators in this

department from embarking in so wild an enterprise as that of the Mexican Pearl Fishery. (Hardy [1829] 1977:448–49)

Unknown and forbidding places must have a compelling allure. Among Sonorans, Hardy's negative findings did little to dispel the idea that mysterious Tiburón was rich in pearls. Writing in 1835, Alexander Forbes, an Englishman living in Mexico, noted that:

It has always been the popular opinion among the Spaniards, that there were immensely rich banks of Pearl Oysters on the shores of an island near the head of the Gulf called Tiburon; but that its inhabitants, who use poisoned arrows, were of such a savage disposition, that no one could approach it without being sacrificed: this originated in or at least was confirmed by the circumstance of some people being killed near it.... [A]lthough the Mexican Republicans have thrown off the Spanish dominion, yet the dominion of early prejudice is not so easily got rid of, and consequently the island of Tiburon is still considered by the Mexican Spaniards as equally rich and perilous as heretofore; although recent visitors, and among others Mr. Hardy, have proved the risk and the riches to be equally apocryphal. (Forbes 1839:73)

Nor were North Americans immune from tales of riches. In 1863, an enterprise calling itself the Pacific Pearl Company incorporated in New York and obtained a concession from the Mexican government to work the putative pearl oyster beds of Tiburón Island. The prospectus of the company assured potential stockholders of high returns because the company planned to fish the beds with a submarine. This vessel, dubbed the *Submarine Explorer*, was to carry not only its own compressed air supply but an on-board air purification system. This would allow its crew of six to stay below continuously for 10 hours, giving them the oyster-gathering potential of 300 conventional divers. With an operational depth of 100 feet the submarine would enable the company to tap deep oyster beds that had not already been depleted. However, the prospectus indicates nothing of the vessel's design, construction, or cost. Not surprisingly, there is no evidence that anything ever came of this scheme (Anonymous 1863:5–7; Kunz 1905:117; Mosk 1941:465).

A plan to exploit the pearl beds of Tiburón Island again surfaced in 1882. This time it was the proposal of a consortium headed by Guillermo Andrade, a Mexican citizen then living in San Francisco. Pearling was to be carried out at various points in the Gulf between Guaymas and the Colorado River, but especially off Tiburón and Ángel de la Guarda Islands. Andrade promised no technological marvels for finding pearls, and the pearling operation was merely a sidelight in a grand development and colonization scheme that involved San Esteban Island as well as Tiburón and Ángel de la Guarda (see Chapter 8). However, the fact that Andrade did not propose pearling as an industry for San Esteban suggests that pearl oysters were not known to occur there.

The mid-nineteenth century was a time of dramatic changes in the pearl industry, the first since the discovery of pearls there in 1533. In 1830, a French trader named Cyprien Combier found that there was a market in Europe for the nacreous interior of the pearl oyster shell, the *concha de perla fina*. Known as mother-of-pearl (or *madre perla*), it came to be made into buttons, knife handles, and many other decorative items. In the next 25 years, the value of the shell more than tripled. This discovery helped greatly to revive the moribund pearling industry because the demand was strictly for fresh shells brought up from the placers, not old shells that lay on the beaches. Pearlers could now dive for the shells themselves, which were a more reliable source of income, in addition to the elusive long shot of recovering a prize pearl (Kunz and Stevenson 1908:245–46; Mosk 1941:463).

The effect of more intense exploitation of the already overworked oyster beds was, of course, further depletion, which prompted the peninsular government in 1857 to enact regulations to conserve the resource. The peninsular coast and islands from Cabo Pulmo near the southern tip to just north of Mulegé (well short of the Midriff) were divided into four districts, only one of which would be worked during a given year. The right to work each individual placer within the district would go to the highest bidder at public auction, a move which gave an advantage to *armadores* with some capital (Lassépas 1859:63; Esteva 1865:25–27; Bancroft 1889:757–60).

Pearling abruptly became a true capitalistic industry with the successful introduction of diving suits in 1874. With these devices, divers could exploit untouched beds well beyond the lung capacity of naked Indians. Profits were instantaneous and enormous. Within a few years, a number of companies formed by politically powerful entrepreneurs had obtained exclusive pearling concessions. By the late 1880s, most of these had merged into a single corporation, the Compañía Perlífera de Baja California. Its work force of nearly 500, including suited divers and crewmen, operated from a fleet of five schooners. The four pearling districts were no longer recognized, and each season the company worked the entire peninsular coast from Cabo San Lucas to the Colorado River, over which it held a virtual monopoly (Kunz and Stevenson 1908:246–48; Mosk 1941:465–66; Townsend 1891:91).

Although big business now dominated the industry, it did not completely replace the traditional diving crews operating from small boats. These crews were able to remain competitive because their labor was cheap. Usually, however, they were not entirely independent of the large companies, who advanced them food for the diving season and purchased their catch of shells and pearls when the season was over (Kunz and Stevenson 1908:249–50).

Thus small-scale *armadores* with tiny boats and a small crew of naked Indian divers continued to scour the placers of the Gulf into the latter part of the nineteenth century. As a method of pearling and as a way of life, it was the direct legacy of the small-time pearling ventures of the two preceding centuries with all its brutal exploitation of Indian divers. Sanford Mosk gives a graphic summary of this life, based on mid-nineteenth century descriptions:

The *armador* owned or rented the boats used, he outfitted them, and he advanced food to the divers during the fishing season. This usually lasted from May to October, when the waters of the Gulf were warm enough for naked diving. The *armadores* employed annually about 500 men, mostly Yaqui Indians from Sonora, who with their families were housed in temporary shore settlements. These reminded [José] Esteva [1865] of prison camps, so closely were the inhabitants watched and so bad were the living conditions in them. Divers were not paid wages, but received a division of the product. Before the mollusks were opened, each diver shared his catch equally with the *armador*. Whatever pearls were found in his portion constituted the gross payment for his services; from this, he had to pay for the food which had been advanced to him, generally calculated at one real per day. The entrepreneur [*armador*] received all the shell, in addition to the pearls from his half of the catch.

This type of organization almost invariably leads to peonage. The diver's debt to the *armador* rarely could be liquidated at the end of the season, and he was bound to work for the same person the following year. Custom gave the employer even the right to sell his divers' services to another *armador*. Permanent debtor status for the diver was easily maintained in the institutional environment of nineteenth-century Mexico. Specifically, the diver usually sold his pearls to his employer, at prices fixed by the latter. It is not surprising to find that the value of his share each year turned out to be less than the value of the food advanced to him. The burden of debt and the tyrannical vigilance under which the divers worked could be shed only by running away, and Yaqui divers frequently escaped to the mainland in their employers' boats. (Mosk 1941:463–64)

These *armadores*, like those before them, concentrated their efforts on the known oyster beds south of Mulegé. It may be that a maverick pearling crew sometimes ventured farther north to look for undiscovered placers in the Midriff region and perhaps even scouted the shores of San Esteban Island. But it is unlikely that they found anything of value, for in the entire history of the industry, there seems to be no indication that San Esteban ever became a recognized pearl fishing locality. Today, all one can find there is an occasional shell of *concha nácar* (*Pteria sterna*) washed up on San Esteban's tiny beaches.

Whaling

For much of the nineteenth century, the northern Pacific Ocean was considered one of the finest whaling grounds in the world, and dozens of vessels set out for these waters each year. Although the vast majority headed for the cold waters off Alaska and eventually the arctic seas, whalers ranged widely in search of unexploited whaling grounds. For a while, the Pacific coasts of Alta and Baja California provided excellent hunting. Although a few vessels rounded Cabo San Lucas and sailed into the Gulf of California, the Gulf never became a recognized whaling ground (Duflot de Mofras [1844] 1937:104; Wilkes 1845:Map opposite p. 457; Maury 1851; Scammon 1874:270; Clark 1887b:Pl. 183). The reason was not a lack of animals altogether but of commercially valuable species in sufficient numbers to make voyages there worthwhile (Gilmore 1957).

Whales were hunted primarily for their blubber, which was rendered into oil and used extensively as a lubricant, in tanning and cordage production, and as fuel for lamps. In time, baleen, the flexible bone from the animals' jaws, also acquired value as a raw material. It was eventually made into a seemingly endless array of items, from buggy whips and corset braces to fishing rods and tongue scrapers (Starbuck [1878] 1964:155–56; Clark 1887a:4–5). Pacific whalers sometimes hunted the bowhead and right whale, and occasionally the sulphur bottom and humpback. The finest oil came from the sperm whale, and it was this animal that first lured whalers into the Pacific. Very occasionally, the intestines of this animal would contain ambergris, the most valuable substance of all, used in the perfume industry and literally worth more than its weight in gold (Scammon 1874:244; Starbuck [1878] 1964:98; Clark 1887a:4–5; Townsend 1935:18; Henderson 1984:162).

Whaling in Pacific waters was dominated first by British and then by New England whalers. The way was led by the *Amelia*, an English ship which reached the Pacific in 1789 (Starbuck [1878] 1964:90; Henderson 1972:16). It was quickly followed by several New England whalers coming around the horn of South America and by British vessels entering the western Pacific by way of the Indian Ocean and Asia. In 1793, H.M.S. *Rattler* explored as far north as the southern tip of Baja California, and in 1795, the English whaler *Resolution* put in for supplies at San José del Cabo. In 1799, some two dozen British vessels were operating in the vicinity of Baja California (Bancroft 1884:731, 737; Henderson 1972:16–21, 1984:161).

By the 1820s, the North Pacific was primarily the domain of whalers from the United States, who used the Hawaiian Islands as a base of operations. In the next two decades, a well-defined seasonal round evolved which took them to arctic waters in the summer and back to Hawaii when the ice began to form in autumn. In the winter, they would either head south or cruise for sperm whales in the deep water some 10 to 50 miles off Baja California. During this time, crews became increasingly aware of the California gray whale (*Eschrichtius robustus*), called "scrag whales," which summered in the northern Pacific, migrated southward along the coast of California, and wintered in the shallow bays and lagoons on the west coast of Baja California. Though ignored at first, curiosity about California gray whales began to mount as more valuable species became scarce. In the winter of 1845–1846, two Connecticut whalers, the *Hibernia* and the *United States*, sailed into Bahía Magdalena on the Pacific side of Baja California and captured 32 grays. They found the dark-colored oil to be of inferior quality and the bone nearly worthless. Moreover, pursuing these ferocious animals in shallow waters was dangerous business which eventually earned gray whales the name "devil-fish." But as sperm whales declined and the price of oil escalated, whaling for grays in the winter off-season could turn at least a small profit (Clark 1887a:12, 23; Henderson 1972:82–85, 1984:162–66, 178).

The following winter eight whalers appeared in Bahía Magdalena, and during the next 25 years, the quest for these animals became intense. The lagoons were visited each year by whalers from San Francisco, New England, and even Europe (Bancroft 1888:529; Henderson 1984:164, 172). Along the peninsular coast "shore stations" sprang up when it was discovered that gray whales could be hunted directly from shore in small boats during their annual migrations (Scammon 1874:247). In the winter of 1857–1858, Charles M. Scammon discovered an unexplored lagoon where gray whales calved and were especially vulnerable. During the next four seasons the slaughter in Scammon's Lagoon was enormous (Clark 1887a:23–24; Henderson 1972:136–37, 1984:167–68).

Before long, whalers learned that California grays also calved in the quiet lagoons of mainland Mexico and northward in the Gulf as far as southern Sonora. In 1862, Jared F. Poole sailed his bark *Sarah Warren* up the Gulf to hunt gray whales in Bahía Altata in northern Sinaloa, and he returned again the next year (Henderson 1972:165–66, 211). But how many others followed him is not clear. So far as is known, about two dozen whaling vessels sailed past Cabo San Lucas during the main era of gray whaling. Some of these apparently did fish the southern Gulf (Turner 1871:302) though many turned southward after passing the cape (Henderson 1972:175–77, 1984:168–69). By 1870, the U.S. Consuls in La Paz and even Guaymas had noted that whalers had sometimes called at these two ports during the previous 30 years (Elmer 1865; Alden 1866; Turner 1871:302), but it may be that most were looking more for places to resupply and trade than places to hunt whales (Buffum [1850] 1959:142; Taylor [1869] 1971:111, 117; Findlay 1870:122).

Although Scammon remarked that gray whales had been seen in large numbers near Bahía Adair at the head of the Gulf, it is unlikely that they were ever hunted there. Probably they were seen not by whalers but by schooner captains ferrying supplies up the Gulf to Ft. Yuma from San Francisco, Scammon's home port. During the early years of gray whaling, the animals were so accessible in the calving lagoons on the west coast of Baja California that there was little point in hunting them in the Gulf at all. By the end of the bonanza period of the 1850s and 1860s, the slaughter had so reduced the population everywhere that there would have been even less reason to make a long and arduous voyage in search of a few survivors in the remote upper Gulf. Entrepreneur Guillermo Andrade did propose whale hunting as one of his many Gulf enterprises in 1882 and even as late as 1892 (Velázquez 1882; Anonymous 1892), but he probably knew almost nothing about the real prospects, and he certainly never carried out the idea.

After 1865, whaling for grays declined sharply. They had not been very numerous to begin with, and two decades of intense hunting had decimated the population (Henderson 1984:176, 181). By the 1870s, changes in the marketplace had also made the pursuit of gray whales largely uneconomical. With their inferior oil and nearly worthless whalebone, they had been profitable only because they could be taken cheaply and in large numbers. But during the 1870s, a more valuable oil was beginning to flow from the petroleum wells of Pennsylvania (Starbuck [1878] 1964:110; Ellis 1991:167). The decline in gray whaling in the late nineteenth century allowed the population to partially recover until the 1920s and 1930s, when whaling from floating factory ships again nearly decimated them. Since about 1940, their numbers have been on the increase (Gilmore and Ewing 1954; Gilmore and Mills 1962).

Among the few whalers that did cruise northward in the Gulf, it seems that at least one may have spent a considerable time in the Midriff region. During their visit to the Seris in 1932, writers Dane and Mary Coolidge were told a remarkable tale of whalers who once came to Tiburón Island. The Seri who narrated the story, Santo Blanco, also illustrated it for the Coolidges with several drawings. Throughout the narrative, Blanco characterized the sailors as "Giants," which is a common Seri literary convention for indicating that the event took place a long time ago. As the Coolidges recorded it, the whalers:

> had white hair and were so big it took two *fanegas* (bushels) of tobacco to fill their pipes. They came in a big ship, in which they lived all the time, and went out in boats to kill whales. When they speared one, a man would pick it up and put it on the ship.
>
> They cooked the whale meat in an enormous iron pot, ate it[,] and drank the oil. They did not drink mezcal, but smoked lots of tobacco. This was in the time of the Antigua Seris, before the Yoris [Europeans] came. They wore hats so big it took twelve men to lift them, and had a liquor of their own. They would not sell this liquor—they drank it themselves. It is said they were very happy when they were drinking, and they sang ... when they were drunk. (Coolidge and Coolidge 1939:246–47)

As to their ship, Santo Blanco told the Coolidges that it:

> "... was so big that four whales would not fill it. The men sat in front and behind, but not in the middle of the boat....
> "... Their paddles were so big that each stroke would push them half a league.... They did not row backwards—they paddled forward. They had no sails on their small boats. Two men paddled—one on each side.
> "There were many men and one woman in the ship, and they told the Ancient Seris there were many more like them in their country. They lived in big houses, by the sea....
> "... The Giant Woman was the wife of the Captain. She was whiter than the men and had red hair. She had big braids down her back. She was dressed in thick clothes, and a big cloak or mantle went over her back. Her carrying-basket was so big, they could cut a whale in two and she would put one-half in her basket.
> "The story says their shoes were very big and wide, but when they went hunting they took off these shoes and wore sandals. They hunted on the mainland—they would have turned the Island [Tiburón] over if they had hunted there [because of their great weight]. They always slept in their boat and had no camp on shore. They went hunting very early in the morning. All

the weapons they had were bows and arrows and spears." (Santo Blanco, in Coolidge and Coolidge 1939:251–54)

Blanco said that the whalers came only once. Even though they stayed in the vicinity of Tiburón Island for 16 months:

"The Seris were afraid of them. All except the Old Wise Woman, who talked with them. They took four families of Seris away with them, who were all afraid to go. The Giants [whalers] promised to bring them back when they returned; but they never came back." (Santo Blanco, in Coolidge and Coolidge 1939:251)

Although the Coolidges were unaware that the Seris may have pulled their legs by fabricating some of the stories they told them, this narrative may well have been based on a real incident. If these sailors were gray whalers, their visit to Tiburón probably would have taken place during the 1850s or 1860s. This would place the event within about 80 years of the time it was told to the Coolidges, nearly within the span of living memory. The statement that there was a woman on board is especially interesting, for it was not unusual for North American captains to bring their wives with them (Henderson 1972:131). On the other hand, there is little chance that the whalers were actually hunting with bows and arrows, one of the points that led the Coolidges to the fanciful conclusion that these visitors must have been pre-Columbian Norsemen (Coolidge and Coolidge 1939:255–56).

Sea Lion Hunting

The quest for oil during the nineteenth century was not limited to whales, for a commercially marketable oil could also be obtained from several other blubber-bearing marine mammals. In fact, it was not uncommon for Pacific whalers to return to their home ports with a cargo consisting of both whale oil and "elephant oil." The latter derived its name from the elephant seal, which was the first of these animals to be systematically slaughtered, but eventually it included oil from harbor seals and California sea lions as well (Scammon 1874:130, 135; Henderson 1972:103–4).

Elephant seals were sufficiently numerous and so vulnerable that they quickly became prime targets. In some cases, crews of whaling ships split into two groups, with one group going ashore to kill seals while the rest of the crew cruised the nearby waters for whales (Henderson 1972:103–4). It took only about 20 years of relentless hunting to drive these animals to the brink of extinction (Busch 1985:186–87).

The California sea lion was abundant not only on the Pacific side, but also in the Gulf of California. Its oil, though inferior to that of the elephant seal, was still of a commercial grade and thus made hunting these animals a profitable pursuit (Scammon 1874:135). In 1852, the *Zoroaster*, the first whaler known to have set sail specifically for the Gulf, returned to San Francisco having spent its time hunting sea lions (Starbuck [1878] 1964:498–99). During the next decade, North American whaling vessels occasionally showed up at La Paz and Guaymas with cargoes of "seal oil" (Elmer 1865:146, 1867:777; Anonymous n.d.b). But sea lion hunting could also be pursued profitably detached from whaling, thereby eliminating the heavy capital investment of a large sailing vessel. For this reason, most sealing in the Gulf took on an entirely different character from its counterpart on the Pacific side of the peninsula. It became a predominantly Mexican enterprise, carried out on a small scale by crews consisting of a few men who operated from small boats.

Sea lions were especially numerous in the Midriff region, and these animals had long been targets of opportunity for European sailors. Probably the first European sea lion hunt in the Gulf took place in 1615, when the crew of the Cardona Company's pearl fishing expedition killed a large number of animals on Patos Island, off the north end of Tiburón Island. They found that the oil made an excellent tar for their ships as well as fuel for their lamps (Cardona [1627–1632] 1974:102). In 1826, the intrepid Lieut. Hardy stopped not only at Patos Island to hunt sea lions, but also at San Esteban, where he saw so many animals that he named it "Seal Island" (Hardy [1829] 1977:279–80, 295–96). The great numbers of sea lions in the Midriff continued to impress visitors into the middle of the nineteenth century. Passing by the San Lorenzo chain in December of 1850, Lieut. George Derby noted that "Immense quantities of seals are found upon these, as well as most of the other islands in the gulf" (Derby 1852:9).

According to Frederick Fitch, an engineer who worked in the Midriff region with the Jecker-Torre Survey in the late 1850s:

> About many of the islands in the northern part of this Gulf immense numbers of the common hair-seal (*Phocidae*) [more likely, the California sea lion] abound, and so unused to the presence of man, that they could not be made to move out of your way on landing. I have seen the beach of Los Angeles Island [Ángel de la Guarda] lined for miles with them, basking in the sand. I mention this simply with the idea that they might be made an important source of revenue. (Fitch 1875:61)

Similarly, in the early 1870s, the crew of the survey ship U.S.S. *Narragansett* found an abundance of sea lions on the beaches of San Jorge Island near the head of the Gulf (Belden 1880:137).

For sea lions to have been as numerous as these observers suggest, the Midriff islands must still have been beyond the range of most hunters up to the early 1870s. To the south, however, uncontrolled hunting had begun to take a heavy toll by midcentury. Although sea lion hunting was never anything but unorganized activity undertaken by individuals in small boats, the animals were such easy prey that the slaughter was prodigious. In 1856, the Mexican government began taking steps to curb excessive killing by implementing a concession system that granted exclusive hunting rights to only a single entrepreneur at any one time. The initial concession was awarded to one Manuel Múgica, giving him a monopoly on rights to hunt sea lions "on the coasts and islands of the Gulf of California" for a period of eight years (Maza 1893:630). This was followed by similar exclusive awards to other individuals. But monopolies and government restrictions on hunting were seldom heeded, and the animals were often shot in great numbers (Bassols Batalla 1961:142; Lluch Belda 1969:4).

By the 1880s, hunting had unquestionably extended to the Midriff islands. In the summer of 1884, a single vessel from Mulegé that cruised the upper Gulf, including the Midriff islands of San Pedro Mártir, San Lorenzo, and Ángel de la Guarda, shot 287 animals (Ramos 1887:155–56). Judging from figures of oil production, the annual slaughter of sea lions at this time must have been at least 500 animals.

Nor were sea lions any longer naïve to the threat posed by humans. By then, successful hunting had to rely heavily on stealth. The hunters in their small boat would try to approach a colony of animals while they were sleeping. A large male sea lion stood guard over the colony, so the best marksman among the hunters would try to shoot it before it could sound the alarm. If they succeeded in killing the guard male, the hunters could easily approach the remaining animals, which were groggy from sleep, and club them to death (Ramos 1887:155).

Hunting sea lions continued in the Midriff in the 1890s (Anonymous 1899:34), and by then there is documentary evidence that San Esteban was one of the islands where these animals were taken commercially. In 1894, a Mexican military expedition to Tiburón Island enlisted as their guide a sea lion hunter named Luis Henríquez, who was working around San Esteban Island at the time. The military commander noted that Henríquez had made his living hunting sea lions and sharks around the Midriff for some 25 years. Unfortunately, he did not record how much of this took place around San Esteban itself, or whether other hunters also operated in the island's vicinity (López 1894). Modern Mexican fishermen believe that the first Mexicans to visit San Esteban Island were sea lion hunters. The Seris also believe that Mexican sea lion hunters exploited San Esteban Island, and they relate a story about a confrontation between Seris and Mexican sealers that they think took place there in the late nineteenth century (see pp. 261–62).

San Esteban certainly would have been a good hunting ground, for it has supported a large number of sea lions at least since the time of Hardy's visit in 1826. However, hunting there may not have been intense or continuous, for in 1918, after the peak years of hunting, government inspector José Zárate found San Esteban still well-populated with the animals (Zárate 1920:79). In the 1980s, census data showed that the island was a major rookery that supported between 3,500 and 4,500 sea lions, around one-quarter of the entire Gulf population (Le Boeuf et al. 1983:79–80; Bourillón et al. 1988:193).

The profitability of sealing, and consequently the intensity of hunting, depended on the demand for sea lion products, especially in foreign markets.

Initially, the most valuable part of the animal was the blubber. Compared to the much larger elephant seals, however, the yield of oil was relatively low, and the blubber of three to four sea lions was needed to produce a barrel of oil (Scammon 1874:135; Ramos 1887:156). In 1877, the oil from an average-sized male brought between six and nine dollars on the U.S. market. But, as with whale oil, the demand for sea lion oil was eroded by the increasing use of petroleum products in the last decades of the nineteenth century (Elliott 1887:473; Busch 1985:202). By 1886, the value of the oil from an average male had dropped to around three dollars, prompting one contemporary commentator to succinctly remark that "There is now very little profit in this business" (Elliott 1887:473–74).

But sea lions proved to be valuable for more than just their oil. As the price of oil began to decline, a modest market developed for the hides, which could be used in the production of glue (Scammon 1874:135; Busch 1985:201). At the same time, a much greater demand was emerging for the "trimmings," which could be sold on the Chinese market in San Francisco. These parts included the gall, which was used medicinally; the genitalia, prepared both as soup and processed into a youth potion; and the teeth, from which ornaments were fashioned. The whiskers, sometimes elaborately mounted with silver or gold, served as toothpicks and cleaners for opium pipes. Thus as oil prices fell, sea lions continued to be slaughtered merely for the trimmings and sometimes the hide, with the remainder of the animal being left to rot (Elliott 1887:474; Ramos 1887:155; Lluch Belda 1969:5; Busch 1985:201–2).

Despite the increasing use of petroleum, sealing could still bring small profits if the oil could be produced cheaply enough, and a small export market continued into the late 1910s (Zárate 1920:77–78). In 1921, a scientific expedition found a band of sea lion hunters camped on San Pedro Mártir Island (Slevin 1923:57). In the 1930s and 1940s, a market developed for sea lion meat, which was made into feed for animals. There are reports of sealers hunting and rendering oil on Ángel de la Guarda Island in the 1950s and 1960s (Bahre 1983:296; Le Boeuf et al. 1983:77), and a decade later, a Guaymas company was producing it as a diluting agent for shark liver oil (Lluch Belda 1969:115). Local poaching of sea lions continued in the Midriff into the 1980s.

Fishing

Before the commercial overfishing of recent decades, edible fish were among the greatest resources of the Gulf. Yet prior to the twentieth century, there is no indication that fishing played more than a minor role in the lives of the European residents of the Gulf, either as a subsistence activity or as a commercial resource (Huey 1953). Indeed, the historic record frequently indicates starvation in the midst of abundance; several of the early attempts to settle Baja California, beginning with Cortés's Santa Cruz colony, foundered for lack of food. The first Jesuit mission communities also faced recurrent bouts of star-

vation, but at least in some cases, subsistence fishing helped the Jesuit fathers
weather critical periods (Burrus 1967:66; Crosby 1994:77–78). For a time, Indians from Mulegé apparently supplied fish to the nearby missions with some
regularity (Sales [1794] 1956:87). The missionaries were unquestionably familiar with the food resources of the Gulf, for their treatises on the natural history
of the region contain descriptions of sea life and remarks about their edibility
and flavor (Venegas [1759] 1966a:47–48; Barco [ca. 1770s] 1980:233–47;
Clavigero [1789] 1971:67–77). But fishing techniques at this time were apparently not very effective, and throughout the Jesuit period, the mission settlements relied primarily on foods shipped in from the Mexican mainland (Baegert
[1772] 1952:37–38; Crosby 1994:286).

Little seems to have changed after the departure of the Jesuits. Scattered
comments during the nineteenth century suggest that subsistence fishing added
little to the diet, even for those living in coastal villages. Sea lion hunters and
others who made their living on the Gulf itself may have engaged in some fishing for their own consumption, though apparently even pearl divers subsisted
largely on a diet of dried beef and maize (Baegert [1772] 1952:45; Wise
1849:321; Esteva 1865:7). Whatever its role, subsistence fishing was apparently
strictly a local activity.

One would expect that commercial fishing might have prompted considerable maritime exploration, for fishermen bent on harvesting large quantities for
sale might be strongly motivated to comb the far reaches of the Gulf in order
to locate the best fishing grounds. The commercial potential of the Gulf fisheries was obvious even to the early explorers. When Sebastián Vizcaíno set sail
for the Gulf in 1596, his royal license authorized him to fish for tunny, codfish,
and sardines, as well as for pearls, and one-tenth of his catch was to be delivered
salted and barreled as the Crown's share (Wagner 1930:197–98). Forty-two
years later, Pedro Porter y Casanate cited the possibilities of establishing a fishing industry when he petitioned the Crown for a license to explore the Gulf
(Mosk 1931:171). But neither Vizcaíno's nor Porter's schemes seem to have
produced results, and there was apparently little commercial fishing in the Gulf
during the next two centuries.

By the mid-1820s, some fishing for profit was taking place around Guaymas,
and a good supply of fish was getting as far as Hermosillo (Bourne 1828:566).
On the peninsula, Loreto sometimes produced a small quantity of salted fish for
market during the 1850s, on the order of 300 pounds in some years, probably
aided by the nearby salt deposits on Carmen Island (Lassépas 1859:90). In the
1860s and 1870s, the Mexican government issued regulations intended to en-
courage the industry throughout the nation (Bancroft 1888:527–28). During
this period, a number of trading vessels from San Francisco arrived at Guaymas
with cargoes of "fishing tackle" (Anonymous n.d.b), but it is hard to tell what
this gear was used for because, in both Spanish and English, it was common to
speak of "fishing" for whales, seals, and pearls, as well as for fish. The same is
true for vessels said to be on "fishing" cruises. By the 1880s and 1890s there was
some interest in fishing for shark (Velázquez 1882; Anonymous 1892; López

1894), and there is evidence that at least sometimes this extended to the waters around the Midriff islands.

But most commercial fishing remained a sporadic and largely local activity until the early twentieth century. The reason lies in the problem of rapid spoilage in a hot climate. Extended cruises were probably impractical until ice became available and cheap, so that large quantities of fish could be preserved long enough to get them to salting and drying facilities or canneries on shore. In the 1880s, Guillermo Andrade proposed setting up fish processing facilities in the colonies he expected to establish on the Midriff islands, presumably to open up the rich regional fishery to commercial exploitation (Hendricks 1967:102; Anonymous n.d.a). But even around Guaymas, with its large population and its bay "ever alive with fish" (Ober 1884:653), fishing remained desultory at best. As two ichthyologists who had come to Guaymas in 1887 to make a scientific collection of fish put it:

> Although Guaymas is a considerable city, containing about ten thousand inhabitants, there is no regular fish market. The reason for this does not lie in the scarcity of fishes in the bay, for great numbers of the best of food fishes abound.
>
> The extremely warm climate renders the keeping of fish even for a short time a matter of great difficulty, and the high price of ice makes its use impracticable. Otherwise the Bay of Guaymas might be made to furnish an abundance of a choice article of food. (Evermann and Jenkins 1892:123)

The situation was much the same in Baja California in March 1889, when the U.S. Fisheries steamer *Albatross* visited La Paz:

> But little fishing is carried on at La Paz. There are three or four Italians who occasionally visit the islands in the bay for that purpose, and bring a few fish to market. Their trips are made with no regularity, but only when they have need of a little money. They use dugout canoes, and the fish that are not disposed of fresh are split and salted, and afterwards exposed for sale in a very uninviting condition. The markets are very simply arranged. A common table set on the side of the street and covered with half a dozen dirty and bad-smelling fish compose the fish dealer's stock in trade. All the fish, both large and small, are split down the back, and the heads are left on. In the case of the salted ones[,] the flesh is gashed crosswise in order that it may absorb the salt quickly, which is essential to its preservation. Several years ago a French fisherman supplied the town with fish, but he has since gone to Guaymas. (Alexander 1892:468)

And a few days later, after crossing the Gulf, the crew of the *Albatross* found that:

> The fish market at Guaymas is but little superior to that at La Paz. The French fisherman formerly resident at La Paz and several Italians supply the town with fish. Three-fourths of a cent per pound was the standing price for all kinds of fish during our stay at the place. Shipments are sometimes made to the interior of the State and frequently to the southern part of Arizona. Gen-

erally 3 and 4 cents a pound are realized from such shipments. (Alexander 1892:469)

By the time the *Albatross* returned to the Gulf in 1911, Mexican sloops and small schooners had begun to fish the waters off Tiburón and other Midriff islands (Conn ca. 1909) though perhaps infrequently (Williams 1911:101) and with little effect on the commercial fishing industry overall:

> The population of the region is quite limited[,] and while there is desultory fishing at all towns and villages, there are no fish markets worthy of the name. The methods of handling the catch are crude. Fresh fish must be sold promptly as ice is not available[,] and there are no fishing boats fitted with wells in which fish can be transported alive. Much of the catch is roughly salted and is uninviting. (Townsend 1916:447)

The Gulf also produced edible oysters. Unlike fish, they could be stored easily and shipped live, and consequently there developed a considerable export market for them. During the late 1860s, oysters were gathered around Carmen Island, transferred to tanks, and shipped live by steamer 1,700 miles to San Francisco. Often only about half the oysters survived the trip, but the North American entrepreneur who personally accompanied each shipment was able to sell the survivors at a substantial profit (Bell 1870:373–74).

Guaymas also provided an outlet for oysters of reputedly excellent flavor (Ober 1884:653). These came from the mouth of the Río Yaqui, 20 miles south of Guaymas, where Yaqui Indians gathered them by hand and transported them to town by canoe. At the time of Lieut. Derby's visit in 1850, they were being sold to foreign vessels anchored in Guaymas harbor for a dollar a bushel, but they were not eaten by the local Mexican populace (Derby 1852:6). In the 1880s, the Indians were receiving one dollar per thousand oysters (Alexander 1892:442; Townsend 1916:447). During this time, they were shipped to the United States, and an oyster cannery was even established at Guaymas. By 1889, the cannery had failed, but Guaymas oysters had achieved "a wide reputation, even as far as the great centers of our Eastern cities. Arizona and New Mexico markets are flooded with the bivalve, that is sent in quantities by rail" (Forbes [1893]:41).

Beds of edible oysters were known to exist in other parts of the Gulf, and it was rumored that there were some off Tiburón and Ángel de la Guarda Islands (Anonymous n.d.a). For the most part, however, there was not much exploitation of oysters outside the Guaymas area (Alexander 1892:471; Rathbun 1894:196–97; Townsend 1916:447).

Sea turtles were yet another maritime resource. At one time, these animals swam throughout the Gulf in great numbers, and they were especially common in the Midriff region, where they served as one of the staple foods for the Seri Indians. In the Gulf, the first Europeans to make extensive use of these animals may have been the French buccaneers who sat out the hurricane season of 1688 in Bahía Pichilingue, near La Paz (Gerhard 1963:6). During the next 200 years,

sea turtles were at least an occasional source of meat for mariners and for In-
dian residents of Gulf communities, but the meat was generally disdained by the
Europeans living there (Revere [1849] 1947:232; O'Donnell 1974:50–52;
Crosby 1994:286).

For turtle hunters, the problem of spoilage is less a limiting factor than fish
spoilage is to conventional fishermen. Sea turtles can be taken live and, if turned
on their backs and well shaded from the sun, they can be kept alive and immobile on a boat or at a shore camp for many days. This has long been known to
sailors who would often stop to capture turtles in quantity, and then set sail with
a supply of meat that would stay fresh for a considerable time (O'Donnell
1974:23–30, 37–50). It also facilitated the emergence of sea turtle hunting as a
commercial industry in the Gulf, for it enabled turtle hunters to make extended
trips to productive hunting grounds and return to their home port with a supply of live animals for sale. Commercial sea turtle hunting has been mainly a
twentieth century enterprise, but its beginnings extend back at least as far as the
1870s, when canned turtle meat briefly became an export item from Guaymas
to the United States (Willard 1875a:848, 1878:730; Garrison 1877:758). It is
not known when sea turtle hunters first began to exploit the rich grounds in the
Midriff region, but they were certainly operating around Tiburón and other
islands by the beginning of the twentieth century (Anonymous 1899:34;
Townsend 1916:445).

SIX

Pursuing the Peso (II):
The Harvest of the Land

Maritime Trade

Much of the navigation in the Gulf during the nineteenth century was carried out in the interest of commercial trade. However commerce, especially with foreigners, developed gradually and only toward the end of the Colonial period. During Jesuit times, mission vessels crisscrossed the Gulf, bringing supplies from the mainland to Loreto, and then ferried them up and down the peninsular coast for distribution throughout the mission chain. But this was an in-house operation run by the Jesuits themselves primarily to meet their own immediate needs. Few commodities were exported to Spain, and Spanish policy prohibited trade between its American colonies and foreign powers. Foreign vessels that showed up along the coast were considered, often rightly, to be pirates or smugglers.

By late Colonial times, the threat of pirates had subsided, and Spain's extreme isolationist policy lost most of its virtue. In remote regions such as Baja California, local people welcomed visitors and goods from the outside world. Even in the mid-eighteenth century, the Manila galleons that touched each winter at Cabo San Lucas put ashore not only to attend to the sick and make repairs but also to carry on a brisk if illegal trade with the mission community. Small domestic coasting vessels also occasionally appeared and found a market among the mission residents (Bancroft 1884:467–68; 1889:706–7).

The first friendly foreign trader to reach the Gulf was probably the Dutch vessel *Hervating*, which arrived at Cabo San Lucas late in 1746 with a crew ill from scurvy. The Jesuits received them hospitably, trade flourished, and the Dutchmen stayed a month. They were not so well received when they later tried to put in on the mainland, where the Spanish authorities regarded them as pirates. No other foreign trader tried to stop on the peninsula for the remainder of the Jesuit period (Gerhard 1963:9–10; Crosby 1994:337–38).

By the late eighteenth century, whalers had discovered the northern Pacific whaling grounds, and some began to test the Spanish ports as places to resupply. Whaling cruises were voyages of great length, and no vessel could be away from its home port for two to five years without resupplying. Thus in 1795, the English whaler *Resolution* stopped at Santo Tomás for supplies, though it greatly displeased the Governor, who reiterated the ban on foreign trade and the danger of piracy (Bancroft 1884:731). This official reaction was not entirely unreasonable. Some of the most brutal raids on coastal towns during the previous 200 years had been perpetrated by English pirates and privateers, and in the closing years of the eighteenth century, the Spaniards were living under the threat of British intervention in the Americas. Although not automatically considered enemies or traders, many early whalers were indeed heavily armed, and they did engage in a great deal of trading. Consequently, the line between whaler, trader, and privateer and hence resupply, illicit commerce, and piracy was sometimes a fine one (Bancroft 1884:731–37; Henderson 1972:16, 21). Over the next two decades, whalers occasionally met with overt hostility from the Spanish authorities, but most were granted permission to resupply in Spanish ports with a minimum of harassment (Starbuck [1878] 1964:187, 195).

Probably the first authentic Yankee trader in the Gulf was William Shaler, who arrived in July of 1804, after a long voyage by way of China. He dropped anchor at Guaymas, where the Spanish authorities treated him with civility but barred contact with the populace. After a month there, Shaler set sail for Baja California, apparently crossing the Gulf in the vicinity of the Midriff islands. A day later, he sailed northward to Bahía de los Ángeles, where he careened his ship. Though the bay itself was deserted, the sailors were befriended by the Dominican missionary from nearby San Borja, who paid them a number of visits and brought them fruit from the mission. A month later, on October 1, they weighed anchor for Mazatlán, where they were again prevented by the authorities from engaging in trade. After a brief crossing to Cabo San Lucas, they left the Gulf and headed for Central America (Shaler 1808:144–45).

Although Shaler's narrative does not provide a detailed account of his movements, he explored enough of the upper Gulf to form some clear impressions of it:

On the [Baja] California side, there are a great number of ports and commodious bays: few of them afford water; but fish are generally plenty and good, and in several there is an abundance of pearl oysters. On the eastern side is situated the fine fertile province of *Sonora*, with many rivers, but no ports for vessels of burthen, except Guimas, ... which is large and commodious. (Shaler 1808:159)

Shaler saw the Midriff as a desolate, though not especially hazardous, region:

Above Guimas the coast is barren, and affords no water; above the latter [Guaymas], this gulf is covered with an immense number of barren islands: the navigation is, however, good among them, and there is no danger out of sight. (Shaler 1808:159)

His observations of the human condition of the region gives an equally drab picture:

> The inhabitants of [Baja] California were formerly very numerous. In the journal of a voyage performed by ... father Consag, a jesuit, in 1746, to explore the gulf of California ... it is remarked, that all along, wherever they passed, they found great multitudes of people. I have touched at a great number of the same places in the course of my voyages to this country, which are now solitary and desert; not a soul is to be seen, except now and then a straggler from the neighbouring missions.... At present, Lower California is nearly depopulated: no mission there numbers above 350 Indians; not more than three exceed 250; and the greater part have less than fifty persons....
>
> ... From San Borja down to San Josef del Cabo, there is not an establishment worth notice; even Loreto, the capital, produces nothing. (Shaler 1808:152, 156)

Despite Shaler's bleak assessment, foreign traders gradually began to appear in and around the Gulf, among them wandering merchantmen from the United States. Many of their captains had been involved with the Northwest Coast sea otter trade and were accustomed to smuggling as well as to legitimate commerce. Occasionally, they showed up at Loreto and Guaymas, where they were not always welcomed by local officials. In 1821, one unfortunate North American captain did time in the Guaymas jail for smuggling (Bancroft 1889:630, 707; North 1908:61; Ogden 1941:76–81, 155–68).

By the first decades of the nineteenth century, the center of gravity for this nascent maritime commerce had shifted from Baja California to the mainland side of the Gulf. Toward the latter part of the previous century, the collapse of the Jesuit missionary enterprise and drastic population loss among the Indians had thrown the peninsula into a long social and economic decline. While San José del Cabo, La Paz, and Mulegé remained active as ports of entry for the sparsely populated peninsula, the mainland towns of Mazatlán and Guaymas emerged as the principal commercial ports for the region (Bartlett [1854] 1965:466; Lassépas 1859:66–68; Voss 1982:43; West 1993:94–95). Mazatlán dominated the commerce because of its excellent location on the Pacific coast and its access to a large population base. Guaymas was inconveniently tucked away far up in the cul-de-sac of the Gulf, but it quickly became the major port of entry for goods destined for northwestern Mexico.

At the same time, the Colonial government began to ease many of the oppressive restrictions on trade with foreigners. Guaymas was officially opened to foreign vessels in 1811 and declared a free port for a brief time in 1814 and again in 1820 (Stevens 1963:45–46). After Mexican Independence in 1821, commerce in the Gulf became routine and sometimes brisk. For about three years, Guaymas remained a free port and commerce blossomed. During this period, it was common to see 20 vessels in Guaymas harbor, and the port collector later recalled a time in 1824 when there were 28 vessels there at once (Bourne

1828:563; Cummings Cherry, in Browne 1869a:647). The establishment of the Guaymas customshouse in 1823 or 1824, intended to raise revenue for the new nation, soon ended this initial boom. When Lieut. Hardy and Col. Bourne arrived early in 1826, trade had fallen off badly, and only one brig and a few small schooners lay at anchor (Bourne 1828:563). But this depression proved to be temporary, and commerce at Guaymas was soon on the increase. A good measure of its success is the town's population, which tripled between 1828 and 1845 from less than 1,000 to more than 3,000 people (Velasco 1850:53).

During the first half of the nineteenth century, much of the maritime traffic in the Gulf consisted of a lively coasting trade, which was handled mainly by small Mexican vessels that shuttled cargoes among the settlements in the Gulf and other port towns along the west coast of Mexico (Ward 1828:464; Hardy [1829] 1977:243, 246; Forbes 1839:63, 294–95). International commerce was primarily the domain of foreign vessels. Some of these were traders from South America and Europe, but the majority were merchantmen from the United States who specialized in bringing in cargoes from San Francisco (still part of Mexico at that time). Once in the Gulf, they would often double for a while as coast traders, ferrying local products among the coastal settlements—mainly San José del Cabo, La Paz, Loreto, Mulegé, and Guaymas—before returning to Alta California (Halleck 1850:606; Cunningham 1958; Voss 1982:36–38).

But throughout the first half of the nineteenth century, Guaymas was the end of the line for nearly all merchant vessels heading north up the Gulf. Most had no reason to sail farther. For foreign merchantmen, the important destinations were the ports of entry, principally La Paz on the peninsula and Guaymas on the mainland. For Mexican coasting vessels, trade opportunities were mainly concentrated in the populated region from Guaymas and Mulegé southward, since there were no towns on either coast farther north.

Nevertheless, Mexican coasting vessels occasionally did venture northward through the Midriff and into the upper Gulf (Halleck 1850:607). Though there were no settled ports, a sparse population lived on the ranches and tiny settlements of the interior. For these people, the Gulf provided the easiest access to commercial goods, and traders who showed up from time to time at Libertad and Bahía de los Ángeles often found a small but eager market for their wares.

Maritime commerce in the Gulf flourished during the second half of the nineteenth century, but under conditions that were hardly tranquil and orderly. Merchantmen were often exasperated by excessive tariffs and by erratic customs regulations. North Americans, in particular, complained bitterly that customs practices arbitrarily seemed to favor Europeans. Moreover, corruption was rampant, and legitimate traders found their cargoes competing with enormous quantities of contraband goods that routinely slipped in and out through the same customshouses that charged them such high tariffs. And the ports themselves suffered greatly from the political and economic chaos that pervaded northwestern Mexico throughout much of the period. Guaymas endured bombardment and blockade by U.S. naval forces in 1847 and 1848, followed by threats of invasion by the United States in 1858 and 1859 and by Britain in 1862 and occupation by the French in the 1860s (see Chapter 7). The port was even beset with raids by pirates and held for ransom in 1870 and 1872 (Halleck 1850:610; Mowry [1864] 1973:49; Willard 1870; Garrison 1873:51; Martínez 1960:350–52; Stevens 1963:48–49; Acuña 1974:104–5; Voss 1982:179–80).

International trade in the Gulf was seriously disrupted by the 1846–1848 war with the United States, and the little commerce that continued during that time was taken over by the English and French (Voss 1982:110). But these were brief interruptions. After the close of hostilities, trade relations with the United States resumed and soon thrived, especially with the rapidly developing new state of California. Over the next three decades, around 30 to 40 foreign merchantmen called each year at Guaymas, and of these, the vast majority were North American. Even the capture of Guaymas by pirates in 1872 failed to put much of a dent in foreign trade, for that year the port received 22 ships from the United States and four European vessels (Alden 1866:747; Willard 1871:296, 1879:954; Garrison 1873:686; Bancroft 1889:763). Foreign shipping through Guaymas continued to expand through the turn of the century, though after the completion of a railroad link in 1882, goods moving between Guaymas and the United States were increasingly carried by rail.

But just as during the first half of the century, most of the commercial traffic in the Gulf after 1850 consisted not of foreign vessels but small Mexican craft engaged in the coasting trade. Compared to transportation by land, coastal shipping was quick and cheap and thus was an essential element of regional commerce. By 1850, enough goods were being ferried across the Gulf between Guaymas and Mulegé to employ 10 small sailing vessels plus a number of launches and canoes (Espinosa 1854:123; Lassépas 1859:68). During the 1870s, there were typically about 170 coasting vessels entering and clearing the port of Guaymas each year (Willard 1871:296, 1879:954; Garrison 1873:50–51). And for coastal traders, the railroad that eventually connected Guaymas with the United States proved to be a boon to business. Mexican export goods and raw materials brought to Guaymas on coasting vessels could now be sent directly to the United States by rail, while North American and European products arriving by rail from the United States were reloaded on outbound coasting vessels for shipment to other Mexican ports. So good was this business that in 1887 fully 296 Mexican coasting vessels called at Guaymas (Willard 1888:594). And as commerce increased, the town itself continued to grow. Population estimates for the decade of the 1870s vary wildly, ranging from around 5,000 to almost 15,000. But between 1850 and the end of the nineteenth century, it is clear that Guaymas at least doubled and perhaps tripled in size (Pérez Hernández 1872a:73; Hamilton 1883:29; Gracida Romo 1985:30; Ruiz 1988:19).

By the 1850s, Guaymas was no longer the normal end point for commercial vessels in the Gulf as appreciable numbers of merchantmen began to sail northward through the Midriff on their way to the head of the Gulf. The catalyst that opened the upper Gulf to commercial navigation was the 1846–1848 war with the United States, with the subsequent need to supply Ft. Yuma and the newly created Arizona Territory by sea in the absence of a reliable overland route.

*Figure 6.1   Central Guaymas and a portion of Guaymas Harbor,
probably late nineteenth century. The Plaza de Armas is the area of trees at the
extreme right center, just to the right of the cathedral tower. The large three-masted
ship (center) is the Mexican warship* Demócrata *or its sister ship* México.
(Courtesy Huntington Library, San Marino, California [CL Pierce 9508].)

Before long, large sailing vessels and steamers were making several runs a year
from San Francisco to Cabo San Lucas and then up the length of the Gulf to
the mouth of the Colorado River, where a shipyard was built and where passengers and freight transferred to river steamers for the last leg to Ft. Yuma (see
Chapter 7). Coasting vessels also began traversing the Midriff with some frequency, for the first coastal settlements were starting to appear in the upper
Gulf. San Felipe, on the peninsular side, was established sometime in the 1850s
or 1860s (Taylor [1869] 1971:34; Anonymous [1870] 1965b:38), and on the
mainland side, the harbor at Libertad was opened as an officially recognized port
for the coasting trade in 1874. But this flurry of activity in the upper Gulf did
not last. The Southern Pacific railroad, which connected Arizona with southern California in 1877, quickly replaced most shipping past the Midriff by sea.
By 1890, Guaymas was again the northernmost port for nearly all commercial
vessels (Willard 1890) (Figure 6.1).

There was also a clandestine side to trade that drew merchantmen north of
Guaymas. Smuggling was a major enterprise throughout the nineteenth century. Not only did contraband enter and exit through ports such as Guaymas,
but goods were illegally landed and picked up on remote beaches. Apparently,
one of the favorite haunts for smugglers was Bahía Kino. Here, it was said, large
vessels from England, South America, and even China discharged entire cargoes

in exchange for silver and copper bullion. From Bahía Kino, the contraband goods were hauled to the lucrative Hermosillo black market and to other towns in the northern part of the state (Poston 1854:12; Browne 1869b:249).

But while there were many commercial voyages into the upper Gulf during the second half of the nineteenth century, most of the available information about them deals with matters of economic interest. We know virtually nothing of what these travelers may have seen as they sailed and steamed their way past San Esteban and the other Midriff islands.

From Gold to Guano

When Cortés dispatched the first of his three expeditions into the Gulf in 1532, it was in search of the fabled cities of gold to the north. Of course, none of these ill-fated ventures found either cities or gold, and with the failure of the subsequent Coronado expedition, the myth of golden cities faded. Entrepreneurs bent on making quick fortunes shifted their sights from gold to pearls as the most realistic source of wealth in the north. Yet the hope of finding fabulous deposits of precious metals remained and, for a fortunate few, was eventually fulfilled. The first prospectors entered eastern Sonora during the late 1630s and quickly discovered respectable deposits of silver. By midcentury, a number of productive silver mines had been put into operation. Gold, mostly in the form of placer deposits, was not found until the latter half of the eighteenth century, though its discovery precipitated a sizable gold rush. The placers were located in the northwestern part of the state, and some of the best were near Caborca and Cieneguilla, on the fringes of Seri territory. But the mining regions of Sonora were almost entirely confined to the northern, eastern, and southern portions of the state. Precious metals were never discovered anywhere near the heart of the Seri coast (West 1993:44–50, 79–91; Radding 1997:36–37).

Baja California proved much more barren. About 1748, Manuel de Ocio, who had already amassed a fortune in pearls, opened the first silver mine at Santa Ana, south of La Paz. But after some initial success, production at this and other mines fell off, and silver mining in the region did not again become profitable until the middle of the nineteenth century. Gold was not discovered on the peninsula in significant quantities until well into the nineteenth century (Clavigero [1789] 1971:347; Smith 1860:420–21; Taylor [1869] 1971:160; Bancroft 1889:755–56; Martínez 1960; 388; Aschmann 1967:259; Crosby 1994:325–28, 360, 365, 387).

The most valuable metal proved to be a massive deposit of copper ore on the peninsular coast opposite Guaymas. Between about 1866 and 1868, ball-like chunks of high-grade copper ore, called *boleos*, were discovered in the area, and over the next 15 years or so the deposits were worked by a succession of small operators. In 1885, after a thorough survey of the region, a French company obtained the concession for the deposits and prepared to extract the ore on an industrial scale. It soon opened several mines, built a smelter, and founded a company town and port. The town was named Santa Rosalía, and the entire mining district became known as El Boleo (North 1908:139–41; Aschmann 1967:259–61; Huycke 1970:33–42). Regular shipping in and out of the port began almost immediately, but because the operation was located well south of the Midriff, vessels that serviced El Boleo never sailed within sight of San Esteban Island.

The islands of the Gulf showed even less promise, although persistent rumors of gold and silver (and eventually copper) kept hopes alive until the beginning of the twentieth century (Ramírez 1884:350–51; Anonymous 1899:32–34). There was one brief success in 1881 when a small vein of gold and silver, discovered on San Francisco Island just north of La Paz, was worked profitably for about five years by a German named Federico Ernst (Anonymous 1899:32–33; Lewis and Ebeling 1971:245). By this time, most of the rumors were directed toward the two largest islands, Ángel de la Guarda and Tiburón (Hardy [1829] 1977:98–99; Browne 1869a:635; Anonymous [1870] 1965a:33; Pérez Hernández 1872b:43; Johnson 1894; Anonymous 1899:34; Bowers 1909:168; Anonymous n.d.a; Wilkins 1939:159–64; Steinbeck 1975:224). Their sheer size coupled with their remote position in the Midriff region had left them among the least explored of the Gulf islands. Moreover, the evil reputation of the Seris discouraged serious prospecting expeditions to Tiburón Island, enabling tales of riches in gold and silver to be easily perpetuated with little chance of being discredited (Derby 1852:8). Among these were classic stories of "lost mines":

> The mineral resources of the island [Tiburón] consists of gold, silver[,] and copper veins, but none of these have been worked. There is a vein of silver which has assayed in San Francisco at $6,000 a ton. The prospector, who was an Indian, died and all trace of it has been lost. (Anonymous 1897b:73)

Even the participants in Governor Izábal's campaign, who spent eight days harassing Seris on Tiburón in 1904, left the island believing that:

> in the interior of the Island, there are mines or placers of gold, and in its waters there are pearl shells. This is demonstrated by the fact that the Seris have repeatedly come to Hermosillo in times past to exchange or sell gold dust and pearls. (García y Alva 1905–1907)

Some of those who claimed to have personally been to Tiburón must have taken great delight in recounting their stories in the form of tall tales, as did one J. Bulwer Clayton:

> Now, Mr. Editor, I am probably the only white man who ever put his foot on Tiburon Island and lived to tell about it. I was wrecked there in 1867, coming over from Santa Rosalia in a pearl boat to Guaymas, and every man of the crew was killed and eaten but myself, and I would have been eaten, too, but for the scurvy which I had got up in British Columbia, and was given up

to die by the doctors when I was wrecked on Tiburon, and I owe my life to that same fact as the Indians cured me with herbs so that they could kill me afterwards....

Now, Mr. Editor, I was on Tiburon Island eighteen months, and I know what I talk of when I say that there is more gold there than in all the rest of Mexico. I saw idols and gold ornaments among the Indians which they got out of a cave in the middle of the Island, and an old woman of the Ceris told me that the cave was full and that they were brought there a long time ago by Aztec Indians from the south. There are rich placers in the south end of the Island[,] but as the Indians watched me closely[,] I got very little chance to prospect. (Clayton 1895:8)

Clayton's departure from the island was especially inventive:

I escaped by lashing the trunk of two good-sized trees to the sides of a big turtle that towed me over to the Sonora side. Tom Keefe of your town [Los Angeles, California] is the only witness I have of the truth of this, if he is still alive. Phil Fox is dead and they are the only two who could prove it. (Clayton 1895:8)

But not quite everybody told a tale of great riches:

Some years ago a Mexican named Amago [probably José G. Moraga, who was actually from California (see p. 222)], who owned an interest in the San Juan mine in Lower California, determined to thoroughly prospect the island [Tiburón]. He disguised himself as a priest and was duly escorted to the Tiburon and properly introduced in his holy capacity by a Seri Indian who was working at the Encinas ranch. The Indians received him with all respect and veneration, for the Seris have all pretended to embrace the Catholic religion. Amago remained on the island for thirty days, during which time he married the Indians[,] baptized their children[,] and industriously prospected their island. He found copper and traces of silver, but not a particle of gold, and he is prepared to swear that Tiburon Island is a good place for prospectors to keep away from. (Anonymous 1897[?])

According to the same writer, for a short period after 1880, when the government reduced the Seri threat by removing 150 Indians from the vicinity of the island:

Tiburon was overrun by practiced prospectors and no El Dorado was discovered. Other parties of experienced prospectors have visited the island at different times and it may be stated as a fact that it has been examined from one end to the other without a trace of gold being found. (Anonymous 1897[?])

And contrary to García y Alva, "The Indians have never been seen in possession of any gold or silver" (Anonymous 1897[?]).

Nevertheless, rumors of gold persisted. Unfortunately, not all who attempted to prospect there returned unscathed. One story claims that:

> in 1879 two prospectors, while digging for water [on Tiburón Island], found placer gold at a depth of six feet. After working for ten days, panning out about eight thousand dollars in gold dust and nuggets, they were discovered and ambushed by the [Seri] savages, but managed to escape with their lives.
>
> Later they returned with a small party, but as none of them were ever seen again, it is believed they fell victims of the Seri blood-lust and were massacred on their arrival. (Bowers 1909:168)

According to newspaper reports, only one member of a party of five gold prospectors who landed on Tiburón in January 1896, escaped (McGee 1898:121). In July 1905, three of the four members of Thomas Grindell's well-documented prospecting expedition succumbed to thirst before they could even cross the channel to Tiburón Island (Hoffman 1983). Two months later, while the lone survivor of this expedition was grimly struggling toward Guaymas, a search party led by Grindell's brother Edward found the remains of Henry Miller and Gus Olander (also rendered Orlander and Olinger), who had sailed for Tiburón Island at the beginning of the year to prospect for pitchblende (Grindell 1907:380–81; Bowers 1909:172–73; Miller 1972:84–99; King 1989:247–48). It was not until 1909, when Fayette Jones and his party success-fully crisscrossed a substantial portion of Tiburón Island, that the myth of gold there was finally laid to rest (Jones 1910). A Mexican government expedition to the Midriff in 1918 confirmed that none of these islands was likely to contain economically valuable deposits of precious metals (Zárate 1920).

Though generally lacking in precious metals, a few of the Gulf islands were found to contain deposits of mineral resources of economic value if they could be extracted in bulk quantities. One of these resources was ordinary salt. Extensive deposits occur on two islands, Carmen and San José. These islands have been known since at least 1633, when they were visited by Francisco de Ortega and given their present names. Though salt has been extracted commercially from both islands, the salt works of Carmen Island have always been the more important. This island lies conveniently just off shore from the old Jesuit mother mission of Loreto, and its enormous deposit of nearly pure sodium chloride has been mined more or less continuously since the first missionaries arrived on the peninsula. As the eighteenth century historian Clavigero described it, with only modest exaggeration, the great salt bed:

> extends for so many miles that the end is not seen with the eyes; it appears to the observer as an immense plain covered with snow. Its salt is very white, crystallized, and pure, without a mixture of earth, or of other foreign bodies. Although it is not so hard as rock salt, it is broken with picks, and in this manner it is cut into square cakes of a size such that each laborer can carry one of them on his back. This work is carried on in the first and last hours of the day, because at other times the reflection of the rays of the sun on it is so bright

that it dazzles the workmen. Although all the merchantmen of Europe might go there to load salt from that salt bed, they never could exhaust it, not only because of its great size but principally because all that salt which is taken from it is reproduced at once. When not more than seven or eight days have passed after the quantity necessary for loading a boat has been dug out, the excavation is rapidly refilled with new salt. (Clavigero [1789] 1971:30–31)

Throughout Jesuit times, the missionaries tried to obtain government authorization to extract Carmen Island salt commercially to help support the mission chain, but without success (Dunne 1968:156–57; Gerhard and Gulick 1962:209). Though they amply fulfilled their own needs, exploitation on a commercial scale did not begin until the 1850s when the California gold rush created a sudden and very great demand. Over the next two decades, Carmen Island was the principal source of salt shipped to San Francisco. It was also transported to mainland Mexico for use in processing silver ore and often simply loaded on board passing vessels as cheap ballast (Espinosa 1854:123; Anonymous 1864:2–4; Bell 1870:372–73; Gerhard and Gulick 1962:209; Henderson 1972:235–39; Ewald 1985:176). In 1867, 30,000 tons a year were being shipped out at $18 a ton, making the North American concessionaire, Ben Holladay of San Francisco, a wealthy man. The labor, as was customary, was provided by imported Yaqui Indians, who worked long hours six days a week for 75¢ a day. These men would dig the salt with crowbars, cracking it into large "cakes" which were further broken up and carted to the beach. Here the salt would be loaded into sacks weighing from 75 to 130 pounds, which the Indians would then carry into the sea, often up to their armpits, to load in waiting boats. Despite the long hours of hard work, during the summer months the biting gnats near the shore were so vicious that at the end of the day the Indians would walk two miles into the mountains to sleep (Anonymous 1868[?]).

Since then, the Carmen Island salt works has passed through a series of Mexican and foreign owners. During the first quarter of the twentieth century, it was apparently run by an English firm. Eventually, it was acquired by a Mexican company, Salinas de México, which has continued operations into the present (Anonymous 1864:4; Townsend 1916:425; Slevin 1923:68; Ewald 1985:176–77).

Farther north, San Marcos Island has been a source of gypsum since the early 1700s, when Father Juan Basaldúa quarried translucent sheets of the material for use as windows in the church at Mulegé (Gerhard and Gulick 1962:211; Lewis and Ebeling 1971:303). Commercial quarrying was underway at least sporadically by 1869, when 600 tons were shipped to San Francisco (Henderson 1972:237). At this time, blocks of the material were cut from the quarry by hand and pushed over a cliff to the beach below. From here, they were ferried by dory out to schooners anchored offshore. However, ownership disputes frequently interrupted the work, and it was not until 1925, when a Mexican subsidiary of the Kaiser Corporation named the Compañía Occidental Mexicana acquired rights to the deposits, that steady extraction on an industrial scale began. Nearly all of the gypsum is shipped to the United States for use in building materials (Kirchner 1983:39–41; Gerhard and Gulick 1962:210–11).

The only other mineral resource of the Gulf islands that has proved to have important commercial value is phosphatic guano, the accumulated excrement of sea birds (and in some places sea lions). This substance occurs in commercially significant quantities on a half dozen or so small rocky islands, most of them in the Midriff and upper Gulf. These tiny islands, too small to support ground predators, have long served as traditional breeding grounds for sea birds, which visit these sites in enormous numbers. Over the millennia, countless nesting birds have capped these safe havens with thick layers of guano. In the mid-nineteenth century, European farmers found that this nitrogen-rich material made an excellent fertilizer. Guano soon began to be surface-mined and exported, mainly to Europe, from various parts of the world. It was not long before the guano deposits of the Gulf islands were discovered, and enterprising companies moved quickly to obtain concessions from the Mexican government to strip the islands of this marketable resource.

The initial guano mining operations began not in the Gulf but rather on the Pacific coast of Baja California, where whalers had just begun to wreak their havoc on gray whales. The first concession went to an American concern which called itself the Mexican Guano Company. It started its operations around the beginning of 1857 on tiny Elide Island, north of the bay that was soon to be known as Scammon's Lagoon. The company established a barracks on the island for its workers, who were brought in from San Francisco. Within three years, some 28,000 tons of guano, which had initially covered the island to a depth of 10 or 12 feet, had been stripped off, as had the accumulations on several other guano rocks in the region (Scammon 1869:128; Taylor [1869] 1971:162–63; Henderson 1972:104–6, 234).

Well before the deposits of these islands had been exhausted, companies began to turn their attention to the guano islands in the Gulf. Four islands proved to have sufficient deposits to be mined profitably. One of these, San Jorge or "George's" Island, lies near the head of the Gulf. The other three, Patos, Rasa, and San Pedro Mártir, are all located in the Midriff region. With the exploitation of these islands came a major increase in maritime traffic in the Midriff. As colonies of laborers were established, food, water, and equipment had to be shipped in on a regular basis, while guano bound for Europe and San Francisco was shipped out. Except for the trip to San Pedro Mártir, most of the vessels involved in the guano trade would have sailed directly past San Esteban Island.

The first of the Gulf islands to be mined for its guano was probably the rocky outcrop of Patos Island. This island (not to be confused with another island of the same name on the west coast of the peninsula, mined for guano about the same time) lies deep in the heart of Seri territory, a mere six miles north of Tecomate, the most important Seri camp on Tiburón Island. One of the initial attempts to exploit the island met with disaster, although through no fault of the Seris. In the summer of 1858, the full-rigged ship *John Elliot Thayer* (Figure 6.2), which had been trading between San Francisco and Liverpool, sailed up the Gulf to take on a load of guano. The vessel anchored off the south side of Patos and began to take on its smelly cargo. But on September 13, fire broke

Figure 6.2 The John Elliot Thayer *in 1854. Painting by D. McFarlane.*
(Courtesy Peabody Essex Museum, Salem, Massachusetts [No. 24828].)

out on board the partly loaded vessel, and the ship sank. The crew managed to get south to Manzanillo, on the Mexican west coast, where they sent word of the catastrophe to San Francisco. Captain Pousland reported that the fire had been deliberately set by a disgruntled crewman by the name of Philip Richard. Richard was apprehended and sent to Guaymas in irons and from there to Boston, where he was bound to stand trial for arson. Although he entered a plea of not guilty, a newspaper correspondent reported that "Richard, who claims to be a Frenchman, is rather a hard-looking customer, and, it is said, asserts that this is not the first ship he has set on fire" (Anonymous 1858). The loss of the ship and its cargo were estimated at $100,000 (Peterson 1992:149–50; Walt Peterson 1992:pers. comm.).

According to their own oral history, the Seris were not entirely bystanders to the guano mining on Patos. They recall the time when great sailing ships came to Patos Island and say that they supplied the sailors with meat, fish, and firewood. The *John Elliot Thayer* is well remembered as the ship that burned and sank off Patos the year Juan Tomás was born. Around 1965, Roberto Herrera described the incident:

> The sailing ship was said to be very big … and also fairly old. It leaked somewhat. The Seris didn't know who the sailors were, nor where they came from. They say that the sailors were friendly and treated the Indians well. They gave them food and gifts. (Mary Beck Moser 1997:pers. comm.)

Herrera said that the sailors also hired Seri men to help them load the guano. They brought it down to the beach in wheelbarrows, down a wide ramp that was reinforced at the sides with rocks. One of the Seri men was put in charge of the other Indians and his position went to his head. He was given new clothes and shoes and a hat, too. When he was paid, he would throw handfuls of his money to the other Indians. But the loading job was never finished:

> [The sailors] had a mule aboard to haul up buckets of water from the hold. One day, one of the sailors threw his cigarette stub into the mule's hay and went ashore, leaving the ship alone. The hay caught fire, and the ship burned and sank, the mule burning to death. The main mast broke off at the base and floated to Tiburón Island, where it lay for a long time. Finally, one of the Indians took a big hunk of it and carved out a dugout canoe, and he was able to carry four turtles in it. (Mary Beck Moser 1997:pers. comm.)

As for the Seri who was put in charge, Herrera wryly noted that when the ship burned, he was out of a job, and he found himself as poor as he had ever been.

Another Seri, Ramona Blanco, recalled seeing the masts still poking up out of the water around the turn of the century. Apparently, about that time some Seris began to dive to the wreck, which lies in comparatively shallow water, and salvage pieces of bronze which they would carry inland to Costa Rica Ranch and trade for livestock. Other Seris still dive there from time to time (Mary Beck Moser 1997:pers. comm.). In recent years, scuba diver Walt Peterson and several other North Americans have also explored the wreck, which they say is still easily recognizable (Peterson 1992:149).

Shortly after the turn of the century, the Seris are said to have been involved in another episode of guano mining on Patos. So the story goes, around 1906 a small brigantine out of San Diego named the *Blakely* was in the Gulf looking for a cargo of guano to haul back to the fertilizer plants in California. The vessel turned up at Tiburón Island, where the crew encountered some Seris who were suffering from rheumatism. One Seri man had discovered a cure, which was to sleep on a seal lion skin, but there were no skins readily available:

> There were some seals on the other side of the island, but the Indians lacked guns suitable for the job—and they quickly found that there were a couple of rifles aboard the brigantine. They also found that the crew of the vessel detested the slow, hot, filthy job of digging guano and loading it aboard. It didn't take long to set up a deal: If the Blakely's people would shoot them some seals, they would load the ship with guano, and quickly.
>
> So the Blakelians loaded their guns and headed for the seal-rookery. It didn't take them long to shoot enough seals to handle Tiburon's rheumatism problem. The Indians, true to their word, tackled the cargo with such vim that, before long, all you could see of the Blakely's two masts was their upper parts, above a cloud of yellow guano dust.
>
> The job was done with amazing speed. In an atmosphere of mutual satisfaction[,] the crew of the brigantine washed down their decks, loosed sail and

took in their anchor, standing across the Gulf to round Cape San Lucas and begin the long beat, up the coast for San Diego. (MacMullen 1964)

Soon after mining began on Patos Island, guano was also removed from San Jorge Island. One period of intense activity was in late 1861, when three vessels touched at Guaymas while carrying out more than a thousand tons of guano from "George's I." (Alden 1861). One of these vessels, the ship *Ashland* under Master Edward Moore, brought home the reality of the Civil War to North Americans living in remote northwestern Mexico. The *Ashland* had just spent a month and a half at San Jorge Island loading guano. On October 24, 1861, when she made a routine call at Guaymas on her way out of the Gulf, the vessel's steward jumped ship and sought asylum at the U.S. Consulate, in order to escape the alleged cruelty of the captain. Captain Moore, a Secessionist from New Orleans, refused to recognize the authority of a Union consulate, and demanded that Vice-Consul Farrelly Alden return his crewman. Alden reported later that when he refused the captain's demand, Moore and his "burly mate" stormed into the consulate, drew a loaded pistol, and threatened to kill both the steward and the Vice-Consul. Alden seized the barrel of the gun in one hand and a heavy object in the other, and the consulate erupted in a wild melee. Amazingly, nobody had been seriously hurt when the police arrived and carted Captain Moore off to jail. The *Ashland* was sold a month later, and on January 4, 1862, she set sail for Mauritius with her cargo of San Jorge Island guano and Charles Scammon as her new Master (Anonymous 1861; Alden 1862).

Guano was also mined on San Jorge in 1863 and in 1866. In August of 1866, Guaymas customs authorities seized the bark *Frances Palmer* on trumped up charges that it was loading guano at San Jorge Island without a license. This seizure occurred on the eve of the evacuation of the French troops who, in support of Maximilian's Empire, had been occupying Guaymas for a year and a half. Apparently, the customs officials had been collaborators in the service of the French and now stood in mortal fear of retribution when the occupation force departed and Mexican control was reestablished. The *Frances Palmer* offered a timely means of skipping town, and on September 13, the day before the French exodus, the customs officers slipped out of Guaymas aboard the vessel (Fergusson 1863; Conner 1866a, 1866b).

San Jorge was evidently deserted when the U.S.S. *Narragansett* anchored there at the end of 1873 and again in early 1875, for the crew knew only that the island's guano had previously "been worked to some extent" (Belden 1880:137). Mining may have resumed shortly thereafter. When the Gulf of California Phosphate Company acquired the concession to Rasa Island in 1873, it also acquired the rights to San Jorge from the previous concessionaires, and one report claims that 1,700 tons were removed from San Jorge in 1876 (Hutchinson 1950:129). As on other guano islands, the miners have left a legacy of their activities in the form of rockpile walls and terraces all over the island (Murray and Poole 1965:68–69).

Some of the most extensive guano mining operations in the Gulf took place on Rasa (or "Raza") Island. Today, this low-lying basaltic platform, only one-quarter square mile in area, is a rookery for some 350,000 birds, and one of the only breeding sites presently used by elegant terns and Heermann's gulls (Anderson 1983:249; Bourillón et al. 1988:168; Velarde G. 1989). As recently as 1940, nesting birds may have numbered more than a million (Walker 1965:27). After the U.S.S. *Narragansett* stopped at the island in the spring of 1875, the ship's surgeon, Thomas Streets, remarked that:

> At the time of our visit (April) [actually, March 18–19], immense numbers of the birds were congregated there, preparatory to laying their eggs, which, however, they had not begun to deposit. We may safely say, without exaggeration, that there was a bird on every square foot of the ground, and others were continually hovering about overhead. Their incessant noise deadened all other sounds. (Streets 1877:26)

Over the millennia, the incredible numbers of nesting birds had built up a layer of high-quality guano over much of the island. As a result, Rasa was the first Gulf island to be exploited for its guano on a truly industrial scale.

Until 1873, two men from Mulegé held the government concession to Rasa's guano, though their mining activities there must have been very modest. In that year, the concession for Rasa (as well as San Jorge Island) was transferred to an English firm called the Gulf of California Phosphate Company, which incorporated in Liverpool for the express purpose of mining Rasa Island guano. At the same time, the company contracted to sell and deliver between 5,000 and 10,000 tons of guano per year to a firm in Hamburg, Germany, for a five year period beginning January 1, 1874. At the end of five years, the contracts were scheduled to terminate, and the company would dissolve itself (Anonymous 1873).

The Gulf of California Phosphate Company was clearly out to make money quickly and efficiently, and it lost no time in transporting laborers and equipment to the island and getting its operation under way. By the end of the year, guano was already being shipped out, for in early December of 1873 when the U.S.S. *Narragansett* first arrived at Rasa, they found "The German bark Henrietta Hein at anchor taking in cargo" (*Narragansett* Deck Logs 1873–1875).

Nine months later, some 2,000 tons had been shipped to Germany (Willard 1875a:845). When the *Narragansett* returned to the island in March 1875, the ship's surgeon, Thomas Streets, was told that 10,000 tons of guano had been removed out of an estimated total deposit of some 70,000 tons (Streets 1877:26; Belden 1880:114–15; Hutchinson 1950:130). In 1878, in accordance with its original plan, the Gulf of California Phosphate Company wound up its affairs and voted to dissolve itself (Anonymous 1878f).

The dissolution of this company did not end guano mining on Rasa, though what went on there over the next several years is uncertain. By 1887, the island was being worked by the Mexican Phosphate and Sulphur Company of San Francisco, a company that had also begun extensive mining operations on San Pedro Mártir Island. During 1889, five vessels touched at Guaymas on their way to Rasa Island with supplies for the mining activities (Willard 1888:590; Anonymous n.d.b). In June 1890, it was the company supply ship *M. Romero Rubio* that sailed to San Esteban Island to rescue two Mexicans who had been wounded by Seris (see pp. 243). By then, the annual tonnage had fallen off considerably, though some guano extraction continued on Rasa into the 1910s (Willard 1890, 1891; Muñoz Lumbier 1919:23; Villa Ramírez 1976:19).

To the modern visitor, the only phenomenon that rivals the spectacle of Rasa's bird populations during breeding season is the peculiar presence of hundreds of human-made cairns and long low walls of piled rocks. All the islands that were mined for guano have piled stone structures on them, but on no other island are they so conspicuous and numerous. One count based on an aerial photograph estimated the number of structures at 11,200 (Murray and Poole 1965:133), and these features cover a large portion of the island's surface. The finest structures were built with sufficient skill and precision of form to suggest to some observers that they must have been the work of trained stonemasons. They have generated such widespread curiosity that it is worth describing them in some detail.

The cylindrical (or "conical") cairns are the most striking features. They are typically about five to seven feet in diameter at the base and taper slightly toward the top, which generally has a diameter a foot or two less than the base (Figure 6.3). The majority are between three and five feet high. Some were built entirely of large rocks. Most, however, have only an outer skin of large rocks one course thick that encapsulates either a rubble core of small stones and pebbles, or a mixture of large rocks and pebbles. These cairns were built by piling the outer course of large rocks first and, as the wall progressed upward, periodically filling the interior with rubble. A few were never completely filled and still have two or three courses of outer wall standing above the level of the rubble fill, which gives them the appearance of having been built as containers for rubble (Figure 6.4).

The peculiar forms and sheer number of structures on Rasa have spawned several theories of their origin and purpose, some more credible than others (Murray and Poole 1965:133; Murray 1967:70–71; Lewis and Ebeling 1971:331; West and West 1984:64; Peterson 1992:145). Some have logically attributed the cairns to the guano miners. One explanation is that they were piled up by the workers in order to get at the underlying guano and perhaps to make shoveling easier. Another theory is based on the fact that the birds prefer to nest on smooth soil. It proposes that the miners were intent on removing rocks from the ground, which would create more nesting space and which would in turn create more guano to be mined in the future. Though the motives differ, these two theories suggest that stacking rocks into concentrated piles was simply the most efficient method of getting them out of the way. Another idea is that the structures were built as anchors for canvas sun shades used by the miners.

Mexican egg collectors have also been credited with construction of the cairns. Toward the end of the nineteenth century, a market for tern and gull eggs developed in the peninsular copper-mining town of Santa Rosalía, and

Figure 6.3   Rasa Island stone cairns. April 1993.

Figure 6.4   Rasa Island stone cairn with a rubble core. April 1993.

enterprising individuals began coming to Rasa each spring to harvest eggs in com-mercial quantities. The scale of egg collecting increased so rapidly that humans soon became dangerous predators. Eventually, settlements as far away as San Felipe, Hermosillo, Guaymas, and even La Paz became markets for Rasa eggs. Although the number of eggs laid by the birds was enormous, the number harvested by col-lectors also became enormous, eventually reaching half a million a year. By 1964, the nesting populations were so threatened that the island was finally given federal protection as a migratory waterfowl sanctuary (Walker 1965:29; Lindsay 1966a:10; Bahre 1983:302; Bourillón et al. 1988:172–73).

According to the egg-collecting theory, even long before this practice reached its most destructive level, egg gatherers would have been wise to en-courage the birds to lay as many eggs as possible. The limiting factor on egg production would have been available nesting space, which needs to be soft sandy ground. Since much of Rasa's ground is rocky, egg collectors might have removed surface rocks and stacked them into the cylindrical piles in an effort to increase nesting space and hence egg production. By helping the birds, the egg collectors would also have been acting in their own economic self-interest.

Rational as this practice might have been, the indications are that egg gath-erers did not look with an enlightened eye to their long-term economic future. As collecting increased over the years, gatherers became aware that the birds could not indefinitely survive the pressure of their activities, yet none was willing to quit collecting as long as eggs were available (Walker 1965:27). Moreover, the spaces created between the cairns have only marginally increased nesting area and egg production. For the most part, the ground exposed by cairn build-ing is not the sandy soil that the birds prefer, but a pavement of loose stones. Nesting density between cairns is less than about 15 percent of that in the open sandy areas, and because there are fewer adults in these stony areas to chase away predatory gulls, the loss of young chicks there is much greater (Enriqueta Velarde G. 1992:10, 1993:pers. comm.).

There also seems to be an old folk legend that attributes Rasa's cairns to the Seris. The Seris are said to have used Rasa "as a sacred burial ground, a sort of cemetery annex of Tiburon Island" (Lewis and Ebeling 1971:331) and that "a monument was always erected over a tomb by the burial party which had paddled across the Gulf [to Rasa] in sort of a nautical funeral procession" (Murray and Poole 1965:133).

Among their many ways of disposing of the dead, the Seris often did heap rocks on a grave to discourage coyotes and other predators from disturbing the body (McGee 1898:287–91; Bowen 1976:47–48). However, there have prob-ably never been any terrestrial predators on Rasa (apart from humans), other-wise birds would not nest there. Moreover, the effort required to carefully construct a neatly-fashioned monument would not be in character for the prag-matic Seris. Nor would the prospect of a long paddle to Rasa to bury someone, since the Seris are anxious to get rid of their dead quickly. Indeed, a Seri once told Walt Peterson that the burial ground idea was untrue (Peterson 1992:145). Yet it is by no means unreasonable to suppose that the Seris may have visited

Rasa from time to time for other purposes (McGee 1898:49). It is less than 25 miles from both Tiburón and San Esteban Islands, and in the spring, the virtually limitless supply of birds' eggs might have been a powerful lure. Thus the folk legend continues on a different tack:

> Later, goes the story as it is told in *Sonora*, [after the Seris had been building stone structures as burial markers], the [Seri] egg-gatherers discovered that the birds favored the ground near the monuments where the soil had been laid bare and was therefore more easily accessible. As a result each [Seri] gatherer, as though in tribute to the birds for their heaven-sent gift of eggs, built one monument upon his annual return to *Raza*.... Of course, stone-stacking made egg harvesting just that much easier, so whether the poachers were really helping the birds or merely helping themselves is a point that will long be argued. (Murray and Poole 1965:133)

There is an even more unlikely legend that would account for the structures:

> During the Spanish [actually, Mexican] Revolution of 1910, the Yaqui Indians had built these walls and piled conical heaps of stone nearby to hurl down on their aggressors in an attempt to hold their island camp. (West 1963:376)

Egg collectors, Seris, and revolutionaries aside, there is good evidence that the structures were built in conjunction with guano mining. Bedrock outcrops and large undisturbed boulders bear a conspicuous horizontal crusty ring of remnant guano around them at the level of the original deposits (typically 6–9 inches above the present exposed ground surface). Below the ring, the basaltic rocks show a whitish discoloration due to chemical reaction with the guano, while the dark natural cortex is exposed above the ring. Many of the rocks that make up the cairns have a totally whitened surface, indicating that they were once completely buried in the guano. Others bear the crusty ring that indicates partial burial, and these rings are oriented randomly within the structure. Clearly, none of these rocks could have been stacked in cairns until they had been removed from within the guano matrix.

The spacing of the cairns and the long walls also reinforce the idea that the structures themselves are largely a byproduct of stripping the ground surface. The cairns typically stand between about 8–12 feet from one another. This is a convenient and efficient working distance for someone intent on clearing the ground of rocks with the least walking. In most cases, the long walls occur in sets that are parallel to each other and similarly spaced, again suggesting a separation determined by body space while clearing the ground.

Originally, much of Rasa's surface must have been a boulder field in which the rocks gradually became buried in the accumulating guano. By the time mining began, the island's surface must have resembled an incredibly dusty cobblestone street. According to the crew of the U.S.S. *Narragansett*:

The surface guano is collected in the form of dust and shipped in bags. The layer succeeding it is composed of "clinkers," which require crushing before using. These "clinkers" are richer in the phosphates than the pulverized guano and are more easily gathered and shipped. (Belden 1880:114)

To mine the guano below the dust layer must have required extracting the rocks from the guano matrix as much as extracting the guano from the rocks. After breaking up the guano, dislodging the rocks and chipping off the guano adhering to them, the rocks would have to be disposed of. Rather than haul them to the shore and dump them, it would have been much more efficient to stack them, either as cairns or as walls, in areas that had already been stripped of their guano layer.

What is most perplexing is that none of the three scientists who visited Rasa in the late nineteenth century—Thomas Streets, Edward Palmer, and Guillermo Krull—even mention the presence of stone structures, although they all indicate that the original surface was strewn with rocks (which, despite all the structures, is still true today). When Streets saw the island in early 1875, less than two years after mining had begun, some of the rocky surface was still blanketed with guano:

The formation of the island is a black volcanic rock, entirely destitute of vegetation. Through the long series of years during which these birds have made it a breeding-place, there has been going on a chemical reaction between the acids of their excrement and the bases of the rock, which has resulted in the formation of a new substance, composed largely of a tri-basic phosphate. This now forms (or did form) a thick layer, covering the whole surface of the island. On breaking open the bowlders, a sharp line of demarkation can be seen extending into the body of the rock showing the depth of the chemical reaction. The altered rock being a softer material than the original is easily pulverized and worn off by the constant attrition of the birds' feet during their breeding-season. In this way, the inequalities of the surface of the rocky islet have been smoothed over. (Streets 1877:26)

Palmer, who spent one day there in February 1890, saw the island after most of the blanket of guano had been removed. Still, he describes the island as:

being covered with a deposit of guano, [and] it has a whitish appearance. The island is exceedingly rocky, except a few low places which seem to have been subjected to the action of large volumes of water; these spots produce a few varieties of plants which are usually found upon alkali soil (some of the same plants were found on the rocky surfaces also). (Edward Palmer, in Vasey and Rose 1890:79)

Krull, who was there sometime prior to 1894, noted that:

The island is crossed from south to north by rocky ridges up to one hundred feet elevation, which merge to the south. They encircle several plains, of which three in the northwest are lagoons. It is more than six kilometers in circumference, the ridges are covered with blocks of dark rock, all encrusted and covered with ... hard phosphate.... The guano ... covers the plains to a thickness of 6 to 18 inches, [and] underneath is sandy soil that is dark or carbonate, and is contaminated with much clay, iron and gypsum. (Krull 1894:313)

The stone structures are such a dominant aspect of the landscape today that it seems remarkable that none of these trained observers thought to make note of them (assuming, of course, that they existed at the time of their visits). The fact is, however, that even trained observers tend to report only what interests them. Many of the scientists who have been to Rasa more recently have written eloquently of the birds and said nothing of the cairns. In one such instance, ornithologist Griffing Bancroft wrote an entire chapter about Rasa without a single mention of the island's cairns (Bancroft 1932:336-47).[98]

The last of the Midriff islands to be exploited for its guano was San Pedro Mártir. This lonely volcanic rock rises more than 1,000 feet out of the middle of the Gulf, 21 miles southeast of San Esteban (Figure 6.5). The exploitation of San Pedro Mártir's guano is connected with one of the more notorious land development schemes of the time, perpetrated by the International Company of Mexico. The company had its beginnings in 1881, when a wealthy North American promoter named George H. Sisson met the well-connected Luis Húller in Mexico City, and the two decided to become partners in speculative ventures. The meeting was well timed, for two years later the enactment of the new Colonization Law of December 15, 1883 enabled foreigners to acquire huge tracts of vacant land for colonization and development (see pp. 173–75). Taking advantage of the new law, Húller and Sisson formed the International Company, backed eventually by 20 million dollars in U.S. capital, and acquired title to 18 million acres in northern Baja California. Edgar T. Welles was named company President, Sisson was Vice President and General Manager, and Húller, in whose name the government contracts were awarded, was "Resident Director" in Mexico City. In addition to land, the company, through Húller, acquired concessions for a number of ancillary enterprises. One of these was a contract to exploit the Gulf islands for guano, which gave the International Company control of both San Pedro Mártir and Rasa Islands. To this end a subsidiary company, the Mexican Phosphate and Sulphur Company, was organized in San Francisco, and its field office was established in Guaymas (Willard 1887a:880, 1888:593; Bancroft 1889:730–36; Martínez 1960:444–49).

Plans to begin work on San Pedro Mártir must have moved quickly, for the company was already shipping guano by the summer of 1885, evidently without adequate preparations. On July 21, the ship *Ellen Goodspeed* limped into Guaymas from San Pedro Mártir with a partial cargo of guano and no anchor. She had been loading guano destined for Hamburg for a week when a fierce gale developed, and the vessel began to drag anchor. The ship was being blown rapidly to shore, and the only way to save her was to hoist sail, cut the anchor

Figure 6.5   San Pedro Mártir Island, looking west. May 1984.

chain, and head for open water (Willard 1885a). The insecure loading situation at San Pedro Mártir may have been one of the reasons Sisson himself spent two months at the start of the following year on an inspection tour of the Gulf guano islands. Shortly after he returned from the trip, he sent a letter to company president Welles with a staccato message:

> The Phosphate Company this day signed charter for schooner American Boy, to carry and establish moorings at San Pedro Island, to enable large vessels to load in safety throughout the year, said moorings costing about $5,000, but deemed indispensable to the energetic handling of products, and she brings back guano for this market. Advices by to-day's mails from the islands very satisfactory. (Sisson 1886)

For the next three years, San Pedro Mártir was mined intensively. Of an estimated 50,000 tons of marketable guano, approximately 2,000 tons had been shipped to Europe on the *Ellen Goodspeed* by the end of 1885, and another 8,000 tons by the end of the following year. In 1887, the company was working on Rasa as well as San Pedro Mártir, and the quantity of guano shipped to Europe reached its high point of around 15,000 tons. Additionally, the company had now begun shipping recently deposited "soft" guano to San Francisco. By 1888, most of San Pedro Mártir's valuable guano had been removed (Goss 1888:241) and the company's total production that year apparently fell to about 5,800 tons (Willard 1885a; 1887a:876, 880; 1888:590, 593; 1889:38).

The International Company proved to be a short-lived venture. In November 1888, an agent named Manuel Sánchez Facio was sent by the Mexican government to inspect the company's operations, and he found it riddled with fraud, deceit, and contract violations (Sánchez Facio 1889). The company was soon under such pressure from this and other problems that by May 1889, it had sold its interests to a newly-formed British firm, the Mexican Land and Colonization Company, Limited (Anonymous 1889). The Mexican Phosphate and Sulphur Company, using the same name but now under British ownership, continued to extract guano from San Pedro Mártir and Rasa until about the end of 1891, though by that year production had dropped to less than 1,000 tons for both islands (Willard 1891). The guano concession then transferred into Mexican hands and by 1918 had passed to yet another concessionaire (Zárate 1920:76; Martínez 1960:450–52).

Almost nothing is known about the daily operation of the guano mines and the life of the men whose job it was to dig the putrid substance. The small glimpse that has been preserved comes mostly from the observations of ornithologist Nathaniel Goss, who visited San Pedro Mártir in 1888, the last year the island was worked under the U.S. concession. From its field headquarters in Guaymas, the company operated a small steamer, the *M. Romero Rubio*, flying the Mexican flag, which was used exclusively to bring food, drinking water, and other supplies to the workers on San Pedro Mártir and Rasa (Willard 1887a:876–77; 1888:590, 593). Goss took the steamer to the island on March 15 and returned to Guaymas on the 28th. At that time, the company seems to have had a total work force of some 300 men on all the islands in its concession (Bancroft 1889:733) On San Pedro Mártir, Goss found that:

> The Company has a large force of Yaquie Indians collecting the guano that has formed a crust on the rocks of from one to four inches in thickness…. One hundred and thirty-five Indians were on the payroll and many had their families with them, and in working and climbing over the isle, they were continually disturbing and often robbing the birds. In this respect, however, the Indians are not as destructive as the white race, and as the Company feeds them well, seem to care but little for the eggs. (Goss 1888:240–41)

Writer Peter Mathiessen, who visited the island almost 100 years later, suggests a very different kind of work force in citing the:

> small stone platforms constructed by convicts who were sent out here during the late nineteenth century to harvest guano; the platforms—probably foundations for small huts—have been taken over by blue-footed and brown boobies. (Mathiessen 1984:129)

Mathiessen may have gotten the idea that the workers were convicts from the oral traditions of present-day Gulf fishermen. These men tell of a San Pedro

Mártir very unlike the one Goss saw, which they portray as a sort of Mexican Devil's Island. They say that during the Porfirian era, up to around 1910, the people sent out to mine the guano were political prisoners, and that almost nobody ever came back. It was a way of emptying the jails. At least half the men sent out there were Indians, and nobody had their families with them. Since most of the guano was on the steep cliffs, stone walls were built on them to catch the guano chipped off by a man working above them. Though Goss found the Yaquis to be "expert climbers" (Goss 1888:244), modern fishermen say that many people fell from these cliffs to their death. Disease, often from the bad drinking water shipped in, killed others. The prisoners were poorly fed, and few people lived more than five years. When a man died, he would be buried by a fellow prisoner. There is a cemetery on the island with a lot of graves that attest to all the people who died there. Sometimes, say the fishermen, the prisoners were even harassed by the Seris, who would paddle out in their balsas and rob them (Elfego Briseño 1982 and 1987:pers. comms.).

It may be that working conditions on San Pedro Mártir changed drastically between the time Goss was there and the years just before the 1910 Revolution. In mainland Sonora, the period the fishermen describe was the time of greatest persecution of the Yaquis. As a solution to the endless armed conflict with Mexicans over traditional Yaqui lands and to supply labor to the booming henequen plantations in Yucatán, the Sonoran government began rounding up Indians and forcibly deporting them en mass to the south:

> Yaquis, along with Mayos, Opatas, and Pimas, were regularly rounded up on the haciendas, placed temporarily in jails in Hermosillo and Guaymas, and shipped by boat to San Blas in Nayarit. From there they were herded on foot across Mexico, either to be dropped off in northern Oaxaca or pushed on to Vera Cruz for final shipment to Yucatán. In these places the forced labor system reached its most inhumane.... Direct and often brutal physical punishment, chiefly whipping, was relied on to break men's spirits and reduce them to acceptance of the rigid work regime and the very low standard of living....
>
> ... One set of rumors which developed indicated that Yaquis died in large numbers soon after arrival in Yucatán, unable to survive the brutal conditions of the peon life with no hope for the future. (Spicer 1980:160–61)

It is possible, of course, that the Yaqui work force on San Pedro Mártir was never made up of deported prisoners and that the two themes have become intermingled in the oral traditions of modern fishermen. But it is certainly plausible that of the thousands of Yaquis who were deported, some may have been condemned to end their lives in forced labor breaking up guano on that barren rock. Interestingly, there is a Seri belief that Rasa Island was used for a time as a penal colony (Peterson 1992:145), which may be related to the idea that it was Yaquis who built the cairns there.

The physical legacy of mining on San Pedro Mártir is still very clear. Much of the mining was done on the cliff faces around the perimeter of the island.

Figure 6.6
Rock wall and
platform on a
cliff face, San
Pedro Mártir
Island.
May 1984.

Many of the stone terraces, whether built to serve as work platforms, surfaces to catch guano mined from above, or perhaps to increase nesting space and guano deposition (Lindsay 1966a:9), still cling precariously to these cliffs (Figure 6.6). Elsewhere, terraces and trails remain clearly defined. Many of the stone houses in the village where the miners lived are still standing (Figures 6.7 and 6.8). Whoever the miners were, it could not have been pleasant to live out one's life in the extreme isolation of this desolate rock, with the blinding glare of the sub-tropical sun reflecting off the white guano, the pervasive acrid stench, guano dust in every breath, the cacophony of nesting birds during the spring, and in summer the sweltering heat and omnipresent *bolbito* gnats.

Figure 6.7   Part of the guano miners' village, San Pedro Mártir Island. May 1984.

Figure 6.8   House in the guano miners' village, San Pedro Mártir Island. May 1984.

Guano mining in the Gulf has continued sporadically through much of the twentieth century (Zárate 1920; Bahre 1983:301–2). With most of the old accumulations of petrified guano removed during the initial years, attention has turned more to the fresh guano laid down each spring as birds return to breed. In the 1940s, the Mexican government created a federal corporation to try to revive the industry and sent two scientists into the Gulf to investigate the prospects (Osorio Tafall 1944; Vogt 1946). Their recommendations ranged from immediate protection of the birds from human interference to capping the summit of San Pedro Mátir with concrete in order to increase nesting area (Vogt 1946:115).

Much of this sporadic interest has been directed toward Patos Island. It was mined for a short time in 1910, but the operation could not be made profitable, and by 1918 the concession for Patos and the other Midriff guano islands had again changed hands (Zárate 1920). According to Roberto Herrera, sometime in the 1940s, a group of North Americans came to Patos and built a house with a cement floor. Although they had planned to mine the island, he said they found a better deposit on an island farther north, and so they pulled out without doing any work (Mary Beck Moser 1997:pers. comm.). Herrera may have been speaking of the activity that took place in 1945 or 1946, when the island was virtually stripped of vegetation, and the Peruvian cormorant was introduced in an effort to revive the industry (Gentry 1949:100; Felger and Lowe 1976:25). Even as late as the 1980s, an occasional fishing panga would show up at Patos and haul off a load of guano to sell (Peterson 1992:149).

Mescal Aguardiente

San Esteban island had neither gold nor guano, but it did have one terrestrial resource of sufficient interest to have caught the eye of late nineteenth century entrepreneurs. This was its vast stands of agave, readily available for harvesting and distilling into *mescal aguardiente*, the tequila-like Mexican national liquor. One plan to exploit this resource got under way in the spring of 1877.

The little that is known about this brief business comes from a series of cursory public notices in two of Guaymas' many short-lived newspapers. In its notices of arrivals and departures from the port, *El Triunfo de Sonora* reported unceremoniously that on May 14, 1877:

> the Domestic pilot boat "Herminia" of 37 tons displacement, [departed] for San Esteban Island carrying equipment and supplies for the wine business, with its Captain Tomás Valenzuela, a crew of 5, and passengers José de la Cruz, Tiburcio Encinas, Jesús Duarte, and 14 Indians. (Murillo 1877:4)

The sketchy story picks up again on December 1, when the Guaymas City Council considered the request of Francisco Tápia to be allowed to introduce mescal liquor, produced at his distillery, into the city without restriction. For the privilege, Tápia offered to pay a fee of 10 pesos per month. The Council denied the request, so Tápia tried again the following week, this time offering to pay 15 pesos per week. After some discussion, the Council agreed to grant Tápia a liquor concession for a six month term (Anonymous 1878a:4, 1878b:2).

There is no indication that Tápia's operation had anything directly to do with San Esteban Island, but his concession must have set a precedent for others in the mescal business, including the San Esteban entrepreneurs. Two weeks later, at the City Council meeting of December 22, José de la Cruz, the man who had taken distilling equipment to San Esteban the previous May, and his partners David Spence and Pedro J. Camalich, requested:

> that they be granted the same concession for the introduction of mescal that was made to Citizen Francisco Tápia, offering to pay eight pesos monthly. The request was agreed to on the condition that the petitioners pay fifteen pesos each month like Tápia, and only for a term of six months. (Anonymous 1878c:3)

These concessions must have been attractive, for at its next meeting:

> Citizen Juan A. Robinson, the younger, requested that he be granted for the next January, February and March, the same concession as that of Francisco Tápia and the promoters of San Esteban Island, to freely introduce his mescal liquor. (Anonymous 1878d:3)

Robinson's request was granted, but the price was quickly escalating, for his concession would cost 20 pesos a month. The rush to get into the distilling business may have been due partly to a market that briefly opened up north of the border. In his annual report for 1878, the U.S. Consul in Guaymas noted that exports from his district to the Territory of Arizona "consist principally of flour, cattle, tobacco, and mescal (spirituous liquor produced from the root of a species of cactus)" (Willard 1879:950).

Twice more the San Esteban entrepreneurs approached the Guaymas City Council. On February 22, 1878:

> Citizen Pedro Camalich appeared showing that the Treasury is collecting from him for the month of December the fifteen pesos of monthly payment required of the promoters of San Esteban Island, for the introduction of its mescal liquor; as the concession was agreed to on the 22nd of December, he does not believe it just that [the Treasury] collect from them for the entire month. (Valencia 1878:1)

The Council's decision on this was not recorded, but on March 29:

> Citizens P. J. Camalich, José de la Cruz and David Spence showed that, since last February 11, they suspended their "wine business" from San Esteban

Island, requesting therefore that there be collected from them only the fifteen peso monthly fee for the months of December, January and the indicated [portion] of February. — The request was approved. (Anonymous 1878e:1)

And so ended the first known Mexican enterprise on San Esteban Island. Whether the workers encountered any Seris on the island is, of course, not revealed in these brief notices. A few years later, there emerged another proposal to harvest agave and distill mescal on San Esteban. But this was a minor sidelight in one of the many great development schemes proposed by promoter Guillermo Andrade, whose enthusiastic plans for San Esteban, Tiburón, and Ángel de la Guarda Islands are the principal subject of Chapter 8.

SEVEN

Might Makes Right:
The 1846–1848 War and Lingering U.S. Designs on the Upper Gulf

The U.S.-Mexican War of 1846–1848

War came to the Gulf in 1846. Its causes were complex and varied. The precipitating event was the annexation of Texas by the United States in 1845, and the first shots were fired along the Texas-Mexico border the following spring. But it was Alta California and its neighboring territories, not Texas, that were the central focus of the war. The Mexican population of California was sparse and only tenuously connected with the political and cultural forces in Mexico City, and the remote federal government had left the province poorly protected. By the 1840s, California was becoming increasingly Anglicized as English-speaking settlers began to migrate westward across the Great Plains in ever greater numbers. In Washington, fears were mounting that the British were looking on vulnerable California with covetous eyes. But perhaps the fundamental factor that encouraged the war was the ground swell of belief among North Americans in the self-serving doctrine of Manifest Destiny. This was the conviction that the United States was bound to rule the entire continent from the Atlantic to the Pacific, and that this in itself was justification for pushing aside any impediment that stood in the way. A few decades later, the main impediment to that vision would be Native Americans, but in the 1840s it was Mexico.

Although late in 1845 the Polk administration made overtures to purchase California and New Mexico, there was little doubt that the U.S. government intended to annex a huge piece of Mexico's northern territory, whether by purchase or by force. Thus when Mexico declined to negotiate, U.S. military forces had already been positioned and put on alert. On the West Coast, the U.S. Navy's Pacific Squadron had been given secret orders to capture all major ports in Alta and Baja California if war broke out. A series of skirmishes along the boundary between Texas and Mexico erupted in the spring of 1846, and on May 13 the United States declared war on Mexico.

At the official outbreak of the war, the United States moved quickly to take possession of Alta California. On July 7, Commodore John D. Sloat captured Monterey, the capital, and took possession of the territory for the United States. Though some resistance continued into the beginning of the following year, by late August, Alta California was basically in North American hands. This left the Pacific Squadron free to sail southward where, according to instructions, it was to protect the new acquisition by blockading the ports of western Mexico and the Gulf, interrupting commerce, capturing Mexican vessels, and gaining undisputed control of the sea from San Blas northward. This task could be carried out without undue fear of the Mexican Navy, which had only three schooners and a brig in service in the Pacific. But the objectives for Baja California, whether it was to be merely blockaded or captured and annexed, were ill-defined from the outset and became increasingly problematical as the war progressed (Cardenas de la Peña 1970b:Documento 30; Scheina 1970:46; Yates 1975:221–22; Nunis 1977:17–21, 60–62).

The first U.S. warship entered the Gulf in the middle of September 1846. At the beginning of that month, in the opening offensive against the Mexican coast, the U.S. sloop of war *Cyane* under Commander Samuel Dupont (or Du Pont) had staged a raid against San Blas which captured two Mexican vessels and destroyed the port's gun emplacements. From there the *Cyane* sailed directly for the Gulf. Arriving at La Paz on September 14, the North Americans were received hospitably despite their capture of seven vessels, including one of the Mexican Navy schooners, in the harbor. The Governor and the populace, long isolated and neglected by Mexico City, were receptive to the prospect of a change in nationality. Here the *Cyane* was joined briefly by the U.S.S. *Warren*, which had just captured a second Mexican warship in Mazatlán. Two weeks later, the *Cyane* set sail up the Gulf in search of the two remaining schooners of the Mexican Navy's Pacific fleet, rumored to be operating to the north. After unopposed visits to Loreto and Mulegé, the *Cyane* crossed the Gulf and on October 6 sailed into Guaymas harbor, where the two schooners and a merchant brig were discovered. But here there was a garrison of Mexican troops, and the reception was different. To avoid capture and reuse by the Americans, the Mexicans burned the two warships and prepared to defend the brig. The *Cyane* began shelling the troops, and a full-scale battle ensued. In the end, the brig was captured and burned, the Mexican Navy had lost its only warships in the Pacific, and the opening salvo in the war in the Gulf of California had been fired (Dupont 1882:420–21; Bancroft 1889:665; Cardenas de la Peña 1970a:146–67; Nunis 1977:19–21).

From Guaymas, the *Cyane* continued on to Mazatlán where it imposed a temporary blockade on the port. In November, it returned to Alta California for reprovisioning, making one peaceful stop en route at San José del Cabo for water. Despite the Guaymas incident and despite the fact that not a single U.S. warship or soldier had been stationed in the Gulf, the lack of resistance the *Cyane* had met with on the peninsula lulled the United States into a false sense that Baja California had been both pacified and conquered (Chamberlin 1963:51; Nunis 1977:18, 21).

It was not until the following April that another U.S. naval vessel cruised up the Gulf, and it was July before the first troops were garrisoned at La Paz. By then, a resistance movement had been organized in Mulegé by Captain Manuel Pineda, who had crossed the Gulf from Guaymas with a cadre of officers and munitions. Moreover, anti-American sentiment had spread throughout much of the peninsula. On October 1, Pineda's militia attacked a landing party from the U.S.S. *Dale*, which had been dispatched to Mulegé to assess the strength of the resistance movement. Nobody was killed in the battle, and the *Dale* weighed anchor the next day. In the south, hostile action erupted three weeks later in San José del Cabo. The tranquillity on the peninsula was drawing to an end (Martínez 1960:355–63; Chamberlin 1963:53; Cardenas de la Peña 1970a:147–48; Craven 1973:62–68; Nunis 1977:33).

Because most of Pineda's supplies were arriving by sea, U.S. commanders decided to interrupt his supply lines by blockading Mulegé. In La Paz, the American-owned schooner *Libertad* was chartered and armed. Under the command of Lieut. Tunis A. M. Craven, the *Libertad* was sent up the coast to patrol the waters off Mulegé for enemy shipping. Craven's one success was the capture of the Mexican sloop *Alerta*. Acting on information wrested from a sea lion hunter, Craven sailed north and found the vessel some 25 miles above Mulegé. He took her without resistance after her crew jumped overboard and swam ashore rather than fight. But three weeks after it began, the blockade of Mulegé was lifted, and the *Libertad* sailed to Guaymas, which was now in the hands of U.S. forces (Bauer 1969:211–13; Craven 1973:69–75; Nunis 1977:33–34). Though the patrol had sailed farther up the peninsular coast than any other U.S. vessel, it had turned around well short of the Midriff islands.

At the time the *Libertad* set out, it was already clear that Guaymas was the main source of supply for Pineda's forces and that the port would have to be captured to prevent reinforcements from reaching him. On October 17, three U.S. warships, the *Congress*, *Portsmouth*, and *Argo*, rendezvoused in Guaymas harbor and ordered Col. Antonio Campuzano, the garrison commander, to surrender the port. Campuzano refused, and early on the morning of October 20, the three warships opened fire. An hour later, a white flag appeared in the heavily damaged town. Campuzano, it turned out, had realized that he lacked the armament to repel an invasion, and he and his soldiers had left town during the night.

With the harbor blockaded and their cannons trained on the town, the North Americans had succeeded in cutting Guaymas off from Mexican shipping. But they had not seen the last of Campuzano, whose soldiers infiltrated the town by night and repeatedly harassed the invading forces over the next several months. The U.S. warships responded by shelling the port, so that by the time the war ended, few buildings in the entire town stood undamaged (Bancroft 1889:667; Bauer 1969:214–19; Cardenas de la Peña 1970a:148–49).

With the blockade of Guaymas in the fall of 1847, the war in the Gulf had begun in earnest. As the fighting escalated around Guaymas, Pineda's troops in Baja California marched southward, and a series of bloody battles were fought in the towns of the south. Military action in the Gulf, however, was almost totally confined to the region from Guaymas and Mulegé southward because that was where the towns and people were concentrated. The coast to the north was essentially uninhabited by Europeans, and U.S. forces, at least, concluded that the few harbors to the north that were occasionally visited by coasting vessels were of little commercial or military importance (Halleck 1850:607). But while blockades were not warranted north of Guaymas, these harbors could be utilized by small vessels intent on ferrying war materials across the Gulf, and there was no question that some vessels were doing just that. Early in 1848, when intelligence reports of Mexican activity to the north began to reach the U.S.S. *Dale*, the ship then on blockade duty at Guaymas, the officer in command, Lieut. Edward Yard, dispatched a series of patrols northward to investigate. On February 13, Yard reported to Commodore Shubrick:

> Having reason to suspect that there might be some vessels on the coast to the North I had the Launch fitted and provisioned for a cruise, and placed under charge of Lieut. Stanly, with orders to proceed up the coast, examining the numerous bays and anchorages, and in the event of finding any vessels in them or hovering on the coast, whether enemies or neutrals, to send them to this port. After an absence of three days, he returned, having gone up the coast some forty miles [approximately to Tastiota], where he found at anchor the released Brigantine "Mazatlea," Vial, Master. He found her papers correct [and so he did not detain her]....
>
> ... On Lieut. Stanly's return he captured a sloop rigged launch from Mulejé, laden with Panoche (sugar of the country) and dried fruit, and brought her in.... I immediately dispatched the launch again to the same quarter, in hopes of catching another boat, expected from the other side, and she returned after an absence of three days without success. I again sent her off, and ... [she] returned without having fallen in with any thing.
>
> Lieut. Stanly has been almost constantly employed on boat service, and has been exceedingly zealous, and useful in the performance of this duty. (Yard 1848a)

No sooner had Lieut. Yard completed his report than new intelligence arrived indicating renewed Mexican activity north of Guaymas. Two days later, on February 15, he again ordered Lieut. Stanly to patrol northward, this time all the way to the Midriff:

> Having heard of a vessel being on the coast to the North discharging cargo, and another likely to arrive there for the same end, I availed myself of the Sch[n] Libertad's being here, to charter her for the purpose of making an examination in that quarter.... Having armed and manned her, I put her under the charge of Lieut. Stanly with orders to proceed along the Coast to the Northward as far as the Island of Tibaron. (Yard 1848b)

Seven days later, Lieut. Stanly was back in Guaymas, and he reported to Lieut. Yard on an encounter with the Seris:

> In obedience to your order of the 15th inst. I took command of the Schooner 'Libertad' with 16 men & Boatswain James H. Polley, and took an eye sketch of the coast as high up as the Island of "Tiberoni" and gave the intermediate harbors a close overhauling. I found the chart (a Spanish chart published at Madrid in 1826) erroneous in its positions of rocks and harbours, and in not pointing out a shoal of several miles in depth near the harbor 'Tastiota' where I found the Schooner 'Magatlito,' 'Veal' Master. I meet on board of her two Mexican officers whom I took prisoners, but having no accomodations on board the Libertad & being bound higher up the coast, I paroled them....
>
> At 5 oclock on the 18th inst. I anchored in a snug harbor on the Southern coast of 'Tiberoni' opposite a villiage of huts an[d] hoisted a white flag at early light. The inhabitants retired to the hills whooping their war cries. I dispatched Mr Polley with 6 men and a flag on shore. He found the villiage deserted, and my hope of communication proving abortive he returned to the boat, when the warriors ran to the beach and fired their arrows at him. I then went myself but could not induce them to come nearer than the flight of their arrows, which are armed with poison. (I afterwards learned that they recognise a *cross* as the only symbol of peace.) I did not deem it necesary to destroy their town or disturb their provisions of shark, Boats of reeds, etc., etc. (Stanly 1848)

During the war, other American naval personnel certainly heard about Tiburón Island and the Seris (Revere [1849] 1947:230–31), but Lieut. Stanly's voyage was probably the only foray of the North American forces to actually visit the Midriff islands. Among the Mexican vessels that successfully escaped the U.S. blockade, it is certainly possible that a few sailed as far north as the Midriff in order to run supplies across the Gulf unmolested. If they did, they achieved a double success by also evading the U.S. naval intelligence network.

Even before Lieut. Stanly's men were dodging Seri arrows, an armistice had been officially declared with the February 2 signing of the Treaty of Guadalupe Hidalgo. However, it was some time before the news reached the Gulf, and the Congresses of both countries still had to ratify the treaty. Before that could be done, the precise terms of the territorial settlement had to be worked out. As negotiations dragged on through the spring, the U.S. naval forces remained in the Gulf, and it was widely assumed on both sides that Baja California and a portion of Sonora would be among the territorial concessions to the United States. Indeed, Commodore Shubrick had won the neutrality of many residents of the peninsula on this assurance, evidently due to a careless misinterpretation of a message delivered by President Polk to Congress on the importance of the peninsula to the United States (Nunis 1977:36–37, 60–61). But the final terms of the treaty left Baja California with Mexico, and many peninsular residents who had chosen not to resist U.S. forces, now fearing for their lives in the hands of the Mexican patriots, had to be evacuated to Alta California when the last

U.S. troops left the peninsula on September 6 (Gerhard 1945:423–24). For Mexico, the retention of Baja California and Sonora was an important victory in the face of an enormous territorial defeat. For the United States, it meant not only that important territory had not been acquired, but that there would not be an American port on the Gulf of California.

Filibusters and Annexation Schemes

Many North Americans had assumed it a foregone conclusion that Baja California would be among the lands ceded to the United States, and they were stunned to learn that the peninsula had been omitted (Chamberlin 1963; Nunis 1977:61–70). Six years later, Americans were equally incredulous that the new boundary between Arizona and Sonora established by the Gadsden Purchase took a sudden jog northwestward, skirting the head of the Gulf and again depriving the United States of a port there. For many years afterward, prominent politicians and businessmen in Washington, Arizona, and California spoke out publicly in favor of pushing the border farther south, whether peaceably or by force. And many outraged citizens with an unswerving belief in Manifest Destiny and a disdain for international law were convinced that the failures of the statesmen should be rectified by more aggressive means. As a result, a long succession of schemes were hatched to forcibly invade Baja California and parts of Sonora in order to "liberate" these regions, annex them, or even establish them as independent nations (Conner and Faulk 1971:179–83; Acuña 1974:11–12; Voss 1982:113–15). Most of these schemes were long on talk and short on action. But during the 1850s, a few filibustering expeditions actually took to the field, and one even succeeded in briefly taking possession of Mexican territory.

Perhaps the most notorious of the filibusterers were William Walker and Henry A. Crabb. In 1853, Walker and a tiny band of 45 armed adventurers sailed to Baja California, where they managed to capture La Paz and occupy the town for several days before being driven out by Mexican forces (Martínez 1960:373–38; Woodward 1966). Four years later, the Crabb expedition marched across the border into Sonora, but these invaders did not enjoy even temporary success. Crabb and his 69 armed followers were met by a well-prepared Mexican force as they tried to enter Caborca, and those Americans who survived the ensuing seven-day siege were summarily executed (Forbes 1952; Acuña 1974:29–37).

One filibustering expedition ended with a disastrous voyage past the Midriff islands. This venture had its beginnings in 1852, when a disaffected Frenchman from California named Gaston de Raousset-Boulbon led a band of compatriots into Sonora to establish a mining colony. Raousset-Boulbon believed he had both legal authority and support for the project. He had obtained financial backing from the Mexico City banking house of Jecker, de la Torre y Compañía, and the support of the federal government, which hoped the colony would provide a buffer against Apaches and aggressive North Americans. The venture was also expected to be profitable, for among the shareholders were President Arista and other high Mexican and French officials (Wyllys 1932:71–76). But Raousset-Boulbon was unaware of the deep-seated local conviction that only Sonorans had the right to exploit their state's resources and that the federal government, which Sonorans increasingly mistrusted, had no business selling off the wealth of their state to foreigners (Acuña 1974:54). State officials, further aggravated by Raousset-Boulbon's heavily-armed entry into Sonora and haughty disregard for existing colonization laws, moved quickly to contain him. The infuriated Raousset-Boulbon responded by marching his men to Hermosillo, and after overrunning the poorly defended town, began laying plans to capture Guaymas. But at this point his luck failed, for Raousset-Boulbon fell gravely ill and his followers began to desert him. He negotiated a truce that allowed him and his remaining men to leave Sonora without retribution, thus ending the incident for the time being (Wyllys 1932:104–36).

But two years later, a vengeful Raousset-Boulbon returned to Sonora as a filibusterer. He and a band of comrades sailed up the Gulf in the small schooner *Belle*, running guns to a sizable French force that was already in Guaymas. For nearly two weeks General Yáñez, commander of the Mexican troops in Guaymas, tried to negotiate with the French but to no avail. Fighting erupted on July 13, and this time it was the French who retreated in disarray. Even before the battle ended, some 30 of the Frenchmen beat a hasty retreat to the *Belle* and tried to escape northward toward the Colorado River and the sanctuary of the U.S. border. The overcrowded vessel apparently managed to sail past the Midriff islands unscathed, only to be wrecked at the head of the Gulf with no known survivors. As for Raousset-Boulbon, on August 12, 1854, he met his end in front of a Guaymas firing squad (Bancroft 1889:673–92; Soulié 1927; Wyllys 1932:190–224; Acuña 1974:11–12; Voss 1982:117–19).

During the 1850s, there were also North Americans who sought to acquire Mexican territory by less forceful means. One of these, Charles D. Poston, became interested briefly in the Midriff region. Operating on erroneous reports that the Gadsden Purchase would give the United States all of Sonora, Poston and a group of followers set out for the Gulf in February of 1854, intent on locating and purchasing a harbor which could serve the presumptive new U.S. possession as a port and a railhead. The place he settled on was the bay of San Juan Bautista (Bahía Kino), and he promptly entered into a potentially lucrative partnership with some Mexicans who owned land in the region. Poston's long-term plans included building a city at Bahía Kino and a breakwater extending across the Canal del Infiernillo that would connect Tiburón Island with the mainland. However, he quickly abandoned the scheme when he learned that the land acquired under the new treaty would not extend the U.S. boundary even as far as the head of the Gulf (Poston 1854:9, 13–18; Love 1978:408–10).

Though Poston spent several months exploring Sonora, it is unlikely that he ever actually visited Bahía Kino, the very place where his fortune was to have been made. His description of the area (and of the nearby Seris), though detailed, is filled with just the sort of errors that come from second-hand information (Poston 1854:8–12; see also Browne 1869b:247–50). Indeed, with the Walker expedition and other filibusters still very recent events, there was good reason why Poston did not explore Bahía Kino and its environs personally:

> The bay of San Juan Bautista has never been surveyed by the Spanish or Mexican Governments[;] consequently no accurate information could be obtained of its capacity or soundings. The unsettled condition of the Government in Sonora and the continual fear of Filibusters making a landing on their coast rendered it impossible to procure liberty to cruise in the Gulf at this time[,] and an especial order of the Government made it a capital offence for any Foreigners to be caught prowling about the coast or harbors. (Poston 1854:11)

A succession of harebrained filibustering schemes continued to be proposed over the next several decades (Martínez 1960:453–55; Hager 1968). The fact that tiny bands of armed adventurers could invade Mexican territory more or less at will and that these expeditions were considered just and heroic by a sizable portion of the U.S. public, drove home to Mexicans just how vulnerable the northwestern frontier was to the North American territorial appetite (Blaisdell 1962:23–24; Acuña 1974:26–28). Though none of these schemes ever received official sanction from the U.S. government, influential North Americans at the highest levels of government and commerce openly and repeatedly advocated annexation by purchase or seizure throughout the 1850s and 1860s. In the U.S. Congress, calls for annexation of Baja California continued well into the twentieth century (Acuña 1974:57–58; Voss 1982:141–42; Chamberlin 1949).

The Gulf Route to Arizona Territory

One of the principal reasons the United States had been anxious to secure a port on the Gulf of California was to provide an efficient and inexpensive supply route to its newly acquired Territory of Arizona. Settlers coming into the territory would clearly be dependent for some time on merchandise from the outside. More importantly, the wealth of Arizona lay in its mineral resources, and to establish a mining industry would require bringing in tons of heavy machinery and establishing a means of exporting raw or partially refined ores. These heavy cargoes could be transported by wagon only with great difficulty and expense, but shipping by sea was relatively easy and cheap. A port on the upper Gulf would not only minimize the distance and expense of the overland segment of a freight route, but if it were in North American hands, it would avoid customs difficulties and the added cost of import and transit tariffs.

Although the 1848 treaty did not provide North Americans with the desired port, one of its provisions did guarantee the United States unrestricted access to its new territories by way of the Gulf and the Mexican-held portion of the lower Colorado River. This guaranteed access was reaffirmed six years later in the Gadsden Treaty. While not the ideal solution from the North American point of view, it gave the United States an important supply route into the interior. But supplying the mines of Arizona turned out not to be the most pressing concern. The discovery of gold in California the same year the war ended created a much more urgent need to bring supplies to the lower Colorado River itself.

The immigrants who flooded to the gold fields of California in 1849 came by the thousands. Many opted for the recently blazed Gila Trail down through New Mexico and westward along the Gila River across southern Arizona. To enter California, these hardy souls had to cross the Colorado River. One of the few places where this could be done was at its confluence with the Gila, a place called Yuma Crossing, and a lucrative ferry business was established there around March of 1850. With thousands of fortune seekers converging on this bottleneck, clashes with local Quechan Indians were inevitable. This prompted the government to send a detachment of army troops to keep the peace at this critical spot. Thus in November of 1850, about 100 soldiers under Major Samuel P. Heintzelman arrived at the crossing and established Camp Independence, the forerunner of Ft. Yuma.

It was clear from the beginning, however, that maintaining troops at the crossing would not be an easy task. The detachment would be totally dependent on the outside for food and all other commodities, and it was recognized that there were no practical sources of supply anywhere close by. San Diego, little more than 200 miles to the west, would have been a logical source were the wagon road to the Colorado River not so difficult. But this route lay across a miserably hot and inhospitable desert that offered inadequate forage for the wagon teams and little water for man or beast. Without a practical land route, the alternative approach was to supply the prospective outpost by sea. Although nine times as long, the idea was to send provisions by ship from San Francisco, around Cabo San Lucas, up to the head of the Gulf, and then on up the lower Colorado River some 170 winding miles to Camp Independence (Smith 1850; Leavitt 1943a:1–3; Kemble 1963:138–40; Faulk 1969:7–8).

This idea was not entirely novel, for in the late 1770s Father Francisco Gárces suggested the possibility of supplying missions along the lower Colorado River by ship from the Gulf (Gárces [1775–1776] 1900:494). And while unconventional, it was sufficiently obvious that it prompted two independent proposals for sea expeditions to the head of the Gulf to survey the region and assess the feasibility of the route. One proposal originated with Boundary Commissioner John Bartlett, the U.S. official responsible for establishing the new United States-Mexico boundary. Bartlett's proposal was sent to the government on October 31, 1850 by Navy Lieut. I. G. Strain, whom Bartlett recommended should lead the expedition. The objective was to explore and survey the upper Gulf and the Colorado River as far as the army post. To get there, Lieut. Strain proposed that the four boats belonging to the Boundary Commission be shipped to Guaymas, manned with navy personnel, and sailed northward through the Midriff into the upper Gulf (Bartlett [1854] 1965:162–68, 602–4). But neither

*Figure 7.1   Lieutenant George Horatio Derby (1823–1861), photographed about 1846.
(Courtesy Bancroft Library, University of California, Berkeley [Portrait No. 2].)*

Bartlett nor Strain knew at the time that the War Department had already dispatched Lieut. George H. Derby of the Corps of Topographical Engineers (Figure 7.1) to reconnoiter the entire sea and river route from San Francisco to Camp Independence.

Derby had been assigned the military transport schooner *Invincible*, and on November 1, 1850, the day after Strain submitted the Bartlett proposal, Derby's expedition sailed out of San Francisco Bay. The vessel put in at San Diego to take on rations for Heintzelman's troops, who had already begun their overland march to Yuma Crossing. Here, Derby also picked up copies of Lieut. Hardy's *Travels in the Interior of Mexico* and a chart of the Gulf by James Imray, the only two navigational aids for the Gulf then available. The *Invincible* left San Diego on November 15, touched briefly at Cabo San Lucas on the 23rd, and beat its way up the Gulf against a heavy gale, arriving at Guaymas harbor on November 29. In Guaymas, Derby consulted with English expatriot Thomas Spence (known locally as Tomás Espence), a long-time resident and experienced navigator, who had assisted Hardy in 1826 and had personally sailed on several occasions into the Midriff region, including a circumnavigation of Tiburón (see pp. 235–37). Leaving Guaymas on December 6 in the face of another heavy gale, the *Invincible* was blown across the Gulf to Tortuga Island. The next day, the wind abating, she worked her way up the coast of the peninsula into the Midriff region. On December 10:

> we passed the island of "San Juan Pedro Martyr," the longitude of which we determined to be 111° 54'. The island is a barren rock, about five miles long, situated nearly in the middle of the gulf. Far beyond, to the northeast, we saw the rugged outline of the celebrated island of Tiburon. This island has long been known as the abode of the Ceres Indians, a small tribe of about five hundred, who are represented as extremely hostile, and invariably opposing any attempt at landing; they are said to be armed with poisoned arrows. A rich bed of pearl oysters is said to exist between this island and the coast of Sonora, and there are accounts of rich gold mines upon the island; but as no one is ever known to have landed there, it is difficult to understand how the fact was ascertained. We should have landed and attempted an examination of the island, but the wind being contrary compelled us to lay over to the [Baja] California shore, and we passed it in the night. (Derby 1852:8)

The following day the *Invincible*:

> passed the island of San Estavan, which presents an exceedingly wild and sterile appearance, resembling the generality of the gulf coast on the [Baja] California side. The appearance of the water between this island and that of San Lorento led us to suppose that we were on soundings, but on trying the deep sea lead we found no bottom at one hundred fathoms. (Derby 1852:8–9)

Just how much of San Esteban Derby saw is not clear, for the *Invincible*, struggling against a north wind, followed a circuitous course as it entered the Midriff region. In his navigation table, Derby noted only that at 10:30 A.M. on December 10 the "island of San Estefan bore north-northeast 8 or 10 miles" (Derby 1852:24). His sketch of the island (which he failed to identify by name) was probably made at about the time of this note, for it seems to depict the sea cliffs of the south and west coasts from approximately this perspective. From this side and at this distance, it is extremely unlikely that any sign of human activity would have been visible, and indeed Derby makes no mention of any.

The *Invincible* continued on to the head of the Gulf and started up the Colorado River. But the vessel was able to navigate only about 30 miles before it was stopped by shallow water. After making contact with Heintzelman, the rations brought for the garrison were unloaded and hauled laboriously by wagon the remaining distance to Camp Independence. On January 29, 1851, the *Invincible* weighed anchor and headed down river for the Gulf. The schooner again sailed past San Esteban Island on February 2 or 3, but Derby made no specific record of it. The expedition reached Guaymas on February 5, and on March 6 the *Invincible* dropped anchor in San Francisco Bay (Derby 1852:27–28).

Although Derby had only been able to navigate a fraction of the way to Camp Independence, he concluded that the route up the Gulf and the river was entirely practical. From his high point, a direct and hence relatively short road could be built and supplies hauled to the post by wagon. But a far better solution would be to transfer the cargo directly from ocean-going vessels to river steamboats having a sufficiently shallow draft to steam all the way to the garrison. As Derby succinctly put it, a single river steamer could haul more to the post in a day than 100 wagons could in a week (Derby 1852:20).

The commercial potential of a supply route by river was quickly recognized by one of the Yuma Crossing ferrymen, George A. Johnson, who contracted with the army to deliver supplies to the garrison. Johnson hoped to sail most of the way up river and then, rather than use steamers, pole the remaining distance in two flatboats. By late February 1852, the transport *Sierra Nevada*, provided by the army, had brought Johnson up the Gulf and about 70 miles up river. But the flatboat scheme was a failure. One boat sank with its cargo, and the other delivered supplies to the post (recently renamed Ft. Yuma) only about as fast as they were consumed.

In November of 1852, the first river steamer was put into operation by James Turnbull, who assembled the vessel from parts freighted to the mouth of the river by the U.S. transport vessel *Capacity*. Christened the *Uncle Sam*, it arrived at Ft. Yuma with its first cargo on December 3, after a 15 day trip. But success was fleeting. The vessel was seriously underpowered, and while Turnbull was in San Francisco purchasing a new engine, the *Uncle Sam* sank, putting Turnbull out of business.

Turnbull's failure gave Johnson a second chance. Johnson shipped parts for a new steamer to the head of the Gulf on the brig *General Viel*. By January 1854, the vessel had been assembled and named the *General Jessup*, and it was soon put into operation. With its success, Johnson put additional vessels into service. He then built a shipyard and dry dock named Port Isabel near the mouth of the river

*Figure 7.2   Port Isabel, at the head of the Gulf of California.
Photograph probably taken in the 1870s. (Courtesy KLVX Steamboats on the
Colorado Collection, University of Nevada, Las Vegas Library [No. 0156–0091].)*

in order to maintain his growing fleet (Figure 7.2). The Gulf and the Colorado River quickly became the main supply line for Ft. Yuma (Sykes 1937:24–26; Mills 1941:259–61; Leavitt 1943a:4–7; Kemble 1963:141–43; Sykes 1976; Lingenfelter 1978:8–16).

The rapid appearance of mines and communities along the Colorado River north of Ft. Yuma raised the question of how far the river-based supply route could be extended. To make this determination, the army planned another exploring expedition to the head of the Gulf and as far up the Colorado as it was possible to navigate. The officer assigned to lead the expedition was Lieut. Joseph C. Ives of the Topographical Engineers.

This time, the trip up river would be made in a 50-foot steamer which Ives had shipped disassembled to San Francisco. There it was loaded on board the schooner *Monterey*, which set sail for the Gulf on November 1, 1857. A week of easy sailing brought the expedition members to Cabo San Lucas, where they sat out a week of dead calm. When the air finally stirred:

what breeze there was blew *down* the Gulf, and we had to beat slowly up against it, making sometimes little more than twenty miles in the twenty-four hours. When near the end of the voyage the long-wished-for wind indeed came, and then it blew a gale, and for twelve hours a sea was running that occasioned, in the deeply laden schooner, considerable apprehension for the

safety of the property of the expedition, to say nothing of its members. (Ives
1861:22–23)

But to Ives the slow ascent of the Gulf was not without interest, and he was
especially impressed by the islands of the Midriff. Though he does not single
out individual islands, his lyrical but astute description may well be based on a
careful look at San Esteban:

> North of Guaymas these islands are more numerous, and in one place, with
> narrow channels between, extend across the Gulf in an uninterrupted chain,
> presenting wild and abrupt outlines, as though formed by spouts of lava hurled
> up from mammoth submarine craters, and hardened in the air before falling.
> They are by no means destitute of vegetation, but appear to be uninhabited,
> and the unbroken solitude adds to their desolate grandeur. It is probable that
> upon many of their surfaces no human foot has ever trodden. They appear,
> indeed, almost inaccessible, though among the rugged cliffs an occasional
> break affords a glimpse of some green valley or cool sheltered glen inviting
> to the eye, or a narrow vista momentarily opens to view dark and mysterious
> looking recesses, suggesting the notion, in this region teeming with mineral
> wealth, that there may be among those secluded nooks places that it would be
> well worth while to explore. (Ives 1861:23)

At the head of the Gulf, Ives assembled the river steamer, which he christened
the *Explorer*, and with one of George Johnson's pilots at the helm, started up
river on December 31. To his consternation, a short distance above Ft. Yuma
Ives met Lieut. James L. White and Johnson himself returning from virtually
the same exploratory voyage for which Ives had been commissioned. Though
he had been scooped, Ives proceeded up river, ending his exploration at Las
Vegas Wash, around 350 miles above Ft. Yuma and some 70 miles farther than
White and Johnson had ascended. Though Ives received most of the credit,
together the two expeditions had clearly demonstrated the practicality of supplying communities throughout western Arizona via the Gulf and the Colorado
River (Sykes 1937:20–23; Leavitt 1943a:8–10; Woodward 1955:69–104; Lingenfelter 1978:17–21; Walker and Bufkin 1979:39).

With the establishment of the sea route from San Francisco to the Colorado
River, vessels for the first time began to pass by the Midriff islands on a regular basis. The real beginning of this traffic was in 1855 when five vessels made
the round trip, and it continued unabated until 1877, when the railroad from
southern California reached Yuma and obviated the need for the sea route.
Between 1855 and 1872, some 217 voyages were made. During much of this
period, there were at least 10 trips annually, reaching a record 24 voyages in
1866 (Leavitt 1943b:168–74; Kemble 1963:143–44). In the early years, most of
the vessels were private sailing ships chartered by the U.S. Army to transport
troops and supplies, but as Arizona rapidly gained civilian population commercial runs increased. By the 1860s, many of these vessels were also shuttling

passengers and cargo between La Paz, Guaymas, and other major Gulf ports on their way to and from the head of the Gulf. Although most were North American vessels, Mexican merchantmen occasionally extended the coasting trade to the mouth of the river (Leavitt 1943a:10, 1943b:162; Kemble 1963:145).

By the 1860s, steam began to replace sails on the long run from San Francisco to the mouth of the Colorado River. The first of these ocean-going steamships was the *Uncle Sam* (not to be confused with the river steamer of the same name) which the army chartered in 1859 to carry troops to the military posts on the river. Another steamer, the *Santa Cruz*, followed a month later, and the *Panama* made one trip to the river in the early 1860s. At least two trips were made by the steamer *Oregon* in 1866 and one by the *Continental* in 1869 (Mills 1941:257–58; Leavitt 1943a:10, 169–73; Kemble 1963:145). But it was not until 1871, when George Johnson placed the steamer *Newbern* in regular service that sailing vessels began to be phased out of the Gulf run. With the addition of the *Montana* in late 1873 and the *Idaho*, which replaced the *Montana* after it caught fire in late 1876, the voyage from San Francisco to the Colorado River was handled almost exclusively by Johnson's steamers. In April 1877, when the Southern Pacific reached Yuma, the railroad bought out Johnson's river operation in order to eliminate competition. Johnson continued to operate his ocean-going steamer service from San Francisco to ports on the Gulf, though only as far up as Guaymas. With freight coming into Yuma by rail, there was no longer much reason for the San Francisco steamers to sail north of Guaymas, nor for river steamers to descend below Yuma (Mills 1941:273–74; Leavitt 1943b:161–63; Woodward 1955:118–19; Kemble 1963:151–52).

Though no longer served by the San Francisco steamers, the route to the head of the Gulf was not yet abandoned entirely, for there was one community on the lower Colorado River that still needed a transportation link. This was Colonia Lerdo, an agricultural colony between Yuma and the mouth of the river that had been founded in 1874 by entrepreneur Guillermo Andrade and his partner Thomas Blythe (see pp. 177–79). Partly to fill this void, toward the end of 1877, these two men established their own steamship line, the Línea Acelerada del Golfo de Cortés, with the intention of providing regularly scheduled service between Gulf ports and Colonia Lerdo (García and Andrade 1877; García 1878). They purchased the steamer *Coquille* for the Gulf portion of the route and a small steam launch to navigate the river. In July 1878, the new line was running (Hendricks 1978:141–42). The venture, however, was not a great success. By the end of September, the *Coquille* had made only three irregular trips. A year later, the steamer, now renamed the *General Zaragoza* and flying the Mexican flag, was serving Gulf ports as far north as Guaymas but had abandoned the final leg to the Colorado River. Although the Lerdo colony endured at least into the 1890s, after 1881 not even an occasional steamer ventured north beyond Guaymas (Willard 1879:951, 1880:432, 1885b, 1888:592). After three decades, the more or less regular voyages through the Midriff had ended.

Between Derby's 1850 exploration and the end of scheduled steamship service in 1877, almost 300 voyages were made to the head of the Gulf by U.S.

vessels, plus a smaller but unknown number of trips by Mexican coasting vessels. Since each voyage was a round trip, vessels passed through the Midriff more than 600 times during this 27 year period. In the peak year of 1866, this was an average of nearly one vessel a week. The normal routes through the Midriff seem to have passed directly by San Esteban Island. In August 1859, the Brig *Floyd* sailed through the channel between San Esteban and San Lorenzo Islands on its way to deliver troops to Ft. Yuma (Hussey 1859). Most vessels, however, probably traversed the channel between San Esteban and Tiburón Islands, the most direct line from Guaymas to the upper Gulf. This was the route recommended by Tomás Robinson in his report on the feasibility of opening a port of entry at Libertad (Robinson 1863:271). An 1868 map prepared by the Lower California Company shows the "San Francisco and Colorado River Steam Boats" traversing this channel (Anonymous 1868), and it was also the projected route for the steamship line established by Guillermo Andrade and Thomas Blythe (Anonymous 1874:map).

With this volume of traffic, many people must have had a passing view of San Esteban, but it is doubtful that they would have seen much more than the same distant sea cliffs observed by Lieutenants Derby and Ives. Sailing vessels blown off course or forced to tack against the wind may have occasionally steered close to shore, but ships on a schedule, bound for somewhere else, would otherwise have had little reason to approach the island. For steamships, there would have been no reason whatever to stray from midchannel, a distance of at least four miles.

A Port on the Northern Gulf

Important as the Colorado River route was, it still did not fully meet the supply needs of Arizona. During the early years, service was irregular and unpredictable, with long delays in the arrival of vessels the rule rather than the exception. Until steamships took over the leg from San Francisco to the mouth of the river, sailing vessels still had to beat their way either up or down the Gulf, against the prevailing winds, during most of the year. The trip was occasionally accomplished in just under 20 days, but adverse conditions could draw it out to nearly two months (Mills 1941:257; Leavitt 1943b:154; Kemble 1963:144). Nor was the river any easier to navigate, even with steam vessels. Trips always had to be coordinated with favorable tides and flood stage. In the fall, the water level often dropped to a depth of little more than two feet, difficult for even the exceedingly shallow draft of the river boats. Moreover, there was no predictable course that could be followed from one trip to the next, for navigable channels appeared and disappeared literally overnight. Foundering on sand bars could create major delays, and one captain claimed to have once been stranded on a bar for 52 days. At times, hundreds of tons of cargo sat piled up at the mouth of the river unable to be shipped higher (Sykes 1937:30–32; Mills 1941:263; Leavitt 1943a:11, 156, 160–61).

The other major shortcoming of the river route was that it put supplies ashore a great distance from Tucson, the largest emerging town in the Territory, and the rich mining district that surrounded it. Getting supplies from Yuma to this part of Arizona required adding a two week wagon trip onto the already difficult river passage. Although Tucson came to depend heavily on this supply line, many North American observers believed that the vital southeastern region could only be served efficiently by a much closer port, which would have to be located on the Sonoran side of the upper Gulf (Mills 1941:266–67).

The only established port on the Sonoran side of the Gulf capable of serving the needs of Arizona was Guaymas, and at the end of the war it immediately became the port of entry for goods bound for southeastern Arizona (Gracida Romo 1985:41). A good road led from Guaymas to Hermosillo and on to Tucson, and cargoes arriving from San Francisco by ship would be loaded on wagon trains in Guaymas and hauled northward. This route was far shorter than overland routes within the United States, and it avoided many of the problems of the Colorado River route. But it still involved an overland haul of some 350 miles and it required transporting goods through Mexican territory which, from the North American viewpoint, created expensive and frustrating customs problems. If a port could be established on the *upper* Gulf, far to the north of Guaymas, the overland distance to Tucson could be greatly shortened. And, so went the thinking of many, a port to serve U.S. interests should be a U.S. port. Thus in the long run, the unrestricted access to the Colorado River provided by the 1848 and 1854 treaties did little to quell North American interest in acquiring more Mexican territory.

Although Mexico had no intention of giving up more territory to the United States, the idea of opening a port on the upper Gulf was also attractive to the Sonoran government, if for different reasons. From the Sonoran perspective, a northern port was essential to the development of the rich Altar district in the northwestern part of the state. Although the region had great potential wealth in both minerals and agricultural products, overland transport was inefficient and expensive. A nearby port would provide an economical way of shipping the region's products to market (Robinson 1863:264–65; Ruibal Corella 1985:164).

There were only two natural harbors in the northern Gulf that had much potential. One was called Lobos and the other, some 20 miles to the south, was known as Libertad. Both were uninhabited and for a while they were often confused with each other. Of the two, Lobos was the least suitable though it was apparently the first to be formally evaluated. In 1853, the government of Sonora commissioned Thomas Spence of Guaymas to explore Lobos harbor as a potential site for a port (Poston 1854:20), and the following year, Andrew B. Gray considered its possibilities as a railhead, though he did not actually visit the bay (Gray 1856:56).

The harbor of Libertad was a much better prospect. It was also a site with fresh water, an essential resource if a town was to be established, and it had good access to the Altar valley. Libertad had been used now and again since Jesuit times, and its existence was widely known in both Sonora and the United States. Coasting vessels sometimes went there as, perhaps, did smugglers. Because it was an obvious possibility, in 1861 the Governor of Sonora appointed a scientific commission, this time headed by Tomás Robinson of Guaymas, to conduct a survey of the harbor and its surroundings and assess its suitability as a port and town site. The commission promptly carried out its mission, producing not only a map of the bay but also a plat of the projected town, with streets named and locations designated for major facilities, including wharves, a customshouse, railroad depot, hospital, theater, and jail. It even explicitly recommended that vessels coming from Guaymas should pass through the Midriff by way of the channel between Tiburón and San Esteban Islands (Robinson 1863).

A year later, the United States followed with a survey of its own. In September of 1862, the U.S. Army ordered Major David Fergusson to survey the bay at Libertad and assess the feasibility of transporting supplies from there to Arizona. Like Robinson, Fergusson found the harbor an excellent prospect for a commercial port. He also noted that the harbor was already in occasional use, for the previous year a large vessel stopped there and picked up a cargo of copper ore. Moreover, a fine wagon road to Caborca had already been established. The entire route overland to Tucson from Libertad seemed faultless and was far shorter than the road from Guaymas. Since Bahía Libertad was often confused with Bahía Lobos to the north, Fergusson made a separate trip to Lobos, which he judged promising though not as outstanding as Libertad (Fergusson 1863:2–7, 22).

Despite these strongly positive assessments, there was no development of Libertad for several years. It is possible that the Sonoran government dragged its feet for fear that the United States might attempt to annex that part of the state in order to acquire the port. Certainly there was no shortage of rhetoric to this effect at the time. General James H. Carleton, who forwarded Major Fergusson's report to the War Department, sent an accompanying note asserting that:

> This is a report of great importance, as showing how much cheaper supplies can be gotten for Arizona ... *via* Libertad, than from Indianola, Texas, or from Kansas City. The report is of still greater importance when considered with reference to the political and commercial geography of our country. It shows how practicable it is to make a railroad from the Rio Grande to the gulf of California and thus to the Pacific. It shows why the southern confederacy wish to hold the Territory of Arizona and wish to have a part of the State of Sonora. It shows how very important it is for us to purchase from Mexico, before it becomes a possession of, say, France, a strip of territory which will give us so fine and accessible a port on the gulf of California.
>
> When the vast mineral resources of Arizona ... have become better known ... then the government will see that a port on the gulf of California should be ours, at any cost. (Carleton 1863)

The next year Sylvester Mowry, a former army officer turned Arizona promoter, asserted that "The natural outlet for the productions of Arizona must be through a port on the Gulf of California, and the acquisition of California necessitates the possession of Sonora" (Mowry [1864] 1973:16).

A year later Richard C. McCormick, Secretary of the Territory of Arizona wrote that the economic development of Arizona:

> is somewhat retarded, as is the prosperity of the whole country, for the want of an American port upon the gulf of California, by which route goods and machinery might be speedily and economically received. The great oversight of the United States in the failure to acquire such a port when it might have been had without difficulty or expense is keenly and constantly deplored, and it is the hope of every one living in or interested in Southern Arizona that our Government will, by negotiation, (if coming events do not afford other means) soon secure either the port of Libertad or Guaymas, or both. Indeed, the geographical relations of the State of Sonora to Arizona and our access to the Pacific are such that its acquisition seems little less than a matter of duty. (McCormick 1865:140)

While the development of Libertad remained in limbo, coasting vessels continued to make sporadic use of the harbor (Carron de Fleury 1869; Willard 1869:645), though for small vessels the trip through the Midriff always entailed some risk. Part of that risk turned out to be Seri attack. In January 1862, the sloop *Esperanza* left Guaymas bound for Libertad with a crew of four and a cargo that included a quantity of sugar and 13 cartons of women's shawls. When the vessel failed to arrive, a Mexican search party headed down the coast as far as Tiburón Island but failed to find any trace of the missing sloop. Later, the shawls began showing up among Seris on the mainland, who had purchased them from their kinsmen on Tiburón. An investigation disclosed that the *Esperanza* had been taken by Seris in a surprise attack, its crew killed, and its cargo stolen (Redondo 1862).

Finally, in 1873 the Mexican Congress authorized the expenditure of $15,000 pesos to develop the port of Libertad (Lerdo de Tejada 1873). On July 16, 1874, the federal government declared it open, but only to the coasting trade, not as a port of entry for foreign vessels (Lerdo de Tejada 1874; Willard 1874b). Although Libertad quickly became a routine stop for steamships bound for the Colorado River, little real development ever took place. When the U.S.S. *Narragansett* surveyed the bay at the end of 1873 and again in early 1875, the only structures there were a few houses standing behind the beach, one of which was used as a customshouse (Belden 1880:140). In late July of 1878, when the steamer *Coquille* arrived at the head of the Gulf, she still:

> had aboard a lot of freight for Altar, which was to have been landed at Port Libertad. But on arriving there, no one appeared to receive it, and it was brought along [to the Colorado River], to be discharged on the down trip. (Anonymous 1878g)

Interest in Libertad dwindled when railroads connected southern Arizona with California in 1877 and then with Guaymas in 1882. Not only did rail offer a more efficient means of conveying goods to Arizona than had the steamers, but for Sonorans the railroad from Guaymas also established a transportation link within reach of the Altar district. Although a scheme emerged in 1883 to run a spur line to Libertad (sometimes still called "Lobos"), nothing ever came of it (Willard 1884a:229, 1887a:878). By 1881, with the complete abandonment of the Gulf route to the Colorado River, Libertad reverted to little more than an occasional stop for domestic coasting vessels. In 1890, U.S. Consul Alexander Willard remarked that Guaymas was now the final destination even for Mexican coasting vessels "as there are no ports open to traffic north of Guaymas" (Willard 1890).

Foreign and Domestic Warships in the Gulf

During the uneasy peace that prevailed in northern Mexico throughout much of the nineteenth century, naval vessels on patrol occasionally entered the Gulf of California and called at the major ports. Toward the end of the century, most of the warships in the Gulf were Mexican, but in earlier decades the majority were U.S. and British. For the United States, the primary mission of these peacetime patrols was to protect the American merchant fleet and safeguard American lives and property in foreign countries, both afloat and ashore (Goldberg 1973:41). To accomplish this task worldwide, the U.S. Navy divided its warships among several regional fleets.

Despite the internally unstable and sometimes threatening political conditions in the region, visits to the Gulf by U.S. warships were neither frequent nor regular events. The unit designated to patrol the west coast of Mexico was the far-flung Pacific Squadron, which was responsible for the entire Pacific Basin. During the period between 1850 and 1889, this squadron was rarely assigned more than 10 vessels, and it often had to make do with only three (Johnson 1963:214–23). With so few vessels to serve this enormous arena, it is little wonder that U.S. warships rarely showed up in the Gulf more often than once a year. In 1871, U.S. Consul Willard complained that there had been not a single U.S. naval vessel in Guaymas in nearly 2½ years (Willard 1871:301, 1872:904). The following year brought only one brief visit from the U.S.S. *Saranac*, even though the port itself had been captured and held for ransom by pirates twice in the space of a few months (Garrison 1873:686). In 1873, there were two calls by U.S. warships, but during 1874 only the U.S.S. *Narragansett* on survey duty stopped at Guaymas (Garrison 1873:686; Willard 1874a:828, 1875a:846). The banner year of 1875 brought four visits from U.S. naval vessels in addition to the *Narragansett*, but thereafter no more than about one a year. In 1884, Willard again noted that no U.S. warship had appeared at Guaymas for three years, and it was another two years before one finally arrived (Willard 1875b, 1884b, 1887b).

Occasionally, the U.S. government sent a warship to the Gulf to deal with specific threats to its citizens. The most dramatic instance was the appearance of the sloop-of-war *St. Mary's* at Guaymas in 1858 and 1859, in response to the tense situation created by Charles P. Stone and the Jecker Survey of Sonora (see pp. 169–71). Similarly, in 1874 the U.S.S. *Saranac* was dispatched to La Paz to investigate problems involving North American mining operations in the vicinity (Robeson 1874:8, 32–33; 1875:8–9, 30). But for the most part, U.S. naval vessels touched at Gulf ports only during their irregular and infrequent patrols.

On the peninsular side of the Gulf, La Paz was a more frequent stop for U.S. warships. In part, this was because in 1866 the U.S. Navy had acquired a concession for a coaling station at Bahía Pichilingue, only about 10 miles from the port. La Paz was also situated much closer to the mouth of the Gulf and the more important ports to the south. Guaymas, nearly 300 miles farther up the Gulf, was all the more remote from these centers of activity. Beyond Guaymas, North Americans did acquire a number of economic interests, including George Johnson's shipyard at Port Isabel, guano mining concessions on the Midriff islands of San Pedro Mártir and Rasa, and a silver mine at Bahía de los Ángeles. But with few people and no real towns, there were apparently no international incidents in the upper Gulf, and therefore little need for a naval presence there. For U.S. patrols, Guaymas seems to have been the end of the line.

During the middle years of the nineteenth century, some of the international commerce in Guaymas was handled by British interests, which were accorded the protection of the Royal Navy. When John Russell Bartlett visited the port in early 1852, the steamer H.M.S. *Driver* was detailed to the Pacific coast and made regular monthly calls at Guaymas (Bartlett [1854] 1965:479). However, these frequent patrols did not last, for by the 1870s visits by British warships had apparently become as irregular as those of the U.S. Navy. In 1870, three British men-of-war came to Guaymas, but the port was not visited by another British warship until late 1873, when three vessels appeared in the space of two months (Willard 1871:301, 1872:904, 1875a:846).

Like the North Americans, British naval officers did their share of saber rattling under the guise of protecting their citizens. Early in 1862, English merchants in Guaymas, protesting the legality of a new tax on commerce, appealed to their government for assistance, and the H.M.S. *Mutiny* under Captain William Graham was dispatched to investigate the situation. After unsuccessfully demanding that the tax be rescinded, Captain Graham captured a Mexican pilot boat believed to be carrying a cargo of silver, with which he apparently intended to reimburse the merchants for taxes already collected. The incident came to a head when 100 British troops were landed to prevent Mexican officials from making another tax collection. But when the Mexicans responded with a threat of force, Graham backed down, removed the troops, and departed (Acuña 1972:75–77).

French warships on peacetime patrols also occasionally visited the Gulf, but it was during the Intervention years of 1861–1867 that the French Navy showed up in force. In 1864, the French emperor Napoleon III installed Austrian archduke Maximilian as emperor of Mexico. Though this dramatic change in governance was supported by a sizable fraction of the Mexican populace, resistance was strong, forcing France to send its own military forces to occupy Mexico in support of the fragile puppet empire. The French Navy was already active along Mexico's west coast by 1862, and the first hostile action broke out with the arrival of four French warships at Acapulco at the beginning of 1863. Off and on during the next three years, the French maintained partial blockades of most of the west coast ports, and some were occupied by French troops. Although the United States regarded the French presence as a serious threat to its own interests in Mexico, the French wisely kept the major ports open to U.S. commercial vessels. Since the United States was also preoccupied during much of this period with its own Civil War, it was willing to maintain an uneasy policy of neutrality toward the Intervention (Gilbert 1955:36–37; Acuña 1972:83–84).

Apparently, Baja California saw little of the French, though warships put in briefly at La Paz in July 1864 and again late in 1865 (Martínez 1960:395; Acuña 1972:81). Guaymas, however, was another story, for France saw mineral-rich Sonora as a special prize, and realized that its deep and bitter internal political divisions would make it easy prey. At the beginning of 1864, a French warship briefly blockaded Guaymas, and other ships appeared there in May and July. On March 29, 1865, a squadron of four vessels landed an occupational force of 1,200 soldiers and a section of artillery at Guaymas (Bancroft 1889:696; Gilbert 1955:33; Acuña 1972:80, 85). Backed by French troops and widespread popular support, Sonoran Imperialist forces succeeded in taking control of much of the state over the next few months. But in France, support of Maximilian was beginning to weaken in the face of the obvious failure of the Mexican Empire, and French soldiers were needed for more pressing international problems. Over the next year, as French troops were gradually withdrawn and the Navy recalled, Sonora began to be retaken by Republican forces, led by Governor Ignacio Pesqueira, in a series of bloody battles. By October 1865, the occupational force in Sonora had been reduced to a single battalion in Guaymas. Nearly a year later, on September 14, 1866, the French pulled out of Guaymas completely.

The transition to Mexican governance in Guaymas was effected relatively peacefully when Pesqueira's forces entered the town three days later. However, thousands of Mexican supporters of the French cause had already fled for their lives, including some Guaymas customs officials who made their escape in a guano vessel they had seized on a phony charge (see p. 125). Two leaders of the Imperialist faction also tried to escape across the Gulf in a small French schooner but were apprehended in mid-Gulf, returned to Guaymas, and executed (Conner 1866a, 1866b; Bancroft 1889:697; Acuña 1972:92).

For the Mexican Navy, operations in the Gulf were seldom peaceful, for when there were no foreign wars, the region seemed almost perpetually plagued by internal strife. In the 1840s, the navy had maintained a small Southern Fleet that operated along Mexico's Pacific coast. In 1846, at the outbreak of war with the United States, this fleet consisted of three schooners and a brig. When the war moved into the Pacific, these vessels were among the primary targets of U.S. warships. After one was taken at Mazatlán, the remaining three were encountered in the Gulf, one at La Paz and two at Guaymas. By November 1846, all four Mexican warships had been captured or burned.

Figure 7.3   The Mexican Navy warship Demócrata *in 1914.
(Courtesy U.S. Naval Historical Center, Washington, D.C. [NH 93619].)*

For the next three decades, Mexico's naval presence on the west coast seems to have consisted mainly of small civilian vessels temporarily chartered for specific duty. In 1854, the schooner *Suerte* was enlisted to cruise the Gulf near Guaymas in an unsuccessful attempt to intercept Gaston de Raousset-Boulbon's filibustering expedition (Wyllys 1932:193). Three years later, an armed pilot boat was patrolling the west coast to discourage pirates. But during the Intervention years of the 1860s, when the French blockaded Guaymas and other west coast ports, the Mexican Navy had no warships in the Pacific capable of mounting a resistance.

Mexico did not establish its Pacific Fleet until 1874, when the Navy commissioned an English firm to construct two 151-foot steamships of 663.5 tons displacement. These gunboats (*cañoneros*) were armed with five cannons each, christened the *Demócrata* (Figure 7.3) and the *México*, and placed in service the following year. In early 1876, both vessels steamed into Guaymas, bringing 200 troops to quell unrest in the region. U.S. Consul Willard remarked that these were "the first regularly armed national vessels of the Mexican Navy" to enter Guaymas harbor in recent memory (Willard 1876a, 1876b; Dios Bonilla 1962:418; Cardenas de la Peña 1970a:186, 211; 1970b:46, Documento 49, 58).

Around 1882, the gunboat *Juárez* joined the fleet, and in 1888, the *México* was converted into a training ship. But the *Demócrata* remained on line into the twentieth century, and saw much of its service in the Gulf. Frequently, the government made temporary additions to the small Pacific Fleet by commandeering civilian vessels, which were used mainly as troop transports. Thus in the spring of 1880, the *Demócrata* was assisted by Guillermo Andrade's commercial steamer *General Zaragoza* in carrying troops from Mazatlán and Guaymas to San Felipe in the upper Gulf, to help crush the antigovernment insurrection led by Manuel Márquez de León (Martínez 1960:401–42, 529–30). By 1890, the navy had acquired its own transport vessel, the steamer *Oaxaca*, though the government still continued to make use of civilian vessels from time to time (Dios Bonilla 1962:423–32; Cardenas de la Peña 1970b:46).

In addition to dealing with civil unrest, from the 1880s to the first decade of the twentieth century, the *Demócrata* and *Oaxaca* were used extensively in military actions against the Yaquis and Seris, usually operating out of Guaymas. During the Yaqui wars, the *Oaxaca* was frequently employed to deport Yaquis to the south, while the *Demócrata* became notorious as one of the ships that carried Yaqui prisoners into the open Gulf, where they were thrown overboard (Turner 1969:31; Hu-DeHart 1984:167). Campaigns against the Seris took both vessels, as well as others, to Tiburón Island. In 1890, the *Demócrata* transported 50 soldiers to Tiburón Island on a reprisal mission against the Seris for the wounding of two Mexicans off San Esteban Island. In 1894, the government borrowed the civilian steamer *M. Romero Rubio* to transport troops to Tiburón to punish the Seris for the murders of North Americans Robinson and Logan (Anonymous 1896a, 1896b). Three years later, a similar military expedition sailed for Tiburón on the civilian steamer *Río Yaqui* to investigate the disappearance of the North Americans Porter and Johnson (Nieto 1897; MacMullen 1968:G-2). Late in 1898, the *Oaxaca*, freshly overhauled, made a trial run to the east coast of Tiburón, and this time shore parties succeeded in establishing peaceful contact with a large group of Seris (Cerisola 1898). In 1904, the *Demócrata* and the civilian vessel *Bernardo Reyes* brought Governor Izábal and a large contingent of soldiers from Guaymas to Tiburón to carry out the last formal military campaign against the Seris. Toward the end of its career, during the 1910s, the *Demócrata* lay at anchor in Guaymas harbor, having been relegated to service as a floating jail for political prisoners taken during the Mexican Revolution (Zavala 1984:93).

EIGHT

Concessions for Capitalists:
Colonization and Development Schemes for the Midriff Islands

During the second half of the nineteenth century, the Mexican government, through its Secretaría de Fomento, Colonización e Industria (roughly, the Department of Development), opened up vast tracts of public land and resources in northwestern Mexico for investment and development. Although these lands and resources were to remain as part of the Mexican nation, federal policy made it possible for foreigners to own these holdings outright and reap whatever profits they could accrue from them. For North Americans who had long coveted the region, the government's policy was a bonanza which triggered a flood of land speculation and promotional schemes, some honest and some laden with fraud. Among the schemes was a plan by an entrepreneur named Guillermo Andrade to develop the supposed resources of and even establish settlements on the islands of Tiburón, Ángel de la Guarda, and San Esteban.

These schemes had their roots in Mexico's disastrous relations with the United States. In little more than a decade, between the 1836 secession of Texas and the end of the war with the United States in 1848, Mexico had seen more than half its sovereign territory lost to its land-hungry northern neighbor. In 1854, the international boundary was pushed still farther south by the Gadsden Purchase. But in the United States, the continuing inflammatory rhetoric of Manifest Destiny gave Mexicans little reason to think that even these huge acquisitions would end the North Americans' seemingly insatiable territorial appetite. The point was driven home by the filibusters, albeit unsuccessful, of Walker, Crabb, and Raousset-Boulbon. Thus in the mid-1850s, Mexicans were acutely aware that their hold on the redrawn northern frontier was tenuous and was continually threatened by North American dreams of further annexation (Voss 1982:113–15).

From the perspective of Mexicans living in the northwest, there were three serious problems that kept the region at risk. The most fundamental was the sparse population of Baja California and Sonora, which was both insufficient for defense against armed invasion from across the border and inadequate to develop the mineral and agricultural resources of the region. At the end of the war with the United States, almost all of the tiny population of Baja California was concentrated in the south, and much of the peninsula was virtually uninhabited. In 1851, the population of the entire peninsula was only about 7,000 (Deasy and Gerhard 1944; Martínez 1960:409; Aschmann 1967:25–26), and despite rapid growth, even by 1880 it had not reached 25,000 (Lassépas 1859:47; Taylor [1869] 1971:139–40; Martínez 1960:409). Sonora's population during this period was much larger, with most estimates placing it between about 90,000 and 130,000 people (Velasco 1850:54; Pérez Hernández 1872a:73; Riva Palacio 1877:460; Voss 1982:110–17, 183; West 1993:Figure 41) or slightly higher (Ruibal 1985:156; Gracida Romo 1985:29). But in a large state even this many people amounts to sparse settlement, and several times Sonora's population underwent sharp declines. Many people immigrated to Alta California, drawn by the lure of the gold fields, while others moved to Arizona Territory to escape Sonora's endless political turmoil. Most importantly, there were too few people to resist the devastating raids of the Apaches. Ranches, mines, and entire settlements were abandoned across the whole northern frontier of the state, leaving the region vulnerable not only to further Apache raids, but to North American territorial ambitions as well (Acuña 1974:7–8, 13–14, 100–102, 107, 118–19; Voss 1982:67–72, 110–12; Holden 1990:582).

The isolation of the region from potential federal assistance was a second problem, for there were no speedy means of communication and transportation between Mexico City and the northwestern frontier. Ships plied the Mexican west coast and the Gulf of California, serving the few port towns, but once people and supplies reached the ports, it was often difficult to transport them farther. Especially in Baja California, roads were inadequate or nonexistent, and there were no railroads anywhere in region.

More basic still was uncertainty about the federal government's commitment to preserving the territorial integrity of the northwestern frontier, for it was unclear whether the federal government was able or even willing to mount a military defense of the region. In Sonora, state authorities had long received promises of federal assistance in dealing with the terrible Apache problem, but little help had ever materialized. Moreover, the government in Mexico City seemed bent on sabotaging Sonora's own attempts to address its problems. As early as 1850, the Sonoran legislature had tried to deal with its underpopulation by enacting a colonization law designed to bring settlers into the state. But the law was declared unconstitutional by the federal government, which claimed sole authority to set colonization policy for the entire nation. At the same time federal policy, which encouraged the emigration of French nationals from Alta California, had brought in little more than adventurers, culminating in the invasion of Gaston de Raousset-Boulbon (Wyllys 1932:9–33; Voss 1982:116–19). The federal role in sanctioning Raousset-Boulbon's contract with the banking house of Jecker, de la Torre y Compañía in Mexico City to exploit Sonora's mines suggested to many people in the northwest that government officials in Mexico City, in attempts to raise capital or profit personally, were as likely to sell off the region and its resources as to defend it. It is little wonder, then, that Sonorans did not welcome the next Jecker contract, approved by the federal government in 1856, which would have transferred title to huge tracts of Sonoran territory to North American financiers.

The Jecker Contract for the Survey of Sonora

Sonoran misgivings aside, the 1856 Jecker contract to survey Sonora seems to have represented a step in evolving federal policy aimed in part at protecting the frontier. Since most North American interests in the region were economically motivated, it was believed that one way to stave off outright annexation was to allow North Americans to develop the region without the necessity of annexing it. Thus foreign capitalists might be permitted to own land and profit from its resources, but the land itself would remain part of the Mexican nation. Foreign investment would be essential if there were to be any economic development of the region, since Mexico simply lacked sufficient capital. Of course, any influx of money from abroad would be beneficial to the country. And an economically developed northwest with heavy North American vested interest in the status quo, it was reasoned, would be less of a target for annexation in the future.

The contract for the survey of Sonora was one of three such contracts negotiated between Jecker, de la Torre y Compañía and the Mexican government. The other two, about which little is known, were for surveys of Baja California and the Isthmus of Tehuántepec (Lassépas 1859:244–45; Sánchez Facio 1889: 41; Maza 1893:641–45; Pacheco et al. 1893). Central to these and all subsequent contracts was the concept of *terrenos baldíos*, the lands that were to be made available to foreign investors. Although often referred to simply as "idle" or "vacant" lands, it was widely understood that the concept was much broader:

> The lands improperly called in Mexico "terrenos baldios," waste lands, are not only those that are uncultivated, but include all those that are the property of the Government.... [T]he lands that belong to the nation are the lands of the former Jesuits and Franciscan Missions; the lands of the former presidios or military stations now abandoned; the lands occupied by the different barbarous tribes, enemies of the white race, that have not subjected themselves to the general laws of civilisation; and lastly, the lands which, although they may be of private individuals, have no legal title conformable to Mexican laws. (George F. Henderson, in Lower California Company 1870:15)

This generally accepted interpretation meant that the most disenfranchised groups, peasants and Indians, were vulnerable to eviction from their traditional lands. Some peasants did lose their lands by being unable to produce legal titles, but contrary to conventional wisdom, this seems to have been the exception rather than the rule (Holden 1990:581, 592–99). Indians, however, did not fare as well. Eventually this policy encouraged developers to embark on a wholesale appropriation of the fertile agricultural lands of the Yaqui and Mayo Indians, fueling a series of destructive wars with these two peoples. And since the Seris were counted among the "barbarous" Indians at the time, their traditional territory, including Tiburón and San Esteban Islands, became fair game for development.

The principal figure in the banking house of Jecker, de la Torre y Compañía (which later became J. B. Jecker y Compañía) was Juan B. Jecker. Born in France in 1810, he had immigrated to Mexico early in the century but continued to maintain strong ties with his native country. This, coupled with his involvement in the Raousset-Boulbon affair, led Sonorans to regard his company's continuing activities with deep suspicion.

The basic contract for the Jecker survey of Sonora was signed on December 19, 1856. It obligated the company:

> to send to the State of Sonora one or more scientific commissions, with the object of reconnoitering all the waste lands, mark their limits and bounds, form particular and general plans of them, and make the most exact descriptions possible of their climate, productions, and advantages for commerce and agriculture. (Ramón de la Cueva, in Lower California Company 1870:16)

The contract further stipulated that this work was to be completed within three years. All expenses were to be born by the company and none by the government. But as compensation for the survey, the company would be granted absolute ownership of one-third of the "waste lands" mapped. The other two-thirds would belong to the federal government. Should the government decide to sell any of its land, the Jecker Company was to have first option. Finally, the federal government would order the Sonoran civil and military authorities to give all possible assistance to the survey (Maza 1893:641–43).

By March 1857, the Jecker Company had taken on three partners in the venture. Two were Mexican, political insider and former Secretary of Hacienda Manuel Payno, and financier Antonio Escandon. The third was North American Joseph B. G. Isham of San Francisco. Isham's role was twofold. First, he was charged with assembling the scientific commission that was to conduct the survey. Secondly, he was responsible for raising the capital to fund the commission's fieldwork. To do this, he was empowered to organize a company of foreign investors either in the United States or Europe. In return for fronting the operating capital for the survey, the investors would receive a portion—up to half—of the one-third of the *terrenos baldíos* that would be assigned to the Jecker Company. The remainder of the Jecker lands were to be divided equally among the four partners (Lower California Company 1870:15–20, 35–36).

The structure of the scientific commission was also clearly spelled out. The principal positions consisted of three engineers and their assistants, a geologist, and a "draughtsman" and his assistant. All were to serve under the Chief of the Commission, who would coordinate the fieldwork, oversee the preparation of maps and descriptive reports, represent the commission to the Mexican authorities, and communicate results to Jecker and Isham. The headquarters of the commission was to be established in Guaymas (Lower California Company 1870:23–30).

Figure 8.1
Charles P. Stone (1824–
1887) as a brigadier
general. Photograph
probably by Mathew
Brady, middle 1860s.
(Courtesy Massachusetts
Commandery Military
Order of the Loyal Legion
and the U.S. Army
Military History
Institute, Carlisle
Barracks, Pennsylvania
[No. 111-B-3803].)

Isham fulfilled his responsibilities promptly. By May 8, 1857, he had put together the scientific commission and shortly afterwards had organized a company consisting of five San Francisco investors. By November 1, these men had put up $70,000 in advance money for the fieldwork and committed themselves to an additional $230,000, payable via Isham to the Chief of the scientific commission, as needed.

It was during this time that the main player entered the unfolding drama. This was Captain Charles P. Stone (Figure 8.1). Although Stone acknowledged that he "did not understand the Spanish language," Isham designated him to act as his agent in Mexico and conferred upon him full power of attorney. Soon after, Stone was given similar authority by Jecker, Escandon, and Payno. But most importantly, he was appointed Chief of the Commission that would conduct the actual survey (Lower California Company 1870:25, 32–43).

The project began to unravel almost immediately. The financial arrangement proved to be completely unstable. In February 1858, four of the original California investors sold out to the fifth member, who defaulted on his obligation to the commission two months later, leaving Jecker and his three associates to cover $36,000 in accumulated overdrafts and with no financial backers to fund continuation of the survey (Lower California Company 1870:47–49). By then, however, the field survey itself was already in deep trouble, for a serious political confrontation was developing between Stone and the Sonoran government, one which propelled Mexico and the United States to the brink of another war.

On November 18, 1857, Stone sent an advance party into Sonora to begin surveying the northwestern part of the state. These men worked until the following April, when they proceeded to Guaymas to meet up with Stone and the main body of the commission. Meanwhile, Stone completed preparations in San Francisco and sailed on March 16, 1858, with the remainder of the commission personnel, arriving in Guaymas on April 13. Two days later, Stone sent a letter to Sonoran Governor Ignacio Pesqueira requesting that he order the state's civil and military authorities to put themselves at the commission's disposal. But Sonorans, who had little respect for the authority of the government in Mexico City or the Jecker Company, were not about to aid an intrusion of North American surveyors so that their state could be sold to other North Americans. Pesqueira's polite but firm reply the following day not only refused the state's official assistance but prohibited the commission from continuing its survey. The Sonoran legislature moved swiftly to support the Governor's action, ruling the Jecker contract invalid (Lower California Company 1870:69–71; Acuña 1974:56–57, 64).

The standoff quickly escalated into an international crisis. Stone, who apparently had a singular disdain for diplomacy, brazenly ignored the Sonoran government and proceeded with the survey. In fact, Stone seems to have seldom passed up an opportunity to alienate Sonorans with arrogant and offensive behavior. As tensions mounted, the United States government ordered the warship *St. Mary's* to Guaymas, and in December of 1858, in a taunting display of gunboat diplomacy, the vessel's captain, Charles H. Davis, appointed Stone Acting U.S. Consul for Guaymas. The investors who still held a financial stake in the Jecker survey began lobbying hard with both the U.S. and Mexican governments to intervene, militarily if need be. The press in the United States was once again calling for annexation of Sonora, an action which Stone strongly recommended and President Buchanan was indeed considering. And the Sonoran press asked whether Stone's inflammatory behavior might not be intended to provoke an incident which the United States could seize upon to declare war (Stone 1858; Rose 1859; Acuña 1974:57–59).

On May 18, 1859, Pesqueira gave Stone and his men 40 days to leave the state. Though Stone backed down and retreated to Arizona Territory, his departure merely set the stage for a new confrontation. In October, rumors of the survey's return coupled with the reappearance of the *St. Mary's* at Guaymas triggered an outpouring of anti-American hostility. At the U.S. Consulate, Vice-Consul Farrelly Alden lamented that:

> whilst the coat of arms over the [consulate] entrance was spat upon and wantonly defaced, the flag has been shot at repeatedly from the surrounding eminences, the balls whizzing into the consulate enclosure to the imminent danger of the inmates, whilst night is made hideous with cries of "muerto a los Americanos."…

Since Capt. Stone and his Survey were driven out of Sonora, defenseless Americans have been stoned in the public streets of Guaymas at mid-day, and now that the Commission is about to return I am unoficially informed by those high in authority, that it will not be permitted to enter Sonora, will be expelled by force, and should it gain a footing, the small surveying parties will be cut off in detail by assassins. (Alden 1859)

Pesqueira had already fortified Guaymas with 80 dragoons. The *St. Mary's* new commander, William D. Porter, landed 100 men and two pieces of artillery in Guaymas and threatened to blockade the port. The final showdown came on November 18, 1859, when Guaymas citizens rioted against the U.S. Consulate and tore down its flag. To Porter's threatened bombardment of the city, Pesqueira countered that such an act would obviate all responsibility on his part for North American life and property within the state. Finally comprehending the intensity of anti-American sentiment in Sonora, Porter capitulated and sailed away (Acuña 1974:57–64; Voss 1982:142).

The departure of the *St. Mary's* defused the diplomatic crisis, but it did nothing to resolve the disposition of the Jecker survey. For years afterward, Jecker and other investors filed legal claims for possession of the *terrenos baldíos* that had been surveyed, along with damages for lost capital. In 1868, Isham sold his interest to the Lower California Company, another syndicate of North American investors, which continued to press for damages and possession of these lands. From this company, claims to the lands were taken up by two Mexican entrepreneurs, Carlos Quaglia and Luis García Teruel, who had acquired the commission's accumulated maps and some 75 field notebooks. In 1885, the Mexican government acquired these documents and agreed to compensate the two men with 20 percent of the lands surveyed or an equivalent parcel somewhere else in Mexico (Mowry [1864] 1973:99; Lower California Company 1870:78–81; Pacheco et al. 1893).

From the fragmentary information available, it would appear that the territory covered by Stone's engineers was vast. According to Lower California Company documents, some 11,500,000 acres were surveyed (Anonymous n.d.c). Only a small fraction of this total was surveyed legitimately by the advance party that preceded the arrival of the commission's main contingent in April 1858. Although formally barred from continuing the survey from this time on, Stone did not hesitate to send his men into the field, especially after the protective arrival of the *St. Mary's*. Within a month after the survey had been officially banned, commission engineers had surveyed some 36 miles of coast around Bahía Adair and were busily mapping a large ranch on the outskirts of Guaymas. By August, one field party was surveying the coast south of Guaymas, while another was working to the north along a 100-mile stretch of coastal plain opposite Tiburón Island. By November, the survey had been extended to the fertile valleys of the Ríos Yaqui, Mayo, and Fuerte. Stone estimated that before the following spring of 1859, he would have the entire Sonoran coast mapped inland to a depth of 30 or 40 miles (Mowry [1864] 1973:100–101; Lower California Company 1870:65–66).

For its work along the Sonoran coast, the commission had acquired at least two vessels, one of them an armed brig named the *Manuel Payno* in honor of Jecker's partner. These vessels also enabled the survey teams to map the Gulf islands. By mid-May of 1858, a field party had surveyed San Jorge Island near the head of the Gulf, and in November, Stone dispatched a team to San Pedro Nolasco Island, just northwest of Guaymas, and to the guano island of San Pedro Mártir in the Midriff (Lower California Company 1870:66). It is clear that the survey made a reconnaissance of Tiburón Island and mapped Tortuga Island on the peninsular side of the Gulf, for these were among the Jecker documents eventually turned over to the Mexican government (Pacheco et al. 1893: 1007). In September 1859, three months after the commission had been ordered out of Sonora, Stone's men were still hard at work in the Gulf. On September 6, after dropping troops off at the mouth of the Colorado River, Andrew S. Hussey, Master of the brig *Floyd*, was working his way down the Gulf in the channel between San Lorenzo Island and the peninsula when he:

> Saw a Sail Boat under the land standing off. with colors union down. Stood in shore and got her alongside. It proved to be a boat belonging to Capt. Stones party surveying the Gulf. They were out of provisions. with which we Supplied them. and continued on beating down—at noon outside of the Islands [i.e., he was now south of San Lorenzo]. (Hussey 1859)

A day later, off San Pedro Mártir Island, Hussey:

> saw a Brig to the SE. Standing up the Gulf—at noon was boarded by an Officer from Surveying Brig San Bernardino. Belonging to the Party of Capt Stone who is Engaged in Surveying Part of Sonora. and the Gulf. and about which there is a controversy Going On. and he and Party were driven from Guaymas. They were in want of potatoes of which I had none to spare. and leaving him we continued beating down off the island of San Pedro Martyr. (Hussey 1859)

Hussey's encounters suggest that after the expulsion, Stone's men tried to avoid detection by Sonoran authorities by renaming their brig, dispensing with flags, and shifting their fieldwork away from the Sonoran mainland. It was probably during this period that the survey of the Gulf islands and the peninsula was carried out. And this portion of the fieldwork must have been fairly thorough. Engineer William Denton later wrote that the commission members had ultimately managed to survey much of the Gulf coasts and many of the islands north of Mulegé (Sánchez 1889:43). Similarly, later remarks by Engineer Frederick Fitch (1875, 1886) indicate that he had acquired considerable firsthand knowledge of the Midriff islands. In a description of the Gulf in which he mentions Ángel de la Guarda, Tiburón, and "San Estevan" Islands by name, Fitch confidently asserts that:

> None of the islands are inhabited, if we except the southern end of Tiburon, where a few miserable Ceres Indians maintain a scanty livelihood by fishing.

A solitary, scanty spring furnishes them with water. No attempt has ever been made to cultivate any of the islands of this Gulf, for the reason that water is not to be found on them in sufficient quantities for irrigation. With the exception of a limited supply on the northern part of Los Angeles Island [Ángel de la Guarda] and that mentioned as existing on Tiburon, no other island in the Gulf contains a drop. (Fitch 1875:61)

Whether Fitch or other members of the commission ever actually went ashore on San Esteban Island is not known. As for the survey itself, Stone's men continued to work at least until late 1860, nearly a year and a half after their Chief had been expelled from Sonora (Sánchez 1889:43). Engineers Fitch and Denton later settled in Fuerte, Sinaloa and La Paz, Baja California, respectively, and for many years continued to practice their profession in northwestern Mexico. Captain Stone, meanwhile, shifted his energies to the American Civil War, and despite a turbulent career, rose to the rank of Brigadier General.

Federal Colonization Laws

Although Sonorans had managed to block the parceling of their state to the Jecker interests, the publicity generated by this debacle had, if anything, left northwestern Mexico even more vulnerable to North American adventurism than before. With its vast tracts of *terrenos baldíos*, the region's acute under-population was still its primary problem. To the government in Mexico City, the situation in the northwest was merely a special case of undesirable population distribution that existed in much of the country, and in the early 1860s, the federal government began to develop a strategy for encouraging settlement of *terrenos baldíos* throughout the nation. Though there were many antecedents, in 1863 it enacted the first of several landmark pieces of legislation that were to become known collectively as the "colonization laws," which defined policy for bringing people (and later capital) to the nation's *terrenos baldíos*.

The "Law of July 20, 1863," as it was formally titled, resembled the 1862 Homestead Act of the United States. It enabled individual Mexicans to "denounce," or file claim on, up to 2,500 hectares of *terrenos baldíos* and purchase the parcel from the government at a nominal cost. Two major conditions were imposed on claimants. One was a requirement for a professional survey of the land in question. The other was the settlement requirement itself, which stipulated that, for four months per year for 10 years, each 200 hectares was to be inhabited by at least one person (Maza 1893:729–35; Hendricks 1967:7–10; Hale 1989:235).

This initial attempt to populate *terrenos baldíos* met with little success. One of the stumbling blocks was that the federal government had little real knowledge of what lands qualified as *terrenos baldíos* and whether they were actually able to support settlers. Without better information, colonists could not be effectively recruited. Yet it was believed that any government attempt to launch a comprehensive survey of these lands would be prohibitively slow and expensive (Coerver 1977:52, 1979:211).

Twelve years after it was enacted, the 1863 law was superseded by the Law of May 31, 1875, which in turn was replaced by the Law of December 15, 1883 (Maza 1893:826–28, 936–45). These later laws made two fundamental changes in the way colonization was to be accomplished. The first and most important change was that the new laws once again attempted to fund economic development and colonization with private capital. This was to be accomplished by taking the process of claiming and settling the land out of the hands of individual homesteaders and turning it over to private companies, which could be made up entirely of foreign investors. As with the Jecker contract, the federal government was again offering both Mexican and North American capitalists an opportunity to reap big profits from Mexico's *terrenos baldíos*. But this time Sonora put up little resistance, for by 1880 the state government was firmly controlled by the dictatorial hand of Mexican President Porfirio Díaz.

The new procedures required each colonization company to enter into a contractual agreement with the federal government to establish a colony within a specified length of time. It also required that a bond be posted to ensure that the contract was fulfilled. As its first obligation, the company would be responsible for surveying and producing maps of the lands targeted for development. Many contracts required the company to recruit and transport the settlers to their new location and provide them with construction materials, farming equipment, and other supplies sufficient to maintain the colony until it could become self-supporting. The laws authorized that any colonist be permitted to purchase up to 2,500 hectares of land from the company at a nominal price. Both the company and the colonists would be subject to Mexican law but exempt from most taxes (Bancroft 1889:729–30; Maza 1893:826–28, 936–45; Hendricks 1967:10–11; Coerver 1977:52–53, 1979:211–12; Hale 1989:235–37).

What the investors were promised in return for their capital was, of course, land. Just as in the Jecker contract, in compensation for the task of conducting its survey, the colonization company was to be granted outright ownership of one-third of all the *terrenos baldíos* it had surveyed. But the new laws also gave companies the option of purchasing an additional one-third from the government. For both Mexican and foreign investors, this was an effective lure. Between 1881 and 1889, colonization companies, many of them backed by North American capital, may have acquired through survey compensation and purchase options title to as much as 27,500,000 hectares, amounting to nearly 14 percent of the total land area of Mexico (Coerver 1977:54, 1979:215).

The second basic change was that the later laws were intended to attract not only Mexican settlers but also foreign colonists as well. The important role of immigrants in the economic development of the United States was well understood, and it was assumed that industrious foreigners, specifically Europeans, would exert a progressive influence on Mexican colonists. Some colonies might even be made up entirely of foreigners except in politically sensitive areas such as frontier regions and islands, where Mexican nationals were to comprise a minimum percentage of the new population (Maza 1893:826; Coerver 1977:52, 1979:312–14). The one principal upon which everybody agreed, however, was that North American capital must not be accompanied by North American colonists. Part of the purpose of the new colonization policy was to protect Mexico's territorial integrity, and the government had no intention of recreating the very same demographic conditions that had led to the secession of Texas in 1836 (Bancroft 1888:488–92; Coerver 1979:210–11; Voss 1982:205; Hale 1989:234–38).

Whether the wholesale transfer of land to foreign interests succeeded in defusing North American annexation schemes is impossible to guess. If it did, it was the only success of the colonization program. Not only did the program accomplish little in terms of its other objectives, but it ended up exacerbating some of the country's existing problems. Because the *terrenos baldíos* were mostly lands completely unsuited to agriculture, few colonists ever settled them, and most of those who tried eventually abandoned them. The majority of the colonization companies proved to consist of land speculators and promoters rather than developers, and little in the way of economic development ever occurred. Moreover, the program fell victim to corruption and fraud. Contracts for some of the more promising tracts were awarded to colonization companies whose principal investors were the President of Mexico and his close relatives and advisors (Coerver 1977:57–60, 1979:265–67; Holden 1990:592). Some foreign companies conducted grossly inadequate surveys, sold lands to which they had no title, and misrepresented their holdings and activities to both the Mexican government and their own investors (Sánchez 1889). To what extent peasant farmers and small landowners were dispossessed is less clear (Holden 1990), but there is little doubt that the program tended to further concentrate land in the hands of the wealthy and powerful. In the end, the colonization program had the effect of exacerbating the inequities in land distribution that were gradually leading toward revolution (Tannenbaum 1933:141–43; Powell 1968:22; Coerver 1977:54, 1979:213–15; Hale 1989:237).

But the long-term social consequences were probably of no interest, nor for that matter, clearly foreseen by those who stood to profit by the policy. For entrepreneurs like Guillermo Andrade, the colonization program was welcomed as a legitimate way to make a lot of money. And one of the *terrenos baldíos* Andrade proposed to colonize was San Esteban Island.

The Saga of Guillermo Andrade

In 1882, Mexican citizen Guillermo Andrade (Figure 8.2) and his wealthy North American partner, Thomas H. Blythe (Figure 8.3), formed a company whose purpose was the economic development and colonization of the islands of Tiburón, Ángel de la Guarda, and San Esteban. Farming, raising livestock, mining, fishing, pearling, and other industries were to be established, and each island would have its own village of self-sufficient colonists. As it turned out, their scheme foundered not so much because the islands had insufficient re-

Figure 8.2
Guillermo Andrade
(ca. 1834–1905).
(Courtesy Sherman Library,
Corona del Mar, California.)

sources to support these enterprises, but because of plain bad luck and insur-
mountable legal problems that derailed the venture before the first colonist ever
arrived. Much of this legal tangle has been pieced together by William O.
Hendricks (1967), whose work remains the single comprehensive source on
Andrade's activities.

For a man of Andrade's prominence, surprisingly little is known about him.
He was born in Hermosillo sometime between 1833 and 1835 and was educated
in the finest schools of Spain and France. He returned to Sonora at age 24 to
manage the family sugar plantations. In 1863, he immigrated to California,
settling in San Francisco, where he became a businessman and banker. Eventually, he moved to Los Angeles, where he served as Mexican Consul (Tout
[1931]:43; Hendricks 1967:36–37).

Just how Andrade became interested in acquiring and developing *terrenos*
baldíos in Sonora and Baja California is not known, but he was unquestionably

724½ Market St.   *Imperial*   San Francisco.

Figure 8.3
Thomas H. Blythe
(1822–1883).
(Courtesy Huntington
Library, San Marino,
California [PF 6932].)

in an excellent position to do so. San Francisco in the 1870s was a prime place to find investment capital, and it was a city where interest in Mexico's resources ran high. By retaining his Mexican citizenship, Andrade held certain legal advantages which enabled him to acquire territory that was off limits to non-Mexicans. And personal connections with some of the highest federal officials in Mexico City could not help but be an asset.

Andrade's first colonization project, and in some respects his most successful, began to take shape late in 1873. With several associates to provide start-up capital, he formed a plan to acquire and develop a large tract of *terrenos baldíos* below the international border in the delta of the Colorado River. Here the group would establish a community of colonists who would harvest the area's enormous stands of wild hemp and farm the rich delta land. In November of 1873, a suitable location for the colony was found, and in December, in accordance with the Law of July 20, 1863, the process of "denouncing," or filing claim on the land was begun. In January 1874, Andrade and his 15 associates formed the company that was to build the settlement, bring in the colonists, and support the operation until it was self-sufficient and profitable. The company, descriptively named the Compañía Mexicana Agrícola, Industrial y Colonizadora de Terrenos del Colorado, was organized under Mexican law, legally domiciled in Guaymas, but actually headquartered in San Francisco, where the majority of the associates resided. Late in 1874, the company added 13 new stockholders. The most important of these, both to the fortunes of the company and to Guillermo Andrade personally, was Thomas H. Blythe.

By early 1875, the project land had been surveyed and mapped and the results sent to the Secretaría de Fomento, Colonización e Industria, which granted its approval. In addition to the delta land, the company acquired small tracts encompassing two ports on the Gulf of California, George Johnson's Port Isabel (renamed Puerto Isabel) near the mouth of the Colorado River, and San Felipe, on the Baja California side. When the process was completed in 1876, the company held title to some 340,000 acres for an outlay of about $27,000 pesos. The project was diplomatically named Colonia Lerdo, in honor of the President of Mexico, and the settlement was to be called Ciudad Lerdo.

Unlike many promoters who created empty speculative ventures, Andrade and his partners promptly set about fulfilling their legal obligations. By October 1874, more than 200 colonists had been settled and were cutting hemp. But in the spring of 1877, a devastating flood swept through the delta, totally destroying the town and carrying away 5,000 tons of cut hemp. Losses to the company were estimated at $233,000. Not wishing to risk more money, most of the investors pulled out, the settlers abandoned Lerdo, and the project lay in ruins (Hendricks 1967:37–54, 1976:48).

Andrade, however, was a man of irrepressible optimism, and he was unwilling to abandon his cherished enterprise. Lacking sufficient funds to resurrect Lerdo on his own, he persuaded Thomas Blythe, perhaps the wealthiest of the company stockholders, to finance a rebuilding project. This established the first of what was to become a series of partnership agreements between the two men. In this, as in subsequent ventures, Blythe's role was to supply the capital, while Andrade would use his time and energy, his Mexican citizenship, and his excellent political connections, to create profitable enterprises. Whether as a matter of principle between honorable men, inattention to protocol, or casual neglect, the terms of their partnerships were never recorded in writing, a mistake for which Andrade paid dearly for the rest of his life.

To begin reviving the Lerdo project, Blythe purchased from former associates most of the outstanding shares in the Compañía Mexicana, giving him and Andrade controlling interest. In January 1878, Andrade signed a new contract with the Secretaría de Fomento which obligated the partners to establish 200 families on company lands within five years. Once the resettlement was complete, the company was free to operate the colony as a profit-making enterprise (Hendricks 1967:78–83, 1978:140–41).

Andrade and Blythe realized that the colony would need an efficient transportation link with the outside world. This was not a new concept, for the company's 1874 progress report had proposed establishing its own steamship line to connect the colony with Guaymas and other Mexican Gulf ports (Anonymous 1874). But Blythe's money breathed new life into the old idea, and one of the first joint ventures of the new partnership was to found their own Gulf shipping and passenger line. In November 1877, the Mexican government approved a contract for a separate Andrade-Blythe company called the Línea Acelerada del Golfo de Cortés. With this official blessing, Blythe purchased a steamship for the Gulf and a smaller steam launch to run from their tract at Puerto Isabel at the head of the Gulf on up the Colorado River to Colonia Lerdo. The vessels were put into service the following July (García and Andrade 1877; García 1878; Hendricks 1967:93–95; 1978:141–42).

In addition to the steamship line, Andrade and Blythe negotiated a separate contract to build a wagon road from Lerdo to Ft. Yuma, thereby providing an overland connection between their colony and the Southern Pacific Railroad, which was about to reach Yuma. This road would also link the railroad with Puerto Isabel, the terminus of their new steamer route, and with this connection they hoped to realize great profits by halving the shipping time between Guaymas and San Francisco. At the same time, Andrade and Blythe succeeded in nearly tripling their Lerdo holdings. By November 1882, the Compañía Mexicana controlled some 914,000 acres of delta land extending on both sides of the Colorado River in an unbroken tract from the international border to the Gulf of California (Hendricks 1967:73–75, 1978:144–45).

It was within this heady atmosphere of cheap and easy land acquisition that the scheme to colonize the islands of Tiburón, Ángel de la Guarda, and eventually San Esteban, arose. The precise origins of the islands venture are obscure, for very little information about it has come to light (Hendricks 1967:93). Possibly, the idea materialized in connection with the Andrade-Blythe steamship line, for the vessel's route through the Midriff would take it into the channel between Tiburón and San Esteban Islands and past the eastern shore of Ángel de La Guarda (Anonymous 1874:map). Timing may also have been a factor, for in 1880, a little more than a year before the scheme was formalized, a military expedition had removed 150 Seris from the coast opposite Tiburón Island, perhaps convincing Andrade that the islands were now "safe" for settlement (see pp. 240–42).

For the Midriff islands venture, Andrade and Blythe took on two partners and formed yet another company. One of the new partners was Manuel Romero Rubio, a powerful lawyer who was the father-in-law of President Porfirio Díaz and soon to become a cabinet minister in the Díaz regime. The other was Agustín R. González, a senator and later a cabinet minister. Within this new framework, Blythe himself became a silent partner, whose task would be to provide the lion's share of the capital. The company, organized on January 5, 1882 in Mexico City, was called the Compañía Mejicana Colonizadora e Industrial (Velázquez 1882). Its objectives were summarized in the preamble to its articles of incorporation. In this document the partners asserted that:

> in the Gulf of Cortéz, lying between Sonora and Baja California, there exist resources of great public wealth which have experienced truly disastrous

exploitation and have been neglected to the point of complete destruction, because nobody has cared to conserve them. [We, the aforementioned individuals], desiring to establish an enterprise [that] can put an end to these evils, have become partners in order to form a corporation represented by stock which can raise all the capital necessary to initiate, in a structured and reliable way, the breeding and cultivation of the pearl oyster in the most accessible parts of the Gulf and Coast and especially on the islands of Tiburón and Ángel de la Guarda. [The Company] will [also] exploit all the shellfish, sharks, whales and sea lions and will breed and raise on the aforementioned islands horses of European and American breeds, as well as Angora goats and cattle of the best breeds and other natural and manufactured products to which these islands lend themselves. In order to realize this idea of reconciling the public interest with the private, it is proposed that the islands be colonized, giving preference to Mexican colonists residing in Arizona and San Francisco, and that the Government be given, as rent and compensation, a portion of the harvest of pearls and sea foods. [Because the] natural markets [for these products] are foreign, [the Government] should seek [to encourage developing] the shortest and most rapid communication by means of railroad connecting Puerto Ysabel with the closest and most convenient railroad beyond the international boundary. With these goals [the] founding partners are setting themselves up as a Company. (Velázquez 1882)

On January 17, 1882, less than two weeks after the new company had incorporated, Andrade signed a contract with the Secretaría de Fomento that authorized the company to go ahead with its colonization plan for Tiburón and Ángel de la Guarda Islands (Andrade and Fernández 1882). Its main provisions, as paraphrased by William O. Hendricks, required that:

Within three months, and at its own expense, the company was to begin surveying and marking off the lands of the islands of Tiburón and Ángel de la Guarda. It was to complete this work within two years of the contract date, and, in accord with Article Six of the law of May 31, 1875, the company was to be given one-third part of the lands surveyed as compensation for the work performed. An additional one-third, destined exclusively for colonization, was to be appropriated to the company at the current tariff price, payable in four annual installments. When the surveying of the lands had been completed, the company was to submit its maps for the approval of Fomento, which would select the one-third portion of the lands reserved to the nation.

The lands to be colonized were to be subdivided into lots no larger than 50 hectares and apportioned among the colonists, with no one person being allowed to own a larger holding.... The company was to sign individual contracts with the colonists for acquiring ownership of lands and to grant the colonists 10 years, beginning two years after their establishment, in which to pay for them. Also, by contract, the company was to provide the poor colonists with foodstuffs, tools, farming implements, animals for work and for breeding, and materials for the construction of their homes.

The company promised to establish at least 100 families on the land within the first five years and to establish the balance necessary for the appropriation of all the lots within the next five years. Of the 100 families, two-thirds were to be of European origin, the rest Mexican. To be established, a family must have built a house and started to till the soil....

... Transporting the colonists to Tiburón and Ángel de la Guarda was to be in the hands of the company, and at its expense. In compensation, the government promised to pay 35 pesos for each person over seven years of age transported....

Both the company and the colonists were to be considered Mexican, with the colonists having the same rights and obligations as all Mexicans and being subject to the tribunals of that country to the absolute exclusion of all foreign intervention. At no time and under no circumstances could the company transfer, alienate, or mortgage the concessions of the contract, nor admit as an associate any foreign government or state.

The company promised to create new industries on the islands, to dry, salt, and can sea foods, and to establish, within two years, ranches for breeding cattle, thoroughbred horses, and Angora goats. Any coal or marble discovered on its lands and any mines or quarries established by the company were part of its property. All farming equipment, animals, and machinery introduced to the colonies were to be free from duty for 10 years. Sea foods, as with all items of export from the colonies, could be taken to any port of the country free from duties. (Hendricks 1967:99–103)

In addition, the company was granted two general concessions that would enable it to engage in pearl fishing, oyster gathering, whaling, and sealing along the entire mainland coast from Sinaloa to the Colorado River (Hendricks 1967:103–4).

Thus the contract provided admirably for the interests of both the company and the government. For the company there would be lucrative concessions, subsidies, exemptions, and of course land—half of it at no cost, and the remainder at the nominal tariff of 12 centavos per hectare for Tiburón Island and half that for Ángel de la Guarda (Hendricks 1967:9). For the government, there would be an influx of foreign capital without intervention by a foreign power. The foreign-born colonists would provide a model of industry as they were absorbed into the Mexican social and legal milieu. Most importantly, the contract required settling a minimum number of families and limited the size of the parcel that could be owned by any one colonist. This insured that the company would settle a large number of small-time farmers rather than a few large landowners since, after all, a fundamental purpose of the government's colonization policy was to populate the vulnerable northwestern region of Mexico.

With contract in hand, the company's first order of business was to survey the two islands, and this task was underway by mid-April of 1882. But a minor hitch developed when it was reported to Andrade that the two islands lacked enough wood for the needs of the colonists. Fortunately, it was also reported that sufficient wood could be obtained on a nearby island called San Esteban.

And so on April 18, three months after the original colonization contract, Andrade petitioned the Secretaría de Fomento to add San Esteban Island to the lands to be colonized:

> After finalizing the contract last January 17 with the Supreme Government of the Nation, through this Department which you so ably represent, for colonization of the islands of Tiburón and Ángel de la Guarda in the Gulf of Cortés, I have been informed by persons who know these islands well that they are devoid of shrubs and trees which the colonists will most certainly need for fuel and for building fences and corrals in order to raise cattle and horses which we are obligated to import in compliance with article 24 of the contract. [I am also informed that] a few miles to the south of Tiburón Island, between it and San Lorenzo Island, there is to be found an island called "San Esteban," which in spite of its being small contains some lumber for the uses I have indicated, and, additionally, various veins of limestone, a material also indispensable for constructing the houses of the colony.
>
> I ask that you to be so kind as to obtain from the citizen President of the Republic the concession for this, so that the Company I represent may proceed at once to survey and mark the boundaries of the aforementioned island of "San Esteban," under the same conditions, procedures, and concessions which were stipulated for the islands of Tiburón and Ángel de la Guarda in the aforementioned Contract of January 17 of the present year. (Andrade 1882)

A month later, the Secretaría de Fomento granted Andrade's request:

> The President of the Republic, heeding the reasons expressed in your petition dated April 18, has agreed sufficiently with what you have said to grant you authorization to colonize the island of "San Esteban" in the Gulf of Cortés, under the same conditions that were stipulated in the contract finalized last January 17 for the colonization of the islands of Ángel de la Guarda and Tiburón, without altering the terms of the latter. [And it is also the President's will] that the lumber of the aforementioned island be exploited in accordance with the existing regulations that apply to this material. (Fernández 1882)

In fact, Andrade's agents were not "persons who know these islands well," for San Esteban has no more wood than Tiburón and no limestone whatever. But it was now one of the islands to be colonized, and so the company proceeded to survey it. By early autumn, the surveys of Tiburón and San Esteban had been completed, and in October, maps of both islands were sent to the Secretaría de Fomento for approval (Figure 8.4). On November 25, the government sent word to Andrade acknowledging their receipt (Hendricks 1967:106).

The government processed the Tiburón claim first. At the beginning of December, the Tiburón map was certified accurate, and on December 4, 1882, as payment for the survey, the Secretaría issued a document giving Andrade and his associates title to one-third of the land on Tiburón Island. Based on the

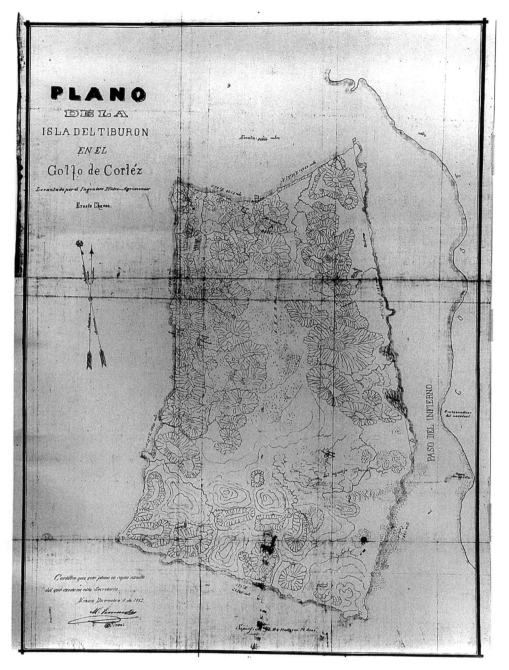

Figure 8.4   Certified copy of Guillermo Andrade's 1882 map of Tiburón Island, drawn by Erasto Chávez and submitted to the Secretaría de Fomento in Mexico City. (Courtesy Sherman Library, Corona del Mar, California.)

survey's own calculation of the area of the island (which underestimated its size by more than 20 percent!) the company's share was figured to be 32,015 hectares (González and Pacheco 1882).

Early 1883 must have been a time of great satisfaction for Andrade and Blythe. The Midriff islands project was proceeding smoothly, and Colonia Lerdo was back on its feet. The settlement at Lerdo had been rebuilt, an initial contingent of Italian colonists brought in, crops planted, and engineers had begun developing an irrigation system. Although Blythe's health was not good, his letters to Andrade expressed optimism, and in early April, he planned a personal inspection trip to Lerdo. But on April 4, according to Andrade's later testimony:

> Mr. Blythe took a bath at 5:00 P.M. and, on coming out, suddenly dropped dead without leaving either a will or instructions for the continuation of our enterprises.... (Guillermo Andrade, in Hendricks 1967:110)

In an instant, the partnership that had thrived on a word and a handshake had vanished.

Blythe's estate was valued at more than two million dollars. Without a will, the estate was thrown into probate court, and it is no wonder that nearly 200 people claiming to be heirs emerged from the woodwork. Not until 1900, after 17 years of legal wrangling, including three trips to the United States Supreme Court, did Blythe's only daughter emerge as the sole heir, and it was another 12 years before all the remaining challenges were finally defeated (Hendricks 1967:111–14, 212).

For Andrade, Blythe's death was a disaster because he had been counting on Blythe's money to cover their contractual obligations to the Mexican government. He believed these funds should now come from Blythe's estate, but in the absence of written partnership agreements, Andrade could not provide documentary proof of Blythe's commitment to finance their projects. Nor could he afford to wait for litigation to run its course, for unless sustainable colonies could be established in the allotted time span, the lands would revert to the government and the projects would be lost.

On November 16, 1883, Andrade filed a petition with the Superior Court of the City and County of San Francisco detailing his verbal agreements with Blythe, outlining the terms of the contracts, and explaining the urgency of the situation. In it he asked for funds from the Blythe estate to enable him to travel to Mexico City, where he hoped to work out arrangements to preserve their joint ventures (Andrade 1883). Despite the lack of written records, the court recognized that some form of partnership between the two men had been a matter of common knowledge and that Andrade was entitled to sufficient funds to hold on to the contracts until the estate could be settled (which the court then believed would require no more than a year or two). And so in December 1883, the court made $10,000 available to Andrade, who boarded a stagecoach for Mexico City to do what he could to keep the projects alive (Hendricks 1967:114–18).

Thanks to his connections with Romero Rubio and former President Díaz, Andrade was able to successfully plead his case directly to President Manuel González and his ministers. When he returned to San Francisco three months later, he had resolved the most urgent matter, the approaching deadline for full colonization of the Lerdo project, with a two year extension on the time limit. He had also managed to consolidate the Midriff islands project. For all three islands, he secured title to the one-third due the company for performing the surveys, plus title to another one-third of each island which he acquired by exercising his purchase option. For Tiburón and San Esteban, he also arranged a lease for the remaining one-third held by the government. Thus he arrived back in San Francisco with rights to virtually all the land on Tiburón and San Esteban Islands, and two-thirds of Ángel de la Guarda (Hendricks 1967:119).

The title document for San Esteban Island, issued on February 25, 1884, certified the total area of the island, as calculated by Andrade's survey, to be 4,452 hectares (about three percent too high). It granted the company immediate ownership of one-third of the island as payment for the survey. The second one-third was arranged as a mortgage to be paid off in four annual installments, with payment of the first installment giving ownership to the company. This was the land to be used specifically for colonization. The government reserved, as its one-third, land on the south side of the island. It also retained an encircling strip of shoreline 20 m wide, measured from the high tide line, which was to be kept available for public use (González and Pacheco 1884).

The agreement to lease the government's one-third of San Esteban was spelled out in a separate contract. It was to run for nine years at a rent to the company of $250 pesos annually. It gave the company access to the entire tract except for 50 hectares which would be set aside for public use. The company was expected to utilize the land to establish industries as proposed in the previous agreements, but all improvements would revert to the government at the end of the lease (Pacheco and Andrade 1884).

The $10,000 from Blythe's estate had temporarily secured the Midriff islands project by producing titles. But these titles carried with them the obligation of making good on the colonization contacts. The cost of establishing the colonists fell squarely on the company, and this effectively increased Andrade's financial burden. Although he had bought time, it would be years before the enterprise would produce profits, and in the meantime, still more expenditures would be necessary.

In 1885, Andrade's fortunes took a turn for the worse, and he began to lose control of his paper empire. Early in the year, the government announced its intent to recover lands whose titleholders had failed to settle colonists, and defaulters were given 30 days to make their defenses. Although Andrade had settled 74 of the required 200 families in the Lerdo colony, he had to scramble to insure that those lands would not be repossessed. Because of map errors and other problems, the government inadvertently reassigned some of Andrade's lands to another developer, a matter that required considerable untangling. As the Blythe estate proceedings dragged on, Andrade was forced to seek yet another two-year extension for the Lerdo colonization contracts. By September, an agent in Germany had found 50 families willing to settle there, but the agent drowned before the would-be settlers ever left Europe.

As the situation deteriorated, Andrade asked the court for permission to sell some of the properties he held with Blythe in order to raise capital to support the remaining holdings. Since even selling property would require money, he requested $20,000 from the estate to cover sales costs. With court approval of both requests, Andrade sailed for England, where he hoped to find buyers, but he returned empty-handed. With even the revised colonization deadline steadily approaching, Andrade desperately cast around for settlers from the United States and managed to find 30 families willing to come to Mexico. But all of these efforts were expensive, and before long, he had spent more than $12,000 above and beyond the $20,000 that had been granted by the court (Hendricks 1967:120–32).

The legal tangle continued until Andrade's death in 1905. In the intervening years, he sold many of his holdings. But Andrade remained the true entrepreneur, for despite the endless problems with his existing properties, he continued to acquire new lands and enter into new colonization contracts until shortly before he died.

And what of San Esteban and the Midriff islands scheme as Andrade's empire was gradually crumbling? On August 10, 1885, Andrade and the Secretaría de Fomento signed a slightly revised contract for the Midriff islands project, probably intended to bring it into compliance with the latest federal colonization Law of December 15, 1883 (Pacheco and Andrade 1885). The one notable feature of the new contract is that it spelled out just how the 100 families Andrade was required to settle were to be distributed among the three islands. Tiburón Island, the most habitable, was to receive 20 families. San Esteban, with a miniscule four percent of Tiburón's land area and far fewer resources, was to have 10 families. The remainder—a full 70 families—were to be settled on Ángel de la Guarda, the most sterile and waterless of the three. Apparently, Andrade and the government were most optimistic about the places for which they had the least information.

The revised contract underscored the fact that Andrade could retain title to his three islands only if he could colonize and develop them. By now it must have been clear that the capital to do this would have to come from some source other than Blythe's estate, which was sinking ever deeper into the legal quagmire. Characteristically, Andrade approached the problem of raising money by attempting to create a new company, to which all properties and concessions currently held by the Compañía Mexicana would be transferred. The new venture was aimed exclusively at North American investors. It was called the Gulf of Cortez Land and Fish Company and was to be incorporated in California. The prospectus, known only from a hand-written draft copy, was not dated, but it was clearly drawn up sometime during the mid- to late 1880s. The objectives of the company were to colonize and exploit the supposed resources of Tiburón, San Esteban, and Ángel de la Guarda Islands and the surrounding Gulf. Specifically, the company would run livestock, establish distilleries, mine precious metals and guano, set up fish canning factories, gather oysters, hunt sea lions, and fish for pearls (Anonymous n.d.a:1).

The prospectus stipulated that the new company was to be formed by a syndicate of not more than eight persons. These members would provide $50,000 in start-up capital, sufficient to launch two of its planned enterprises as pilot projects. One of these was to harvest at least "one cargo" of edible oysters to test their marketability. The other was the "prompt erection of distillation works on the Island of San Estevan." Once these operations were judged successful, the members would raise another $100,000 through the sale of stock to inaugurate the rest of the projects. Ultimately, the prospectus called for the issue of six million dollars in common stock, half of which would supply working capital for the company's enterprises. The other half, three million dollars, would be used to buy out "the original owners and grantors" of "the Mexican Company," who still held the concession for the islands. In other words, a million dollars each was to go to Manuel Romero Rubio, Agustín González, and Guillermo Andrade.

The prospectus, of course, was written in an enthusiastic and authoritative style aimed at convincing the potential investor that the islands offered a high-profit low-risk opportunity to make a lot of money. But it also provides an extraordinarily revealing glimpse of what people like Andrade, operating at a distance, thought they knew or were willing to speculate about the three islands and their resources:

The Tiburon Island

Is situated in the Gulf of California about 100 miles from the City of Guaymas and 75 miles from Hermosillo, and about one mile from the main land.

It is 18 leagues long and from 6 to 7 wide, with 8 springs of flowing water, which, with a small outlay, can be made to furnish an ample supply of water for all required purposes, by the construction of reservoirs on selected sites.

The island is covered by a growth of nutritious grasses of several varieties. The principal and most abundant are the *orregano* and *sabria*. These grasses impart to the flesh of the beeves and milk and butter of the cows a peculiarly delicious and much esteemed flavor. The beeves fattened on them bring enhanced prices for market purposes.

On the authority of the following named gentlemen[:] El Sr. Don Dioniso Gonzales, Jesus Moreno, Feliziano Aviza, and Doct^r Rubio[—]well-known agriculturists and stock-raisers of the State of Sonora—at least 25,000 head of cattle could be kept in good condition on this island alone, without cultivation of the soil or sowing of grasses for sustenance—the wild nutritious and native grasses that are indigenous to the soil, being sufficient. The above-named gentlemen speak from personal observation and investigation—they having several years ago expended Ten Thousand dollars in exploring this island with men, animals and supplies, intending to form an extensive stock ranch; but upon examination they ascertained that they had no title to the property, which was vested in the General Government, and, ascertaining that the Government would not sell, the plan was withdrawn.

Recently, the Government has granted the right to utilize these Islands for colonization purposes as herein stated.

The Springs.

On this island are several, as follows:

1st — The Carriscal [Carrizal], which forms a small arroya through which its waters flow and disappear at a point near the beach.

2nd — The Coyote, is a strong spring and flows from its source into the sea, a distance of several miles (at all seasons of the year).

There are six others whose names are unknown.

Senor Don Pascual Encinas, a large and well-known landholder and stock-raiser, permits me to state that he knows the island well, and that it is not only his opinion but that of the best informed judges that this island is peculiarly adapted for stock purposes. The ranges are good, well grassed, and water in abundance.

Gold is said to have been found on this island in several places, specimens of which have been brought to and seen in Guaymas, but from its isolated position it has never been explored by the Gambusino (prospector). It is, however, believed to be rich in mineral wealth.

This island is not heavily timbered, but contains ranges of mesquit and chapparal sufficiently large for all domestic or steam purposes. The mesquit is very nutritious and a favorite food for stock.

The island is sufficiently well watered for all stock purposes.

2nd The Island of San Estevan (St. Stephen.) is situated 9 miles in a South-easterly [actually, southwesterly] direction from the Tiburon. It is nearly round. It's diameter is about 15 miles — its circumference 45 miles.

The riches and values of this island consist in the Maguey plant, with which it is densely covered. From this plant is distilled the celebrated Mexican national drink known as *aguardiente mescal*. The number of barrels of mescal that could be distilled from the present growth of the Island would be enormous and almost incalculable. Mexico is at present not producing sufficient mescal to supply the demand; in consequence the price is rapidly advancing. There is no industry in Mexico to-day so profitable as the distillation of this product.

The conditions of the contract and grant are such that all the products of these islands are admitted free of all duties, both State and Municipal, to all the ports of Mexico, for a period of 10 years. The internal revenue duties on mescal in Mexico, both State and Municipal, are now $12.^{00} for each barrel of 20 gallons, from which we are exempted. The rebate of all duties from this island gives its mescal product a great advantage over the mescal produced in any other part of Mexico, and large profits can be realized. The three islands are virtually free ports and subject to no import or export duties.

3rd — The Island of the "Angel de la Guarde" (Guardian Angel.)

Of this little is known, it having been less explored. Its principal resources, so far as known, consist in its mineral wealth. It is said to contain gold, silver and copper. Large metaliferous veins coursing Easterly and Westerly through the island, are said to exist, but not sufficiently explored and developed to prove their values. This island may reasonably be expected to contain fertilizers, as it is near the Raza Island, from which guano has been shipped.

In the surrounding waters the seal and sea-lion are found in abundance. Turtles, several varieties of fish, lobsters, mussels, &c. &c. abound in its waters adjacent to the shores. (Anonymous n.d.a)

The prospectus goes on to specify the major conditions imposed by the Mexican colonization laws and the previous contracts Andrade had signed with the Secretaría de Fomento. As always, one-third of the lands would remain with the government. Another one-third, to be used for colonization, would be purchased at the going rate of 4 cents per acre. However, the remaining one-third of all lands and privileges were to be granted directly to Andrade himself "in consideration of certain expenses incurred in surveying the three islands." The document closes with a radiant summary of all the profitable industries in which the shrewd investor would have a share. Nowhere does it mention Indians on any of the islands.

Evidently, Andrade did not get far with the Gulf of Cortez Land and Fish Co., for in 1892 he tried to organize still another company. Aimed also at North American investors, it was called the Gulf of Cortez Fishing Company. Curiously, its articles of incorporation make no reference to the three islands or to colonization, but instead focus exclusively on the waters of the Gulf. The company's purpose was:

> to engage in the fishing and exploitation of Oysters, Seals, Sharks, Whales, and all other kinds of fish and shell fish, pearls, shells and everything that lives in and inhabits the water, and for the establishment and Cultivation of oyster and pearl oyster beds in the Gulf of Cortez and in all the estuaries and coasts from Tecapan to the mouth of the Colorado River. (Anonymous 1892)

According to this document, the value of the capital stock that had been "actually subscribed" was $10 million, all shares being held by the seven San Francisco men who made up the company's Board of Trustees. One of the seven was Andrade himself, who is credited with holding nearly one-third of the company's stock, with a nominal value of around $3 million.

For the most part, what happened during the next five years can only be inferred. There is no indication that the Gulf of Cortez Fishing Company was any more successful than its predecessors had been. It is also clear that Andrade was not able to colonize the islands, though he was apparently able to engineer still more extensions of time. The Secretaría de Fomento, however, did not have unlimited patience. On April 10, 1897, Andrade renegotiated a third and final contract for the Midriff islands and the various concessions. It reaffirmed most of the fishing and pearling rights, and it greatly softened the terms of his obligation to colonize Tiburón Island, probably because the most recent legislation, the Law of March 26, 1894, had largely discarded colonization requirements for new contracts (Hale 1989:237). For Tiburón, the number of families that Andrade now needed to settle was reduced to 10, their nationalities could be Mexican, European, Japanese, or Chinese, and eight more years would be allowed for him to accomplish this. But for San Esteban and Ángel de la Guarda, this was the end of the line. In the first article of the new contract, all titles to land on these two islands held by Andrade through the original Compañía Mexicana Colonizadora e Industrial were gently, but unequivocally, revoked:

> Although the Company which Guillermo Andrade represents has done everything possible on its part to fulfill all the obligations that it incurred in the above-mentioned Contract of January 17, 1882 and its modifications of August 10, 1885, nevertheless it was not possible for [the Company] to carry out some of [the Contract's] stipulations; but taking into consideration that this was due to extraneous causes beyond [the Company's] control, the two contracting parties have agreed by mutual consent to revalidate that concession, subject to the penalty of the Company losing to the Federal Treasury ownership of the two-thirds parts of the islands Ángel de la Guarda and San Esteban, without retaining for itself any [portion] of them; but at the same time, under the condition that there be established a subsidized guarantee of colonization, [the Government and the Company agree to revalidate the Contract] for the two one-third parts of Tiburón Island which [the Company] had acquired. As a consequence [of these revocations] it is now necessary to return to the Department of Fomento the titles which were issued to [the Company] for the lands of the first two islands for cancellation, making sure that the new agreement is signed and returned the same day. The Company, meanwhile, will remain the sole owner of the two one-third parts of Tiburón Island, but with the guarantee of ownership being contingent upon the establishment of colonies on that island. (Fernández Leal 1897)

For Sale: Tiburón Island

The forfeiture of Andrade's titles to San Esteban and Ángel de la Guarda effectively solved the problem of colonizing those two islands, and of course, ended Andrade's connection with San Esteban. But it did not free Andrade entirely of his Midriff islands scheme, for there still remained the vexing question of what to do about Tiburón Island. Tiburón had turned into an albatross, and Andrade was gradually becoming more interested in ridding himself of this continuing headache than in trying to colonize the island himself.

In California, where Andrade was living, there were not only potential buyers for Tiburón but in the mid-1890s, the island was also receiving plenty of publicity. Much of the press coverage was generated by the disappearance of several North Americans there, presumably killed at the hands of the Seris (see pp. 247–55). The sensational reports of these "outrages" spawned, on the one hand, a number of swaggering proposals for retaliatory expeditions to "conquer" the island and "tame" or exterminate the Seris. On the other hand they generated a renewed interest in acquiring the island in order to exploit its supposed wealth (McGee 1898:122). Of course, anybody intent on acquiring or exploiting the island would have to negotiate with Guillermo Andrade, the man who still held title to it.

*Figure 8.5
John Bradbury, photo-
graphed ca. early 1890s.
(Courtesy Bancroft
Library, University of
California, Berkeley.)*

The first of these North American schemes actually predates Andrade's final contract with the Secretaría de Fomento by a little more than a year. It was
proposed late in 1895 by a group of wealthy and influential southern Californians who called themselves the Tiburon Conquest Company. The main financier was a young man known as Col. John Bradbury (Figure 8.5), who was
enthusiastically profiled in the gossipy Los Angeles society weekly *The Capital*:

This is probably the wealthiest young gentleman in Los Angeles, and he
probably enjoys the possession of wealth as much and in as rational a manner
as any man in California. He spends his money like a gentleman, as he is, and
in a quiet, unostentatious way. Col. Bradbury is the reverse of the gilded youth,
in the common acceptation of the term, and had he not inherited wealth would
have accumulated it by his own efforts. Just now the Colonel is devoting himself to the pleasures of life in a refined way, but he is ambitious, and we pre-
dict will in after years strive for the attainment of some end that will make him
famous. He is a thoroughly good man of business, for one so young, a pleasant companion and a thoroughbred. He has been prominently before the

people through the newspapers, but he has treated all chaffing with a good-natured indifference. The CAPITAL likes Col. Bradbury and thoroughly approves of him. (Anonymous 1895c:10)

An unnamed "agent" had been workinig on behalf of Bradbury's group in Mexico City, and by early December, his efforts had succeeded in securing for the company a concession for Tiburón Island—or so its members thought. This agent, whom *The Capital* appropriately characterizes as "one of the best known men in Los Angeles" (Anonymous 1895a:9), may have been Andrade himself, certainly the person best suited to arrange with the Mexican government for a transfer of titles.

Andrade must have painted a picture of Tiburón Island to the prospective concessionaires in his usual idealistic terms:

It is about six times as large as Catalina Island, and is rich and fertile of soil; with good harbors, and with mineral resources vast and valuable....

... A conservative estimate places the value of this island at $5,000,000, without at all taking into account the value of the gold, silver, copper, coal and other minerals which are said to exist upon the island....

One of the objects the company has in view is to establish a great resort, and lines of steamers will be put on from both Yuma and Guaymas. The climate being delightful, the island will soon become one of the noted resorts of the world. The island is teeming with game, and this will be protected. In fact game, and games, will be imported there. The agricultural possibilities will be developed to the fullest extent, and mining will also be a great industry. (Anonymous 1895a:9)

Before developing Tiburón Island, however, the company would have to deal with the resident Seri Indians who, by every recent account, would not take kindly to an invasion of outsiders. It was, after all, barely more than a year since San Francisco journalist R. E. L. Robinson and his partner James Logan had been killed there by Seris (see pp. 248–53). It is not clear whether the company ever did develop a strategy for economic development. But there is no doubt that it did lay plans for a quasi-military invasion to round up and rid the island of Seris. *The Capital* saw the pending campaign as a dashing adventure and provided its readers with a lurid portrayal of the Seris and the fearless men who would subdue them:

it has long been known that a grant of the island would be made to any company that would conquer it and annihilate the Indians. This is the leading clause in the concession.... In these piping times of peace nobody has dared to tackle the proposition. Some who considered it were deterred from fear; others because they had conscientious scruples against shedding the blood of these Indians.... These Indians are blood-thirsty, murderous, and crafty, and not only murder and mutilate, but devour those so unfortunate as to fall into their hands. Any good God-fearing man would be doing work in the cause of humanity by assisting to rid the earth of these unspeakably cruel creatures. It is as much a duty to kill them as it is a duty to kill a mad dog that is running at large and threatening humanity....

... Only men of proven fighting qualities will be enrolled, and many of them will come from Texas, New Mexico and Arizona. There are estimated to be only forty grown male Indians on the island, but in such esteem do the conquerors hold the prowess of this handful that a company of three hundred fighters will be enlisted to go against the Indians. The troops are to be under the command of Col. I. H. Polk, who will come up from Mazatlan for that purpose, and will hereafter be known as General. The troops will mass at Guaymas, and take boats from there to the island. They will be armed with Manlicher rifles and the latest improved small arms. Several small pieces of artillary will also be taken along, as well as horses. The commissary department will be the care of Col. Walter S. Moore, and the troops will be fed as troops were never fed before. The money for this expedition will be put up by Col. Bradbury and other wealthy gentlemen, and a large amount will be required to carry it to a successful termination. Each soldier who enlists for the war is to receive $250, which is of itself $75,000, and the arms and provisions and transportation will cost at least $150,000. In addition, each soldier who is alive when the island is conquered is to receive a deed to one hundred acres of good land. If a soldier is killed, the land and his wages go to his widow or other heirs. This will give the island a population from the day it is conquered, and care will be taken in the selection of the men to see that they will make good citizens after the war is over.

It is the intention of the Tiburon Conquest Company, as the new corporation is called, to establish a little government—a republic—of its own, and have a protectorate extended over it by the United States. To this, Mexico, it is understood, has consented....

This is one of the best and most favorable schemes of this century, and the men who are actively engaged in pushing it are just the people to bring it to a successful conclusion. It only requires money and nerve, and both requisites are represented to a marked degree in the different members of the company. That the expedition is to be attempted is now a fixed fact, and the CAPITAL will have a war correspondent on the ground. (Anonymous 1895a:9)

After providing such passionate support, *The Capital* was chagrined to learn that all the manpower and firepower was intended to be used not to slaughter the Seris once and for all in the name of civilization, but merely to round them up, hopefully without firing a shot. Once captured, they were to be relocated on Ángel de la Guarda Island, which at that time was still one of Andrade's holdings (Anonymous 1895b:1). Moreover, praise for the venture was hardly universal. The proposed expedition was the topic of much local discussion, and in many quarters it had became a subject of scorn. The *Los Angeles Daily Times*, which had broken the story in the first place, was unmerciful in its mockery of both the venture and its youthful promoter:

After Col. John Bradbury made his tour of the world in ninety days, or thereabouts, he had achieved a proud eminence which nothing but hard cash and plenty of it, made possible. But even as Christopher Columbus, Pizarro, Cortez, Bougainville and Cook, Col. John Bradbury, having discovered a number of places which had hitherto been considered by him as mere spots of ink on a map, now thirsts for glory which will place his name on a par with that of the celebrated voyagers who have been mentioned above.

Col. John Bradbury is going to discover Tiburon, the gruesome island on which the inhabitants are supposed to eat guests.... It might be alleged that Tiburon has already been discovered, but that is entirely a mistake, due to a great extent to the carelessness with which American writers sling about the great United States language. Tiburon has never been discovered, but the Tiburonese have, on several occasions, discovered gentlemen of gringo, or Spanish extraction on the island, who having no visible means of existence, were promptly disposed of on the spit....

First and foremost after the gallant Colonel, who be it understood, goes merely for relaxation and to lose that blase feeling which a trip around the world superinduces, comes the Hon. J. Downey Harvey....

The next man of importance, if not as important as any of the rest, is [Col.] Walter S. Moore, chief of the [Los Angeles] fire department.... As an after-dinner speaker there is none to beat the colonel [Moore]. What a proud distinction it would be for him in after years to be able to tell his friends that he made the post dinner talk at Tiburon to the admiring Ceris while Col. Bradbury and the Hon. Harvey were quietly reposing in the stomachs of the attentive hosts....

This expedition will certainly fill the cup of Col. Bradbury's greatness, which has been filling fast. First of all, he became proprietor and editor-in-chief of the Herald; then lieutenant-colonel on the staff of Gov. Budd; next he made the tour of the world in ninety days or somewhat more; then he went to his mines in Mexico and returned without being sunburned, and now he is going to discover Tiburon! Some people are born fortunate and rich. (Anonymous 1895d:9)

As if the *Times* piece were not enough, the venture was ridiculed in a tall tale about Tiburón that even sneaked its way into *The Capital* itself as a letter to the editor by one J. Bulwer Clayton (see pp. 118–19). *The Capital*, however, was unflinching in its defense of Bradbury's character and the righteousness of the expedition:

There is a great deal of talk regarding this proposed expedition and in the opinion of the CAPITAL Col. Bradbury is engaged in a laudable undertaking. The minds of very few rich young men run in such channels, poker, "red neck," fast horses and footlight favorites usually occupy the thoughts of such youngsters. Col. Bradbury is made of different stuff, however, and the people who are now poking fun at this expedition would be loud in their plaudits were it to be attempted by an older man. The colonel and his associates will not only attempt this capture of Tiburon but will carry it to a successful termination. (Anonymous 1895b:1)

But the Tiburon Conquest Company never set foot on Tiburón Island, for both prudence and legal problems with the concession intervened. As a journalist later remarked:

Colonel John Bradbury and others seriously contemplated organizing an expedition for the conquest of Tiburon, but the true nature of both the Seri Indians and the island being revealed to them, coupled with the further fact that the concession of the island had already passed to General Andrade, caused them to drop the matter. (Anonymous 1897[?])

Though the Tiburon Conquest Company had bowed out, glowing reports of the island's supposedly fabulous resources continued to appear (Anonymous 1897b:72–73) and others were eager to take up the challenge. Soon afterward, according to the same journalist, "Jesse Grant of San Diego tried to get a concession to the island and sailed south to conquer it. He could not get the concession and did not land at the island" (Anonymous 1897[?]). At about the same time:

Mr. W. J. LYONS, of Hermosillo, Sonora, has secured a concession for the exploration of the island, and ... next November [1897] he will fit out an expedition for that purpose. It seems that the island is rich in grasses and furnishes excellent pasturage for cattle; that the mineral resources are also considerable, consisting of gold, silver, and copper veins, none of which, however, have been worked. The waters surrounding the island teem with fish and crustaceans. (Anonymous 1900:34)

The most flamboyant of Andrade's potential buyers entered the picture in 1902. This was an extravagant self-promoter named Abram Henson Meadows, better known as "Arizona Charlie" Meadows (Figure 8.6). Growing up on a homestead in Arizona Territory, the young Meadows first spent time as a scout for General Crook. Later, he became the promoter of the only bullfight ever staged in the United States (for which he was jailed), joined Buffalo Bill's Wild West Show, and in Dawson City, Yukon Territory, became the founder-publisher of the *Klondike News* and the builder-owner-impresario of the Palace Grand Theater (Jones-Gates 1980).

In 1902, Meadows sold his Yukon enterprises at a handsome profit and moved to Los Angeles, where he immediately achieved notoriety by throwing money from his taxi to people along the street. It was here that he met Guillermo Andrade, who by then was living in Los Angeles and who succeeded in interesting Meadows in "conquering" and colonizing Tiburón Island. It was not the first that Meadows had heard of the island, for he had been interviewed in 1893 by R. E. L. Robinson of the *San Francisco Examiner*, who had invited Meadows to join his ill-fated 1894 expedition to Tiburón. But now the timing

Figure 8.6
"Arizona Charlie" Meadows
(1860–1932), photographed in
1892. (Courtesy Jean E. King and
the Western History Collection,
Denver Public Library, Denver,
Colorado [No. 14574].)

was right, and Meadows hatched a plan to tackle Tiburón Island (King 1989: 221, 227). As reported in the *Dawson Daily News*:

> Arizona Charlie will show the world that knight-errantry is not dead. Never was a bolder, or possibly more quixotic, adventure planned than that which the former government scout, southwest cowboy, Indian fighter, wild west showman, and Alaska gold digger, proposes to lead into that one bit of primeval savagery that remains on the western hemisphere—Tiburon island, in the Gulf of California.
>
> Arizona Charlie has organized a company of twenty men, most of them his former companions on the Arizona ranges, with which he proposes to invade Tiburon island, overcome the savage Seri Indians, prospect the mountains for gold and silver and copper, which it is said exist in the interior of the island, where no white man has yet reached, and, if successful, establish on the island a great stock raising industry. (Anonymous 1902)

One of Meadows's sources of information on the riches of Tiburón was W. J. Lyons, the same man who had reportedly secured a concession to the island a few years earlier. As Meadows tells it:

I have lately met Dr. Lyons, who was a member of Prof. McGee's party that was on the island some years ago and who, I believe, is from the only expedition that ever returned from the island. He says it is undoubtedly rich in gold, silver and copper and that he has seen some beautiful large colors (nuggets) that the Indian women trade with the settlers which indicates that there is placer also. Dr. Lyons says he saw the assay from a piece of gold quartz that assayed $8,000 to the ton and that the governor of Sonora has a copper specimen almost pure, both of which were brought off the island by women and children who trade among the settlers near Hermosillo. Dr. Lyons says that McGee would not let any of the party go into the interior and they could not learn much. (Meadows 1902)

In fact, Mr. Lyons had most certainly not been a member of McGee's expedition (Fontana and Fontana 1983:25). It is difficult to tell whether this report was Lyons trying to deceive Meadows or Meadows deceiving himself, but such misinformation unquestionably made good press for the folks back in the Yukon. In either case, by August, Meadows was deeply involved in preparations for his expedition and aiming for an early September departure:

> The cowboy knight is now spending his time between San Francisco, Los Angeles and Yuma, collecting stores and arms and making preparations for the trip to Tiburon island. He has a boat under construction at Yuma that will carry his little army of invaders down the Colorado river and out on the Gulf of California to the island.... [I]t will be a veritable little battleship. Two five-inch rapid-fire Maxim guns will be mounted on the deck, and in the armory will be Mauser rifles, Mauser rapid-fire pistols and shotguns.... Each man will have his own rifle as well, and brace of revolvers and hunting knife—ornaments that from long habit with them have become indispensable even when on peace missions. Brave men have sailed to Tiburon before, but never in as large numbers and never as well prepared for the conquest.
>   But for all the warlike preparations, Arizona Charlie thinks that there will be very little fighting to do. He is confident that his large force will overawe the Indians and that they will be glad to make peace.... "I don't expect to have to do much fighting to gain possession of the island, and if I succeed I will buy the land. I have an option on the island from a high Mexican official, who holds it as a concession from the government." (Anonymous 1902)

The "high Mexican official" was, of course, the Mexican Consul in Los Angeles, Guillermo Andrade. On August 6, 1902, Meadows wrote a letter to a friend in Dawson City in which he outlined some of the terms of his option (essentially the conditions specified in Andrade's contract with the Secretaría de Fomento) and his financial plan. The letter was published on August 23 in the *Daily Klondike Nugget*:

> Now this island contains over 300,000 acres of land. I have bought two-thirds of it and the other one-third belongs to the government and I have the refusal of a lease on it for ten years with an option for renewal. I am to pay $50,000

for the two-thirds in ten yearly payments, and am to put ten families or residents on the island within two years. I am to give 15 per cent of the mining interests to the governor of Sonora, Gen. Andrade and two Mexican bankers in Nogales. That is, of what is found on the first expedition; after that the whole mining interest will be held by the forty shareholders. From all the information I can get this is an ideal stock ranch, rich in mineral and valuable for pearl fishing. I have a party here who has just sold several million acres of Mexican land to eastern capitalists. He says he would have no trouble in floating this concern with a valuation of at least a million dollars if we can give a favorable report of it....

I propose to pay the entire expense from [the] starting point, San Pedro or Yuma, to the island and return.... [A]ll of us will be interested alike one-for-tieth each [i.e., each person will acquire one-fortieth interest] ... which will cost five hundred dollars each. I would propose immediately after we have shown the world that the Indians are tamed or all good Indians, to incorporate under the Mexican laws with such high officials as the governor of Sonora, and Gen. Andrade (Mexican consul at Los Angeles) as two of the directors, for at least a million shares at $1 each or double that amount if we find any good mineral.... [With] the advantage of free advertising in the press (which gives so much attention to this remote and interesting island) we can handle the stock if we don't like it ourselves, at a profit of $20,000 to $40,000 on an investment of $500. (Meadows 1902)

In September, Meadows decided to make a preliminary scouting trip to Tiburón. He and part of his heavily-armed band set sail on the sloop *Elia*, captained by Gus Olander (variously spelled Orlander and Olinger), and they did indeed reach Tiburón Island. They spent about two weeks there, circumnavigating the island and going ashore at half a dozen places. For all the armament, they found the Seris to be wary but not hostile, and their visit passed without incident (Bowers 1909:168, 171–72; King 1989:233–34).

With the success of this trial run under his belt, Meadows began preparations for the full expedition, scheduled for the following January. For this extravaganza, he issued a personal invitation to President Theodore Roosevelt, who prudently declined to join the party. But the expedition never materialized, for Mexican President Porfirio Díaz seems to have intervened by blocking the sale of the island (King 1989:230, 234). As a result, Meadows pulled out of the deal, and Andrade remained stuck with the titles and colonization contracts for Tiburón Island.

A little more than two years later, on April 10, 1905, eight years after the last contract had been signed, Andrade's final deadline for establishing 10 families of colonists on Tiburón Island passed. On September 17 of that year, Guillermo Andrade died.

Andrade's Midriff Islands Scheme in Retrospect

Looking back from the present, it is easy to write off Andrade's entire Midriff islands venture as little more than a naïve fantasy that was doomed to failure from the beginning. Even at the time, there was ample sentiment to this effect, for the court that handled the Blythe estate eventually refused to advance Andrade any more money on the grounds that the schemes were fundamentally chimerical (Tout [1931]:44). There is little doubt that there was a measure of self-delusion in these projects, the result of insufficient information and excessive optimism.

In the case of San Esteban and Ángel de la Guarda, it seems clear that Andrade was willing to incorporate these islands into his colonization plan knowing virtually nothing about them. In the Gulf of Cortez Land and Fish Company prospectus, he openly admitted he knew little about Ángel de la Guarda and was relying on hearsay. As for San Esteban, he was apparently unaware of its very existence when he signed the initial Gulf islands contract in January 1882. By April he had heard of the island, but even his agents knew little about it, for he added it to his concession in order to make use of essentially nonexistent resources. Later that year, Andrade's agents must have at least sailed around San Esteban in order to perform their survey for the Secretaría de Fomento, though it is possible that they constructed their map without ever seeing the interior of the island. The San Esteban map has not been located, but it is fairly clear that the companion map of Tiburón Island was produced with little if any shore time. In the mid- to late 1880s, when Andrade tried to form the Gulf of Cortez Land and Fish Company, he still did not seem to know just where San Esteban was with respect to Tiburón Island or how small it really was. At least by then, he had learned what entrepreneurs in Guaymas already knew some 10 years earlier, that if San Esteban had any commercial value at all, it lay in its stands of agave (see pp. 138–40). It is unlikely that Andrade ever personally visited San Esteban.

From today's perspective the very idea of colonizing San Esteban, even with just 10 families, seems patently absurd. The greatest obstacle to settlement would have been the scarcity of water. Even allowing for the likelihood that there was more water in the nineteenth century than there is today (see pp. 415–16), it still would have occurred as widely scattered bedrock pools and brackish springs or shallow beach wells. Water in this form might easily have sustained 10 families of highly mobile Seris, who were accustomed to using such water sources, but not Europeans attempting to establish a permanent village. Whether sufficient water could have been obtained from excavated wells is a moot question. There is certainly no indication that the Compañía Mexicana ever intended the San Esteban colony to be dependent on shipments of water and other necessities from the outside, as was the case for the guano mining operations on Rasa and San Pedro Mártir Islands.

Much the same can be said of Andrade's vague plans for Ángel de la Guarda, which, by his own admission, were based mostly on hearsay, and not even very much of that. And some of the "information" available to Andrade at the time was utterly fanciful, such as one published piece in which only the "many hills" and "abundant fishery" have any basis in reality:

> *Ángel del la Guarda....* It has many hills, although not very high, excellent waterholes, rich forests, fertile farmland, two minerals not yet exploited, and

a multitude of animals like deer, wild bulls, mountain goats, pheasants, rab-
bits, jackrabbits, wild turkeys, [and] a rich and abundant fishery on its coasts.
This island is a real treasure. (Pérez Hernández 1872b:43)

But Tiburón Island was another matter, for by 1882 Tiburón was not entirely
unknown territory among Sonorans. Some had been to the island during military expeditions against the Seris, while others claimed, at least, to have gone
there to prospect for minerals. Nor was Andrade the first person to envision
raising stock on the island. The idea had been proposed at least as early as 1793
(see pp. 89–90), and long before that, Guillermo Stratford, who had personally
been on Tiburón in 1721 with Father Ugarte's expedition, wrote that the island
had "good plots of farmable land" (Stratford [1746] 1958:63). Some time around
1850, Don Pascual Encinas (see Figure 10.1), who had already established a
thriving ranch on the mainland across from Tiburón, personally scouted the
island's ranching potential. His first foray lasted only a few hours, but Encinas
went back later with a large party, including horses transported by steamer, and
explored the island for two or three days (McGee and Johnson 1896:132;
McGee 1898:111). Although he did not pursue the idea of running livestock
there, he was favorably impressed, and his is probably one of the more genuinely authoritative opinions on whom Andrade relied in proposing his ranching schemes. According to McGee (1901:373), Andrade himself actually took
a first hand look at Tiburón, and a newspaper article, probably written in 1897,
confirms that "Some years ago General Andrade, with twenty men, went to the
island and surveyed it" (Anonymous 1897[?]).

But by the late 1890s, optimism about the ranching potential of Tiburón lay
chiefly with those farthest from the scene, and Sonorans by now generally held
more realistic views. In November 1898, the recently-overhauled Mexican Navy
transport ship *Oaxaca* made a trial cruise to the east coast of Tiburón Island. On
the basis of a few hours ashore at a single location, the officer in charge of the
landing party, Captain Alejandro Cerisola, sent a rosy report of the island's
economic promise to Mexico City (Cerisola 1898). Cerisola's assessment immediately prompted President Porfirio Díaz (who, it will be remembered, was
the son-in-law of Andrade's former partner, Manuel Romero Rubio) to personally recommend that the Sonoran government carry out a thorough exploration
of the island's ranching potential. Of course, Sonora's governor, Ramón Corral, formally acceded to the President's directive, but with great politeness, he
also informed Díaz that:

Tiburón Island is not unknown, nor would it [the proposed exploration] be
the first time it would be explored. On various occasions this has been done,
having been found that its land is of little use because of its mountainous [char-
acter] and because of scarcity of water. The few waterholes that exist are of
very little volume and scarcely sufficient for the few Indians that inhabit the
island. Subsurface water has not been found, which would be necessary [for
settlers] to remain on the island for a long time.

The land is very rugged, producing some grasses and a few maguey [agave] plants, which is one of the foods that the Indians make use of: the vegetation is generally of shrubs, [and] there are neither great forests, nor woodlands, and according to all reports that have been collected from these same Indians[,] it rains very little on the island, which is in accord with what happens on the adjacent mainland coast, a few kilometers away, where rains are very scarce. (Corral 1898)

Within three weeks, Corral had received notification from the federal government that the directive to explore the island had been retracted.

Ultimately, the greatest stumbling block Andrade would have faced in trying to settle colonists on Tiburón might not have been a hostile environment so much as hostile Seris. This might not have been the case in January 1882, shortly after the 1880 roundup of Seris, when he first proposed the Midriff islands scheme. But by the 1890s, the situation had changed entirely. The Seris were back on Tiburón, and it was during this decade that some of the most notorious killings of outsiders took place there. Andrade was surely aware of these incidents, which were at least as widely publicized in California, where he was living, as in Sonora. By the time the final colonization contract was signed in 1897, the absurdity of trying to settle even 10 non-Indian families amidst the hostile Seris must have been obvious even to Andrade, whose plight had become fair game for journalistic ridicule:

General Andrade's Cannibals
They Are Tenants of an Island of His
but He Doesn't Collect Rent

General Guillermo Andrade, who used to be Thomas Blythe's partner in Mexican land schemes, counts among his possessions Tiburon island.

His title is as perfect as elaborate legal documents can make it, but anybody who wants an island can have this one cheap. The drawback to its possession is that it is inhabited by a strong tribe of cannibals who prefer the flesh of white men who come there to almost any dinner dish....

From all accounts an Apache is a high-toned, peaceful gentleman compared with the men of Tiburon. The Mexicans have at intervals essayed the subjugation of the Tiburon islanders and other Indian tribes have warred with them, but the little cannibal nation is there yet, stealing from the mainland, shooting those who come to the island and carrying off the women of neighboring tribes....

Anybody who thinks he would like to buy an island well stocked with superstitions and cruel, fierce cannibals has only to negotiate with General Andrade. The General is at Ensenada just now, but he has an office on California street in this city. (Anonymous [ca. 1895])

NINE

Rediscovering the Midriff:
Cartography and the Beginnings of Science in the Upper Gulf

Mapping the Midriff

The nineteenth century was a peculiar time for the cartography of the Midriff islands. On the one hand, several comparatively accurate maps appeared, beginning with an 1825 government map and culminating in the U.S. Hydrographic Office charts of 1877. Though none of these represents the Midriff islands with complete accuracy, the best ones depict all the major islands, place them approximately in their correct positions, and refrain from inventing nonexistent islands. On the other hand, a steady stream of highly inaccurate maps continued to appear. To varying degrees, these maps misposition the islands, distort their shapes, omit them altogether, or add imaginary islands. That such misinformation could persist so long is strong testimony to how poorly the region was known, at least in official circles, even in the final decades of the century.

The half-century between the expulsion of the Jesuits and Mexican Independence seems to have been a time of little progress in charting the upper Gulf. In 1825, the government of the new Republic published a map based on information accumulated by the Spanish Navy during Colonial times (Figure 9.1; see also Barrera Bassols 1992:246). This map depicts the southern Gulf with fair detail and accuracy, but beyond Mulegé and Guaymas the detail falls off. The Midriff islands are represented crudely but roughly correctly in shape and position, with San Esteban and San Lorenzo labeled together as the "Islas de Salsipuedes." Above Tiburón Island, the poorly-known upper Gulf is indicated by only a bare outline.

The lack of reliable and accessible maps at this time had posed a problem for Lieut. Hardy, who was sent to investigate the pearl fishing potential of the Midriff and upper Gulf. During the course of his exploration, Hardy compiled his own map, which turned out to be somewhat different than, if not an im-

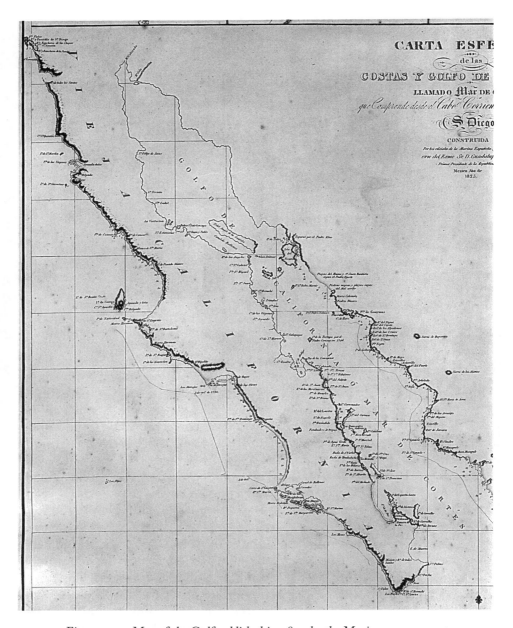

Figure 9.1   Map of the Gulf published in 1825 by the Mexican government,
titled Carta Esférica de las Costas y Golfo de Californias....
(Courtesy Bancroft Library, University of California, Berkeley [F1246 1825 M3].)

provement over, the Mexican government's 1825 map. His portrayal of the head of the Gulf is slightly more accurate while his representation of the Midriff region is perhaps a bit less so. Nevertheless, Hardy's map was better than many that were produced during the next several decades (Hardy [1829] 1977:map).

One of the most significant—and infamous—maps to appear in the middle of the nineteenth century was published in 1847 by John Disturnell. It was of great importance because it was the map attached to the Treaty of Guadalupe Hidalgo, which ended the war between Mexico and the United States, and it was used as the geographical basis for drawing the new boundary between the two countries. But the map contained serious errors in the region where the international line was to be established. This precipitated a series of major boundary disputes that were not resolved for another eight years (Rittenhouse 1965:5). The Disturnell map was equally flawed in its representation of the Gulf and especially the Midriff region (Figure 9.2; see also Rittenhouse 1965). Though Tiburón and San Lorenzo Islands are recognizable and labeled, San Esteban is missing entirely. As if to compensate, four imaginary islands were inserted off the south coast of Tiburón Island.

Yet not all maps at this time show the Midriff in such fanciful terms. Another 1847 map, this one by Sherman and Smith, gives a fundamentally accurate picture of all the major Midriff islands (Figure 9.3). This map found its way into the schoolroom where it was used to illustrate *Olney's School Geography*. Ironically, while statesmen were locked in negotiations over the spoils of war with the error-ridden Disturnell map, school children were seeing the geography of the Midriff in largely realistic terms.

Little changed during the next two decades. One of the best representations of the Midriff was an 1864 ethnographic map of Mexico compiled by Manuel Orozco y Berra. It erred in positioning San Esteban Island a bit too far to the northwest and in giving San Lorenzo Island a small counterclockwise twist. Otherwise, the locations, shapes, and relative sizes of the islands are fundamentally correct (Orozco y Berra 1864; see also Ruiz Naufal et al. 1982:313). However, the most interesting aspect of this map is the ethnographic classification of the region, which was indicated both by labels and by color coding. Tiburón Island and the adjoining Sonoran coast are shaded pink to indicate Seri territory. Ángel de la Guarda and San Lorenzo Islands are given the blue shading of the peninsular regions occupied by the Cochimí. But San Esteban Island is neither labeled nor colored, implying either that it was thought to be uninhabited, or that it was simply unknown territory.

Somewhat less accurate was an 1863 map by Ulises Lassépas and Roberto L. D. Aumaile. By and large, the Midriff islands are correctly positioned, although their shapes, including that of "S. Estevan I.," are badly distorted (Lassépas and Aumaile 1863). One of the worst but most widely circulated maps was produced in 1864 by Ernesto de Fleury, a Frenchman who served as Sonora's state engineer during the French Intervention (Voss 1982:152). To his credit, Fleury included some of the lesser Midriff islands missing from other maps, and identified them by name. Thus it is one of the first maps to show the islands of

Figure 9.2   Detail of John Disturnell's 1847 Mapa de los Estados Unidos de Méjico.... *(For the full map, see Rittenhouse 1965.) (Courtesy Bancroft Library, University of California, Berkeley [F1226 1847 D38].)*

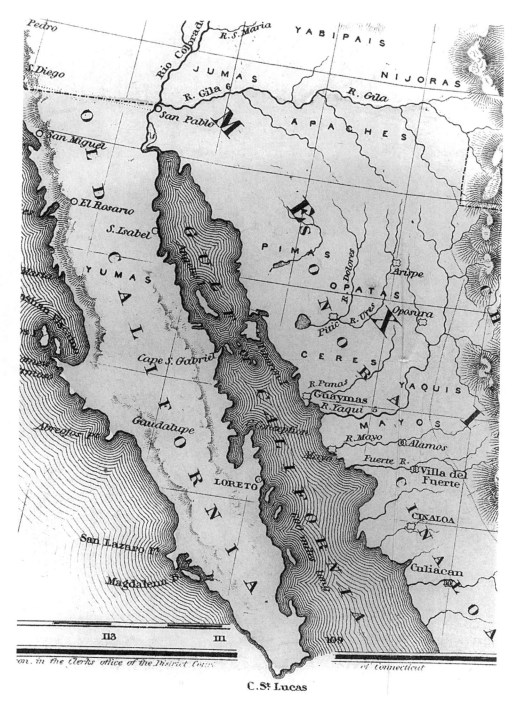

Figure 9.3 Detail of Sherman and Smith's 1847 Map of the United States, Canada, and a Part of Mexico. (Courtesy Buffalo Bill Historical Center, Cody, Wyoming [MRL Coll.].)

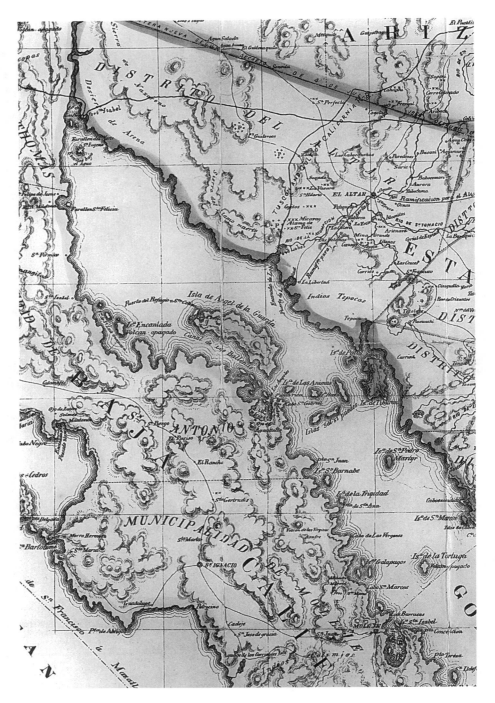

Figure 9.4 Detail of the 1881 edition of Ernesto de Fleury's 1864
Nuevo Mapa de los Estados de Sonora, Chihuahua...., *revised by Warren Holt.*
(For the full map, see Ruíz Naufal et al. 1982: 303.) (Courtesy Bancroft Library,
University of California, Berkeley [No. 990563].)

Patos, Rasa, and Partida (mislabeled "Ánimas"). Fleury apparently created Rasa and the "Islas Sal si puedes" from the four imaginary islands that Disturnell had placed south of Tiburón, by moving them to the northwest and rotating the group 180 degrees. Although this was an improvement over Disturnell's map, it left Fleury with a nonexistent large island lying off Tiburón's west coast. The coastlines of all the islands are mostly imaginary, and to make matters worse, many of the major geographical features on the adjacent mainland and peninsular coasts are badly distorted and misplaced. The map was evidently a commercial success, though, for it was republished as late as 1881. Although this was a revised edition, all the original errors in the Midriff region survived unscathed (Figure 9.4).

It was probably not critical for academics, school children, or even government officials to have an accurate knowledge of the Midriff islands. But for sea captains who were responsible for the safe passage of their vessels, crews, passengers, and cargo, it was a different matter. It was essential for sailors to have accurate information not only about the coastline and islands, but also the water depth and hazards such as shoals and submerged rocks. While there must have been an extensive body of navigational information passed among mariners by word of mouth, this would be no substitute for reliable printed charts and coast pilots. By midcentury, the most faithful sources were the various editions of James Imray's charts and *Sailing Directions for the West Coast of North America* (Imray 1849, 1853), compiled from Spanish surveys, observations of English and French naval officers, and especially, Lieut. Hardy's observations in 1826. Imray's representation of the Midriff region is substantially correct. The islands lie in their true positions and their overall shapes and relative sizes are rendered with fair accuracy, although Ángel de la Guarda is graced with several extra islets. "S. Estevan" is even shown with its distinctive shingle spit protruding from the southwestern corner.

By 1870, a considerable fraction of the traffic in the Gulf consisted of North American merchant vessels coming from San Francisco and other West Coast ports, and this included the ships making the long run up the length of the Gulf to the Colorado River. With such a large stake in Gulf navigation, in 1872 the U.S. Congress allocated funds to the U.S. Navy's recently created Hydrographic Office to conduct the first comprehensive survey of the region. Although by this time the era of regular voyages to the head of the Gulf was almost at an end, the survey was intended to accurately map the entire route of these vessels. Not only was it charged with fixing the positions of points of land, but also with taking soundings in order to provide the basis for a comprehensive hydrographic chart (Robeson 1874:8; Nelson 1971:17–18).

The vessel the Navy assigned to carry out the survey was the U.S.S. *Narragansett*, a 186-foot wooden hull steam-powered sloop (Figure 9.5). For close-in work and establishing shore stations, the *Narragansett* was to carry three small boats, one of which was a steam-powered launch, fitted with a removable boiler, named the *Rattler*. The officer placed in charge of the expedition was Commander George E. Dewey, who later achieved fame in the Philippines during the Spanish-American War (Figure 9.6). Dewey was glad to accept the survey

Figure 9.5   The U.S.S. Narragansett *at Mare Island Navy Yard, San Francisco Bay.*
The small boat under the bow may be the steam-powered launch Rattler, *used for close-in survey*
work in the Gulf. Photograph probably taken between 1873 and 1875.
(Courtesy Benjamin Kohn and the U.S. Naval Historical Center, Washington, D.C. [NH 93242].)

Figure 9.6   George E. Dewey
(1837–1917) as a naval
lieutenant, early 1860s. (Courtesy
U.S. Naval Historical Center,
Washington, D.C. [NH 50591].)

assignment, for he had just requested sea duty in order to take his mind off the recent death of his young wife just five days after the birth of their son. The fieldwork kept Dewey occupied for two years, from 1873 to 1875 and required two separate voyages to the Gulf. Apparently, the assignment afforded him the distraction he needed, for Dewey later wrote that:

> Two years in the Gulf of California means practical isolation; and survey-ing in that hot climate, as we used to keep at it from dawn to dark, was hard work. It was with pleasant anticipation of seeing my little son and the home country that I received my orders detaching me from the *Narragansett* in the spring of 1875. (Dewey 1916:149)

The *Narragansett* set out from its base in San Francisco Bay in the fall of 1873. By the end of November, the expedition had rounded Cabo San Lucas and worked its way up the coast of Baja California to the Midriff. Before dawn on December 1, the vessel passed through Salsipuedes Channel, between San Lorenzo Island and the peninsula, arriving the following day at Bahía de los Ángeles. After two days there taking soundings, they backtracked to Rasa Island. On the 6th, they departed Rasa and sailed southeast, passing about a mile from San Pedro Mártir Island, and put in that evening in Guaymas.

On December 11, the *Narragansett* sailed from Guaymas bound for the up-per Gulf, passing around the eastern and northern sides of San Pedro Mártir and again through Salsipuedes Channel. Monday December 15 was spent at anchor in Bahía Refugio at the northwestern tip of Ángel de la Guarda Island, where a survey party went ashore. For the next 10 days, the expedition worked its way up to the head of the Gulf and began to descend on the Sonoran side, spend-ing Christmas at anchor at Libertad, and anchoring the following afternoon in the lee of Patos Island before beginning a survey of Tiburón Island. Early the next morning, December 27, the steam launch *Rattler*, under the command of Master W. R. Harris, left the ship for a surveying run through the Canal del Infiernillo. Meanwhile, the *Narragansett* sailed down the west coast of Tiburón, around Punta Willard, and through the channel between San Esteban Island and the southwest coast of Tiburón. Early that afternoon, the ship anchored next to Punta Monumento at the southern tip of Tiburón Island. Here, a sur-vey party went ashore and established a camp in order to facilitate measurements needed to fix the position of the island. In view of the tales Dewey and his crew had heard of the Seris, the shore party was armed and wary, as were the Seris they encountered. As H. M. M. Richards recalled some 40 years later:

> It was evident that the natives were surrounding the camp during the en-tire night so a strict watch was kept, and the morning came without mishap. It was far from our purpose to excite any aggressive action on their part so every effort was made to avoid hostilities and to show the Indians that our errand was of a peaceful character. They seemed to grasp this fact and, on their part, merely kept in touch with us. In the course of the day one of them was

seen to show himself openly. In the hope of persuading him to enter the camp one of our seamen grasped his rifle and started towards him, but he had hardly advanced a few paces when the savage drew the arrow in his bow to its head and kept it there as a menace towards further approach. The seaman then dropped his gun, in token of amity, and took a step or two further when again the bow came up as a warning, whereupon a handkerchief was displayed and waved, and several trinkets laid upon a rock while the sailor retired a short distance, but all without avail. (Richards 1913:85–86)

Richards, who was a member of this shore party, had his own surprise encounter. As he was walking near the beach, he was startled by a Seri who:

suddenly loomed up before me. He was truly a veritable giant with his more than six feet of height ... and as naked as the day he was born save for a breechcloth, or covering, of some material which I failed to recognize. I must have looked like a pigmy to him. Fortunately, he seemed to be on a peaceable errand, or else was taken as much by surprise as myself, so we parted without further effort towards acquaintanceship. (Richards 1913:85)

On the morning of December 28, the *Rattler* returned to the ship, having been out overnight, and having unexpectedly:

intercepted some of the Indians on one of their boats or balsas, who, realizing that they could not escape, allowed themselves to be overhauled. Among them was one of their women, the only one clad of the number, who had over her a covering of pelican skins.... [I]t was such a curiosity that every effort was made to secure it as a relic. Of course verbal communication was impossible, but a profuse use was made of the sign language, and various plugs of tobacco, knives, etc., were offered in exchange but without avail, and finally the party was allowed to proceed on its way. (Richards 1913:85)

For the rest of the day, the reunited expedition remained at anchor off Punta Monumento, and then departed early the following morning.

The next three days were spent working around Alcatraz Island and Bahía Kino where, on New Year's Eve, the *Rattler* took a survey party ashore. On January 1, 1874, the *Narragansett* weighed anchor and sailed for Guaymas, and 18 days later departed for Acapulco and points south. Although they had had some interesting encounters with the Seris, they had only been in the vicinity of Tiburón for two days and had not crossed the channel to San Esteban Island (*Narragansett* Deck Logs 1873–1875).

On December 1, 1874, Commander Dewey again maneuvered the *Narragansett* out of San Francisco Bay on its final cruise to the Gulf. Working their way up the peninsular side as before, the expedition reached the channel between San Lorenzo Island and the peninsula on February 19, 1875. For the next five days the *Narragansett*, along with the *Rattler* and the other two launches, surveyed around Ángel de la Guarda Island. On the 25th, they departed for the head of the Gulf and gradually circled around to the mainland side, stopping to map "George's Island" (San Jorge Island) on March 12 on their way down the coast. On March 18, they crossed the Gulf to Rasa Island, where they landed a shore party and spent two days surveying. The *Narragansett* left Rasa the morning of the 20th and arrived that afternoon at their old anchorage next to Punta Monumento, at the southern tip of Tiburón Island.

No survey work was undertaken on the following day, being Sunday. But at 6 A.M. Monday March 22, the *Rattler*, under Master Harris, set off to survey "Tiburón Passage," returning at 5 P.M. That evening, the crew coaled and watered the *Rattler* for two days' work, and the next morning, March 23, "The 'Rattler' left the ship at 6.00 to run lines of soundings" (*Narragansett* Deck Logs 1873–1875). Early the following morning, March 24, the *Narragansett* left Tiburón Island, sailing past the mouth of Bahía Kino and heading southeastward, coming to anchor at Tastiota. Meanwhile the *Rattler*, which had been away overnight, caught up with the *Narragansett* at 2:30 that afternoon, March 24.

Although the deck logs fail to specify exactly where the *Rattler* went between March 22 and 24, it must have been during this interval that Master Harris and his survey team steamed to San Esteban and circumnavigated the island, taking soundings as they went. Most likely, this comprised the March 22 day trip through "Tiburón Passage," but the possibility cannot be ruled out that they went to San Esteban on the 23rd, camped on the island overnight, and then steamed hard to catch up with the *Narragansett* the next day. What is clear is that sometime in this short period, the coast of San Esteban was surveyed and described at close quarters for the first time by trained engineers. The soundings show that the *Rattler* circled the island within a few hundred feet of shore, close enough to give the survey party a good look at the character of the coastline, and enabling them to determine the island's approximate shape and sketch in the most prominent coastal features.

While Harris was away with the *Rattler*, surveyors at the *Narragansett*'s anchorage at the southern tip of Tiburón were gathering topographic data for San Esteban. From Tiburón they shot two sets of elevations, one set to the highest summit of the island, and the other to Male Mountain. The two heights obtained for the island's summit (designated "S. Pk Esteban") were a disparate 1,557 and 1,987 feet, which Hydrographic Office cartographers later averaged to 1,772 feet for the published chart. Dewey's men had better luck with Male Mountain (called "N. Pk Esteban"), obtaining more consistent elevations of 1,418 and 1,478 feet, which were averaged and rounded off to 1,450 feet (Anonymous 1875a, 1875b). This topographic data, coupled with Harris' survey, enabled the Hydrographic Office to compile the first substantive and approximately accurate description of San Esteban's shoreline, which was published in its 1880 coast pilot:

> San Esteban is a barren, rocky island lying 7¾ miles south of the south-western point of Tiburon. It is 4 miles long north to south, about 3 miles wide,

and from 1,000 to 1,800 feet high. On its eastern side, a mile from the south-east point, is a rock 25 feet high [El Monumento], a quarter of a mile from the shore, to which it is connected by a rocky reef. Just north of this rock and reef is a gravel beach, from which a valley [Arroyo Limantour] slopes toward the interior of the island. From the south-western part a low shingle spit [El Cascajal] makes off three-quarters of a mile, the soundings on either side of it increasing rapidly. The remaining shores of the island consist of almost perpendicular bluffs, varying in height from 100 to 500 feet, with short stretches of gravel and shingle beaches intervening. (Belden 1880:145–46)

During the 3½ days the *Narragansett* remained in the vicinity of Tiburón Island, the crew again encountered Seris, and this time they were able to establish friendly relations with them:

They are reputed to be exceedingly hostile and to use poisoned arrows in opposing the landing of strangers on what they consider their domain, but during the stay of the *Narragansett* in the vicinity they were very friendly. At first they were shy and made threatening gestures, but soon finding that our intentions were peaceable, became friendly and returned our visits to the shore by frequent and lengthy calls on board ship. (Belden 1880:145)

On one of these amicable shipboard calls, expedition artist Hector von Bayer obtained what are probably the first two photographs ever taken of the Seris (Figure 9.7). Their balsas were of special interest to the expedition members, who not only described and sketched them but also managed to purchase one "for a pint of alcohol, largely diluted with water, and a couple of pairs of old trowsers" (Belden 1880:145).

Although Seris were very much in evidence on Tiburón Island, there is no indication that Harris and his survey team saw any sign of human activity on San Esteban. Based on what Dewey's surveyors had seen (and heard from Mexican sources) they reported that:

During the greater part of the year Tiburon Island is resorted to by the Seris (or Ceres) tribe of Indians, who inhabit the adjacent main-land, and their huts and encampments may be seen in many places along the shore, principally on the eastern side of the island. (Belden 1880:145)

Considering the fascination of the expedition members with these people, had Harris and the crew of the *Rattler* seen any hint of Seris on their excursion to San Esteban, they surely would have noted it.

On March 25, the *Narragansett* steamed the short leg from Tastiota to Guaymas, and on July 7, 1875, dropped anchor in San Francisco Bay, its survey mission completed. The data must have been forwarded immediately to the Hydrographic Office in Washington, which managed to print an error-ridden preliminary chart of the Midriff region by the end of the year (Anonymous

Figure 9.7   Seri Indians on board the U.S.S. Narragansett *at Punta Monumento, Tiburón Island, photographed in March 1875 by Hector von Bayer. This is one of the two earliest known photographs of the Seris. The image reproduced here was printed from the shattered and mold-damaged glass plate negative, then digitally enhanced and restored by Kevin C. Horstman. (Courtesy Richard S. Felger and the National Anthropological Archives, Smithsonian Institution, Washington D.C. [No. 4278-B].)*

1875c). In its final form, published in September 1877, many of the initial errors had been corrected. The sheet covering San Esteban (Anonymous 1877) became the first map to depict the shoreline and near-shore topography of the Midriff islands with both good accuracy and detail (Figure 9.8). Three years later, the Hydrographic Office released its Publication No. 56 (Belden 1880), the accompanying coast pilot, which presented a precise written description of the Gulf coastline and islands, including San Esteban (see pp. 213–14).

The *Narragansett* survey marks the beginning of modern cartography of the Midriff islands, but it did not end the Hydrographic Office's efforts to supply accurate navigational data for the region. Seriously underfunded and lacking a vessel dedicated to survey work, for many years it requested that all U.S. Navy vessels should undertake surveys whenever the opportunity arose, and most captains complied (Nelson 1971:19). At the beginning of the 1880s, two vessels contributed to this effort in the Midriff region. One of these, the Coast and Geodetic Survey steamer *Hassler*, commanded by Lieut. Henry E. Nichols, sailed into the upper Gulf to establish magnetic declinations for compass navigation (Nichols 1881). The *Hassler* steamed northward out of Guaymas on De-

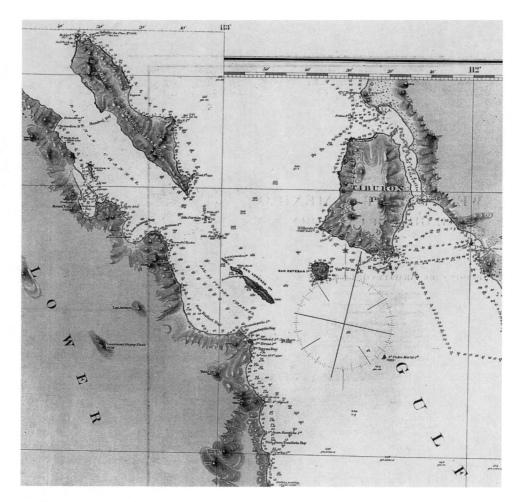

Figure 9.8   Detail of the 1877 first edition of the U.S. Hydrographic Office's Map 620, Sheet II, compiled from U.S.S. Narragansett *survey data. (Courtesy Library of Congress, Geography and Map Division, Washington, D.C. [No. 904965].)*

cember 28, 1880, passing San Pedro Mártir in the afternoon, and then cruised slowly toward the channel between Tiburón and San Esteban Islands. At 4:20 A.M. the next morning, it was between the two islands and "passing through large patches of whale feed," probably bioluminescent plankton glowing from the disturbance of the ship in the predawn darkness. Rounding Punta Willard at 7:30 A.M., the *Hassler* proceeded northward:

> through several stormy tide rips to the W^d of Tiburon Id.... [and] ... At 2.30 [P.M.] came to anchor in Freshwater Bay [Bahía Agua Dulce].... At 3.00 sent a boat with officers armed to inspect landing.... At 4.15 boat returned. (*Hassler* Deck Logs 1880–1881)

The *Hassler* remained anchored in the bay off Tecomate for 2½ days. Three times during their stay "Observation Parties" went ashore, armed because of the evil reputation of the Seris. On December 31, an observation party returned to the ship about 5:30 P.M.:

> leaving 4 men with Lt. Swinburne and Ensign Coffin on shore [a]s a guard on account of the reported hostility and treachery of the Ceres Indians. (*Hassler* Deck Logs 1880–1881)

It may be that there were few Seris left on Tiburón at this time, for earlier in the year the Mexican military had rounded up about 150 people on the adjacent mainland coast and deported them to Pueblo de Seris, outside Hermosillo. But probably the ship's crew did not know this. Although Lieut. Swinburne and his men saw no Seris that night, guard duty at Tecomate must have been a tense and not very festive way to spend New Year's Eve.

On the morning of January 2, 1881, the *Hassler* sailed to Patos Island and on to the head of the Gulf. After cruising southward on the peninsular side, the vessel rounded Cabo San Lucas and sailed northward, arriving at San Francisco Bay in April (*Hassler* Deck Logs 1880–1881).

Four days before the *Hassler* returned to San Francisco, the U.S.S. *Ranger*, under Commander J. W. Philip, embarked on a cruise that took it into the Gulf, where it made soundings to supplement the work of the *Narragansett*. As the *Ranger* proceeded up the Gulf, it made a line of soundings as far as San Pedro Mártir Island. From there, on June 28, 1881, the vessel passed northwest through the channel between San Esteban and San Lorenzo Islands, but the crew took no data. Later in the afternoon, having reached Ángel de la Guarda, they began to take soundings again. The *Ranger* then sailed nearly to the head of the Gulf before turning southward, stopping on July 7 at the Pichilingue coaling station near La Paz on its way toward Acapulco (Anonymous 1881; *Ranger* Deck Logs 1881).

The 1877 and later editions of the Hydrographic Office charts soon became the basis for most maps of the Gulf. WJ McGee used it to compile the map of "Seriland" which appears in his monograph on the Seris (McGee 1898). For this publication McGee's topographer, Willard D. Johnson, made major changes in the interior features that had been depicted in the Hydrographic Office chart. But since neither McGee nor Willard had ever been near San Esteban, the topographic features shown on their map bear little resemblance to reality.

A few other late nineteenth century maps were based on obsolete sources of data. One such map, produced in 1882 under the direction of W. R. Morley, Chief Engineer for the Sonora Railway Company, not only perpetuated all the errors of the 1864 Fleury map, but added yet another imaginary island to the Midriff region (Morley 1882). An official state map of Sonora by Chas. E. Herbert, dated 1885, puts the islands in their correct positions but imparts an unnatural blocky shape to Tiburón and San Esteban Islands (Herbert 1885; see also Brown Villalba et al. 1982:568). Curiously, Hubert Howe Bancroft relied chiefly on older inaccurate maps of the Gulf to illustrate his *History of the North Mexican States* (Bancroft 1884, 1889:666), even though the Hydrographic Office chart was by then available. And although Lieut. Nichols, who commanded the *Hassler*, would surely have had a copy of the Hydrographic Office chart, the sketch map that accompanies the report of his magnetic survey has San Esteban totally out of position, lying half way between Tiburón and Ángel de la Guarda Islands (Nichols 1881).

One nineteenth century map was made specifically of San Esteban Island. It was commissioned in 1882 by entrepreneur Guillermo Andrade, who had received a concession from the Mexican government to colonize San Esteban, Tiburón, and Ángel de la Guarda Islands (see Ch. 8). As a condition of his contract, Andrade was required to produce a map of each island and submit them to the federal authorities in Mexico City. Andrade complied, and the government acknowledged receipt of all three maps. A copy of the Tiburón map has survived (Figure 8.4), but neither the San Esteban nor Ángel de la Guarda maps has been found. One interesting aspect of the Tiburón map is that it shows few inland features that are not visible from the coast, suggesting that Andrade's surveyors spent little if any time on shore. Whether they bothered to go ashore on San Esteban is not known, since the map of this island has not been located.

Scientific Research in the Midriff

Scientific investigation of the Gulf with approaches that are familiar today began during the nineteenth century. But if science is viewed in a broader historical context, its antecedents, at least, go back much earlier, and it is not always possible to meaningfully distinguish science from prospecting, natural resources exploration, cartography, or even voyages of discovery. In fact, the early Spanish exploratory voyages of Ulloa, Vizcaíno, Ortega, and others, though motivated by hope of personal gain, were also very much voyages of basic geographical investigation. The royal contracts that governed seventeenth-century pearling expeditions routinely required these navigators to compile charts and descriptions of the natural resources and inhabitants of the regions they visited. Although initially the information they gathered was strictly classified in order to protect potential wealth, it is these voyages that have given us our earliest views of not only the geography but also the natural history and ethnography of the Gulf region.

For the contemporary literate public, it was the eighteenth century Jesuit missionaries to Sonora and especially Baja California who provided the first published and hence generally available accounts of the natural history of the region. Many of these tireless souls penned descriptions of the country in their letters and reports, in some cases in great detail. These missives enabled two colleagues in Europe, Miguel Venegas and Andrés Burriel, to assemble and publish the first comprehensive treatise on the social and natural history of the region, entitled in its 1759 English translation *A Natural and Civil History of*

California (Venegas [1759] 1966a, [1759] 1966b). This was followed by Father Johann Baegert's firsthand *Observations in Lower California*, with editions published in 1771 and 1772 (Baegert [1772] 1952), and Francisco Clavigero's *History of (Lower) California* (Clavigero [1789] 1971), the latter based on the detailed but unpublished social and natural history compiled by peninsular missionary Miguel del Barco. On the Sonoran side of the Gulf, Ignaz Pfefferkorn's *Sonora: A Description of the Province* first appeared in 1794 (Pfefferkorn [1794] 1989). These works, however, deal mainly with the land surrounding the Gulf and have little to say about the natural history of the islands, especially those of the Midriff.

Though the Jesuits were often keen observers and writers, most were not collectors of specimens. The exception was Father Francisco Inama, who arrived on the peninsula with an academic background in natural science, a strong avocational interest in zoology, and a microscope and dissection tools. While stationed at Comondú, west of Loreto, Inama undertook a prolonged and detailed anatomical study of rattlesnakes, and engaged in frequent discussions of his results and other scientific matters with his southern neighbor and fellow naturalist, Father Miguel del Barco at San Javier (Crosby 1994:255).

During the nineteenth century, natural history remained a descriptive science, but one in which the study of specimens collected in the field played an increasingly central role. Great emphasis was placed on the identification and careful description of new taxa, and to accomplish this, large numbers of specimens from exotic locations were needed. But the collections that formed the basis for these studies were often assembled not by the scientists who performed the taxonomic analysis but by others. Some of these fieldworkers were more or less professional collectors, though many were competent amateurs. The nineteenth century was still a time when education meant cultivating a broad range of knowledge and interests, and it was common for travelers to take a lively interest in local flora and fauna and assemble important scientific collections.

Collecting in the Gulf region began as the result of a special botanical survey of New Spain commissioned by Carlos III. This royal project enabled a self-styled naturalist named José Longinos Martínez to spend the first half of 1792 traversing the length of Baja California, erratically collecting botanical and zoological specimens. He did not visit any of the islands (Simpson 1938:ix-xii; DuShane 1971:12-15).

During the first half of the nineteenth century, France, England, and the United States all launched maritime exploring expeditions, some of them ambitious multiyear projects that were global in scope. In part, their objectives were mapping, hydrography, and other navigation-related pursuits. But these expeditions were also staffed with at least one naturalist charged with making collections and observations on the natural history of the places visited. Among the vessels dispatched were the French frigate *Venus* and the British vessel H.M.S *Sulphur*, both of which touched at Cabo San Lucas in the late 1830s (Petit-Thouars [1841] 1956:104-13; Belcher 1843). At the end of 1849, another British vessel, H.M.S *Herald*, explored the Gulf as far as Mulegé and Guaymas (Seamann 1853:152-58). The U.S. Exploring Expedition was staffed by nine scientists, but although it was at sea from 1838 to 1842, it did not enter the Gulf at all. The first major botanical collection from the Gulf was taken between December 1841 and February 1842 by Russian naturalist Il'ia Gavrilovich Vosnesenskii, who accompanied the ship *Nasnedlik Aleksandr* to Carmen Island, where the Russians obtained salt for processing furs in their colony at Sitka, Alaska. Vosnesenskii collected 360 plant specimens, representing 113 species, on Carmen Island and in the vicinity of Loreto. Though he shipped the collections to St. Petersburg, they wound up in storage unstudied (Carter 1979:31–32). Neither Vosnesenskii nor naturalists from any of the other expeditions of this period sailed as high as the Midriff region (Taylor [1869] 1971:113–19).

During the next three decades, a number of naturalists and scientific expeditions worked around the margins of the Gulf. Foremost among these were the members of the U.S. and Mexican Boundary Survey operating at the head of the Gulf (Emory 1857); the eccentric John Xantus de Vesey, who collected botanical and zoological specimens at Cabo San Lucas (Madden 1949:97–151; DuShane 1971:15–19); Lassépas (1859), who conducted a resources survey of the peninsula for the Mexican government; J. Ross Browne (1869a), who conducted a similar survey on behalf of North American land speculators; and Edward Palmer, whose 1869–1870 botanical collecting around Guaymas and on Carmen Island foreshadowed his extensive work in the Gulf region in later decades (McVaugh 1956:43–45). During the French Intervention, a Commission Scientifique du Mexique undertook a reconnaissance of the mineral resources of Mexico, which extended into Sonora and the peninsula as far as Guaymas and La Paz (Guillemin Tarayre 1869). Even Capt. Charles P. Stone, head of the infamous Jecker Survey of Sonora:

> caused numerous collections to be made in the northern part of the Gulf, chiefly opposite Guaymas. Of these a portion, consisting principally of shells, have been received [by the Smithsonian Institution] during the year [1860], and prove to be of much interest, not only in themselves, but as completing the history of Cape St. Lucas and Mazatlan species. (Baird 1861:68)

In the 1880s, there was an explosion of scientific interest in the region, and a sizable force of scientists and collectors descended upon Sonora and Baja California. Some field trips were privately funded, while others operated under the auspices of the U.S. National Museum and the California Academy of Sciences, which sponsored a long series of expeditions to the peninsula (Nelson 1922:141–45; Johnston 1924:973–77; Irigoyen 1943b:377–78; van Rossem 1945:7–16; Felger 1976; Lindsay 1983:10; Cody 1983:210). Between 1880 and 1900, some 200 publications emerged from this work (Trujillo 1967:58–77). From Mexico, the federal government sponsored an expedition to the peninsula in 1884 to assess the geology and natural resources of the region (Ramos 1887). In the 1890s, the Muséum d'Histoire Naturelle in Paris engaged Leon Diguet to collect botanical specimens from the peninsula, where he undertook some of the early archaeological studies of burial caves as well (Johnston

1924:975). In late 1900, Diguet also managed to visit both Ángel de la Guarda and Partida Islands, and on the latter captured the two type specimens of the fish-eating bat *Pizonyx vivesi* (Reeder and Norris 1954:83-85). But apart from brief excursions, few scientists working on either side of the Gulf extended their investigations in any significant way to the islands, and fewer still to the islands of the Midriff.

Among the rare scientific observers who did visit the Midriff islands were U.S. naval officers, for the Navy often sanctioned a wide array of scientific investigations in addition to their assigned missions (Nelson 1971:20-21). The ship's surgeon, because of his medical training, was most frequently the officer who doubled as naturalist, and many of these individuals collected valuable plant and animal specimens from exotic localities. During the 1873-1874 cruise of the U.S.S. *Narragansett*, Surgeon Edward Evers collected a modest number of plant, animal, and mineral specimens, but apparently only from the Pacific coast of Baja California (Evers 1873, 1874). However Thomas Streets, who served as ship's surgeon during the *Narragansett*'s 1874-1875 cruise, made floral and faunal collections from several localities in the Gulf (Streets 1877). Three of his collecting sites were on the Midriff islands of Rasa, Ángel de la Guarda, and Tiburón. Unfortunately, he did not join the crew of the ship's boat *Rattler* for its brief excursion to San Esteban Island.

When the U.S.S. *Hassler* embarked on its magnetic survey of the Gulf in 1880, it came equipped with a dredge, and its captain, Lieut. Henry Nichols, used every opportunity to take marine samples during the cruise. Two of its hauls were taken as the ship rode at anchor off Tecomate, on the north end of Tiburón Island, and others were taken at Patos Island (*Hassler* Deck Logs 1880-1881). Among the fish collected during the Gulf portion of the *Hassler*'s cruise were three previously unknown species (Jordan and Gilbert 1882).

Marine research took a major leap forward when the U.S. Fish Commission steamer *Albatross* was placed in service in August 1882. This was the first government ship ever built and equipped specifically as a research vessel (Figure 9.9). Her construction was supervised by Commander Zera L. Tanner, who commanded the *Albatross* for more than 12 years. During its 40 years of service, the vessel participated in a wide spectrum of studies in marine biology and oceanography, conducted on board by some of the most prominent marine scientists of the period (Rathbun 1894; Tanner 1895; Nelson 1971:19-20).

The *Albatross* sailed into the Gulf of California three times prior to the turn of the century. In 1888 and 1891, it sailed only as high as Guaymas. But the 1889 cruise took the vessel to the mouth of the Colorado River to investigate the relationship between these two bodies of water and marine organisms (Rathbun 1894:131, 196-97; Fraser 1943a:5). After leaving Guaymas on March 23, the vessel steamed northward taking soundings, serial temperatures, and specific gravity measurements as it passed between San Esteban and Tiburón Islands. After nearly a week in the upper Gulf, it turned southward, again passing between San Esteban and Tiburón Islands, and arrived at Guaymas on the 30th. Though many of the measurements and collections were made at sea, shore parties landed and collected at a number of locations, including the north end of Ángel de la Guarda, where several chuckwallas and two rattlesnakes were

Figure 9.9   The U.S. Fish Commission research vessel Albatross.
(Courtesy U.S. National Archives, Washington, D.C. [No. 19-N-13141].)

captured, in addition to intertidal organisms. No other Midriff islands were visited by shore parties (Tanner 1892; Rathbun 1894:196).

Only a few civilian scientists visited the Midriff islands during the nineteenth century. One of these was W. J. Fisher, who had been the naturalist aboard the U.S.S. *Tuscarora* in 1873. Fisher obviously saw field collecting as a potentially profitable business, for in April of 1876 he chartered the small schooner *Harvest Queen* and set out from San Francisco on a trip to the Gulf "to collect seals, birds, fishes, mollusks, crustecea, radiates, etc., for sale or exchange" (Lockington 1882:113). He cruised up the east coast of Baja California, collecting at localities as far north as Bahía de los Ángeles and possibly the northern tip of Ángel de la Guarda Island. Fisher's few terrestrial specimens were of little interest, but by using a dredge, he obtained a number of new and little-known marine organisms. Eventually, he turned over much of his shell collection to the U.S. National Museum, and some specimens may have gone to the California Academy of Sciences. But Fisher seems not to have kept careful records, and these specimens "were left by him in such a confused condition that they can rarely be identified as his" (Cooper 1895:36). Moreover, his attempt at natural history entrepreneurship ended in financial disaster (Stearns 1879, 1895:139–43; Lockington 1882; Cooper 1895:36–37; Fraser 1943a:4).

In March 1888, Nathaniel S. Goss made a two week trip to San Pedro Mártir Island to observe and collect birds. At that time, the island was being actively mined for its guano, and Goss found only three nesting species. Upon his return to the United States, he donated half his specimens to the U.S. National Museum (Goss 1888).

One of the most prodigious collectors of the time was Edward Palmer (Figure 9.10). On field trips extending over more than 50 years, Palmer collected an estimated 100,000 plants, many new to science, plus innumerable faunal, archaeological, and ethnographic specimens. Most of his collecting was done in the American Southwest and especially northern and western Mexico, where he returned again and again. He collected for many different herbaria, museums, and agencies, and under the auspices of some of the foremost botanists of the day (McVaugh 1956:v-ix, 3–7).

Palmer's first work in the Gulf region was at Guaymas in late 1869. Before he left the area, he made a point of visiting the Seris living at Pueblo de Seris near Hermosillo, and he collected briefly on Carmen Island on his way home. He returned in 1887, 1889, and 1890, collecting on both sides of the Gulf (Johnston 1924:974; McVaugh 1956:43–44, 93–100). One of his destinations on the 1887 trip was Bahía de los Ángeles, where he took time off from botany to excavate a burial cave (Wilson 1890:127–29; Massey and Osborne 1961). In October of that year, Palmer sailed to San Pedro Mártir Island, where he found only 19 species of plants during a stay of two weeks (Watson 1889:37; McVaugh 1956:230–31). In February 1890, Palmer again returned to San Pedro Mártir, presumably as a passenger on the company steamer making one of its supply runs to the guano mines. This voyage enabled him to visit Rasa Island as well but gave him only a day to collect on each island (Vasey and Rose 1890:63, 78–80; McVaugh 1956:230–31).

Archaeology in the Gulf region also had its beginnings in the late nineteenth century. Except for Edward Palmer's excavations at Bahía de los Ángeles, these investigations were confined to the southern peninsula and Espíritu Santo Island, where a series of burial caves and rock art sites were explored by Hermann ten Kate and Leon Diguet (Massey 1966:47; Hovens 1991). There was also, however, an extraordinary 1893 report of archaeological remains on Ángel de la Guarda. The man who claimed to have observed them was one of the owners of the San Juan mine at Bahía de los Ángeles, José G. Moraga, likely the same man who impersonated a priest some years earlier in order to prospect Tiburón Island (see p. 119). Moraga described the remains to the U.S. Consul in Guaymas, J. Alexander Forbes, who in turn relayed Moraga's story to the State Department (Forbes [1893]:27–29). Moraga told Forbes that he had often sailed past Ángel de la Guarda, where he had seen what appeared to be a road. Since he believed the island had never been inhabited, he wondered if the road led to a mine, and resolved to explore it. When Moraga landed on the island:

> he found a well macadamized road that seemed to have been made with great care. The road commences at the beach and leads to the interior. As he fol-

Figure 9.10
Edward Palmer
(1831–1911) in the field
in Sinaloa, 1891.
(Courtesy Hunt Institute
for Botanical Documenta-
tion, Carnegie Mellon
University, Pittsburgh,
Pennsylvania.)

lowed along the road, he admired the work of ancient art, and found that all
the prominent points on the mountains near the road were fortified; and as
he turned, he saw a great number of these fortifications, that overlook the
roadway, seemingly intended to prevent the advance of an enemy. The fortifications are of nothing but stone.... No mortar was used, but the large stones
used are well shaped. He continued on this mysterious road for more than six
miles.... [I]n going over mountains and ravines he noticed many plots of
ground that resembled graves, because each had the shape of a parallelogram,
with stones well and evenly laid over the plot. Here he found a coin that has
on one side hieroglyphics on the upper half, and the date in Arabic numbers,
1288; while on the reverse it has a double triangle, thus: [Forbes's drawing

resembles a Star of David]. Continuing on his course, he suddenly came upon a place where he counted 166 habitations built of stone. They are not made with mortar, but the stone is well cut, and laid over one another, making a good substantial wall. All of them are round, and on an average about fourteen feet in diameter. Some have doors, and others have a place where those who lived in them would go into them over the top....

Mr. Moraga assures me that there is no water on the Island, and that he did not find any traces of arrows, pots, or other utensils of the people who must have inhabited the said place; neither could he see any marks of fires, nor any indications that the said habitations had been covered over with roofs. (Forbes [1893]:27–29)

With an admirable display of interest tempered by cautious skepticism, Forbes concluded that Moraga's "description of these ruins, if such they can be called, is somewhat curious, and may deserve investigation for the benefit of the Smithsonian Institute" (Forbes [1893]:29).

A year later, R. E. L. Robinson's party, en route to Tiburón Island, heard of the road (which by now was attributed to the Aztecs) while they were ashore at Bahía de los Ángeles. When they departed, they detoured to Ángel de la Guarda for a look, but were unable to spot it from their sloop:

Since daylight have been sailing along the shore of the Bay looking for evidences of the Aztec road but have found none.... None of us have gone ashore on this portion of the island and we have perhaps overlooked the road. If we get a fair wind tonight we will go direct to Tiburon and investigate this later. (Robinson 1894:35)

Two days later, May 25, 1894, Robinson's party landed on Tiburón Island, and the day after that, Robinson and his companion James Logan were dead (see pp. 247–53). Whatever structures Moraga actually saw, word of strange remains on Ángel de la Guarda quickly became established as regional lore. Half a year later and on the other side of the Gulf, WJ McGee was told of "a stone roadway 9 miles long, a cemetery, [and] a village of 178 stone houses" by Sonoran rancher Pascual Encinas (McGee 1894:November 4). "Arizona Charlie" Meadows, who had known Robinson, referred to them in a 1902 newspaper interview (King 1989:221). Rex Beach heard about them during a fishing trip in the Gulf around 1920 (Beach 1927:266), and in 1921 the scientists of the California Academy of Sciences expedition unsuccessfully searched for them at the southeast tip of the island (Slevin 1923:69). As late as 1930, Griffing Bancroft remarked disdainfully that "Rumors and tales of flowing water and weird occupants [on Ángel de la Guarda] circulate all over the Gulf and even find their way into print" (Bancroft 1932:354).

Had the Smithsonian launched an archaeological expedition to Ángel de la Guarda, as Forbes suggested, it is uncertain what it would have found to correspond with Moraga's "macadamized road." But it unquestionably would have found dry-laid stone structures, which are conspicuous features on that part of the island. As for Moraga's coin, there is little doubt that it was a common, and contemporary, Moroccan 2 or 3 *falus* piece. The "double triangle" is the seal of Solomon, and the startling 1288 date is based on the Mohammedan calendar (*Anno Hegira*). Year 1 in this system corresponds with A.D. 622, when Mohammed fled from Mecca to Medina, and each year contains only 354 days. Hence Moraga's 1288 coin was actually minted in A.D. 1871, only about 20 years before he found it (Krause and Mishler 1994:1468–69, 2127). Nor is its presence on Ángel de la Guarda a great mystery, for it has been a widespread practice among sailors and other travelers to pick up common low denomination coins as cheap souvenirs or good luck pieces, often passing them on to others, or eventually losing them far from their country of origin.

Archaeology on the Sonoran side of the Gulf began with WJ McGee's 1894 and 1895 expeditions to the Seris. Although these were primarily ethnographic investigations, McGee interpreted, no doubt correctly, the archaeological sites his party encountered as old Seri camps. Throughout his report, descriptions of these remains are interspersed with his account of contemporary Seri material culture (McGee 1898).

In an important sense, ethnography in the Gulf region began with descriptions of peninsular Indians by the earliest Spanish pearling expeditions. In most of Baja California, the ethnographic record of the aboriginal inhabitants ended with the virtual extinction of those peoples by the late eighteenth century. For Sonora, descriptions of Seri culture began in the seventeenth century and flowed more or less continuously through the nineteenth century. The majority of these, however, describe displaced Seris located outside their traditional territory, often under hostile or heavily Europeanized conditions. This lends special importance to the reports of observers such as Iturbe (Cardona), Ortega, Salvatierra, Ugarte, Kino, and Hardy, who visited the Seris on their own turf, on the Sonoran coast and Tiburón Island. In the nineteenth century, the emerging interest in the natural history of the Gulf also extended to ethnography and especially linguistics. A number of Mexicans as well as North American and European scientific visitors to Sonora took time off from their principal pursuits to arrange interviews with Seris. These superficial encounters, conducted in the safety of Mexican communities, succeeded in obtaining short vocabularies of the Seri language and limited cultural data (McGee 1898:84–108). However, it was not until WJ McGee's expeditions that a scientific investigation was organized with Seri ethnography as its principle objective.

In most respects, McGee's first visit to the Seris in November 1894 was little different from previous superficial studies. It was undertaken as an unplanned side trip during an expedition to study the Tohono O'odham (Papagos), and his contact with the Seris, spanning about a week, took place in the thoroughly Mexican setting of Pascual Encinas's Rancho San Francisco de la Costa Rica (Figure 9.11). But McGee was fascinated by what he saw, and the following year he outfitted an expedition specifically to conduct further interviews at the Encinas's ranch and to make a collection of Seri material culture for the Bureau

Figure 9.11   William John McGee (1853–1912), with notebook and revolver, poses with Juan Chávez, one of the Seris camped at Costa Rica Ranch. Photograph by William Dinwiddie, November 1894. (From McGee 1898.)

of American Ethnology. Unfortunately, his timing could not have been worse, for a series of armed skirmishes and hostile government actions had greatly damaged Seri-Mexican relations in the intervening year. When McGee arrived in early December, the Seris had long since fled the ranch to Tiburón Island. Unwilling to give up, McGee had a makeshift boat constructed, and he and a dozen men boldly crossed the Canal del Infiernillo to Tiburón Island in pursuit of the elusive Seris (Figure 9.12).

Figure 9.12   The first anthropological expedition to Tiburón Island. WJ McGee's camp at "Sandspit Rancheria," looking across the Canal del Infiernillo toward the Sierra Seri on the Sonoran mainland. Photograph by J. W. Mitchell, December 1895. (Courtesy National Anthropological Archives, Smithsonian Institution, Washington, D.C. [No. 4283-A-2].)

McGee's journal (McGee [1895] 1983) graphically records their eight harrowing days on Tiburón Island. For the first three days the party was fearful of being marooned, for their rickety boat, sent back to the mainland for supplies, had been unable to recross the channel. By the time it finally arrived, nearly everyone's shoes had been literally torn to shreds by the island's sharp rocks, and some were wrapping their lacerated feet in canvas. Most of their days were consumed by exhausting trips to the nearest waterhole for water, which they drank about as fast as they could haul it, and their nights were spent alternately standing guard against the threat of Seri attack (Figure 9.13). The desperate mood of the expedition is reflected in McGee's names for some of their camps: Camp Thirsty, Camp Disappointment, Camp Despair. On December 28, with food and water nearly gone, the party took advantage of a temporary lull in the stormy sea and managed to retreat across the channel to the mainland.

But for McGee, the ordeal was not yet over. In the afternoon, he set out alone on the long walk to Bahía Kino, expecting to return with badly needed food and water from the support party that was to meet them there. But neither men nor supplies were anywhere to be found. In desperation, McGee turned inland and grimly set out across the desert for Costa Rica ranch, walking through the night, accompanied only by the unrelieved terror that Seris might be stalking him and patiently waiting for the right moment to kill him. Just before sunrise, McGee

Figure 9.13   Armed anthropology. Samuel C. Millard stands guard at McGee's "Sandspit Rancheria" camp, Tiburón Island. Photograph by J. W. Mitchell, December 1895. (Courtesy Special Collections, University of Arizona Library, Tucson [No. 6780].)

stumbled into the courtyard of Costa Rica ranch. It had been "Fifty-two miles ... over terrible walking, the last 17 hours without sitting down. I have had some hard tramps before, but this is the hardest" (McGee [1895] 1983:55).

During their eight days on Tiburón Island, the expedition failed to encounter a single Seri, perhaps a mixed blessing considering the hostile state of affairs. As a collecting trip, however, the venture was a success, for McGee hauled back to the mainland some 300 pounds of artifacts. Reflecting the ethics of the time, McGee was evidently not troubled by the fact that many of the items he collected were Seri personal property, taken from camps only temporarily abandoned. In keeping with the naturalist tradition, he managed to find time to collect a number of plant and animal specimens and take copious notes on the natural history of the island. In this, he was not the first, for 51 years earlier Thomas Spence of Guaymas had made brief notes on the geography and animals he had seen on the island while rounding up Seris for Colonel Francisco Andrade. But McGee's observations, both on Tiburón and the mainland, were detailed and extensive, which enabled him to put together a comprehensive physical description of the entire Seri region (McGee 1898:22–50). He even included a short remark about San Esteban Island (McGee 1898:49), though he had not visited it.

As to ethnography, McGee's only Seri interview of the second trip was conducted on January 3, 1896, with a thoroughly Mexicanized Seri living in Hermosillo (Fontana 1971; Fontana and Fontana 1983). Two years later, this fleeting contact and his brief interviews with Seris at Costa Rica ranch in 1894 became the nucleus for his classic 344-page monograph on the Seris (McGee 1898).

Commenting on the brevity of McGee's actual contact with live Seris, Bernard Fontana wryly observed that "Rarely in the annals of anthropology has so much been written based on so little field work"(Fontana 1971). But as Fontana also noted, McGee's monograph encompasses much more than just Seri ethnography. In addition to the comprehensive natural history, McGee included a detailed human history of Seri-European contacts which was a tour-de-force of documentary research that has had few equals since. Though the ethnology itself is deeply flawed by today's standards for its excessive speculation and rigid adherence to a unilinear evolutionary perspective (Kroeber 1931:18–28; Hinsley 1981:240–44), McGee's study nonetheless marks the beginning of modern Seri ethnography, and his voyage into the Gulf stands as the first and by far the most daring anthropological investigation ever undertaken on Tiburón Island.

As the nineteenth century drew to a close, all of the Midriff islands had been charted, and a few had been visited by trained naturalists. As for San Esteban Island, however, it was still scientifically unknown territory. The century ended without a single person having set foot there in the interest of science.

TEN

Punishing the Seris (II):
Mexican Military Expeditions to Tiburón Island

The nineteenth century brought little change in Seri-European relations. Throughout the 1800s, periods of relative tranquillity gave way
to new cycles of raids and retaliatory expeditions. As ranches began to
encroach on traditional Seri territory, the conflict increasingly took the form
of small but deadly skirmishes between Seris and Mexican cowboys. The government also continued to mount formal military expeditions aimed, as always,
at rounding up and containing, punishing, or exterminating the Seris once and
for all. A few of these campaigns brought soldiers to Tiburón Island. One of
them, the Seris say, resulted in the extinction of the San Esteban people.

Seri raids had continued to plague European settlers as the eighteenth century drew to a close (McGee 1898:80–81; Kessell 1975:85–90). Late in 1798,
the Spanish authorities contemplated sending a military expedition to Tiburón
Island in July of the following year. It was believed that 250 Seri warriors, along
with their families, were holed up on the island, and the Spaniards were bent on
exterminating them. The plan for the campaign was devised by Pedro de Nava,
the Commander in Chief of the Interior Provinces. It called for a force of 300
soldiers, supplemented by a contingent of auxiliaries, to be transported to the
island by a frigate and three launches brought up from Guaymas. Although the
expedition would be supported by 100 cavalrymen, they would not be taken to
the island. Nava, it seems, had been misled by an elderly Hispanicized Seri into
thinking that the terrain was too rough for horses and that there were neither
trees nor grasses on Tiburón for pasturage (Nava [1798] 1999:449).

It would therefore be up to the foot soldiers to scour the island's shores and
burn balsas to prevent the Seris from escaping. They would then fan out in three
columns over the entire island to hunt down the trapped Indians. Significantly,
Nava also proposed that:

At the time of the attack ... two or three canoes for [pearl] divers should be
stationed with armed men on the west side of Tiburón to prevent the natives

fleeing punishment from passing over to the three small islands about six or
seven leagues in that direction. The landing crafts can occupy themselves in
the same procedure while the operation lasts on the island. The operation will
continue until we are certain that all of the inhabitants have been either im-
prisoned or killed....

Once the Tiburón expedition is accomplished and everything is paid for,
I believe that the three islands mentioned previously and those farther out
named Salsipuedes and San Agustín should be scrupulously reconnoitered.
Then, certain that no enemy remains in that area, all our attention should be
devoted to the Apache frontier. (Nava [1798] 1999:450)

Nava was obviously confused about the geography and nomenclature of the
Midriff region. The "three small islands" are presumably San Esteban and the two
islands of San Lorenzo, which at the time were often referred to collectively as the
"Salsipuedes" islands, while "San Agustín" is simply the name Father Kino had
mistakenly applied to Tiburón Island. Despite the confusion, Nava clearly believed
that San Esteban and the neighboring islands served the Seris as refuges, though
nothing in his remarks suggests that he thought any Indians lived there.

Although troops did amass on the coast the following summer, the expedition never crossed to Tiburón Island (Arrillaga [1802] 1999:453). Yet in Baja
California, Interim Governor José Joaquín de Arrillaga was convinced that this
threatened invasion had provoked the Seris into scouting the other Midriff islands as possible places of refuge. Worse still, he believed that the Seris had
already used these islands as a staging ground for a raid on the peninsula in 1802
and that they might use them to launch additional attacks. As he explained to
the Viceroy in November 1802:

The reverend father minister of the mission of Santa Gertrudis advised me
... that on the nineteenth of [September] he gave permission to an Indian to
go to the beach in the early evening with some women. Five apparently unknown Indians appeared, struck him, and took his clothes. The Indians wanted
to do the same to the women, but fortunately they fled with the darkness of
night, although some of the women's clothing was also taken.

[The reverend father] sent another two Indians at the beginning of October in search of shells for lime. The [unknown Indians] killed one of them.
The other fled after seeing his companion wounded. Nonetheless, they pursued him as he fled and gave him three nonfatal blows. This Indian also did
not know the malefactors. He knew only that they wore the clothes of the
Indian maltreated in the incident of [September] 19, and those of the women
who were in his company. He also noted that there were six in the group....

...[Later], two of the malefactors came at night to scout the mission. But
the vigilant soldier saw them and shot at them. The following morning he followed their tracks with some Indians from the mission, but he could not find
them because they had taken to the hills and rocky ground....

My speculations are that they could be Indians from Tiburón Island, situated on the coast of Sonora. Three years ago, the Sonoran troops attempted an expedition to the island. They gathered on the coast, where they remained for part of the summer of 1799. The expedition was not carried out because the Indians knew of the superior size of this force.

Without a doubt, the Indians wanted to reconnoiter the islands close to the coast of this peninsula as a retreat [in order to] avoid similar surprises. For this reason, they have come and performed the evil deeds to which I have referred.

There is not the least doubt that this [development] will have disastrous consequences because this coast is completely defenseless. They will continue to make hostile incursions by way of the nearby islands as they please or when the weather is moderate and as they gain knowledge of the water holes afforded by the various islands between Tiburón and California Antigua. (Arrillaga [1802] 1999:452–53)

Four months later, in March 1803, Arrillaga again wrote the Viceroy to tell him that the threat of further Seri attack would increase in May, when the Gulf calmed, and that both Santa Gertrudis and San Borja, directly across the Gulf from Tiburón Island, were vulnerable. And again, he implicated the Midriff islands as Seri points of departure for raids:

Because the coast [of the peninsula] extends for a great distance and there are various islands, some farther away than others, situated along it running from south to north like the coastline, the Indians can travel with impunity among them all as they please, although some [of the islands] do not have water. Likewise, they can disembark wherever it suits them. They could be driven away if there were adequate vessels for this purpose, but there are not. (Arrillaga [1803] 1999:454)

The solution, argued Arrillaga, was to eliminate the problem at its source, which he took to be Tiburón Island:

For next year, that is in the month of May 1804, if it please Your Excellency, consult with the commandant general of the Provincias Internas on the most appropriate means of exterminating once and for all that nation which has caused so much harm.... In 1799, the commandancia general arranged an expedition to attack Tiburón Island, but ... it did not take place because some English ships entered the gulf.

Such an expedition demands the greatest secrecy, however. The one formed in 1799 failed because the Seris and Tiburones learned, even before the troops gathered at the coast, that they were going to be attacked. It is to be expected that they will not trust us, and I believe this is the reason for their coming to scout this coast last summer. Moreover, I believe that they have made many balsas as a precaution. (Arrillaga [1803] 1999:454)

Arrillaga's fears of continuing Seri raids on the peninsula may have been well founded. In 1824, Fray Francisco Troncoso wrote that Tiburón Island:

> has more than 1000 barbaric inhabitants, enemies of the [Baja] Californians, and it has often occurred that, on cane balsas ... they cross over to invade this mission [of Loreto], killing and robbing some of those from there. It would be very advantageous to reduce these islanders, and relocate them to San José del Cabo. (Troncoso 1849:18)

Both Arrillaga and Troncoso had naturally assumed that the Seris perpetrating the raids were from Tiburón Island, because that is the island the Seris were known to inhabit. If, as Seri oral accounts suggest, the raiders were actually members of the San Esteban band, rather than island-hopping Seris from Tiburón Island, there is probably no way that these two writers would have known it.

Arrillaga's pleas for help may have resulted in some official consideration of an expedition to Tiburón, but apparently no immediate action was taken (Bancroft 1889:628). In 1807, however, Seri raids on Sonoran settlements prompted Governor Alejo García Conde to assemble a force of 1,000 men in Guaymas in preparation for a new invasion of the island. But troubles between Spain and France seem to have interfered with the expedition, and as in 1799, the troops probably never set foot on Tiburón. In any event, it was the last Spanish plan to invade the island before Mexico won her independence (Velasco 1850:132; McGee 1898:83).

During the years from 1825 to 1832, Sonorans were preoccupied with an extended revolt of the Yaqui Indians, whose leader Juan de la Banderas hoped to enlist the Seris and other Indians as allies. In August 1826, Banderas captured a large shipment of Mexican supplies, part of which he hauled to the Seri coast opposite Tiburón Island as inducement for the Seris to join his cause. The Yaquis were met on the coast by a Mexican force, but in the ensuing battle, the Mexican troops were unable to prevent the rebels from ferrying the goods across the channel to the Seris on the island. A few Seris seem to have joined the Yaqui cause, but their role was evidently not a large one (Hardy [1829] 1977:395–97; Forbes 1957:343–45; Spicer 1980:130–34).

By the early 1840s, Seri raids were on the increase, and the Sonoran government found itself under heavy public pressure to mount a reprisal. The response came in the summer of 1842, when General José Urrea drew up plans for a combined land and sea expedition to Tiburón Island. The troops were to be led in the field by Captain Victor Araiza, and this land force was to receive naval support from the schooner *Sonorense* and some launches. The entire expedition was to be personally commanded by General Urrea.

Following his initial instructions, Araiza led his men northwest to Tastiota, where he was under orders to await Urrea and the ships. After much waiting, and with no sign of either the general or the vessels, the exasperated Araiza took the campaign into his own hands and marched his soldiers to Carrizal, near

Bahía Kino. Here he managed to surprise an unsuspecting group of Seris, killing 11 of them, including women and children, and taking four children captive. But Araiza's impulsive attack proved to be both a military and public relations blunder. Not only had he failed to subdue the Seris, but his action was widely condemned by the Mexican community as cruel and inhumane (Velasco 1850:124–25; Voss 1982:101–2).

In reaction to the Araiza fiasco, Acting Governor Francisco Poncé de León authorized a second, and more ambitious, joint land and sea expedition to Tiburón Island. Its purpose was to round up the Indians and relocate them in Pueblo de Seris, on the outskirts of Hermosillo, where it was thought they could be kept from causing trouble. The entire operation was placed under the command of Colonel Francisco Andrade, who would lead the land force of 30 cavalry and more than 220 infantry. In charge of the naval auxiliary was pilot Thomas Spence (known locally as Tomás Espence) of Guaymas, whose fleet consisted of a chartered 12-ton schooner, two armed launches, and a rowboat. Setting out from Guaymas on August 11, 1844, Spence's vessels arrived six days later at Bahía Kino, where they rendezvoused with the advance guard of Andrade's forces (Andrade 1850:175–76; Spence 1850:164).

Their first concern was for water, for both Andrade's men and Spence's sailors had already exhausted their supplies. While mules were dispatched to the spring at Carrizal, Spence crossed the channel with a detachment of five soldiers to try to locate a water supply on Tiburón Island. As Spence and his sailors searched in vain, the soldiers managed to find a water hole, but it was surrounded by Seris who immediately attacked them. So thirsty were the soldiers that they each drank, one at a time, while the others held off the Indians. Eventually, they beat a retreat, having killed two Seris, but they were unable to bring any water with them. That night they regrouped with Spence and his sailors on shore and the entire party, with raging thirsts, sailed back to the mainland. To their relief, Andrade's mules returned from Carrizal the next day with water.

On August 21, Spence began ferrying troops, animals, and supplies over to Tiburón, and a base camp was established at a good waterhole on the eastern side of the island (which they named Aguaje Andrade). From here, Andrade sent his soldiers out on patrol to various parts of the island in search of Seris. Meanwhile Spence, his ferrying task completed, was free to set out on a different mission. Leaving the schooner and one launch with the troops, he set sail on August 26 in the other launch with eight men, a cannon, and five rifles, and headed northward into the Canal del Infiernillo with the intention of circumnavigating the island (Spence 1850:167).

On the 27th, Spence reached Tecomate, where he found the well-known waterhole, a Seri camp, and skeletons of stolen horses, but no Indians. Here, acting on Andrade's orders, he initiated a policy of burning Seri huts and balsas wherever he found them, hoping to force the Indians into surrender by destroying their means of subsistence. From Tecomate, he sailed around the northwest point of the island, and for the next two days cruised along the cliffs of the western shore, finally reaching Bahía Vaporeta:

On August 30 we arrived at a very large bay on the west side of the island, and at the back of it we found many huts and fresh signs of Indians. I went ashore with four men, leaving the others on board. I scouted the tracks and followed them until we came to a very wide swale [where] we captured a woman who had been bitten by a rattlesnake; this was about two or three miles from the beach. I had two of the men carry her and one of the others carry the rifles of their companions, leaving me with only one man for defense. We walked in this manner the distance to the launch without being bothered, [despite] there being more than forty or fifty Indians hidden in the bush. At times it was difficult to get the sailors to follow me, because they were afraid that the Indians would cut off our retreat to the launch, but finally they took courage at seeing that nothing had happened to us. As soon as I put the woman in the launch, I cured her with a little aguardiente [liquor], lacking anything else. The reason I captured her was so that she might show us the water holes, and reveal to us where on the island the Indians were hidden.

With the tides having changed in our favor and a wind springing up, I departed and continued cruising to the opposite side of the bay, about two leagues from our point of departure. With a telescope I spotted a group of Indians [hiding] with their heads sticking out of the grass. I decided to attack them and headed for shore. As soon as they realized that we had seen them, they rose up with their customary shrieks, limbered their bows, and came running to the beach getting ready to attack me. There were around twenty or thirty of them, and at the same time we could make out another party of about forty Indians coming toward the beach from the place where we captured the woman. These [Indians] joined the others, forming two lines and waiting for me, with arrows in their bows, making a thousand gestures and shouts. I placed the launch between the two lines of them and, at a distance of half a pistol shot, dropped anchor and uncovered the cannon. As I was taking aim, an Indian knelt down in front of us with an enormous wooden cross. I held my fire and asked what he wanted. He replied, "Peace."

I invited the ringleaders on board and seventeen of them came. They agreed unconditionally to place themselves at the will of the government and [agreed] that they would all have to leave the island. I gave them a letter to be taken and presented to Colonel Andrade. In all there were seventy-four armed men, in addition to women and little children who were in the shelter of a hill.

[With] this business concluded ... I continued cruising the coast until the first day of September at six in the afternoon. At the southwestern point of the island we came to another great bay, and since we had no water we went to the back of it with the hope of finding some. [When we] arrived on shore, we encountered an Indian with his wife and young child. I seized them but they were unable to speak a word of Spanish. I made him understand that we wanted water, and I sent him off with a cask, taking the precaution of keeping his wife and son as hostages. I gave them food, and around eight in the evening he arrived with the water, and with him came thirty to forty Indians asking for peace. I made them all bed down on the beach until daybreak, and then I sent them to fill my water barrels, dispatching with them two sailors to find out where [the water] was. When they returned I offered them peace under the same conditions as the others, and [gave] them a letter for Andrade. As I [now] had enough water, and was at the southern point [of Tiburón], not far from my point of departure on the island, I took on board one of their worst ringleaders, one who had committed many killings, some sick women, and a few young children. On the 3rd [of September] I arrived at the spot where I had set out, having circumnavigated the island in a period of nine days [and] having, during this time, burned seventy-four huts, ninety-seven balsas, and pacified one hundred four Indians with their families. (Spence 1850:167–69)

Because so many of the Seris were willing to surrender to the Mexican forces, the expedition ended with few Indian deaths. Just how many were rounded up, however, is unclear. Andrade indicated that around 210 Indians were taken prisoner while Spence put the total number of captives at 510 (Andrade 1850:180–81; Spence 1850:169; McGee 1898:90). Whatever the number, from the Mexican perspective, the roundup of so many Seris made the campaign a great success, even though most of the captives were women and children. The prisoners and soldiers were soon transported to Bahía Kino and marched to Hermosillo. While Andrade and his men received a hero's welcome, the adult Seris were deposited in Pueblo de Seris and their children, taken from them, were distributed among Mexican families throughout the city. Predictably, this solution was no more effective than in the past, and within weeks, both children and adults began to escape to the coast. Before the end of the year, the old pattern of raids and reprisals had resumed (McGee 1898:91).

Though Spence's circumnavigation of Tiburón Island had taken him within eight miles of San Esteban, he did not go there. Since the entire purpose of the expedition was to capture and remove Seris from their island refuge, he must not have thought any Seris would be there or he surely would have crossed the channel and tried to find them. Yet it is hard not to wonder whether he actually did encounter some San Esteban people on Tiburón Island in the docile folk he found near Punta Willard. If so, Spence was certainly unaware of the distinction.

The next punitive expedition to Tiburón Island was the direct result of one of the most notorious incidents in Seri-Mexican relations. This was the abduction of the young Mexican woman Dolores (Lola) Casanova. On February 23, 1850, a caravan that included Casanova and several members of her family was traveling along the road from Hermosillo to Guaymas when it was attacked by a band of about 20 Seris. In the ensuing fight, 13 of the Mexicans were killed and seven, including the young Lola, were carried off as captives. Most accounts maintain that Casanova was taken as a wife by the leader of the attackers, a Seri man called Coyote Iguana (also known as Jesús Ávila), and that she lived for some time afterwards among the Seris.

The kidnapping of Lola Casanova was such a sensational event that the entire episode has become deeply enshrined in both Seri oral tradition and Mexican legend (Lowell 1970). Many Seris today claim descent from Casanova and Coyote Iguana through their son, Victor Ávila. However, they also believe she was later recaptured and returned to Sonora by a Mexican military expedition. In most Mexican versions (which includes romantic novels and even a motion picture) she lived out her life among the Seris, though it was also rumored that she secretly returned to her family and was quietly sent off to live with relatives elsewhere (Lowell 1970:158).

But legends aside, the attack on the Casanova party and its aftermath were documented at the time by the Mexicans who were directly involved. A small military force was immediately sent out from Guaymas in search of the Seri attackers and their captives. When it returned empty-handed, the Sonoran government launched a formal campaign against the Seris, consisting of more than 100 men and two vessels, under the command of Col. Cayetano Navarro. The government provided additional incentive by offering a bounty of $150 pesos for each dead Seri warrior and $50 pesos for each captive (Parra and Astiasaran 1850).

The initial action took place on March 12, when Navarro's forces clashed with some Seris at a place called Batamote. But the Mexicans were determined to pursue the Seris to Tiburón Island, where they believed Casanova and the other captives had been taken. By late March, Navarro had established his troops at the Carrizal waterhole near Bahía Kino. Early on Thursday, March 28, an advance party led by Sergeant José Gallegos crossed the channel and made a landing on Tiburón Island. At 3 P.M., after most of the soldiers had dispersed, a lone balsa appeared at the landing place, paddled by Coyote Iguana himself. Gallegos conferred with him through his interpreters and immediately departed for the mainland to report to Navarro. According to Navarro, the Seri leader had told Gallegos:

> that he wanted peace ... and that the interpreters should return the day after tomorrow to take possession of the captives.... He offered to assemble his people in order to deal with me [Navarro] about peace.... Since he was not in the action at Batamote, he believed the captives whom they left there were dead. The others were on the far side of the Island, and he would bring them on Saturday [March 30] and deliver them to the interpreters. (Navarro 1850a)

When Coyote Iguana appeared on Saturday, he was again alone. Explaining that the balsas needed to bring the captives were far away, he promised that they would be delivered early Sunday morning. But by this time, Navarro had lost his patience, and so before dawn on Sunday, March 31, he ordered his entire force to the island to search for the Seris and the remaining Mexican captives. One detachment was sent immediately across the island while another set out that evening by launch to reconnoiter the north coast. Early Monday morning, Navarro himself led the main force toward the southwest coast. About eight miles from the coast, he encountered a friendly Seri who told him that an entire ranchería of Indians was camped at a large waterhole not far away and intended to escape. According to the Indian:

> twenty-some adult men and twice that number of women and children ... were thinking about embarking to the Island of the West. In view of this situation ...

I chose two detachments of 25 infantry [and] placed them, with their respective commanders, under the direction of Matéo [a Seri guide], with orders to track them [the Seris] down to the departure point for the aforementioned Island of the West. (Navarro 1850a)

The island that lies to the west (actually southwest) of Tiburón is, of course, San Esteban, and this is probably where these Seris intended to hide out. How many of them actually got there is uncertain, but at least a dozen were captured the next day near *Xapij* waterhole in Arroyo Sauzal, before they ever reached the coast.

Over the next two weeks, the detachments sent to the other parts of Tiburón also managed to capture or kill a few Seris. On April 7, Navarro and his troops clashed with some Seris on tiny Dátil Island, just off the southern tip of Tiburón. By the time this skirmish was over, the Mexicans had executed five Seri men by firing squad, taken two women prisoner, and left an elderly woman stranded on the island to die of thirst (Navarro 1850b, 1850c).

By the middle of April, the various detachments had returned, and the entire expedition had regrouped and sailed back to the mainland. Navarro briefly considered taking his soldiers up the mainland coast north of Tiburón Island, where some Seris had reportedly fled. But by this time, troop morale and logistic support had begun to deteriorate, so instead he drew the campaign to a close.

Navarro's report to the Governor, submitted April 24, included an annotated list of the 12 Seris killed or executed and the 32 captured, perhaps in anticipation of the government bounty offered at the inception of the campaign (Navarro 1850c). But he said little of the Mexican captives whom the expedition had set out to liberate in the first place. Navarro did report the grim news that Lola Casanova was dead. On the day his troops crossed to Tiburón Island, hostile Seris had let him know through his interpreters that she had been executed a few hours after the March 12 action at Batamote, in retribution for the death of a Seri woman who had been wounded in this skirmish (Navarro 1850a; 1850c). However, without her body, Navarro had no proof of this, and hence was merely repeating what the Indians had told him. It would not be farfetched to suppose that the Seris, discovering the importance of Casanova to the Mexicans, fabricated her death in the hope that the soldiers would have no reason to continue the campaign.

Navarro was cautiously optimistic that the expedition had subdued the Seris and made the road from Guaymas to Hermosillo safe for travelers, but Seri depredations quickly resumed. Within a year, he proposed another military operation, this time with adequate preparation and supplies. It was to consist of 100 infantry and 20 cavalry, and provisioned for three months (Navarro 1851). Although the Sonoran legislature authorized the campaign, including the use of two vessels that would enable the force to land on Tiburón Island, the expedition apparently never materialized.

By this time, ranches had begun to push the Mexican frontier west and northwest from Hermosillo to the fringes of the Seri coast. The first and most famous of these was the Rancho de San Francisco de la Costa Rica, founded in 1844 by

Figure 10.1
Pascual Encinas (ca.
1819–1903), cofounder of
the Rancho San Francisco
de la Costa Rica, with
WJ McGee in the
background. Photograph
by William Dinwiddie,
November 1894.
(Courtesy National
Anthropological Archives,
Smithsonian Institution,
Washington, D.C.
[No. 4277-B-8].)

two brothers, Pascual and Ignacio Encinas (Figure 10.1) (Thomson 1989). For a while, Seris and Mexicans coexisted in relative peace on this new frontier. But good relations did not last, for Seris began to steal livestock for food, and the Encinas' cowboys began to kill Seris in reprisal. The Seris responded in kind, and a vicious cycle of mutual killings between about 1855 and 1865 is thought to have wiped out around half the Seri population (McGee 1898:109–14).

By the late 1870s, Seri numbers and range had been greatly reduced, and in some formerly dangerous places, such as the road from Guaymas to Hermosillo, there had been no incidents in many years. But the ranches springing up along the Seri frontier, from Caborca to Tastiota, were a different matter (Corral [1885] 1959:257–59). Early in 1879, a French traveler and scholar named Alphonse Pinart intended to visit the Seri coast but upon reaching Caborca was dissuaded by the news that Seris had recently sacked a nearby ranch, killing more than a dozen Mexicans (McGee 1898:106–7, 116). This and other incidents about the same time persuaded Governor Luis E. Torres to order yet another military expedition to capture the Indians and remove them to Pueblo

*Figure 10.2   Ramón Corral (1854–1912), formerly Governor of Sonora,
photographed in 1904 as the new Vice President of Mexico. (Courtesy Huntington Library,
San Marino, California [CL 249 (61)].)*

de Seris. As recounted five years later by Torres's successor, Ramón Corral
(Figure 10.2):

> Periodically, these savages have rebelled, and not only to rob cattle that can
> be found within their range, but also to kill the residents of the coastal ranches.
> In 1880 they carried out one of their revolts; [and] the State Government saw
> the necessity of initiating a campaign against them. It was successful in seiz-
> ing as prisoners about one hundred fifty of them, among them men, women
> and children, who were brought to this capital [Hermosillo]. In order to pre-
> vent their returning to their old life of disorder, they were placed in a kind of
> reservation in the Pueblo de Seris. A chief for them was appointed from this
> same tribe, [and it was his duty] not only to guard them and maintain order,
> but he was also the interpreter with whom the authorities could communicate.
> With a subsidy that was paid by the Federal Government and with assistance
> from the State's revenues, they were given an abundant daily ration of meat,
> corn, and beans to live on. It was like this for several months and the Govern-
> ment was busy searching for a way to use these Indians in a manner which,
> while rendering some service to agriculture, would gradually create [among
> them] a habit and taste for work. But all the training projects on this matter
> remained entirely unrealized. Then one night they revolted, tying up and
> almost assassinating the chief who had been appointed for them, and fleeing

to the coast to rejoin the rest of the tribe and follow their nomadic and savage life. (Corral [1885] 1959:258)

It was the last time the Sonoran government tried to forcibly resettle the Indians in Pueblo de Seris, and the Seris may have had compelling reasons for trying to escape:

Seris believe that on at least one occasion [during the incarceration] Mexicans expressed their hatred for Seris by poisoning the rations; when some Indians became gravely ill and a few died, the rest managed to escape. Only a few remained behind to become absorbed into the Mexican population. (Spicer 1962:113)

Some modern Seris have connected this incident with the last of the San Esteban people, thinking that the few who had survived the roundup and initial killings were incarcerated at Pueblo de Seris, where they fell sick and died (see pp. 27–29). However, the 1880 campaign seems to have been entirely a land operation carried out on the mainland coast directly across from Tiburón Island. Apparently, soldiers never crossed the channel to Tiburón, much less San Esteban. This makes it very unlikely that the campaign had anything to do with the extermination of the San Esteban people, although it is conceivable that a few of them might have been inadvertently included among those who were relocated.

The 1880 roundup did not, of course, end the conflict. As Seris escaped back to the coast, the old pattern of raids and reprisals resumed along the frontier and continued throughout the 1880s. Federal troops as well as cowboys were sometimes sent out in pursuit of marauding Indians, frequently leading to pitched battles and often dead Seris. But the towns and roads were no longer threatened, and officially, the government considered the raids of minor importance (Corral [1885] 1959:258–59; Troncoso 1905:18).

One person who rejected the government's tranquil portrayal of the period was Roberto Thomson Encinas (Figure 10.3), a Sonoran who was in a unique position to evaluate these times. Thomson was a grandnephew of Pascual Encinas and knew the reality of conditions on the frontier at first hand. He had spent part of his youth at Costa Rica ranch and had once ridden with ranch cowboys in pursuit of a Seri raiding party, a reprisal that had cost three of the cowboys their lives (Thomson 1931:138). He had also seen wanton brutalization of the Indians at the hands of ranchers and government. In the 1910s, he took up the Seri cause, became a government liaison agent to the Indians, and over the next two decades became a familiar visitor and a friend to the Seris. Though he was no ethnographer, these experiences gave him a good knowledge of both Mexican and Seri perspectives on that era. According to Thomson, the two decades from 1880 to 1900 were an especially dark period for the Seris. With a silent nod from official circles, a bounty of $3 pesos was placed on each male Seri head. Atrocities were committed as Seris were hunted for sport as well

Figure 10.3   Roberto Thomson E.(1888–1969) poses with Seris at Bahía Kino, 1935.
Back row, left to right: *Juan Tomás, Chico Romero, Roberto Thomson, Antonio Herrera.*
(Courtesy Arizona State Museum, University of Arizona, Tucson [No. Pix-1212].)

as profit, and whole families were wiped out. Thomson maintains that detailed information on this period is very hard to come by. Civil authorities sometimes knew little of what was actually happening, and official reports are often so truncated and vague as to be of little value. Moreover, Mexicans who were participants in these events would seldom reveal much about this portion of their lives, and some would distance themselves from these incidents by attributing their own actions to their forebears (Thomson n.d.).

Vague and possibly incomplete reporting seems to extend even to the largest formal military action of this period. It began in June 1890 as a skirmish of little consequence, but it immediately escalated into a formal punitive expedition to Tiburón Island. This in turn triggered a major revolt of Seris on the mainland that took government troops nearly half a year to quell. The incident that precipitated these events was an armed clash off the coast of San Esteban Island between Seris in a canoe and the crew of a Mexican sloop. The official Mexican version of the skirmish was first reported in a telegram sent on June 3 to Governor Corral by Lieut. José Urgell, commander of the Guaymas garrison:

> The steamer "Romero Rubio," which arrived today from Rasa Island, brought two wounded individuals. According to what they said, they were in an attack which the Seri Indians staged on the domestic sloop "Playa Colorada," on which they were crew members. The boat was anchored off the

North part of San Esteban Island when it was attacked. According to what they told me, ten Indians attacked, and they were armed with Winchester carbines. (Urgell 1890)

The two sailors, José Dolores Lucero and Cirilio Talamante, were taken to the Guaymas public hospital. Although they had sustained only "Slight wounds in the arms" (Aguilar 1890), the government response was immediate and forceful. But it was also, according to the one available official account, ineffective. As Governor Corral reported to the Sonoran legislature:

On account of this [incident], the commanding general of the region ordered the gunboat 'Demócrata,' with 50 men aboard from the 27th Battalion, under the command of Captain Alberto Méndez, and with an interpreter that I sent from this capital, to look for the Seris of Tiburón. The forces disembarked on that island but all the efforts they expended trying to find the Indians were useless, and they returned to Guaymas without obtaining results. (Corral 1891:368–69)

But Roberto Thomson recounts this episode quite differently. As to the original skirmish, he says that:

The Seri version of this same incident is as follows: "As is our custom, we had gone to that island [San Esteban] in two pangas in order to obtain sea lion oil and hides, giant iguanas, and agave heads. All at once the 'Playas Coloradas,' which had not spotted us before, showed up next to us. And then they began to shoot, wounding three of us before we succeeded in getting ourselves to safety."(Thomson n.d.:4)

According to Thomson, Guaymas citizens, incensed by the wounding of the two sailors (which the Indian account fails to mention), were out for Seri blood, and the government's reprisal was anything but a failed exercise. The *M. Romero Rubio*'s mercy mission to retrieve the wounded Mexicans was undertaken with great public display, which Thomson believed was intentionally calculated to "inflame passions against the Indians in order to immediately launch a large-scale offensive on Tiburón" (Thomson n.d.:4–5). The well-armed expeditionary force, Thomson maintained, was quickly organized by Brigadier General Nemesio Carrillo and soon set sail for Tiburón Island, where troops, led in the field by Captain Alberto Méndez, were landed. With considerable disdain and sarcasm, Thomson portrays their actions on the island as:

cruel, ostentatious, treacherous and inhumane. With great demonstrations of force, they positioned themselves in such a narrow part of the sea [the Canal del Infiernillo] that it was impossible for the Indians to leave, approach, or to catch a fish to eat. And the drinking water was surrounded by soldiers so that nobody [among the Indians] could drink without their consent. Patrols were kept moving throughout the island and during all hours, with bugle calls, drum rolls, trumpets, and cornets; [and also] with brigades of signalmen with flags and numerals and artillery salvos etc. etc. Apparently, this was done to terrify the Indians and reduce them to peace. But increasingly, they climbed to the mountain peaks, while the women and children hidden in the canyons were chewing roots in order to reduce their hunger and thirst. Day after day, and week after week, the bold conquerers waited with club in hand in order to crush their victims, but the Indians preferred death to surrender.

[So] the astute hero [Captain Méndez] changed tactics, abandoning this location and leaving [the Indians] free to obtain fish and drinking water. And permitting a smile to cross his face, he replaced the drum rolls and martial bugle calls [with] music and popular songs. He held foot races along the beach and horse races and regattas by the sea shore. There was much to eat, and many very cordial civilities were extended toward the Indians who, little by little, began to poke their heads out of the bushes. When he gained their confidence, he invited them to take part in the sports. Since they were good at running, they won prizes in the races, nor did they put in a bad performance in the rowing regattas. Among the men who stubbornly refused to surrender were many of great agility and strength, which [would have] enabled them to compete well, but their distrust kept them away from the fiestas and banquets, which day by day were being expanded. One fine day, amid enthusiasm and happiness, the sport took a new twist and ! BANG ... [Captain Méndez] closed the trap and ensnared nearly one hundred of them. These unfortunate individuals could not free themselves as did [some of the] others who, though wounded and battered, broke through the cordons of soldiers.

Once the Government's forces had triumphed, they proceeded to load the prisoners on board ship, taking precautions. Just in case, the large vessels were escorted by the small ones, the guards were redoubled, and the fleet weighed anchor at dusk. At the latitude of Punta Monumento the famous Coyote Iguana threw himself into the water, leaving behind as prisoner in the boat his pregnant Lola Casanova ... and here for prudence or perhaps for respect we are leaving some lines blank: [seven blank lines follow, ending the account of the expedition]. (Thomson n.d.:5–6)

Thomson was apparently trying to achieve a literary effect by liberally embellishing his narrative of the campaign with romantic images, including the extravagant reference to Coyote Iguana and Lola Casanova. But the context of this description makes it clear that Thomson was relating history as he understood it, not fiction, and he was very much aware that his account directly contradicted the official line. It is unfortunate that Thomson chose to end with a dramatic flourish of blank lines rather than reveal what became of the hundred Seris taken on board the vessel, for in general terms, the roundup he describes resembles the one the Seris believe wiped out the San Esteban people.

Whatever actually happened during the Tiburón campaign, the Seris living on the mainland were clearly outraged, for they responded with a major insurrection. On June 30, after riding to Hermosillo from their Costa Rica ranch, Pascual Encinas and his son Ignacio appeared in person before Governor Corral to alert him to the situation. As Corral summarized it:

> the Seris who were working for them [the Encinas family] have fled from their jobs and joined with others in that territory who are entirely wild. They have formed a group of fifty or sixty men, the majority of whom are equipped with firearms, many of them repeating [rifles]. Don Ignacio Encinas with some fifteen men that he recruited from among his cowboys went to look for them. They found them near the sea and invited them to return to the ranch, offering them provisions, clothing and good treatment; but they refused and went into hiding in a mountain range on that coast.... These events, according to Sr. Encinas, must have occurred three or four days ago.
>
> According to the reports given by the Encinases, who are completely reliable, the Indians know about the expedition that the steamer "Demócrata" undertook among the islands of the Gulf. They [the Indians] swear to having seen the vessel and the soldiers who went ashore on the coast of this District, and it seems that this has contributed to the uprising of the aforementioned Seris—perhaps because of fear or perhaps because they were only waiting for a pretext to do it. (Corral 1891:369)

Fearing that these renegade Seris would begin attacking the isolated frontier ranches, Corral asked General Carrillo to send troops to Costa Rica as a show of force to convince the rebels to lay down their arms. Carrillo assigned the mission to Captain Alberto Méndez and his 50 soldiers of the 27th Battalion—the same outfit that had just carried out the Tiburón campaign that triggered this new insurrection. Though they had barely disembarked from the *Demócrata* in Guaymas, Méndez and his troops quickly remobilized and established themselves at Costa Rica ranch. But this move did not bring peace. A skirmish in mid-July left three soldiers wounded and six Seris dead, prompting the government to launch a new offensive. In mid-October, a combined force of 25 cavalry, 20 cowboys, and 10 Tohono O'odham (Papagos) auxiliaries under First Adjutant Luciano Enríquez set out in search of the Seris. The Indians were found on October 24 near Bahía Kino and were willing to discuss peace, until they realized they were being surrounded. In the ensuing battle, two Seris died, and the rest fled to join their kinsmen on Tiburón Island. But by the end of the month, the Indians, facing a winter of limited resources on the island, began to surrender themselves to Enríquez.

Thinking the entire tribe was finally in check, Corral ordered Enríquez to take the first comprehensive census of the Seris. The process was started in early November, as the first Indians began to turn themselves in at Costa Rica ranch. Most people came of their own accord, but Enríquez had to dispatch the leader of the rebellion, José Paulino de la Cruz (known as El Cojo "The Cripple"), to Tiburón Island to bring back five recalcitrant families that had refused to surrender. By about December 8, Enríquez concluded that for all practical purposes the Seris had been subdued, and he declared the census finished, having collected 192 names along with age, birthplace, marital status, and other data (Monteverde 1891). Though the census is a surprisingly rich record of Seris who were alive in late 1890, it is not a complete inventory, for one of the people missing from the list is Porfirio Díaz, the Seri who had lived among the San Esteban people as a boy.

After the census, the Seris were distributed among the coastal ranches to serve as wage laborers and to be instilled with Mexican ideals of law and morality. In Governor Corral's estimation, the Seri problem had finally been resolved (Corral 1891:368–71). Reflecting this belief, in January 1891 the official government weekly, *La Constitución*, which had briefly reported the events as they had unfolded during the summer and autumn (Anonymous 1890a, 1890b, 1890c, 1890d), published an extended retrospective of the insurrection, the campaign to quell it, and the resulting census (Anonymous 1891). Although this article purported to give background information about the cause of the revolt, starting with the wounding of the two sailors, not a word was written of the *Demócrata's* punitive expedition to Tiburón Island. Indeed, by the 1930s the entire episode had been reduced to historic trivia, which a standard history of the state dismissed in a single sentence:

> About the middle of the same month of July [1890] the Seri Indians who were situated in exile on Tiburón Island carried out an uprising which, with little force, was stifled. (Villa 1937:426)

In fact, the "Seri problem" had not been entirely eliminated, though it was viewed as only a minor annoyance compared to the massive military operations against the Yaquis that were to consume the Sonoran government for the next two decades. In addition to continued skirmishes between Seris and Mexican ranchers along the frontier, some of the incidents of the 1890s were heavily publicized for their involvement of U.S. citizens. In 1894, a flamboyant lawyer-turned-journalist R. E. L. Robinson (Figure 10.4) embarked with four companions on an expedition to Tiburón Island to prospect, pursue old rumors of buried treasure, and find out about the Seris at first hand. For Robinson and one of his party, George F. Flavell, this was apparently not the first attempt at such a venture. In April of the previous year Flavell, who was also known as George Clark and "Clark the Trapper," had sailed solo in his home-built 25-foot skiff *Dart* from Yuma to Guaymas and Mulegé and back, looking for sources of furs and plumage. From Bahía de los Ángeles he had detoured across the Midriff "in order to take a squint at Tiburon island" (Anonymous 1893a). He must have taken his squint at close range, for he discovered that:

> The Indians on Tiburon island are a dangerous lot and I had a close call from them. They are armed with repeating rifles, have boats and will tackle anything that comes in sight. (Flavell 1893)

Figure 10.4
R. E. L. Robinson
(1864–1894).
(Courtesy Arizona
Historical Society, Tucson.)

In July, following Flavell's return, Robinson and three others seem to have embarked on the *Dart* on their own voyage to the Gulf (Anonymous 1893b). The details of this trip are not known, but it is clear that they too chose not to land on Tiburón. However, these trips must have whetted their respective appetites. For the 1894 expedition, a rather clumsy sloop of around 32 feet was built and christened *Examiner* (Figures 10.5 and 10.6), evidently named for the San Francisco newspaper with which Robinson had been affiliated. In mid-April, Robinson and Flavell, with James Logan, Morgan O'Brien, and Charles Cowell, hoisted the *Examiner*'s sails and set out down the Colorado River from Yuma, bound for notorious Tiburón Island (Anonymous 1894[?]a; Carmony and Brown 1987:6–7).

As they sailed through the upper Gulf, the party weathered a succession of furious squalls, calms, and even waterspouts. Two of the men were perpetually seasick, and when they reached Bahía de los Ángeles, Cowell defected over disagreements with Robinson that threatened to erupt in violence. But on May 23, the four remaining adventurers steered for Tiburón, which they were determined to explore, or as Robinson prophetically put it, "leave our bones bleaching on its hills" (Robinson 1894:36). Putting in at Tecomate on the 25th,

*Figure 10.5
R. E. L. Robinson's
party aboard the
Sloop* Examiner *at
Yuma, Arizona,
ready to set sail for
the Gulf. April
1894. (Courtesy
Grand Canyon
National Park
Museum, Grand
Canyon, Arizona
[No. 22550].)*

*Figure 10.6
Detail of the previous
photograph. The
man standing at the
mast is thought to be
George Flavell
(1864-ca. 1901);
this is the only known
photograph of him.
(Courtesy Grand
Canyon National
Park Museum,
Grand Canyon,
Arizona
[No. 22550].)*

they established seemingly excellent relations with a group of Seris camped there. Flavell even spent the night with them, eventually dozing off while the Indians sang and danced until dawn.

The next morning the party split up. Although well aware of the Seris' murderous reputation, Robinson and Logan abandoned caution and set out with five Indians to hunt deer. Flavell stayed in the Seri camp to exercise his tattooing skills on some of the Indians, while O'Brien, who was sick, remained on board the *Examiner*. Two hours passed. Then three shots rang out, and the Seris in camp suddenly became agitated. Realizing something was amiss, Flavell beat a hasty retreat to the *Examiner*. Then more shots, Logan's voice calling out, and silence. Flavell and O'Brien realized their companions were probably dead, and they feared they would soon see Seri boats coming out to get them as well. Worse still, it was dead calm. In desperation, the two men set to poling and rowing the *Examiner* away from Tiburón, working nonstop most of the day and part of the night. Finally a breeze sprang up, and they were able to hoist their sails and make for Guaymas (Flavell 1894b:41–50; Robinson 1894:36–40; King 1989:221; McGee 1898:117–19).

When they reached Guaymas, Flavell and O'Brien reported the incident to the Mexican authorities and to U.S. Vice-Consul Charles Hale, who in turn advised the State Department. Though of little real importance to Sonorans, the intense anti-Seri sentiment, sensational press coverage, and the international character of the incident made an official response necessary. Consequently, General (formerly Governor) Luis Torres authorized an expedition to Tiburón Island to investigate the incident and punish the guilty Indians (Anonymous 1894–1897).

The main force of this campaign consisted of 50 infantrymen under the command of Lt. Colonel Luis López. On June 22, they set sail from Guaymas on the merchant steamer *M. Romero Rubio*, eagerly lent to the cause by its owner, Sr. Lilovier, whose family had been killed by Seris some years earlier. Simultaneously, a cavalry detachment was to be dispatched to the coast to prevent the Seris from escaping from the island to the mainland. Accompanying the main expeditionary force was George Flavell, who later gave U.S. Vice-Consul Hale a detailed chronicle of the campaign (Flavell 1894b).

According to Flavell, the expedition reached Bahía Kino on the morning of June 23, and the troops spent this day and the next looking for signs of Seris on the mainland coast. On the 24th, the land force appeared, consisting not of a cavalry unit but 26 of Pascual Encinas's cowboys, who turned around and headed home when they were "told their help was not wanted" (Flavell 1894b; Hale 1894a). At 9 A.M. on June 25, Flavell, Lt. Colonel López, and 46 soldiers landed on the east coast of Tiburón. During the next two days, they marched some 25 miles north and west around the coast, passing recently occupied camps and burning huts and balsas, but never straying far from shore and never catching sight of any Seris. Skirting around the northeastern tip of the island, they reached Tecomate on the 26th, where they met the ship. That evening they searched briefly for signs of Robinson and Logan but found nothing. According to Flavell, the next day the soldiers rested while the colonel and the captain of the *M. Romero Rubio* sailed to Patos Island to spend the day hunting.

From here the expedition made a detour to San Esteban Island. At dawn on June 28, everyone:

> went aboard. Weighed anchor and started around the NW point of the island with a dog barking on the beach we had left. We coasted the W coast of Tiburon and bore off to San Esteban island which lays SW. 8 miles distance where we met Louis Henriques, a seal fisher who agreed to show us the trail to the stronghold of the Indians, which was 9 miles in the intierior of the is-land [Tiburón].
>
> Anchor was weighed [at San Esteban] at 2^{am} and at dawn we were close to the island [Tiburón]. Anchor was cast. Part of the Troop was landed but as there was no fresh sign, went aboard again after being on the beach ½ hour. Moving 5 miles farther down the coast, anchor was cast again where about 10 men was landed to investigate. Dogs were on the beach when we landed 9^{am}. In the mouth of the Cañyon was a village capible of accomidating a 100 Indians and in good condition. A well beaten trail lead to the intierior which we followed ¼ of a mile. There were foot prints which had been made in less than an hour [earlier]. The captain (of the troop) said it was no use going any far-ther. We returned to the ship and the orders were given to sail to Guaymas with out any explanation whatever. The anchor was again raised after it had layed on the bottom 1 hour. Louis Henriques was taken back to his boat at San Esteban island and then the steamer was headed for Guaymas, where we ar-rived a couple of days later [on July 1]. (Flavell 1894b) [punctuation added]

Flavell was thoroughly disgusted with the expedition, which he considered an unmitigated farce:

> He [López] never left the beach one foot farther than was absolutely necessary, nor was any one else allowed to do so. He returned to the steamer as soon as possible.... The truth of it was, everything was done to avoid a skirmish. We fooled around between the Tiburon and the mainland *41 hours*, tooting the cor-net to let them [the Seris] know we were there. When a landing was made old shacks and rafts were burnt, the Colonel trying his marksmanship on coyotes, and everything *possible* was done to scare the Indians away. (Flavell [1894?])

Lt. Colonel López portrayed the events quite differently in his official report of the expedition, which he submitted to General Torres. Contrary to Flavell, he presented a picture of a professionally conducted operation during which his troops "scoured the island for a period of five days" (Anonymous 1894[?]c), investigating camps and waterholes, and searching the area where Flavell said the killings had occurred. Finding no trace of North American corpses nor live Seris on Tiburón, López:

made three smoke signals on one of the mountains, [which was] recognized by the Captain of the ship as a signal for him to come to the place where he would find me. At about 12 A.M. [noon] the ship arrived, and we set out from [Tiburón] Island for Patos Island, following [the suggestion of] one of the guides. He said that the Indians travel to this place or to San Esteban Island, which are the closest [islands to Tiburón]. I arrived at Patos and reconnoitered it quickly and without any difficulty, because it is small and has only one mountain in the center. Not having found anything there, I proceeded toward San Esteban, and upon our arrival there I met a fishing boat belonging to Don Luis Henríquez, a man who makes his living from hunting sea lions and fishing for sharks. I was able to talk with this gentleman, and it became clear to me that he had spent twenty-five years reconnoitering all these places [the Midriff islands] and that he knew some waterholes [on Tiburón] where we could find the Indians. We agreed to set out at one in the morning, in order to arrive at the coast of Tiburón before dawn so we could land without being seen. All this took place punctually. We arrived on shore at the agreed hour and approached a *ranchería*. (López 1894)

But this camp and another they visited shortly afterward, like all the others seen previously, were deserted, and López concluded that the Indians were not to be found. Since supplies were by now nearly depleted, he called a halt to the campaign, and the expedition returned to Guaymas. As to his North American guest, it is clear that López had no more respect for Flavell than Flavell had for López. Throughout his report, López refers coolly to Flavell only as "*el americano*," and concludes with an assessment of the man and his suspected motives:

Permit me to expose to this Authority the American who accompanied us and who claims to be a companion of those assassinated by the Indians. I have a slight suspicion that he may have made use of a trick in order to get the forces of the federal Government to enter the Island to help him with his schemes. He certainly did not take a great interest in anything other than exploration, always hanging around at my side, taking down information about all the terrain, [and] carrying with him his personal notes. Right away, on the first day we landed, I happened to read the title of some reports he was writing, which said "*The Exploration Continues*." Besides, this man made great friends with one of the officers of my force, and he let slip to him the remark that in Nogales there was a company, with ten thousand dollars in gold, for the purpose of coming to explore Tiburón Island, and that he would return to the island within six months. Furthermore, he told me that they [he and his friends] had remained for 24 hours in the camp where the events [that supposedly led to Robinson and Logan's deaths] had taken place, and that they had entertained themselves by tattooing the Indians with jabs of a needle and ink. This shows that this man must be very low class, for his entire body is tattooed with blue dots, forming various figures. He also revealed that the Indians have twenty dollar coins recently minted in the United States; from this one can reasonably presume that he had brought money [to pay] for an exploration of Tiburón Island. This is only my assumption, not having more information to place before your superior knowledge. (López 1894)

Given the sensational nature of the events, it is not surprising that Sonora was rife with differing accounts of the fate of Robinson and Logan and the resulting military expedition to Tiburón Island. Ethnologist WJ McGee, who visited Costa Rica ranch only a few months afterward, reported that he heard "various conflicting accounts of the affair" (McGee 1898:119), including a Seri version, and his summary of the retaliatory expedition differs markedly from both the Flavell and López versions (McGee 1898:120). Meanwhile, General Torres, the man who had ordered the retaliatory expedition, noted that no sign whatever had been found of Robinson and Logan, and consequently he expressed much doubt that the two had really died at the hands of the Seris. There was even widespread speculation that Robinson, in keeping with his flamboyant character, was alive and pulling a scam, hiding out among the Seris in order to create a sensation when he reappeared (Anonymous 1894[?]b; Johnson 1894). Flavell, of course, proclaimed no doubt about the fate of his companions and was publicly outraged that neither Mexico nor the United States was willing to go to greater lengths to avenge their deaths. But the incident was of little real consequence to either government, and a *pro forma* response may have been entirely appropriate. Lacking Flavell's passionate personal interest and suspecting his real motives, it may be that López intentionally refrained from risking the lives of his troops and pointlessly worsening Seri-Mexican relations merely to avenge a North American adventure that had been foolhardy in the first place.

For the Seris, the year 1895 was traumatic because of the deportation of about a dozen people, not just to Pueblo de Seris, but to permanent exile in southern Mexico. The circumstances of this action are not clear. McGee states vaguely that after his first expedition had left Sonora in November 1894:

the Indians became restive and soon withdrew beyond the desert. In the course of the ensuing winter a group returned to the neighborhood of Costa Rica, where, by aid of strategy, seven warriors ... with the families of four, were arrested, taken to Hermosillo, tried, and, according to oral accounts, banished. (McGee 1898:120)

Documentary sources state that, these prisoners were then taken from Hermosillo to Guaymas, where they were put on board the military transport vessel *Oaxaca*. On October 14, 1895, Governor Corral sent the ship's captain a list of the deportees, which totaled 17 people — 12 Seri men and women, plus five Yaquis (Luna 1973:43). Two days later, U.S. Vice-Consul Hale, who by now had no love for the Seris, reported that:

The Government has just commenced a good enterprise. They have just embarked 17 of those thieving murdering Seris Indians from Tiburon Island, the tribe who murdered Robinson and Logan in May 1894. They are to be transported to the extreme southern part of the Republic. (Hale 1895b)

To put it mildly, the Seris were "Irritated by this action ... [and] resumed the warpath, displaying special animosity toward the residents of Costa Rica" (McGee 1898:120).

After the Robinson-Logan incident, stories of killings on Tiburón abounded. At the end of 1894, a rumor circulated, later declared false, that the Seris had killed a member of another North American party that landed on the island (Hale 1894b, 1895a; McGee 1898:120). A year later, newspaper accounts told of a party of five gold prospectors who had gone to Tiburón Island, of whom only one escaped (McGee 1898:121). But it was the sensational events surrounding the 1897 disappearance of two more North Americans, George K. Porter and John Johnson, that again brought official response. Porter operated a San Diego curio store which sold sea shells, bird feathers, and other tourist items popular at the time. Apparently, he was also an accomplished smuggler (Anonymous 1897[?]). To further both businesses, he made frequent trips south along the coast and into the Gulf on his Chinese junk *World*, with Johnson as crew. In August 1897, Porter and Johnson put in at Guaymas to obtain a permit to go to Tiburón Island. The permit was denied and the two men were strongly warned away from the island. Shortly thereafter, they set sail from Guaymas and were not heard from again (Anonymous 1897[?]; McGee 1898:121–22; MacMullen 1968).

However on October 21, Martín Méndez, captain of the Mexican schooner *Otila*, reported to the authorities in Bahía de los Ángeles that he and his crew had seen the *World* being ransacked by Seris near the southern tip of Tiburón Island. Events began to unfold for Méndez the night of October 5, when strong currents forced the *Otila* to anchor off Dátil Island, a mile from the southern point of Tiburón. At daybreak the next morning, four Seris appeared and tried unsuccessfully to lure the sailors ashore to Tiburón. When they began firing on his vessel, Méndez retreated, and the *Otila* sailed for San Esteban Island. After six days (of unrecorded activity) at San Esteban, bad weather forced them to run for Tiburón, and they again anchored near the southern point. The next morning two Seris appeared in a canoe, and the sailors chased them northward some four miles, where they recognized the *World*, surrounded by 100 Indians taking things from it. Being fired upon, badly outnumbered, and assuming that the *World*'s crew had already been killed, Méndez realized he could do nothing but report the incident (Anonymous 1897a; Legrand 1897).

When the news reached Mexican and U.S. officials in Guaymas, the wheels of government were again set in motion. Governor Corral sent a military force to Costa Rica ranch to find out directly from the Seris what had happened. The account the Seris gave, in which Porter killed five Indians before succumbing to a volley of arrows, quickly made lurid newspaper copy (McGee 1898:122). The government, acting through the federal judiciary, ordered an expedition to Tiburón Island to investigate the alleged murders, and if possible, apprehend the guilty Indians. On November 12, a detachment of 50 troops, accompanied by Guaymas District Judge R. F. Nieto, sailed for Tiburón on the commercial steamer *Río Yaqui*, returning to Guaymas five days later. According to Nieto's guarded report to U.S. Consular Agent Frank M. Crocker, the soldiers made:

> a meticulous reconnaissance of the entire island in search of Porter and Johnson, who could not be found, [but] the broken and partly burned remnants of the "World" were found and brought to this port, along with some personal effects of the vessel's crew, which are being identified by the Court.
>
> As to the manner in which these acts were carried out, and whether Porter and Johnson were victims of a maritime disaster or a crime by the Indians, as is supposed, I am unable to inform you because [determining] that is the objective of the ongoing investigation. But I take the liberty of advising you that you should be skeptical of the fantastic and exaggerated accounts that the local press and that of your country publish regarding the event. (Nieto 1897:2)

One of the more responsible newspaper accounts noted that Judge Nieto and the troops were on Tiburón Island only two days and did not penetrate the interior. They encountered no Indians, but at one of the camps they must have come close, for they discovered a fire still burning and a brand new litter of puppies. The soldiers found the *World*'s nameplate, its logbook, several novels, two old shoes (not mates), and some small articles, but no trace of the two men themselves. Nieto later concluded to General Torres, with admirable judicial restraint, that there was simply no evidence of how Porter and Johnson died, who killed them, or for that matter, whether the two men were even dead (Anonymous 1897[?]). As with the Robinson-Logan affair, there was little point in risking lives to pursue the Seris in this matter, and it quickly faded from official interest (McGee 1898:122).

In the United States, however, the Seris did not fade from popular interest. The disappearance of North Americans on Tiburón Island and the failure of the Mexican and U.S. governments to adequately punish the Seris aroused a wave of righteous indignation. Several adventurous North Americans proposed to take the law into their own hands and launch private expeditions to Tiburón to conquer the Seris once and for all and, not incidently, assess the island's economic potential. Most of these proposals went nowhere. But in September 1902, a heavily-armed expedition from the United States, led by "Arizona Charlie" Meadows, actually landed on Tiburón Island (see pp. 195–98). Fortunately, the invaders were much more interested in reconnoitering the island's economic resources than killing Seris. Each group found the other to be cautious but not basically hostile, and the visit passed without bloodshed (Bowers 1909:171–72; King 1989:233–34).

The final military expedition to Tiburón Island took place during the last days of 1904 (Moser 1988). It is one of the few for which there exists a detailed record from both a Mexican participant, Federico García y Alva (1905–1907, 1988), and from Seri oral history (Herrera Marcos 1988), along with many garbled summary accounts. This time the campaign was directed not only against the Seris, but also against some Yaquis who had fled to the island. The immediate events that precipitated the action probably began inland from the Seri coast at La Máquina ranch. When the Mexican ranch owner caught a Yaqui worker clandestinely butchering one of his cows, he killed the Indian. News of the murder spread to Yaquis near Guaymas, who came to the ranch and killed the Mexican owner in reprisal. These Yaquis fled to the coast and took refuge among the Seris on Tiburón Island. Together, the Yaquis and some Seris then staged a raid on the mainland in which an elderly Tohono O'odham (Papago) man was killed (Moser 1988:471). With war against the Yaquis raging in southern Sonora and anti-Seri sentiment still strong, it is not surprising that the Sonoran government was determined to punish the offenders.

The expedition to Tiburón was conceived on a large scale and was personally led by Governor Rafael Izábal. A force of 160 soldiers was supplemented by some 42 mounted Tohono O'odham auxiliaries and 40 cowboys, under the field command of Commander Luis Medina Barrón. Including the Governor himself and an assortment of his friends, the expedition totaled some 262 men. On December 22, the infantry and the Governor's party boarded the gunship *Demócrata* and sailed from Guaymas. They were followed by the small steamer *Bernardo Reyes* which ferried the cowboys and Indian auxiliaries from the mainland. By noon of December 24, the entire expedition was in place on the east coast of Tiburón Island (Figure 10.7). Later the same afternoon, the forces fanned out and began their search for Indians (García y Alva 1988:475, 478).

According to García y Alva, the campaign resulted in one major encounter, in which 11 Seris and four Yaquis died, and probably two lesser skirmishes. A few balsas were burned, camps looted, and a number of Seri women and children were taken captive. Though they spoke almost no Spanish, the captive women were interrogated and told by the Governor that the Seris would not be harmed if they turned over the renegade Yaquis (Figure 10.8). One woman was then released to carry the message to the other Seris on the island. The extent of miscommunication was obvious three days later, on December 29, when two women appeared at Tecomate, where Izábal and part of the Mexican force had moved. They carried a pole from which dangled several Yaqui straw hats and eight severed hands—"four men's, three women's and one of a child" (García y Alva 1905–1907).

As Lt. Colonel López may have done 10 years earlier, Governor Izábal took the next day off to go hunting on Patos Island. Meanwhile, Seri leader Juan Tomás had been located and had promised that the entire tribe would surrender and present themselves to the Governor for relocation within six months. On December 31, having declared the campaign a success, Izábal and his forces boarded the two ships and arrived back in Guaymas on January 1, 1905 (García y Alva 1905–1907, 1988:481–92).

In contrast to the hunting party atmosphere conveyed by the Mexican account, the Seri version (Herrera Marcos 1988) portrays a deeply tragic episode. From the Seri perspective, the assaults on their camps were unprovoked and came as a complete surprise. The only soldiers recalled in the Seri account are

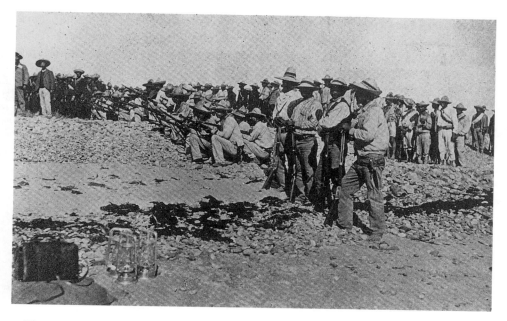

Figure 10.7 *Mexican forces assembled on Tiburón Island during the last formal campaign against the Seris, December 1904. (From García y Alva 1905–1907.)*

Figure 10.8 *Sonoran Governor Rafael Izábal (1854–1910) (seated at right) interrogates captive Seri women on Tiburón Island, December 1904. (From García y Alva 1905–1907.)*

the Tohono O'odham auxiliaries, who attacked camps throughout the island. In addition to the people killed, both men and women were taken prisoner, and they were incarcerated under guard in a stone enclosure. Here the Governor threatened to kill all the captives unless they brought in the Yaquis. And among the Yaquis were innocent families who had fled the ranches where the trouble had taken place. When the Mexicans finally left for Guaymas, they took many Seri women and children with them. With the help of the Yaquis, who understood that the Seris had been forced to kill their kinsmen, the Seri women were later released and allowed to return to Tiburón Island (Herrera Marcos 1988).

IV.

San Esteban Island in the Twentieth Century

If the nineteenth century was a time of change in the Gulf as a whole, the twentieth century has been a time of change for San Esteban Island. In many respects, it was during this century that the island was truly discovered by the outside world. The purported demise of the San Esteban people late in the nineteenth century left the island uninhabited, and nobody has replaced them as residents. But a variety of people have come to visit. In the twentieth century, San Esteban has become a destination for a multicultural mix of Seris, Mexicans, and North Americans, and a place of multiple, if sporadic, uses.

By the turn of the century, Seris from Tiburón Island and the Sonoran mainland were occasionally traveling to the island to gather agave and chuckwallas. More recently they have come there to hunt sea turtles, to fish, and even just to look at the island as sightseers. Most twentieth century Mexican visitors have been small-scale commercial fishermen, who come to the island in pangas, fish or hunt sea turtles in its waters, and camp on its beaches. North Americans have generally been much more recent visitors. Many come as sport fishermen or ecotourists, and most of the latter arrive as passengers aboard natural history cruise ships. By and large, these people spend little time on shore.

Science on San Esteban has been entirely a twentieth century endeavor, and one that has involved both Mexicans and North Americans. Since the first scientific expedition arrived in 1911, the island has been studied by topographic surveyors, prospectors, and an array of scientists interested in investigating the island's natural and cultural history. And San Esteban is not without its dark side, for there are indications that it has sometimes been used in the illicit drug trade.

Despite the diversity of recent visitors, few people, including scientists, have stayed on the island for very long or have explored more than a small fraction of it. San Esteban at the end of the twentieth century is no longer an unknown island, but neither is it one likely to have revealed all its secrets.

ELEVEN

Toward Peaceful Coexistence:
Seris, Mexicans, and North Americans on San Esteban Island

After the San Esteban People: Modern Seri Visits[99]

The Seris today say that their own ancestors may have been partly to blame for the extinction of the San Esteban people. When the Mexicans came to punish the Seris for raiding, the guilty Indians may have falsely implicated the San Esteban people as the raiders. But when these innocent folk were rounded up and then brutally exterminated, the other Seris were horrified. They say that the shock of what happened, coupled with a fear of the lingering spirits of these people, was so great that nobody wanted to go to San Esteban for a long time afterward.

How long they stayed away is uncertain. Seri accounts indicate that they were once again visiting San Esteban by the end of the nineteenth century. This was a time when Mexicans were also coming to the island. With hatred between the two groups running high, it is little wonder the Seris remember some of their early trips primarily for the hostile encounters that took place.

One of the best remembered of these incidents was a confrontation with Mexicans who were hunting sea lions on San Esteban. The story revolves around a man named Nantes. Long ago, Nantes had been living at *Sacpátix*, a camp on the eastern side of Tiburón Island. But food began to get scarce, and when he could no longer find turtles or clams, Nantes decided to take his family to Hermosillo to live. There he acquired a house. It was while he was living in Hermosillo that he first heard that Mexicans from Guaymas were beginning to sail to San Esteban to hunt sea lions and render their blubber into oil. When Seris traveled to Hermosillo to trade, they would stay at Nantes's house, and that is how the other people learned of the sea lion operation.

The Seris say that a number of men were working at one of these Mexican sea lion camps on the western side of San Esteban when some Seris in a boat appeared unexpectedly. A group of Yaqui Indian laborers were working on shore cooking down the sea lion blubber. The Mexicans were in a boat, with the boss seated in the prow holding a rifle. The boss yelled at the Yaquis to keep on working and not to mix with the Seris. Then he told them he was going to shoot the Seris. Although the Seris were doing no harm, the man began to shoot into their boat. One Seri, Guadalupe Astorga, grabbed his rifle, but there was too much smoke from the Mexicans' rifles to see. So he waited until the smoke cleared enough to make out the forms of the Mexicans, and then he fired, hitting the boss in the chest. The boss was a well-dressed man who wore a watch with a chain in his vest. The Seri bullet hit the watch chain and drove it right into the man's chest, killing him. A second bullet passed clear through the boss and into another Mexican who was rowing the boat, killing him as well. One of the Yaquis then said "Don't shoot anymore, the boss is dead."

Later, when news of the deaths of the two Mexicans circulated, the Yaquis spoke out in defense of the Seris, saying that they were not to blame for the killings. When the incident was related to Nantes in Hermosillo, he exclaimed with typically wry Seri humor, *"Pti iqui matósni"* "Pelicaned together" (i.e., "Two birds killed with one 'stone'") in recognition of Astorga's outstanding marksmanship (Mary Beck Moser 1987:pers. comm.).

A different account of this incident omits the sea lion operation and partly reverses the roles. In this version, it was Astorga and some other Seris who were on shore, along with several Yaquis, when some Mexicans appeared in a boat. The Mexicans told the Yaquis to leave. They would not, and the Mexicans started shooting. Unfortunately for the two Mexicans, the outcome of this version is much the same (Mary Beck Moser 1981:pers. comm.).

During this same period, the Seris say that one time a group of men went to San Esteban to gather agave. While they were on the island, they saw a boat arrive with three Mexicans on board, a young man and two older ones, who had apparently come out to hunt sea lions. One of the Seris, Luis Torres, said to the others "Let's kill them," and they did (Mary Beck Moser 1980:pers. comm.).

On another occasion, it is said that a group of Seri men who had just arrived on San Esteban discovered that a party of Mexicans were already there. In this case, the Seris contented themselves with puncturing the water cans of the Mexicans (Mary Beck Moser 1980:pers. comm.).

The smoldering hostility between Mexicans and Seris flared up in yet another incident on San Esteban. Chico Romero (see Figure 10.3) told Richard Felger and Mary Beck Moser about:

a small group of Seri who survived four or five days of summer heat by drinking agave juice.... This event occurred at about the turn of the century, when Chico was a child. He told of five men and a boy who, arriving at San Esteban Island, left their wooden boat on the beach and went inland to harvest *heme* [agave]. Mexican fishermen happened along and set their boat adrift. Marooned on the island, they drank agave juice to stay alive while they constructed a raftlike boat or balsa from bundles of agave flower stalks. Fearing that the young boy, Juan Marcos (deceased ca. 1919), might not be able to survive much longer on the agave juice, the men sent him along with Manuel Encinas (deceased ca. 1931), who paddled the makeshift balsa to the opposite south shore of Tiburón Island for help. They landed at *Hant Copni* 'land carpenter-bee,' near *Cyajoj* (Arroyo Sauzal at the coast). (Felger and Moser 1985:223)

According to Manuel Encinas's son Antonio Herrera (see Figure 10.3), there was no one to help at *Hant Copni*, and so Encinas had to walk some 20 miles or more to a camp called *Haanc* on the east coast of Tiburón, where he found some Seris (Map 1.4). From here, a rescue party set out for the southwest coast of Tiburón, and then from there to San Esteban where they rescued the stranded men (Mary Beck Moser 1980:pers. comm.).

In early May of 1922, Juan Tomás (see Figure 10.3) told Edward H. Davis of a similar desperate plight. Davis understood that this had just taken place, although it may have been a retelling of the earlier incident in slightly altered form:

> The chief said that a day or two before, some of his men had a fight with some sailors (Mexicans) on the Island of San Estevan four or five miles off the south west corner of Tiburon. Nobody was killed, but the two boats, the wealth of the Island, had drifted away and were lost, leaving eight men marooned on the Island. They had gone there to gather *mescal* to make drink to celebrate a wedding to come off soon. These[100] men were five days without water. They sent up frantic smoke signals every day. At last they were seen, and help went for them in the only remaining boat on the Island. They were rescued. (Davis 1965:178)

The purpose of most twentieth century Seri expeditions to San Esteban Island has been to gather food. As McGee noted (McGee 1898:191), eggs and young birds are one of the island's resources, but the Seris today say that the main reason people went there has always been to collect agave, and to a lesser extent, chuckwallas and iguanas. By the 1910s, this was known to outsiders as well. In November 1918, a Mexican government party exploring for natural resources saw recent footprints on San Esteban, which they attributed to Seris who had come there to collect agave (Zárate 1920:80–81).

In 1978, María Antonia Colosio vividly recalled a voyage to San Esteban she experienced as a little girl, just after the turn of the century. It was spring, and the group went by balsa, departing from the southwest coast of Tiburón Island. She said she was so terrified of this dangerous trip that she ran and hid from her father:

> We were on two balsas that were tied together, side by side. We were going to ... what's it called, the mountain out in the sea? I didn't want to go. We were going to *Coftécöl* [San Esteban Island]. They had put blankets and water on, jugs as big as this [gesturing, indicating a large water vessel]. Since the jugs were full of water, they were tied in place. Plants were stuck in the mouth of the jugs, and the jugs were in carrying nets. I didn't want to get on, but my father caught me and put me on. After he caught me and put me on, he tied

me behind a blind man who went along to paddle. Then I cried a lot, but he didn't pay attention to me. That's how we went to *Coftécöl*. It was so dangerous when we almost entered the area called *Ixötáacoj* [Big Whirlpool]. The sea just swirled and churned. The wind wasn't blowing but the water was choppy. It just churned, it was dangerous. The sea was going around. Everything just roared. The children and old women all cried. The old man Pozoli just said, "We'll land really soon." As we were going to land, he sang to the shore. And it seemed we landed right away. The men paddled with all their strength, and we landed near the rocks. (Felger and Moser 1985:131–32)

Despite the fears of young María and the genuine hazards of such a trip, expeditions to collect agave on San Esteban were fundamentally joyous occasions because of all the food they produced:

The first person to sight a returning boat would call out, "Here come the Mountain Travelers!" (San Esteban is mountainous), whereupon pandemonium would break loose. As their boat neared the beach, the men would stop paddling and begin throwing cooked *heme* [agave] hearts into the eager outstretched hands. Sometimes a spiny-tailed iguana called *heepni* (*Ctenosaura hemilopha*) was tossed ashore with the century plants, causing much screaming and laughter. (Felger and Moser 1985:222)

Although whole families occasionally made the voyage to San Esteban, as in the case of María Antonia's trip, it was more usual for only a group of men to go. In the early twentieth century, the total Seri population was so small (less than 200) that people still remember the individual men who most often made the trip. At first, it was mainly Ramón Montaño, José Torres, Jesús Ibarra, and Chico Francisco. By the 1930s, it was Antonio Herrera and his son Roberto Herrera, Nacho Romero, José Romero, José Torres, and Luis Torres.

The Seris say that San Esteban agave is most flavorful in January, but that ripe plants can be found at any time of year (Felger and Moser 1985:222). People do recall trips to the island during different seasons, but they greatly preferred to go there in April or May. The trip was much less dangerous during this period, after the fierce winter storms and before the violent squalls (*chubascos*) and hurricanes of summer. In the early days, expeditions departed from the southwest coast of Tiburón Island. By the 1930s, many Seris were living near Bahía Kino, and so that became the usual point of departure. People knew the entire San Esteban coastline, but their destination, at least for winter and spring trips, was almost always *Pajíi* camp (El Monumento) on the east coast (Map 1.1). Sometimes contrary winds would force the party to land at *Xnitom* (Playa del Faro) on the northeastern corner of the island, but the group would usually push off the next day for *Pajíi*. The travelers would stay on the island only a short time, usually no more than three or four days. Roberto Herrera recalled a trip that lasted only two days because they had failed to bring enough water to stay longer. Prior to the 1930s, when metal containers became generally available, water had to be brought to the island either in pottery ollas or in turtle or deer stomachs. Evidently, the Seris of this period did not attempt to rely on any of the island's water sources. For springtime trips, this would be wise policy, because spring is the dry season when the bedrock pools would most likely be waterless. In addition to water, people would bring with them a knife, rope to tie chuckwallas to carrying sticks, and perhaps a blanket.

Agave can be found in abundance on north and east facing rocky slopes throughout the island, but the Seris say that not all plants are of the same quality. Those with a noticeably "oily" film on the leaves are said to be bitter and were passed over, whereas very fibrous plants, called *heeme quims* "fringed San Esteban agave," are considered the most savory (Felger and Moser 1985:222). They note that plants growing near the coast are generally not of very good quality, so the men would hike up Arroyo Limantour and seek out the more desirable plants growing on the rocky slopes above the arroyo.

Although Felger and Moser (1970:164, 1985:222) were told that San Esteban agave was harvested by a distinctive (but impractical) procedure, they were probably harvested in essentially the same manner as *A. subsimplex* and other species that occur elsewhere in Seri territory. In this standard procedure, the plants were first severed from the roots at ground level with a wooden chisel or pry-bar. One end of the instrument, shaped into a cutting edge, was placed against the base of the plant and the other end was pounded with a rock to sever the roots. If the edge became dull, the bar could be used to pry up the plant (Felger and Moser 1985:225). Next, the plant was turned so the root faced the worker, and the leaves were cut off at their base, working from those nearest the root to those next to the inflorescence (Felger and Moser 1985:Fig. 17.6). Those leaves sheathing the incipient flower stalk were the last to be cut off, serving as a convenient handle to grip the plant during earlier stages of defoliation. One leaf, however, on the side of the plant would be left attached. Split in half with its ends tied together, it would serve as a built-in handle for carrying the large heart. This lone leaf was not removed before roasting.

San Esteban agave was roasted in the same manner as other species from Tiburón and the mainland:

> A deep pit was dug in the ground and a fire built in it. When it had burned down, the agave hearts were piled, top down, on the bed of coals. Flat rocks were placed over them and the rocks covered with earth to a depth of about 5 to 10 cm. Another fire was then built on top of that, the resulting bed of coals covered with more earth, and the hearts left to bake overnight.
>
> On the following day the agave hearts or cores were removed from the pit. They were blackened from contact with the coals. Beneath the charred surface the pulp was brownish in color and rather firm in texture. (Felger and Moser 1985:225)

The cooked hearts were then mixed with sea turtle fat and eaten. It is said that they had a coconut-like flavor (Felger and Moser 1985:222).

Because people did not go to San Esteban very often, when they went they would usually gather a large number of agave hearts. Though it is said that more than 100 hearts might be harvested during a single trip, this is no doubt an exaggeration. Hearts of the San Esteban agave are so big that it does not take many to provide a large amount of food. If the gatherers felt they could afford the time, they would bake the hearts before leaving, using large pit ovens dug into the bottom gravels of Arroyo Limantour. However, if they had not brought sufficient drinking water, or if the party feared an adverse change in the winds that could leave them stranded on the island, they might decide to depart with the raw hearts and cook them elsewhere. Indeed, at least a dozen large pit ovens are still visible near *Cyaxoj* camp on the southwest coast of Tiburón, the point of departure and return for many of the early expeditions. But sometimes people did get briefly stranded on San Esteban and would go ahead and bake the agave there while waiting for the winds to change.

Although people often walked a mile and a half or so up Arroyo Limantour to find the best agave plants, they came back to the beach at night to camp. In part, this was a matter of convenience, since their boats and drinking water were there. However, they did not like to go very far inland for fear of the lingering spirits of the massacred San Esteban people. The "spookiness" of the island was less frightening near the shore.

While agave was the central focus of trips to San Esteban, the Seris also made use of the island's two large terrestrial animals. These are the piebald (blotched) chuckwalla (*Sauromalus varius*) and the spiny-tailed iguana (*Ctenosaura hemilopha*), both of which were considered savory fare (Figures 1.5 and 1.6). When disturbed, chuckwallas scurry for the protection of their burrows, but it is a simple matter to dig them out. The Seris say that one can still see places on the island where people have dug down to extract these creatures. Chuckwallas and iguanas often served as food while the group was camped on the island. They were also taken back to Tiburón or the mainland to be eaten there (Felger and Moser 1985:222). Sometimes they were kept alive for the trip back, but their backs might be broken in order to keep them immobile and prevent them from climbing out of the boat. They were usually prepared for eating by throwing them on a fire whole and roasting them.

San Esteban possesses a number of other plants, animals, and even minerals that the Seris have viewed as resources, but only a few of these were utilized, and usually incidentally. The voyage to San Esteban was a major undertaking, and the Seris considered it worthwhile to go there because its agave and chuckwallas could not be found anywhere closer. But other resources which were not unique to San Esteban were exploited only if it were convenient to do so.

One such resource was sea birds. Sometimes people would capture pelicans, terns, cormorants, gulls, and other birds during organized night-time hunts. On dark moonless nights, the men would sneak up to within about 150 feet of the sleeping birds. Then they would light torches and charge, clubbing the birds while they were still confused from sleep. In this way, it is said that a few men could kill several hundred birds (Felger and Moser 1985:50).

The eggs of gulls and other sea birds were also sometimes gathered (McGee 1898:191). This was a food source available in the spring, the time of year when the Seris say most trips were undertaken. Apparently, eggs were of greatest interest around the turn of the century.

The succulent fruit of the *pitahaya agria* cactus (*Stenocereus gummosus*) was a prized food among the Seris (Felger and Moser 1985:256–57), and it is the only cactus fruit they recall gathering during trips to San Esteban (Figure 1.4). Possibly, it was valued more for its liquid content than as food, for the fruit ripens later than most cacti and would have been available for "off-season" travelers coming in the heat of summer and fall.

A great many sea lions inhabit the island's beaches. Though easily killed and reputedly a major food source for the San Esteban people, the present Seris say that they themselves have not hunted these animals for a long time. Sometimes, however, they would capture a pup and bring it back to Tiburón as a pet.

During one early trip to San Esteban, Guadalupe Astorga was astounded to come across a fat goat which, of course, he immediately shot for food. He and his companions had never seen goats on the island before, and they wondered how it had gotten there. They figured that it had lived mainly on agave leaves, which would have provided a source of liquid. Since a desert bighorn can tear open a barrel cactus with its horns to get at the liquid, Astorga reasoned that a goat could probably do the same to agave leaves. Roberto Herrera, who told of this incident, thought it happened about 1915. A few years before this, probably around 1910, he said, some Mexicans came out to San Esteban for a year or so to harvest agave to make liquor. He thought they probably brought goats with them for food, and the animal Astorga shot must have been one that had escaped. The scarcity of water on the island would not have been a problem for it, for as Herrera noted, goats are perfectly capable of living for long periods without fresh drinking water.[101]

In the old days, Seris who visited San Esteban sometimes quarried a red hematite from an outcrop that faces the sea, north of Playa Limantour. It was ground and made into a red paint called *xpaahöj* and used for decorating pottery (Bowen and Moser 1968:107). It was valued because it was the only known deposit of red ochre that did not change color when it was fired. It was probably used mainly prior to the 1930s, for by then Seri pottery had been largely replaced by metal containers.

The *xpaahöj* may also have been the red pigment the Seris were using for face paint around 1930. In 1929, Edward H. Davis described this pigment as a dark red rock from San Esteban that resembled jasper. It was burned in a fire and then ground into powder on metates (Davis 1929:132-33). Three years later, the Coolidges apparently saw it in the form of hard round balls which they describe as an "iron oxide" from San Esteban (Coolidge and Coolidge 1939:200).

Davis (1929:106,132) noted that powdered gypsum was the white pigment used for face paint, and that it too was gathered on San Esteban. Much later, Roberto Thomson, the Mexican who was both Davis's guide and a government agent for the Seris, made the curious passing remark that a white rock from San Esteban (presumably gypsum) was first mixed with eggshells, perfumed, and then worn by the Seri women (Thomson 1969:41).

A long time ago, Seris visiting the island also made use of the red-brown jasper that outcrops on El Monumento, next to *Pajíi* camp. Old Loreto, who was born around 1880, said that chunks of El Monumento rock were called *cmaam yapópt* 'woman her-striking-against' and were used especially to make arrow points. She said that this rock was heat treated by leaving it in a fire overnight so that in the morning it flaked easily.

Up to the 1940s, the lure of agave still occasionally enticed people to San Esteban. But that ended as Seri life began to undergo profound change. The establishment of the village of El Desemboque about 1937 shifted the focus of Seri activity far to the north, greatly increasing the distance to San Esteban. Many people began to settle into a pattern of semisedentary residence in the new community. As Mexican storekeepers moved in, packaged commercial foods began to replace gathering as the basis of subsistence. Even with the introduction of more seaworthy boats and eventually, outboard motors, agave was no longer of sufficient economic value to make the now much longer trip to San Esteban worthwhile. The last two agave gathering expeditions took place in September 1947 and June 1949, possibly at the request of anthropology graduate student William Smith, who accompanied both parties.

As cash became increasingly central to the economy, Seri interest in San Esteban shifted from collecting agave to hunting sea turtles. Sea turtles have long been a prized and staple food for the Seris (McGee 1898:186–90; Malkin 1962:6–7, 54; Smith 1974; Felger and Moser 1985:42–49), and the sale of turtles to Mexican buyers has probably provided an intermittent source of cash since the 1920s. But early in the century, turtles were not normally a sufficient reason to go all the way to San Esteban because they could be found in great numbers along the shores of Tiburón Island and the mainland. The earliest remembered trip to San Esteban specifically to hunt sea turtles took place around the beginning of the 1940s. Fernando Romero, who was a teenage boy at that time, was a member of the hunting party. He says that instead of bringing the turtles back live they butchered the animals right there on the island. By leaving the carapaces and bones behind, they could bring back a lighter load of just meat.

In the 1950s, the commercial market for sea turtles boomed. The Seris found that they could sell large numbers to Mexican fish buyers who drove their trucks to Desemboque. As the commercial appetite for sea turtles escalated in both Mexico and the United States, so did the intensity of hunting, by Mexicans as well as Seris (Figure 11.1). Sea turtle populations close to the mainland quickly declined, and trips to more distant hunting grounds became necessary to assure a catch. In the 1950s, San Esteban Island became an important destination for Seri turtle hunters (Malkin 1962:22–23).

The Seris were never more than minor players in the commercial turtle hunting business. By the early 1960s, intensive hunting throughout the Gulf in conjunction with relentless egg harvesting in southern Mexico had overwhelmed the animals. As their populations collapsed, so did sea turtle hunting as a viable commercial enterprise. By the early 1980s, all five species of sea turtle in the Gulf had become scarce, and some were on the verge of extinction.

*Figure 11.1   Bahía Kino fisherman Emilio García hunting sea turtles
near Playa del Faro, San Esteban Island. July 1967.*

As turtle hunting declined among the Seris, hook-and-line fishing gradually
replaced it as a source of cash (Malkin 1962:31). Though people quit going to
San Esteban to hunt sea turtles, the boats and motors that had made those trips
practical also made occasional fishing expeditions to the island economical.
Today it is still a long way to go, but present-day Mexican fishermen report that
one or two parties of Seris show up on the island nearly every year to fish. Although there has been no overt violence between Mexican and Seri fishermen
in many years, when the two groups arrive on San Esteban at the same time, they
establish separate camps and generally avoid each other.

In the past few decades, some entirely different motives for Seri trips to San
Esteban have surfaced. Recently, a few individuals have gone out to the island
as guides with North American friends. Some people have even been there as
"tourists." During the summer, a time of poor fishing, Seri fishermen occasionally go to San Esteban and other places in the Gulf simply for something to do.
Those who made one such trip in 1966 found a small pottery olla near the
northeastern corner of the island, which was later turned over to the Museo y
Biblioteca de Sonora in Hermosillo. In 1982, two Seri families, each in a separate boat, circumnavigated the island just to see it, not bothering to go ashore.
A year later, two other families in their boats went out and spent three days on
the island, as one of the participants put it, "just for the fun of it" (Mary Beck
Moser 1982, 1984, and 1995:pers. comms.).

All Seris today know of San Esteban, although less and less of its role in Seri history is being passed on. Perhaps this is why some people are now able to visit the island in a spirit of curiosity more than apprehension. Even in the 1980s, however, many Seris continued to regard the island as a dangerous place because of its great spirit power. For this reason, James Hills of Tucson has been cautioned by a number of Seri acquaintances not to go there. But he has gone out three times despite this advice, and on one of these trips, he was accompanied by a Seri friend. Hills says that his companion felt it important to sing at several stages of the trip to insure safety. It was especially important when leaving Tiburón, when entering the fierce current called *Ixötáacoj* "Big Whirlpool" that runs through the channel between the two islands, and before making landfall on San Esteban. As he explained to Hills, some of the songs concern a huge snake that once spanned the channel, with its head anchored on Tiburón, its tail on San Esteban, and its body arched over the channel between like a rainbow. In the old days when people tried to cross over to San Esteban, the snake would drop its body onto the travelers and kill them. Later, the snake went under water, and people today know it is there because of the dangerous current that runs between the two islands. But even though he took the precaution of singing, Hills' Seri friend was uneasy about going ashore. One of the things a person should never do on San Esteban, said Hills' friend, is throw rocks in the water, as this will cause the snake to create the terrible current that will suck you under. One should also refrain from shouting, as this will help prevent evil things from happening while on the island (James Hills 1983 and 1995:pers. comms.; Hills 1989:40).

Mexican Commercial Fishermen

As far as the Mexican government was concerned, when Guillermo Andrade lost his title to San Esteban in 1897, the island reverted back to the public domain. So far as is known, nobody has since tried to acquire title to the land or concessions for its rather limited resources. As public land, however, the island has remained available to any Mexicans who might find a use for it. Since the turn of the twentieth century, the one group that has maintained a consistent interest in the island has been small-scale commercial fishermen. These are not the operators of the large trawlers that run up and down the Gulf, but Mexicans who fish from 20- to 25-foot open pangas, powered by outboard motors, who go ashore on San Esteban and the other islands at night to camp (Figure 11.2). A number of these men have been working the Gulf waters long enough to have accumulated some ideas about the human use of the island in recent decades. A few have integrated what the old timers have told them with their own experiences into a patchwork oral history of San Esteban from the late nineteenth century to the present. These oral accounts, of course, are sometimes at variance with the equally sketchy written record (see Appendix B).

Figure 11.2 Conchita, *a modern fiberglass panga and its owner,*
Bahía Kino fisherman Feliciano "Chano" Cota (standing). Photograph taken on the
southwest coast of Tiburón Island, with San Esteban in the background. January 1983.

Almost all the fishermen say that it was hunting sea lions for their oil that first brought Mexicans to San Esteban. Most say that the base of operations was on the northern side of the island on the beach that has since become known as Playa La Freidera (Frying Place Beach) (Map 1.1; Figure 1.10). Some people believe that hunting may have begun around the time of World War I, though others think it probably started much later. At that time, sea lions inhabited all the beaches on the island, so it was a simple matter to shoot them and haul their carcasses back to La Freidera. Here the sea lions were "fried" in pit ovens on the beach, which several fishermen (erroneously) believe are still visible today. The oil was extracted and the remains discarded except for the hide, which sometimes could be sold.

One fisherman says that sea lion hunting was a summertime enterprise involving as many as 20 men in four boats. Most of the men were from Baja California where the business was headquartered. He says that some may have been *vagabundos*, the itinerant fishermen who at that time roamed the Gulf in canoes and makeshift pangas, living mostly on what they could catch (see Murray and Poole 1965:138–41, Murray 1967:83–84). The operation ran continuously throughout the summer, but the crews rotated so that nobody had to stay on the island more than a month. The men cheered up their stay by drinking mescal liquor, which they distilled in camp from the island's agave. Wages were a peso a day, and this was at a time when the peso was worth a dollar.[102] According to this account, once the oil was extracted, it was poured into 5-gallon containers, taken to Bahía de los Ángeles on the Baja California side of the Gulf, where it was delivered to Antero Díaz, the man said to be in charge of the operation.[103] Here the oil was sold to the Americans and loaded on sailing ships bound for San Francisco, California (Elfego Briseño 1982 and 1987:pers. comms.).

Another fisherman agrees that some of the sea lion hunters were from Baja California, but he thinks that most were probably Yaquis who came out from Guaymas. In the old days, he says, sea lions inhabited all of San Esteban's beaches, even Playa Limantour. Consequently, the hunters fried the blubber on several beaches, including San Pedro and El Cascajal, not just La Freidera. Some of the oil may have been taken to the peninsula, but most was sent to Guaymas (Severiano León 1980 and 1987:pers. comms.).

There is no clear consensus on how long the sea lion industry lasted. The prevailing view seems to be that it continued until sometime around World War II. One man says that the operation at Playa La Freidera continued until about 1955. A similar enterprise, he says, persisted on San Pedro Mártir Island until about 1965, and the oil from there was shipped to Guaymas. Another man agrees that hunting continued until the 1960s, when the Midriff islands came under government protection.

For Gulf fishermen, the discovery about 1936 that shark livers are a rich source of Vitamin A was an event of major proportions. Prior to that time, the market for sharks was a limited one. The fins could generally be sold for soup, the oil was sometimes used locally to make soap and process leather, and occasionally the best cuts of meat could be passed off as coming from other fish (Byers 1940:23; Walford 1945:1). But by 1938, the demand for shark livers was so great that shark fishing took over as the dominant activity in the Gulf:

> There is hardly a bay or sheltering island in the Gulf of California or on the open coast that does not support one or more shark fishing camps. Though individually these are small enterprises, the sum of their effort is impressive.
>
> Shark fishing camps are composed of several men, sometimes with their families, equipped with sailing dugouts or skiffs and necessary fishing gear. Two to several men operate one boat. Boats and gear may be owned by the fishermen themselves, or wholly or in part by investors living ashore. Fishermen put to sea daily, weather permitting, leaving early in the morning and returning in mid-afternoon with their fare of liver, flanks, and fins of sharks. These are salted, the liver stored in cans, the flanks baled, the fins piled or sacked. From time to time, the collected products are hauled by burros or sailed in canoes to various ports visited by freight boats or served by railroads. At the larger ports, like … Guaymas are refrigeration facilities. Fishermen operating from these ports land livers fresh, which are then iced, frozen or chemically-treated for shipment to the United States. (Walford 1945:1)

The value of the livers was based primarily on their vitamin content, and it was quickly discovered that there is great variation among different species and between males and females. Coupled with fluctuation in prices at the market place, a kilogram of raw liver brought anywhere from about $3.50 to $7.00 pesos. During the early 1940s, a shark fisherman might earn between $300 and $500 pesos per week (Irigoyen 1943a:39).

San Esteban Island is well known to modern fishermen for its sharks, and they say that shark fishing was an important activity there during the boom years. Some think that there was a direct connection between sea lion hunting on San Esteban and the rise of shark fishing there. The sea lions that lived on the beaches attracted sharks, and so when the market for shark livers developed, the fishermen were in turn attracted to San Esteban for the sharks. One man estimates that shark fishing began around 1912 and ended about the time of World War II. As with sea lion hunting, the most important entrepreneur of the shark industry, he says, was Antero Díaz in Baja California. Although the most valuable part of the animal was the liver, people usually saved the fins, which were sold for soup, and sometimes the skin and meat. Sharks were most abundant in the summer, so naturally shark fishing was a summertime pursuit. He says that the catch was processed on San Esteban in order to avoid having to haul the entire carcass back to the mainland.[104]

Most Mexican fishermen believe that the Seris were the first people to come to San Esteban to fish, perhaps beginning shortly after the turn of the century. It is thought that they came out initially to hunt sea turtles, which at one time abounded near the island. But back then, the Seris did not make the long trip very often because sea turtles could usually be found much closer to the mainland. The fishermen say that the Seris are still only occasional visitors, coming mainly in the summer, and sometimes using the island only as an overnight stop on their way to Baja California. They camp on the same beaches as the Mexicans, and if they venture inland it is only to gather firewood. The fishermen have no notion that any Seris ever lived on San Esteban.

The Mexican panga fishermen who have come to San Esteban in the late twentieth century have mostly been men who live in Bahía Kino, though sometimes people show up from Baja California. The island itself serves mainly as a place to camp while fishing the local waters, and as a convenient stopover if they are heading for other fishing grounds. Sometimes they will stop at San Esteban to fish for a day or two on their way home from San Lorenzo or Tiburón Island, especially if the fishing in those places has not been good. Fishing off San Esteban is done with lines, for it is not a place where nets can be used. The main catch during the 1980s was *cabrilla* (grouper) or sometimes shark, which was caught in the summer. However, San Esteban has a reputation as a rather poor fishing ground. It is also said to have the worst weather of any of the islands. When a storm comes through the area, it is always more severe on San Esteban, and people sometimes get stranded on the island for days at a time. Because of the mediocre fishing and bad weather, the island has never been a very popular destination. It is visited mainly by a few "regulars," people who will make the trip three or four times during the winter and another two or three times in summer. But many fishermen avoid the island completely.

In the 1970s, divers discovered that sea turtles overwintering on the sea floor off the shores of San Esteban could be easily captured, and for a brief period the island became the scene of intensive turtle hunting by both Mexican and Seri fishermen (Felger et al. 1976). In the 1980s, after the turtles gave out, San Esteban became known among Mexican fishermen primarily as a place to dive for scallops and lobsters. The usual diving party was made up of four fishermen equipped with wet suits and a compressor rigged with a length of simple hose to supply air for the divers. One man says he would come to San Esteban because scallops and lobsters were often not so deep there as they were at the other islands. Nevertheless, he would routinely descend 60 feet and often found it necessary to dive as deep as 115 feet to find productive scallop beds. He knows well the risk of diving to this depth, for he has been hospitalized with nitrogen narcosis, and he knows two men who are now permanently crippled from "the bends." Two or three days of diving would usually deplete the beds. If no others could be found nearby, which was often the case, the divers had no choice but to leave San Esteban and search elsewhere (Elfego Briseño 1982:pers. comm.).

By about 1990, the scallop beds off San Esteban had become thoroughly depleted, and fishermen turned to diving for sea cucumbers, which could be sold in Southeast Asian markets. By 1993, it was not uncommon to find 20 or more sea cucumber fishermen working the island at one time (Alberto Lucero 1993:pers. comm.).

Fishermen and divers working the waters off San Esteban usually stay for two or three days at a time. They nearly always make use of one of the two traditional camps where pangas can be beached and shelter found from storms. The winter and spring camp is on the eastern side of the island at El Monumento, where a cove offers a protected beach where pangas can be beached. Here a small cave provides shelter even in the worst weather, though it is so small, uncomfortable, and prone to rockfall from the roof that people resort to it only in severe conditions. Until the late 1980s, fishermen would normally camp in the open near the cave. They slept in a series of beach-cobble windbreaks, which were adequate to stave off most of the north winds of winter (see pp. 363–64, Figure 13.21). These windbreaks remained standing over many years, though extra walls and various furnishings came and went as different fishing parties remodeled to their tastes and needs. By 1993, however, the windbreaks had been destroyed and abandoned (see Figure 13.22), and the fishermen had switched to sleeping in simple floorless tents. These tents take the form of a basic A-frame, with the framework constructed of agave stalks lashed together and a tarp tied on for the covering.

During the summer, fishing activity traditionally shifts to San Pedro camp on the western side of the island. Here a cove and a sheltered beach give protection from the violent southerly storms that sweep the Gulf at that time of year. Like El Monumento, there is a small overhang to which fishermen can retreat if a *chubasco* or hurricane is brewing. San Pedro camp has not been as elaborately furnished as El Monumento, partly because it is only used in the hot season, and partly because, in the past, far fewer fishermen worked in the summer. Although a major revival of summer shark fishing in the Midriff began about 1990, San Pedro has not had much increase in use. For the most part, fishermen working near San Esteban in the summer prefer to camp elsewhere, and the widespread use of powerful motors makes campsites on other islands easily accessible (Alberto Lucero 1993:pers. comm.).

Occasionally, fishermen have camped on other parts of San Esteban's coast. One such place is Playa El Cascajal at the southwestern corner, and another is Playa La Freidera on the northern side, but neither location is considered a normal camping site.

The Mexican fishermen are, by virtue of their profession, intimately familiar with San Esteban's coastline and the surrounding waters, but most of them know little of the island beyond the immediate area of the camps. Sometimes a man will walk up one of the smaller hills near camp to check the wind. If the group has run short of food or water, a man may be sent up a hill to keep a lookout for a passing vessel, which the others can then intercept in their panga in order to borrow supplies. Firewood always needs to be collected, but this task usually does not require more than a short walk from camp. Generally, the only exploration of the island comes as a product of boredom. When the winds blow for days on end, it is impossible to fish or dive or even to leave the island for home. For some people, hiking up the valley becomes a way of alleviating the monotony of lying around camp reading, listening to the battery-powered radio, and making conversation with men they know all too well from years of working together. From El Monumento, some fishermen have walked part way up Arroyo Limantour, though apparently not more than a mile and a half or so. This is about the distance to the petroglyphs at *Icámajoj Zaaj*, which are occasionally the objective of a hike. Sometimes chuckwallas are captured along the way to bring back to camp or to take home. Hiking from San Pedro camp is much more arduous, since one must first ascend several hundred feet straight up the steep gravel slopes to the pass above. Now and then somebody will make the climb, and a few men have continued a short distance over the pass into the valley beyond. While most fishermen are only casual hikers, one man is reputed to be a dedicated explorer and has hiked all over San Esteban and other Gulf islands out of curiosity and interest. He is said to be a careful and astute observer who has learned a great deal about the natural history of the islands (Elfego Briseño 1982:pers. comm.).

Casual hiking over the years has led to the widely held view that water can sometimes be found on San Esteban. Most fishermen have never seen water themselves, but they have heard that it collects in bedrock pools after a big rain. One man has heard that water can be found during the summer in the arroyos that drain into the lower Arroyo Limantour. According to another man, water in bedrock pools can sometimes persist for many months, although he says a relentless wind may quickly evaporate it.

One aspect of the island about which the fishermen have learned very little is the archaeology. This is probably due both to the limited scope of their exploration and the inconspicuous nature of most of the remains. The only features that everyone knows about are the petroglyphs at *Icámajoj Zaaj*, and most people know that one of the figures (which has recently disappeared) depicted a sailing vessel (see Figures 13.15 and 13.16). Though apparently all the fishermen know of this site, very few have actually seen it, and they uniformly refer to the figures erroneously as "paintings" (*pinturas*). It is common knowledge that the petroglyphs are Seri, and one man was actually shown the site by a Seri friend. However, nobody knows why the figures were created or what they "mean."

Some fishermen also know that there are large pits laden with charcoal up the valley from El Monumento, but very few have seen them personally. Most people speculate that the pits were the places where sea lion hunters long ago cooked the blubber into oil. One man, however, suspects they were built to bake agave hearts, perhaps by *vagabundos* attempting to use the hearts to distill mescal. At least one man knows of the circular rock-walled structure on the pass above San Pedro camp, but he does not know who built it or why—only that it has been there for a long time (Elfego Briseño 1982:pers. comm.).

Like the Seris, some of the Mexican fishermen feel a strong sense of uneasiness about San Esteban which they do not experience on the other islands. One fisherman who took scientists into the Gulf in the 1950s and 1960s did not like going to San Esteban, though he had no such reservations about any other island (Charles H. Lowe 1995:pers. comm.). Another man characterizes San Esteban as a "spooky" place and says he often has nightmares at San Pedro camp. Sometimes fishermen see a "phantom light" at San Pedro while they are approaching the camp at night from the sea. The light appears to be the campfire of other fishermen who are already on shore, but when they approach the beach the light vanishes (Elfego Briseño 1987:pers. comm.). No one has an explanation for this phenomenon.

North American Sport Fishermen

For an island reputed to have few economic resources, it is ironic that nearly all early twentieth century visitors to San Esteban—Seri agave harvesters and Mexican sea lion hunters and fishermen—came for straightforward economic reasons. But resources need not be defined strictly in terms of making a living. Thus the island has gradually acquired value to other kinds of people for other reasons, and the use of boats with increasingly powerful motors has made the island accessible to a broader spectrum of people.

Of the new kinds of visitors, the vast majority have been North American sport fishermen. The pioneers of this new group were California "angler-yachtsmen" who began to explore the Gulf north of Guaymas shortly after the turn of the century (Townsend 1916:452). Exactly when these people first began to fish off San Esteban is not known, but one North American sport fisherman tested the waters around Tiburón Island less than four years after the last military campaign there. This was Charles Conn, who sailed from San Diego to Tiburón in 1908 on his yacht *Comfort* (Conn ca. 1909). In addition to fishing, Conn went ashore on Tiburón, where he took a number of photographs of Seris and a photograph of perhaps the first Caucasian woman (apart from the captive Lola Casanova) to set foot on the island. About the same time another sportsman, E. A. Salisbury, was making periodic hunting and fishing trips to Tiburón in his power boat *Wanderer* and establishing friendly contact with Seris in the vicinity (Williams 1911:100).

Other North Americans gradually followed. In 1921, Western novelist Zane Grey declined an invitation to hunt and fish on Tiburón from "Arizona Charlie" Meadows (King 1989:307). In 1922, Y. L. Holmes obtained a concession for 6,000 acres of land at Bahía Kino and built a rustic but comfortable hunting and fishing lodge that became known as the Kino Bay Club. Over the next decade or so, lifetime memberships in the Club were sold to wealthy sportsmen both in Hermosillo and the United States. North American members were flown in from Nogales by the Club airplane, and promotional literature noted that members living on the East Coast of the United States could be fishing or lounging at the lodge 24 hours after leaving home (Anonymous 193[?]; Browne ca. 1931). By the late 1930s, the Kino Bay Club had folded, presumably a casualty of the Great Depression.

Though short lived, the Kino Bay Club drew attention to this part of the coast as a logical point of embarkation for the Midriff islands. The dirt track connecting Bahía Kino with Hermosillo (dubbed "a fine road" by one enthusiastic Kino Bay Club member) helped stimulate a new market outlet for Mexican commercial fishermen and spawned the small fishing village of Bahía Kino. The paving of the road in 1953 made this portion of the coast accessible for serious development, and a number of Mexicans from Hermosillo built vacation homes along the beach north of the old fishing village, which was increasingly referred to as Kino Viejo (Old Kino). Soon after, North Americans began to migrate toward Bahía Kino in some numbers, attracted by the natural beauty of the region, the excellent boating and fishing, and the relative proximity of the new beach community to the Arizona border. In the postwar climate of affluence and leisure, some of these visitors decided to stay. Their vacation and retirement homes began to spring up alongside those of the Mexicans, and they gradually became the dominant faction in the new community, today referred to as New Kino.

Sport fishing at San Esteban is closely tied to the emergence of New Kino. Sport fishermen, unlike Mexican commercial fishermen, usually go out just for the day. Nearly all of these people own inboard cabin cruisers, typically around 24 feet in length. They launch at New Kino, which is just close enough to San Esteban to make a day trip there practical. On rare occasions, a boat from Bahía de los Ángeles or other ports may show up at San Esteban, but these are usually yachtsmen on extended cruises who are just passing through the area.

For the North American residents of New Kino, boating and sport fishing is the centerpiece of life. This was underscored in 1977 by the founding of the Club Deportivo de Bahía Kino, a vigorous organization that promotes boating, sport fishing, and a wide range of social activities. The majority of the 800 or so active members are North American residents of New Kino, but club membership also includes many nonresidents who vacation in Kino and a small con-

Figure 11.3   Eldon Heaston (1924–1988), one of the founders of the Club Deportivo de Bahía Kino and Rescate 1. *December 1980.*

tingent of Mexican sport fishermen. It was also a group of New Kino people who formed the marine rescue unit known as *Rescate 1* (Rescue 1) during the early 1970s (Figure 11.3). This organization monitors the disposition of boaters throughout the central Gulf by VHF radio, and over the years, it has been instrumental in averting many potential boating disasters.

North Americans who bring their boats to Bahía Kino on short vacations generally try to get out to fish each day the weather is stable. Permanent residents, having more time, seldom launch more frequently than once a week. Nearly everyone considers the trip to San Esteban a long one. With calm seas, most sport fishing boats need between 1½ and 3 hours to reach the island, and many people feel this is just too much travel time. Besides, they say, most of the fish that occur off San Esteban can be caught much closer to Kino. But those who have been there say the long trip is sometimes worth it because the fishing there is often fairly good. One man knows a spot where yellowtail can almost always be caught. During one year, red snapper was especially abundant along the eastern shore of the island and that brought a lot of fishermen out. It is said that bottom fishing is usually quite good, but it can only be done during the half moon when the strong currents that sweep past the island subside. One long-time resident of New Kino says that good weather at the height of the fishing season may bring as many as three or four boats to San Esteban each day (Eldon Heaston 1984:pers. comm.; Robert Jarratt 1984 and 1987:pers. comms.).

Strictly speaking, North American fishermen come to the waters surrounding San Esteban, not to the island itself, and few people have ever set foot there. The main reason for this, of course, is that they come to fish, not to explore, and

Figure 11.4   Buckshot, *a North American sport fishing boat,*
anchored off Playa Limantour. On this trip it brought archaeologists and field equipment
to San Esteban, with the help of a rubber dinghy. December 1980.

there are no shelling beaches to entice people ashore. Moreover, landing poses a
logistic problem for most New Kino boaters. Unlike Mexican fishing pangas, which
can be beached, the cabin cruisers piloted by most North Americans must lie at
anchor (Figure 11.4). The only way for people to get in is by dinghy, and most
boaters neither own a dinghy nor care to tow one. Staying overnight, whether to
extend a fishing trip or to explore the island, is not usually considered a realistic
option, for the consensus is that the island has no secure anchorage for large boats.
Yet a few people have stayed there overnight. One man, who used to come out with
his son during the summer, would anchor at San Pedro camp and sleep out on his
boat. Another man has anchored overnight at El Monumento while diving for lob-
ster. Virtually the entire New Kino community, however, considers San Esteban
to be the worst place of all the Midriff islands to get benighted in bad weather. As
two well-seasoned skippers put it, they would far rather run in the dark for Tiburón
or Kino than try to anchor off San Esteban (Eldon Heaston 1981:pers. comm.;
Robert Jarratt 1987:pers. comm.). In some instances, boaters have had no choice,
as with an Arizona man whose engine quit, forcing him to spend New Year's Eve
of 1981 nervously anchored off El Monumento. Far more frightening was Ray
Cannon's "Voyage of Terror," in which he and a companion barely managed to ride
out a raging nighttime *chubasco* in the inadequate lee of El Cascajal, coming through
it with losses of just four anchors and a dinghy (Cannon 1966:97–100). In September
1990, a scientific research group from the Arizona-Sonora Desert Museum was not
so fortunate when their boat, anchored off Playa Limantour, was hit by Tropical
Storm Norbert (see pp. 312–13).

Despite poor anchorage and potentially violent weather, a few North American sport fishermen have been ashore on San Esteban briefly at "The Big Valley" (lower Arroyo Limantour), "The Sandspit" (El Cascajal) or at "Herm's Cove," the name used by a few old-timers for San Pedro camp. Most of these people say they went ashore hoping to see one of the famous chuckwallas or just "to have a look around." Having spent so little time on the island, it is not surprising that nobody seems to be aware of any archaeological remains. Apparently, no one has ever heard that Seri Indians might once have lived there.

Scuba Divers, Ecotourists, and Drug Runners

The turbulent years of the 1960s brought about changes in attitudes and values in many realms of life. Perhaps none were more profound than the heightened awareness and appreciation of the natural environment. For the first time in many decades, significant numbers of people worldwide began to perceive the natural order as something of great intrinsic beauty to be valued for its own sake, not merely for its utility for human exploitation. The coasts and islands of the Gulf of California were quickly recognized as among the few places that had largely escaped the onslaught of civilization (Bahre 1983). Their stark scenic beauty and extraordinary biological diversity made them excellent destinations for people wishing to experience an unspoiled bit of nature.

Among those who are interested in observing the Gulf rather than exploiting it for profit are scuba divers. Those who have been to San Esteban say that the diving is excellent, especially near the reef that extends out from the northeastern corner of the island (Peterson 1992:146). However, the island is not well known to the diving community because of its remoteness. In January 1982, four divers from Phoenix came out for a day and a half, camping overnight on Playa Limantour. They said they had a good time diving but that the trip to San Esteban was just too far to be worth it.

Wildlife photographers, both amateur and professional, have also been lured to the Gulf and a few have ventured out as far as San Esteban. Most have been interested in photographing the island's chuckwallas or its resident sea bird and sea lion colonies (Cadieux 1969; Anonymous 1985a; Fisher 1985:24, 1988:78).

One visitor to the Gulf with a unique interest in local wildlife was the epicure of natural foods, Euell Gibbons. According to a Bahía Kino fisherman who served as his guide, Gibbons spent the better part of an August day in 1972 investigating San Esteban for edible plants and animals (Elfego Briseño 1982:pers. comm.). Although he reported on his Gulf trips in two of his books (Gibbons 1964, 1973), he makes no mention of delectable finds on San Esteban.

New values also bring new opportunities for the entrepreneur. Renewed popular interest in the natural world is no exception, for it has spawned a whole new industry of organized ecotourism. In the Gulf, the predominant form of this concept is the natural history cruise ship (Anonymous 1985b). Unlike the self-indulgent gastronomic extravaganzas popularized by television, the tour companies operating in the Gulf generally try to provide an educational experience

Figure 11.5   Ecotourism on San Esteban Island.
Passengers returning to the Lindblad Sea Lion *after a morning on shore.*
March 1993.

by enabling their passengers to learn about the natural environment of the region. These vessels make their stops at remote bays and uninhabited islands instead of tourist ports, and passengers take in the local wildlife instead of the shopping (Lindblad et al. 1985). Many cruises are staffed by professional scientists who present scheduled lectures and serve as guides, and it is not uncommon for well-known scientists to sign on as paying passengers (Lindsay and Lindsay 1981). Cruise sponsors frequently include prestigious museums, conservation organizations, and scientific institutions such as the Smithsonian Institution and the California Academy of Sciences (Anonymous 1981b, 1985b, 1989; Peterson 1992:13–14).

One commercial company, Lindblad's Special Expeditions, first began bringing passengers to San Esteban in 1981, and since then its vessels have stopped there six to eight times each year between December and April (Peter Butz 1994:pers. comm.). One of these visits was in January 1982, when the company's 70-passenger *Pacific Northwest Explorer* appeared shortly after dawn off El Monumento. Once anchored, some 50 of its passengers were quickly ferried to shore in Zodiac inflatable motorboats. For three hours, these visitors explored the lower reaches of Arroyo Limantour, intent on seeing some of the island's famous chuckwallas. Unfortunately, the morning was unusually cold, gray, and very windy, and apparently nobody saw any of these warmth-loving lizards. According to one of the naturalists, on this cruise Captain Lindblad himself was on board, and the passenger list included the legendary evolutionary biologist George Gaylord Simpson. By contrast, in March 1993, the 70 passengers of the company's vessel *Sea Lion* went ashore on a warm, sunny, and thoroughly beautiful day when the chuckwallas, iguanas, birds, and other creatures were out in force (Figure 11.5).

A form of ecotourism that requires a much deeper level of personal commitment is one in which the customer pays for the privilege of signing on as a field assistant to help collect data for a legitimate scientific project. As with tours, the logistic arrangements such as transport, meals, permits, and so forth are usually handled professionally, which leaves the client free to concentrate on the scientific project at hand. Unlike conventional tours, the fieldwork may be rugged and demanding, and the participants are not passive observers but make genuine contributions to the research objectives.

In the mid-1980s, the Arizona-Sonora Desert Museum in Tucson launched just such a venture to San Esteban Island to study the endemic chuckwallas. Billed as one of the Museum's "Desert Watch" research expeditions, four separate field trips for the project were scheduled over the course of a year. To facilitate the trips, the Desert Museum contracted out the logistic arrangements to a professional travel company. Accommodations at the island itself were to be on board a "very comfortable" 120-foot yacht, though Museum notices did not hedge about the demands of the fieldwork itself (Anonymous 1985c:10; Lawler 1992:24). The scientific objectives of the project were to obtain normal physiological data and identify pathological disorders that occur in the wild among the island's chuckwallas. In addition to its intrinsic scientific value, this information would serve as baseline data to improve management of captive populations, such as those at the Desert Museum. The project was grant-supported and was to be codirected by two members of the Museum scientific staff in collaboration with a Mexican colleague. No animals were to be removed from the island, and extreme care was to be taken to insure minimal stress on the sampled animals and no disruption to the island habitat. In the end, only one such trip materialized, but from a scientific standpoint it was successful (Anonymous 1985d:14; Howard E. Lawler 1985, 1986, and 1995:pers. comms.).

Many of the people who visit the Gulf, either on cruise ships or as paying field assistants, would not be able to go there any other way. The reasons for some include age or physical limitations, but the greatest barrier is often simple lack of knowledge of how to put together a wilderness expedition. For such individuals, packaged alternatives can be richly rewarding experiences. But others believe that no setting can be construed as "natural" in the presence of large numbers of visitors who bring the trappings of civilization with them and stay only a few hours. For these individuals, the natural world should be experienced by blending in with it, not overwhelming it, and by taking sufficient time to come to know it. A wild setting is something to be experienced alone or shared with a few close companions.

The last four decades have produced a number of ecologically-oriented outdoor schools that attempt to impart this attitude to their students while teaching them various wilderness skills. Some of these schools offer sea kayaking and sailing courses in the Gulf. Although most of these courses stay clear of the difficult currents and winds of the Midriff islands, kayaks and small sailboats are occasionally seen there (Peterson 1992:55–58; Suzy Messer 1997:pers. comm.). One of these institutions, the Wyoming-based National Outdoor Leadership School, offers regularly-scheduled sailing courses that traverse the Midriff on the peninsular side and make use of anchorages on Ángel de la Guarda, Salsipuedes, and San Lorenzo Islands. In 1993, a pair of instructors from this school sailed to San Esteban on a scouting trip, but the island has never been incorporated into the regular course itinerary (Terri Watson 1993:pers. comm.; Mark Van Winkle 1997:pers. comm.).

Because of its remoteness and largely pristine condition, San Esteban has been a superb destination for those seeking unspoiled isolation, and a number of individuals have gone there in this spirit. One person who has explored the island is Tucson photographer Richard Fisher, who conveys this perspective in a richly illustrated book on northwestern Mexico (Fisher 1988). Another is James Hills, whose academic background in anthropology and geography (Hills 1973) has been supplemented by many years of close contact with the Seris as a trader. Hills first decided to go to San Esteban because of "an intense curiosity about the island due to its place in Seri history" (James Hills 1987:pers. comm.). Two of his trips were made in an old-style wooden plank panga which he purchased from a Seri. He did this in an effort to experience what the voyage was like for the Seris who went out there before the introduction of fiberglass boats and high-horsepower motors. David Yetman, who accompanied Hills on both trips, has written vividly of their experiences during the first of these voyages. The small motor they used was almost unable to cope with the waves and currents as they crossed the channel from Tiburón Island. A storm that whipped up after they arrived slammed their boat into the rocks of Playa Limantour, punching a hole in its side. And the group ran out of drinking water before the storm had abated enough for them to leave the island (Yetman 1988:155–65). Hills says that the second trip was less scary, except when the motor mount fell off the back of the panga and the motor was almost lost. But despite these incidents, Hills regards these trips as eminently successful, for the near disasters have given him an intense appreciation of just how risky the trip to San Esteban was for the Seris in the early days (James Hills 1986 and 1987:pers. comms.).

Among those who have visited San Esteban out of interest in its natural history, few were more widely known than Alexander "Ike" Russell (Figure 11.6). Because he was a highly skilled bush pilot and well acquainted with the scientific community, Russell flew many scientists to isolated research sites throughout the Gulf region. He also kept a large deisel-powered boat (christened *Ofelia*) in Guaymas, which he used as an alternative means of travel to the Midriff islands. Between the late 1950s and 1970s, Russell made a number of trips to San Esteban, often taking scientists there, and often staying for several days at a time. He was a careful observer and he used his time ashore to explore the island. In fact, Russell was one of the first people to discover and record archaeological remains on San Esteban (Bowen 1976:36).

There is also a sinister side to San Esteban's recent history, for it is rumored among Mexican fishermen that the island was used for a while by drug runners working for "the Mafia." Little is known about this shadowy business, if in fact it did occur. During the height of the drug trafficking era of the 1970s, much of northern Mexico was an open corridor for the smuggling of illicit drugs into

*Figure 11.6   Alexander "Ike" Russell (1916–1980) at Bahía Vaporeta,
west coast of Tiburón Island. January 1976.*

the United States. Remote and uninhabited localities were carefully sought out as drug transfer points, and the Gulf of California was an ideal place for transfers to be made. In an attempt to curb this growing problem, the Mexican Navy stepped up its patrols of the Midriff waters and established three military outposts on Tiburón Island, each manned by a squad of Marines equipped with semiautomatic rifles.

Mexican fishermen say that it was the makeshift airstrip hacked out during the 1970s that attracted the drug runners to San Esteban. The airstrip was built innocently enough by a Tucson man, and a Bahía Kino fisherman says he was involved with its construction. The man who wanted it built was interested in chuckwallas, not drugs. The fisherman says he took the man and two youths who were with him out to the island by boat. They built the airstrip entirely from scratch, spending about a week clearing away the brush and rocks. Then a plane landed and picked up the man and his companions. He says it was some time later that the potential of this remote airstrip was discovered by the drug runners. They would bring cargoes of marijuana to San Esteban by boat and transfer it there to airplanes, which would then make the final run across the border. But the drug operation apparently did not last long. Mexican authorities caught wind of it and sent out some soldiers. Rather than set up another military outpost, they simply piled large boulders and dug a series of trenches across the airstrip, making it suicidal to try to land there. The airstrip has not been used since, and vegetation is gradually returning to cover this scar on the landscape.

Putting the airstrip out of commission ended the alleged drug flights out of San Esteban, but it did not quite sever the island's connection with drugs. In 1988, the residents of New Kino watched in awe as a man by the name of Carlos Enrique Tápia A. bought up the better part of a city block and began constructing a house that was clearly designed to fill the entire lot. Awe turned to dismay and fear when the 10-foot high and foot-thick concrete wall went up around the perimeter, and construction workers began to tell of underground living quarters, along with the indoor tennis courts, swimming pool, and billiards hall that made up the house's 20 rooms. As Tápia and his associates flamboyantly began "spreading money around Kino like it was beach sand" local people began to suspect that he might not be just the building contractor he said he was (Hernandez 1989).

Then in late September 1989, while Tápia's "fortress" was nearing completion in Kino, the U.S. Drug Enforcement Agency pulled off a raid on a warehouse in Los Angeles, California. The agents turned up 20 tons of cocaine said to be worth two billion dollars on the street, probably the biggest bust in the agency's history. About the same time Tápia disappeared.

Six days later, on the morning of October 5, a special team of Mexican Federal Police staged a dawn helicopter raid on San Esteban Island. They found Tápia and seven others hiding out in a humble tent. After his arrest, a spokesman for the Federal Police identified Tápia as a major figure in a Mexican cocaine cartel, and the residents of New Kino breathed a big sigh of relief (Hernandez 1989).

TWELVE

Rediscovering San Esteban Island:
Modern Cartography and Scientific Field Research

Survey Parties and the Cartography of San Esteban Island

After the brief visits to San Esteban (or the waters surrounding it) by the survey crew from the U.S.S. *Narragansett* in 1875 and by Guillermo Andrade's agents in 1882, there do not seem to have been any further attempts to map the island until the middle of the twentieth century. The first modern surveyors known to have set foot on San Esteban were sent by the Secretaría de la Defensa Nacional to gather basic topographical data. This expedition, led by Cleofas Méndez, arrived in March 1958 with the intent of establishing a survey station on the highest peak of the island. Their ascent up the mountain was a long haul:

> To reach the [survey] station, I departed from Bahía Kino by boat, going 63 kilometers until I arrived at the north side of the Island. Here there is a small rocky beach [where] one disembarks from a panga. Continued on, with the equipment carried by [the] men, (southwest) up the nearest canyon for a duration of 4 hours, [until] I arrive at a small pass. From this place the highest part of the hill is visible, sloping down to the southwest. After a stretch of 1½ hours, I arrive at the highest part, which is where the station is found. The trip takes approximately 6 hours by foot. (Méndez 1958)

The peak they had climbed turned out to be Male Mountain, some 200 feet lower than Pico San Esteban, the highest point on the island (see Figures 1.3 and 13.2). But it was on this summit that they set up their survey station and installed three benchmarks, along with an azimuth marker placed some two thousand feet away. The main benchmark was engraved "ESTEBAN 1958," and its position was established as 28° 43′ 33.3290″ north latitude, 112° 35′ 36.8260″ west longitude, and its altitude 485.8 m (1,594 feet), determined trigonometrically (Méndez 1958; Anonymous 1982).

With so much time spent climbing to the survey station, the surveyors were forced to spend at least one uncomfortable night on the summit of Male Mountain:

> The weather that prevailed during the occupation of the station was hot by day and cold during the night [with] strong winds from the north—at the station there is no place for camping nor firewood to burn. Water is obtained in Kino, the boat to transport one is obtained in Guaymas. (Méndez 1958)

There seem to have been at least two subsequent visits to the island by government surveyors. According to a Bahía Kino fisherman who has frequently guided visitors in the region, two federal surveyors and a pair of government prospectors spent three days on San Esteban about 1973 or 1974. The surveyors were interested in measuring altitudes while the prospectors searched for uranium. The guide, who brought the party to the island, did not accompany them during the day. He said that the surveyors later told him that they had climbed three peaks and set benchmarks in cement.[105] The prospectors, meanwhile, apparently found nothing of interest (Elfego Briseño 1982:pers. comm.).

A third survey party came to the island in 1980 or 1981. Their visit is known not from documentary sources or oral accounts, but archaeologically from the artifacts they left behind. The surveyors established their base camp at the foot of Male Mountain, where they cleared sleeping areas and built a small circular hearth of stones. On the summit, they may have constructed a cairn and three windbreaks. Both sites are strewn with essentially the same artifacts, including food containers, dry cell batteries, and other tools of the surveyors' trade (see pp. 362–63).

Despite these ground surveys and the availability of aerial photographs and satellite imagery, some peculiarities remain in the cartography of the Midriff region. In one case, the problem is nomenclature. A 1992 world atlas published by *The Times* of London depicts San Esteban correctly but identifies it as "S. Sebastian" Island (Anonymous 1992:Pl. 115). Most other lingering errors involve San Esteban's shape. For sailors, the 1877 Hydrographic Office chart of the Gulf was good enough that, with relatively minor revisions, it has continued to serve as the standard navigational chart up to the present time. It is now produced by the U.S. Defense Mapping Agency, and the most recent edition, the 61st, was published in 1984. Yet the slightly distorted shape of San Esteban on the original Hydrographic Office chart has never been corrected (Anonymous 1984).

Two current map series that cover the Midriff region at a scale of 1:250,000 give a more accurate representation of the island, and these also provide topographical information. The best of these is the Joint Operations Graphic (Air) map series, designed for aircraft pilots. Though originally prepared and published by the U.S. Department of Defense, it is now also printed and distributed by the Mexican government through its Comisión de Estudios del Territorio Nacional (CETENAL). The sheet entitled "Isla de San Esteban, México" gives the most detailed contours for the island of any available map, though the scale is small (Anonymous 1976a). The island also appears on the "Isla San Esteban" sheet of the Mexican government's 1:250,000 series, published in 1980 by the Secretaría de Programación y Presupuesto (SPP) (Anonymous 1980a). This map provides less topographical information, and it places four nonexistent islets just off San Esteban's shore.

The SPP has also embarked on an ambitious project to compile topographical maps of the entire Republic at a scale of 1:50,000. But how San Esteban Island will be dealt with in this series is not clear, for Tiburón Island has not fared well so far. Two of the sheets, entitled "Punta Chueca" and "Bahía Kunkaak," cover a stretch of the Sonoran coastline opposite Tiburón Island, the Canal del Infiernillo, and the territory to the west of the Infiernillo where Tiburón Island is situated. But there is not a hint of Tiburón Island on either of these maps, not even an outline. The space the island should occupy is represented in blue as empty water, as if the Canal del Infiernillo extends indefinitely westward into a featureless Gulf. With some searching, the explanation for this omission can be found in small print: "The islands not represented in this chart, for lack of geodesic and photogrammetric information, will be included in the second edition" (Anonymous 1980b, 1980c). As of 1998, the San Esteban sheet has yet to be published.

Science Comes to San Esteban Island

The first scientists to set foot on San Esteban Island arrived in 1911 on board the U.S. research vessel *Albatross* (Figure 9.9). Their visit was a short one, for the ship dropped anchor at 1:30 on the afternoon of April 13, and departed for Guaymas at 8:30 the following morning. But these few hours were sufficient to collect or note many of the dominant plants and animals, including several entirely new species and subspecies. By the time the *Albatross* departed, San Esteban was no longer a complete blank on the scientific map.

The voyage was a cooperative venture of the American Museum of Natural History, the New York Zoological Society, and the United States National Museum, which contributed the funding and part of the scientific staff, and would house most of the specimens collected. The *Albatross* was provided by the U.S. Bureau of Fisheries in return for oceanographic data and information about the Gulf fishery resources. Publication of the scientific results was authorized by the Commissioner of Fisheries.

The *Albatross*, under the command of Commander G. H. Burrage, left San Francisco on February 23 and picked up the scientific staff two days later in San Diego. The scientists were Charles H. Townsend, who directed the expedition, botanist J. N. Rose, mammalogist H. E. Anthony, ornithologist P. I. Osburn, conchologist Paul Bartsch, ichthyologists L. M. Tongue and W. L. Schmitt from the Bureau of Fisheries, and modeler James Bell. Departing San Diego on February 28, the expedition steered for Guadalupe Island and spent the next three weeks investigating the Pacific coast and islands of Baja California. On March 25, after a stop at San José del Cabo, the *Albatross* turned northward into the Gulf (Townsend 1916:399–404).

On April 10, the expedition reached Ángel de la Guarda Island, its northernmost destination in the Gulf, where the day was spent collecting both terrestrial and marine organisms. The next day, the vessel sailed to the southern tip of Tiburón Island. After spending the remainder of the 11th and all of the 12th there:

> The 'Albatross' left Tiburon Island at 11 o'clock on the morning of April 13, arriving at San Esteban Island at 1:30. Almost upon landing we began to obtain specimens of two species of large lizards, one a *Sauromalus*, the other apparently *Ctenosaura hemilopha*. They occurred in shallow depressions under large stones and were usually detected by their tails, which were not always drawn in out of sight. They were captured easily by turning the stones, which were not generally too large for a couple of men to handle. Forty-seven specimens in all were captured alive, the largest being thirty inches long. The *Sauromalus* proved to be new to science. Two rattlesnakes (*Crotalus molossus*) were also secured and a few mice and birds, while the botanist obtained a new century plant (*Agave dentiens*). A new species of mouse obtained here has been named *Peromyscus stephani*. San Esteban is about 4 miles in diameter, exceedingly rough and mountainous, with a height of 1800 feet. It lies 8 miles S. W. of Tiburon, is without fresh water and is uninhabited. (Townsend 1916:427–28)

During the hours the *Albatross* lay at anchor off the east coast of San Esteban, the crew used the boat dredge and fired five shots of dynamite in the water, securing, among other marine organisms, a new species of sting ray (Osburn and Nichols 1916:144–45). By the next morning, they had discovered that San Esteban is sometimes a hazardous place to lay over:

> The flow of the tides is very strong in this part of the Gulf. During the night the ship dragged anchor somewhat on the ebb tide. When we left for Guaymas at 8:30, the anchor came up minus a fluke which had broken off. The tide was running fiercely, and with half a gale of wind also in our favor, we started for Guaymas under sail and steam. Passing San Pedro Martir Island at noon, where it was impossible to make a landing on account of the weather, we reached Guaymas after dark. (Townsend 1916:428)

From Guaymas the vessel sailed southward, stopping at four of the peninsular islands before rounding Cabo San Lucas and steaming to San Francisco, where the expedition ended on April 28.

Throughout the voyage, oceanographic data were gathered on a regular basis, and extensive collections of marine organisms were obtained by dredging, seining, and exploding charges of dynamite. Although shore parties had little time on dry land—never more than two days and often only a few hours—these excursions were extremely productive. During the two months of the expedition, including work on the Pacific side of the peninsula, the collections of terrestrial organisms:

> included 804 specimens of birds representing 143 different species; 259 specimens of mammals of 59 species, ten of which proved to be new to science; 446 speci-

mens of reptiles, of 47 species eight of which are new. A number of living reptiles were brought to the New York Zoölogical Park. A small but important series of insects was obtained and a very large collection of invertebrates.

The botanist, with assistance from the crew, made large gatherings of plants, obtaining about 1800 specimens. The collection of cacti was the most important of its kind ever brought from Lower California, and more than a thousand living specimens were sent safely to the New York Botanical Garden. Many of the plants have been described as new to science and there are many still to be studied.... Most of the century plants brought back by the expedition proved to be new species. (Townsend 1916:400–401)

Upon their arrival in the United States, these collections were turned over to specialists, and within a few years most of the organisms collected, and especially the type specimens of new species, had been described in the scientific literature. For San Esteban Island, this taxonomic work produced the first descriptions of several of its most conspicuous endemic forms, the piebald (or blotched) chuckwalla (*Sauromalus varius*) (Schmidt 1922:641–43), the whiptail lizard (*Cnemidophorus estebanensis*) (Dickerson 1919), the white-footed mouse (*Peromyscus stephani*) (Townsend 1912), the giant rainbow cactus (*Echinocereus grandis*), and the agave (*Agave dentiens*, now *A. cerulata* subsp. *dentiens*) (Trelease 1912; see also Gentry 1978:43–44). It was also suspected, correctly as it turns out, that the black-tailed rattlesnake collected on San Esteban might be subspecifically distinct (Schmidt 1922:697–98), and it has since been designated *Crotalus molossus estebanensis* (Klauber 1949:104–6). Other organisms taken at this time have also been subsequently reclassified as taxonomically distinct.

It was this pioneering voyage of the *Albatross* that effectively opened the Gulf of California to systematic scientific study. During their four weeks in the Gulf, the scientists were able to go ashore and collect on nine islands. Some, like San Esteban, had never been seen by scientists, while others had been barely touched. Though only a fraction of the islands were visited and the collections far from exhaustive, they provided basic data sets of great interest and clearly demonstrated the biological diversity of the region and the high level of endemism among certain groups of organisms. Equally important, the organization and itinerary of the *Albatross* cruise came to serve as the model for most of the large-scale scientific expeditions that followed.

In 1918, seven years after the *Albatross* cruise, the first Mexican scientific party landed on San Esteban Island, though it was not a planned visit. Like most Mexican expeditions, this reconnaissance was directed not toward basic science but rather toward identifying economically useful biological and mineral resources, including petroleum. It was sponsored by the federal government through its Secretaría de Industria, Comercio y Trabajo and was carried out by a party of four under the leadership of Inspector of Industries José C. Zárate. Accompanying him was José María Gallegos of the Secretaría de Agricultura y Fomento in Hermosillo. The other two members were Francisco Ramonet, a maritime customs administrator who held guano mining concessions to San

Pedro Mártir, Patos, Rasa, and San Jorge Islands, and his friend Luis C. Gaxiola of Guaymas. The vessel chartered for the cruise was the 20-ton American steamer *Frolic*, which carried a four-man crew (Zárate 1920:74–75).

The expedition set out from Guaymas on November 26, 1918, and planned to visit each of the islands in Ramonet's concession. The first stop was San Pedro Mártir, where the party spent a day assessing the economic value of the guano reserves and the difficulties that would be faced mining and shipping it. They also made note of the island's enormous potential resources of edible fish and sea lions (Zárate 1920:75–78). On November 28, they left San Pedro Mártir, intending to steam to San Lorenzo Island, but they soon found themselves battling a gale rising out of the northwest. Changing plans, they steered for the shelter of San Esteban Island, where they found only scant protection from the developing storm:

> minutes after 7 [P.M. on the 28th], the wind detached the anchors, and for more than two hours we went struggling to try to cast anchor again. About 4:30 A.M. on the 29th, it was necessary to cast [the ship] adrift, and it was not until some three hours more had passed that we were again able to secure an anchorage. (Zárate 1920:80)

After this hard night, the expedition stayed put on San Esteban for the day and used the time to reconnoiter the island. The next night was equally trying for Zárate and Gallegos, who decided to paddle into shore to try to capture a young sea lion. As they neared the beach, the stormy sea suddenly swamped their canoe. Fearing they would be drowned, they abandoned the canoe and frantically jumped to shore. But now they were unable to get back to the *Frolic* until the tide ebbed at dawn, so they passed what must surely have been a miserable night stranded on the beach (Zárate 1920:80).

The *Frolic* left San Esteban on the morning of the 30th, intending to sail to Patos Island, but:

> the storm was not subsiding, and the sea we encountered was extremely rough because of the excessive violence of the wind and the strong currents, which probably originated from the Río Colorado. Our intention was to go to Patos Island, but the bad weather completely prevented us from this, forcing us to find shelter in the nearest cove on Tiburón island.... We arrived at this cove [near Punta Willard] the same day, the 30th, at 9:40 A.M., remaining anchored in it until the 2nd [of December]. We left for Patos island at 4:10 A.M. on this day. The NW wind never ceased to blow for a moment, to such a degree that we were on the verge of giving up this trip. (Zárate 1920:81)

With such ferocious weather, the *Frolic* stayed only about three hours at Patos, while the expedition members hastily assessed the island's guano resources for Ramonet. Then the ship ran southward through the Canal del Infiernillo, anchoring late that afternoon in a cove at the southern tip of Tiburón

Island. After a day at this anchorage, the *Frolic* steamed southeastward, and the expedition ended shortly thereafter in Guaymas.

Despite the terrible weather and forcibly altered itinerary, the expedition members spent their days exploring the islands, noting the rock types, vegetation, wildlife, and other resources. They spent three days exploring Tiburón, keeping well armed to take advantage of hunting opportunities as well as for protection against a possible hostile confrontation with the Seris. Though they inspected recent Seri camps, they saw no Indians. As to Tiburón's resources, they judged the island well suited for agriculture and cattle grazing, needing only tanks and reservoirs to supply water, and they recommended launching a more intensive study (Zárate 1920:81–83).

Although the expedition spent only a day at San Esteban, Zárate wrote a careful physical description of the island, particularly the area around Playa Limantour, and noted the island's volcanic origin:

> San Esteban is an island formed from volcanic ash, rocks, breccias, and debris; it extends about 6½ kilometers from North to South, [and has] a radius of about 4,800 meters. Its greatest elevation above sea level is 540 meters. Toward the East, at a distance of about 800 meters from its SE extremity and approximately 400 meters from the beach, there is a rock 9 meters high [El Monumento]. Extending North from this rock, [there] begins a pebble beach composed of rounded rocks of greatly varying sizes. This [beach] serves as the beginning of an extensive, gradually sloping valley, which terminates toward the middle part of the island. Its [the island's] coasts are generally formed by cliffs of ash and other volcanic substances. They are all nearly vertical and reach varying heights, from about 35 to 170 meters. There are some long stretches of beach composed of large rounded rocks (typically excellent places for sea lions, which are not scarce on this island, to spend the night). (Zárate 1920:79)

Zárate also commented on the island's agave (maguey), which he realized might constitute a food source for visiting Seris:

> There is an abundance of small maguey on the South [side] of the island.... We encountered recent human footprints in the trails that exist among the agave stands, and they appear to belong to Seri Indians who come from Tiburón to gather maguey. One would suppose that they do not utilize it to make mescal [liquor], for lack of the necessary equipment. Probably they are limited to harvesting the heads of these magueys, and it is this that they surely eat. (Zárate 1920:80–81)

Zárate concluded that the agave, while useful to the Seris, could not be effectively exploited as raw material for a Mexican fiber industry, in part simply because the rugged terrain of the island would make collecting the plants too hazardous a task. Apart from the sea lions, the expedition members saw little on San Esteban that had any obvious economic value.

In 1921, the California Academy of Sciences organized a large scientific expedition to the Gulf. This institution had a long-standing research interest in the region and had sponsored many of the initial scientific investigations of Baja California during the late nineteenth century. It had also lost the extensive collections from these trips in the 1906 San Francisco earthquake and fire (Nelson 1922:143–44). The 1921 venture was the first of the Academy's expeditions to focus specifically on the Gulf islands. Its purpose was:

> to make as comprehensive and thorough study of the fauna and flora of the islands in the Gulf, and of localities on the adjacent mainland, as time, funds, and weather conditions would permit. This would include, of course, the making of as extensive collections in the various groups as possible. (Slevin 1923:55)

The Academy expedition was patterned after the highly successful *Albatross* cruise 10 years earlier. The eight-man scientific party, led by Joseph R. Slevin, included specialists in botany, herpetology, ornithology, mammalogy, entomology, and paleontology. Two of the members were Mexican scientists representing the Museo Nacional de México. The group assembled in Guaymas, where the 22-ton motor schooner *Silver Gate* had been chartered for the trip. On April 16, the expedition got under way (Slevin 1923:56).

It was something of a whirlwind trip, both literally and figuratively. High winds and heavy seas often prevented landings and forced changes in the itinerary. During the 87 days of the cruise, the *Silver Gate* covered more than 1,800 miles. In addition to stops at many points on the peninsular and Sonoran coasts, the expedition visited every major island and many of the minor ones, 36 in all. About half the islands, mostly the smaller ones, were investigated for a day or less. But this enabled the scientists to spend parts of several days collecting on some of the larger islands, often at different localities, and on separate occasions. For two days, April 19–20, the *Silver Gate* lay:

> anchored off a large valley on the east side of San Esteban Island. The country was extremely rough, and dry, and cut up into small washes and cañons not unlike some of the country in our own southern deserts. One is at once struck by the great number of immense chuckwallas (Sauromalus) on San Esteban scattered about in the cactus patches, and by the large rock iguanas (Ctenosaura) sometimes seen sunning themselves on the tops of the giant cacti. (Slevin 1923:57)

On July 10, the expedition ended as the *Silver Gate* sailed into Guaymas (Slevin 1923:70–72).

This expedition was important for a number of reasons. The cruise of the *Albatross* 10 years earlier had been invaluable as a voyage of initial exploration. But the itinerary of the *Silver Gate* was much more inclusive, enabling its staff to make collections at most of the islands not visited by the *Albatross* and to make more thorough collections at islands where the *Albatross* did stop. Moreover, it had expanded the breadth of investigation by including a paleontologist and an entomologist. The latter was especially successful in obtaining previously unknown insect and arachnid species, including many on San Esteban (Van Duzee 1923; Cockerell 1923, 1924; Chamberlin 1924). While collecting was the focus of the fieldwork, and the resulting papers were largely descriptive, Ivan Johnston's monumental report on the vascular plants was far ahead of its time by placing the botanical data in a broad ecological and biogeographical framework (Johnston 1924).

The next three decades after the *Silver Gate* cruise were lean years for science on San Esteban Island and the Midriff islands generally. Although vessels of about 50 research expeditions entered the Gulf between 1921 and the early 1950s, the vast majority of these were oceanographic cruises that either stayed south of the Midriff or did little or no work ashore (Schwartzlose and Hendrickson 1983). Much of the terrestrial fieldwork on the Midriff islands during this period was incidental collecting by tourists and sportsmen, or was conducted by small and usually privately funded expeditions with limited scientific objectives. In several cases, the written accounts are too general to determine which islands were visited. Some of the best documented expeditions of the period, such as the 1940 Ricketts-Steinbeck *Western Flyer* cruise, sailed past San Esteban Island but did not stop there, although a few took oceanographic measurements or sampled marine organisms in the general vicinity.

One of the foremost visitors to the Gulf during this period was ornithologist Griffing Bancroft, who made around half a dozen trips into the Midriff region between 1925 and the early 1930s. In 1925, and again for part of the 1930 expedition, he was accompanied by the inveterate ornithologist A. J. van Rossem. On the 1930 trip, Bancroft was in the Gulf from April to June. For five days, between about April 17–21, the party worked on and around San Esteban Island (van Rossem 1930b:220, 1931:239, 1945:15–16; van Rossem and The Marquess Hachisuka 1937:323–25), although this portion of the voyage was not recorded in Bancroft's own semi-fictionalized account (Bancroft 1932). Among the birds collected on San Esteban were new subspecies of black-throated sparrow (*Amphispiza bilineata cana*) and curve-billed thrasher (*Toxostoma curvirostre insularum*), though the latter may have been a stray from Tiburón Island (van Rossem 1930a:207–8, 1930b:223–24; Banks 1969:91–92). Observations of the birds on San Esteban and Tiburón led van Rossem to tentatively propose that these two islands comprise a distinct avifaunal district (van Rossem 1931:238–41). Later he would affiliate the avifauna of San Esteban with the birds of Baja California, although this too was an idea that has not withstood the test of time (van Rossem 1945:24; Banks 1969; Cody 1983:220–21, 224–26).

The expedition's focus on birds did not prevent Mrs. Bancroft from collecting the first specimen of a new subspecies of Sonoran whipsnake (*Masticophis bilineatus slevini*) (Lowe and Norris 1955:93). This discovery shows clearly that the 2½ days of intense collecting by the *Albatross* and *Silver Gate* scientists had by no means revealed all of San Esteban's biological diversity, for this animal is the most common diurnal snake on the island.

The most elaborate private expedition to visit San Esteban Island during this time was one that sailed from southern California on P. J. Pemberton's 65-foot yacht *Petrel*.[106] The scientific party consisted of ornithologist van Rossem, mammalogist William H. Burt, conchologist Herbert N. Lowe, a crab specialist, and Pemberton himself, a collector of reptiles. The cruise lasted 10 weeks, from late November 1931 to the beginning of February 1932, and included stops at most of the major Gulf islands. For five days at the end of December, the party worked around the shores of Tiburón Island, where they were visited by Seris who came out from the mainland. After cruising north to Ángel de la Guarda, they began working southward along the San Lorenzo chain, and on January 11, they spent the day observing and collecting on San Esteban Island (Burt 1932:163; van Rossem 1932:122, 129; Lowe 1933). Here, while van Rossem went after birds, Pemberton collected the first specimen of the common side-blotched lizard (*Uta stansburiana*).

Like many other visits, the *Petrel*'s stay at San Esteban was not without some excitement:

> At the latter island [San Esteban], where we lay at anchor sheltered from the northwest wind, without any warning a fresh current from the opposite direction took the yacht almost aground on the rocks, and but for prompt action of all on board serious damage might have resulted. As it was we bumped two rocks. The tides have a tremendous rise and fall in this part of the Gulf and strong currents run around the islands which[,] with the prevailing swell and the heavy and sudden winds[,] make the Gulf at times a very treacherous body of water. (Lowe 1933:113)

As to the region in general:

> The upper part of the Gulf is one of the most desolate and lonely spots in the world. The islands are waterless and uninhabited, and the coast line of both sides is practically so. We passed but one boat of any description in all the three weeks we were there. (Lowe 1933:113–14)

In the spring of 1944, a recently-formed Mexican company named Guanos y Fertilizantes de México sponsored an expedition to the Gulf and the west coast of Baja California. Its purpose was to study a broad range of biological factors that influence the life cycle of guano-producing sea birds, in the hope of establishing a self-perpetuating guano industry. The company vessel *Gracioso* was dispatched for the cruise. The scientific staff consisted of biological oceanographer B. F. Osorio Tafall, of the Escuela Nacional de Ciencias Biológicas in Mexico City, ornithologist Mario del Toro, and a representative of the Peruvian guano industry (Osorio Tafall 1944:331–32).

The expedition was preceded in February by an airplane flight over the Gulf islands, including San Esteban, as a preliminary reconnaissance for the voyage (Vogt 1946). Two months later, on April 16, the *Gracioso* set out from Manzanillo, returning to Mazatlán to end the cruise on June 23. During their two months at sea, the scientists visited most of the Gulf islands, whether or not they had obvious importance to the company's objectives. Whether they stopped at San Esteban Island is unclear, for nowhere in Osorio Tafall's report is the island mentioned specifically. However, his text and photographs show that they did go ashore on virtually every other Midriff island, and they even photographed some Seris on Tiburón (Osorio Tafall 1944, 1946:opposite p. 96).

In the spring of 1947, George E. Lindsay was invited on a month's cactus-hunting tour of the Gulf islands by Wilson and Lynne Long, who were spending a year roaming the seas on their sailing yacht *Adventurous* (Lindsay 1947). Leaving Guaymas on April 2, the vessel headed north, first to Tiburón Island, and then on to San Esteban, arriving a couple of days later. They stayed only a day, noting the cacti, sea lions, ospreys, gulls, and other wildlife, and they spent the night in the lee of El Cascajal. Though the seas were calm, the water was not entirely tranquil:

> We were about to hoist anchor ... when we first noticed a disconcerting gulf phenomenon. Bill was in the rigging to choose passage out, when he noticed what appeared to be rocks awash in the area through which we had just passed. Then there seemed to be a long reef awash, to our starboard. More on our port! ... Investigation revealed these lines of breakers are common about the islands. The rush of the tides up and down the long gulf results in strong opposing currents which throw up areas of broken water with the appearance of submerged rocks. Even when we knew the reason for the disturbance we avoided the areas whenever we could, and if we had to pass through one we couldn't help peering apprehensively into the boiling depths. (Lindsay 1948a:8)

After sailing as far as Ángel de la Guarda, the *Adventurous* turned south and cruised among the peninsular islands before heading into Mazatlán. Lindsay characterized the trip as more a pleasure cruise than a scientific expedition, but many cacti were collected and specimens deposited in botanical gardens in both Mexico City and Arizona (Lindsay 1948b:35).

During this period, two large-scale institutional cruises of the *Velero III*, sponsored by the Allan Hancock Foundation of the University of Southern California, did stop briefly at San Esteban. In 1931, this institution embarked on a major long-term study of the biologically rich but neglected marine environment lying between the low-tide mark and the hundred fathom line of the eastern tropical Pacific. The two portions of this vast region to receive particular attention were the Galápagos Islands and the Gulf of California. Interest in the latter area stemmed from a 1921 test cruise by Captain Hancock in the *Velero I* that had taken him as far as Tiburón Island (Fraser 1943a:2, 20).

The *Velero III* put scientists on San Esteban's shore on two occasions. On March 27, 1937, P. J. Rempel landed on the south side of the island, and E. Yale Dawson went ashore at about the same place on February 5, 1940 (Fraser

1943b:310, 333, 403; John S. Garth 1983:pers. comm.). Both men obtained small plant collections, later described by Howard Gentry, who summarized what was known of the island's flora in 1949:

> The *Velero III* land plant collections from San Esteban Island, Rempel 6 numbers, Dawson 6 numbers, consist mainly of cactus. The early springs 1937 and 1940, when their collections were made, apparently were too dry for general floral response. The summer-fall flora of San Esteban Island is not known, all collections having been made in the spring.... The known flora consists of 48 species. (Gentry 1949:95–96)

And Gentry noted that for the Gulf islands generally:

> it is clear that botanical exploration has been fleeting.... Except for Johnston's published notes [Johnston 1924] of a general nature, the ecology of the islands has been given only the most cursory attention. The development of the vegetation, the nature of plant communities, the amount of endemism, and the many diverse problems facing the phytogeographer cannot be determined until further careful and less nomadic fieldwork has been systematically done. (Gentry 1949:100)

Small collections of other taxa were made on San Esteban by *Velero III* personnel during both cruises. In 1937, a specimen of the endemic rattlesnake was collected (Klauber 1949:104) and in 1940, naturalist Granville P. Ashcraft went ashore and made a small collection of birds (van Rossem 1945:10).

The Golden Age of Expeditionary Science

The 1950s and 1960s were halcyon days for big science on the Gulf islands, bringing a number of large-scale biological expeditions to the region. Like the model *Albatross* and *Silver Gate* cruises, these were fast-paced and very much "nomadic" voyages that rarely allocated more than a day or two to any individual island. But nearly all included San Esteban in their itineraries. These trips generated sufficiently widespread interest that, like their predecessors, general accounts of the expeditions were published in addition to a wide range of technical papers describing the scientific results.

The first of these ventures was the 1952 Sefton-Stanford Gulf Expedition, led by George E. Lindsay. The eight-man scientific staff, with the exception of Cornell botanist Reid Moran, were all from Stanford University, while the research vessel *Orca* was supplied by the J. F. Sefton Foundation of San Diego. The primary purpose of the trip was to make comprehensive observations and collections of plants, reptiles, insects, and fish. The cruise began on March 26, 1952. In 61 days, stops were made at 23 Gulf islands, in addition to many localities on the peninsula. The expedition arrived at San Esteban early on May

6 and departed the following morning, but in their single day on the island the party succeeded in taking good collections of plants, reptiles, and fish (Lindsay [ca. 1961]:2–4, 61–62).

The next year, the Sefton Foundation sponsored a second Gulf cruise of the *Orca*. The scientific staff this time represented the California Academy of Sciences, the San Diego Zoological Society, and the University of California at Los Angeles, as well as Stanford. It included two members of the previous year's expedition along with herpetologist Joseph Slevin, who 32 years earlier had led the 1921 *Silver Gate* expedition (Arnaud 1970:1–2).

The main segment of the cruise ran from March 9 to April 5. The *Orca* dropped anchor at San Esteban late in the afternoon of April 1 and stayed until the morning of April 3. With a full day available on shore, four of the scientists took the opportunity to hike well inland, some two miles or so up Arroyo Limantour. Meanwhile, paleontologist G. Dallas Hanna investigated some of the sea cliff fossil beds, which he thought to be of possible upper Pliocene age. There were no botanists on this trip, but the herpetologists and entomologists made excellent collections. Hanna collected what proved to be a new subspecies of land snail (Emerson and Jacobson 1964:327–28).

The two *Orca* cruises were highly productive. Of the insect fauna alone, some 6,000 specimens were collected. On San Esteban, about 40 specimens were obtained of a tiny bee fly that proved to be new to science (Arnaud 1970:16–17, Fig. 19). The herpetologists recorded the night snake (*Hypsiglena torquata venusta*) which had not been seen there previously, and what they thought was the first specimen of the endemic subspecies of Sonoran whipsnake, apparently unaware of Bancroft's 1930 specimen. They also captured what they believed to be the third specimen of the endemic black-tailed rattlesnake (Cliff 1954:74–77, 85).

In the spring of 1957, 46 years after the 1911 voyage of the *Albatross*, the American Museum of Natural History launched a second expedition to the Gulf. This time it was on the schooner *Puritan*, which had been made available for a three month cruise by Harry J. Bauer of Los Angeles. The five initial expedition scientists, led by William K. Emerson, were specialists in malacology, invertebrate zoology, invertebrate paleontology, mammalogy, and herpetology. Though they intended to make collections, this trip marked the first serious departure from the emphasis on systematics that had dominated previous expeditions. Its primary objectives:

> were to study the effects of insular isolation on populations of mammals, reptiles, and amphibians and to compare the present and past distributions of the littoral marine invertebrate faunas, particularly the mollusks, stony corals, and bryozoans. (Emerson 1958:1)

The scientists made brief stops at 22 Gulf islands. By May 18–19, when they visited the east coast of San Esteban, the expedition had become primarily a marine biology cruise due to the early departure of the herpetologist and invertebrate zoologist, though mammal trapping and incidental collecting of reptiles

Figure 12.1 The San Agustín II, *chartered for the 1962 Belvedere Expedition and the 1966 Gulf Islands Expedition. Photograph probably by George E. Lindsay, 1962 or 1966. (Courtesy San Diego Natural History Museum, San Diego, California.)*

continued. On June 6, the *Puritan* returned to its home port of Newport, California (Emerson 1958).

The next major expedition to stop at San Esteban was the 1962 Belvedere Expedition to the Gulf of California, sponsored by the San Diego Natural History Museum, and supported by the Belvedere Scientific Fund of San Francisco. A Mexican vessel was chartered for this trip, the 85-foot *San Agustín II* (Figure 12.1), owned and operated by Antero Díaz of Bahía de Los Ángeles (Figure 12.2). Among the seven scientists who signed on for the entire cruise were three veterans of previous Gulf expeditions, Museum Director and leader George Lindsay, Reid Moran, and William Emerson. Botanist Ira Wiggins, soon to publish a monumental compendium of the flora of the Sonoran desert (Shreve and Wiggins 1964), represented the Belvedere Fund. Five others joined the expedition for part of the trip (Figure 12.3), including Ambrosio González C., Chief Investigator of the Instituto Mexicano de Recursos Naturales Renovables. The major collecting emphases were on plants, mammals, birds, reptiles, terrestrial arthropods, and recent and fossil invertebrates (Lindsay 1962:3).

The *San Agustín II* sailed from Bahía de los Ángeles on March 15 and returned April 26, having made stops at 32 Gulf islands. It anchored off El Monumento on the eastern side of San Esteban in the late afternoon of March 21 and

Figure 12.2   Antero Díaz A.(1913 or 1914–1988), owner and captain of the San Agustín II. *Probably photographed during the 1962 Belvedere Expedition or the 1966 Gulf Islands Expedition. (Courtesy San Diego Natural History Museum, San Diego, California.)*

Figure 12.3   Scientists of the 1962 Belvedere Expedition aboard the San Agustín II. *Standing, left to right: Richard C. Banks, Michael Soulé, Don Hunsaker II, Chris Parrish, Ira L. Wiggins, Charles Shaw, and Reid Moran. Seated: William K. Emerson, Dennis Bostic, Charles F. Harbison. Not pictured: Ambrosio González C. Photograph by George E. Lindsay. (Courtesy San Diego Natural History Museum, San Diego, California.)*

departed early on the 23rd, giving the investigators a full day on shore. Moran used the time to climb Pico del Sur and collect plants on its north slopes, which added a number of species to the recorded flora, including two plants otherwise known only from Ángel de la Guarda. Meanwhile, Lindsay discovered a new endemic fishhook cactus, later named *Mammillaria estebanensis*. The herpetologists saw several Sonoran whipsnakes but were unable to capture any, and could not find any black-tailed rattlesnakes, which were still known from only three or possibly four specimens. They did collect live chuckwallas and iguanas for the San Diego Zoo. Emerson worked the Pliocene fossil beds in the marine terrace at the north end of Playa Limantour, and the entomologists found abundant scorpions and insects (Lindsay 1962:14).

As a whole, the trip was extremely productive, with collections numbering in the thousands of specimens. But the expedition was noteworthy for scientific work in addition to collecting and gathering distributional data. Information was obtained about the breeding characteristics of some of the mammals, and the herpetologists spent considerable effort making behavioral studies, even recording lizard behavior on motion picture film. In addition, more than 100 serum samples were taken from some of the reptiles for immunological and electrophoretic studies (Lindsay 1962:42–43).

In the summer of 1964, the California Academy of Sciences organized the Sea of Cortez Expedition, but this cruise went only from La Paz to Loreto and did not enter the Midriff at all (Lindsay 1964). Two years later, however, the Academy joined forces with the San Diego Natural History Museum and the Universidad Nacional Autónoma de México's Instituto de Biología for the Gulf Islands Expedition of 1966. With support from the Belvedere Scientific Fund and the National Science Foundation, this was a lightning trip that visited 13 islands in 10 days. But the expedition limited its range to only the Midriff islands, and one of those visited was San Esteban (Lindsay 1966a, 1966b).

The 12 men who comprised the scientific party represented a diversity of fields, including for the first time a geologist, Richard P. Phillips. George Lindsay again led the expedition, and among the veterans of previous trips was botanist Reid Moran (Figure 12.4). Invertebrate zoologist Alejandro Villalobos F. and his assistant Virgilio Arenas F. represented the Instituto de Biología of the Universidad Nacional Autónoma de México.

On April 19, the expedition set out from Bahía de los Ángeles aboard the *San Agustín II*, with Antero Díaz again at the helm. The vessel reached San Esteban about noon on April 26 and anchored off the east coast. Though the scientists stayed at San Esteban only that afternoon and overnight, it was a particularly interesting visit. Among the animals collected there were the endemic mouse, the introduced rat, and a variety of arachnids, insects, and intertidal organisms (Figure 12.5). The bird collections focused on geographically variable species in order to reassess the avifaunal relationships of the island. Moran obtained eight new plant records. The herpetologists captured five species of lizards, including two specimens of iguana and a chuckwalla. They also encountered some disturbing signs of wanton overcollecting:

*Figure 12.4   Science with a sense of humor. Veteran Gulf of California botanists
Reid Moran (left) and George Lindsay honored on the cover of the*
Cactus and Succulent Journal. *Caricatures by Gerhard Marx, based on a
photograph from the 1966 Gulf Islands Expedition.
(Courtesy Gerhard Marx and the Cactus and Succulent Society of America.)*

Figure 12.5   Raymond Bandar, with cloth snake bags tucked in his waist, sets up an insect flight trap behind Playa Limantour, 1966 Gulf Islands Expedition. The San Agustín II *is anchored off shore. Photograph by Robert T. Orr, April 1966. (Courtesy California Academy of Sciences.)*

These two kinds of giant lizards are much less common than formerly, when they could be observed in great numbers along the arroyo banks. A series of old reptile can-traps were found in the bottom of the large arroyo [Limantour]. These were five-gallon cans, with tops removed, sunk to their brims in the soil. Such traps are used by some biologists to collect specimens. However, many of those which were found had been abandoned without having been filled with dirt, so were acting as perpetual booby traps for lizards for no purpose whatever. All that could be found were filled with soil. (Lindsay 1966b:330–31)

Geologist Phillips, who had been on San Esteban briefly the previous year, sampled the shoreline fossil beds and determined that they lie unconformably on older volcanics. He and Moran also climbed to the summit of Pico Rojo, where they made the first known record of the island's archaeological remains:

At the summit of the peak at about 1500 feet, both Moran and Phillips noted several semicircular to circular walls of loosely piled rock, built apparently by the Indians. These were about 2 or 3 feet high, each structure about 3 feet wide, the open ones facing alternately in opposite directions. (Lindsay 1966b:331)

As they descended the arroyo on the southwestern side of the peak, they found and photographed a fine specimen of the unusual crested form of cardon (Moran 1968:7).

The next morning, the *San Agustín II* weighed anchor and sailed to El Cascajal, at the southwestern corner of the island, where the scientists spent an hour ashore collecting. When they departed for San Lorenzo, they gave a tow to three Mexican fishermen in a canoe who had spent the night on San Esteban en route to Baja California. The expedition arrived back at Bahía de los Ángeles on the evening of April 28 (Lindsay 1966b:333, 337).

The era of the large-scale and highly publicized expeditions came to a close when the 1966 Gulf Islands Expedition dropped anchor in Bahía de los Ángeles. Collectively, these wide-ranging ventures had been exceedingly successful in carrying out basic biological exploration and introducing the scientific community to the biota of the Gulf islands. By the late 1960s, islands such as San Esteban were no longer scientific blanks, but neither were they familiar territory, for the big expeditions had all been fast-moving reconnaissance trips. Only one of the large expeditions had stayed at San Esteban even as long as two days, and the combined observation and collecting time on the island in the 55 years since the *Albatross* expedition amounted to little more than about 10 days. Moreover, most of these expeditions had anchored in the same place, off Playa Limantour, and had explored only a very limited portion of the island.

Shoestring Science, Evolutionary Theory, and Other Recent Trends

In the decades since the 1966 Gulf Islands Expedition, there have been significant changes in the way science has been conducted in the Gulf. One of these, an emerging trend toward small-scale research trips, was already well underway during the heyday of the large high-profile expeditions. These investigations were carried out with no fanfare at all, often by just two or three people or even a lone investigator. Among these intrepid individuals were established scientists, but many were graduate students whose data formed the basis of doctoral dissertations. A few were supported by modest grants, but in many cases the participants funded themselves, which often required them to operate on a shoestring budget. For many of these people, the attraction of the Gulf was not just the science but an opportunity to do research in a largely pristine wilderness of unspoiled beauty, whose scientific resources had barely been explored. And one destination of some of these investigators was San Esteban Island.

The pioneers in this maverick approach were mostly affiliated with the University of Arizona. The main instigator was herpetologist Charles H. Lowe, who began making a succession of fast and furious weekend collecting trips into Sonora shortly after joining the Arizona faculty in 1950. At that time, even the road to Hermosillo was something of an adventure, and only a tangle of rough and unbelievably dusty tracks served as the road to the coastal fishing village of

Bahía Kino. Perhaps the most significant event that made the Gulf and its islands accessible from Tucson was the paving of the Bahía Kino road in 1953.
Thereafter, it was a day's drive from Tucson to Kino, and from there San Esteban could be reached in another six or seven hours (in good weather) in a hired
fisherman's panga. Accordingly, in 1954 Lowe and Kenneth S. Norris expanded
one of these weekend ventures into one of the first out-of-pocket scientific
expeditions to San Esteban Island, where they collected a series of the island's
reptiles (Lowe and Norris 1955). Lowe recalls that his Arizona-bound colleagues in Tucson had not the slightest comprehension of the allure of the Gulf,
and many thought him crazy for even crossing the Mexican border (Charles H.
Lowe 1995:pers. comm.).

By the late 1950s, San Esteban had also become a destination for Richard S.
Felger, then a graduate student at the University of Arizona. Felger's interest was
in the botany of the Midriff region, and over the next two decades, he made a number of field trips to San Esteban and other islands. These were the epitome of low-
profile, low-budget expeditions, usually undertaken with just one or two colleagues
or friends. Transport to the island was often in a Bahía Kino fisherman's panga, in
some cases with only the fisherman as company. Yet his early trips provided data
for his doctoral dissertation (Felger 1966), which remains the definitive study of the
vegetation and flora of San Esteban and several other Midriff islands. Felger continued to pursue research in the Midriff region (e.g., Felger and Lowe 1976; Felger
and Moser 1985), and by the late 1970s, he had been to San Esteban about 10 times
(Richard S. Felger 1983 and 1995:pers. comms.).

Other small-scale trips followed. One such venture was a trip to San Esteban in
April 1963, undertaken by Kenneth S. Norris and William R. Dawson, as part of a
physiological and behavioral study of chuckwalla adaptation to arid conditions
(Norris and Dawson 1964). Between 1962 and 1966, University of Arizona graduate
student Armando Maya spent several months traveling with Mexican panga fishermen or North American friends to San Esteban and other Midriff islands to investigate the natural history of fish-eating bats (Maya 1968:5, 10). In a more formal
grant-supported project, James R. Dixon of New Mexico State University and a
small group of graduate students spent the summer of 1964 on San Esteban and
other Midriff islands studying the dispersal and speciation of insular geckos (Dixon
1966:415). In the late 1960s, University of Michigan graduate student Timothy E.
Lawlor visited San Esteban as part of a dissertation project to assess evolutionary
relationships among the endemic mice of the Gulf islands (Lawlor 1969). Around
1970, Michael D. Robinson re-evaluated the evolutionary relationships and biogeography of the insular chuckwallas, often making use of fishermen's pangas to get
out to San Esteban and other Midriff islands (Robinson 1972). These and other low
profile trips have served as a powerful precedent for fieldwork in the Midriff, for
most of the more recent scientific work on San Esteban has been carried out by
individuals and small groups operating with modest funding , local transportation,
and little publicity.

Throughout the 1960s and beyond, efforts to inventory San Esteban's plants
and animals continued. In 1949, the number of known vascular plant species on

San Esteban stood at only 48 (Gentry 1949:96). By 1966, the figure had risen to 84 (Moran 1966:340) or 88 (Felger 1966:273). Ten years later, Felger and Lowe (1976:21) placed the number at 107, and by 1983 the total had increased to 116 (Cody et al. 1983:59–60). Along with new records of familiar organisms, biologists still occasionally found plants and animals new to science, even some that were conspicuous and common. And progress was not uniform in all fields. In the late 1960s, even bare species lists for some groups of organisms, such as land birds, were seriously inadequate (Cody 1983:210).

Nevertheless, by the late 1960s, taxonomy and distributional studies were largely giving way to theoretically more significant issues of ecological and evolutionary relationships. Forerunner to these was Ivan Johnston's (1924) effort to interpret the Gulf islands in a broad ecological perspective. In the 1950s, Charles H. Lowe (1955) evaluated evolutionary relationships among the reptiles and mammals of San Esteban and neighboring islands, and during the following decade, similar projects were undertaken by others (e.g., Dixon 1966; Felger 1966; Soulé and Sloan 1966; Soulé 1967; Lawlor 1971; Robinson 1972). The first sweeping attempt to synthesize data from the region was the product of a symposium entitled "The Biogeography of Baja California and Adjacent Seas," held in 1959 at San Diego State College and published in *Systematic Zoology* (Vol. 9, Nos. 2–4, 1960). The emphasis, however, was on marine biology and the peninsula itself, and neither San Esteban nor the other Gulf islands were given close attention. But major developments in island biogeographic theory provided the backdrop for a landmark 1977 symposium, held at the University of California at Los Angeles, that focused specifically on the Gulf islands. The resulting volume (Case and Cody 1983) is an important resource both for its theoretical contributions and its data-rich appendices, which present comprehensive inventories of the flora and fauna of all the Gulf islands, including San Esteban. As of 1999, this volume was being updated for a revised second edition.

In recent decades, much of the biological fieldwork on San Esteban has involved detailed investigation of single species, with the endemic chuckwalla receiving the greatest attention. Projects have ranged from studies of life history, physiology, and genetics to investigation of diet and reproductive strategies, and nearly all of this research has been framed in the context of ecological and evolutionary issues (Robinson 1972; Case 1975, 1982; Sylber 1988; Densmore et al. 1994; Lawler et al. 1994). The shift in focus from taxonomy to behavioral questions has been accompanied by a heightened awareness of the chuckwalla as a living creature and an endangered species. This in turn has fostered new ethical considerations among investigators who now commonly go to great lengths to avoid sacrificing or unduly disturbing the animals under study (Case 1982:192; Howard E. Lawler 1985:pers. comm.).

The end of the 1960s was also accompanied by a reduction in the lopsided foreign dominance of research in the Gulf. Up to this time, the majority of fieldwork in the region, both oceanographic and on dry land, had been conducted by scientists from the United States. Although Mexican scientists had accompanied several of the major North American expeditions, there had been relatively few exclusively Mexican studies of the Gulf, and most of these had been resources surveys. Up to this time, San Esteban Island had been visited by only two Mexican expeditions, the 1918 *Frolic* cruise and, less certainly, the *Gracioso* expedition in 1944. Four Mexican oceanographic cruises had ranged as far north as the Midriff in 1942, 1949, 1966, and 1968 (Schwartzlose and Hendrickson 1983), but these were all dedicated to marine biology rather than terrestrial research, and there is no indication that any of them stopped at San Esteban. Though one objective of the Mexican cruise of 1966 was to conduct a census of sea lions, the investigators bypassed San Esteban Island and missed altogether the huge colony of animals there (Lluch Belda 1969:8–11; Le Boeuf et al. 1983:82).

Mexico's decisive entry into the Gulf scientific arena occurred primarily through oceanography, spurred both by new wealth from the nation's short-lived oil boom and the rapid depletion of the Gulf fisheries. In this climate, both government and academic institutions embarked on a series of ambitious research programs. Foremost among the institutional sponsors were the Instituto Nacional de Pesca in Mazatlán, the Escuela de Ciencias del Mar of the Universidad Autónoma de Sinaloa, the Universidad Autónoma Nacional de México's Instituto de Ciencias del Mar y Limnología, the Centro de Investigación Científica y de Educación Superior de Ensenada (CICESE) in Baja California Norte, and the Centro de Investigaciones Biológicas de Baja California Sur. For several years during the 1970s and 1980s, more than half of the oceanographic cruises in the Gulf were Mexican (Brusca 1980:429; Schwartzlose and Hendrickson 1983). Most of this fieldwork was applied science in the national interest, primarily fisheries research and a wide range of marine biology and physical oceanography studies related to fisheries. These studies helped establish that it was not only the fisheries that were in decline but also that the biological health of the entire Gulf ecosystem had become seriously threatened. The problems came not only from fisheries exploitation practices within the Gulf but from economic activities in the surrounding lands as well, including the United States. These realizations quickly brought to the fore some difficult conservation issues which have come to permeate virtually all scientific work in the Gulf up to the present time. The question, both then and now, has been how to protect the integrity of the Gulf's fragile environment and its endangered organisms and yet balance these urgent conservation needs with legitimate economic interests in the Gulf's resources in the context of a rapidly growing nation.

As part of the initial exploration of this problem, a series of five annual conferences that became known as the "Simposio[s] Binacional Sobre el Medio Ambiente del Golfo de California" were held from 1976–1980. These were organized by a number of Mexican and North American institutions and agencies under the general aegis of the Mexican government's Instituto Nacional de Investigaciones Forestales (e.g., Anonymous 1976b; Villa Salas 1979). Participating scientists came from both sides of the international boundary, and topics ranged from assessments of specific organisms and sources of human impact to the prospects of environmental education and the effects of urban planning. The scope of the conferences was regional rather than local, and for this reason, specific Gulf islands, such as San Esteban, figured into the discussions only occasionally (e.g., Hernández García 1979). The first conference, however, which was held in Bahía Kino, included a field trip for participants to neighboring Tiburón Island (Villa Salas 1979:21).

In addition to oceanography and marine biology, Mexican scientists have become involved in terrestrial research on the Gulf islands. Fieldwork on Midriff islands, occasionally including San Esteban, has been conducted by biologists from both Mexico City and Hermosillo, including the Universidad Nacional Autónoma de México, the Dirección General de la Fauna Silvestre, and the Centro de Ecológico de Sonora. And a number of recent projects, not all of them biological, have been collaborative ventures between Mexican scientists and North American colleagues. This has included the archaeological fieldwork on San Esteban reported in the next section of the present book, which was a collaborative effort between Thomas Bowen of California State University, Fresno and María Elisa Villalpando C., of the Centro Regional de Sonora of the Instituto Nacional de Antropología e Historia (see also Villalpando 1989).

Beyond Flora and Fauna

Finally, the end of the 1960s ushered in a renewed interest in scientific fields other than biology. While much had been learned of San Esteban's plants and animals, geological knowledge lagged far behind. Marine geologists had been intensively studying the structure and tectonic history of the Gulf floor since the 1940s, but this work did little to elucidate San Esteban's structural history and petrology. For many decades, the Mexican government, through the Instituto Geológico de México, the Consejo de Recursos Naturales No Renovables, and such academic institutions as the Universidad Nacional Autónoma de México's Instituto de Geología, had been actively investigating the geology and mineralogy of Sonora and Baja California. But seldom did this fieldwork extend to the Gulf islands and never, apparently, to San Esteban. Maps accompanying Mexican geological publications on the region frequently show San Esteban as a mere outline or omit the island altogether.

The researchers aboard the *Albatross* did not comment on San Esteban's geology, but the volcanic origin of the island's rocks has been consistently recognized by scientists since José C. Zárate first noted them in 1918 (Zárate 1920:79). Carl H. Beal, who worked in the region in 1921 for Marland Oil, did not go ashore on the island, but he observed from a distance that:

> Isla San Esteban [is] a very steep and precipitous island.... The mountains from a distance appear to be composed of volcanic and fragmental rocks; they rise to two peaks with elevations of 1450 and 1772 feet, respectively. (Beal 1948:23)

Ivan Johnston, who went ashore in 1921, remarked that San Esteban has "scoriae-covered slopes and much breccia," and he correctly surmised that essentially the whole island is volcanic (Johnston 1924:954). For that reason, he affiliated it structurally (though incorrectly) with the San Lorenzo chain, which he believed (also incorrectly) was almost wholly composed of volcanic rocks (Johnston 1924:954). Though neither the 1939 nor 1940 cruises of the *E.W. Scripps* stopped at San Esteban, the geological map from the 1940 trip labels San Esteban's rocks as early Tertiary volcanics (Anderson 1950:opposite p. 1). A 1956 Mexican geological map identifies the island's rocks as Quaternary *"rocas efusivas"* (González Reyna 1956). Five years later, Zoltan de Cserna showed the island more precisely and correctly (except for age) as made up entirely of late Oligocene to early Pliocene dacites and related volcanics (Cserna 1961). Yet somehow the idea emerged that much of the island is composed of granitic rocks, and this idea was sporadically perpetuated in publications by people who had obviously never been there. One map that appeared in 1976 labeled the island as consisting of Mesozoic granitics (López Rámos 1976). And as recently as 1981, a geological map compiled from Landsat images and aerial photographs, and supposedly field checked, misidentified the entire northeastern one-third of San Esteban as Upper Cretaceous granitics intruded into the island's otherwise Tertiary volcanics (Anonymous 1981a).

The fossil layers next to Playa Limantour were sampled at least three times by members of the big expeditions of the 1950s and 1960s, who all agreed that they were likely of Pliocene age (Emerson and Hertlein 1964:337). Richard P. Phillips was apparently the first geologist to note the island's structural features, though his visits to the island in 1965 with the National Science Foundation Peninsular Ranges Project and the following year with the California Academy of Sciences expedition were both too brief for a detailed analysis (Lindsay 1966:330; Phillips 1968:327; Richard P. Phillips 1983:pers. comm.). Even the enormously ambitious and successful projects to map the geology of northern Baja California and coastal Sonora during the 1960s and 1970s, directed by R. Gordon Gastil of San Diego State University and several North American and Mexican colleagues, failed to shed light on the geology of San Esteban Island. Although dozens of their graduate students swarmed over this huge region, including nearly all the Midriff islands, San Esteban was the one island that was neither visited nor mapped. In the publications resulting from this fieldwork, the northern half of San Esteban appears only incidentally in a simplified map of the Sonoran side of the Gulf, and its composition, characterized as "Cenozoic Strata," is apparently based on Phillips's two brief visits in the mid-1960s (Gastil and Krummenacher 1977:189, Fig. 2). It was not until 1984, when Dana L. Desonie devoted nearly two months to geological fieldwork on the island, that the petrology and structural history were studied in depth, and the ages of the rocks determined radiometrically to be consistent with the Pliocene fossils (Desonie 1985, 1992).

The presumed demise of the San Esteban people in the late nineteenth century did not quite end opportunities for ethnographic fieldwork on the island, for in the twentieth century the mainland Seris continued to visit the island from time to time. In September 1947 and June 1949, anthropology graduate student

Willim Neil Smith accompanied some Seris from El Desemboque on their last two expeditions to San Esteban to gather agave and chuckwallas, trips that may have been undertaken at his request (Bernard L. Fontana 1987:pers. comm.). Unfortunately, Smith's notes and excellent photographs of these trips have never been published.

The ethnobotany of San Esteban Island is known through the botanical fieldwork of Richard S. Felger and the linguistic and ethnographic research of Mary Beck Moser. For two decades, Felger and Moser collaborated on a long-term study of the traditional Seri use of plants, including those on San Esteban Island. The island is discussed in three of their ethnobotanical papers (Felger and Moser 1970, 1974, 1976) as well as their monumental work on Seri ethnobotany (Felger and Moser 1985).

As to archaeological fieldwork, Frederick S. Rogers very nearly became the first archaeologist to visit the island. Rogers accompanied Griffing Bancroft's 1930 ornithological expedition to the Gulf, which worked on and around San Esteban for five days. But the most northerly island Rogers surveyed was San Marcos, about a hundred miles south of San Esteban. Due to prior commitments, Rogers left the expedition in Santa Rosalía, just before the remaining members set sail for San Esteban and the other Midriff islands (Rogers 1930; Bancroft 1932:26).

The earliest known archaeological collecting on San Esteban took place in 1966 when a group of Seris found a small pottery olla at the northeastern tip of the island. They brought it to linguists Edward and Mary Beck Moser in El Desemboque, who turned it over to the Museo y Biblioteca of the Universidad de Sonora (Bowen 1976:Fig. 47e; Mary Beck Moser 1981:pers. comm.). In July 1967, as part of the Arizona State Museum's 1966–1967 archaeological survey of Sonora, Thomas Bowen and Stephen D. Hayden hired a fisherman's panga and spent about 24 hours on San Esteban recording stone circles and other features (Bowen 1976:33, 39–40). This was a year after Reid Moran and Richard Phillips became the first scientists to observe summit structures when they climbed Pico Rojo. About this time, Richard Felger and Alexander Russell learned of the petroglyph cave near *Icámajoj Zaaj* and discovered a set of large agave roasting pits and rock figures that were probably built by Mexican mescal distillers (Alexander Russell 1968:pers. comm.; Richard S. Felger 1983:pers. comm.). The archaeological survey reported here (Chapters 13–15) was conducted between late 1979 and 1987.

Thus the occasional appearance of scientists on San Esteban is no longer remarkable, but getting there still requires negotiating a potentially treacherous sea. While serious problems have been rare, a few recent researchers have been rudely reminded that San Esteban, Tiburón, and San Lorenzo were once known as the "Salsipuedes" (Get-Out-If-You-Can) islands. In the course of about a dozen trips to these three islands, our archaeology group was often unable to depart or return on schedule because of rough seas, and we came to regard delays of two to three days as normal. Once when we were actually picked up on the scheduled day, we learned that this was the first day that any vessel had been able to put to sea since we had been dropped off on San Esteban two weeks earlier. And to witness a severe winter storm or a summer *chubasco* from a fisherman's panga is an experience that will not soon be forgotten.

Similarly, in late March of 1980, rough weather prematurely ended a Midriff islands trip for botanist Reid Moran. Moran had been reluctantly persuaded by a zealous zoologist to go out in an 18-foot "speedboat" that was entirely inadequate for Gulf conditions. He described the unnerving venture in the monthly reports of the San Diego Natural History Museum's Botany Department:

> The boat was beautiful but designed for placid lakes and not very seaworthy, the young men [who drove it] were affable but inexperienced, the boat was overloaded, the leader was much more optimistic than realistic or even sensible, and the result was very educational but dangerous and at times frightening. We launched at Bahía Kino, Sonora, and managed to reach Isla San Esteban. On the 31st we started for Isla San Lorenzo but turned back because of rough seas. That leaves me at the end of the month back on Isla San Esteban. By the next report [for the month of April] I may be able to tell you whether we all drowned. If not, presumably we did. (Moran 1980a)

Happily, Moran did file a report for April:

> The last day of March saw me stranded on Isla San Esteban … feeling very uncertain about prospects for getting home. Next day we made another attempt to reach Isla San Lorenzo but again turned back because of rough seas. By now we were beginning to run short of gasoline, so the following day we went back to Kino Bay. Thus we reached only one island of the three intended. (Moran 1980b)

Moran later concluded that they were lucky to have gotten back to Bahía Kino at all (Moran 1997:pers. comm.). And it is little wonder. On the day he returned, our archaeology group was scheduled to go to San Esteban with a veteran Bahía Kino fisherman, who postponed our trip because of high winds and rough seas. But probably no amount of experience, preparation, or equipment can guarantee protection from the sometimes unpredictable violence of the Gulf. In September 1990, this was driven home to Howard Lawler and his well-organized research group from the Arizona-Sonora Desert Museum that had been studying chuckwallas on San Esteban Island:

> As everyone bedded down for the night [at camp on Playa Limantour], the winds began to increase and lightning filled the skies. Within a short time, the full fury of tropical storm Norbert fell upon the island, lasting most of the night. Survival of the trip participants was in jeopardy since little or no shelter was available. Canopies were leveled by the first gale-force gusts as intense (horizontal) rain blew through the tents, driven by 70 mph winds. Lightning frequently struck the hills near camp and flash flooding and exposure were serious threats.

Everyone was soaked and shaken by the ordeal but luckily, the only injuries were emotional ones. The largest boat, a 22-foot vessel owned by Stephen Hale, capsized during the storm, sustaining major damage to the cabin, hull, and motor, and compromising evacuation from the island in the face of further storm activity. As a result, the remainder of the trip was devoted to insuring personal safety and salvage of equipment. ([Lawler] 1990:4)

Despite occasional adventures, research scientists continue to go to San Esteban, and field data continue to accumulate. Yet as the twentieth century draws to a close, the island may still hold some surprises, even for the biological community. In January 1982, our archaeology group discovered a thriving stand of at least 40 organ pipe (*pitahaya dulce*) cacti near the rarely visited northwestern corner of the island. Previously, this plant had been known from only about a half dozen isolated individuals, some dying. And more recently, the California kingsnake (*Lampropeltis getula*) has been found to be an island resident. It was first discovered from a fleeting glimpse in the early 1980s, then in 1985 from a shed skin, and finally in 1990 from the capture of two live individuals, serendipitously a male and female (Lawler 1990:4, 1992:26–27; Lara-Gongora et al. 1993).

V.

The Archaeological Legacy of
San Esteban Island

*If people lived on San Esteban Island, as modern Seri oral accounts con-
tend, there should be archaeological evidence of their activities. Between late
1979 and 1987, our group made some 10 trips to the island to find out
what remains were out there. Most of this exploration was carried out as
a simple surface survey with very limited objectives. We were interested in
determining just four things: 1) Is there evidence of people having been on
the island; 2) Were any of these people Seris; 3) Did they actually reside
on the island, as the oral accounts maintain, or were they just temporary
visitors; and 4) When were they there? Answering these questions, we
believed, would provide an empirical basis for evaluating whether the San
Esteban people really existed.*

*Of course, we recorded all the remains we encountered, whether or not
we thought they had anything to do with the San Esteban people. Indeed,
a few of the remains can be attributed to Mexicans or North Americans
who have visited the island since the latter part of the nineteenth century.
There are also a few indications that the island may have been utilized by
a very early people, although as yet there is not enough evidence for this
possibility to be properly evaluated. But most of the archaeological record
is probably Seri. While a small fraction of this Seri material is likely the
result of late nineteenth and early twentieth century visits, the majority
is almost certainly earlier, though probably not by much. The remains are
reported in summary form[107] in the next three chapters, sorted out culturally and chronologically to the best of our ability.*

*San Esteban turned out to be a strange place to do archaeology. Not only
are the remains themselves unlike anything we had seen previously, but*

working there provided some unique challenges. Moreover, we voluntarily imposed some major constraints on our activities in an effort to abide by the conservation ethic that has been adopted by nearly all scientists currently doing research in the fragile environment of the Gulf. Hence we attempted to conduct our work with a minimum of impact on the archaeology, observing but not collecting, and leaving the remains as we found them. Although operating in this way severely limits the information that can be recovered, this approach was generally adequate for our limited objectives. These considerations are discussed more fully in Appendix C.

Elisa Villalpando C. has already assessed the archaeology in terms of the cultural ecology of the island (Villalpando 1989). The present book describes the features, artifacts, and ecofacts in greater detail, and discusses how they might have been used, by whom, and when. We shall defer to Part VI the question of whether the archaeological remains are of residents or visitors, and what this suggests about the existence of the San Esteban people.

THIRTEEN

Altering the Landscape:
Archaeological Structures and Features

Habitation Caves

San Esteban is a volcanic island, formed in part from a succession of airfall deposits, pyroclastic flows, and lahars or mudflows (Desonie 1992:128). Over geological time, water and wind have eroded hundreds of caves and overhangs into these soft layered rocks. In much more recent times, some of these caves and overhangs have served as shelters for people.

We recorded 13 caves with clear evidence of occupation (see Figure 16.4). None shows very much surface refuse, but about half of these have enough domestic trash to suggest that they were true habitation sites—living quarters where people returned frequently or resided on a regular basis. The others were probably used less regularly. We also saw, but did not record, about another half dozen small caves that contain only the barest traces of occupation. These were probably nothing more than handy refuges where somebody sought temporary shelter from bad weather, and the only evidence of their stay is one or two fragments of chipped stone, shell, bone, or perhaps flecks of charcoal from a small fire. However, we did record two additional caves that are occasionally used by modern Mexican fishermen (D46 and J16), and a petroglyph cave with no evidence of occupation (G15). They are described later in this chapter.

The people who used caves clearly chose them in part on the basis of convenience. Three are within a few hundred meters of major beaches, and all but one of the remainder are located along the principal arroyos, which constitute natural highways connecting most parts of the island. Most of these caves are conveniently situated at ground level, and only one lies more than about 10 m up a hillside. Though there are many excellent natural cavities weathered into steep slopes high in the mountains, we saw none in remote locations with evidence of more than the most casual and temporary use.

Most of the recorded caves face between south and east, giving full protection from the bitter northwest winds of winter and allowing their entrances to be heated by the winter sun. Two (I42 and I47) face southwest and one (E10) faces northeast, but they too are sheltered from northwest winds by their position in the arroyo bank. One cave (I1) faces north.

Floors are usually fairly level, but the chambers tend to be small and shallow. Most are between 2.5 and 10 m wide at the mouth, 2–3 m deep, and 1.5–2 m high. This makes them large enough for several people to sleep or sit, but they are not always high enough for a person of medium height to stand upright. The largest single habitation cave (A4) is about 30 m wide and 10 m high at the entrance, though it is only a few meters deep. The deepest cave is a narrow level-floored tunnel extending some 12 m into a hillside, much like a mine entrance. This chamber is actually one of about seven that are clustered together (collectively designated L7), and it is unclear from the sparse trash below how many of these chambers were actually occupied. Another cave (G4) has rocky partitions that nominally separate adjacent overhangs, but they are so ill-defined that the site could be considered either a single very large cavity or a complex of several (Figure 1.11).

The people who used the caves often threw their trash out the entrance, and this is where we find most of the surface refuse today. They probably also left trash on cave floors, but if so, little of it remains visible on the surface. The poorly consolidated rock layers in which most of San Esteban's caves formed disintegrate readily, and cave floors are subjected to a continual rain of dust and small chunks from the ceiling. Hence the floor one sees today may have formed very recently, and some caves that today appear uninhabited could contain buried living surfaces. Though unlikely, there is always an outside chance that, like Gatecliff Shelter in Nevada (Thomas 1983:16, 172–76), few or no surface remains could belie deep stratified deposits of cultural material.

Some caves are subject to more catastrophic processes than the steady drizzle of small particles from the roof. One shelter (E10) was created when a multi-ton chunk of the arroyo bank collapsed and slid away from the cavity it left behind. Another cave (I35) has an obvious history of frequent rockfall. It was hollowed out of a mudflow breccia consisting of large rocks tenuously held in a soft matrix. The cave ceiling contains dozens of boulders inexorably weathering their way out. Some, weighing up to around 200 kilograms, hang precariously suspended with two-thirds of their mass exposed. Others already lie on the cave floor. Despite the unmistakable hazard, trash both inside and outside the overhang leaves no doubt that people lived there anyway.

Fires were a normal part of cave life. Although almost all the recorded caves contain charcoal and ash, only two have identifiable hearths. Both are situated just at the edge of the overhang. One of these (at N4) is merely a localized concentration of dense ash and charcoal. The other (at I35) is rimmed by a circle of small stones. It is partly buried by fallen roof material but still contains a piece of a cooking pot, consisting of a large sherd of a Historic Seri pottery olla.

Animal bones are common surface ecofacts at cave sites. Though they are presumably the remains of meals, few are burned, suggesting that fires were used less for cooking than for warmth. By far the most common bones are sea turtle, and these occur at nearly every cave, occasionally in some quantity. Three caves have fish vertebrae and chuckwalla bones, and one contains a crab claw. The most peculiar animal remains were found at I35. When we first visited this cave in 1980, we discovered a chuckwalla carcass that a former inhabitant had very efficiently skinned, much as one would skin a snake. First, the head had been removed and then, with no further cuts, the skin had been turned inside out at the neck and peeled back in a single piece all the way to the animal's hind legs, which in turn had been skinned in the same manner. This was presumably done to get at the chuckwalla's flesh, which of course was long gone. When we returned to the cave in 1984, the carcass was still intact. But strangely, three years later, the skin had completely disappeared, and only the chuckwalla's vertebral column remained.

Shells and shell fragments are much less common than bone and were seen at only six caves. One cave (A4) near Playa La Freidera has about 20 limpet shells. However, these shells appear fresh and may have been carried in by a recent visitor (along with a piece of plastic). At the other caves, it appears as though specific shells were brought in as specimens for a collection, valued for their individuality and not the nutrition of their contents or even their utility as tools. Thus the shells at one cave (E10), located well inland, consist of one *Turbo*, one *Conus*, one *Pecten*, and one broken clam shell. Another inland cave (G4) contains, in addition to a few unidentified fragments, three limpets and one broken piece each of a *Turbo*, a *Pecten*, and an *Arca*.

We saw parts of agave plants at three caves (B2, I1, and I35). Although agave is said to have been a major food item for the San Esteban people, the remains in the caves were not from the edible heart but rather frayed pieces of leaves and cut sections of stalk. One piece of stalk at B2, found crammed into a crack in the ceiling, has two 1-cm diameter holes drilled into it, suggestive of a flute or whistle. A similar object at I35 has four such holes. This cave also has several bundles of stripped agave fiber, perhaps intended for making cord. One of the most interesting ecofacts at I35 is an unmodified piece of reedgrass or carrizo cane (*Phragmites australis*) about 50 cm long. This is the plant from which Seri balsas were made, but it does not grow on San Esteban. The closest source is at the permanent waterhole of *Xapij*, inland from the southwest coast of Tiburón Island (Map 1.4).

A single projectile point was found on the surface outside B5, and two fragmentary points were seen outside I47 (see Figure 14.5). When Elisa Villalpando and Arturo Oliveros excavated cave B2 in 1984, they found about six more small points (Elisa Villalpando 1984:pers. comm.). The presence of projectile points is perplexing since there is literally nothing on San Esteban to hunt with a bow and arrow.

Eight caves also have pottery. Though B2 produced around 200 surface sherds, in most cases we saw only a few pieces. The four sherds at I1 are all Tiburón Plain, thought to be the earliest Seri pottery type. Two sherds at I47

Figure 13.1   Two clearings (B13 right, B14 left) high above the northeastern corner of San Esteban, looking north. B13 length is 2.2 m, width 1.9 m; B14 length is 2.6 m, width 2.1 m. The southwest coast of Tiburón Island is visible in the background. April 1980.

are also Tiburón Plain. All the rest of the pottery we saw at cave sites is Historic Seri, a type which seems to date mostly from the nineteenth century. Three caves (B2, G4, and I47) have painted Historic Seri sherds. One of these (I47) also produced a piece of a Seri ceramic figurine while another (G4) has three sherd disks.

In terms of interpreting San Esteban's archaeology, the most important cave is probably E10, for it is one of the relatively few sites whose surface remains include a wide variety of artifacts and ecofacts. Although far from abundant, the assemblage here consists of shells, bones, flakes, an end scraper, a chopper, metates, a mano, agave knives (see Figure 14.7), and a lone sherd of Historic Seri pottery. Thus E10 provides evidence that all of these items are probably contemporary with each other, chronologically late, and part of ordinary domestic life on San Esteban Island.

Clearings

Clearings, like caves, were probably also habitation sites, and they are among the most numerous features on San Esteban (see Figure 16.4). The majority are nothing more than small oval or circular areas where the ground surface was more or less cleared of large rocks. The ones we recorded are well preserved,

Figure 13.2   Clearing (I55) on the west side of San Esteban, with Male Mountain (Hast Ctam) in the background. Length is 2.6 m, width 1.3 m. Photograph looks northeast. January 1987.

distinct, and almost certainly of human origin (Figures 13.1 and 13.2). However, these may constitute only a fraction of the human-made clearings on the island, for we saw many more such features that might have been intentionally produced, but are not distinct enough to be certain (see Appendix C).

Of the 53 clearings we recorded, we took measurements on 46. The mean size, based on this sample, is 2.4 m long by 2.0 m wide. The largest clearing we saw is about 5 m long and 4 m wide, while the smallest is 1.5 by 0.9 m. Nearly three-fourths of those we recorded occur in obvious clusters, ranging from two to six clearings per cluster, with the constituent clearings no more than a few meters from each other, and sometimes touching. However, the true number of clearings in these clusters could be much greater, because some clusters are accompanied by vaguely defined and hence uncertain clearings which we did not record.

There are some differences in the specific ways clearings were made and the locations chosen for them. In most cases, the rocks removed were simply tossed outside the clearing and are now mixed into the natural surface scatter. In a few instances, some of the rocks were placed around the perimeter, creating a slight rim of small stones. Only one clearing (K7) has a true boulder rim. Generally, only large loose rocks were removed, and no effort was made to dig out embedded rocks or clear the ground of pebbles less than about 2 or 3 cm in diameter. Some clearings, however, have very smooth floors (Figure 13.2). In locations where the ground has an appreciable slope, a level surface was sometimes produced by excavating 10 or 15 cm into the uphill side. Though lying barely below the original ground surface, we discovered that some of these leveled features in north slopes (such as D36–D39) provide a reclining person with superb protection from the northwest winter wind. Many clearings, however, do not seem to be well situated for wind protection, and some are in highly exposed locations, including the top of a knoll (F1–F2) and a shelf just below the summit of the island's highest peak (C4–C8). Another group of clearings (I2–I7) is equally exposed on a pass overlooking the western sea cliffs, though here there is also a circular piled rock enclosure (I8) that might have provided shelter from the wind. What nearly all clearings have in common, whether located on flat ground, sloping hillsides, hilltops, ridges, or high summits, is an unobstructed view of the surrounding landscape.

Like habitation caves, most clearings are accompanied by at least a few artifacts and ecofacts. Although this may consist of nothing more than a few flakes in the immediate vicinity, there is reason to believe that these associations are generally valid, because other kinds of features, such as stone circles, are seldom found with anything at all. Only about half a dozen clearings appear to be lacking entirely in nearby artifacts or ecofacts. Since clearings are strictly surface features, the artifacts that accompany them are also presumably limited to the ground surface.

As with caves, nearly every kind of artifact and ecofact that occurs on San Esteban can be found at clearings, though not necessarily in the same quantities or proportions. Charcoal, for instance, was seen at only 10 of these features, and in very small amounts. We saw sea turtle bone at only one group of clearings and shell fragments at just three. Chipped-stone tools are rare items, and we saw just eight: a spokeshave, an oval scraper, a unifacial chopper, two crude bifaces, and three agave knives. However, most clearings have a few simple stone flakes in the immediate vicinity, and two groups of clearings (I2–I7 and I56–I60) have flakes in comparative abundance (more than 200 at I2–I7 and about 100 at I56–I60). Slightly more than one-third of the manos and metates seen on the island occur at clearings.

Pottery is conspicuously absent from most clearings, but at the three places it does occur, it is abundant (by San Esteban standards). Ten sherds of Historic Seri were seen at B4 while a whopping 90 Historic Seri sherds are strewn about the I2–I7 clearings. About 25 sherds, all Tiburón Plain, accompany the I53–I55 group of clearings. This is the only place on the island where we saw more than two or three sherds of this apparently early pottery type.

Three clusters of clearings are of sufficient interest to single them out briefly. One of these is the I2-I7 group, situated above the sea cliffs on the west side of the island. These clearings occupy an unusually strategic position, because this is one of the very few places in the entire western part of San Esteban where it

*Figure 13.3   Unusual raised "clearing" with retaining wall (P21) in Arroyo Bonito,
east side of San Esteban. Diameter is 2.4 m. Photograph looks southwest. January 1981.*

is feasible to descend the sea cliffs to the shore below. The features here also
include I8, the remains of a more or less circular rock-walled structure similar
to the island's summit enclosures. Probably both aboriginal peoples and recent
Europeans have been here, for the site assemblage includes a button, two snaps,
and a belt clip from a military-style canteen, plus 200–300 flakes, about 90
Historic Seri sherds, five metates, two manos, and an agave knife. In one of the
clearings (I3), rocks have been arranged on the ground to make designs, one of
which seems to be "31."

The third noteworthy cluster of clearings is I53–I55 (see Figure 13.2), near

Another cluster consists of three clearings in Arroyo Bonito (P21–P23) that
were leveled by piling rocks on the downhill side to create a sort of retaining wall
some 30 cm high. Here, "clearing" is not an entirely appropriate term, for while
the interiors are smoother than the surrounding ground surface, they would not
make very comfortable living surfaces (Figure 13.3). Although only three of
these "clearings" were recorded, there may be at least five others in the immediate vicinity that are similar but less well defined. Neither artifacts nor ecofacts
were found nearby.

The third noteworthy cluster of clearings is I53–I55 (see Figure 13.2), near
the sea cliffs that overlook the west side. These three clearings each have a vague
rim, probably created by raking some of the rocks from the cleared area to the
perimeter. Although only the three best defined features were recorded, there
may be as many as 20 barely discernible clearings nearby that could be associated. This is also the location of 14 mano-sized, but apparently unworked

cobbles, whose purpose is unclear. But the importance of the site lies not in the unusual remains, but in the fact that the conventional artifacts are relatively abundant and almost certainly associated with the clearings. These remains include two genuine manos, two metate surfaces, some 20 flakes, about 25 sherds of Tiburón Plain pottery, and a few slivers of charcoal. Together, this site and I2–I7 provide good evidence that clearings, especially those in clusters, were domestic camps and that at least some were used by Seri families during pottery-making times.

The idea that clearings are camp sites is an old one that originated with the fieldwork of Malcolm Rogers in the lower Colorado River Basin during the 1920s and 1930s (Rogers 1939:7–8, 1966:45–47). In this region, Rogers encountered thousands of these features, which he termed "temporary sleeping enclosures" and interpreted as the bedding places of nomadic peoples. On the whole, he found them to be remarkably uniform in technique of construction, form, and size. A few have boulder rims, but the majority are simple clearings with, at most, a slightly raised rim created by raking rocks to the perimeter. Rogers found around 90 percent to be circular rather than oval and typically close to 1.8 m in diameter, seldom exceeding 2.4 m. Only in rare cases were these circles accompanied by any artifacts at all. Since he generally found them on ancient landforms and since they often possessed other indicators of great antiquity, Rogers assigned most of these circles to the ancient Malpais culture, for which Julian Hayden has since proposed dates in excess of 20,000 years B.P. (Hayden 1976:286–87, 1982:582; Dolzani 1988; Reid and Whittlesey 1997:119).

Since the 1930s, clearings have been found throughout most of the Desert West, including Tiburón Island and much of Baja California. They are now widely referred to as "sleeping circles," "sleeping clearings," or "camp clearings" (see Tuohy 1984), and it is assumed that the purpose of removing rocks was to make sleeping more comfortable. And, as Rogers himself was very much aware, not all clearings are ancient. Differences in location, slight differences in form, and especially associated artifacts indicate that clearings in some regions, including Baja California, persisted into late prehistoric and even historic times (Rogers 1939:8, 1966:45–47; Tuohy 1984:45).

The clearings on San Esteban fall easily within this broad category of "sleeping clearings" as recognized in surrounding regions. In construction, they are not much different from Rogers's Malpais clearings, though typically they are about 0.5 m larger, a little more variable in size, more likely to be slightly oval, and they are not confined to ancient landforms. More importantly, they are frequently associated with artifacts, and the presence of Seri pottery at three groups of clearings indicates that these features were probably in use well into the nineteenth century. The age of those without diagnostic artifacts is not known, and one might speculate that some of the many barely discernible clearings, which we did not record, could have great antiquity. But it hardly need be said that vagueness alone is no guarantee of great age. On San Lorenzo Norte Island, about 30 km away, there is a pair of inconspicuous clearings that were made by two Mexican military men who arrived by helicopter and slept in them during a presidential visit to the region about 1981 (Daniel Anderson 1984:pers. comm.)

Figure 13.4   Pit oven (E13) on a terrace of Arroyo Limantour, east side of San Esteban. Dimensions not recorded. Photograph looks southeast. January 1981.

Pit Ovens

We found 19 features that are clearly pit ovens and almost certainly used to bake agave (see Figure 16.2). Of these, 13 are probably aboriginal and are discussed here. The remaining six (D1, D2, D33, E2, E3, and E6) are most likely of Mexican origin and are described in a later section (see pp. 356).

Most of the presumably aboriginal pits have been sufficiently filled in by wind- and water-born sediment that they are now shallow basin-shaped depressions, which are surrounded by a raised rim of dirt and small rocks and look very much like eroded bomb craters (Figure 13.4). Charcoal occurs at nearly all of these features, and at three (D26, D55, and E13) we found pieces of ironwood that had been cut with a metal ax. Three of the pits have sea turtle bones nearby, but none was clearly associated with any artifacts.

The rims surrounding the central depressions were probably formed from the dirt and rocks thrown up out of the hole when the pits were first dug, but they may have been altered each time the ovens were opened to retrieve the baked agave hearts. Rims are circular to slightly oval. Among the 11 we recorded, the mean size is 2.9 m long by 2.8 m wide, measured from crest to crest. The largest (G9) is 4.0 m by 3.5 m, while the diameter of the smallest (D55) is 1.8 m. The height of the rims today is mainly a function of how much erosion they have suffered. One well-preserved rim stands 70 cm above the present ground surface, while most are between 10 and 40 cm high. One is so eroded it is barely visible.

Little can be said about the pits themselves from surface indications. Their present depth depends mainly on how much they have filled in since last use, and the range is from about 50 cm below the ground surface (D27) to essentially zero. In one case (D32), the bottom of the pit has been so thoroughly filled by material eroding from the rim that it now lies 25 cm *above* the level of the surrounding ground surface, though still 25 cm below the rim crest.

Pit ovens are such an important part of the archaeological record that we eventually decided to excavate one in order to determine something about the size and structure of the underlying pit. The one selected was D27, and it provided us with a basis for reconstructing how aboriginal pit ovens were built and used. In this example, the builders first excavated a slightly tapered cylindrical pit, approximately 1.2 m in diameter at the surface and rounded at the bottom. How deep this pit was dug into the original ground surface is difficult to judge because the ground around it was badly disturbed by later episodes of use, but the depth must have been something like 1.0 m. The dirt and rocks from this excavation were probably thrown up around the outside of the hole to form the rim. Next, the bottom of the pit was floored with rocks, typically about 20 cm long by 15 cm wide. More rocks were then carefully stacked up against the sides of the hole, resulting in a completely stone-lined pit. At the surface, the finished oven was about 100 cm long by 85 cm wide, tapering to about 85 by 50 cm at the bottom. From top to bottom, the rock-lined cavity is about 50 cm deep.

At first, the people who built D27 used it for baking with no further modifications. A thick, dense layer of nearly pure charcoal lying directly on the rock floor suggests that wood was piled on the bottom of the oven, ignited, and allowed to burn down to a bed of hot coals. What happened after that cannot be determined from the pit itself because evidence for the rest of the process was destroyed each time the oven was opened. If, as we believe, D27 was built and used by early twentieth century Seris to cook agave, the process would have proceeded in this manner:

> When it [the fire at the bottom of the pit] had burned down, the agave hearts were piled, top down, on the bed of coals. Flat rocks were placed over them and the rocks covered with earth to a depth of about 5 to 10 cm. Another fire was then built on top of that, the resulting bed of coals covered with more earth, and the hearts left to bake overnight.
>
> On the following day the agave hearts or cores were removed from the pit. They were blackened from contact with the coals. (Felger and Moser 1985:225)

The charcoal layer at the bottom of D27 was about 20 cm thick. Above it, we found a thin lens of sterile sand that must have blown in shortly after the oven was last opened. Above the sterile layer was a 10 cm mixture of charcoal, ash, and burned rock, then another layer of nearly pure charcoal, and finally another layer of mixed material that extended to within 15 cm of the top of the stone-lined pit. Evidently, nobody bothered to clean out the oven before it was reused, and it became nearly filled with the detritus from at least two episodes of baking.

Among the Pimas, similar stone-lined pits used for roasting cholla buds would fill up with repeated use in a similar manner, until it was more trouble to clean them than dig a new pit, at which time they were abandoned (Greenhouse et al. 1981:232). In the case of D27, however, even when the original pit had almost completely filled up, the oven was not yet entirely abandoned. A new layer of rocks was placed on top of the burned rubble that filled the original pit, and this became the basin-shaped floor of a much more casual baking area, about 1.0 m in diameter and with no rocks lining the walls. Like the original pit, the fill above the new rock floor consisted of dense charcoal mixed with ashy soil and burned rocks. Whether this baking area was used more than once cannot be determined, but it was eventually abandoned, and the depression that remained gradually filled in with sand and rock eroding from the rim.

The assumption that the San Esteban pits were used to bake agave is based on two principal lines of reasoning. The first is the extremely wide distribution of more or less similar features throughout the U.S. Southwest and most of Mexico, including much of Sonora and the northern part of Baja California. They occur archaeologically in almost all areas where edible agave species grow, and they have been described ethnographically among peoples within this wide area since Colonial times (Bartlett [1854] 1965:291–92; Castetter et al. 1938; Gentry 1972:2–11, 1978:18–20). The second line of reasoning stems from information provided by the modern Seris, who in recent decades have constructed similar pit ovens to cook agave and believe that the San Esteban pits were used for this purpose. The Seris say that during the first half of the twentieth century, people used to go to San Esteban to collect agave. They would walk some distance inland up Arroyo Limantour to gather plants because those near the coast were not very good. Sometimes they cooked the hearts on the island, in the loose gravels of the arroyo bottom near where they collected them. Otherwise, they would bring them back to the southwest coast of Tiburón Island for baking (Felger and Moser 1970:161–64, 1985:222–25; Roberto Herrera 1981:pers. comm.).

On San Esteban, pit ovens are almost exclusively confined to the region where it is said the recent Seris did their gathering and baking. On Tiburón Island, virtually identical pit ovens (to judge by surface indications) can be seen at two well-known Seri camps on the southwest coast where the modern Seris say raw agave hearts from San Esteban expeditions were brought. One of these camps, called *Cyaxoj*, is in an area completely devoid of agave plants, but one can still see more than a dozen ovens. The ovens are all within easy walking distance of the beach, where people returning from San Esteban would have landed. The most distant ones are next to stands of mesquite and ironwood, which were needed in quantity as fuel. According to Roberto Herrera (1981:pers. comm.), the main difference between the ovens on San Esteban and the southwest coast of Tiburón, and those the Seris built elsewhere, is that the former were larger, because the hearts of the San Esteban agave are very large and because people would cook many of them at once.

While all this may seem to belabor the obvious, there have been suggestions that pits in other areas were sometimes used for purposes other than baking agave (Gasser 1982). As noted above, one specific interpretation, based on both archaeological evidence and ethnographic data, is that similar stone-lined pits were also used to roast cholla buds and occasionally reused to cook other foods (Bruder 1977:242; Greenhouse et al. 1981). The Seris are among those who have roasted and eaten cholla buds, including two species that occur on San Esteban island (*Opuntia bigelovii* and *O. cf. burrageana*). However, the ovens in which cholla buds were cooked, as described by the modern Seris, were simple unlined excavations on the order of 30 cm deep (Felger and Moser 1976:266–67), quite unlike the larger stone-lined pits described here. While it is certainly possible that the pits on San Esteban were sometimes reused for cooking cholla or other items, they were most likely built specifically to bake agave.

What is less certain is how many ovens might have been built by Mexicans rather than Seris. Because Europeans in the New World learned how to prepare agave from native Americans, it may not be easy to distinguish a Mexican pit oven from an aboriginal one, especially by looking at the filled-in surface remains. Based on archaeological context and historical data, there is reason to believe that at least six of the ovens on San Esteban are indeed Mexican, as will be discussed in a later section (see p. 356).

Stone Circles and Ashy Areas

If there is one kind of structure that typifies the surface archaeology of San Esteban Island, it is the stone circle (Figures 13.5 and 13.6). These features occur throughout the island, and we recorded 61 of them (see Figure 16.3). The majority are in the loose gravel of arroyo bottoms, but we have seen circles on rocky terraces, hilltops, and plateaus high in the mountains. They all seem to be isolated features, neither clustered together nor apparently associated with any other type of feature. Just over half of those we saw are genuinely circular, while the remainder are slightly oval. Of the 52 we measured, the mean dimensions are 1.7 m long and 1.6 m wide. The two largest (A6 and L11) are both 2.5 m in diameter, while the smallest (I15) is about 70 cm long by 50 cm wide.

Stone circles were built by simply setting rocks on the ground in a roughly circular pattern. The rocks are generally no larger than about 20 cm in diameter, and they were usually placed with a gap of about 20 cm between them. Normally, circles are one rock wide, but in one case (E19) the rocks are doubled up in some places, making part of the circle two rocks wide. Other variations include a circle that was built in a small cave (Q1), and two circles (B14 and K1) that were placed in human-made clearings. The vast majority of the circles, nearly 90 percent, rest on a substrate of loose soil that is laden with charcoal and ash and extends beyond the circle itself. But the rocks that make up the circles are not burned, so it is clear that they were set in place after a fire in or on the underlying loose soil had burned itself out.

Figure 13.5 Stone circle (J11) in lower Arroyo Limantour, looking south-southwest. Length is 2.3 m, width 1.8 m. This circle was tested with a 1-m wide trench. January 1987.

Figure 13.6 Stone circle (L10) near the center of San Esteban, looking east. Diameter is 1.6 m. January 1982.

Only seven circles have no surface charcoal, and in three of these instances, the reason is probably partial destruction (B6) or burial (G3 and L6). The remaining four (B8, D14, K3, and M15) were clearly never associated with fire and were built on consolidated, undisturbed ground. One of these (D14) may be associated with some apparently ancient rock clusters and alignments (see Figure 13.7). What these circles without charcoal represent is uncertain, but it is likely that they are a different kind of feature from those built on ashy soil, related perhaps to boulder-rimmed clearings. One of the circles without charcoal (M15) has two sherds of Historic Seri pottery, but nothing was found with the other three.

Of the charcoal-bearing circles, about 60 percent have neither artifacts nor ecofacts anywhere in the immediate area. Most of the items that occur in the vicinity of the other 40 percent may not be genuinely associated but may simply be part of the thin scatter of material that pervades the island. Such nearby artifacts seldom consist of more than a flake or two, but the inventory does include cobble manos or hammer stones, a metate, a biface, a spokeshave, an end scraper, and several agave knives. We saw pottery near three circles (B7, I10, and I24), all Historic Seri except for a single sherd of Tiburón Plain. Ecofacts, consisting of sea turtle bones or shell fragments, occur in the vicinity of 11 circles.

In addition to circles per se, we found 17 places where large quantities of charcoal and ash are intermixed with loose soil or arroyo bottom gravel but with no circles of stones (see Figure 16.3). These ashy areas appear identical to the material that underlies most circles. In fact, five of them have a few stones showing, which may be remnants of former circles. Arroyo bottoms are susceptible to periodic flash flooding, and when that happens, the stones that make up a circle may be swept away or buried by gravel washing in. It is not uncommon to see charcoal scattered several meters downstream from a circle, and one circle (B7), first seen in 1967 and recorded again in 1980, has since disappeared entirely. In all likelihood, the ashy areas are simply "circles" where the circle itself has been destroyed or possibly, in some cases, never constructed. Like conventional circles, one can sometimes find sea turtle bones, shell fragments, or an artifact or two in the general vicinity of the ashy areas.

During our 1967 overnight visit to San Esteban, we saw three circles. One of these (D14) is among the few that were built on sterile ground and lack any trace of charcoal and ash. The other two (including B7) were conventional circles on charcoal-laden soil. Coming fresh from the Seri mainland, where we had seen more or less similar stone circles that the Seris themselves identified as structures used in the vision quest, we naturally assumed that these three San Esteban circles were Seri vision rings (Bowen 1976:40–41). It is perhaps remotely possible that D14 was constructed for this purpose, but it is now very clear that the vast majority, built on ashy soil, must have been used in some other way. During the intervening years, many Seris have been asked in various ways if the San Esteban circles might be vision rings. While many have said that they are the right shape and size, they are positive that no vision seeker would ever build a fire where he or she would seek a vision, and they are totally baffled by the presence of all the charcoal that accompanies the San

Esteban circles. Moreover, they are quite certain that Seris did not go to San Esteban from the mainland or Tiburón Island to seek visions, and that the San Esteban people sought visions at sea in their balsas, not in circles (Roberto Herrera 1981:pers. comm.; Mary Beck Moser 1981:pers. comm.). Clearly, some other explanation is needed.

On subsequent field trips, we considered several alternative explanations. One of the most attractive was based on the fact that we had seen no evidence of human burials anywhere on the island. The modern Seris seem unsure of how the San Esteban people disposed of their dead and assume that they probably placed the bodies in crevices in the rocks. We wondered, however, whether the ash and charcoal areas might be cremation sites with the circles built afterward to mark the location, perhaps as a memorial, or maybe simply to warn others not to dig up the ground there. Over time, the accumulation of deaths might well account for the number of circles seen, and their wide distribution on the island might result from cremating people more or less wherever they died. If the circles were built as memorials, the few that were placed on sterile ground might even be explained as markers for those who died elsewhere, such as people who were drowned at sea. Clearly, one test of these ideas was whether we could find any calcined human bones around the normal ash-laden circles. Although we realized that all the bone might be hidden underground, the only surface fragments we were able to find were from sea turtles, not humans. Perhaps an even more basic problem is that other Seris, for all their varied ways of disposing of the dead, have apparently never practiced cremation (Bowen 1976:47–50).

Another possibility we considered was that the circles marked former house sites. Though the San Esteban people preferred caves, it is said that they also constructed makeshift shelters of agave stalks, driftwood, and piled branches. When a death occurred among Seris on the mainland and Tiburón Island, the personal possessions of the deceased and immediate family members were removed from their house and the house itself was destroyed, sometimes by burning (Griffen 1959:44; Bowen 1983:244). If a similar custom prevailed among the San Esteban people, the ashy soil might be the remains of burned houses. As in the cremation theory, the circle of stones might have been placed on the ashes to mark the spot. Again, the frequency of deaths over time might easily explain the number of circles, and their wide distribution would correspond with the obvious fact that people utilized the entire island. The practice of removing personal possessions might explain the lack of useful tools at most of the circles and, perhaps, would also account for the sporadic occurrence of waste flakes, bone, and shell—the trash from ordinary living that would not be worth carrying away. But circles always seem to be isolated from each other. Unlike clearings, they do not occur in clusters as one would expect if they were the habitation sites of normally sociable people.

A third hypothesis was that stone circles were ordinary pit ovens for baking agave and had, for some reason, been intentionally filled in and the location marked with a circle of stones. Considering the immense quantity of agave on the island and the modern Seri belief that the hearts served as a staple of the San Esteban people's diet, the number of "bomb crater" pit ovens did not seem nearly sufficient nor widely distributed enough for all the agave cooking that must have gone on. The circles, on the other hand, like both the plants and the litter of the people who ate them, can be found all over the island. It might have been useful to mark the locations of former ovens because the ground would already be loose and digging a new pit in the same spot would be easy. But why an old pit would have been filled in in the first place is not obvious, nor have the modern Seris been able to think of any logical reason why the San Esteban people would have done so (Mary Beck Moser 1982:pers. comm.).

Because we were as perplexed by these circles as the Seris, we decided it was worth sacrificing one to excavation in the hope that it would elucidate their function. In April 1987, we put a 1.0 m wide trench through the center of circle J11 to find out (Figure 13.5). To our surprise, J11 turned out to be not a deep pit oven but merely a shallow, basin-shaped depression about 25 cm deep in the center. It contained a gray mixture of charcoal, ash, silt, and many fragments of small and mostly burned rocks. The fill also contained a chuckwalla leg bone and several small sea turtle bone fragments, both burned and unburned, but no bone fragments that are likely to be human. There were no artifacts and no well-defined contact surface suggesting a house floor at the bottom of the depression, nor was it entirely clear whether the depression had been intentionally excavated before the burning took place.

To be sure that J11 was representative, we took a small trowel to several other circles with surface charcoal and made a small hole in their centers. In each case, we encountered ashy fill below the surface similar to that at J11 and hit sterile soil between 8–25 centimeters below the surface. As a control, we also tested one of the circles that completely lacks surface charcoal and found the soil below the surface to be sterile and undisturbed.

The excavation and testing enabled us to say with certainty that the circles are not filled in "bomb-crater" pit ovens. They seem to make the cremation hypothesis less tenable, though one excavated circle does not allow us to categorically eliminate either it or the burned house explanation. However, the results do suggest a fourth possibility that we had not previously considered — that the circles represent *surface* baking of agave. This was the sole technique used by the Cochimí of central Baja California, directly across the Gulf from San Esteban, and all other groups to the south of them, and it explains why there are no pit ovens in the southern two-thirds of the peninsula (Gentry 1978:20).

Johann Baegert, one of the Jesuits who worked in the southern peninsula during the eighteenth century, notes that the Guaicura method of cooking agave was to "throw it directly on the fire or on hot embers" (Baegert [1772] 1952: 179). Miguel del Barco, Baegert's colleague who worked among the Cochimí, left a wonderfully thorough description of the entire process of gathering, preparing, and consuming agave. Collecting and baking the hearts was the domain of women, and after a day of gathering:

in the afternoon each woman brings back eight or nine mezcales, ... which is some load! They walk with this load sometimes one or two leagues, maybe adding on top of this some firewood for roasting. Near the ranchería they light a fire, into which they throw stones that are not very large. When the firewood has been consumed and the stones have become as red hot coals, they use long sticks to spread the fire and stones a little and they place the mezcales in between, arranged as seems best for the purpose. The whole thing ends up as a pile, which they cover up with the surrounding hot dirt so that the heat is reconcentrated and will not dissipate for a long time. They leave them like that at least twenty-four hours, and more frequently two nights and a day. Then they take it all out well cooked....

When the mezcales are brought out ... and allowed to cool, the woman has a ready supply of food for herself and her family for three days, more or less, according to the number of persons. (Barco [ca. 1770s] 1980:228–29)

This description suggests that a surface oven would produce ashy areas like those that accompany the circles on San Esteban Island. Since Barco does not mention the Cochimí constructing circles on the site of the ovens, these may be a purely San Esteban invention, for which we still have no explanation.

Putting all this together suggests that both recent Seris and Mexicans were probably responsible for the "bomb crater" pit ovens. The stone circles and the similar ashy areas that lack circles were most likely the surface ovens of a different group, presumably the San Esteban people.

There is one stone circle (N5) that does not fit the general pattern. It is of normal size, but it is an incomplete circle and is two to three stones wide. There is charcoal here, but it comes from the burned stump of an ironwood tree still standing in the center of the circle, perhaps the victim of a lightning strike. For reasons unknown, somebody built the circle around the charred remains of this tree.

Rock Clusters, Cairns, and Alignments

From time to time, we encountered places where somebody had gathered unmodified rocks into a definable cluster. Some of these features are haphazard agglomerations of rocks thrown together with little care. Others consist of rocks placed with some deliberation. Many clusters are only one rock high, while others are slightly mounded, some rocks lying on top of others. The latter, if they are relatively high compared with their diameter, take on more of the appearance of cairns than rock clusters. Although there is almost certainly a continuum of form, we did find nine features for which the term cairn seems particularly appropriate.

Of the nine cairn-like features, two (I41 and J14) consist of just three and four rocks, respectively, stacked one on top of the other, European-style. They may well have been built by Mexican surveyors. Three more (unnumbered) consist of two rocks in a stack, and a fourth (M18) is a single rock placed on a boulder. These four are less clearly European, especially since they are not located on useful survey points nor visible from afar. Two cairns (P9 and P24) consist of a large upright slab supported by several slabs piled at the base. Although Europeans have certainly built cairns of similar form, these may not be European because they occur among the aboriginal summit enclosures on Pico Rojo and are not well placed to be effective survey markers. The other cairn (B3) is a pile of about a dozen large rocks, situated on a low ridge, overlooking a beach often visited by Mexican fishermen. As Keith Muscutt (1993:pers. comm.) has pointed out, rockpile cairns such as this occur on promontories all over Mexico, and many are probably the bases that once supported crosses erected by Mexicans.

In addition to these cairns of Mexican and uncertain origin, we recorded about 20 rock clusters that we assume to be aboriginal. Almost none are completely isolated features. Many are grouped into clusters of clusters, others are seemingly associated with summit enclosures, and some occur on saddles or passes with trails nearby.

The most elaborate clustering of rock clusters is the group that comprises D15–D22 (Figure 13.7). These eight clusters are arranged in a rough semicircle, about 10 m in diameter and open to the southeast. The individual clusters that make up the semicircle are all between about 1.0 and 1.5 m in diameter, and the rocks are piled no more than one or two high.

Just east of these clusters, and perhaps associated with them, are several other rock features (Figure 13.7). The most distinct of these, about 15 m away, is D14, one of the stone circles that lacks any sign of charcoal or ashy soil (see Bowen 1976:Fig. 33). Northeast of it is a figure (D13) which consists of three lines of single rocks placed in a sort of open-ended rectangle on undisturbed ground. A possible circle remnant (unrecorded) lies northeast of D13, and just beyond it is a sinuous rock alignment (D12) that may originally have consisted of two

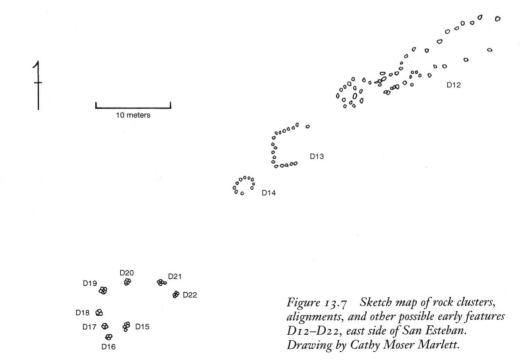

Figure 13.7 Sketch map of rock clusters, alignments, and other possible early features D12–D22, east side of San Esteban. Drawing by Cathy Moser Marlett.

Figure 13.8   Rock cluster of slabs (F4) beside a trail leading over the pass between two major arroyos. Length is 0.9 m, width 0.7 m, height 0.1 m. Photograph looks southwest. January 1981.

parallel lines of rocks. These and several other uncertain figures that are too vague to record all lie on an ancient terrace on the northern side of Arroyo Limantour. Some of the rocks in each of these features have acquired a distinctive buff-colored to orange ground patina on the underside, suggesting that they have rested in their present positions for a considerable time (see pp. 390–92). Because of this, they are among the few features on the island that have the appearance of genuinely great antiquity. Terraces with comparable groupings of rock clusters and ground figures are known on the west coast of Tiburón Island. Similar figures in the Sierra Pinacate, near the head of the Gulf, have been attributed to the ancient Malpais culture (Hayden 1982:584).

Three clusters of rocks (F3–F5) lie within 4 m of each other on the pass that connects Arroyo de las Cuevitas with the northeastern corner of the island. The clusters are a jumble of slabs of local rock, some more or less on end, and no more than about two high. A trail fragment is visible leading over the pass, and there are four Historic Seri sherds and a flake nearby (Figure 13.8).

Much farther down the arroyo to the south, there is a trail fragment leading toward a low saddle that probably served as a shortcut from middle Arroyo Limantour to upper Arroyo de las Cuevitas. On the saddle itself are three rock clusters, E20–E22, all within 4 m of each other. A short distance down the ridge is another cluster (E16) with a few of its slabs standing more or less on end. Alongside this cluster is E11, a single rock slab with a petroglyph in a grid pattern incised on one face (see p. 352).

Another small cluster (J13) that sits in a low point on a ridge does not seem to have a trail associated with it. But the cluster itself is unique because two of the five rocks that comprise it are agave knives, and a third knife lies 2.5 m away. Another aberrant cluster is H11, which lies on a hilltop. It may actually be a group of three or four clusters, but it is too jumbled to be certain.

The remaining five clusters or cairns (P9, P16, P17, P24, and P27) are all part of the summit structure complex on Pico Rojo. One of these (P27) is a simple cluster of unstacked rocks. Two others (P16 and P17) are similar but include a few rocks that lie on top of each other. The remaining two (P9 and P24, noted earlier) can be considered cairns, consisting of an upright slab supported by other slabs at the base.

Apart from the cairns that are most likely modern survey markers or the base of a former cross, the purpose of the clusters and cairns is anything but clear, and they may have been built for a variety of reasons. The modern Seris say that there are piles of rocks where the San Esteban people dug chuckwallas out of their burrows (Felger and Moser 1985:230–31). This might conceivably account for small rock piles in the arroyo bottoms and lower hillsides that chuckwallas generally prefer, but most of those we saw are too deliberate to be the unintended result of hasty digging, and their location mostly on high points is not where chuckwallas are commonly found (Lawler et al. 1994:333). Moreover, rock clusters are not accompanied by holes in which the animals would have burrowed and from which the rocks would have been removed.

Those on prominent passes with nearby trails may well be "trail shrines" analogous to those in southern Arizona, the lower Colorado River Basin, and the Sierra Pinacate (Rogers 1966:51–52; Hayden 1967:336, 339, Fig. 7, 1976:282–83, 1998:29). In historic times, the Yumas and Tohono O'odham (Papagos) often tossed a stone on a growing pile at significant points along a trail, such as a pass or a fork, for luck. According to Edward Moser (undated notes), a Seri might place a stone or stick on a prominent rock alongside a trail, asking the spirit of the rock to make some person give him a gift. On Tiburón Island, McGee's party saw a conical rockpile about 20 feet in diameter and seven feet high near a major trail fork (McGee 1898:289). By comparison, the clusters on the passes of San Esteban are tiny features, but there were surely far fewer people on San Esteban, and for much less time, than on Tiburón or in the lower Colorado River Basin.

Well-stacked cairns strategically placed on ridges or high points have been used by many hunting peoples from the Canadian arctic to the Great Basin as "dummy hunters," intended to look like wolves or threatening humans, in order to help funnel large game animals toward an ambush. On San Esteban, however, there are no terrestrial animals larger than chuckwallas and iguanas. Even if the island had much more fresh water in the past, it is simply too small to have supported a population of game animals such as desert bighorn or mule deer, and the probability of large mammals ever successfully rafting to San Esteban is exceedingly low (Bruce Coblentz 1984:pers. comm.).

Cairns have also been built over graves by many peoples as burial markers. An even more widespread practice, shared by the Seris, has been to simply cover the grave with a mound of rocks or brush to keep scavengers from getting at the body. McGee wrote of Seri burial "cairns," although what he actually describes are simple mounds of small rocks "3 or 4 feet long, two-thirds as wide, and seldom over 12 or 15 inches in height" (McGee 1898:288).

During much of the twentieth century, the Seris continued to heap rocks on graves (Bowen 1976:48). But this practice cannot explain the rock clusters and cairns on San Esteban, which are almost all situated on undisturbed ground that is much too rocky to enable a grave to be easily dug.

Rock clusters and cairns similar to those on San Esteban are also common features on Tiburón Island. One site on the north end of Tiburón consists of about 50 oval mounds of rocks. One mound was dismantled by a visitor who found nothing underneath, and Seris who knew of this site had no explanation for it (Bowen 1976:36). Rock clusters at other sites on both the north end and west coast of Tiburón are apparently associated with rock alignments and other ground figures. At a site near Tecomate (Son I:15:3), there is even a semicircular set of rock clusters closely resembling D15–D22 in form and size, though oriented in a different direction (Bowen 1976:Fig. 29). Like the San Esteban features, this cluster of clusters and associated rock alignments and figures may be ancient. Seris queried during the 1970s about this site were completely unfamiliar with such features and could only speculate that they might be connected with the vision quest (Bowen 1976:37–38).

Rock clusters and cairns have been used by Seri shamans as a means of exercising power over others. Edward Moser (1960 unpublished notes) reports that rockpile cairns represented the chief spirit of an area, and that a shaman who built one might pronounce a curse on anybody who would tear it down. The last incident of this sort occurred in the village of El Desemboque, apparently in the middle 1950s. By then, the authority and practice of traditional Seri shamans had been greatly eroded by competition with Mexican medical personnel and an evangelical Protestant mission. In an act of self-assertion, one of the last shamans, Nacho Morales, built a circular mound of stones about 50 cm high near the mission church and placed a curse on it. He said that anyone who moved the rocks would die and that anybody who spoke badly of him (Morales) would be afflicted with a pain. The other Seris would not go near the cairn for fear of its power. In 1956, a Mexican dismantled it (Edward Moser 1976:pers. comm.; Mary Beck Moser 1997:pers. comm.).

Clusters and cairns occur in parts of Baja California (Ritter 1981:41; Foster 1984:65; Ritter et al. 1984:21), and in some of these areas shamanism may also have been involved in their construction. According to Clavigero ([1789] 1971: 110–15), the eighteenth century Cochimí recognized a deity that periodically came to earth and visited them. These visits were celebrated by feasting and dancing carried out under the direction of a shaman. The shamans wielded enormous power and had the authority to punish and impose "penance" on those who failed to heed their directives. One form of penance involved building rock clusters or cairns up in the mountains:

Not only private individuals but even entire tribes were often subjected to these penalties. Likewise in the punishment of similar sins they were obliged frequently to open some new road in the mountains so that the spiritual visitor could descend with more ease and to erect on it at certain distances some heaps of stones on which he might rest. Perhaps the *guama* [shaman] commanded someone to hurl himself from the cliff of a mountain; and he was obeyed without fail, either willingly or by force. Such was the authority of these impostors over those barbarians. (Clavigero [1789] 1971:115)

Summit Enclosures

Among the most peculiar features on San Esteban are the circular or arc-shaped rock wall enclosures that stand on several of the island's major mountain summits. The two highest points on the island, Pico San Esteban and Male Mountain, each have at least two of these features. There are between three and six on La Fortaleza, at least five on the summit of *Icámajoj Zaaj*, and 15 or more on Pico Rojo (in addition to several rock clusters and cairns). We also found two similar structures on high saddles at the edge of sea cliffs. One of these (I8), an unusually large enclosure on the west side, may be associated with the nearby cluster of clearings (I2–I7). The other (I50) is an isolated enclosure overlooking the precipitous sea cliff between Male and Female Mountains. Except for these, the structures are all on mountain tops, though not all are situated exactly at the summit. On Pico Rojo, four enclosures surround the actual peak, and the rest of the features there, including the rock clusters and cairns, are strung out individually or in groups of two and three for about 70 m along both sides of the narrow summit ridge. On *Icámajoj Zaaj*, there are additional structures on a ridge well below the summit.

Of the summit enclosures we recorded, the mean size is 1.3 m long by 1.0 m wide. The two largest by far (C3 and I8) are 2.6 m long and 2.1 m wide, and 2.5 m in diameter, respectively. The next largest (H10) is only 1.5 by 1.4 m. The smallest (P18) is 0.8 by 0.6 m. In most cases, the walls show no evidence of collapse, and the mean height is about 60 cm. All but three (F12, P25, and P26) have openings, though we measured only 11 (inadvertently omitting those on Pico Rojo). Most measured openings are between 40 and 90 cm wide, varying from 2.1 m at the unusually large C3 to a peculiar but clearly intentional opening of a mere 5 cm at I37.

Most summit enclosures were built by stacking rocks of various sizes, one on top of another, without well-defined courses and without mortar. In the finest examples of construction (e.g., P11, P12, and F11) the walls are only one or two rocks wide (about 30–40 cm) but stand five or six high (up to 90 cm), resulting in graceful and delicate-looking structures (Figure 13.9). Most walls are somewhat thicker and sturdier than this, and some low walls, built of casually piled rocks, are about as thick as they are high. At least one enclosure at La Fortaleza (H8) was built by leaning large slabs, set on end, toward the center against a base of piled rocks (Figure 13.10). Upright slabs were also incorporated to a lesser

Figure 13.9   Summit enclosure (F11) near the summit of Icámajoj Zaaj, looking west-southwest. Diameter is 1.1 m, height is 0.7 m. The walls of this delicate structure are just one course wide. January 1982.

Figure 13.10   Summit enclosure of leaning slabs (H8) on La Fortaleza. Length is 1.5 m, width 1.0 m, height 0.6 m. Photograph looks north-northeast down Arroyo Muerte to its confluence with Arroyo Limantour. January 1982.

extent in some of the enclosures on Pico Rojo. Several structures have walls that incorporate bedrock outcrops. In most cases, interiors were more or less cleared of large rocks but not of small ones, and several of the enclosures on Pico Rojo have rather steeply sloping floors. One structure (P5) was accompanied by a small amount of charcoal. But with the exception of the unusual structure I8, none produced even a single artifact.

Two structures on Pico Rojo (P6 and P7) share a short segment of wall, suggesting they might have been built at the same time. Otherwise, we know nothing of the sequence of construction among the structures at each location, whether they were used at the same time, or whether individual structures had any functional relationship with each other. Nor do we know whether the five mountain summits that have these features were used at the same time.

It is always tempting to interpret rock-walled enclosures in windy places as windbreaks, especially if their openings face away from the prevailing wind. This is the case on *Icámajoj Zaaj*, where the four structures that have openings are all open to the southeast. On Pico Rojo, eight of the 15 enclosures have openings that face between southeast and southwest (Figure 13.11), and on both our visits to the site, we appreciated the fact that these structures block the wind exceedingly well. Among the many enclosures at this site, however, one can find openings that face every direction, even directly northwest. Unless they were built to provide shelter from the wind no matter which way it was blowing, wind pro-

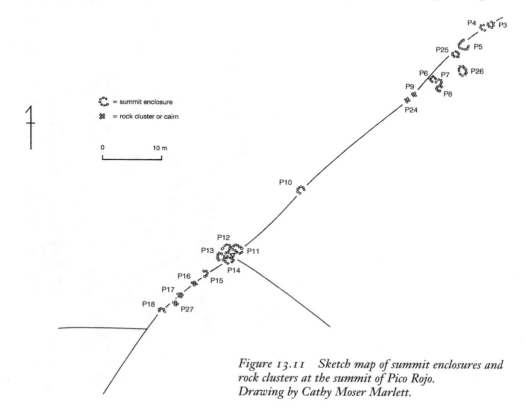

Figure 13.11   Sketch map of summit enclosures and rock clusters at the summit of Pico Rojo. Drawing by Cathy Moser Marlett.

tection must not have been the reason for their construction. Moreover, not every enclosure at every site has walls high enough to offer good wind protection. Those on La Fortaleza provided no shelter at all from the gale force winds that were blowing when we visited the site.

Even if the summit enclosures were built to provide respite from the wind, it still remains to be explained what people were doing on mountain tops in the first place. Though not a specific answer, one obvious possibility is that it had something to do with the view. Each of the summits with structures has a superb vista of a large portion of the island and a direct line of site with each other (Figure 13.12). Three of them are, in effect, located at three corners of the island, giving not only a broad panorama of San Esteban but also a clear view of the sea on two sides. There are no structures on Pico del Sur, at the fourth corner, but virtually everything visible from its summit can also be seen from other peaks with enclosures. La Fortaleza and *Icámajoj Zaaj* are not on the perimeter but offer superb panoramic views of the interior of the island and, conversely, can be seen from nearly all points on the island (Figure 13.13). La Fortaleza also overlooks the only access to the island's interior from the south coast, and Pico Rojo provides a commanding view of the entire southwest coast of Tiburón Island. Because of their locations, one might speculate that these sites had something to do with people monitoring the island and the adjacent sea, and perhaps communicating with each other.

One reason to maintain a lookout might be to guard against hostile intruders. The Seris say that the San Esteban people came to fear outsiders who sometimes came ashore and tried to kidnap people. When strangers appeared on the island, they would retreat into the mountains and drive the intruders away with rocks. In 1746, Father Fernando Consag experienced a similar response by several groups of peninsular Indians who had been brutalized by pearlers. Along the peninsular coast directly opposite San Esteban:

> The people on seeing the canoes took us for divers, and fled up the country; the outrages and brutality of those men having rendered them equally dreaded and detested by all the natives of [Baja] California. (Consag [1759] 1966:312)

At Bahía de los Ángeles, where the Indians had recently retaliated by killing some offending divers, the response to Consag's party was a combination of flight, fury, and concealment:

> These arrogant cowards at the sight of our men, without standing one fire, fled in the utmost confusion, leaving behind them even their wives and children; nor did they stop till they had reached the very summit of the rocks, where concluding they were safe, they skipped, shouted, and made many threatening postures which we did not think worth regarding. We examined all their caverns and retreats, but finding only the women and children, which had unnaturally been left behind, we treated them with all possible marks of tenderness, assuring them that no harm should happen to them; but all our promises were not sufficient to hinder them from running away, and leaving their children. (Consag [1759] 1966:322–23)

Figure 13.12 *View from the summit enclosures on Male Mountain, looking east-southeast at Pico Rojo (left) and* Icámajoj Zaaj *(right). San Pedro Mártir Island is visible on the horizon just to the right of* Icámajoj Zaaj. *January 1987.*

Figure 13.13 *View from summit enclosure F13 (foreground) on* Icámajoj Zaaj, *looking west-southwest across upper Arroyo Limantour to the mountains on the west side of San Esteban. The long bulk of San Lorenzo Island is visible in the middle distance, with the mountains of Baja California on the horizon. January 1982.*

And a bit farther north:

> when they saw that our people put the canoe ashore and leaped on the beach, well armed, they betook themselves to their usual refuge[,] the summits of the mountains. Here they stopped; and our men called out to them. But such was their fear, that instead of entering into a conference, they turned about and fled. (Consag [1759] 1966:329)

Whether the "mountains" to which these Indians retreated were as lofty as San Esteban's high peaks is impossible to tell from Consag's narrative, nor does he indicate whether the peninsular Indians built or used summit enclosures as refuges. But his experience shows that Indians had good reason to keep track of European activity in the Gulf and that flight from strangers was a widespread response. On San Esteban, monitoring the surrounding sea would not have been a straightforward task, however, because the high sea cliffs that surround most of the island make it virtually impossible to view the Gulf from most localities in the interior. Only from these sea cliffs can one survey the Gulf, and the most comprehensive views are from the high summits along this perimeter. These places are thus the logical lookout posts from which to keep an eye out for European vessels. From these vantage points, any ship heading toward the island could be spotted far enough in advance that people in the interior would have time to retreat into the mountains before intruders landed. Putting all this together, one might speculate that the structures on these summits were built as windbreaks for the people maintaining this vigil.

Interpreting summit enclosures as lookout posts might also account for the nearly total lack of artifacts and ecofacts, since the people manning them would likely have descended regularly to camps below. If pearl hunters were the feared intruders, it might specifically explain the near absence of charcoal, because pearling was strictly a summertime activity when lookouts would have no need for the warmth of a fire. However, this would not explain why so many of the structures offer protection against *winter* winds blowing out of the northwest. Moreover, one must ask why there would need to be more than just one or two windbreaks, let alone the 15 on Pico Rojo, and the seemingly associated rock clusters and cairns on that peak, which remain unexplained.

Groups of structures architecturally similar to the summit enclosures of San Esteban are known at several localities on Tiburón Island. One such site (Son M:2:15) lies on the summit of a prominent 200-meter hill near the southwestern corner of the island and possibly within the portion of Tiburón said to belong to the San Esteban people. The unobstructed panorama from this site is unparalleled, encompassing almost the entire Midriff region of the Gulf, from Ángel de la Guarda to San Pedro Mártir Island. Features here include at least 20 arc-shaped or circular summit structures and around 60 rock clusters and cairns, suggesting a greatly expanded version of the Pico Rojo complex of structures. Whether this site was functionally connected with the San Esteban summit sites is, of course, not known. But signaling San Esteban would certainly have been easy, for all five of the San Esteban peaks with summit structures are readily visible from here.

Similar structures are also known from several much less dramatic sites at the north end of Tiburón Island. At one of these, there are more than 30 arc-shaped features, and many were built with the same inward leaning slab technique used on La Fortaleza. Most of the structures on the north end of Tiburón, however, occur not on high summits with commanding vistas but on low hills, and sometimes on the flanks as well as the summits. Though the Seris know of at least one of these sites, they have no explanation for it (Bowen 1976:35–36, Figs. 24–25).

There is one mountain site with summit structures, however, in the north-eastern corner of Tiburón Island, for which there is a Seri interpretation. This interpretation involves the legendary Giants, whom the Seris say inhabited the region long ago (see pp. 403–5). These huge beings are said to have been invet-erate gamblers, and to enhance their luck, they sought spirit power before gam-bling. According to Mary Beck Moser (1987:pers. comm.), during the early 1970s, Roberto Herrera flew over this mountain and saw what he termed "circles of stone" on the summit. He immediately recalled that an elderly Seri from this part of Tiburón had once told him that this peak, called *Inzíime Cacösxaj*, had circles of stones on top and that it was a place where the Giants sought their spirit power. Herrera also remembered a song that spoke about the circles of stones and the sticks used in this gambling:

> The cane gambling sticks, thrown in the air,
> Hit each other and rattle,
> They fall to the ground.
> The gamblers play.
> There is talking during the game
> The circle of stones up high that I made
> The place of the gamblers.

The Seris say that the San Esteban people, like the Giants, were also exces-sive gamblers, and indeed there may be some deeper linkages between the two groups in Seri thought. Perhaps this connection would have led Herrera or his elderly Seri source to interpret the summit structures on San Esteban Island, had they known about them, as gambling places of either the Giants or the San Esteban people.

Talus Pits

The most enigmatic features on San Esteban Island are talus pits. When we first saw them in 1967, we had never heard of such things, and it took some soul searching to convince ourselves that these could not realistically be just random undulations in the talus slopes. Since then, we have seen hundreds of talus pits on Tiburón Is-land, and these features have been recognized by other archaeologists elsewhere,

*Figure 13.14
Talus pit (D53) in a
hillside near Playa
Limantour, looking
east. Length is 1.2
m, width 0.9 m,
depth 0.6 m.
January 1987.*

including Baja California, Arizona, and the Great Basin. On San Esteban, we have actually counted about 250 talus pits and have seen many more.

Talus pits are places in talus slopes where rocks have been removed to create a depression (Figure 13.14). In most cases, the excavated rocks were simply tossed away, and there is absolutely nothing more to these features. Some, however, are slightly more elaborate. The most common embellishment was to pile a few of the rocks on the downhill edge, creating a raised lower rim. On a few San Esteban pits, this rim is two rocks high and has the appearance of a makeshift wall. The fanciest pit we have seen (D52) has a definable rock rim built up all around it *except* on the downhill side, and the rim on the uphill side is a wall three rocks high. Most pits are more or less circular at the rim, though some are distinctly oval. Diameters generally range from about 1–2 m at the rim, tapering toward the bottom. Depths, measured from the downhill lip, almost always fall between about 50 cm and a bit over 100 cm. The largest pits are about 2.5 m in diameter, and the smallest we have seen (D52) is 70 cm in diameter.

Talus pits are difficult to detect from a distance, especially from below. From close up, however, they are often readily visible. In many cases, the rocks inside the pits, exposed when the features were built, are the natural gray color of San Esteban andesite and contrast markedly with the brilliant reddish-brown hue of the heavily oxidized rocks that make up the surface of the talus slope. Other pits have well-oxidized interior rocks that have acquired the same hue as the surrounding talus.

There seems to be little predictability about precisely where talus pits occur, and we have seen them throughout much of the island. Although the talus must be deep to have pits, they can be found in very small slopes as well as the most extensive ones, some of which are more than 0.5 km long and 200 m high. Pits often occur from the bottom to the top of the slope. Small slopes may have only a half dozen pits, while on one large slope, we quit counting after 140 pits, though we had checked only a fraction of the total surface. The pits we noted are in talus slopes that face between northeast and south, but it may be that talus slopes with pits face other directions as well.

Talus pits almost never occur with artifacts or ecofacts. One explanation for this is that small items dropped in or near a pit nearly always slide off the slick rocks and disappear into the depths of the underlying talus, as one can instantly demonstrate with a lens cap. In the very few cases where pits do have apparently associated material, it is usually just one or two flakes or a shell. While some of this could be random scatter, there are rare but unequivocal exceptions. The most clear-cut example is a pit that contains six beach cobbles, two with slight signs of battering, and two shells.

Talus pits have baffled almost everyone who has encountered them. Initially, we seriously questioned whether they could really be human features and searched for natural mechanisms that might produce them. The only possibility we came up with is that they might be holes where cardon cacti once stood. When cardons die, they usually remain standing and undergo most of their disintegration in place, with their roots firmly embedded. However, we have seen dead plants that have fallen over, bringing their roots to the surface, and even live plants are occasionally uprooted by violent winds. In both cases, the roots may lever up buried material and leave a depression. Stones brought up from below can even be deposited in a vague ring around the depression, superficially resembling the piled rocks that surround some of the talus pits. Talus would not be a very firm substrate to anchor a large cardon, and plants on talus slopes might be especially prone to uprooting in a severe storm. Taken together, these considerations suggest that talus pits might be nothing more than the depressions left by many uprooted cardons over geological spans of time.

The problem with this idea is that cardon cacti do not colonize deep talus. They occur on talus slopes only in places where the rocks form a thin veneer over soil. As Richard Felger (1980:pers. comm.) has pointed out, a cardon seed that managed to penetrate through deep talus to underlying soil would receive no sunlight and could not germinate. Thus except in unusual cases, talus pits could not be the legacy of cardon cacti. Besides, cardons cannot build the clearly intentional walls we see on some rims or, on rare occasion, leave artifacts.

There are several imaginable reasons why humans might have excavated pits in talus slopes, and it could be that it was done for more than one purpose. Perhaps the simplest explanation is that they were dug to recover objects dropped on the slope, a possibility that is not quite as simplistic as it first seems. It is astonishing how easily objects slide off talus blocks and how deeply one must dig to have any chance of retrieving them. Over time, people may have dropped a considerable number of objects on these slopes. Compared with other kinds of terrain on San Esteban, talus slopes composed of large blocks are relatively stable surfaces. They may have been used extensively as highways because they are among the least treacherous ways to get up and down hillsides, and this would have been as true for indigenous peoples as for modern visitors. With countless trips up and down the slopes, year after year, the number of times people dropped things and tried to dig down to them would add up. Even so, it is hard to believe that this simple mechanism could account for the hundreds, or perhaps thousands of pits on the island, and especially those with built-up walls.

Another reason people might have excavated pits in talus slopes would be to dig out chuckwallas. According to the modern Seris, chuckwallas were an important food of the San Esteban people, and both the recent Seris and Mexicans have also sought them. When threatened, chuckwallas wedge themselves into their burrows or crevices between rocks and inflate a subcutaneous air sack that makes them difficult to pull out. But they can easily be dug out. Chuckwallas prefer arroyo bottoms and adjoining hillsides, and they will utilize at least the lower portions of talus slopes. Therefore, one might suppose that talus pits could be the holes left over from generations of people digging out hundreds of chuckwallas over a long span of time. While this might account for the unadorned talus pits, it would still not explain the ones with rocks stacked on the downhill side.

There is one well-documented place in the Midriff region where people have unquestionably created talus pits by hunting animals in talus slopes. This is Partida Island, about 50 km northwest of San Esteban. Partida is an important nesting site of both the least petrel (*Halocyptena microsoma*) and the black petrel (*Oceanodroma melania*). It also supports the largest colony of the Midriff's endemic fish-eating bat (*Pizonyx vivesi*). All three species utilize talus slopes as burrows, either for nesting places or day-roosts. For many years, scientists, collectors, and probably tourists have dug pits in these talus slopes in search of animals and eggs. Ornithologist Griffing Bancroft describes his collecting efforts there in 1930:

> Everyone on the boat except Captain, who was above such folly, dug himself a little trench, throwing rocks out by hand. Even Juan and the Partner

[Mrs. Bancroft] caught the fever and soon could be seen standing waist deep, excited by their Easter hunt. As soon as the surface covering [of talus blocks] had been removed signs of life began to appear, and when a depth of two feet had been reached the removal of any flagstone might disclose a bat or a petrel on an egg. (Bancroft 1932:350)

Over the years, collectors have left a large number of unfilled talus pits, enough that Armando Maya, who studied bats there in the 1960s, warned of habitat destruction and recommended restricting access to the island (Maya 1968:92).

Fish-eating bats inhabit nearly every other Midriff island, at least seasonally, and a few islands, including San Esteban, support permanent though vastly smaller colonies (Reeder and Norris 1954:Fig. 1; Maya 1968:Table 1). This raises the question of whether the talus pits on San Esteban might have been created by people digging for bats. If so, these hunters were clearly not scientists or we would have records of them. One might therefore ask whether they could have been the San Esteban people, presumably hunting bats as food.

Today, fish-eating bats on San Esteban (and most other Midriff islands) do not day-roost in talus, probably because of their vulnerability there to predation by the introduced rat (Maya 1968:27-30, 85, 98–99). Humans, of course, are another potential predator. Since both rats and humans are probably late arrivals on San Esteban (see Chapter 15), one might speculate that bats originally day-roosted in San Esteban's talus, that they were hunted there when people first arrived, and that the legacy of this hunting is the talus pits throughout the island. Any bats that continued to day-roost in talus when the rats showed up were wiped out by this vicious new predator, and the small colony that still remains on San Esteban has survived by sleeping in safer places.

Whether fish-eating bats are likely to have served as food for people is another question. Their bodies, the size of large rodents, are big enough to be a worthwhile food item. The San Esteban diet apparently differed somewhat from that of their surviving kinsmen, but Seris today have no recollection of ever eating bats. Some people even regard the animals with fear or revulsion, although these attitudes may reflect recent Mexican influence (Malkin 1962:9, 15–16).

Perhaps the most reasonable conclusion to be drawn from this is that the talus pits on San Esteban could certainly be human creations, that a large number could have been produced in a short time, and that if they were indeed dug to extract animals, the quarry could possibly have been bats more often than chuckwallas.

Talus slopes in the Tucson Basin of southern Arizona sometimes also contain pits. Many of these talus pits, though not all, are very similar to those on San Esteban, and some even have rocks stacked on the downhill rim. John Madsen (1993) has explored at length the possibility that these pits could be Tohono O'odham (Papago) hillside burial crypts. He suggests that in localities where digging was difficult, the Tohono O'odham might place the body in a cleft in the rocks, wall up the downhill side, and roof the crypt with brush weighted down with rocks. In time, the perishable roof, the body, and all perishable grave goods, would decompose and disappear. If the crypt were in a talus slope, all that would remain would be the pit. Sometimes, Madsen speculates, pits might have been excavated in anticipation of mass deaths from Apache raids that never materialized, leaving a hillside of open pits. Small pits might have been intended for children, the disproportionate victims of epidemics, or for cremated remains, as suggested by two small pits with sherds whose interiors revealed minute layers of ash. And, as Madsen aptly notes, some of the southern Arizona open pits might be the work of pothunters (Madsen 1993:97–98).

But when Madsen made a detailed study of 10 selected pits, he failed to uncover evidence of any human remains which, as he points out, could literally have fallen through the cracks. The possibility that talus pits on San Esteban may also have been burial sites is intriguing, since we have found no other evidence of how the dead were disposed of. In the past, the Seris did sometimes place corpses in crevices in rocks, and there are indications that the former Seri bands may have disposed of their dead in quite diverse ways (Bowen 1976:50). In fact, Roberto Herrera speculated that the San Esteban people "probably" placed the body, along with ollas or other possessions, in a cave or crevice in the rocks and then walled it up (Roberto Herrera 1981:pers. comm.). But if pits in San Esteban talus slopes were burial crypts, it must be explained why they are now open and empty. Preservation is good, there are no large scavengers to remove rocks from a walled crypt, and the hundreds of open pits could not realistically be due to looting on this remote island.

One funerary practice that would leave open pits is gathering up the bones for secondary burial. Tradition among some northern California peoples states that warriors were initially interred in talus slopes, and the bones were later exhumed for permanent burial elsewhere, leaving an open talus pit (Eric Ritter 1986:pers. comm.). But this was not likely a Seri custom. One reason Seri burial practices have been so varied is to enable them to get rid of a corpse as quickly as possible, an objective that is totally incompatible with secondary burial. As for Seris killed in battle, they were usually left where they fell (Moser 1970:213).

In the early 1970s, Eric Ritter encountered several "talus depressions" near Bahía de la Concepción in Baja California, and the enigma posed by these features prompted him to explore the subject at length. The peninsular talus pits were not isolated features but seemed to be associated with piled rock enclosures, chipping debris, and prominent trails. Ritter notes that in several parts of the western United States, there are associations between talus pits or rock-walled enclosures, game trails, petroglyphs of game animals, especially desert bighorn, and sometimes the bones of these animals. Hence he logically concludes that most talus pits and piled rock enclosures, including those at Bahía de la Concepción, were probably hunting blinds, most likely for desert bighorn (Ritter 1977:8).

As Ritter implies, in slopes where talus is thin, it is not always possible to make a useful typological distinction between pits with low walls and piled rock enclosures. On Tiburón Island, we have also seen depressions in talus slopes with rock walls that could be classified either way. On the southwest coast of Tiburón, one such intermediate structure at the bottom of a talus slope lies only a few meters from a trail used today by mule deer, and this structure would have made an excellent ambush. Whether ambush might also explain the hundreds of pits on the enormous expanses of talus at the north end of this island is less certain. Desert bighorn apparently never colonized Tiburón Island, suggesting that the pits there would probably have been blinds for hunting mule deer. When threatened, these animals may seek an uphill escape, but they are not as agile as desert bighorn on rocky slopes and will avoid them if possible. A mule deer driven onto a broad talus slope might ascend anywhere, and it would require a very large number of hunters concealed in pits all across the slope to insure that one of them would be close enough to get off a shot. This would account nicely for the large number of pits on the huge talus slopes on the north end of Tiburón Island, but whether the Seris were ever much disposed to staging well-orchestrated hunts with such manpower is far from clear. It would definitely not be a viable explanation for the similar distribution of pits across the large talus slopes of San Esteban Island because, as noted earlier, it is extremely unlikely that San Esteban was ever capable of supporting any game animals at all.

The Seris acknowledge ambush as one of their techniques of hunting game, but they say that this was normally done from blinds made of brush built next to waterholes (Felger and Moser 1985:51–52). There is no recollection of using talus pits for this purpose. In fact, few Seris are even aware of all the talus pits on Tiburón Island. Those who do know of the Tiburón pits are inclined to attribute them to an antiquated form of vision quest rather than hunting. They say that a vision seeker who for some reason chose to spend the final night of the quest on a talus slope might dig a small pit to sit in. The seeker would have brought a special plant juice with him in a small pottery olla, along with a clam shell that would have been used as a paint palette. Each person would have built his or her own pit rather than reuse an existing one.

This is an appealing interpretation for the Tiburón Island pits, in the first place because some of the talus slopes are in places considered appropriate for seeking visions, and secondly because these locations could be used repeatedly, if not the individual pits. Over time, this could result in a great many pits on a single slope. The few pits that contain artifacts usually have sherds or shells, the very items that would have been brought there by the vision seeker. Hence the artifacts lend support for the Seri view that the talus pits on Tiburón Island might have been structures for seeking spiritual nourishment rather than animal protein.

Apparently, the modern Seris are unaware that there are talus pits on San Esteban, so whether they might be inclined to explain them in the same way is a moot question. To the best of their knowledge, the people on Tiburón did not go to San Esteban to seek visions, and the San Esteban people sought visions at sea in their balsas.

The Seri belief that the San Esteban people came to distrust the outsiders who occasionally landed on shore suggests one final explanation of the island's talus pits. It is just barely possible they were used for concealment, not from game animals, but from other people. As noted above, talus pits are almost impossible to see from afar and from below, and a person sitting in one with only his head protruding might be able to watch without being seen. The talus blocks would provide the ideal personal camouflage, making a black-fringed bronze head virtually invisible among the thousands of deeply-shadowed red-brown rocks of the slope. If the summit enclosures were built as lookout posts to warn of approaching intruders, it is conceivable, at least, that talus pits might have been places where people could quickly take refuge and hide. If the threat of outsiders was perceived to be frequent as well as severe, it might not be too far-fetched to imagine that talus pits were constructed in advance in strategically located slopes throughout San Esteban, ready to be used on a moment's notice.

If there is any credibility at all in this interpretation, it might be speculated that some of the talus pits on neighboring Tiburón Island could also have been used as hiding places. When the Spaniards and Mexicans mounted their periodic military invasions of Tiburón Island, most of the Seris fled the island or hid, and the soldiers seldom saw more than a fraction of the population. Sometimes they found people hiding from them in caves, and one wonders if the troops may have occasionally marched right past hillsides where people sat concealed in talus pits.

Artifact and Ecofact Concentrations

We found and numbered 13 locations where there were no structures, but where there seem to be significant concentrations of artifacts or ecofacts. Six of these are nothing more than small chipping sites containing between about 20 and 100 waste flakes, probably left over from the manufacture of a single tool. One of the six (M17) includes two cobble hammers which show battering from the chipping event. Another (P2) was a spot where a typical tabular andesite agave knife was reworked into a smaller tool.

The only chipping site that seems to have been reused on several occasions is conveniently located out of the brunt of the wind and just a short distance from Playa Limantour. This site (D25) probably has between about 200 and 300 flakes and cores, of several different materials. There are also several beach cobbles that might have served as hammers, though we found only one that shows clear evidence of battering. In one spot, flakes are conspicuously clustered around a boulder on which the knapper must have sat as he fashioned a tool.

Two sites (D11 and D35) are located at outcrops along lower Arroyo Limantour where tabular andesite, favored for agave knives, was quarried. Both sites include battered hammer stones as well as chipping debris. Though not recorded as a site, Playa Limantour was almost certainly another source of rock for agave knives, for knives made from its distinctive water-worn gray tabular slabs can be found throughout the island.

One artifact concentration (P19) consists of eight agave knives along a 50-meter stretch of ridge leading toward Pico Rojo. We assume that another artifact concentration (M14) was a camp, even though there is no evidence of clearings, because within an area 50 m in diameter, we found a slab metate, three bedrock metate surfaces, a Levallois-like flake, many waste flakes, and a broken *Pecten* shell. Another site (J12) was apparently somebody's lunch spot for here, on a small level plateau, are about 25 *Turbo* sea snail shells, broken and weathered, and a single flake. Finally, we recorded I17 because it was the place somebody broke a Historic Seri wide-mouthed olla. We found sherds from only the rim and upper one-third of the vessel, suggesting the bottom was salvaged for reuse as a large bowl.

Petroglyphs and Pictographs

We found petroglyphs in two locations. One (E11) is on a ridge that was part of a cutoff route between Arroyo de las Cuevitas and Arroyo Limantour. The lone petroglyph here is a simple rectilinear grid incised on a slab of local rock. It lies next to a rock cluster (E16) built of similar slabs. A little experimenting on another local slab showed that the incised lines are too wide to have been made with a steel knife, but they can be closely replicated with a simple stone flake.

The other petroglyph locality, G15, is near the G4 habitation caves in Arroyo Limantour. The figures are mostly in the ceiling of an overhang that offers excellent protection from wind and rain. The rock here is a welded tuff that is so soft that, with some persistence, one can make grooves in it with a finger. In fact, some of the petroglyphs consist of grooves 5–10 millimeters wide that could well have been executed with the fingers or a small rounded pebble. Most of the elements consist of much narrower incisions, 2–3 millimeters wide. These are too wide to have been made with a metal knife, but a sharp stone flake carves an incision of about this width and form. The remaining petroglyphs consist of holes drilled into the rock, generally about 5–10 millimeters in diameter, and equally deep. Many of these pits seem to be isolated and randomly placed, but some form sinuous lines and apparent clusters, and others occur at the center or end of incised lines.

There is no obvious overall organization to the G15 figures. Though it is difficult to be sure, our impression is that each of the elements was made separately and has no connection with the others. For this reason, we recorded the figures as individual elements, making no attempt to map their spatial relationships to each other. Nor did we attempt to register the large number of poorly defined lines and pits that do not comprise clearly delineated figures, but rather confined our recording to the reasonably distinct glyphs (Figure 13.15).

There is little doubt that both recent Seris and Mexicans contributed to the G15 petroglyphs. Two of the figures are almost surely the personal sign of Luis Torres (d. 1948) (Figure 13.15b), a Seri who is remembered as a man who sometimes came to San Esteban in the early twentieth century. Next to one of his signs is probably the identifying mark of Ramón Blanco (d. ca. 1929) (Figure 13.15c), another Seri visitor. It was not known that the Seris used graphic figures as identifying marks until 1921, when Charles Sheldon made a remarkable solo hunting trip with some Seris on Tiburón Island. During that trip, Sheldon

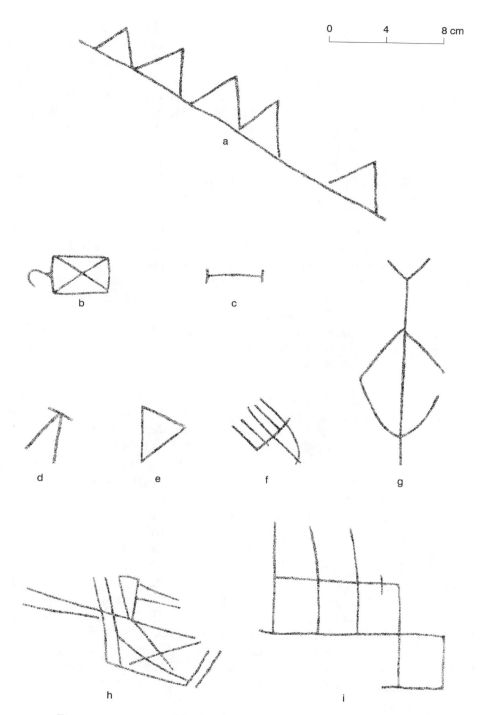

Figure 13.15 Some of the figures on the ceiling of petroglyph cave G15.
In this sketch, each figure has been oriented so that north is up and
the mouth of the cave (south) is down. Drawings by Cathy Moser Marlett.

recorded the personal signs of several people (Sheldon 1979:Fig. 5–29). He rendered the curved tail on Torres's sign facing backwards from the figures at G15, but he may have got it wrong or it may be that Torres made it both ways. Several other petroglyph figures are suggestive of personal signs, but are not recognized by the present Seris (Mary Beck Moser 1996:pers. comm.).

Two or perhaps three sets of initials are likely Mexican. One is simply a capital "R." The other is "AR" inscribed next to what may be "66," seemingly carved by the same hand and possibly indicating the date of AR's visit (presumably 1966, but conceivably 1866). However, it is difficult to be certain that the "66" is not actually "GG," which could be somebody else's initials. There are also a number of "X" figures which could, perhaps, be the initials of people who were not literate.

The line with the connected horizontal zigzag (or pendent "V") incisions (Figure 13.15a) is likely Seri because this was a design often incised on rims of Historic Seri pottery (Bowen 1976:Fig. 50d), including some sherds found on San Esteban. If so, it was probably carved prior to the twentieth century. Another figure could be an inverted version of the same motif with the edge of the rock serving as the pendant line, analogous to the rim of a vessel.

Two figures are clearly representational and could be either Indian or Mexican. One is presumably a human figure. The other is widely referred to as "*El Galeon*" (Figure 13.16). This figure is known to some Seris and most Mexican fishermen, though few of the latter have actually seen it. Del Cover (1993:pers. comm.) identifies the vessel as a two-masted schooner, which was the workhorse of the Gulf all during the nineteenth century and well into the twentieth. Cover notes that the execution of the petroglyph suggests that it was created by someone who was well acquainted with sailing vessels. This could as easily have been a Seri as a Mexican, for the long history of conflict with Europeans would no doubt have made the Seris astute observers of European sailing craft.

Unfortunately, this best-known piece of San Esteban's archaeological record, as well as the personal signs of Luis Torres and Ramón Blanco, disappeared sometime between 1987 and 1993. Though it is hard to tell, there is no indication that they were removed by vandals. The soft rock is riddled with cracks, and *El Galeon* and the personal signs were inscribed near the lip of the overhang. Most likely, the chunk with these unique figures one day simply spalled off.

The combination of drilled pits and incised lines occurs sporadically over a broad region, including the interior of Baja California directly across from San Esteban Island. On the peninsula, the "pit and groove" technique sometimes occurs in the same caves as the famed Great Mural pictographs of giant human figures and animals (Crosby 1984:42–44, 163), though it is not known whether the two forms of rock art are related or contemporary. Some of the pit and groove petroglyphs at G15 are closely similar to peninsular counterparts (Keith Muscutt 1993:pers. comm.).

Both Seris and present-day Mexican fishermen speak of cave "paintings" (*pinturas*) on San Esteban. For the Mexicans, this seems to be mostly a matter of passing along a tradition that does not clearly distinguish petroglyphs from painted

Figure 13.16   The famed petroglyph of "El Galeon." It is 12.5 cm. long from stern to tip of the bowsprit, and 11 cm. high from bottom of the hull to top of the mast. Sunlight just below the hull marks the edge of the cave ceiling. Top of the photograph is north. January 1987.

figures. The Seris are certain of the difference, and they attribute painted figures to both "the ancestors" and to more recent Seri visitors (Mary Beck Moser 1980:pers. comm.). Roberto Herrera remembered seeing red and blue pictographs during trips to the island when he was a young man, probably in the 1930s. They were located at the caves the Seris call *Icámajoj Zaaj*, and Herrera's verbal descriptions and identifications on aerial photographs leave no doubt that either G4 or G15 is that series of caves. Yet we inspected not only these caves but also intensively searched the numerous caves in the surrounding area and found no trace of pictographs.

There were also about 10 pictographs in red paint in two caves, B2 and B5, near the northeastern corner of the island. In 1984, Arturo Oliveros and Elisa Villalpando (1984:pers. comm.) recorded these paintings, which included two anthropomorphic figures and two "X" designs. By 1993, however, only a single small patch of paint was still visible in B2. How much remained in B5 is not known, for a dense thicket of *pitahaya agria* cactus has completely blocked its entrance.

San Esteban is not an island of resistant rock. Most of the caves are cavities eroded into the friable walls of mudflow conglomerates, and nearly all show evidence of continual surface exfoliation and rock fall. In all likelihood, the pictographs at *Icámajoj Zaaj* recalled in Seri and Mexican traditions were readily visible early in the twentieth century and have completely weathered away since then. Much the same seems to be happening currently to the pictographs at B2. There is no telling how many cave petroglyphs and pictographs may have totally disappeared even within the last few decades.

Mexican Features

The archaeology of San Esteban includes a number of features that are probably, or certainly, of Mexican origin. Several of these have already been mentioned, including cairns B3, I41, J14, and perhaps others, plus the designs made of stones in the I2–I7 clearings, and some of the G15 petroglyphs. Some Mexican features, such as those at El Monumento fishermen's camp (D47), were in use until very recently. Others may date from the latter part of the nineteenth century.

Of all the features of probable Mexican origin, none are as curious as those we designated E1–E9, situated on a terrace at the confluence of Arroyo de las Cuevitas and Arroyo Limantour (Figure 13.17). They were partially described previously (Bowen 1976:36–37) from verbal descriptions provided by Alexander Russell, who had first seen them in the 1960s. Three of these features, E2, E3, and E6, are pit ovens with rims of unusually large but very uniform size, around 6.5 m in diameter (Figure 13.18). Not only is this more than twice the diameter of most pit oven rims on San Esteban, but these ovens are also associated with some unusual features seen nowhere else on the island. These are rectilinear patterns of rocks set in the ground (E1, E4, E5, and E7), and a single very deep pit (E8) of uncertain function.

One of the rock formations (E1) is a simple rectangle 5.0 m long by 4.9 m wide. The rocks that constitute it were all set in the ground in neat parallel rows, and they were placed in such a manner that they all tilt in the same direction, down the length of the rows. The same construction technique was used for E9 (Figure 13.19). However, E9 consists of three adjacent but distinct sets of rocks in rows, and the tilt of the rocks in each set differs from the tilt in the other two sets. E4 has a similar rectangular set of rows of tilted rocks, but at this feature the orderly rectangle abuts a second rectangle whose rocks were placed not in neat rows, but more or less at random. Both E5 and E7 are rectangles of haphazardly placed rocks.

The other feature at this site (E8) is a pit, but it is quite unlike any of the partially filled-in agave baking ovens. Here, the pit itself is clearly exposed, and it is a huge unlined hole, about 9.2 m long by 7.2 m wide, with its bottom close to 4 m below the present ground surface. Although there is a modest rim around part of the pit, much of the dirt from its excavation was simply piled in a large mound on the southeastern side.

The only artifacts we found in the vicinity of E1–E9 are a single scraper, a waste flake, and a Historic Seri sherd, which are probably just random scatter. There is a small amount of charcoal at two ovens and a considerable quantity next to the deep pit E8. Two of the ovens are also surrounded by a quantity of

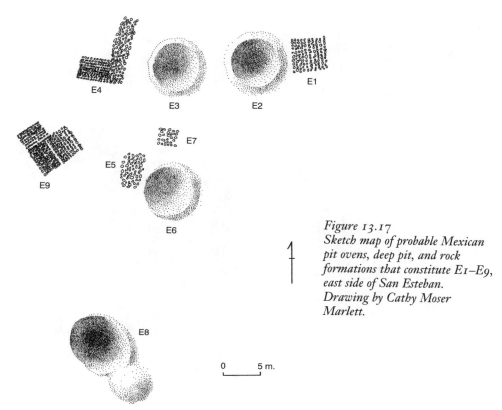

E4

E3

E2

E1

E9

E7

E5

E6

Figure 13.17
Sketch map of probable Mexican
pit ovens, deep pit, and rock
formations that constitute E1–E9,
east side of San Esteban.
Drawing by Cathy Moser
Marlett.

E8

0   5 m.

Figure 13.18   Probable Mexican
pit ovens E3 (front) and E2
(behind), looking southeast. E3
length is 6.6 m, width 6.2 m, depth
1.1 m; E2 length is 6.6 m, width
6.4 m, depth 1.3 m. January 1981.

· 357 ·

*Figure 13.19   Part of probable Mexican rock formation (E9), looking northwest.
Width is ca. 3.5 m. January 1981.*

small vesicular volcanic cinders that were clearly brought in, likely from a source
about 1 kilometer farther down Arroyo Limantour. In two cases, the rectilinear rock formations seem to predate the last use of the ovens, because debris
from the last opening of oven E3 covers some of the rocks of formation E4, and
debris from oven E6 similarly covers rocks in formation E5. Just when all of
these features were last used is not known, but enough time has passed for several plants, including limberbush, elephant tree, cholla, and a cardon to take root
in some of the pit ovens and rock formations, and grow to heights of about 1.5 m.

Nothing like this complex is known elsewhere on San Esteban Island, Tiburón Island, or the Seri portion of the Sonoran coast. For this reason, and contrary to an earlier conclusion (Bowen 1976:37), it seems likely that these features
are not Seri. Perhaps the most plausible interpretation is that this site was part
of a Mexican *mescal aguardiente* distilling operation. Distilling mescal liquor
from agave hearts is a time-honored Sonoran tradition that has gone on with
few changes in basic procedure since Colonial times (Bahre and Bradbury 1980:
393). John Russell Bartlett described the process as it was carried out on the
mainland around 1850:

> A hole is first dug some ten or twelve feet in diameter, and about three feet deep,
> and is lined with stones. Upon this a fire is built and kept up until the stones are
> thoroughly heated. A layer of moist grass is then thrown upon the stones, and on
> this are piled the bulbs of the maguay [agave], which vary in size, from one's head

to a half bushel measure, resembling huge onions. These are again covered with a thicker layer of grass; and the whole is allowed to remain until they are thoroughly baked. They are then removed to large leathern bags, and water is poured on them to produce fermentation. At the end of a week the bags are emptied of the maguay and its liquor, which, after undergoing the process of distillation, is ready for use. (Bartlett [1854] 1965:290–91)

In the 1970s, Bahre and Bradbury witnessed a moonshine mescal-making operation in eastern Sonora. They note that these operations are usually sited near streams or springs because both the fermentation and distilling processes require fresh water (Bahre and Bradbury 1980:395). As to the baking process:

The pit is about a meter deep, and is long and wide enough to accommodate 60–70 hearts. A large fire is made in the pit, and when a bed of hot coals forms, volcanic rocks, which hold heat well, are thrown in to cover the floor.... When the rocks have turned a whitish hue, the maguey hearts are piled onto them in a dome-like heap. The heap is then covered with palm thatch ... or something else that will keep dirt off of the cooking magueys, and tightly sealed with dirt so that no smoke or vapor escapes.... [G]reat care is taken not to let the hearts burn during baking. (Bahre and Bradbury 1980:396)

Whether the E1–E9 ovens are comparable to the Mexican ovens on the mainland cannot be determined without excavation, but these two descriptions suggest a possible function of the rock formations. In the recent past, when Seris baked agave they were not overly concerned about dirt because they could cut away the contaminated surface layer. But as Bartlett implies and Bahre and Bradbury state explicitly, agave hearts for mescal production must be kept dirt free. By the same reasoning, Richard Felger (1980:pers. comm.) has suggested that the San Esteban rock formations may have been built to provide clean places to set down agave hearts, perhaps both before and after they were baked. Interestingly, a broadly analogous practice goes on today in northwestern Argentina, where long parallel rows of similar-sized rocks are used as racks to keep chiles out of the dirt while they are drying in the sun (Jon C. Avent 1986:pers. comm.). The requirement for water may help explain the location of E1–E9, at the confluence of two major arroyos, as well as the purpose of the large deep pit E8, which may have been dug as a walk-in well in a effort to tap subsurface water coming from the two drainages.

Farther down the arroyo is another pit oven, D33, that is even larger than those at E1–E9. Though it is not associated with rock designs, it also has vesicular volcanic cinders strewn around its rim and has what may be a walk-in ramp. Presumably, it too is Mexican.

Two other pit ovens, D1 and D2, are probably also Mexican. They are located on a terrace overlooking Playa Limantour, a few meters from the shoreline. Because these two ovens did not become completely filled with sediment, the upper portions of the pits, with their stone linings, are still readily visible

Figure 13.20   Probable Mexican pit oven (D2) next to Playa Limantour. The stone lining of the central pit, shown here, is partly intact and contains modern trash. Diameter is 2.0 m, depth 1.5 m. Photograph looks north-east. January 1981.

(Figure 13.20). Pit diameters are 2.0 m and 1.5 m, respectively, and the original depths were at least 70 cm

Although D1 and D2 superficially resemble the excavated D27 oven and others thought to be early twentieth century Seri, they differ in several important ways. Size differences may be significant, for the pit diameter of D1 is almost twice that of D27. Although D1 is rimless, the rim of D2, 10 m across, is more than twice the diameter of the largest oven thought to be Seri. More importantly, D1 and D2 were excavated into the hard rocky ground of an arroyo terrace, rather than the soft loose gravel of the arroyo bottom. This must have been a job for metal tools, not the simple wooden digging stick the Seris have used for this purpose until very recently. Moreover, unlike the Seri ovens, D1 and D2 may not be isolated structures. The surrounding area contains a number of features found nowhere else on the island, and which themselves seem likely to be Mexican, or at least non-Seri. These include a U-shaped structure of rocks (D3), a rectangular area cleared by raking (D4), a set of unusual camp clearings (D5 and D7–D10), two rockwall fragments (D6 and D40), and a prominent trail leading up the adjacent hillside (D42).

Two of these unusual features, D3 and D4, are located on the same terrace and about 10 m from the two pit ovens. D3 is simply a three-sided U-shaped cluster of rocks about 4 m long and 2 m wide. The other feature (D4) is a large square clearing about 15 m on a side, created by scraping away surface rocks and raking them into long low piles on the eastern and western sides.

The five unusual clearings (D5 and D7–D10) are about 15 m directly upslope from the D1–D2 ovens. Unlike other camp clearings on San Esteban, these are not merely places cleared of surface rocks or leveled slightly on the uphill side, but genuine depressions excavated to a depth of 10–40 cm. The deepest clearing is also the largest, about 6 by 3 m, and is arc-shaped. The other four are oval in form and smaller, ranging from 2.2 by 1.5 m (D5) to 4.5 by 2.0 m (D8). Small rocks, probably scraped out of the interiors, line the edges of some of the depressions.

One of the two rock wall segments (D6) is located among the clearings. It is a nondescript 2.7 m long linear feature made of rocks piled two high. The other wall (D40) is farther up the hillside. It is an equally nondescript linear feature, only 1.0 m in length but built of rocks piled four courses high.

Near the top of the hillside, where the slope steepens and narrows to a rounded ridge, there is a well-defined trail (D42) which leads to the broad agave-laden plateau above. About 100 m of trail are plainly visible, and the top section consists of some eight or ten switchbacks.

There are also large areas of the hillside above the excavated clearings and below the trail that have no archaeological remains per se, but show signs of heavy disturbance. There is little or no agave growing in these places today, and the ground looks as though it had been badly chewed up. In all likelihood, these places were the scene of extensive agave harvesting in the fairly recent past.

There are several reasons for thinking that the D1–D2 ovens, the E1–E9 structures, probably the D33 oven, and all the apparently associated features are Mexican. The Seris have known about the D42 trail for many years, and they say it was a burro trail, used by Mexicans to bring agave hearts from the plateau above down to the shore, where they were made into mescal. According to Roberto Herrera, the Seris who came to San Esteban for agave early in the twentieth century always harvested plants some distance inland, up Arroyo Limantour, because those near the shore were not so good for food. The hearts were also baked inland, taking advantage of the soft arroyo gravel. As for E1–E9, Herrera had seen this site and was quite sure that these ovens were built by Mexicans to bake plants brought down from the slopes above. He said that Mexicans came to the island to harvest agave only for about a year, sometime around 1910, he thought (Roberto Herrera 1981:pers. comm.; Mary Beck Moser 1986:pers. comm.).

Modern Mexican fishermen think that late nineteenth century Mexican sea lion hunters who frequented San Esteban may have distilled small quantities of mescal for their own consumption. Documentary sources indicate that in 1877, three Guaymas businessmen tried to produce mescal on the island on a commercial scale, for sale in Sonora (see pp. 138–40). On May 14, three Mexicans and 14 "Indians" (presumably Yaquis) sailed to San Esteban to set up the operation. Their attempt failed, and the enterprise folded in less than a year, but it is possible that E1–E9, D1–D2, and other features in this area are the legacy of this venture. If so, E1–E9 may have been strictly a processing location, but it is likely that the crew lived in the vicinity of D1–D2. This would have been the most convenient place because of its ready access to supplies that would have to have been sent to the island by boat. This location may also have had access to water, supplied by a well that tapped into underground flow. In the 1960s, Alexander Russell observed an excavation nearby in Arroyo Limantour, a few hundred meters behind the shoreline, that he thought might have been the remnant of such a well (Alexander Russell 1968:pers. comm.).

Although the unusual features in this area may have been part of the Mexican distilling operation, it is not clear exactly what their functions were. The smoothed surface of the rectangular clearing next to the D1 and D2 pit ovens suggests that this might have been either a work or living area. The purpose of the two short sections of rock wall is totally obscure. The peculiar excavated clearings just up the slope from the two pit ovens most likely would have been sleeping places. Though presumably not Seri, they may well have been Indian, for it is possible that this is where the Yaqui crew camped. These clearings would have offered good protection from winter winds, and in summer, they may have been just far enough up the hillside to catch a cool breeze that would keep the occupants free of the biting gnats that plague the shore. This must have been an important consideration, for the Yaquis who worked the salt fields on Carmen Island in the 1860s were willing to walk about 3 kilometers into the mountains to escape the gnats for a good night's sleep (see p. 121).

Why the 1877 mescal operation on San Esteban folded is not revealed in the few known sources on that enterprise. But if E1–E9 were part of this venture, it is tempting to speculate that it may have failed for lack of sufficient water to process the plants, despite the deep hole they dug (E8). It is also possible that the island's agave could not be made into a commercially viable mescal. Not all species of agave produce high quality spirits (Bahre and Bradbury 1980:395), and it may be that San Esteban's endemic agave, while highly valued as food by the Seris, was found by the Mexicans to yield an inferior and unmarketable mescal.

Most of the remaining features on San Esteban are more clearly Mexican and recent. One of these is I30, a camp used in 1980 or 1981 by Mexican surveyors, located on a flat terrace at the base of Male Mountain. The main feature of the site is a clearing 3.9 m square that was probably used as a sleeping area. Large boulders surround the clearing and bisect it. These boulders would have served nicely to anchor two overlapping 2 by 4 m ground cloths and prevent them from blowing away in the wind. Another smaller clearing lies just to the northeast, and there is a hearth just outside the main clearing. Under a nearby bush is a wooden crate with tin cans and glass jars that mostly contained food items, while more food containers are strewn throughout the camp area. The artifacts that best reveal the identity of the campers are the large dry cell batteries and other items associated with electrical equipment.

The summit of Male Mountain, directly above this camp, was apparently used as a survey station by the same crew, for it is strewn with the same array of rusted cans, glass jars, and battery carcasses. It is also clear that they carried out their work in 1980 or 1981, for in January 1982 we found fragments of the same issue of a Mexican magazine bearing a copyright date of 1980 at both the base camp and the summit. The food containers suggest that the work required the crew to stay at the summit station over at least one night. This may also explain why three of the five rockwall enclosures on the summit (I38, I39, and I40) seem slightly different from summit structures on San Esteban's other peaks and from the two aboriginal-looking enclosures (I36 and I37) that are also situated on Male Mountain's summit. Distinguishing Mexican windbreaks from Indian counterparts is hardly an exact science, and the presence of electrical gear in I38 and salsa jars in I39 does not necessarily mean that any of the structures there were actually built by Mexican surveyors. Yet in subtle and indefinable ways, I38, I39, and I40 seem different from the two enclosures we believe to be aboriginal. We looked closely at this site three times over a span of five years, and each time came to this same conclusion.

While these three windbreaks seem to be of Mexican construction and almost certainly used by the 1980 or 1981 survey party, it is possible that they were built somewhat earlier by a previous Mexican survey party. We know that Male Mountain was climbed by surveyors in 1958, not only from their field notebooks but also from the dated bronze benchmarks they set on the summit in concrete (see pp. 287–88).

Mexican and Seri fishermen have long used two main camps on San Esteban. San Pedro, the summer camp, is on the west side, while the traditional winter camp is at El Monumento on the east coast. Both camps have sheltered coves where pangas can be beached, and each year the fishermen clear a slip of large boulders in the water just below the beach, in order to make landing less damaging to their pangas. Most of the time, the fishermen would camp in clearings behind piled rock windbreaks on the beach, but both camps have caves to which the men can retreat when the weather is especially violent. We recorded the cave at El Monumento as D46 and the clearings in use there in January 1982 as D47.

The cave at El Monumento (D46) is a natural west-facing cavity in the monolith. One look inside shows why present-day fishermen use it only in extreme weather. A small area of floor has been cleared of sharp rocks, but there is no very comfortable place to lie down. Most of the floor is irregular and sloping, with barely enough room for six or eight people (two panga crews) to sit out a storm. Another reason fishermen do not like to stay in the cave is the obvious rockfall danger (Elfego Briseño 1982:pers. comm.). There is wisdom in this, for just around the corner from the cave, the rock that offered the only easily climbable route up El Monumento collapsed sometime between 1982 and 1987.

The camp at El Monumento where the fishermen normally stayed (D47), was about 20 m from the cave. We photographed it in 1981 (Figure 13.21) and formally recorded it in 1982. At that time, the camp consisted of three oval areas cleared of large rocks and protected by piled rock walls. The main living structure, which served as a bedroom, kitchen, dining area, and living room, was a sandy-floored clearing about 3.3 m in diameter. The rocks removed from the floor had been stacked around the perimeter to form an encircling wall about 80 cm high, with an entryway 1.6 m wide on the south. A hearth of small stones was tucked against the south wall next to the entry. This living area was furnished with an old rusted refrigerator lying on its side and a wooden cable spool 75 cm in diameter, both of which served as tables. This furniture was rearranged almost daily.

Adjoining the living room on the east was a slightly smaller sleeping clearing 3.4 m long by 2.3 m wide. Here, sand had been spread over the underlying pebbles to make a more comfortable sleeping surface. The northwest winds were blocked by a piled rock wall on the north side that joined the wall of the main structure. In 1982, the only furnishing in this clearing was a corrugated cardboard box, completely unfolded and spread out, that one man used as a sleeping pad.

Just east of this sleeping clearing was a third cleared area with a sand and pebble floor 1.1 m long and 0.6 m wide. It was protected on the north by another wall of piled rocks. In 1982, other partly destroyed cleared areas and remnant walls from times past were vaguely discernible but were not in regular use.

Five years later, the camp had undergone some alteration. The main structural changes were an increase in height of the wall separating the main living area from the adjacent sleeping clearing and the appearance of several small newly cleared areas, each with its own windbreak wall. The refrigerator and the cable spool, the furniture of the main structure, were gone. Six years later still, in March 1993, the entire camp was gone (Figure 13.22). It may have been obliterated by Hurricane Lester the summer before, and all that remained was a slight circular depression devoid of large rocks, surrounded by a vague rock rim, the vestige of the main rock-walled living area. By this time, fishermen were camping nearby in A-frame tents made of agave stalk frameworks covered with tarps.

There is one other feature that is related to the fishermen's camp at El Monumento. This is a tiny cave a short distance up the hill to the west, where several people, including a Bahía Kino fisherman and a North American, have inscribed their names and dates. The recess under the cave roof is only about 1.7 m wide, 1.0 m deep, and 80 cm high, which is not enough room to sit up. The cave floor extends out slightly beyond the overhang, and to increase the protected space, somebody neatly built two parallel rock walls from the rear corners of the cave to the outer edge of this floor. The cave faces southeast, giving good protection from northwest storms, but even with the walled extension, there is only space for one or two people to lie down. Perhaps this is what motivated one occupant to claim, in a succinct and colloquial Spanish inscription on a rock, a feat of extraordinary sexual prowess during a four day stint in the cave.

The remnant of the fishermen's clearings (D47) at El Monumento has a nearly identical counterpart on El Cascajal at the southwestern corner of the island. This place is occasionally used as a camp, and near the base of the shingle spit is a basin-shaped depression free of large rocks. In all likelihood, this feature (C1) is the remains of a fishermen's camp clearing and windbreak destroyed by storms.

For a few years, there was rock-walled windbreak (D48) about 100 m behind the beach at El Monumento. In November 1980, fishermen from Bahía Kino

Figure 13.21   Mexican fishermen's camp (D47) at El Monumento in January 1981. The stone-walled living/kitchen area containing the cable spool table is just behind the clearing in the immediate foreground. To the left is the rusted refrigerator table. Photograph looks northwest from the base of El Monumento down the entire length of Playa Limantour.

Figure 13.22   Former Mexican fishermen's camp (D47) at El Monumento in March 1993, viewed from approximately the same location as the photograph above. The camp was probably destroyed in August 1992 by Hurricane Lester.

brought Elisa Villalpando and an assistant to the island to continue the survey we had begun the year before. During the entire month there, the wind blew furiously, making fieldwork exceedingly difficult and making it nearly impossible to keep tents standing in camp. Conditions in camp were so bad that the fishermen built this structure to give the archaeologists some respite from the incessant wind (Elisa Villalpando 1981:pers. comm.). The structure they built was a U-shaped windbreak, open to the south, 2.4 m long by 1.5 m wide. It was made of piled slabs and beach cobbles one course wide and 1.2 m high, which was just high enough to provide shelter. In January 1982, the structure was still intact. Two years later, the upper courses of rock had collapsed both inward and outward, reducing the standing wall height to a maximum of about 75 cm. In January 1987, one small segment of wall still stood 75 cm high, but the rest of the walls had been dismantled or collapsed almost to ground level. Inside the original enclosure, somebody had dug a pit about 1.0 m in diameter by about 60 cm deep, and lined it with rocks scavenged from the walls of the windbreak. Three bones in the bottom suggest it may have been used as a barbecue pit. By March 1993, there was little left of the structure except scattered rocks.

Biologists have also left their mark on the island. In 1966, members of the Gulf Islands Expedition found a number of reptile traps consisting of five-gallon cans sunk in the ground. Because the cans had been abandoned without being filled in, they had become purposeless death traps for lizards, and expedition members filled all those they found (Lindsay 1966b:330–31). Either some of the traps were not found or the practice has continued, for we have also seen examples of these devices. In recent years, unknown scientists have also attached metal tags and surveyors' flagging tape to plants and have marked rocks with spray paint. Nearly all of this activity is confined to the lower Arroyo Limantour.

In January 1987, three sets of what can only be described as wind chimes were found hanging from a prominent cardon on a terrace above Playa Limantour. These were homemade devices, each consisting of three or four tin can lids, suspended by a cord from a hand-carved wooden peg that had been driven into the trunk of the cactus. If their intent was to chime in the wind, San Esteban was an excellent place for them. Possibly their purpose was to scare ravens or rats away from somebody's cached food rather than make music for its own sake. By April of the same year, the chimes were no longer ringing. Two had only a single can lid remaining, and on the third only the cord dangled from its peg.

By far the largest feature on San Esteban's landscape was built in the early 1970s, not by Mexicans, but by North Americans. This is the makeshift airstrip behind Playa Limantour. It is said that it was quickly discovered by drug runners, who in turn were soon discovered by the Mexican government. To halt the drug trafficking, the government sent in soldiers who dug trenches and stacked boulders across the strip, making it impossible to use. The strip is still readily visible, though it is becoming less of a glaring scar as vegetation takes it over.

Finally, mention must be made of San Esteban's most technologically sophisticated feature. This is the automated lighthouse at the northeast corner of the island. It is known to Mexican fishermen simply as *el faro* (the lighthouse).

FOURTEEN

Making Simplicity Work:
Artifacts and Ecofacts

One of the most striking aspects of San Esteban's archaeology is the relative scarcity of artifacts compared with the large number of features. Apart from simple stone flakes, the one common type of artifact is the agave knife, and we saw around 200 of these objects. Otherwise, we found only about 60 purposefully made chipped-stone tools, and even some of these are questionable. The remainder of the artifact inventory consists of some 61 manos and metates, a number of battered hammer stones, around 400 pottery sherds (mostly the breakage of just a few vessels), plus about a dozen miscellaneous artifacts. Happily, even modern non-aboriginal trash is scarce.

Normally, one would expect few artifacts to signify little human activity, but on San Esteban that does not square with the abundance of structures. It could be that the island's terrestrial resources simply did not require much material aid to carry out the tasks of daily life. As Porfirio Díaz succinctly put it, the San Esteban people did not have very many possessions. And as modern Seri belief suggests, it may be that so much of life, particularly for the men, was carried out along the beaches and on the water, that much of the material culture has been lost to the sea. Whatever the reasons, the island seems to have comparatively few artifacts in only a limited range of types.

Chipped-Stone Artifacts

ROCKS AND FLAKES

Most of the human-made objects on San Esteban are nothing more than chipping debris, consisting principally of large primary and secondary flakes. This suggests that nearly all indigenous stone working was carried out by simple percussion with a stone hammer. The hammer stones we saw at quarries and flake concentrations are mostly mano-sized water-worn cobbles with battered ends or edges, though irregular battered rocks suggest that almost any fist-sized rock could suffice. Occasionally, we found smaller well-controlled thinning flakes that suggest the use of a more pliable hammer, but experiments showed that similar flakes can be detached with an ordinary hammer stone. Moreover, the only local materials other than stone that could conceivably have been used as hammers are sea lion and sea turtle bone, or perhaps ironwood. There is no naturally-occurring antler on San Esteban, though of course antler could have been brought over from Tiburón Island. A few artifacts may have been finished by pressure flaking, but the main evidence of this technique comes from the rare projectile points, which most likely were brought in from somewhere else.

Several kinds of rock served as raw material. Two of these, a mottled red jasper that outcrops on El Monumento and a blue-gray banded chert from the mountains south of lower Arroyo Limantour, were transported widely and can be found sporadically as waste flakes and tools throughout the island. Flakes and tools of white chert are also widely but sparsely distributed, though the source of this material is not known. A black microcrystalline andesite occurs as nodules in many of the arroyos, and artifacts of this material are similarly widespread but scarce. There is also a yellow chert that outcrops at the top of the sea cliffs on the west side, but we saw artifacts of this rock only in the vicinity of the source. We found no sources of obsidian, though we did see a few small nodules and flakes of this material on the west side. But these six materials account for only a small fraction of San Esteban's chipped stone. By far the majority of the flakes, and nearly all of the agave knives, are made of a slightly siliceous gray andesite. The source of this material is simply the ground surface, for this is the rock that occurs as cobbles, boulders, and blocky or tabular outcrops over nearly all of the island. Although the rock is naturally gray, surface oxidation produces a beige to brilliant red-brown cortex, and flakes of this material may display any of these colors.

The universality of andesite does not mean that rocks everywhere on the island are equally suitable for stone working. The material on the east side tends to break into tabular slabs, some of which make good agave knives but little else, and much of which is not even suitable for that. The west side rock is generally better, allowing a somewhat more controlled conchoidal fracture, which may explain why the scatter of flakes is noticeably denser on this side of the island. But even west side andesite is generally inferior to the jaspers and cherts from which most of the intentionally-shaped tools (apart from agave knives) were made. And this is decidedly backhanded praise for the jasper and cherts, which themselves are full of impurities that cause unpredictable fractures and breakage. The generally poor quality of San Esteban's rocks for sophisticated knapping may in part explain why so few standardized tools were made and in so few forms. But all of these rocks are capable of producing simple sharp flakes, which may have been completely adequate for the majority of cutting and scraping jobs. Indeed, some flakes seem to have edge damage from use or even evidence of slight retouching. With fully-shaped tools hard to make and rock capable of

*Figure 14.1   Biface of local andesite, well used and broken into three pieces.
Original length was 9.3 cm, width 5.1 cm, thickness 1.5 cm. It was found
in a clearing (G6) near the center of the island. January 1981.*

being transformed into sharp flakes as close as one's feet, people may well have
preferred to rely on simple flakes, easily made and as easily discarded after immediate use, for most jobs. There might have been little need for more elaborate tools.

As to the more fully-formed chipped tools that do occur on the island, nearly
all can be placed in nine loose categories. Using mostly traditional nomenclature, these are bifaces, scrapers, planes, Levallois-like flakes, "pointed tools,"
discoidal cores, projectile points, agave knives, and choppers. However, assign-
ing artifacts to even these broad categories may be playing fast and loose with
reality, for it is entirely possible that some of these objects are nothing more than
spent cores that have acquired the superficial appearance of crude tools.

Bifaces

We found about 10 simple bifaces. Most are around 8 cm long and are more or
less leaf shaped (Figure 14.1). They were bifacially flaked, entirely by percussion. Most are of local andesite, though two specimens are made of the local
blue-gray banded chert. Two specimens are so thick and asymmetrical that they
might as easily be considered scrapers. Since there is no reason to think that
these are preforms, they were presumably used as knives.

*Figure 14.2   Domed scraper, unifacially flaked, of El Monumento mottled red jasper.
Length is 7.5 cm, width 4.5 cm, thickness 3.0 cm. It was found close to a
charcoal-bearing stone circle (G17) near the center of the island. January 1982.*

SCRAPERS

At least a dozen artifacts can be loosely classified as scrapers, and most of these are ordinary discoidal scrapers. They were typically made by splitting a nodule of jasper or chert into two halves, creating an oval blank about 4–9 cm long that is flat on one face and rounded or domed on the other. In most cases, the working edge was produced by removing a series of simple unifacial percussion flakes around a portion or the entire perimeter of the object (Figure 14.2). Because the resulting edge angles are rather steep, 65° or so, it may be that these tools were used more as planes than as scrapers.

Two variants on this theme, end scrapers and spokeshaves, were produced by a slightly different technique. Though simple in form, they were carefully and competently made and tend to fit the hand nicely. In both cases, the starting point was a split nodule much like those that were made into discoidal scrapers. However, the working edge was prepared by unifacially removing several adjacent long narrow flakes, possibly by pressure, perpendicular to the flat face. The objects were then retouched by striking off the protruding points at the intersections of these long narrow flake scars where they meet the flat face, thereby producing a smoothly rounded edge. In the case of end scrapers, flaking was confined primarily to one end of the tool, producing a convex working edge. The distinctive concave edges of spokeshaves were made by removing the flakes along one side of the object. We can only speculate that spokeshaves might have been used for straightening and trimming the shafts of fish spears or other wooden tools.

PLANES

We found three objects that bear some similarity to end scrapers, but are so much larger and cruder that it may be more appropriate to classify them separately as planes. Like scrapers, these tools were made from parent rocks split in half, but from local andesite, rather than chert or jasper. The flat face served as the striking platform for removing long flakes along a portion of the edge, but no effort was subsequently made to trim the intersecting ragged flake scars in order to even the edge. They are also thicker compared to their diameter than are scrapers. One specimen is about 8 cm in diameter, about 6 cm thick, and has an edge angle of about 80°. Calling these objects "planes" gives them the benefit of the doubt, for it is entirely possible that these artifacts are merely cores from which a few flakes were struck.

LEVALLOIS-LIKE FLAKES

The relatively sophisticated artifacts in this category seem out of place on San Esteban, but there is no question that they belong here because a few, at least, were made of local andesite. The name for this kind of flake originated with French Middle Paleolithic sites where the technique was first identified, but artifacts made by this technique occur widely in space and time. The half-dozen or so specimens we saw on San Esteban were made by first trimming most of the cortex off a piece of rock so that a substantial portion of the surface consisted of intersecting flake scars. This "prepared" portion of the blank was then struck from the core. The results are fairly thin flakes possessing several flake scars and little or no cortex on one face, but only the single scar of detachment from the core on the other face. During the European Paleolithic, these flakes were carefully retouched into a wide variety of finished tools. On San Esteban, they were evidently used without further shaping, since the edges are generally worn even and smooth.

"POINTED TOOLS"

We encountered about four flakes that are pointed on one end. In some of these, the points may be nothing more than a coincidence of the way the scars of secondary flakes intersect each other at the tip of the object. But at least two specimens appear to have been retouched just enough along the sides to suggest that the pointed end was intentionally produced (Figure 14.3).

DISCOIDAL CORES

The most distinctive chipped-stone artifacts, apart from agave knives, are bifacially-flaked discoidal objects. Most of the 10 or so we saw are made of chert

Figure 14.3   "Pointed tool" of El Monumento mottled red jasper, from the cave site Icámajoj Zaaj (G4), near the center of the island. Length is 9.2 cm, width 6.5 cm, thickness 1.4 cm. It was bifacially flaked, but shows no evidence of use. January 1982.

or jasper. They are relatively small, generally about 4–6 cm in diameter, though a few reach 10 cm. These are among the few artifacts that were completely shaped by flaking around the entire perimeter of the object. The flaking pattern itself is noteworthy because it was created by removing each adjacent flake from the opposite face, producing a wavy edge (Figure 14.4). In some cases, a portion of the flaked edge is slightly worn or battered, suggestive of use, and for some time we casually referred to these objects as minichoppers. However, it is difficult to imagine what tasks could be performed with a wavy edge, particularly on such light-duty objects. It may be that these artifacts are just discarded cores from which flakes had been struck with great efficiency. The edge wear may be intentional grinding by the knapper to prevent shattering the striking platform when the next flake was detached.

Projectile Points

We saw just three projectile points. All three were found at habitation caves, two fragments at I47 and a nearly complete specimen at B5. One of the I47 fragments (Figure 14.5c) is a slightly rounded tip segment that is missing the base. It was skillfully pressure flaked from a mottled white chert foreign to the island. The second I47 fragment (Figure 14.5a) is from a narrow triangular point with a concave base. Originally, it must have been about 5 cm long and just under 2 cm wide at the base. The blank seems to have been a thin flake, and it may have

Figure 14.4   Discoidal core (or light chopper) showing the distinctive flake removal sequence from alternating faces. It was an isolated find near the west side of the island. January 1981.

been finished in part by pressure flaking. The rock, a pink rhyolite of indifferent quality, is similar to material that occurs on both Tiburón and San Lorenzo Islands, either one of which could be the source. The third specimen, from B5 (Figure 14.5b), is missing the tip and one tang, but is similar in form, size, material, and workmanship to the triangular point at I47. Rather than smoothly concave, however, the base is perceptibly tanged, and it could have been reworked from a corner-notched point with a broken base. This point is sufficiently curved on its longitudinal axis that one wonders if it could have survived impact with a target without breaking.

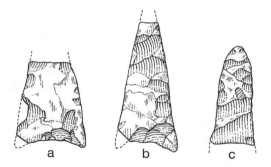

Figure 14.5   The three projectile point fragments found during the survey, all from cave sites. a and c are from I47 on the west side of the island, and b is from B5 at the northeastern corner. Length of b is 35 mm. Drawings by Cathy Moser Marlett.

Villalpando and Oliveros's excavation of B2, a cave a short distance from B5, turned up at least six more points, all near the surface. Some are small triangular concave-base points similar to the two described above (Elisa Villalpando 1984:pers. comm.). Small triangular points with concave bases have a wide distribution in the Desert West, where they are known to be chronologically late.

According to Seri oral history, the San Esteban people did not use the bow and arrow. This makes sense because there was nothing to hunt on their island that needed such a weapon. Even when they periodically retreated to Tiburón Island, where there are game animals, it is said that they did not bother with bows and arrows. Consequently, Roberto Herrera was as perplexed as we were by the presence of points on San Esteban. He suggested that the San Esteban people might have acquired them by trade when they visited the Seris on Tiburón Island, but he was not sure why they would want them. Alternatively, he thought it possible that Seris visiting from Tiburón Island might have brought bows and arrows with them, perhaps from fear of the wild San Esteban folk (Mary Beck Moser 1986:pers. comm.). It is also possible that Seris coming from Tiburón around the turn of the twentieth century brought bows and arrows in case they encountered Mexicans around San Esteban.

All of these explanations are consistent with the archaeological context. All three points are of materials foreign to San Esteban, and the rhyolite of the two triangular points could be from Tiburón. At I47, not only are the points likely imported, but the pottery there was probably made from Tiburón clays, and the Seri figurine fragment at this site is probably also from somewhere else. Modern Seris say they never went as far inland as this cave during their visits early in the twentieth century, so these exotic artifacts must have been carried there by earlier people, either the San Esteban folk or the Seris from Tiburón who occasionally visited them. The point from B5 (and those excavated by Villalpando and Oliveros at B2) could have been brought in by early twentieth century Seris, who occasionally camped in this locality. Of course, it is always possible that the oral accounts are wrong and that the San Esteban people did make limited use of the bow and arrow.

Perhaps the most intriguing alternative is that the San Esteban people simply found the points as surface artifacts on Tiburón or elsewhere and brought them back to the island as souvenirs. If so, they might not even be of Seri manufacture. European military expeditions against the Seris routinely employed large numbers of friendly Indian auxiliaries, armed with bows and arrows, to supplement their own meager forces. In 1750, for example, the Spaniards brought more than 200 Pimas to fight Seris on Tiburón Island, and these Indians used up so many arrows there that a boat had to be sent back to the mainland for more. Assuming that these arrows were stone tipped, it is likely that a large number of projectile points on Tiburón Island, including those that might have been picked up by the San Esteban people as curiosities, were actually made by other Indians of foreign materials.

AGAVE KNIVES

San Esteban has only one kind of chipped-stone tool that is both distinctive and common, and this is the agave knife (Figures 14.6 and 14.7). In all, we encountered approximately 200 of these artifacts scattered throughout the island.

We recorded detailed information on 52 specimens. The mean size, based on this sample, is 13.8 cm long, 11.4 cm wide, and 2.8 cm thick. The largest measured is 17 by 15.5 cm and is 5 cm thick, while the smallest is 10 by 9 cm and is 2.5 cm thick. The vast majority of agave knives were made from tabular slabs of andesite. Although andesite occurs over much of the island, only in certain places does it outcrop in tabular slabs, and not all slabs can be flaked without splitting. Moreover, there was a clear preference for water-worn slabs with rounded corners, perhaps because they could be held tightly without cutting one's hand. Suitable water-rounded blanks can probably be found in many arroyos. But throughout the island, many of the knives we saw were made of the distinctive gray and slick-surfaced andesite that occurs on Playa Limantour.

Blanks for agave knives were more or less rectangular slabs of rock. The cutting edge was generally made by striking a half dozen or so flakes from one end and part of the adjacent two sides. In about 84 percent of the cases, this resulted in a semicircular working edge extending about one-third to half way around the perimeter of the tool. A few specimens have even more cutting edge, and one specimen was trimmed around the entire perimeter. At the other extreme, one knife was made with great efficiency by removing only two flakes from one end. About 65 percent of the sample we recorded had flakes struck from one face only, while the remainder were bifacially flaked. Edge angles are typically less than 45°.

At least one or two agave knives can be found almost anywhere on the island where there is an extensive stand of agave. Twice we devoted a half day to searching dense fields of agave specifically for knives, and each time we found about 15 specimens. This suggests, of course, that they were abandoned where they were used. Although blanks were usually selected with some care and the finished knives carried to the places they were used, it is not surprising they were discarded after use, since experiment shows that it takes less than a minute to make one. They are classic examples of "instant tools," and crude but workable replacements, if needed, could be made from almost any local rock.

And there is little doubt that agave knives work. Late one afternoon, two of us, each armed with a replicated knife, attacked an agave plant. We first cut off the spines, Seri style, to avoid getting stuck by their toxic tips, and then cut off all 48 leaves at their bases. After we got the hang of it, we found that the knives would sever a leaf in less than 10 seconds, and it was clear that a plant could be easily dispatched by an experienced person in not much more than five minutes. Interestingly, we found that a stone knife, with its ragged edge, works better on agave leaves than the smooth blade of a steel knife or machete. However, the

Figure 14.6   Agave knife, bifacially flaked, of tabular andesite. Length is 12.0 cm, width 11.5 cm, thickness 2.5 cm. This is one of eight knives that make up an artifact concentration designated P19, on a high ridge on the east side of the island. January 1981.

edge becomes quite dull in the course of defoliating a single plant and would need periodic resharpening if it were to be used for several plants. We did, in fact, see several clusters of resharpening flakes in agave stands.

Agave knives, or mescal knives as they are often called, occur in North America in one form or another in most regions where edible agave grows (Castetter et al. 1938:52). Yet this does not seem to be the case in Seri country. Although the Seris utilized several different agave species throughout their territory, agave knives appear to be restricted almost solely to San Esteban Island. The only other place we have seen these artifacts is on the southwest coast of Tiburón Island, in the region also said to have belonged to the San Esteban people. But here there is no tabular andesite and only sparse agave of a less desirable species. Knives are correspondingly of different materials and few in number. It may be that the San Esteban people had their fill of agave on their own island, and when they retreated to Tiburón they preferred to eat other things.

The modern Seris have harvested agave with metal knives for decades, and even the old people who visited San Esteban as young men are completely unfamiliar with the distinctive chipped-stone agave knives that litter the island. Roberto Herrera (1981:pers. comm.) said that the San Esteban people must have used stone knives, since they had no metal, but he assumed (incorrectly) that these knives would have taken the form of modern hunting knives.

Figure 14.7   Agave knife, bifacially flaked, of tabular andesite. Length is 13.0 cm,
width 10.1 cm, thickness 2.0 cm. It was found at a cave site (E10) near
the center of the island. January 1987.

CHOPPERS

Choppers comprise a rather poorly-defined residual category, subsuming about
10 specimens that do not easily fit the previous classes of artifacts. Most of these
bear some resemblance to agave knives, but they differ just enough in form to
warrant placing them in a separate category. They tend to be bulkier, less rectangular in outline, and cruder than normal agave knives. Nearly all are unifacial,
with only two or three flakes struck from one side or end (Figure 14.8). Edge
angles are characteristically around 60°, which is a bit steep to be efficient at
cutting agave leaves, though no doubt they could get the job done. It may be
that these choppers are just badly made agave knives, but if so, they certainly lack
the simple elegance that we came to associate with these artifacts.

We also found three choppers that do not bear any resemblance to agave
knives. They are much more like the artifacts of the ancient Malpais Industry
of the lower Colorado River Basin and surrounding regions. This is especially
true for two that are based on tabular blocks of andesite. One of these (Figure
14.9) has a small "beak" projecting between unifacially detached flake scars, and
both have the characteristic Malpais trapezoidal cross-section created by removing one or two flakes from opposite faces of the two ends. Whether these specimens are particularly early, however, is unknown. Elsewhere, Malpais-like

Figure 14.8   Chopper, unifacially flaked, of Playa Limantour andesite.
Length is 13.0 cm, width 9.5 cm, thickness 3.0 cm. This was an isolated find above
the sea cliffs on the west side of the island. January 1987.

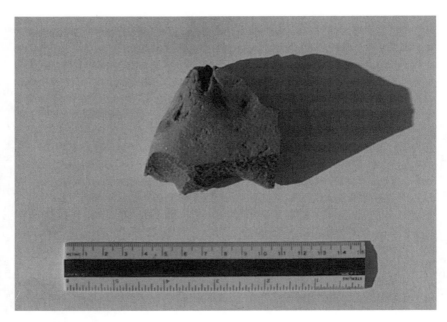

Figure 14.9   Malpais-like beaked chopper of Playa Limantour andesite,
with trapezoidal cross section and fresh-appearing flake scars. Length is 6.9 cm, width 6.6 cm,
thickness not recorded. It was found with several other artifacts near a clearing (B14),
high above the northeastern corner of the island. April 1980.

choppers were in use over a great span of time, and on San Esteban, there are no reliable age indicators that would enable truly ancient specimens to be distinguished from recent ones (see Chapter 15). Given the simplicity of both the Malpais and San Esteban chipped-stone artifacts, it is certainly possible that a few Malpais forms were coincidentally made by the people who used San Esteban in more recent times.

Manos and Metates

Compared to chipped-stone tools, manos and metates are relatively common artifacts. All told, we found 32 manos and 29 metates that show unquestionable signs of use. Because they are in part food processing tools, it is not surprising that we generally saw them at places where people camped, including most of the habitation caves and several of the clearings. Like most of San Esteban's artifacts, there is little about these implements that is either distinctive or diagnostic.

Most manos are natural cobbles of more or less oval form, and suitable blanks can be found by the thousands on beaches and among the bottom gravels of the major arroyos. For the most part, people selected fairly symmetrical cobbles, though a few highly irregular specimens indicate that almost any moderately flat fist-sized rock could suffice. Those we considered to be legitimate manos all show grinding on one or both faces, and several specimens have well-worn faces that attest to heavy and repeated use. However, we also saw at least as many similar cobbles with no clear evidence of grinding at all. It may be that serviceable rocks were so widely available that they were often picked up as needed, used a few times, and discarded before they acquired any macroscopic signs of wear.

Among the 14 clearly used manos we measured, the mean size is 14 cm long, 10 cm wide, and about 6 cm thick. The largest is 19 cm by 17 cm and 8 cm thick. Grinding faces range from cylindrical in cross-section to biconvex and are thus capable of accommodating both flat and basin-shaped metate surfaces. About one-quarter had been worked on both faces, and a few have had their grinding surface intentionally roughened by pecking. Many of the manos were found with their main grinding face down, as if to protect it (Fig 14.10).

Like manos, many of the rocks used as metates are also flat-faced cobbles obtained from beaches and arroyo bottoms. But nearly half the metates recorded are more or less tabular slabs of andesite (Figure 14.11). Apparently, almost any more or less flat surface could be used for grinding, and a few metates are simply grinding surfaces on deeply embedded boulders or bedrock. Of 15 metates we recorded in detail, about half are bifacial specimens, ground on both sides. Probably because metates are generally larger, heavier, and therefore less easily transported than manos, they seem to have been treated less casually. About two-thirds of the metates show extensive wear on their grinding surface(s), providing clear evidence of heavy long-term use. One specimen has a well-developed basin that was worn to a depth of about 1 cm, and another has a grinding surface about half that deep.

Figure 14.10   Bifacial mano of hornblende andesite in situ at the I2–I7 cluster of clearings, west side of San Esteban. Length is 17.5 cm, width 11.5 cm, thickness 3.0 cm. Light grinding is visible on the exposed face and heavy grinding on the buried face. January 1984.

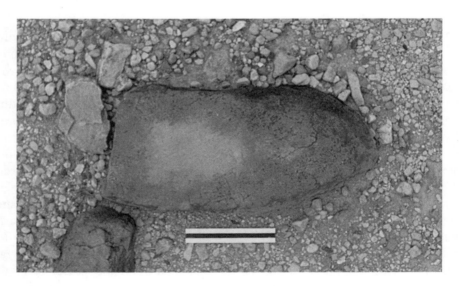

Figure 14.11   Unifacial metate of local andesite in situ at a probable camp (M14) near the west side of the island. Length is 44 cm, width 22 cm, thickness 12 cm. The working surface is a heavily-ground shallow basin. The metate is deeply embedded in the ground, suggesting it was used in place. January 1981.

Apart from bedrock grinding surfaces, the largest metate we measured is 58 by 30 cm and is 8 cm thick. The mean size is about 35 by 23 cm and is 10 cm thick. Grinding surfaces range from flat to basin-shaped. Like manos, a few grinding surfaces have been roughened by pecking. And also like manos, we found most of the unifacial metates lying with their working face down.

Although labeling these artifacts manos and metates carries the implication that they were used to process plant foods, this is surely only one of many uses to which these tools were put. When WJ McGee visited the Seris on the Sonoran mainland in the 1890s, he noted some 13 separate tasks carried out with a single metate-sized flat cobble (McGee 1898:238–39, Pl. 43). Several of the manos and metates we found still retain organic residue on their grinding faces, and a few metates bear traces of a red material, suggesting they were used to grind pigment. The distinction between mano and hammer stone seems to be especially arbitrary, for many manos have battered ends or edges, and some of the hammers found with chipping debris bear traces of grinding on their faces. In a few cases, one or two large flakes were removed from the ends of cobble manos, though it is not clear whether they spalled off as an accident of hammering or were struck off intentionally to convert these manos into crude choppers.

Few if any Seris today still use manos and metates, for they have been replaced by mechanical grinders and pre-processed commercial foods. But in the 1970s, they were still household items for some families, and all of the older women knew how to use them from long experience. At that time, Edward Moser (undated notes) reported that most people distinguished two types of metates and manos based on size and grinding surface, both of which were properties related to use. Large slab metates with flat grinding surfaces served primarily as implements for processing seeds into flour. These metates would be used with either oval one-handed manos or longer elliptical two-handed manos, both of which developed cylindrical grinding faces that matched the flat surface of the metate. Slightly smaller metates with basin-shaped grinding surfaces were used mostly to process softer, wet foods, such as cactus fruit seeds and ironwood beans, which required crushing but were not ground into flour. They were paired only with one-handed manos, which developed biconvex faces that conformed to the metate's basin. When nonfood items needed to be ground, such as paint pigments, dyes, and medicines, metates were turned over and the other face was used. This kept food from being contaminated and produced many bifacial metates.

Nearly all Seri metate and mano blanks were water-worn beach cobbles, and manos were carefully selected to fit specific metates. Metate blanks were often usable with no preparation, but those with uneven surfaces were prepared by chipping. As the grinding surfaces of metates and manos became excessively smooth through use, they were roughened by pecking. Both the initial preparation and later roughening were done with an ordinary rock, not a mano, for fear of breaking it. But according to Roberto Herrera (1976:pers. comm.) this careful handling did not last long. Manos were often heated in a fire and rubbed on the skin to alleviate sore muscles or itching, and because of this, many would suddenly break during later use.

He said that the reason so many metates got broken was because people would heave them at mesquite branches to break them off for firewood.

Yet despite this mistreatment, metates, especially, were considered valuable items, and generally every wife owned at least one of each type. Though blanks were readily available at many beach camps, they had to be carried to inland camps. Since they were heavy, they were generally cached, rather than hauled from camp to camp when people moved. Because of deaths or other factors, some of these cached metates were never reclaimed by their original owners. A few have since been recycled, for in the 1960s and 1970s, Seris who found nice metates at the old camps sometimes brought them home for reuse (Edward Moser, undated notes).

The Seris say that the preferred materials for manos and metates were oval water-worn cobbles of white granitic rock, and this is confirmed by archaeological specimens from both the mainland and Tiburón Island (Bowen 1976:76–79). Since San Esteban has essentially no granitic rocks, grinding implements here were made from local volcanic rocks, and sometimes from irregular chunks rather than water-worn cobbles. Otherwise, there is little about San Esteban's manos and metates to distinguish them either from those the Seris themselves describe or those found archaeologically in other parts of Seri territory.

Pottery

In contrast to most of the Seri region, pottery is relatively scarce on San Esteban Island. We saw only about 400 sherds in some 20 discrete localities, and this probably represents the breakage of just a few vessels. About half the sherds were found at a single site (B2), and almost three-fourths of the total occur at just four sites. Pottery vessels were clearly household items, for we found about 95 percent of the sherds at caves and clearings, the two kinds of habitation sites. But while some pottery occurs at most of the caves, we saw sherds at only three sets of clearings. This could indicate that the other clearings pre-date the appearance of pottery, but it more likely means that we found only three open campsites where somebody had a pot and was unlucky enough to break it.

Apart from two intrusive sherds, the pottery on San Esteban is unequivocally Seri. Though the historical development of Seri pottery is not known in much detail, it appears to have gradually evolved from an initial, hard, well-crafted, and exquisitely thin plain ware into a softer, thicker but serviceable form, before it finally degenerated into the crumbly product that has been made in recent years as a tourist item. The hard and thin early pottery, Tiburón Plain, may have originated in prehispanic times. Its softer and thicker daughter product, dubbed Historic Seri, is the quintessential pottery of the nineteenth century, though it is not clear just when this form began to evolve from the ancestral Tiburón Plain. Historic Seri pottery remained in use until the 1930s, when metal containers became common enough to eliminate the need for native pottery. The few vessels made since then, dubbed Modern Seri, have been produced mainly for sale to tourists (Bowen 1976:53–68).

From a purely typological perspective, about 90 percent of the sherds we found on San Esteban would have to be classified as Historic Seri, and the remainder would be considered Tiburón Plain. Most of the Tiburón Plain sherds are from the breakage of a single vessel at one of the clearings (I55), and the rest is part of the diffuse scatter of artifacts that covers the island. But typology is a poor way of characterizing the Seri ceramic tradition because it does not effectively reflect what was clearly a gradual transition of the earlier pottery into the later form. At least half the pottery on the island is really typologically intermediate between Tiburón Plain and Historic Seri, sharing characteristics of both in varying degrees. This suggests that much of the occupation of the island took place during the period that Historic Seri pottery was evolving into its distinctive late nineteenth century form.

In the small number of cases where we could tell something about vessel form, pots were mostly small wide-mouth ollas with slightly everted rims. A few rim sherds suggest narrow-mouth forms, and we saw one sherd that could be from a bowl. Several of the ollas were decorated with an exterior rim coil about 1 cm wide, positioned either at the lip of the vessel or about 1 cm below it. Some rim sherds have incised fine-line decorations in a horizontal zigzag pattern, like a sequence of connected "V" figures, either pendant from the lip or just below it. In two cases these lines are doubled. A small but surprising number of sherds were decorated with red paint. In one case, it is clear that the decoration consists of alternating straight and zigzag lines descending vertically from the lip. One whole vessel, a small olla found by Seris who were visiting the island in 1966, has a simple rim band of red paint. These vessel forms, decorative techniques, and designs are all typical of Seri pottery from Tiburón Island and the mainland (see Bowen 1976:61–64).

There are several possibilities that might account for the comparative scarcity of pottery on San Esteban. In the first place, the island probably never had more than a small population and perhaps for a relatively short time. Moreover, as the modern Seris tell it, the San Esteban people did not have a great deal of use for pottery. They used it mainly to boil food, but this may not have been a very common practice, for it is said that they ate most of their food raw. For the mainland Seris, pottery ollas were essential for hauling drinking water over long distances. But this was generally done over easy ground. For the rugged terrain of San Esteban, the Seris say the San Esteban people sensibly carried water in nonbreakable sea lion stomachs and stored it in turtle bladders.

It is possible, as one Seri believes, that the San Esteban people did not make their own pottery, but acquired it from other Seris by trade (Mary Beck Moser 1981:pers. comm.). This is not an idea that has occurred to most Seris, who simply assume that the San Esteban people made their own pottery. Another possibility, suggested by Eugenio Morales, is that the San Esteban people made their own pottery but only when they were on Tiburón Island, bringing it with them when they returned to San Esteban (Mary Beck Moser 1982:pers. comm.).

Because of this uncertainty about who made San Esteban pottery and where, we checked the mineral inclusions in a number of sherds to see if we could determine whether they had been made locally. In many cases, there is no way to tell. But some sherds contain biotite mica, a mineral that occurs primarily in clays derived from granitic and other intrusive rocks. Since these rocks are common in much of traditional Seri territory, the pottery found on Tiburón Island and the mainland coast usually contains biotite. San Esteban's rocks, however, contain very little biotite, and most of the small amount that does occur is a surface-altered form included in some of the island's rhyolites (Dana L. Desonie 1996:pers. comm.). Granitic rocks, from which the unaltered biotite in the pottery must be derived, are rare on San Esteban. They can occasionally be found as isolated cobbles among the island's volcanic deposits, having been carried to the surface by the eruptions that created the island. But it is highly unlikely that anyone would have sought out these unusual rocks and laboriously crushed them merely to extract the mica to add to clay for making pottery. This suggests that the sherds on San Esteban that contain biotite must have been made from clays gathered elsewhere, such as Tiburón Island or the Sonoran mainland. Thus it seems clear that some of the pottery, and conceivably all of it, was made somewhere other than San Esteban Island.

Though some of the clays are nonlocal, this still does not tell us whether the vessels were made by the San Esteban people or acquired from other Seris. The comparatively large number of decorated sherds hints at trade, for people worldwide have tended to exchange decorated vessels rather than plain ware. In any case, the pottery that reached San Esteban must have been valued items, for in at least three instances the intact bottoms of broken ollas were salvaged for reuse.

In addition to vessels, we saw three sherd disks at one of the habitation caves (G4). Two are perforated, and all were made from Historic Seri sherds. In the old days, the mainland Seris would make such disks, insert a stick through the perforation, and spin them as tops (Bowen 1976:73).

We also found a piece of a ceramic figurine at one of the caves (I47). It belongs to the most common type (Type 1) found in the Seri area. The Seris remember these items as children's dolls or playthings, although they may have had esoteric functions in the more distant past (Moser and White 1968:Fig. 2, 133–36, 146–53). A second figurine fragment was found during Oliveros and Villalpando's excavations at B2.

Perishable Artifacts

Two of the caves, B2 and I35, each have a cut piece of agave stalk with holes drilled in the shaft. The specimen at B2 is about 50 cm long and has two holes, each about 1 cm in diameter. The other specimen is about 1 m long and has four such holes. We can only speculate that these might be flutes of the kind played by Seri boys (Bowen and Moser 1970:185; Felger and Moser 1985:314).

Also at I35, we found several bundles of agave fiber that might have been intended to be made into cord. This cave also has a piece of vine with strands twisted into a knot-like configuration.

Non-Aboriginal Artifacts

One consequence of San Esteban's remote location and few resources of interest to Europeans is that the island has remained remarkably free of non-Indian refuse. The beaches receive the bulk of the trash influx, much of it the random detritus of the Gulf that floats in and washes up on shore. Fishermen camping at El Monumento and San Pedro continually dispose of small amounts of garbage near camp, but it has not accumulated into a definable trash dump. The agave ovens D1 and D2, because of their proximity to Playa Limantour, have been partly filled with tin cans and bottles discarded by recent visitors. The only places in the interior of the island with significant quantities of modern trash are the surveyors' camp (I30) and summit station on Male Mountain.

A small number of non-Indian artifacts can be found behind the beaches, generally within a few hundred meters of shore. At one cave (B2), we found two cigarette filters and a piece of metal, while another cave (A4) produced a red plastic cap, perhaps from a toothpaste tube. A weathered piece of aluminum foil lies tucked under a rock at an agave oven (E13), while next to another oven (D33) is a rusted tin lid stamped "United States Tobacco Co." Among the waste flakes at D25 is the metal base of a Peters "Victor" 20-gauge shotgun shell. At the I2–I7 clearings, on the west side of the island, we saw a button, plus the two snaps and belt clip from a military-style canteen.

Once beyond this near-shore strip, and not counting the surveyors' trash, there is virtually no trace of recent humans. In many weeks of fieldwork in the interior, we saw only three other items, a rusted meat tin with a slotted twist-key opener, the tongue of an Adidas brand athletic shoe, and a rusted tin can that had been placed to mark the summit of Pico San Esteban.

Ecofacts

Animal bones occur mostly at cave sites. The most common are sea turtle bones, which we found at nearly every cave, and sometimes in modest quantities. Sea turtle bone is also one of the principle components of the thin scatter of cultural material that litters the island. Three caves contain fish vertebrae, and three have chuckwalla bones, including the strange carcass at I35 (see p. 319).

Shells are oddly scarce. Several of those we saw are species of large bivalves, which may have been used as tools or containers rather than as food. In at least two cases, the interior of the shell was apparently stained with red pigment, suggesting they were used for mixing paint (see Felger and Moser 1985:142, 152). Three of the caves with shells have just one or two examples of several different species, almost as if these shells were gathered as specimens for a type collection. Only in one place (J12) did we find a concentration of shells that suggest that the animal inside, in this case a sea snail (*Turbo fluctuosus*), provided somebody with a meal. Today, these gastropods are among the many sea creatures that can be easily gathered among the intertidal rocks of El Monumento, the closest accessible beach to the site.

The bones and shells that occur archaeologically as surface specimens may give a highly distorted picture of the San Esteban diet. According to oral accounts, the San Esteban people relied heavily on a variety of fish, shellfish, and other sea products. It is quite possible that the majority of these were eaten on the spot as they were caught. Bones and shells discarded at sea or along the shoreline would obviously not show up in the archaeological record. One of the animals whose bones are conspicuously missing is the sea lion. In this case, the oral accounts explain the lack of bones by maintaining that these creatures were butchered on the beaches and the bones discarded there, only the meat being carried to inland camps. Thus despite the preponderance of sea turtle bone on the island, these animals were not necessarily a major source of food. Indeed, the Seris say that even though the San Esteban people were expert sea turtle hunters, they disdained the meat and ate it only when more palatable foods were unavailable.

The only potentially edible plant foods we saw in archaeological context were unidentified seeds at one cave (N4). At two caves, we found the inedible leaves of agave plants, which may have been brought in for making cord from the leaf fiber. As noted above, one of these caves (I35) has several bundles of fiber that had already been stripped from the leaves. One of the most interesting plant parts, also at I35, is a piece of reedgrass or carrizo cane (*Phragmites australis*). This is the material from which the all-important balsa was made, and it does not grow anywhere on San Esteban. The closest source, said to have been exploited by the San Esteban people, is the waterhole called *Xapij*, inland from the southwest coast of Tiburón Island (Felger and Moser 1985:309).

A red mineral pigment seems to have been frequently used on San Esteban, for it shows up as pictographs, residue on manos, metates, possibly large bivalve shells, and perhaps on pottery as paint. One source of this material may be the sea cliffs just north of Arroyo Bonito. Here, a red mineral outcrops as almost a powder that dissolves quickly in water and is easily dabbed on almost any surface. Roberto Herrera (1981:pers. comm.) said that the modern Seris have sometimes gathered a red pigment in approximately this location. Apparently, he was not aware that a similar red mineral can be found at a large cave near the northwestern corner of the island. This cave is also the location of a deep yellow mineral that is equally suitable as a pigment. A few ceramic figurines and sherds of Seri pottery have been found with designs in a similar shade of yellow (Bowen 1976:63), but whether this cave was the source of the pigment is not known.

The only other mineral substance we found archaeologically is an unmodified translucent crystal, probably gypsum, about 8 cm long, which is among the surface remains at I47 cave. The Seris often ground gypsum into a powder and used it either as a white face paint or placed it in a cane tube and kept it as an amulet (Kroeber 1931:14–15, 27; Felger and Moser 1985:153, 156). According to Edward H. Davis (1929:106, 132), the Seris' source of gypsum was San Esteban Island.

FIFTEEN

Measuring Time's Passage:
Radiocarbon Dates and
Other Estimates of Age

Assessing the age of San Esteban's archaeological remains is not an easy task. One problem is that much of the island's archaeology consists of isolated surface remains that lack cultural context. In cases where artifacts or features are found together, there is often no way to tell whether the apparent association between them is real. Moreover, many of the island's remains, such as clearings, rock clusters, and most of the stone tools, have little diagnostic value. This is true not only because most of them are very simple in form but also because the types they correspond with elsewhere are generally ones that endured over great spans of time.

It is possible that some of the habitation caves might have stratified deposits, and if so, excavation of these sites might help sort out time relationships. Unfortunately, the one cave site that was partially excavated by Elisa Villalpando and Arturo Oliveros failed to shed much light on chronology, for deposits proved shallow and artifacts scarce (Elisa Villalpando 1984:pers. comm.).

Despite these limitations, a few of the surface artifacts belong to chronologically sensitive types, radiocarbon samples have allowed certain features to be roughly dated, and there are several physical and stylistic cues that provide hints, at least, of the age of some of the remains. These indicators all suggest that the majority of the human occupation, though not necessarily all of it, took place in quite recent times.

The most direct chronological evidence consists of four radiocarbon dates. Surface samples of charcoal were collected at six features: three habitation caves (E10, I35, and I47), two stone circles (E19 and J11), and one summit enclosure (P5). Unfortunately, the samples from E10 and J11 proved to be undatable due to contamination by ^{14}C produced in the nuclear bomb tests of the 1950s. The other four samples produced the following results:

Feature	Obtained Age in Radiocarbon Years (1950 Baseline)	Corresponding Calendar Dates	Sample Number
I35 Habitation Cave	120 ± 60 yrs.	A.D. 1830 ± 60 yrs.	A4725
I47 Habitation Cave	110 ± 70 yrs.	A.D. 1840 ± 70 yrs.	A4723
E19 Stone Circle	80 ± 70 yrs.	A.D. 1870 ± 70 yrs.	A4724
P5 Summit Enclosure	160 ± 70 yrs.	A.D. 1790 ± 70 yrs.	A4712

These results, however, cannot be taken at face value. Calibration studies, in which precisely dated tree-ring specimens are also dated by radiocarbon analysis, have shown that the correlation between radiocarbon content and age is not neat and linear. Most obtained radiocarbon ages are in error by some amount and need to be adjusted with a correction factor in order to approximate the true age of the sample. The problem is particularly complicated for recent samples. During the past 400 years, the atmospheric ratio of ^{14}C to ^{12}C has fluctuated in such a way that charcoal samples of very different age can have precisely the same amount of radiocarbon (Stuiver and Pearson 1986). In practice, this means that a single charcoal specimen with a given radiocarbon content could actually date from any of several different times within this 400 year period and that there is no way to determine which of these times represents the true age of the sample. Thus while the radiocarbon content of the charcoal from I35 superficially implies a calendar date of A.D. 1830, it is equally consistent with six other dates that fall within the past 400 years. After calibrating these seven possible dates and factoring in the statistical error, all we can really say is that there is a 67% probability that the true date of the I35 sample falls either within the interval from A.D. 1673–1754 or the interval from A.D. 1796–1944.

The same considerations apply to the other three radiocarbon dates. Thus the calibrated ranges for the four datable samples (within 1 sigma) are:

I35: A.D. 1673–1754 and 1796–1944
I47: A.D. 1675–1748 and 1798–1943
E19: A.D. 1685–1737 and 1807–1931
P5: A.D. 1655–1890 and 1905–1955

Despite the small number of samples and their broad age ranges, taken together they are significant because they are consistent with each other. At the very least, they indicate that people were living in caves, making stone circles, and using summit enclosures on San Esteban Island sometime during the past 350 years.

Other remains on San Esteban are also indicative of a late occupation. One of these is pottery. Seri pottery originated, probably in pre-Hispanic times, as a hard and very thin ware named Tiburón Plain, and it eventually evolved into a softer and thicker form called Historic Seri. The timing of this transformation is not known precisely, but it was probably underway in the late eighteenth or early nineteenth century. There is little doubt that Historic Seri was the characteristic Seri pottery of the nineteenth century (Bowen 1976:53–68).

Dating specific features with pottery involves some uncertainty, because in many cases it is unclear whether sherds, usually few in number, are genuinely associated with the features or just part of the general artifact scatter. The most convincing associations are at three caves (B2, G4, and I47), two clearings (B4 and I55), a cluster of clearings with an enclosure (I2–I8), and a stone circle (I24). Each of these features or groups of features has at least 10 surface sherds, though in most cases they are probably from the breakage of just one or two vessels. The pottery observed at one of these clearings (I55) is exclusively Tiburón Plain, probably from a single pot. Two of the caves (G4 and I47) each produced two pieces of Tiburón Plain among a much larger quantity of Historic Seri pottery. For the rest of these features (B2, B4, I2–I8, and I24), the pottery is exclusively Historic Seri, suggesting a nineteenth-century occupation.

On a broader scale, the chronological picture provided by the pottery is very clear. On the Sonoran mainland and Tiburón Island, most sites contain large quantities of Tiburón Plain but comparatively little, if any, Historic Seri pottery (Bowen 1976:Tables 10–11). This is consistent with the historic record of a large Seri population in pre-Hispanic and Colonial times that was largely decimated during the nineteenth century, leaving relatively few people as the makers of Historic Seri pottery. But on San Esteban Island the ceramic situation is reversed. Only about 10 percent of the sherds we saw there can be considered Tiburón Plain, while all the rest is Historic Seri (although this includes a large number that are typologically intermediate). This high proportion of Historic Seri pottery would seem to place the main occupation of the island within a span of not much more than 100 years, probably between the late eighteenth and the late nineteenth centuries.

The two classifiable projectile points found at two of the caves (B5 and I47) are probably also comparatively late artifacts. Typologically similar concave-base triangular points are distributed widely throughout the western United States and northwestern Mexico, where they are known by a variety of regional type names. They generally date from late prehistoric to late historic times, and in some areas they were made well into the nineteenth century. Although we do not know whether the San Esteban specimens were made by Seris or how they got to the island, typology suggests they must have arrived there comparatively recently.

A few of the petroglyphs at G15 contain intrinsic hints of their age (apart from initials and other obviously modern and perhaps non-Seri figures). The now-missing representation of the schooner "*El Galeon*" could have been either Seri or Mexican, and it would probably have been carved during either the nineteenth or early twentieth century, when these vessels were active in the Gulf. It may be that the pendant "V" designs are nineteenth century figures since they mimic the incised rim decorations of Historic Seri pottery. Indeed, one might infer that all of the G15 petroglyphs are comparatively recent, simply because the soft rock in which they are inscribed is so prone to erosion and exfoliation that the life-span of rock surfaces at this site may not be very great. This may be even more true of pictographs, some of which were painted on the crumbly walls of caves eroded into old mudflows. Most of the painted figures at B2 have disappeared just since 1984, due to cave wall exfoliation. There is no trace of the *pinturas* that both Mexican fishermen and Seris say decorated the caves at *Icámajoj Zaaj*, even though it is said that some were produced by the Seris who visited the island around the turn of the century. Like petroglyphs, pictographs on surfaces this friable would probably have to be relatively recent to have been seen at all during the present century.

There are circumstantial reasons for thinking the pit ovens on San Esteban are relatively recent structures, but for three of them, there is also evidence in the form of associated firewood that was cut with a metal ax or machete. These are tools the Seris have used for many decades, but they may have been rare items before the latter part of the nineteenth century.

While these artifacts and features suggest a late occupation, our initial impression was that much of San Esteban's archaeology could be ancient because many of the island's artifacts and features closely resemble the early remains in the deserts surrounding the lower Colorado River. This includes nearly all of San Esteban's chipped-stone tool types—bifaces, end scrapers, spokeshaves, Levallois-like flakes, "pointed tools," and perhaps the discoidal cores and some of the choppers. It also includes some of the features, such as clearings, rock clusters and cairns, and rock alignments. Most of these artifacts and features made their initial appearance in the earliest stages of the lower Colorado sequence, termed the Malpais and San Dieguito industries by pioneering archaeologist Malcolm Rogers (Rogers 1939). Though widely acknowledged as early, the actual age of the Malpais and San Dieguito stages has long been a matter of controversy. Debate has intensified as a result of indirect evidence, presented by Julian Hayden and others, which suggests that the Malpais stage in the Sierra Pinacate region at the head of the Gulf, may have had its beginnings anywhere from 20,000 to as much as 70,000 years ago (Hayden 1976:286–87, 1982: 582, 1998:17, 27–29; McGuire 1982:160–64; Reid and Whittlesey 1997:119; see also Dolzani 1988).

But while these tool types and features may have made their initial appearance in the remote past (however early that may have been), many of them persisted more or less unchanged for huge spans of time, in some cases lasting into the historic period (Rogers 1939:18–19; McGuire 1982:161). The critical problem, then, is how to distinguish the truly ancient artifacts and features from those that are typologically similar but much more recent.

As on San Esteban, many of the stone tools in the lower Colorado River Basin and the Sierra Pinacate are isolated surface materials with no cultural context. In these regions, the traditional means of separating chronologically early tools from formally similar late ones has relied on several forms of chemical alteration or coating of artifact surfaces. One of these, characterized as "oxidation" of the surface minerals on artifact flake scars, has long been considered the mechanism by which new flake scars lose their "fresh" appearance. As recently exposed surface minerals oxidize, the scars become discolored and, given enough time, take on the same coloration and texture as the exterior cortex of the rock. For the basalt tools of the lower Colorado and Sierra Pinacate, a consistent and more or less linear relationship has been proposed between degree of oxidation and hence discoloration of the flake scars, and age of the artifact. In these regions, artifacts known to be late by typology or context bear little or no discoloration. Tools of the early San Dieguito industry are more heavily oxidized, while the oldest Malpais stage tools may exhibit flake scars that are oxidized (discolored) to the same degree as the original cortex (Rogers 1939:20; Hayden 1976:277–78).

Color change is also an important aspect of surface alteration on San Esteban's rocks, and it was the strong discoloration on some of the island's typologically early stone tools that initially led us to think that these might also be ancient implements. Much of San Esteban's lithic material, both waste flakes and tools, are made of local andesite, the same rock type that litters much of the island's surface. As undisturbed boulders and outcrops, this material ranges in color from beige to brilliant red-brown and gives the landscape its characteristic ruddy hue. But these colors are confined to the rock surface. Underneath the deeply colored cortex, the andesite is actually a medium to dark gray, and this means that a freshly struck flake will exhibit a gray scar. Indeed, andesite waste flakes on the island are often gray, except where they retain part of the original cortex. But many San Esteban lithic artifacts do not have the gray scars of fresh breakage. Flake scars can be found in all degrees of discoloration, ranging from fresh gray through light beige to the red-brown of undisturbed rock. Applying the Sierra Pinacate-lower Colorado model, this full range of oxidation would imply that people must have manufactured stone tools on San Esteban Island over a very long span of time. Those tools and waste flakes with scars that match the intense coloration of unbroken surface rock should be artifacts of the Malpais industry, and their age should be equivalent to Malpais tools of the Sierra Pinacate and lower Colorado desert.

On San Esteban, however, surface discoloration does not seem to proceed in the steady cumulative manner that has been postulated for the lower Colorado region. Whether this is due to differences in petrology, climate, persistent salt spray, or other factors is not known, but on San Esteban, it seems to be an erratic process that does not correlate in any consistent way with age. The most compelling evidence of this comes from waste flakes. In several locations, we saw clustered debitage that is almost certainly the product of single chipping events, yet these waste flakes may display nearly the full range of color, from the gray of fresh fracture to the deep red-brown of unbroken rock. More revealing still, we encountered a number of individual waste flakes on which discoloration varies over the length of a single scar. And agave knives, which we suspect for other reasons to be a late tool type, have flake scars ranging from natural gray to the red-brown of the unaltered cortex. Clearly, none of this could happen if oxidation were a gradual, orderly, and cumulative process. This in turn implies that color change is not a reliable indicator of age for stone artifacts on San Esteban, and that strongly discolored tools may not be particularly early. This is not to say that there are *no* chronologically early artifacts on San Esteban, for some may well be ancient. It simply means that at present we have no reliable way of distinguishing them from typologically similar late ones. As Rogers himself remarked long ago (Rogers 1939:18–19), in the absence of surface alteration or context, there is often no way to determine if specimens of some of these long-lived types are chronologically early or recent.

We also found that talus pits differ in the degree to which the exposed rocks have undergone color change. Some pits are relatively easy to spot from above because the previously buried talus blocks still retain their natural gray color, providing a measure of visual contrast with the red-brown of undisturbed talus. The exposed rocks of other pits are discolored to the same degree as the surrounding undisturbed rocks. Since it is clear that the discoloration rate of flake scars is unpredictable, there is not much reason to think that it is any more reliable as an indicator of the relative age of talus pits.

In the lower Colorado River Basin and surrounding areas, several other physical properties besides oxidation have been proposed, often contentiously, as indicators of age for both tools and features. These include the depth of embedment of tools and features in desert pavement and the accumulation of desert varnish (rock varnish), ground patina (a manganese-poor form of varnish), and caliche deposits on flake scars and the constituent rocks of features (Rogers 1939:19–20; Hayden 1976:275–80, 1982:581–82; Dorn 1991, 1994; see also Bierman et al. 1991; Beck et al. 1998; Dorn 1998; Malakoff 1998). On San Esteban, however, we see very little evidence of these processes, which indicates either that they do not operate to a significant degree on the island or else that there are few remains old enough to exhibit them. The lone exception is the series of rock clusters and alignments that comprise D12–D22. Some of the rocks in these features are moderately well embedded in the ground surface, and the undersides of some bear a well-developed buff-colored to orange patina which, in the lower Colorado region, may signal great age. Whether a patina-age relationship holds for San Esteban is something that needs to be established empirically, but since the features themselves are similar to Malpais structures, it is certainly possible that the D12–D22 figures are ancient.

Under certain conditions, lichens can be used to date archaeological features. In places were reliable growth curves can be established, lichenometry can often provide reasonably accurate chronometric time scales (Matthews 1994). Lichen growth rates, however, are highly sensitive to microenvironmental factors, which greatly reduces the prospect for lichenometric dating on an island as environmentally diverse as San Esteban. Even so, lichens can provide a rough suggestion of relative age for some of San Esteban's summit enclosures.

Because lichens grow on the north face of rocks, when rocks are moved by humans and reoriented with a different side to the north, established colonies should die and weather off while new ones form on the new north side. If so, the structures on Pico Rojo may be relatively old, for the lichens there seem to be confined to north faces of rocks that make up the structures and are more or less equivalent to the lichens on undisturbed local rocks. In contrast, some of the enclosures on *Icámajoj Zaaj* still have remnant patches of apparently living lichens on rock faces that no longer point north. Moreover, lichens at this site have not become well established on the new north faces of these rocks. While it is impossible to be sure that conditions for the death and weathering of old lichens, and establishment of new colonies are equivalent at the two sites, on the face of it, the structures on Pico Rojo should be older than those at *Icámajoj Zaaj*. How much older is impossible to tell, for if the radiocarbon date from P5 at Pico Rojo is reliable, the absolute ages of both sites may not be very great.

We also noted that a few features, primarily pit ovens and stone circles, have large shrubs or cacti growing in them. Since these plants could not have taken root until after the feature had been last used, we supposed that the present height of the plant might be a measure of its age, thereby providing a useful minimum time since the last use of the feature. Unfortunately, the growth rates of most of these plants are not known or are known to be more closely related to the sporadic availability of water than the simple passage of time. One of the most intriguing candidates, a 1 m high cardon in the center of an ash-laden circle (I43), turns out to be no more than about 40 years old (Raymond M. Turner 1987:pers. comm.). The botanical evidence suggests that few if any of the plants we saw growing in features took root before about 1900.

Despite the appearance of antiquity created by the strongly discolored flake scars of some typologically early stone tools, the predominant subjective impression imparted by San Esteban's archaeology is one of recency. This is particularly true of the island's structures. With the exception of pit ovens, most structures are neither eroded, filled in, overgrown, nor fallen. Thus the fragile piled-rock enclosures that stand on the summit of Pico Rojo remain in pristine condition. Cairns may look jumbled, but they are not collapsed structures. The rocks that make up stone circles generally rest on top of, but are not embedded in, the loose ashy soil underneath them, and they look as if they had just recently been placed there. Many clearings appear as though they had been freshly swept clean of rocks. In one area of D25, waste flakes are not dispersed but are still tightly clustered around a particular rock on which (presumably) a man sat as he chipped a tool. Certain habitation caves convey the impression that their occupants slipped away moments before we showed up, imparting a subjective sense of recency that borders on the surreal. And conversely, comparatively few features give the impression of age common to other regions with similar but demonstrably older structures. Subjective impressions are not evidence, of course, and there is no question that they can be totally misleading. But they are also hard to ignore completely. It is certainly possible that most of San Esteban's remains *look* recent because they *are* recent.

To summarize, it appears that the main occupation of the island, at least, was late. However, the evidence of chronology is both slender and spotty, for we have no empirical age determinations at all for the majority of the island's individual artifacts and features. Moreover, the remains that imply chronology, including the radiocarbon samples, come from the surface, and this can obviously create a bias toward recent material. At sites such as habitation caves, where cultural sequences might be revealed in stratified deposits, we know little of what lies below ground.

A few of the surface remains, though undated at present, offer hints of an older occupation. The most intriguing of these are features such as D12–D22, and perhaps some of the stone tools, which suggest the island might have an early component. But whatever ancient peoples there may have been, most of the human activity seems to be much more recent. An indigenous group, almost certainly Seri, was evidently making extensive use of San Esteban Island sometime within the past 350 years or so, and prior to the twentieth century.

VI.

Did the San Esteban People Really Exist?

The previous chapters have related what the modern Seris say about the San Esteban people, outlined what Europeans knew (or at least wrote) about San Esteban Island and its vicinity, and described the surface archaeology of the island. What must now be considered is whether this information is sufficient to determine whether the San Esteban people really existed, and if they did, why they seem to be completely missing from the European documentary record.

One way of approaching this issue is by posing four questions: 1) Are the Seri oral accounts credible as a source of historic information, 2) Does the island itself have sufficient resources to actually sustain a small human population, 3) Is the archaeological record more likely one of a resident group or merely of casual visitors, and 4) Are there plausible mechanisms by which a group living on San Esteban Island could have eluded the written record?

The first three questions are the subject of Chapter 16, and the fourth is addressed in Chapter 17. Having considered these questions, Chapter 18 suggests how the San Esteban people might have been related to the Seris as a whole.

SIXTEEN

Traditions, Resources, and Archaeology:
Could People Have Lived on San Esteban Island?

The Seri Oral Accounts as History

The question of whether oral traditions qualify as "history" is as old as anthropology itself (Fontana 1969:367). At the heart of the matter is whether nonliterate peoples are capable of preserving accurate information about themselves or others over long spans of time. This is a particularly thorny problem when native traditions are at odds with documentary accounts of the same events. In short, are oral accounts capable of telling us what "really happened"?

The early extreme views on the veracity of oral traditions, ranging from uncritical acceptance to hypercritical *a priori* rejections, have largely disappeared. Today, the issue takes a much more sophisticated form, but it continues to inspire theoretical interest and has generated a large literature. Here it may be useful to touch on a few points in order to provide some perspective on what the Seris say about the San Esteban people.

To begin with, one might ask whether the Seri accounts are likely to be deliberate fabrications. In part, answering this is a matter of determining whether the Seris might have ulterior motives in telling about the San Esteban people.

There are many reasons why native peoples may wish to fabricate or distort information they share with outsiders, and most of these have become enshrined in the anthropological literature as cautionary tales. Ironically, one of the most common motives for deceit stems from good personal relations between the questioner and the people with whom he or she is working, especially when the rationale behind the anthropologist's quest for information is not fully comprehended. Under such conditions, and guided by the best of intentions, people may try to please the visitor by telling him what they believe he or she wants to hear. In some cultures, the obligation to please the listener is institutionalized into a powerful code of etiquette and routinely takes precedence over communicating "the truth" as the people see it.

Motives for fabrication can also be more blatantly self-serving. Informants who are paid for information may manufacture material in order to prolong their employment. People have been known to make up stories to give meddlesome outsiders what they want to hear simply to get rid of them. And in one famous case, an entire Yąnomamö village conspired to manufacture kinship data that avoided revealing taboo information about deceased relatives, while simultaneously making anthropologist Napoleon Chagnon the butt of a five-month-long practical joke (Chagnon 1983:19–20).

The Seris have also been known occasionally to hoodwink inquisitive outsiders. Two such victims were writer-adventurers Dane and Mary Roberts Coolidge, whose book *The Last of the Seris* tells of the six weeks they spent with the Seris around the old Kino Bay Club in 1932. As late as the 1970s, Seris who still recalled the Coolidges' visit intimated that some individuals may have had considerable fun concocting misinformation for these visitors (Mary Beck Moser 1997:pers. comm.)

Though it is hard to be sure that the San Esteban accounts have not been fabricated for the benefit of non-Seris, the circumstances under which the information has been gathered makes this unlikely. The material has come from several different people, principally three men, but corroborated by others as well. Though details sometimes differ, there is general agreement on who the San Esteban people were and on the main features of their culture and history. Agreement among different sources is not an ironclad guarantee against conspiracy, as Chagnon discovered, and too much agreement should send up a red flag. But there is no obvious motive why the Seris would wish to manufacture or conceal information on this rather esoteric but benign subject.

Although Seris expect to be paid for information, it is improbable that the accounts of the San Esteban people have been fabricated to create or prolong employment. Were that the case, they could easily have invented much more bogus information than the limited knowledge they claim. Nor is there any indication that the accounts have been devised as a means of dealing with individuals who must be humored or have been pegged as gullible. Much of what the Seris know they have told to several different outsiders over a span of many years, and in some cases, the information has been given unsolicited. The most extensive body of data was collected not by casual visitors but by their own neighbors, linguists Edward and Mary Beck Moser who, at the time, were already long-term residents of the Seri community of El Desemboque and semi-fluent speakers of the Seri language (see Appendix A). While this in itself does not insure reliable data (Vansina 1985:113), most of the Seris with whom the Mosers have worked over the years have understood the importance of accuracy in their linguistic work, and it is unlikely that these same people would switch gears and practice deceit in relating oral traditions. The fact that a few Seris have been identified as unreliable sources helps validate the reliability of others.

As to the crucial boyhood reminiscences of Porfirio Díaz, these recollections are unique, and there is, consequently, no means of cross-checking them. But so far as is known, Díaz had no ulterior motives in telling about the San Esteban people, and some of what he recorded on tape was information other Seris have known for many years. One person who was long familiar with much of what Díaz knew about these people was Roberto Herrera, the Mosers' principal linguistic coworker for more than three decades, a man of established integrity and astuteness, and their close friend. To the extent of his knowledge, Herrera generally confirmed what Díaz had to say, and it is unlikely that he would have remained silent had he believed that Díaz was manufacturing data for the benefit of the tape recorder.

If we assume that the accounts of the San Esteban people have not been made up from scratch, then the next important question is whether they are accurate records of these people and their culture. The answer to this hinges largely on the reliability of what Porfirio Díaz said about them, since he is the source of so much of the information. Because Díaz's knowledge purportedly came from his experience among them as a child, this becomes a question of the reliability of eyewitness testimony and the childhood reminiscences of elderly people.

This is a difficult issue, not only in the Seri case, but for any historical event. Ultimately all history, written or oral, is based on eyewitness accounts and peoples' memories. On the one hand, first-hand accounts of what people have directly experienced are the very best sources of information because they are the most direct link to the events themselves. On the other hand, in some important ways, they are inherently unreliable. Jan Vansina has summarized the problem:

> Eyewitness accounts are supposedly the fountainhead of all history....
>
> [But even in] the best of circumstances, even the best of witnesses never give a movielike account of what happened, as all accounts of accidents show. Eyewitness accounts are always a personal experience ... and involve not only perception, but also emotions. Witnesses often are also not idle standers-by, but participants in the events. Furthermore, an understanding of what happened cannot occur through mere data of perception. Perceptions must be organized in a coherent whole and the logic of the situation supplies missing pieces of the observation....
>
> ... To sum up: mediation of perception by memory and emotional state shapes an account. Memory typically selects certain features from the successive perceptions and interprets them according to expectation, previous knowledge, or the logic of "what must have happened," and fills the gaps in perception. (Vansina 1985:4–5)

When eyewitness testimony takes the form of reminiscences from childhood, as was the case with Porfirio Díaz's recollections, other distorting factors may come into play:

> Reminiscences are bits of life history. Everyone holds such reminiscences. They are essential to a notion of personality and identity. They are the image of oneself one cares to transmit to others. Reminiscences are then not constituted by random collections of memories, but are part of an organized

whole of memories that tend to project a consistent image of the narrator and, in many cases, a justification of his or her life....

Here we see the full power of memory at work. Events and situations are forgotten when irrelevant or inconvenient. Others are retained and reordered, reshaped or correctly remembered according to the part they play in the creation of this mental self-portrait....

... Childhood memories should portray objects or people as larger than actual size, and the meaning attributed to childhood memories should correspond to the understanding of a child of that age in that culture and in that situation. (Vansina 1985:8–9)

The list of factors that can influence the faithfulness with which a person's experience is communicated to a listener is a long one. For elderly speakers, childhood reminiscences can be distorted by the cognitive dysfunctions that often accompany aging. Probably all people modify the content of the message according to what things they or their audience consider interesting, and both content and tone may vary depending on the effect the speaker wishes to have on his audience. There may be culturally-defined forms of delivery and rules of etiquette that shape the message, and content may depend upon how messages function in social context. And of course momentary factors, such as whether the speaker is feeling well, can alter the message. These are factors that potentially affect the reliability of *all* eyewitness testimony, and they are often difficult to take into account or control. And yet despite these problems, in most cases there must be a large measure of accuracy in eyewitness accounts:

Thus from the very first step, valid for all messages, oral or written, the hypercritical analyst can already deny validity to an eyewitness account. In strictest theory such an analyst would be correct. In practice, as we know from daily experience, he is wrong. For if our observations and their interpretation were so uncertain, we could not function at all. We would not remember nor efficiently act on remembrance for the situation we find ourselves daily involved in. (Vansina 1985:5)

For the Seris, there have never been any systematic studies of the conventions that govern how people tell of their experiences, and we know little of the specific factors that might have influenced Díaz's memory or how he portrayed the San Esteban people. When his recollections were recorded on tape, there was apparently nothing to indicate to either the North Americans or the other Seris present that there might be anomalies in what he said or how he said it. In the absence of corroborating information, there is little we can do but take Díaz's recollections at face value, assume that Díaz was probably about as reliable as most elderly people reminiscing about their childhood, and recognize that any such testimony is subject to many potential sources of error.

Although much of what is known comes from the recollections of Porfirio Díaz, some of the events associated with the San Esteban people took place before Díaz was born. Knowledge of these events is not the reminiscences of anybody recently living, but has been passed down through generational levels by word of mouth as true oral traditions. It includes the various ideas about the origin of the San Esteban people, the story about the death of *Cöimáxp*, the account of the people who emigrated to Baja California, and the tale of the men who went to Baja California to raid. Some incidents, most notably the round-up and extinction of the San Esteban people, are comparatively recent but were not witnessed by anybody still living. Other traditions, particularly the origin traditions, deal with events that must be much older. These accounts raise fundamental questions about whether people like the Seris can accurately preserve information over spans longer than a lifetime, in the absence of writing.

As with eyewitness testimony and personal reminiscences, there are many mechanisms that can result in omissions and distortions in narratives that are passed down through the generations (Vansina 1985:17–24). And yet, there are many cases in which it has been possible to directly compare traditions with documentary records, and these show that many societies are quite capable of preserving information with substantial accuracy over long periods. This is not to say that native and documentary sources will portray an event in the same way, for their perspectives are often dramatically different. Nor is there necessarily agreement on every detail, especially when different versions are recounted by different individuals. But there is no question that many native traditions are legitimate accounts of events that happened a long time ago. A Cherokee tradition known as the "Tsali tale" describes the well-documented round-up of a group of Indians by the U.S. Army in 1838, and a clearly valid account of the incident (but from the Cherokee perspective) was collected in 1961, 123 years after the event (Kutsche 1963). Similarly, a Makah tradition that describes the kidnapping of several men in 1810 by a passing ship was recorded from four different people 130 years later (Blinman et al. 1977). In Canada, the well-documented destruction of an Abenaki village in 1759 by English troops was recounted in considerable detail by an elderly Abenaki woman in 1959, exactly 200 years after the incident (Day 1972). Four Hopi versions of the 1680 Pueblo Rebellion, recorded between 1902 and 1967 (hence between 220 and 287 years after the fact), still preserved a detailed record not only of the events themselves but also of causes and motives (Wiget 1982). These and other examples indicate that many peoples are capable of preserving reliable information via oral tradition to a depth of at least two long lifetimes after the events, while genealogies may be accurate to 500 years or so. And under certain circumstances, oral traditions may do a better job of preserving information accurately than written sources (Sturtevant 1966:29–31; Vansina 1985:189, 192–93).

There are three cases in which it has been possible to compare Seri traditions with written accounts. One of these is the 1904 military campaign to Tiburón Island (Moser 1988). The Mexican version was written by a participant, Federico García y Alva, shortly after the expedition concluded. A Seri version was recounted by Roberto Herrera in 1973, 69 years after the event. Herrera's great-grandfather had been killed in the conflict, and Herrera learned about the campaign from his paternal grandfather. The Mexican and Seri versions of events correspond on many points, but the Seri tradition has a much narrower perspective, probably because the Indians were unaware of the total scope of the expedition (Moser 1988:471). Most striking is the difference in tone of the two accounts. In the Mexican version, the campaign has the air of a sporting event, while the Seri tradition understandably depicts it in much more tragic terms.

The events surrounding the 1858 burning and sinking of the ship *John Elliot Thayer* off Patos Island are also known from both documentary and Seri accounts (see pp. 122–24). In this case, a Seri version was related by Roberto Herrera 107 years after the fact. As with the 1904 campaign, the accounts correspond closely on major points but are very different in perspective, reflecting clear and predictable cultural differences in what the two groups considered important and memorable. The North American accounts are directed primarily toward the aftermath of the event and especially in establishing legal responsibility for the loss. The Seri version focuses on the ship's activities while at Patos, in which the Seris themselves were important participants. Obviously, the Seris would neither have known about nor been interested in the legal issues after the ship sank and the sailors left.

The capture of the Mexican girl Lola Casanova, which took place in 1850, is known from both Mexican and Seri oral traditions as well as from official documents written at the time of the incident (see pp. 237–39). In this case, the Seri traditions were recorded in 1964, 114 years after the fact. The sources of the Seri traditions are Roberto Herrera and Jesús Morales (Lowell 1970), both of whom were also important sources of information about the San Esteban people. Although there are unresolved discrepancies among the Seri, Mexican, and documentary versions of the Casanova story, Edith Lowell concluded that the:

> Seri oral tradition appears to reflect historical events more accurately and completely in this instance than does the better known Mexican version which has been influenced by romantic literature. (Lowell 1970:158)

This is not to say that Seri traditions are flawless journalistic records, or that they are free error and exaggeration. For example, the tradition that describes the extinction of the San Esteban people may combine elements of two quite separate military campaigns (see Note 93). But based on many cases involving a variety of subject matter, Felger and Moser (1985:108, 171) have found that the Seris are generally able to tell about historic events to a depth of 120 years or so with good accuracy. Because Edward and Mary Beck Moser began recording Seri traditions in the 1950s, accurate data may be available for some events that took place as early as the 1830s. Thus the evidence from many societies, including the Seris themselves, suggest that reliable information can reasonably be expected in the traditions about the San Esteban people, extending at least as far back as the early decades of the nineteenth century.

But to take this issue one step further, the fact is that many societies have oral traditions that do not correspond with their documentary counterparts, and some narratives may not make much logical sense to Euro-American audiences. This casts the question of whether oral traditions can be depended upon as sources of historical "truth" in a somewhat different light. Put another way, in these instances, are oral traditions failing to tell us what "really" happened?

First, it is important to be clear about whose "historical truth" we are concerned with. Probably all peoples distinguish stories they regard as factual or "true" from others which they acknowledge to be imaginative or fictional. But while the general categories of fact and fiction may be more or less universal, the criteria on which people assign events to one category or the other can differ markedly and lead to very different views of what is historically valid. What is believable as historical "truth" in one culture may not be at all credible in another:

> Western historians and Navajo historians do not agree on what is important and what is not. Western historians, and especially the archaeologists, believe that Navajos migrated into the Southwest from the Great Plains several hundred years ago. Some Navajos believe just as firmly that they emerged *in situ* from underground, and that any talk of recent migrations from the Plains is nonsense. Archaeologists say they are right; Navajos say they are right. The anthropologist might argue that each is right in terms of the rules of his own game. (Fontana 1969:370)

Here, Fontana rightly frames the issue in terms of cultural relativism by recognizing that each culture defines historical truth in a way that is consistent with its own world view, which itself is not subject to empirical testing. Native views have often been termed "folk histories" in order to distinguish them from their Euro-American counterparts. To anthropologists who study folk histories, the question of what "really happened" is often irrelevant, for the important thing is to understand truth as the people themselves define it (Hudson 1966:53–56, 64–66; Fontana 1969:369–70; Fogelson 1989:134–35). What the Seris say about the San Esteban people, as recorded in Chapter 1, is folk history (or folk ethnography) in this sense. And there seems to be no doubt that the Seris consider what Porfirio Díaz recalled and the traditions that accompany his reminiscences to be factual accounts, not merely imaginative stories.

But even attempting to understand how historic truth is conceived in folk histories is by no means a straightforward matter. Among other things, most traditional societies, if not all, divide the historic past into two or more broad epochs (Hudson 1966:56–61; Vansina 1985:23–24, 176–77). One of these usually encompasses the recent past that includes specifically remembered events and people still recalled as individuals. The other epoch is much more remote and consists of personages and events far removed from the memory of living people. Although this epoch is usually thought of as chronologically remote and preceding the other in time, in some world views (notably the "Dreamtime" of Australian societies) it persists into the present as a shadowy realm that exists alongside the recent epoch. What is important is that societies usually apply different standards to what kinds of things are considered to be "factual" or "true" in these different realms. Often the remote epoch is characterized by marvelous beings and events which are accepted as entirely credible, though they would be dismissed as fictional or impossible were they claimed to be part of the recent epoch. As Charles Hudson (1966:61) has pointed out, this kind of inconsistent treatment of the past has had an important counterpart in Western culture. Until the mid-nineteenth century, when the new concepts of uniformitarianism and evolution enabled people to conceive of a scientifically accessible past of almost infinite duration, most Euro-American historians and scientists accepted the literal truth of miraculous events, so long as they occurred in the realm of "Biblical times" and not "historic times."

The Seris divide the past into at least two epochs. One is the familiar realm of the recent past in which specific people and events are recalled in individual terms. It is the epoch that includes the events that have been directly compared with documentary sources, and as noted above, it has a time depth of at least 120 years.

The Seris also recognize a more distant epoch. It was during this period that the Seris first appeared as a people, but it is known primarily as the time of the Giants, called *Xica Coosyatoj* 'Things Singers.' These huge beings have demonstrably been a part of Seri oral tradition for a long time, for Father Adamo Gilg wrote about them in 1692 (Gilg [1692] 1965:50). It is said that the Giants inhabited coastal Sonora and Tiburón Island, as well as the peninsula of Baja California and that they continued to live in the Midriff region for a while after the Seris appeared on the scene. The Seris have numerous traditions that recount the exploits of these beings, and they are able to describe many aspects of Giant culture (Griffen 1959:19). As it turns out, much of Giants' culture, and even their speech, is fundamentally Seri. Certain material items ascribed to the Giants that are unknown in contemporary Seri culture are known archaeologically, from historic documents, and in some cases are actually remembered by elderly people if the right questions are asked. What this suggests is that the remote epoch, the domain of the Giants, serves as a kind of long-term memory bank for outmoded aspects of Seri culture and events no longer of current interest. Although the Seris maintain that the Giants were not Seris, ascribing things to the Giants nevertheless seems to be a metaphorical way of referring to aspects of their own past, and sometimes a past that is not very distant in time (Moser and White 1968:146–47; Bowen 1976:106–8; Sheridan 1996:188).

Though there are no giant beings today, the Seris seem to find no difficulty in conceptualizing the Giants as fully corporeal and very "real" figures. Like their enormous size, many of their abilities and exploits were superhuman. Thus they sometimes wore strings of large perforated grinding stones across their chests as body armor, and they had no need for balsas because they were able to wade the Gulf between Baja California and Sonora. In this more remote realm of the Giants, the Seris are evidently willing to allow as "true" things that they would not accept as credible in the recent past of living memory.

Seri accounts of the San Esteban people tie firmly into the Giants traditions on one very important dimension. This is language. Giants' speech and that of the San Esteban people are known today from only a few fragments, but in both cases the words recalled are simply archaic forms of Seri language. Both dialects were apparently characterized by sharp pitch contours which the Seris perceive as "musical," and today they refer to both San Esteban and Giant speech as "singing talk" (Bowen 1976:106). To the Seris, the connection may be logical because the San Esteban people, like the Giants, are viewed as anachronisms from the past. It is said that they were the original Seri inhabitants of Tiburón Island and that they maintained their "backward" and "primitive" ways right up to the time of their demise. From a linguistic perspective, it is also reasonable that a small group living in isolation might have retained an archaic dialect of Seri language. This has happened elsewhere, as in some of the isolated Hispanic communities of northern New Mexico, where certain old forms of Spanish are still spoken.

There could be a more general connection between the Giants and the San Esteban people in the consistent portrayal of the latter in terms that are just a bit larger than life. Compared with ordinary Seris, they seem to be physically larger, stronger, possessed of greater endurance, better as swimmers, balsa paddlers and turtle hunters, fiercer as fighters, more reckless as gamblers, and generally wilder and crazier. Thus it is possible that they are just enough removed, both chronologically and conceptually, from living Seris that they are beginning to slip over the boundary from the category of recent past into the more remote epoch of the Giants, where things take on inflated proportions.

On the other hand, it is possible that this oversized characterization is merely the exaggerated perspective of a child—the young Porfirio Díaz—trying to comprehend the very large world of adults. And it is certainly not inconceivable that the San Esteban people really *were* an intimidating bunch by any Seri standards. But apart from language and perhaps the exaggerated scale of the people, the Seris today seem to place the San Esteban people primarily, if not wholly, within the recent epoch of well-remembered individuals and events. And by all indications, they consider the accounts of these people to be historically "true" by the same criteria they apply to events that fall within living memory.

But even if the accounts are "true" by Seri standards, there remains the question of whether they are also credible in terms of the canons of Euro-American historiography. Because native traditions are generally written down and published by Euro-American researchers for Euro-American audiences, this is usually the implicit meaning behind the question of whether they are "historically valid." It is also a reasonable question if one's goal is to integrate native traditions into a broader Euro-American historical context.

On the simplest level, the credibility of the San Esteban accounts must be judged by whether they are plausible in terms of the kinds of beings, events, and relationships that a Euro-American world view permits. From this perspective, it is clear that the accounts do contain a few elements, such as certain shamanistic powers, that would likely be dismissed as incredible. But apart from a few specifics and the slightly larger-than-life portrayal of the people, probably little of what is said about the San Esteban people violates basic Euro-American criteria for plausibility.

But to say that the accounts are plausible or "could have happened" is still an important step short of saying that they are an authentic record of what "really did happen," as defined in Euro-American terms. The favored way of authenticating native traditions is, of course, by comparing them to documentary sources. Here we come full circle. While the documents that form the basis of Euro-American history are sometimes accorded near-sacred status, they are, after all, ultimately nothing more than eyewitness accounts, reminiscences, and hearsay written down, and many of the factors that distort unwritten accounts apply equally to those that are eventually put to paper (Fontana 1969:367; Vansina 1985:6). Thus oral accounts that do not neatly fit into a documentary context are not thereby proven false. Indeed, in the best of circumstances, discrepancies between documentary and oral history can actually be an asset, for they may offer complementary perspectives, each supplying detail the other leaves out. By so doing, they may provide a richer view of the past than either can yield by itself.

But for the San Esteban accounts, the traditional Euro-American idea of validation by comparison with documentary sources is a moot issue, since no written record of the San Esteban people has yet been discovered. In order to assess the historical "truth" of these accounts in Euro-American terms, we must look to other kinds of information entirely.

The Habitability of San Esteban Island

The San Esteban people could not have existed as they are described unless the island itself had sufficient resources to support a small population. The two critical resources would have been food and water. Without these commodities in adequate supply, the island would not have been habitable, and the accounts of the people could not possibly be "true" according to Euro-American historical standards.

One might suppose that the documentary record, which includes a number of statements by Europeans about the habitability of San Esteban and other Midriff islands, would be an important source of evidence. Taken at face value, European comments provide a bleak picture, for they generally proclaim these islands uninhabited or uninhabitable. However, context sometimes makes it clear that what these statements seem to say so unambiguously to a modern reader is not what their authors meant to convey. A prime example is a 1729 letter written by Father Nicolás de Perera, which contains a detailed description of Tiburón Island. Perera spoke fluent Seri, and he had learned quite a bit about the island from conversations with a mission Indian who had originally lived there. When he wrote the letter, he had just returned from the Sonoran coast as part of a military expedition that had persuaded 151 Seris, who lived on Tiburón Island, to relocate in the mainland missions. This expedition gave Perera not only a firsthand view of Tiburón from across the channel, but also enabled him to find out more about the island from the Seris who had just come from there. Yet despite all this, in his letter Perera declared Tiburón Island "uninhabitable":

> The island is about thirty leagues in length, as we saw from a red hill on the shore of the sea nearest to it. The terrain is not only rugged by nature but uninhabitable. All that one can see on it are mountains and hills without a single plain. The report the island Seris gave us proved that this is true. They say it is extremely barren, without any piece of ground that could be cultivated. There is only some grass among the cliffs, which barely supports mule deer, jackrabbits, and squirrels. That is the only game they have to eat....
>
> Along with the lack of food is the lack of water. On the whole island, which as I have told Your Reverence, is made up of two rancherías, there are only two water holes. They are so small that when I asked the Seris if the canoes could be supplied with water from the island, they replied that if three barrels were taken, no water would be left.... I consider this to be quite true, because what the islanders say agrees with what the Indian [from Tiburón] in the pueblo told me before. (Perera [1729] 1999:128–29)

This letter illustrates three problems with European assessments of habitability. One is that when Europeans declared terrain to be "uninhabitable," they often tacitly meant uninhabitable by "civilized people" (*gente de razón*), that is, settled Europeans who required an agricultural subsistence base. Nomadic "wild" Indians who were able to subsist by foraging, such as the Seris, were not "people" in the same sense, and consequently did not figure into their assessments. Secondly, it shows that the testimony of Indians, even when corroborated, could be a poor basis for judgment. As Thomas Sheridan has pointed out (Sheridan 1999:128–29n44), the Seris were shrewd enough to deliberately underrepresent the resources of Tiburón Island, knowing that doing so would help protect it from European invasion. And thirdly, Perera's letter illustrates a common tendency among Europeans to consider observation of the Midriff islands from afar as sufficient basis for judging their habitability. Thus despite the frequent air of authority, documentary sources that pronounce San Esteban or other Midriff islands as "uninhabitable" may not be reliable assessments.

For any of the Midriff islands, food resources are obviously a major factor in determining their habitability. Particularly for San Esteban, the key to evaluating food resources lies in recognizing that they consist not only of terrestrial plants and animals but also the resources of the sea. Because of the abundance of the latter, people trying to live on San Esteban probably would seldom have found lack of food a serious problem. Drawing on both Seri oral accounts of the San Esteban people and direct observation, Felger and Moser (1985:92) conclude that the island's plant food resources numbered about 25 species:

> The San Esteban century plant (*Agave cerulata dentiens*) was unquestionably their most important food plant. It is abundant on the island, and unlike other species of century plant, edible plants can be obtained at any time of the year.

Other important food plants on the island are *cardón* (*Pachycereus*), ironwood (*Olneya*), and *pitaya* [*pitahaya*] *agria* (*Stenocereus gummosus*). *Pitaya agria* is particularly abundant. Dense stands of *Amaranthus watsonii* may occur at any season of the year. (Felger and Moser 1985:98)

Plant foods, however, were not always dependable:

During a period of fifteen years we observed several years in which there were no protein-yielding plant crops available on San Esteban Island or the adjacent south shore of Tiburón Island. We concluded that these people [the San Esteban people] sustained themselves primarily with animal-derived foods, and that during the frequent extended droughts virtually their entire source of protein and lipid was derived from animals. (Felger and Moser 1985:98)

But this was not likely a problem. While some protein and lipid was available from chuckwallas, much more could be derived from sea animals, primarily sea lions, sea birds, fish, and sea turtles, all of which were available in large numbers. Given the extent and variety of the entire spectrum of food resources, Felger and Moser conclude that "The San Esteban people obtained a rich supply of food from the land and sea" (Felger and Moser 1985:98).

The other critical resource, fresh water, is another matter. Regardless of the abundance of food resources, an inadequate water supply would have made the island uninhabitable, and that would settle the question of whether there ever was a resident population. But determining whether sufficient water existed is neither a simple nor straightforward task. In fact, one could legitimately turn the question around and argue that to establish that a population *did* live on the island would be *de facto* proof that the island possessed enough drinking water, regardless of how scarce fresh water appears today. Gerhard and Gulick have done just that for historically documented Monserrate Island, off the Baja California coast, about 220 miles southeast of San Esteban. Though waterless today, "At one time Monserrate must have had fresh water, as it was inhabited by Indians as late as 1717" (Gerhard and Gulick 1962:207).

The problem of fresh water can be approached from several perspectives. In the first place, to say that people "lived on San Esteban" does not necessarily mean that they spent every day of every year there. Secondly, thorough exploration of the island may reveal a greater potential water supply than is immediately apparent. Thirdly, people can obtain water indirectly from plant and animal sources, and the quantities can be substantial. Fourthly, it is possible that the total water requirements of some populations are not as great as the customary intake of Europeans. And finally, the apparent scarcity of fresh water on San Esteban Island today may not be indicative of its availability in the past. Each of these factors needs to be evaluated in turn.

The answer to the first point is very clear, for the Seri oral accounts state explicitly that the San Esteban people did not spend all their time on the island. The accounts indicate that San Esteban was only marginally habitable due to a water supply that was neither large nor dependable over the long term. When the supply failed, the people were forced to abandon San Esteban for the southwest coast of Tiburón Island. What the accounts do not specify is how frequently this occurred and how long they would be away. Nor do the accounts indicate whether water failure on San Esteban was a sporadic occurrence or a predictable event that took place each year during the dry season.

To say that the people "abandoned" San Esteban, however, overstates the significance of these shifts in residence. The Seris maintain that the southwest coast of Tiburón was also a place that "belonged to" the San Esteban people and, hence, was part of their territory. For most nonagricultural peoples, frequent movement within a traditional territory has been the standard response to normal fluctuations in supplies of food, water, and other resources, and the movements of the San Esteban people between San Esteban and Tiburón can be seen as simply an example of this widespread pattern. All Seris moved around a great deal, and there is nothing inconsistent in the Seri view of San Esteban Island as the "home" of the San Esteban people, the place they "were from," and the idea that they might have spent considerable time elsewhere. How much time they spent on Tiburón is not known, but it is obvious that a population that made only part-time demands on San Esteban's water supply could have gotten by on a smaller total water output over the course of a year.

But annual output is only part of the problem. For a people to have resided on the island even for part of the year, water must have been available in sufficient quantity to sustain the population over some minimal period of time. Only five water sources are mentioned by the present Seris, and four of these are now known only by tradition. Judging from now-vague descriptions, it is not clear whether these sources could have supported very many people for very long. The one purportedly permanent source, a spring near the southwestern corner of the island, has largely, if not completely, dried up. In the 1960s, Richard Felger and Alexander Russell were able to coax only a slight flow from this spring, and our attempts to find water there in the 1980s met with no success at all.

Yet the true picture may not be entirely bleak. As Aschmann notes (1967:61) for nearby Baja California, even springs with low output were able to support a comparatively large number of Cochimí Indians. Moreover, in the course of archaeological survey, we encountered many potential water sources in the form of tinajas, or bedrock pools, that are fed by runoff. We recorded around 15 of the largest and most convincing of these, most of which have clearly defined water stains. We made note of about an equal number of others that are either less certain to hold water or are too small to have been of great importance. Some of the well-defined tinajas seem to have benefited from intentional enlargement or modification of upstream channels that would direct runoff into the pool more efficiently, both of which were common Seri practices (Felger and Moser 1985:84–85). A few are partly or completely shaded, which would greatly reduce the rate of surface evaporation.

Assessing just how useful these water sources might have been to humans is more difficult. None of our fieldwork was conducted during the main rainy season, so we did not actually see water in any of the most convincing tinajas and therefore cannot be completely certain they hold water. All of the pools are irregular in shape and most are partly filled with debris, making their capacity hard to measure. It is also difficult to gauge how leakage through cracks and porous rock would affect their ability to store water for long periods. Considerable loss must also come from evaporation, even in winter, when nearly continuous winds sweep over the island. During a typical sunny but windy January, in 1984, we watched about 15 gallons of water that had accumulated in a shallow unshaded pothole disappear in the space of a week.

Yet the potential of these waterholes is clear. One of the largest is a totally shaded bedrock pool on the north side of the island (Figure 16.1). Although it lacks a well-defined water stain, its capacity must be at least 500 gallons. If we assume that it does fill to the top and discount loss through evaporation and seepage, this tinaja could sustain a population of 100 people, each consuming two quarts a day, for about 10 days. Nearby, there are at least four smaller probable tinajas, which altogether would give this small portion of the island a potential storage capacity of around 1500 gallons. Making the same assumptions, these five waterholes could supply 100 people with two quarts of water a day for about four weeks. And if rains periodically refilled them before they were completely emptied, it is possible that they alone could have supplied the water needs of a small population for several consecutive months.

There are clearly a great many assumptions here. But even so, our observations suggest that there is probably more fresh water on San Esteban, at least at some times of the year, than there appears to be at first glance.

In gauging the habitability of a place, Europeans often fail to realize that fresh water is not the only substance that can satisfy human fluid requirements. Liquids derived from plants, and even animals, can be used to supplement a scarce water supply, and peoples in arid environments have often relied extensively on such measures. For Seris on the mainland and Tiburón Island, the barrel cactus (*Ferocactus wislizeni*) has frequently served as an alternative source of liquid, sometimes for long periods. In one remembered instance, in the spring of 1928, it is said that about 10 families who were camped a long way from a waterhole subsisted for an entire month on liquid from the trunk of the barrel cactus (Felger and Moser 1985:85, 264; see also Davis 1929:125). The fruit of certain cacti also provides a seasonally available liquid. Although the Seris tend to think of cactus fruit more as a food than a fluid source, the juice has clearly been a valued component. For Seris on the mainland and Tiburón Island, the most important fruits were those of the organ pipe (*pitahaya dulce*) cactus (*Stenocereus thurberi*). In the old days, the fruit was harvested mainly so its juice could be fermented into wine. It was also used as emergency liquid. In an incident that took place about 1900, a group of Seris fleeing from enemy attack kept a newborn infant alive for about eight days with juice from the fruit of the organ pipe (Felger and Moser 1985:260, 245–47).

There is no information about whether the San Esteban people utilized liquid from cactus fruit as a water substitute, but it would clearly have been an

Figure 16.1 Well-shaded probable tinaja about 1 km inland from Playa La Freidera, north side of San Esteban. Rocks above the pool appear to be artificially arranged to channel runoff. At the time of the photograph the pool was dry and filled with sediment. April 1980.

option. Although there is no barrel cactus on San Esteban Island and relatively little organ pipe, liquid could have been obtained from the *pitahaya agria* (*Stenocereus gummosus*) and cardon (*Pachycereus pringlei*). Both plants grow in abundance on San Esteban as well as elsewhere in Seri territory, and the Seris say that their fruits were heavily exploited in the past, often for making wine from the juice. More recently, James Hills has heard Seris say on several occasions that one does not need water in places like San Lorenzo Island when *pitahaya agria* fruit is available. On Tiburón Island, he has seen people during the heat of September refuse water for a day or so, preferring to obtain fluids from organ pipe fruit (James Hills 1983:pers. comm.). Across the Gulf, the eighteenth century Cochimí were able to go for several days without water when pitahaya fruit was in season (Baegert [1772] 1952:23), and people relying on pitahayas for fluids could travel to waterless places that otherwise could not be visited at all (Aschmann 1967:59).

The reported use of liquid from agave leaves as a water substitute is more problematical. The Seris say that this toxic liquid could be made marginally potable by roasting the leaves before extracting it. They recall at least one incident around the turn of the century when several men stranded on San Esteban in the summer heat survived four or five days on the juice of roasted agave leaves, though they feared that it might soon kill a small boy who was with them (see pp. 262–63). It may be that some degree of tolerance of this liquid is acquired, for the eighteenth century Jesuit and Franciscan missionaries wrote that the Cochimí of Baja California were routinely able to consume agave juice in place of water for periods of several days, and occasionally as long as two weeks (Aschmann 1967:60). Padre Linck remarks that the Europeans did not have the same ability: "Our Indian friends chew a maguey-like leaf and can do without water for two or three days—a feat we were unable to match!" (Burrus 1967:38).

It could be that some species of agave from Baja California are less toxic than the San Esteban plant, which might account for missionary reports of Indians in some parts of the peninsula surviving months or even years on agave juice. But many of the more modest claims involved Cochimís who would likely have utilized *Agave cerulata cerulata*, a peninsular subspecies closely related to the San Esteban agave *A. cerulata* subsp. *dentiens*, whose leaf fluid would likely be similar in potability (Gentry 1978:42, 44).

Sea turtles provided an emergency liquid for the Seris. The blood and body fluids drained from a large turtle were left to stand for several hours, allowing the hemoglobin to settle out. The resulting clear serum could then be consumed in lieu of water. However, sea turtle serum is far from ideal as a water substitute. Though less saline than sea water, it still has appreciable salt content, and the proteins it contains probably require water to metabolize. Consequently, while it may have gotten people through emergency situations, it was not a substance that could be ingested for very long (Richard Felger 1983:pers. comm.; Felger and Moser 1985:85–86; Bert A. Tribbey 1989:pers. comm.). Still, one wonders whether the San Esteban people might have made more frequent use of sea turtle blood than other Seri groups. The oral accounts maintain that even though these people were expert turtle hunters, they disdained the meat, raising at least a remote possibility that they hunted sea turtles more for their liquid than for their flesh.

The San Esteban people are said to have subsisted heavily on fish and other sea foods. Although the Seris make no mention of fish blood, spinal fluid, or the fluid contained in fish tissues as sources of potable liquid, one might speculate that these substances could conceivably have played some role. However, opinion on whether these fluids are even capable of serving as water substitutes has been sharply divided. One proponent of fish flesh as a source of liquid, the French physician Alain Bombard, maintains that many common species contain between 70 and 80 percent water. To demonstrate the value of this resource, Bombard made a 65-day solo crossing of the Atlantic living entirely off the sea, and for 43 of those days he derived his entire fluid intake from fish flesh (Bombard 1953:24–25, 212–13).

Bombard's claims have been seriously questioned, in some cases on the grounds that fish fluids contain enough proteins that the water content would be completely used up metabolizing them (Anonymous 1969:3–6; Anonymous 1985e:281). Although this objection may fail to distinguish the liquid in muscle tissue from the protein-laden blood and spinal fluid, other critics have noted that one cannot turn fish flesh into water merely by eating it, for this would result in a high protein intake that would unquestionably require water to metabolize. The alternative, separating the liquid, is not a simple task. Even for Bombard to make this work, the liquid had to be extracted from the flesh with a mechanical press, and he needed six to seven pounds of fish per day to fulfill his fluid needs. For the San Esteban people, catching this much fish may not have been a problem, but it is not clear how they might have extracted the liquid content other than the free fluids.

More contentious still is the question of whether sea water could have been used by the San Esteban people either as an occasional substitute for fresh water or to extend a limited supply. Among physiologists, there seems to be universal agreement that drinking sea water exclusively and in quantity will result in death from kidney failure within a few days. The literature of shipwrecks and air crashes at sea is replete with grisly accounts of people who tried to drink sea water to assuage a raging thirst, only to suffer increased dehydration, delirium, and death. But there is less consensus on whether this is the inevitable outcome if sea water is ingested in limited quantities under specific conditions. In fact, there is a small body of anecdotal literature that indicates no damage or even some benefits from limited and well-controlled consumption of sea water.

This too is a position that has been championed by Alain Bombard, who calculated that one could get by for about five or six days drinking only sea water, provided the quantity was strictly limited, and provided this regimen was begun before becoming dehydrated (Bombard 1953:25). For 14 days during his solo crossing of the Atlantic, Bombard consumed no liquid other than sea water. During an earlier experiment in the Mediterranean, he and a companion spent six consecutive days drinking only sea water, with no serious discomfort or apparent ill-effects (Bombard 1953:93, 212–13). Other incidents are also suggestive. The crew of a military aircraft that ditched in the Pacific in 1942 ingested large quantities of sea water when their plane sank. Probably because they were well hydrated at the time, they suffered no ill-effects, even though they had no fresh water for the next five days (Trumbull 1943:53). In some cases, the salt in sea water may actually prove beneficial. The crew of the *Kon-Tiki* expedition found that the only way they could successfully quench their thirst was by cutting their drinking water with 20 to 40 percent sea water (Heyerdahl 1968:101). Others on planned voyages have discovered that they could cook with sea water, either undiluted or mixed with fresh water (Lee and Lee 1980:149–51).

Whether sea water can be consumed safely under any circumstances seems to be an emotionally-charged issue. Many commentators reject Bombard's claims as untrustworthy and dismiss other anecdotal evidence as a seriously misleading guide for anybody who might actually be faced with the prospect of drinking sea water. This is probably wise policy, since most people confronted with such a dilemma would be castaways in desperate straits, and even Bombard concurs that sea water is quickly lethal if not ingested with great care under controlled conditions. Hence most military and civilian survival manuals have taken the position that almost any consumption of sea water is dangerous and should be meticulously avoided (Anonymous 1956:135; Anonymous 1969:3–6; Anderson 1978:147; Lee and Lee 1980:120; Craighead and Craighead 1984: 276; Anonymous 1985e:280–81).

Whether the San Esteban people ever used sea water to extend a limited supply of fresh water is purely a matter of speculation, for there is no mention of such a practice in the Seri oral accounts. What we do know, however, is that they did drink sea water in a more esoteric context. In the San Esteban version of the vision quest, a man would set out alone in his balsa for four days and nights, and during this time, he would drink a mixture of sea water and iron-wood bark. It is said that this concoction made him slightly drunk and that sea animals would appear and come to him. This in turn raises the more general question of whether the wild and crazy behavior that the Seris today attribute to the San Esteban people might have been related to ingestion of sea water. The appearance of sea animals to San Esteban vision seekers is consistent with the hallucinations and delirium experienced by shipwreck victims who try to quench their thirst with sea water. Bert Tribbey (1989:pers. comm.) has noted that if the San Esteban people ingested sea water on a frequent basis, their bodies might have rapidly accumulated dissolved heavy metals such as lead and mercury, and that these substances in turn might have triggered erratic mood swings and behavioral changes. Of course, it could be that their wild behavior was caused by nothing more exotic than cactus fruit wine. It is said that the wine made from the *pitahaya agria*, which is abundant on San Esteban, was especially powerful (Felger and Moser 1985:247).

To summarize, cactus fruit could have played a major role in extending a meager water supply for the San Esteban people. But sea water, fish fluids, sea turtle blood, and agave juice are more problematical. While they all might have served occasionally as emergency water substitutes, it is doubtful that these substances would have made a fundamental difference in the habitability of San Esteban Island.

Looking at the problem from a different perspective, one might ask whether some unusual physiological or behavioral characteristics might have enabled the San Esteban people to function with an abnormally low intake of fluids. Modern Seris have certainly impressed many outsiders with their ability to forego liquids. Charles Sheldon, who hunted with Seris on Tiburón Island in 1921, suffered through a very thirsty night at a dry camp while his companions seemed not to mind at all. These Seris told Sheldon that they were quite capable of going waterless for two days with little discomfort (Sheldon 1979:119, 140). More recently, James Hills, who has made several trips into the Gulf with Seri friends, has been amazed at how little water they drink, especially compared with North Americans. In the extreme heat of summer, when Hills has had to consume huge quantities of water, Seri companions have often been satisfied by an occasional sip of a heavily-sugared soft drink. In his experience, the Seris seem to have very few worries about water (James Hills 1983:pers. comm.).

Anecdotes such as these certainly show that modern Seris, and probably the San Esteban people before them, have been able to get by on a low fluid intake, at least in the short term. It may be that low intake is compensated in part by low fluid loss from the body. This in turn could be the result of many factors, ranging from life-long acclimatization to heat and drought to straightforward behavioral and cultural practices that conserve body fluids. It may also indicate that the Seris are more willing to tolerate the discomfort of thirst than are most North Americans. But whatever specific factors enable the Seris to forego liquids in the short term, if a water deficit is incurred it must eventually be made up, and it is doubtful that basic Seri metabolic requirements for fluids are significantly less than those of other populations. If the Seris have been able to get by with less water intake over the long run than some other groups, it is probably due much less to underlying physiological mechanisms than to conservation measures. Even such obvious practices as minimizing physical exertion and seeking shade during the heat of the day can greatly reduce water loss from the body, which would reduce the need for fluids and help extend a scant water supply. Whether such measures might have made a significant difference to people trying to live on San Esteban Island is impossible to estimate.

Perhaps the most important factor to bear in mind in judging the habitability of San Esteban is that the island's condition today may not be indicative of what it was like a century or two ago. Climate and hydrology change over time, and it is possible that the island was a much wetter place when the San Esteban people purportedly lived there. In arid environments, even a small absolute increase in rainfall constitutes a large percentage gain, and the effect on both the surface and subterranean water supply may be exponential (Richard S. Felger 1986:pers. comm.). The output of existing springs may increase markedly, and water may appear in places that were formerly dry. Some of the more dramatic effects may occur in bedrock pools fed by runoff. Because they are often supplied by many converging channels, a slight increase in rainfall spread over a large catchment area can amplify the volume of water reaching the pool manyfold.

Assessing past rainfall on San Esteban is nearly impossible because no climatic records have ever been kept on the island. The only way this factor can be addressed is to extrapolate from rather distant regional data. Moreover, even where records have been kept, instrumented data seldom cover much more than the past hundred years, and rainfall for earlier periods must be reconstructed from tree-ring data. Thus records that extend much beyond the past century are available only in places that have climate-sensitive trees.

The closest regions for which long-term rainfall data are available are southern California and Arizona, some 250 miles or more north of San Esteban (Meko et al. 1980; Meko and Graybill 1995). The records of both places are complex and do not lend themselves to easy generalizations. Although there have been many fluctuations between wet times and droughts throughout the past 300 years, these records do suggest two things. One is that rainfall tended to be relatively high during the second half of the nineteenth century. The other is that the second half of the twentieth century, based on data so far, may be the driest half century since A.D. 1700 (Meko et al. 1980:599; Turner 1990:474–75; Meko and Graybill 1995:614–15).

Whether these general climatic conditions apply to San Esteban Island in particular is anybody's guess. They do reinforce the testimony of the modern Seris, who say that early in the twentieth century water was more or less permanently available from the now-dead spring at the southwestern corner of the island. They also suggest that recent assessments of San Esteban's habitability have been made during an unusually dry period and hence may not accurately reflect the availability of water during the time the San Esteban people were purportedly living there.

James Hills (1983:pers. comm.) has astutely observed that North Americans who have little ability to find desert water sources, no knowledge of water substitutes, and are unaware of the Seri capacity to make do with very little water, may greatly underestimate the habitability of places like San Esteban Island. Especially if it were wetter in the past, the island might not have been nearly as inhospitable to the San Esteban people as it appears today from a Euro-American perspective. And most importantly, the San Esteban people would never have been limited solely to the water resources of that island, for they always had the option of paddling to Tiburón Island, where water was available permanently and in quantity.

Visitors or Residents?

Even if San Esteban had resources sufficient to support a small band of people, that in itself is not proof that anyone actually lived there. The archaeological record, as described in Chapters 13–15, clearly shows that people utilized the island. The radiocarbon samples, projectile points, and pottery all indicate that much of this took place fairly recently, and the pottery suggests that these people were Seris. But were they residents or merely visitors? Is the archaeology consistent with a small but semi-permanent population that used the island as its home base, congregating there whenever there was enough water to do so? Or does it indicate a pattern of recurring visits of limited scope by people who came from, and returned to, somewhere else?

We may approach this question by considering the possibility that the island's archaeology is the result of short-term visits. We do not know exactly what form such trips might have taken, and there is little doubt that different kinds of visits might have created different patterns of material remains. But certainly one realistic model would be based on the visits we know actually did take place. These are the turn-of-the-century trips to San Esteban made by Seris coming from Tiburón Island (and later from Bahía Kino). Until recently, the specifics of some of these ventures were still within the memory of living people (see Chapter 11).

From what the Seris today recall, these trips must not have taken place often. Probably they did not go to San Esteban more than once a year, and it appears that several years might pass with no trips at all. One reason people did not go more frequently was that these trips were considered major undertakings, and there was always risk involved in crossing the channel. Most expeditions that did go to San Esteban were small-scale affairs. They may never have consisted of more than a dozen people or so, and the number of participants seems more often to have been half a dozen or fewer. Most of the time only men would go, although on at least some occasions women and children went along as well. Normally, voyages were made in the spring, but at least one summer trip (which nearly ended in tragedy) is recalled.

When people arrived at San Esteban they always camped at *Pajíi* (El Monumento), on the south end of Playa Limantour (Map 1.1). Even if adverse winds forced them to make landfall and camp initially on the northeastern corner, they would soon move on to *Pajíi*. They would often collect chuckwallas and iguanas to eat while they were there, but during remembered trips they always brought their own drinking water. Although the reason for making the trip in the first place was to exploit San Esteban's special resources, only a few items were actually sought. These were primarily agave, chuckwallas, iguanas, and birds' eggs. Sometimes people would also collect mineral pigments. Most of these resources were available near the shore and close to camp, though to find the best agave the visitors had to walk a mile and a half or so up Arroyo Limantour. Often this is where they baked the agave hearts as well. But people say that they did not wander much farther afield than this and that they always returned to their shore camp at night to sleep. As a result, they made use of only a small portion of the island. The supply of water they had brought and the weather usually set limits to the length of the trip, which rarely, if ever, lasted more than a few days.

Trips such as these would have left only limited archaeological material and on only a small slice of the island. One might expect to find evidence of the main camp, possibly some hint of the alternate camp, and perhaps some indication of agave collecting. In fact, the main evidence we have of these known visits are pit ovens for baking agave, which occur only in lower Arroyo Limantour, precisely where the Seris say they concentrated most of their activity (Figure 16.2). Three of these pits are associated with firewood that was cut with a metal ax or machete. It is possible that some material remains at the northeastern corner of the island are from the alternate Seri camp. There is no evidence whatever of Seri visits at *Pajíi*, for storms and several generations of Mexican fishermen camping in the same spot have obliterated whatever traces there might have been.

Clearly, trips conforming to this pattern could not possibly have produced the full archaeological record we see on the island today. Even if carried out over hundreds of years, ventures of this sort would not have resulted in either the variety or the island-wide distributions of San Esteban's features and artifacts. It is, of course, possible that Seri expeditions of the more remote past were not as narrow in scope and that they once made greater use of the island when they came to visit. Perhaps the Seris' present knowledge of the entire San Esteban

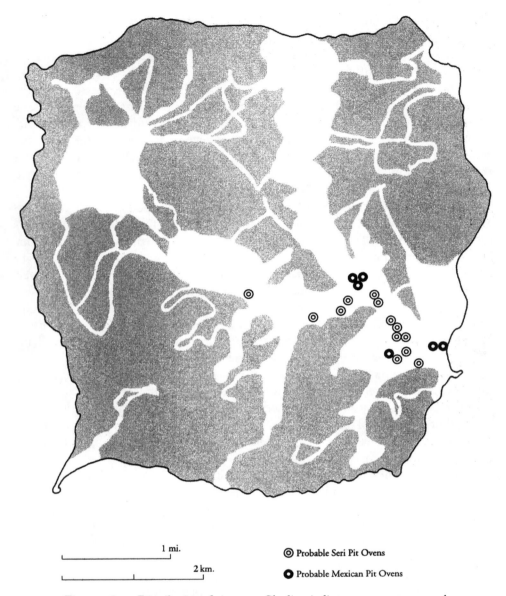

1 mi.

2 km.

◎ Probable Seri Pit Ovens

● Probable Mexican Pit Ovens

Figure 16.2   Distribution of pit ovens. Shading indicates areas not surveyed.

coastline and their names for its features originated from earlier, more wide-ranging expeditions. Such trips might also explain their vague recollection of waterholes said to lie in the interior of the island.

But in order to account for the archaeology visible today, these hypothetical earlier visits must have been vastly different kinds of enterprises than those known historically. They must have been large and broadly-based expeditions that enabled the participants to range all over the landscape, utilizing the interior as much as the coasts, and generating the thin but widespread scatter of artifacts and ecofacts that pervades the island. And these visitors must have come with agendas totally unlike the limited motives of the turn-of-the-century Seris. Their demand for agave hearts must have been prodigious, for the wide dispersal of agave knives indicates that they must have scoured the entire island for suitable plants, including steep slopes and high mountain ridges. They must have cooked the hearts wherever they collected them, often a long way from shore, and by a now-forgotten surface roasting process, thereby producing the broad distribution of charcoal-laden stone circles (Figure 16.3). They must have camped all over the island, including remote ridges and high mountains, to account for the more than 50 recorded sleeping clearings and the dozens of possible faint ones that we did not record (Figure 16.4). Moreover, they must have stayed for long periods or used some of these clearings time and time again in order to have generated the accompanying domestic trash, especially well-worn metates and manos. These visitors must not have shared the modern Seri disdain for occupying caves, for they presumably would have been the people who produced the occupational refuse at the 13 habitation caves recorded throughout the island (Figure 16.4). And some of these expeditions must have encouraged more esoteric pursuits than are recalled today, for some of the visitors must have climbed the island's highest peaks and constructed the many rock wall enclosures and rock-pile cairns that adorn their summits.

Material remains this varied and widely distributed can be expected of a resident population, but they are a lot to ask of visitors who came to San Esteban only for short stays. It is no doubt possible to construct scenarios of expeditions that might have produced all these remains, given sufficiently large parties coming to the island often enough, staying long enough, and behaving very differently from recent Seri visitors. But one must ask at what point expanding the parameters of hypothetical visits to an extent that would adequately account for the archaeology becomes just another way of describing a small and mobile, but resident population, that sometimes shuttled back and forth to the southwest coast of Tiburón Island.

There is one class of artifact that provides both direct and compelling evidence that a small population did indeed reside on San Esteban. These artifacts are metates. We found 29 of these implements, nearly all of them at caves or clearings, the places where people camped. Some occur at sites along the shore, where true visitors such as the twentieth century Seris have stayed, but the majority, 21 of them, were found at camps in the interior. San Esteban metates are made exclusively of indigenous andesite, ruling out any possibility that they

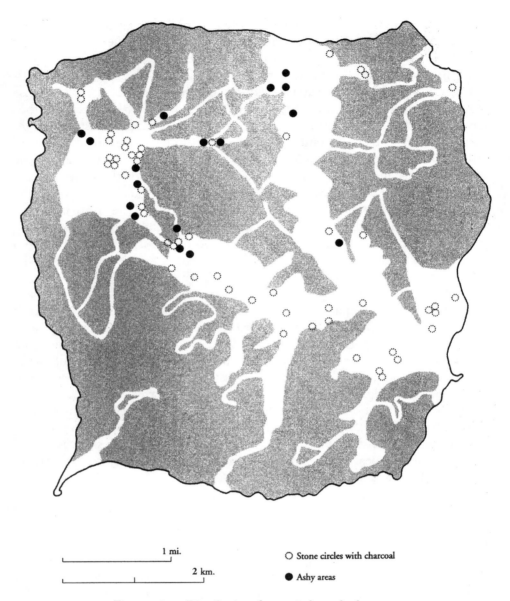

○ Stone circles with charcoal

● Ashy areas

*Figure 16.3   Distribution of stone circles and ashy areas.
Shading indicates areas not surveyed.*

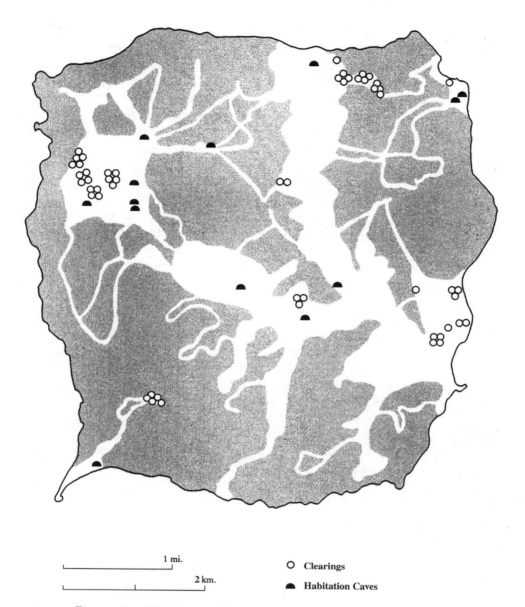

Figure 16.4 *Distribution of living sites: Habitation caves and clearings.*
Most of the clearings are located above and behind the sea cliffs, in the interior of the island.
Shading indicates areas not surveyed.

might have been brought to the island from somewhere else (in fact, three are metate surfaces on deeply embedded boulders or bedrock). This means that all the grinding on these tools must have taken place entirely on San Esteban. And for many of the metates, this was a lot of grinding, because about two-thirds of the specimens we recorded have working surfaces that can only be described as heavily worn. One specimen has a basin that has been ground to a depth of 1 cm and the basin of another metate is about half that deep. How much grinding it took to produce the heavy wear on these implements is difficult to estimate, but the time involved could not have been trivial, for San Esteban andesite is fairly hard rock. Well-worn metates of hard rock are not likely to be the legacy of people who merely visited the island.

During the 1970s, metates could still be found in Seri households in the mainland community of El Desemboque, and some of these showed wear comparable to the well-worn San Esteban specimens. Though no longer in regular use, their owners recalled that the wear on these implements was the result of many years of continual service. Because these modern metates are made of granitic rock, they are not strictly equivalent to the andesite metates of San Esteban. But since both granite and andesite are resistant materials, the modern Seri specimens suggest that the extensive wear on the San Esteban metates was also the product of many years of regular use.

One might speculate that the heavy wear on the San Esteban metates was produced by a constantly changing stream of temporary visitors coming to the island over many generations, each reusing the same few implements. If so, it would be contrary to Seri custom. In the remembered past, metates have always been the personal property of individual women, and the owner has generally been the only person who used her metate(s). In fact, when a woman died, her metate was often buried with her. Although recent Seris have sometimes been willing to recycle metates found at old camps, even reclaimed metates became permanent property and did not subsequently change hands. Thus it seems more plausible that each of the well-worn San Esteban metates represents the continuous work of one woman during the course of a single lifetime.

And the wear on these implements was almost certainly produced by women. The Seris consider food processing with the metate to be women's work, as it is more or less universally. If need be, Seri men are not averse to taking over many tasks customarily performed by women, but apparently this does not extend as far as using metates. Seri women who were asked about this in 1984 uniformly laughed at the idea of men using metates, no matter what the circumstances, and said that men do not know how to grind. Seri men said that it is just not something a man would do, even in a place like San Esteban (Mary Beck Moser 1984:pers. comm.). Thus to attribute the well-used San Esteban metates to visitors and remain consistent with Seri culture, one would have to propose an enormous number of visits to produce the extensive wear and assume that women were regular members of these expeditions. While both conditions are certainly possible in principle, it is far simpler to suppose that San Esteban has well-worn metates because women, as well as men, lived there.

SEVENTEEN

Eluding the Written Record:
A People Without a History

If the Seri oral accounts are plausible sources of historic information, if San Esteban Island was once habitable, and if the archaeology of the island is consistent with people living there, then the remaining question is why we seem to have no written accounts of these people. Or stated more precisely, are there credible explanations for how a small population living on San Esteban Island could have eluded the documentary record? In fact, there are many mechanisms that might have made these people virtually invisible to European record-keepers. Though Seris on the mainland were all too familiar, Seris on the islands were not, and we may begin by reviewing briefly what the Europeans knew, or at least wrote, about the islands they believed the Seris utilized.

Marcos de Niza may have heard rumors of island-dwelling Indians when he passed through Sonora in 1539, but the real discovery of island Seris should probably be credited to Juan de Iturbe, who personally saw them on Tiburón Island in 1615. The second contact likely occurred in 1636 during Francisco de Ortega's probable visit to Tiburón. Though both men wrote of their encounters, their observations probably had little impact since their reports were not public documents. The first published notice appeared in 1645, when Father Andrés Pérez de Ribas stated that Seris inhabited an (unnamed) island in the Gulf of California. Over the next 300 years the conventional wisdom that there were Seris living on an island was repeated by nearly everyone who wrote about them. Though not all writers identified the island by name, most did, and if there has been any universal belief about the Seris, it has been that they were the people who lived on Tiburón Island.

Writers have been less unanimous about whether Seris made use of any other Midriff islands. A few, such as Lieut. Hardy ([1829] 1977:437) and the French traveler Duflot de Mofras ([1844] 1937:110), opined that they lived only on Tiburón. From the end of the seventeenth century onward, however, a number of Europeans stated or implied that Seri activity was not limited strictly to

Tiburón. Most frequently, these are nonspecific statements that the Seris utilize "islands" in the Gulf (e.g., Venegas [1759] 1966b:47, 48). For such vague statements, it is impossible to guess which particular island or islands other than Tiburón the writer had in mind, or precisely what the Seris did there. In many of these cases, the writer's acquaintance with the Seris and Midriff geography was only by hearsay and so tenuous that reference to plural "islands" probably has no real significance.

Eighteenth century writers occasionally did refer to a second Seri island by name, and this name was almost always San Juan Bautista Island. Since there is no island known by this name today, its identity has puzzled a few later commentators. WJ McGee (1898:75, 78) speculated that it might be San Esteban, as did the annotators of a recent edition of Father Nentvig's *Rudo Ensayo* (Nentvig [1764] 1980:78). In both cases, the speculations were probably prompted by ethnographic knowledge of recent Seri visits to San Esteban. The San Juan Bautista Island that Nentvig and his contemporaries had in mind was almost certainly not San Esteban, but Alcatraz (or Pelican) Island, a small islet that the Seris have known well. It lies less than two miles from mainland Sonora in the middle of the body of water known today as Bahía Kino, but which was referred to in the eighteenth century as Bahía de San Juan Bautista. Though the name of this island was familiar to many early writers, few had any real knowledge of what or where it was. Father Nentvig erroneously depicted it as equivalent in size to Tiburón Island. He also placed it nine leagues (23 miles) southeast of Tiburón Island and two leagues (5 miles) from the coast, nowhere near its real location (Nentvig [1764] 1980:78; map). Father Francisco Alegre, in describing how Seris escaped from soldiers in 1761 by paddling to San Juan Bautista Island, gave for its location the approximate position of San Pedro Mártir Island (Alegre [ca. 1780s] 1960:441). While it is certainly possible that the Seris sometimes went to San Pedro Mártir, it is more likely that Father Alegre, who had never set foot in Sonora, got the island's name right but its location wrong.

Connections in the historic record, even tenuous, between the Seris and San Esteban Island are rare. One writer, Matias de la Mota Padilla, stated explicitly in 1742 that the Seris inhabited San Esteban. But it is hard to give this assertion much credence since he also claimed that they lived on five other islands (two of them unrecognizable) as well as in Bahía de la Concepción in Baja California (Bancroft 1874:604–5; Cook de Leonard 1953:19). There are, however, some clues that a few Jesuits suspected that the Seris occasionally made use of San Esteban. The earliest hint comes from Father Adamo Gilg, who had personally visited the Seri coast in Sonora. In his 1692 letter, he refers to Tiburón Island as "the Seri island" (Gilg [1692] 1965:50) and "the big island SERA" (Gilg [1692] 1965:45). But Gilg twice mentions Seri "islands" (Gilg [1692] 1965:41), and he ponders whether there could be Seris living on other Gulf islands (Gilg [1692] 1965:48). Gilg's map, drawn from personal observation, shows with considerable accuracy just two islands, and these are unquestionably Tiburón and San Esteban (Gilg [1692] 1965:41, map).

Nine years later, Father Juan María de Sonora reiterated the contemporary belief that Seris were capable of crossing the Gulf, and he implied that they did so by way of San Esteban and San Lorenzo Islands. But he makes no mention of any island being inhabited by Seris other than Tiburón (McGee 1898:67). The most convincing, if indirect, written indication that Seris at least visited San Esteban is Father Salvatierra's 1710 statement that mainland Seris had told him of water on San Esteban. Though Salvatierra did not believe them, the only way the Indians could have known this is if some Seris had actually been to the island.

Two comments indicate that by the turn of the nineteenth century, some Europeans suspected that Seris might be using San Esteban as a refuge to escape military pursuit. As part of a 1798 plan to invade Tiburón, Pedro de Nava warned that canoes should be stationed on the west side of Tiburón to intercept Indians fleeing to the islands farther west. In 1802, Governor Arrillaga speculated that this invasion plan, though never carried out, had prompted the Seris to reconnoiter the islands west of Tiburón as potential retreats and as staging areas for attacks on the peninsula. A year later, he noted that Seris could utilize all the Midriff islands at will, even though some had no water. During the 1850 invasion of Tiburón, Col. Cayetano Navarro wrote of sending troops to block Seris from escaping to the "Island of the West," presumably San Esteban. Shortly before the end of the century, Seri visits to San Esteban were confirmed by documents describing the 1890 armed clash with Mexicans from the sloop *Playa Colorada*, and by WJ McGee's ethnographic inquiries (McGee 1898:49, 220).

Thus the written record indicates that between the late seventeenth century and the end of the nineteenth, Europeans gradually became aware that Seris made occasional use of San Esteban. But so far as the record is presently known, there is no evidence whatever that Europeans thought that any Seris lived there (Sheridan 1999:10). This returns us to the question of whether there are reasonable mechanisms that might have excluded the San Esteban people from the documentary record.

Perhaps the most basic answer lies in the fact that for some 300 years, few Europeans ever sailed as far north as the Midriff islands. Until the middle of the nineteenth century, most travel in the Gulf was associated with pearl fishing, the Jesuit missionization of Baja California, and to a lesser extent trade. In the first hundred years after Ulloa's epic 1539 voyage, only about half a dozen expeditions are known to have sailed as high as the Midriff. Most of these were exploratory voyages in search of pearls, and they firmly established that the best prospects for pearl hunting were in the southern half of the Gulf. Consequently, during the pearl fishing boom that followed, nearly all of the activity was concentrated well south of the Midriff region. This must have been almost as true for illegal pearlers as for licensed expeditions. While illegal pearlers might have had good reason to avoid the main centers of activity and search for more remote oyster beds, they could not have operated for long in regions where there were no pearl oysters. Only briefly was there any productive pearling in the Midriff, in the 1720s along the Sonoran coast north of Tiburón Island and on the peninsular coast opposite the Midriff in the 1740s. People working these regions undoubtedly scrutinized the Midriff islands, including San Esteban, but they could not have found many pearls or it would quickly have become public knowledge, and the islands would have been overrun with pearl seekers.

Similarly, the Jesuits and their staff made countless Gulf crossings in support of the Baja California mission chain, but nearly all of these voyages took place far south of the Midriff. Supplies generally left the mainland from ports in Sinaloa and southern Sonora, and less frequently from the Río Yaqui and Guaymas. The initial peninsular destination was always Loreto, and from there goods would be redistributed to the outlying missions, either by land or by sea. Only for about 15 years, after San Borja was founded in 1752, did the Jesuits move supplies through the Midriff, often in simple canoes, and there is every reason to assume that the sailors making these supply runs hugged the peninsular coast, putting San Lorenzo Island between themselves and San Esteban. For a while after the Franciscans and Dominicans took over, supplies were intermittently sent northward along this maritime route, but there is no indication that these voyages strayed far from shore.

Trade in the Gulf did not begin to assume much significance until the early nineteenth century. Even then it was confined almost exclusively to the southern Gulf, for there were no coastal settlements north of Mulegé and Guaymas. Perhaps the most graphic illustration of the range of European navigation in the Gulf prior to the mid-nineteenth century is an 1825 Mexican government map of the Gulf. This map shows considerable detail up to the Midriff, but only an outline beyond (Figure 9.1).

Until the mid-1800s, there were not only no real incentives to sail into the Midriff, but there were also very good reasons to stay out of the area, for navigation there could be exceedingly dangerous. The Gulf as a whole was often a difficult sea for early sailors to negotiate. Contrary winds could prevent ships from ever leaving port for weeks on end or blow them far off course. At other times, ships were stranded by prolonged calms. Voyages that required only a day or two under fair conditions would sometimes take weeks when the weather turned. Sudden storms of extraordinary violence made the Gulf not only a difficult, but sometimes a terrifying place, especially for early sailors whose vessels were often poorly constructed and totally inadequate to withstand the fury of these tempests. Shipwrecks, with loss of life and property, were commonplace. The Jesuits, who had some of the worst boats but kept the best records, lost an average of about one vessel a year to shipwreck during their early years on the peninsula, and over their 70 year tenure they wrecked or wore out about 20 transport vessels (Chapman 1920:51; Dunne 1968:370). Their experiences with storms, shipwrecks, and concomitant lost supplies and drowned men, as recounted by such contemporaries as Venegas ([1759] 1966a) and Clavigero ([1789] 1971), are powerful tales of terror and tragedy, even allowing for the customary exaggeration of the day. But if the Gulf in general was sometimes perilous, the Midriff could be worse. Here, even in mild weather, powerful currents, cross-currents, and countercurrents, coupled with unpredictable shifting winds, could make sailing ships as helpless as floating corks. Vessels sometimes found themselves hopelessly trapped by the currents, unable to leave the region for days or even weeks at a time. Conditions were worst in the vicinity of Tiburón, San Esteban, and San Lorenzo Islands, and for this reason, by the mid-seventeenth century, they became known as the "Salsipuedes" (Get-Out-If-You-Can) Islands. And as Father Ugarte found out in 1721, when storms hit this region their fury could be almost unbelievable.

There were undoubtedly voyages into the Midriff of which we have no knowledge. But the known records suggest that until the nineteenth century, decades often passed without a single European expedition to the upper Gulf. According to W. Michael Mathes (1992b:xiv), even Baja California, the main destination of early navigators, was reached only 17 times between the first sighting in 1533 and the Jesuit entrada in 1697. A standard coast pilot of the Colonial period, published in 1734, contains navigational data for the entire world, including the Pacific coast of the peninsula, but does not even mention the Gulf (González Cabrera Bueno [1734] 1970). Few observers mean few opportunities to observe any people who might have been on San Esteban. Of the known Colonial period navigators who did sail as far as the Midriff, some never went anywhere near San Esteban, while others simply passed it by. Others still, caught by storms or currents, were preoccupied simply with saving their ships and their lives. Those who did mention the island left only the barest of commentary. Francisco de Ulloa, who discovered San Esteban in 1539, merely assumed the island was uninhabited. Father Salvatierra, passing by it in 1709, noted its rugged appearance, possible ore-bearing rocks, and could not imagine that it had any water. Father Ugarte and William Stratford thought they saw shells on its shore in 1721, and Manuel Correa briefly noted its size and appearance after sailing around the island in 1750. Similarly, Lieut. Hardy commented only on the island's size, appearance, and abundance of sea lions during his 1826 visit.

Soon after the war between Mexico and the United States, European navigators became regular and frequent visitors to the Upper Gulf. Physical conditions in the Midriff were, of course, unaltered, and from time to time ships and lives were still lost. But by the 1850s, vastly improved sailing vessels, nautical skills, and especially the accumulated knowledge of local conditions had made the Gulf, and the Midriff, a fundamentally less hazardous place. The advent of steamships freed some navigators from the grip of its formidable currents and winds, if not from the peril of its furious storms. Most importantly, there were now powerful incentives to sail into the upper Gulf. One was the need to supply Ft. Yuma by sea, and between 1850 and 1877, this alone resulted in nearly 300 round trip voyages through the Midriff to the very head of the Gulf. At the same time, the upper Gulf region was undergoing a vast economic transformation. Industrial-scale guano mining brought men, supply ships, and cargo vessels to some of the Midriff islands on regular schedules. Promoters embarked on grand development and colonization schemes, which generated government and private surveys of the region. Economic activity on both sides of the upper Gulf prompted the opening of San Felipe and Libertad as commercial ports, and steamships and small coasting vessels began to bring goods and passengers to the region. Sea lion hunters and egg collectors began to exploit the islands. The political chaos that plagued northwestern Mexico occasionally brought warships to the Midriff. And even the beginnings of scientific study of the Gulf brought people into the region. In short, from about 1850 until the purported extinction of the San Esteban people late in the century, a large volume of traffic passed through the Midriff.

Many of these vessels must have sailed past San Esteban. It is doubtful that many sailors tried to run the treacherous shallows of the Canal del Infiernillo, between Tiburón Island and the Sonoran mainland. Some may have traversed the channel between San Lorenzo Island and the coast of Baja California, out of sight of San Esteban. The only other options would have been the channels on either side of San Esteban. Both were used, and the few available records suggest that the channel between San Esteban and Tiburón, the most direct path from Guaymas to the upper Gulf, was the major shipping lane. Assuming this to be the case, why then do we apparently have no reports of people on San Esteban?

One reason is that sometimes there may not have been anyone there to be seen. According to the Seri accounts, during times when the water supply ran out, the San Esteban people took to their balsas and paddled over to the southwest coast of Tiburón Island, where they stayed until the rains came and refilled the waterholes on San Esteban. We do not know whether these relocations took place every year, nor whether their stays on Tiburón lasted for days, weeks, or months. As Richard Felger (1980:pers. comm.) has speculated, it is possible that the San Esteban people actually spent more time on Tiburón Island than on San Esteban. Certainly any Europeans cruising the San Esteban coastline or going ashore during one of these dry periods would not have seen any people there. This could be one reason Lieut. Hardy, whose shore visit in early August 1826 may have coincided with the height of the dry season, saw no one. The fact that both 1874 and 1875 were intense drought years (Thomson 1989:33) may also explain why surveyors from the U.S.S. *Narragansett*, who steamed around the island in late March of 1875 after a year of little rainfall, saw no sign of people. Moreover, anybody who did go ashore in drought times might not even have seen much material evidence of absentee residents. The Seri accounts maintain that the San Esteban people had only a very simple material culture, and this belief is reinforced by the archaeological record. What remains today is so unobtrusive that it has proved nearly invisible to recent visitors, even to most scientists despite their well-honed observational skills.

The oral accounts also suggest that early experiences with hostile intruders may have predisposed the San Esteban people to avoid contact with strangers who came to the island. The documentary record shows that this was certainly a common response of other Seris, who were notorious for being able to flee unseen, keep track of intruders while staying out of sight, or simply vanish into the mountains. Escape and concealment proved to be effective techniques for evading military campaigns on both Tiburón Island and the mainland, and many Spanish and Mexican military expeditions were hard pressed just to find Seris to fight. As Col. Domingo Elizondo put it, writing in 1771 after four frustrating years of guerilla warfare against the Seris:

It is regrettable and lamentable that all the care, persistence, vigilance, and fatigue have not been sufficient to confront the enemies. They understand that concealment and flight are the only ways to avoid perishing at the hands of the soldiers. (Elizondo [1771] 1999:320)

And soldiers were not the only Europeans from whom the Seris hid. In 1895, even ethnologist WJ McGee was unable to make contact with Seris on Tiburón Island, though he found camps where ashes from their fires were still warm. It may be that many visitors to Tiburón who thought the island abandoned (e.g., Jones 1910) were under silent scrutiny the entire time they were there.

On San Esteban, avoiding intruders would have been even easier. Not only were there probably far fewer visitors, but the rugged terrain offers superb opportunities for concealment. Hiding from vessels cruising offshore would have been as easy as ducking behind a boulder or a cardon cactus. As speculated earlier (pp. 350–51), talus pits might conceivably have provided the San Esteban people with effective places to conceal themselves from casual shore parties. Retreating into the mountains would have made them invisible to all but the most thorough explorers. To fully appreciate the effectiveness of determined hiding, one need only recall the poignant story of Ishi, whose tiny band of Yahi Indians was completely surrounded by California settlers, and yet managed to live undetected for almost 40 years (Kroeber 1961).

Another reason European navigators who sailed and steamed through the Midriff may not have observed people on San Esteban is because their ships were poorly positioned to detect human activity there. In the first place, all the larger vessels probably would have steered the safest and most direct course through the middle of the channel, whether on the east or the west side of the island. Sailing in midchannel on the east side of San Esteban would have put ships about four miles from shore, while those on the west side would have been around seven miles away. Experience today shows that one must be within about half a mile of shore to detect any activity there. Sailors cruising this close would have been capable of seeing Indians there, but in all likelihood the San Esteban people would have spotted the approaching vessels well in advance and hidden. Thus even though it is said that the San Esteban men spent much of their time fishing from shore or from their balsas, they may have been able to disappear long before most Europeans ever got close enough to observe them.

Furthermore, passing sailors would have seen almost nothing beyond the beaches. Those running the channel on the south and west sides would have faced almost continuous sea cliffs (Figure 17.1). Those passing on the east and north would have found a less precipitous coastline breached in places by drainages (including Arroyo Limantour), but even here there is no real view into the interior of the island (Figure 17.2). Although the Seri say that the San Esteban people had important camps along some of the beaches, most of the archaeological remains, including most habitation sites, lie inland behind the sea cliffs. Hence much of the activity on San Esteban would have been completely hidden even from sailors cruising close to shore. All of these considerations may

Figure 17.1   The sea cliffs on the south coast of San Esteban, as they would appear from ships passing between San Esteban and San Lorenzo Islands. May 1984.

Figure 17.2   Even the gentler east coast of San Esteban, visible from ships in the channel between San Esteban and Tiburón Island, hides the interior of the island. January 1981.

help explain why such keen observers as Lieutenants Derby and Ives, sailing past San Esteban in 1850 and 1857, saw no signs of people.

There are additional factors that may have reduced the likelihood of sailors noting people on San Esteban. Some of the larger vessels, with no need to anchor for the night, probably passed San Esteban in darkness. Crews of ships traversing the Midriff in rough weather would have been busy manning their vessel rather than looking for Indians, and any passengers probably would have gone below. It is also likely that many of those who sailed past San Esteban in favorable conditions were neither on the lookout for Indians nor much interested. In fact, it is entirely possible that sailors sometimes *did* notice people on San Esteban's beaches or off shore in balsas, and simply made no record of it. To career sailors, it would have been common knowledge that Seris inhabited Tiburón Island, and no doubt many who had logged time in the Midriff had seen Indians around its shores. With Tiburón Island just a few miles away, sightings of Indians on or around San Esteban would not likely have raised any eyebrows, for the natural assumption would probably be that they were merely Seris visiting from Tiburón. And sometimes this may have been correct, for the oral accounts speak of visits to the San Esteban people by their neighbors on Tiburón. In any case, sightings of Indians around San Esteban might have been a curiosity, but probably not worthy of written note.

The converse of this is that some of the Seris that Europeans saw along the southwest coast of Tiburón Island could have been San Esteban people, since this too was part of their territory and the place to which they retreated when the water ran out on San Esteban. Thus it may be that some of the docile Indians that Thomas Spence encountered near Punta Willard in 1844, or the "few miserable Ceres Indians" that Frederick Fitch saw on the "southern end" of Tiburón around 1860 (Fitch 1875:61), were actually from the San Esteban band. Of course, there would have been no reason for Spence, Fitch, or other European observers to suspect that these Seris were members of a separate group.

This raises the question of whether *any* Europeans who might have encountered Seris on San Esteban would have recognized them as distinct. During the Colonial period, Europeans were well aware that the Seris were divided into a number of autonomous bands, and distinctions among them were drawn routinely, if not always accurately. But Seris were rarely distinguished by nineteenth century Sonorans. In part, this may reflect the disintegration of the bands themselves. According to the Seris today, disease and warfare increasingly decimated the population. Without sufficient numbers to sustain the bands as functional entities, the band structure collapsed, and with the exception of the San Esteban people, the Seris began to operate as a single group (Moser 1963:24–26). But it probably also reflects the fact that contact between Seris and nineteenth century Mexicans was almost entirely superficial and communication between them poor. Though there may be one exception (see p. 439), it is doubtful that very many Mexicans would have heard from any Seri sources about a still-independent band of their San Esteban brethren.

Thus in the atmosphere of conflict that prevailed throughout most of the nineteenth century, Sonorans generally regarded all Seris as potential enemies. If the oral accounts are correct and a military expedition rounded up and massacred the San Esteban people, it is quite possible that neither the soldiers, the commanding officer, nor the government had any idea of who those people were. The Seri accounts differ as to whether the roundup took place on San Esteban or Tiburón, but even if it happened on San Esteban Island, the soldiers probably just assumed that these Indians were ordinary Seris from Tiburón Island and the mainland. This suggests that documentation of the extinction event, if eventually found, is not likely to establish whether the Seris who met their demise were the San Esteban people of the oral accounts.

Unfortunately, the Europeans most likely to have encountered people on San Esteban are those least likely to have written about what they saw. These would not be the masters and crews of large sailing vessels and steamers, but the men who plied the Gulf in small sloops, skiffs, and canoes, the forerunners of today's panga fishermen. Not only were they readily capable of sailing close to shore, but they had to anchor or beach their boats at night, either on the mainland or the islands. Some, such as prospectors and perhaps moonshiners, would have had strong motives to go ashore and explore the islands thoroughly. Others, such as sea lion hunters, egg collectors, and possibly turtle hunters and small-scale fishermen, earned their livelihood around the margins of the islands, but they all needed shore camps for sleeping and processing their catch. Others still, the people known as *vagabundos*, who wandered widely throughout the Gulf subsisting mostly off the sea, also needed safe havens where they could put ashore for the night. All of these folk had a vital interest in knowing the coasts and islands well and whether there were Indians living there who might perceive them as a threat. But they were also men whose occupations did not require them to write about what they knew. In fact, some of these people, including smugglers, pirates, and the unlicensed pearlers of earlier times, operated outside the law and would have made every effort to insure that their movements were neither noticed nor reported. And until the twentieth century, the vast majority of those who made their living in the Gulf were illiterate and would not have been able to write about their experiences had they wished. Their knowledge would have been communicated by word of mouth, and mostly among themselves, since they were the only people to whom such information would have been of real value.

Nobody knows how many of these people may have visited San Esteban, or what the full spectrum of their reasons for going there might have been. Since they did not write about themselves, the little we know about them comes from what others wrote, and that was not much. Many of the glimpses we have of these folk comes from the letters and journals of travelers, who sometimes described them as part of the local color, and from government agents who were occasionally dispatched to assess the economic resources of the Gulf. But these descriptions are uniformly superficial. While they sometimes provide quick sketches of how these folk made their living, they reveal little of where they went and nothing of what they may have known about places like San Esteban Island.

Only a handful of written records are known that link these itinerant folk with San Esteban Island, and the only reason most of these records exist is because they involve incidents of official interest. Thus we know that the sloop *Playa Colorada* was anchored off San Esteban when its crew clashed with Seris in 1890, because the incident triggered a military reprisal. But we do not know why the sloop was there in the first place. We know that Luis Henríquez hunted sea lions on San Esteban in 1894 because he served as a guide when Mexican troops investigated the disappearance of two North Americans on Tiburón. The reason the schooner *Otila* spent six days at San Esteban in 1896, according to its captain, was to avoid confronting agitated Seris on Tiburón, following the disappearance of two more North Americans. But we do not know why the *Otila* chose to pass the time at San Esteban rather than somewhere else or what its crew did there. Of the known visitors, those most likely to have encountered Seris on San Esteban were the *mescal aguardiente* distillers who apparently spent several months on the island in 1877. But since we have no substantive reports of this operation, we can only wonder about what these people might have seen.

Visits to San Esteban by people such as these folk, who did not write about their movements may be just the tip of the iceberg. It is entirely possible that in this unwritten shadowy world of unlicensed pearlers, sea lion hunters, and *vagabundos*, it was common knowledge that Indians lived on San Esteban Island. But if so, that knowledge has not been passed down to the present, for the rather jumbled oral traditions of contemporary panga fishermen, the cultural heirs of these nineteenth century folk, make no mention of San Esteban ever being inhabited.

Perhaps the people least likely to know if there were Indians on San Esteban were nineteenth century historians, geographers, and other intellectuals. Because field ethnography as an academic pursuit was unknown in Mexico at the time (and in its infancy elsewhere), nearly everything that scholars wrote about the Seris was second-hand information, often gleaned from travelers who themselves had had only fleeting contact with Seris, and usually in thoroughly Mexicanized settings (McGee 1898:94–108). This sometimes created a vicious circle, for when travelers described the Seris, they were sometimes merely repeating what the scholarly community said about them. To Mexican intellectuals in the second half of the nineteenth century, the Seris had largely become curiosities. As a result, the scholarly papers of the period concentrate on a few sensational topics such as Seri arrow poison, and do little more than perpetuate the widespread and grisly, but totally fanciful, notions of how it was prepared (e.g., Carron de Fleury 1869:114–15; Fenochio 1873; Orozco y Berra 1880:102). As to where the Seris lived, nineteenth century historians and geographers simply reiterated what everyone knew, that the Seris inhabited the Sonoran coast and Tiburón Island.

History is always highly selective in terms of what gets recorded. People write only about those things they consider important or interesting and ignore the rest. If rumors about Seris on San Esteban Island surfaced from time to time, it may simply be that nobody among the literate considered it important enough to bother mentioning.

This raises the question once again of why the Jesuits failed to note people on San Esteban, for they were not only well-educated and prolific writers, but were among the few Europeans who would have had a vital interest in such people. After all, the purpose of their profession was to save souls, and this manifestly included the Seris.

It is possible that the reason they did not record Seris on San Esteban is because there might not have been any Indians living there at that time (see Chapter 18). But even if there had been, the Jesuits were not really in a good position to find out. The missions where most of the Jesuits lived out their lives were in the interior of Baja California and Sonora, not on the coasts. A few of the padres did a great deal of exploring, but most of it was on dry land. The one Midriff island the Jesuits knew had resident Indians was Tiburón Island. Though in need of salvation, the sole visit to these people was made by Father Ugarte, who landed at Tecomate three times during his 1721 odyssey, but only briefly. Though Ugarte sailed past several other Midriff islands he did not explore any of them. When he was in the vicinity of San Esteban, he and his crew were too distracted by illness and storm to consider going ashore.

Only one other Jesuit was ever in the vicinity of San Esteban. This was Father Salvatierra, who sailed past it in 1709 and also failed to land. Though he had been told by Seris at Bahía Kino that the island had fresh water, he dismissed this as unlikely when he saw its arid and rugged landscape. There is no indication that he was told of people living there, but if he could not believe there was water he surely would not have believed there could be Indians. In any case, Salvatierra was in a hurry to return to Loreto. Not only did he forego a landing on San Esteban, but he made no attempt to visit Seris on Tiburón Island, where he knew they were living.

The one Jesuit to actually search for Indians on any Midriff island was Father Linck, who made a brief reconnaissance of Ángel de la Guarda in 1765 after he heard rumors of fires there. He found neither Indians, nor any sign of them, nor water, and concluded the island was uninhabited.

For the Jesuits, the best potential source of information on the whereabouts of native people might have been the pearl hunters. But it is doubtful that the missionaries ever learned much from these people. They generally considered pearlers to be extremely destructive to their evangelical work, and though the Jesuits tried to control them, they also had as little to do with these people as possible. With relations so poor, whatever the pearlers might have known about Indians in places like San Esteban Island, they would not likely have passed on to their Jesuit adversaries.

Perhaps Salvatierra's reaction to San Esteban offers an important insight into the assumptions and conclusions of others who sailed past its imposing mountains and sea cliffs. When Salvatierra saw the island, he had already spent 12 years in Baja California. He was thoroughly familiar with the rugged and arid landscape of the peninsula, and he also knew that enough water existed there to support small numbers of Indians. If a man of his knowledge and perspective could sail directly past San Esteban and dismiss Seri reports of water out of hand, one wonders how many less experienced travelers also wrote off the island as uninhabitable, failed to go ashore, and never imagined that people might be living there.

There is one further mechanism that could help account for the documentary silence about people on San Esteban Island. This is intentional suppression. By its very nature, this is a difficult possibility to evaluate, and one that should not be proposed lightly. But such measures are not unknown, and deliberate suppression would effectively explain the most glaring hole in the documentary record. This is the silence surrounding the June 1890 military expedition, when the gunboat *Demócrata* with 50 soldiers was sent to the Midriff islands to punish the Seris for wounding two sailors from the sloop *Playa Colorada*. Though the official claim was that the soldiers did not find any Indians, one unofficial commentator who described the operation maintained that the troops took nearly 100 Seri prisoners (see pp. 244–45). What happened to those prisoners is not revealed, but the *Demócrata* expedition provides the closest match in circumstances and timing with the campaign the Seris believe wiped out the San Esteban people. The expedition was never even mentioned by the government weekly *La Constitución*, which normally reported such actions, and in contrast to most other campaigns against the Seris, the original reports seem to be unavailable for public inspection. It is certainly possible that, as officially claimed, the expedition accomplished nothing and an embarrassed government preferred not to parade its failure in public. But it is hard not to wonder whether this might have been the expedition that, intentionally or unintentionally, exterminated the San Esteban people. Especially if it were later realized that the Seris who were wiped out were an innocent group, an official policy of silence might well have been adopted to conceal the blunder. If so, this would certainly not be the first or the last time a government tried to cover up a massacre.

To summarize, there are a number of mechanisms which may have contributed to the apparent absence of documentation of the San Esteban people. If they did indeed escape the written record, their lives would be a classic example of what Raymond Fogelson has termed, with eloquent irony, "nonevents," and they would by no means have been the only Indians without a documented history:

> The reality and practical significance of uneventful history was forcibly brought home to me when I took temporary leave from the leisure of the theory class to testify before Congress on procedures for federal Indian recognition. A group petitioning for recognition must document, mainly through written records, that it is descended from historically known Indian tribes, has kept its Indian identity over time, and has "maintained tribal political influence or other authority over its members as an autonomous entity through history to the present." Documented information fulfilling these requirements is often difficult to obtain, and the minimal data available are frequently hard to interpret. Many of these groups did not get inscribed in the documentary record, and thus for purposes of federal recognition they have no history. One possible reason that the documents are silent on the existence of these groups is a deliberate adoption of a low-profile invisibility as a defensive strategy to avoid possible discrimination, persecution, conscription, and perceived threats to their autonomy. They might avoid census takers, distance themselves from

federal, state, or local authorities, refuse to send their children to schools, and not engage in events that were likely to be reported by newspapers. Thus the lack of an authenticated history for many of these groups begs fundamental questions about the authority of history: Who determines it? Who sets the criteria? or, in a literal sense, Who *possesses* history? (Fogelson 1989:141–42)

While it seems clear that the San Esteban people have no history in this sense, we are still left with the most fundamental question: History or no history, did the San Esteban people ever really exist? The only honest answer is that we do not know, nor are we ever likely to find out for sure. Logically, no amount of documentation of Midriff history that fails to mention these people can prove that they did not exist, for one cannot prove a negative. Finding a document, or even many, that substantiate the presence of Seris on San Esteban will probably not settle the matter either, for it is not likely that written records would distinguish between a resident people and visiting Seris from Tiburón. Making this critical distinction probably would have required much more prolonged and astute observations than most pre-twentieth century Europeans would have been either able or inclined to make. Perhaps the most compelling kind of evidence would be a report by the Seris themselves which described a separate band living on San Esteban. In fact, this is precisely the way the idea entered the anthropological literature in the first place (Griffen 1959:46; Moser 1963). But this brings us around full circle to the question addressed earlier, of whether Seri beliefs about the San Esteban people can be accepted as valid in terms of Euro-American historical standards.

A conventional way of dealing with this kind of ambiguity is to appeal to the principle of parsimony. One version of this principle states that one should give preference to the simplest interpretation that accounts for the known facts. Yet even this guideline is not always easy to apply because it is often unclear which of two competing interpretations is actually the simplest. Interpretations that appear simple on the surface may be riddled with hidden assumptions that make them anything but simple. And especially in the realm of human affairs, simple interpretations may turn out to be merely simplistic.

In the case of the San Esteban people, it may seem superficially simpler to accept the negative documentary record at face value and conclude that the reason the San Esteban people do not figure into it is because there never was any such group. But to adopt this position, one would be obliged to convincingly show that the Seri oral accounts are either fabrications or baseless mythology. More importantly, one would have to explain how the island's archaeological remains could reasonably have been produced by a succession of brief visits. On balance, it may be simpler to regard the Seri oral accounts as more or less historically valid in Western terms, to interpret the archaeological remains as that of Seri residents rather than visitors, and acknowledge that there are many mechanisms that could have excluded the San Esteban people from the documentary record. Though ultimately a matter of judgment, it seems much more likely that the San Esteban people did exist, and that the Seris are recounting history when they tell about these people.

EIGHTEEN

Unknown People:
Who Were the San Esteban People?

 If the San Esteban people did exist more or less as the Seri accounts portray them, then one might ask who, exactly, were they? How were they related to the Seri people as a whole?

Although this too can probably not be answered with certainty, one plausible scenario has already been presented. This is the story of the origin of the San Esteban people that was recounted by Roberto Herrera and related in Chapter 1. Herrera's account maintains that the ancestors of the San Esteban Seri were the original inhabitants of Tiburón Island. For a long time, Tiburón Island was the only place these people lived, and at that time, they were its sole inhabitants. Later, well-armed Seris from the mainland began to invade Tiburón, and the people who were already there were relatively defenseless against them. Although the two groups did not actually fight, the mainland people began to take over the island. The original residents were gradually pushed southward to the southwest coast and eventually onto San Esteban Island. Thereafter, Tiburón was primarily the domain of the Seri newcomers, and the original inhabitants of Tiburón Island became known as the San Esteban people.

The Europeans, of course, say nothing about the San Esteban people, and there is no indication that they were aware of a gradual population replacement on Tiburón Island. Yet over the duration of the Colonial period, the Europeans may have inadvertently chronicled such a process. Toward the end of the eighteenth century, the way they described the island and its inhabitants began to undergo a fundamental change, and in a manner that is consistent with Herrera's account.

Shortly after the Europeans first came in contact with the Seris, they realized that these Indians were not a single unified people. Throughout most of the Colonial era, European writers regularly distinguished at least three major groups. Two of these, the Salineros and Tepocas, lived along the mainland coast while the third, referred to as Tiburones, were the people who inhabited Tiburón Island (Sheridan

1999:9) Europeans also knew that these groups differed not only in residence but also in character and in the nature and degree of contact they had with Europeans. The Seris whom the Spaniards came to know and loathe, as many documents state explicitly, were mostly Salineros and Tepocas, for it was mainly these people who moved inland to exploit the missions and raid the towns and ranches. While European writers repeatedly disparaged the depredations of these two groups, they wrote comparatively little about the Tiburones, with whom they had much less contact. When they said anything at all, they generally portrayed them as a peaceable folk who kept to themselves in the isolated fastness of Tiburón Island. In 1729, for example, Father Nicolás de Perera remarked that the Tiburones "are good people, without malice and free from the wickedness of those of this shore" (Perera, [1729] 1999:130). And about 20 years later *Visitador General* José Rafael Rodríguez Gallardo, who was no friend of the Indians, characterized the Seris as "a barbarous and treacherous nation except for those who have not left the island of Tiburón" (Rodríguez Gallardo, in Sheridan 1999:13).

But the documentary record also indicates that the Tiburones did not have their tranquil island to themselves for long. By 1700, 50 years after the Salineros and Tepocas took to raiding, these two groups had already begun to use Tiburón Island as a refuge from Spanish reprisals. And in 1750, it was the large number of hostile Seris holed up there that provoked a major military expedition to the island. For the next 20 years, Tiburón served as a principal retreat for Seri guerilla fighters, and a proposed 1798 invasion of the island was aimed at annihilating the 250 warriors and their families whom the Spaniards believed were living there. Thus by the end of the eighteenth century, mainland raiders and warriors had been making extensive use of Tiburón Island for over 100 years, and the Europeans were coming to think of the island, probably correctly, as more the domain of hostile Seris than the home of docile Tiburones.

By this time, the long recognized distinction between the mostly peaceable Tiburones and the hostile mainland Seris was also beginning to blur. As late as 1770, Col. Domingo Elizondo had clearly understood that the Tiburones were not the enemy and, in fact, had rarely ever left their island homeland. When a group of hostile Seris came to surrender in that year:

> Three Indians from Tiburón Island [also] presented themselves ... and implored that no expedition be carried out against them. They explained that their nation never left their island, that they were unhappy, and that they never bothered anyone. In view of these [facts], they begged to be allowed to live freely in their country because they had been born there. They promised that they would not set foot on our coasts. They were granted the favor of their security on condition that they not leave their island for the coasts of the province of Sonora. (Elizondo [1771] 1999:329)

But toward the end of the Colonial era, European documents begin to refer increasingly to the Tiburones as hostile Seris. For example, Pedro de Nava's 1798 plan to invade Tiburón Island was drawn up:

with the idea of exterminating the families of our declared enemies, the rebellious Seris, Tiburones, Tepocas, and Cimarrones who take shelter on Tiburón Island, where they think they are safe from the punishment of our arms. (Nava [1798] 1999:449)

Probably by then some Tiburones had indeed become hostile, having been caught for over a century in the crossfire between Spanish military forces and their own Salinero and Tepoca kinsmen from the mainland. It would be astonishing if this were not the case, for Spanish soldiers bent on reprisal probably did not often discriminate between innocent Tiburones and guilty raiders. Around 1731, some of the disillusioned Tiburones who had escaped from the Pópulo mission may have joined with the Tepocas to help drive Spanish pearl hunters from the placers near Tiburón Island. The Seris who sacked the short-lived mission at Carrizal and murdered Fray Gil de Bernabé in 1773 are thought to have been disaffected Tiburones, but it was also friendly Tiburones who immediately apprehended the culprits in an effort to preempt a potentially disastrous Spanish reprisal. Thus while some individuals may have become rebels, it does not necessarily follow that the Tiburones as a group underwent a wholesale transformation of character. More likely, later documents were beginning to reflect the profound change in the demographic composition of Tiburón Island, and the meaning of the term "Tiburones" was adjusted to refer to any Seri currently living there. By that time, probably the majority of people living there *were* aggressive Salineros and Tepocas who had come over from the mainland as more or less permanent refugees. Thus in the late eighteenth century, it was probably not the original Tiburones who were the hostile Seris on Tiburón, but the newcomers who were displacing them.

By 1821 when Mexico won its independence, the names "Tiburones," "Tiburón Indians," and "Seris" were being used indiscriminately to refer to any people on the island, and the conventional wisdom was that all Indians who lived there were hostile. But there was at least one Mexican who did not accept this simplistic view. This was Pascual Encinas, the cofounder of the famed San Francisco de la Costa Rica ranch. Encinas probably had more direct contact with the Seris than any other Mexican of his day, and he had made friendly visits to Tiburón Island on at least two occasions. According to McGee:

> About the middle fifties it became apparent [to Encinas] that the Seri were dividing into a parasitical portion clustered around the rancho (as their forebears gathered around Populo and Pueblo Seri long before), and a more independent faction clinging to their rugged ranges and gale-swept fishing grounds; and it became evident, too, that the thievery of the dependent faction would soon ruin the rancho if not checked. (McGee 1898:111)

What Encinas apparently had not considered is the possibility that by the 1850s the Seris were *already* divided into these two factions, and that this division had perpetuated itself since at least the late eighteenth century. It may well be that the "parasitical portion" were the amalgamated descendants of the Salinero and Tepoca raiders, as McGee implies, but it seems equally probable that the people who kept to themselves in their "gale-swept fishing grounds" were the descendants of the Tiburones of Colonial times.

Although McGee was willing to report Encinas's observation and was fully aware of the distinctions among Seri groups drawn by early writers, he himself did not accept the idea that any group might have been reclusive and peaceable, for that would have contradicted his theoretical model of the natural savagery of all Seris. But it is much more likely that Encinas and the early writers were correct in their views. Reading between the lines a bit, it is not hard to interpret the documentary record of Seris on Tiburón Island and the modern Seri tradition about the origin of the San Esteban people, as related by Roberto Herrera, as complementary accounts of some of the same events. If so, it would make the historically-known Tiburones the ancestors of the San Esteban people.

Putting these two sources together gives us a plausible scenario for the emergence of the San Esteban people. In this reconstruction, their ancestors, the peaceable Tiburones, would have been the original inhabitants of Tiburón Island. After the Europeans arrived on the mainland, other Seris living along the coast, mainly Salineros and Tepocas, began to raid the new settlements. When the Europeans responded with military force, the Seri marauders began to seek refuge on Tiburón Island. As the cycle of raids and retaliations escalated, the influx of aggressive mainland Seris eventually overwhelmed the resident Tiburones. These retiring folk, or some portion of them, disposed to avoiding conflict with other Seris and Europeans alike, were gradually displaced toward the "gale-swept" southwest coast, the harshest and most remote quarter of Tiburón, and ultimately onto San Esteban Island itself. By this time most Europeans (excepting Pascual Encinas) had lost track of the Tiburones, and simply assumed, incorrectly, that they had merged with the hostile Seris now living on Tiburón Island. But the other Seris knew that these people had managed to maintain their identity. They were now known as the San Esteban people, and they continued to live on San Esteban Island, largely in isolation, until their extinction.

This reconstruction goes a long way toward reconciling the Seri oral accounts with the historic record. One of its strengths is that it brings the San Esteban people of Seri tradition out of the realm of mystery—the people that no Europeans ever saw—and provides them with a credible identity within the context of the historic record. Moreover, it suggests that the displacement of the Tiburones southwestward probably did not gain much momentum until the late 1700s, which in turn suggests that they may not have begun to actually reside on San Esteban Island until sometime around the beginning of the nineteenth century. This is consistent with the archaeological record, which seems to indicate a late, and rather short, occupation of San Esteban. And perhaps equally importantly, it helps account for the lack of documented sightings of people there. While Seris may have made occasional visits to San Esteban for centuries, the total span that the San Esteban people would have actually lived there would amount to not much more than 100 years or so. For some 250 years after Francisco de Ulloa first sailed past the island, there would have been nobody living there for Europeans to see.

Ironically, the ancestors of the San Esteban people were probably the first Seris the Europeans ever encountered, for they would have been the people living on Tiburón Island when Juan de Iturbe stopped there in 1615. Later Spanish documents, such as Perera's letter and Elizondo's report (quoted above), suggest that the San Esteban people, in their Colonial period guise as Tiburones, may have had just a bit more contact with Europeans than the Seri accounts would suggest. But that would have been before they really became the people of San Esteban Island. Once relocated on rugged and remote San Esteban, a small population of erstwhile Tiburones determined to keep to themselves would probably have had little problem minimizing contact with outsiders. Even though it is said that some traveled widely in their balsas, the places they explored were uninhabited or very sparsely populated, and their human contacts on these excursions were probably limited to a few hit-and-run raids in Baja California early in the nineteenth century. By the late nineteenth century, after three or four generations of people had lived in solitude on San Esteban, earlier experiences with the Spaniards, including their horses and firearms, may have faded from the collective memory. The people who were finally rounded up and wiped out might well have been the naïve and innocent folk that are portrayed in the oral accounts, as told by the modern Seris.

Appendix A:
Sources of the Seri Oral Accounts

Chapter 1 is based primarily on the knowledge of three individuals. Much of it comes from the recollections of Porfirio Díaz (18??–1959) who is thought to have lived among the San Esteban people as a boy. Díaz's memories have been supplemented by information supplied by two other Seris, Roberto Herrera Marcos (1916–1988) and Jesús Morales (1904?–1975). A small amount of additional information has been contributed by other Seris.

The single most important body of data is an interview with Porfirio Díaz that was recorded on tape by linguists Edward Moser (1924–1976) and Mary Beck Moser (b. 1924). This session took place in 1958, in the Mosers' home in the Seri community of El Desemboque. The circumstances of the interview were not written down at the time, but they are remembered by Mary Beck Moser (1995:pers. comm.). On the day the recording was made, Edward Moser and Roberto Herrera were discussing the former band structure of the Seris, a subject they had worked on together many times previously. Apparently, the topic of the San Esteban band had been raised, and it was probably Herrera who suggested asking Díaz, the recognized authority on these people, to come to the Mosers' house and tell about them. Díaz was a neighbor who lived just a short distance away, and he agreed to come over. Because he was both blind and frail from age, his wife Juana usually helped him get around, and she accompanied him as he walked to the Mosers' house. Consequently, the people who were present at the recording session were Díaz, his wife Juana, Roberto Herrera, Edward Moser, and Mary Beck Moser.

Díaz, like everyone in the village, knew of the Mosers' linguistic and ethnographic work, so the idea of talking about the Seris and their past was not new to him. He was also generally familiar with what a tape recorder did and was aware that what he said was being recorded. Díaz also knew that he would be paid for his services, which was not only the Mosers' policy with all Seris who shared linguistic and ethnographic information with them but also is a customary aspect of Seri culture for virtually any service that Seris perform for each other. He was a willing informant, and Mary Beck Moser believes that there is no reason to doubt that he spoke accurately and truthfully to the best of his ability. He answered questions freely and without hesitation, explaining things that were not self-evident, occasionally at some length. However, he tended not to volunteer information that was not solicited nor to elaborate beyond what was asked. This was very much in character, and probably neither an artifact of the recording setting nor of the topic under discussion. Díaz was simply not a naturally gregarious person, and at his advanced age, it was an effort for him just to talk. Indeed, at times he spoke so slowly and with such difficulty that some of his words are hard to understand (Mary Beck Moser 1995:pers. comm.).

The tape is about 37 minutes long. Most of it consists of Díaz speaking, though his wife Juana sometimes interjected comments. He spoke entirely in the Seri language. Because of his labored speech and because in 1958 the Mosers were not yet fully fluent in Seri, Roberto Herrera facilitated the interview by asking some of the questions and, at certain points, by helping translate and clarify Díaz's replies.

Díaz died the following year, leaving Roberto Herrera and Jesús Morales as the two principal sources of information about the San Esteban people. Both men were related to Díaz, and consequently much of what they knew about these people, they had learned directly from Díaz and other relatives who had known them first hand. Herrera's maternal grandmother was Díaz's sister Angelita, and Herrera had lived in Angelita's household for many years after his mother died. Morales was the son of Díaz's first cousin (Díaz's mother's sister's son's son). Moreover, Herrera and Morales had a strong natural interest in the San Esteban people, for throughout their lives both men maintained a deep commitment to learning and preserving traditional Seri culture and history.

For Moser, Herrera continued to be an important source of information about the San Esteban people, primarily because they worked together on Seri language analysis on almost a daily basis for nearly two more decades. The San Esteban people were among the vast array of subjects that arose naturally during the course of their long linguistic collaboration, and what Herrera said about them worked its way into Moser's ever-expanding file of data on Seri band structure and history. Moser's notes contain less information from Morales not because Morales knew less than Herrera, but because he worked with Moser only occasionally as a consultant, rather than as a regular coworker.

The description of the San Esteban people that comprises Chapter 1 was compiled almost entirely from Edward Moser's file of notes (which included transcriptions from the taped interview with Porfirio Díaz). Although Moser maintained an avid interest in Seri ethnography and traditional history, his principal concern was language analysis. Probably for that reason, his ethnographic notes are often spare. Some he compiled and typed, but many consist of brief sentences or even phrases, hurriedly translated into English and jotted down on 3 by 5 inch slips or sometimes just tiny scraps of paper. Though most of his data on the San Esteban people came from the Díaz tape or conversations with Herrera and Morales (and he undoubtedly knew which), he seldom indicated the source of the information with his notes. He assembled his data enough to publish a brief sketch of the San Esteban people (Moser 1963:24–26), but he never had the opportunity to organize the information more fully into the comprehensive account he had hoped someday to produce. The notes were, of course, intended for his own use, and they were made available for the present work by the kind permission of Mary Beck Moser.

Because Moser's notes consist mostly of isolated statements and fragmentary remarks, the major task of Chapter 1 has been to piece together these bits into a coherent description of San Esteban culture and history. To do this, it has been necessary to impose an arbitrary organizational framework on the information and, so to speak, add a lot of connective tissue to Moser's skeletal data. The challenge has been to create a narrative that, on the one hand, is a truly Seri description of the San Esteban people and, on the other hand, contains enough context and explanation so that ideas make sense and flow logically from one to the next. Happily, it has been possible to relate much of the story in the same words Moser used to record it. Retaining the idiosyncratic phrasing of Moser's often hasty transcriptions is one important way of insuring that the narrative accurately reflects what the Seris actually said about the San Esteban people. Sometimes, however, it has been necessary to depart from Moser's wording because of ambiguities or contradictions in his notes. Mary Beck Moser has been able to resolve many of these problems, and in these cases the narrative follows her wording. Moreover, by consulting with Seris who still remembered traditional history she has turned up additional information that bears on the San Esteban people. This newer material has been incorporated into the story and credited to her.

Much of the material derived from non-Seri sources that has been added to flesh out Moser's notes has been identified as such so that it will not be confused with information that comes from the Seris themselves. Hence published information incorporated into the narrative is accompanied by the appropriate citation, and all commentary on what the Seris have said has been relegated to endnotes. Despite these measures, however, it should be emphasized that Chapter 1 is not a pure Seri text but rather a loose compilation of many fragmentary texts set in an artificial framework. The price of casting these bits into narrative form is that the reader will not often be able to distinguish what the Seris actually said from the matrix in which their remarks are imbedded.

Appendix B
Sources of the Mexican Fisherman's Oral Accounts

The oral accounts of the Mexican fishermen, related in Chapter 11, come mostly from conversations with about a dozen and a half individuals between 1980 and 1987. Much of the information was gathered while chatting informally with these men at their camp at El Monumento, on the eastern shore of San Esteban. Usually the setting, the timing, and the mood of these conversations were such that note-taking on the spot would have been inappropriate, if not rude. Consequently, the information from these casual talks was written down later, though usually immediately afterward.

Few of the fishermen were inclined to say much about the history of the island, not because of any intrinsic aversion, but because it is not of particular interest to most of them. As a result, not much was volunteered, and most of their ideas were given in response to direct questions. Generally, one of the fishermen would act as spokesman for the (typically) four-man crew, relating briefly what he knew about the topic queried, while the others would listen and occasionally express their agreement, make additions, and sometimes offer alternative views. Most of the men were not able to provide more than fragmentary information about the history of the island, and their accounts do not really form coherent narratives. Yet conversations with different panga crews over several years show that there is a small corpus of widely shared notions about the local past. For these reasons, the oral traditions related here are mostly a composite sketch derived from a number of different people. Since most of the fishermen showed no desire for formal introductions or an exchange of names, the identity of these men was generally not recorded, and it is not possible to credit their contributions individually.

Yet a few panga fishermen do have a strong interest in and knowledge of the region's history. We were fortunate to have encountered two such people, Elfego Briseño and Severiano León, and both men told us about San Esteban's past in considerable detail. The most extensive information was provided by

Briseño, who maintains a keen interest in the natural and human history of the Midriff region and has made a point of talking about the "old days" with fishermen of previous generations. He shared his knowledge with us at length on several occasions in January 1982, when both his crew and ours were camped on San Esteban, and again in his home village of Bahía Kino in January 1987. León was one of the fishermen who expertly transported us to and from the island, and on several of these occasions, he told us about the region's history from the stern of his panga. Because his mother is Seri, his perspective on the region's past is probably unique among Bahía Kino fishermen. The contributions of both Briseño and León are credited in the text.

Appendix C
An Experiment in Minimalist Archaeology

Conducting archaeological fieldwork on San Esteban Island proved to be a strange but deeply rewarding experience. The island itself places some unusual demands on fieldwork because of its remote location and rugged terrain. The archaeological remains present other challenges, for in many respects they are unique, unlike even the archaeology of neighboring Tiburón Island. And our reasons for going there were not those of more conventional archaeological projects. Unusual circumstances require unusual methods, and for that reason it may be useful to describe how we conducted the fieldwork.

The most important consideration is that we went to San Esteban with a clear, but very modest, objective—to find out if the island's archaeology could provide a material basis for evaluating whether the San Esteban people actually existed. To this end, we hoped to answer just four specific questions. First, is there evidence of people having been on the island? Secondly, were any of these people Seris? Thirdly, did they actually reside on the island or were they just occasional visitors? And fourthly, when were they there? Because these are very simple questions, we envisioned a very simple project, to be conducted as a low-tech surface reconnaissance and carried out quickly and cheaply by just three or four people. Accordingly, in late December 1979, four of us were dropped off by boat on San Esteban for a two week survey of the island.

A small-scale project proved to be an excellent approach. Because of the difficulty getting to and from the island and because every ounce of food, water, and equipment must be brought in, a larger project would have been logistically unwieldy. Surface survey was an appropriate procedure since many of the remains, though not all, lie on the ground surface. However, there was much about the island that we had no way of anticipating. For all practical purposes, nothing whatever was known of the island's archaeology, and we had little advance information about what to expect for working conditions. As it turned out, the archaeology was so unlike anything we were familiar with that it took most of the first trip just to shed our preconceptions and come to terms with what we were actually seeing. And it immediately became apparent that the island's terrain was not conducive to either a speedy survey or one employing conventional techniques. We would have to work out our own way of proceeding, and it was obvious that a number of return trips would be necessary.

In all, we made some 10 separate trips to the island (plus trips to San Lorenzo Island and the southwest coast of Tiburón Island). The first visit had, in fact, already occurred much earlier. This was a fleeting 24-hour stay in the sweltering heat of July 1967, but it was both too brief a trip and too hot to have been of much use. Beginning in December 1979, all subsequent trips were made in the relative cool of winter and spring, and each lasted between about seven days and a month. The final working trip was in April 1987, though an opportunity for a casual three day visit materialized unexpectedly in March 1993. The earlier trips provided data for Elisa Villalpando's thesis and subsequent monograph on the cultural ecology of the island (Villalpando 1984, 1989).

Many archaeologists will be dismayed to learn that we conducted the survey without employing statistically-based sampling techniques. Given the profession's obsession with such matters in the late 1970s and early 1980s, having foregone formal sampling strategies no doubt places our project somewhere between heretical and contemptible. But fieldwork on San Esteban is not like surveying on the Sonoran mainland, or southern Arizona, or even Tiburón Island. Once we realized what we were up against, we concluded that there were several cogent reasons for dispensing with a formal sampling strategy. A few comments on this are appropriate.

First of all, any statistically-based sampling procedure must assume that the potential units to be sampled are accessible. On San Esteban Island, this is a tall order. The island itself can only be reached by boat, and once there, all travel is by foot, without the benefit of roads or trails. Since all supplies, including such heavy commodities as drinking water, must be brought in by boat, it is expedient to camp close to shore. At most of the beaches where it is possible to get ashore, access to the interior is blocked by mountains or sea cliffs. The only place one can off-load supplies, camp, and have good access to the interior of the island is on the east coast at Playa Limantour. From here, much of the island can be reached via the major arroyos, though not necessarily quickly. The west side, for example, is only about four miles away as the raven flies, but on foot, it is a full two hour march by the fastest route. Getting from the major arroyos to more remote localities consumes even more time. In winter, generally the season we could arrange to be in the field, daylight lasts only 10 hours, which means that more than half the day may be eaten up just getting to and from a remote locality to be surveyed. Setting up temporary camps in the interior, as we did on two occasions, can speed up access to some remote areas, but the time required to backpack in supplies, which must include every drop of water for drinking and cooking, results in little net gain in survey time. Thus, no matter what sampling strategy is employed, it is hard to circumvent the fact that just getting access to some of the sample units would be a time-consuming process that would leave comparatively little time for survey.

The second problem is the terrain itself. Though it may take time, it is a straight forward hike to most regions of the island so long as one is free to pick the easiest routes, usually along the major arroyos (Map 1.1). But getting from the major arroyos to a particular patch of ground, such as a quadrat selected by chance, and then surveying it, may be a different story. As almost every visitor has noted, San Esteban is a rugged and mountainous island (Figure 1.1). Much of the terrain consists of weakly consolidated volcanic flows which have eroded into steep unstable slopes. Some are blanketed with tephra or loose rocks that give way like ball bearings, while others merely crumble under foot. The ridges that separate these slopes often consist of shattered outcrops, and the sea cliffs are largely inaccessible. Vegetation rarely stabilizes the steep terrain but often defends it with the characteristic xeric armory of thorns and spines. The smaller arroyos, potentially good pathways, are generally choked with trees and shrubs. Much of the island's gentler ground is covered with luxurious fields of agave plants bearing toxic needles at the tip of each leaf. And a few areas are completely closed off by impenetrable forests of *pitahaya agria* cactus.

The wind compounds the inherent unfriendliness of the landscape. In winter, it can blow unabated for days on end and with sufficient force to make walking a challenge, even on level ground. It is usually worse higher up, and the unpredictable buffeting of staccato gusts can throw one off balance and make unstable terrain particularly precarious. On San Esteban, there is special reason to exercise caution under adverse conditions because medical attention can be more than a week away when winter storms completely isolate the island from the outside world.

Difficult terrain is nothing new to many archaeologists, but it usually does not comprise the majority of their sampling universe. On San Esteban, most units defined by any statistically-based sampling strategy would likely fall in areas that are either hard to reach or difficult to work, and this would make the time and effort required to conduct such a survey prodigious. Despite this unencouraging prospect, in November 1980, Elisa Villalpando divided the island into 76 quadrats and made a valiant attempt to survey a 25 percent random sample. But the combination of difficult terrain and almost ceaseless gale force winds proved overwhelming. It was impossible to work at all in some of the quadrats, and others could be only partially completed. At the end of an exhausting month, Villalpando had been able to survey only a fraction of the designated area (María Elisa Villalpando 1980:pers. comm.; Villalpando 1989:40). Thereafter, the problems of terrain, weather, and access, coupled with time constraints and risk factors, all strongly encouraged us to keep decisions over where to survey in our own hands, rather than relegating them to chance as part of a statistically-based sampling strategy.

By concentrating on the more manageable parts of the island, we were ultimately able to cover about 35 percent of the landscape (Figures 16.2–16.4). Much of this ground was surveyed with fieldworkers spaced no more than 10 m apart. Although we did not follow a rigorous sampling procedure, we made certain that we visited nearly all portions of the island and investigated every type of terrain and physiographic feature. Naturally, coverage was best on the eastern side of the island because of quick access from camp. For the most part, we concentrated on gentler landforms, such as arroyo bottoms, terraces, floodplains, alluvial fans, foothills, the lower slopes of mountains, and talus slopes. But to insure that we did not miss certain kinds of remains entirely, we made a concerted effort to extend the survey to even the most difficult terrain, in those parts of the island we were able to reach. In so doing, we climbed the six highest peaks and many minor ones, traversed ridges, ascended or descended steep gullies, and even conducted systematic transects that covered the entire length and breadth of some steep mountain slopes. If not representative in a statistical sense, we would claim that the survey was as extensive and inclusive as was practical.

The unusual conditions of fieldwork on San Esteban are limited not just to terrain and logistics but extend equally to the archaeology. One of the island's curious properties is that the cultural landscape is dominated by structures rather than artifacts. Though San Esteban has an area of only about 16 square miles, and though our survey covered only about one-third of the island's surface, we recorded more than 275 individual features, not including talus pits which occur by the hundreds, if not thousands.

Artifacts, on the other hand, are nowhere abundant, not even at habitation sites. Most consist of little more than simple waste flakes. Except for agave knives, fully-shaped tools are scarce. But what is even more notable is the way these artifacts are distributed over the island. Although there are some clearly discernible concentrations, for the most part, they are scattered widely in a thin veneer, seemingly at random. This suggests that few activities were limited to specific locations, that most tasks requiring tools could be, and were, carried out almost anywhere. On an island small enough to traverse in a single day and with many resources fairly evenly distributed, this is perhaps expectable. But for the archaeologist, it increases enormously the difficulty of assessing associations among artifacts and features. The general scatter makes it hard to be certain that artifacts that do occur together (on the ground surface) actually "belong" together as the product of interconnected activities. Some of the apparent concentrations could be the product of unrelated events that took place by chance in the same location. In short, there is often no way of knowing whether items found in the same vicinity had anything to do with each other.

Among features, determining associations is equally problematical. Many structures occur in isolation and are unaccompanied by artifacts. But some are found in groups, such as the rockwall enclosures and cairns on several of the island's high peaks. In one case (Pico Rojo), some 20 structures are clustered within 70 m of the summit, but there are few clues to indicate whether they were built and used collectively and, hence, comprise a culturally meaningful unit, or whether they were constructed separately, perhaps by different individuals, at different times, and conceivably for entirely different purposes.

The isolated occurrence and dubious association of so many of the remains give the archaeology of San Esteban a strongly "non-site" character (Schiffer and Wells 1982:370–71; Thomas 1990:245–46). Usually, the site concept signifies a localized concentration of remains, at least some of which are associated with each other as the products of interconnected activities. The island does have some "sites" according to conventional notions, and these include habitation caves and clusters of sleeping clearings strewn with trash. But it is difficult to characterize the more common solitary features and isolated artifacts as "sites" without seriously overextending the normal meaning of the term. And in many cases, applying the site concept to remains that *are* spatially clustered, such as the summit structures on Pico Rojo, would risk implying a functional interconnection among these features for which there is little real evidence.

The non-site character of the island's archaeology was so striking that we had abandoned the site concept altogether by the end of the first field trip. Thereafter, we recorded each individual feature as a separate entity with its own identifying letter and number. The letters were used to designate arbitrary geographical areas surveyed, while the numbers were given sequentially to each feature recorded within that area. Concentrations of artifacts were treated as features, while isolated artifacts were recorded without the formal designation of letter and number. In Chapters 13–15, the term "site" is used sparingly and only when it can be done without violating its conventional meaning.

We also discovered that for several types of features, there was little prospect of obtaining counts and distributions that would be meaningful for quantitative analysis. This is because many features that consist of patterns of rocks on the ground, such as ground figures, rock clusters, clearings, and to some extent stone circles, cannot be consistently and reliably distinguished from natural mimics. Much of San Esteban's landscape is heavily and randomly strewn with rocks. Ground figures, rock clusters, clearings, and circles made by humans were all created by rearranging the surface rocks, thereby producing a perceptible pattern in the otherwise random scatter. But a truly random natural scatter can include distributions of rocks that may be perceived as patterns by the archaeologist, much as people for millennia have found patterns in the random positions of bright stars in the night sky that "form" constellations. When the pattern has a distinctive symmetry, or consists of rocks that have been turned over, or occurs clustered with other features, or is accompanied by artifacts, one can be fairly confident that it was created by humans. But some of the seemingly patterned arrangements of rocks on San Esteban are vague, asymmetrical, and isolated. Whether these should be construed as man-made features or as natural distributions of rocks from which normal perceptual processes create the illusion of pattern, is ultimately a matter of individual judgment.

Clearings pose special problems. Those that are rimmed with rocks, occur in clusters, or are associated with artifacts, are almost certainly man-made. But others seem to occur singly and without artifacts, and some of these are so indistinct that they are visible only at certain times of day in oblique lighting. Features this vague verge on the imaginary, and there is no dependable way to tell the difference. Natural processes also have a way of producing well-defined mimics of clearings. Agave plants usually reproduce vegetatively from the roots, and as new clones appear, they typically form a small oval ring of plants the size and shape of man-made clearings. Because the plants act as a silt trap, the interior becomes a surface that is relatively free of rocks. Once the plants have died off (or been harvested) there may be no sure way of distinguishing these natural rock-free ovals from clearings made by people. Furthermore, while some of these features may have been created by botanical processes, in certain cases people may have taken them over and used them.

Because we were asking only the most basic questions of the archaeology, we operated cautiously and recorded only well-defined features that we are reasonably confident were made or used by people. In so doing we passed over a large number of vague and uncertain features, some of which may actually be of human origin. Thus our conservative approach may greatly underestimate the number of features on the island and may have missed a disproportionate number of chronologically early ones—those most likely to be indistinct. Had we adopted an aggressive recording policy, we probably would have erred by including in the inventory many natural and imaginary features that were not human constructions. Either way the game is played, there is little assurance that the obtained counts would approximate cultural "reality" in a way that would make distributional and quantitative analyses very meaningful.

Finally, it should be acknowledged that we chose to constrain our fieldwork in ways that are not entirely customary. In part, this was an ethical consideration, shaped not only by concerns that had been emerging within the archaeological community, but also by the strong conservation ethic that has governed nearly all scientific work in the Gulf in recent years. As all archaeologists are well aware, excavation physically destroys sites as surely as does the pothunter or the bulldozer. The same is true of collecting artifacts from surface sites, and in both cases, once this has happened the site is gone forever. The difference between the pothunter, the bulldozer, and the archaeologist is, of course, that the latter comes away with information about past peoples, and it is the retrieval of this information that usually justifies the damage inflicted on the site.

The virtue of controlled collecting or excavation is obvious when it takes place just ahead of the bulldozer that is ripping up the landscape for a pipeline or a parking lot, because the cultural information that is salvaged by the archaeologist would otherwise be irretrievably lost. But it is quite another matter when the archaeological remains reside on the uninhabited and (for the moment) unthreatened wilderness of San Esteban Island. In this kind of setting, the price of archaeological information is much greater, and it is important to ask how much unprovoked site destruction is justifiable for the information that will potentially be realized.

There is also an aesthetic dimension to this question. We found ourselves dazzled by San Esteban's stark and wild landscape and deeply moved by the sheer beauty of this isolated little chunk of wilderness. A significant part of that beauty derives from the human component—both the near absence of any trace of recent humans and the remarkably pristine remains of the people who were there earlier. It is not merely that there are a few undamaged sites, but rather that the archaeological record of the entire island is essentially intact. In some cases, sites looked to us as if their occupants had stepped out only minutes before our arrival, and the impact of this eerie sensation was profound. As a result, San Esteban was just not a place where we were willing to conduct archaeological business as usual.

So the problem was how to gather the information we needed without destroying the fragile beauty of the island and its extraordinary archaeological record. Our solution was mixed, but it leaned heavily toward preservation, often at the expense of information. Surface survey can be compatible with the goal of minimal disturbance but only if it is conducted with no collecting (Davis 1978). Accordingly, we picked up and handled artifacts only to record and photograph them, and then replaced them on the ground and left them as we found them. This is a time-consuming way to run a survey, and it limits the information that can be obtained, but these were tradeoffs we considered worthwhile. And since our questions about the island's prehistory were very basic, it was also an approach that was nearly sufficient for what we needed to know.

Nearly, but not quite, for it became clear that two important kinds of features simply could not be understood without testing. Accordingly, on the final trip to the island, after much soul-searching, we reluctantly put a test trench through one pit oven and one stone circle, and we made small trowel holes in several other circles to confirm the results. Flotation samples were taken from the two excavated features, though they were subsequently lost by the specialist to whom they were given for analysis. We collected one artifact, a partly restorable olla, because it lay in a vulnerable position, and turned it over to the Instituto Nacional de Antropología e Historia Centro Regional de Sonora in Hermosillo. We also collected six surface charcoal samples in order to obtain a minimum set of radiocarbon dates. And we sacrificed an agave plant in order to test the efficacy of agave knives (using replicas). Otherwise, the archaeology of San Esteban remains essentially as we found it, and we are hopeful that we have not created any lasting impact on the environment from our many weeks of living and working on this magnificent island.

Appendix D

An Informal Gazetteer
of San Esteban Island

There are no published maps that provide names for San Esteban Island's geographic features. Yet many of the island's features have been named, and these names are in common use among the various groups that visit the island. This informal gazetteer is not intended as a complete list, for we made no systematic effort to canvass every special interest group that makes use of the island. Nor should it be considered a definitive list, for much of the information comes from only a few individuals, some of whom may not have been true authorities on the subject.

The mix of Seri, Spanish, and English names reflects the multicultural use of the island during the twentieth century. Nearly all the names are current, though the Seris believe that most of the names they use today were also used much earlier by the San Esteban people. Most of the Seri names were originally recorded by Edward and Mary Beck Moser in the 1950s and 1960s. The remainder of the "established" names are those of Mexican fishermen. The majority designate coastal features, for fishermen spend little time inland. This lack of names for interior features was something of a handicap for our archaeological survey, and we found it necessary to make up names for a wide variety of features (e.g., Villalpando 1989:Fig. 14). The few made up names that are included here are the ones that refer to features mentioned in the present book.

Names are keyed to Map 1.1 except for features whose locations are uncertain. Within each category of feature, the list moves counterclockwise, starting at El Monumento on the east coast. For features with more than one name, the first one listed is generally the one most used in this book. Numbers in brackets indicate the source of the names:

[1] = Bahía Kino panga fishermen
[2] = Baja California panga fishermen
[3] = Seris
[4] = North American sport fishermen
[5] = Archaeologists (names coined during this project)

Coastal Features

1. El Monumento (The Monument) [1,2]

Pajíi 'Flint' [3]

This famous landmark stands on the southern end of Playa Limantour. It is almost a sea stack, but it is still attached to the shore. From the northwest, it resembles a larger-than-life beached whale some 150 feet long and 30 feet high. The Seri name refers to the bands of mottled red jasper in the rock.

The beach next to El Monumento is the winter camp of both Mexican and Seri fishermen. There is a protected cove in the lee of the rock where pangas can be beached. The rock itself has a small and uncomfortable cave to which the men retreat in extreme weather. The Seri refer to this cave as *Pajíi Zaaj* 'Flint Cave.'

2. Playa Limantour (Limantour Beach) [5]

This is the shingle beach on the eastern shore where the lower Arroyo Limantour empties into the sea (see No. 25). It is about ¼ mile long, making it the largest beach on the island.

3. Turtle-Shell Slide [5]

Hast Ano Ctamcö Quih Hant Yamíxojoj 'Mountain on Men [Are] Place Slid Down [plural]' [i.e., "Place Where the San Esteban Men Slid Down"] [3]

This is a slope of volcanic ash above a sea cliff just north of Playa Limantour. It is said the San Esteban men played a lethal game of "chicken" by sliding down this slope in inverted sea turtle carapaces.

4. [Name unknown] [3]

This is a deposit of red ochre, located just north of the turtle-shell slide. The Seris say that it is the only ochre they know of that can be applied to pottery and not change color upon firing.

5. Punta Pedregosa (Big Boulders Point) [2]

Baja California fishermen apply this name to the prominent bulge in the middle of the east coast. It refers to the many large boulders that make up the beach.

6. Playa del Faro (Lighthouse Beach) [1]

Punta Fueste [meaning uncertain] [2]
Xnitom [gloss unknown] [3]

These names refer to the beach and point just south of the automated lighthouse (*el faro*) near the northeastern corner of the island. The name "Fueste" used by Baja California fishermen may be a corruption of "Noreste" or "Fuerte." The Seris say this area was an important camp of the San Esteban people. Today, it is a place where both Mexican and Seri fishermen sometimes beach their pangas and camp temporarily in poor weather, but it is not considered a normal camp by either group.

7. Playón (Large Beach) [2]

Baja California fishermen apply this name collectively to Playa La Freidera (No. 9, below) and the several tiny beaches along the eastern half of the north coast.

8. *Zaaj An Cooxp* 'Cave Inside White' [3]

This cave is said to be in the Playón area of the north coast, where a conspicuous white volcanic tuff is exposed. The Seris say people once lived in it. Today, there is no trace of a cave. The cliffs throughout this area are composed of soft rocks that are vulnerable to wave erosion and slumping. In all likelihood, the cave has been destroyed in recent decades by natural forces.

9. Playa La Freidera (Frying Place Beach) [1]
Hant Haizj 'Land Mashed' [i.e., "Mud"] [3]

This is the large shingle beach on the north coast. It is more than 1/8 mile wide and constitutes the only major break in the sea cliffs on this side of the island. It is a place where fishermen caught by summer storms can beach their pangas and find some protection. The Seris sometimes camped here, but Mexican fishermen do not consider it a normal camping place. Bahía Kino fishermen call it "La Freidera" because it was once a place where sea lion hunters brought their catch and cooked the animals to render the blubber into oil. The origin of the Seri name is not known.

10. La Ventana (The Window) [2]

This is a hole in the sea cliffs near La Freidera that can be seen from a panga near shore.

11. Cabeza del Caballo (Horse's Head) [2]
(See No. 20, Male Mountain).

12. Playa Lobera (Sea Lion Beach) [2]
Coiij 'Tubular' [3]

Playa Lobera is a small shingle beach under the sea cliffs near the northwestern corner of the island. It is not clear why the Mexican name should single out this particular beach, for sea lions inhabit nearly all of San Esteban's beaches. The Seri name refers to the spiral appearance of a mountain there, as well as a camp that was probably located on this beach.

13. *ZAAȷ HAPÉSXÖ* 'CAVE HIDDEN' [3]

This spectacular cave some 200 feet deep has been hollowed out of the dark red ashy cliffs at the northwestern corner of the island. The Seri name is nonspecific; it is simply the generic term for a vision cave. Unlike the typical small shallow overhangs on San Esteban, this cave is large, visually impressive, and conveys a sense of leading deep into the bowels of the earth. However, it is not clear that Seris have ever sought visions in caves on San Esteban, and it may be that this cave is known not for any remembered use but for its obvious potential as a place to seek visions. There is no trace of human activity inside but ample evidence of catastrophic rockfall along with a steady drizzle of powdery volcanic ash from the ceiling.

14. CAMPO SAN PEDRO (SAN PEDRO CAMP) [1,2]

Insóc Yaahit "Where Black Skipjack Is Fished" [3]
Herm's Cove [4]

San Pedro is the summer camp of Mexican and Seri fishermen and is the only sheltered beach on the west side of the island. The landmark is a large rock monolith barely connected to the shore, much like El Monumento on the east coast. There is a cave in its base, which the Seris call *Zaaj An Cheel* 'Cave [gloss unknown].' The camp, however, is in a cove about 1/8 mile south of the rock. Here an overhang in the sea cliffs offers some protection against summer rainstorms. The Seris say that people once lived under this overhang. The English name for the cove is used by a few long-time North American residents of New Kino. It refers to a North American sport fisherman who liked to anchor here overnight and fish with his son.

15. *HASCAM CAACOȷ QUIH AN IHÁZQUIM* 'BALSA LARGE THE PUT-INSIDE' [3]

This name refers to one of about half a dozen sea caves near Campo San Pedro, but it is not clear which one. It was named because a San Esteban man once paddled a large balsa into the cave and hid there during a time of danger.

16. PLAYA EL CASCAJAL (PEBBLE BEACH) [1]

Punta Baja (Lower Point) [2]
Coftécöl Iifa 'Chuckwalla-large Peninsula' [3]
The Sandspit [4]

This peninsula is the most conspicuous coastal feature. It is a low shingle spit about ¼ mile long, built up by opposing currents that run along the southern and western sides of the island. The Seris say the beach just to the east was an important camp of the San Esteban people. Today, Mexican fishermen occasionally camp there because it is a place where pangas can be beached, but it provides little protection from storms. It is a poor anchorage for larger boats.

17. Punta Sur (South Point) [2]

This name designates the southeastern corner of San Esteban.

Mountains

18. Pico Rojo (Red Peak) [5]

This steep-sided mountain dominates the northeastern part of the island. Its talus slopes lend it a distinctive ruddy hue which sometimes turns a brilliant deep red in the fading rays of sunset.

19. Female Mountain [5]

Hast Cmaam 'Mountain Female' [3]

Female Mountain consists of a complex series of ridges that culminate in a high point. Viewed from most perspectives, it is a comparatively massive and rounded mountain of gray rock. To the Seris, its rounded form suggests femininity and hence its name.

20. Male Mountain [5]

Hast Ctam 'Mountain Male' [3]
Cabeza de Caballo (Horse's Head) [2]

Male Mountain is the major peak in the northwestern corner of the island. From the upper Arroyo Limantour, it is a striking reddish pyramid. Compared to Female Mountain, its pointed shape and greater height suggest masculinity to the Seris, and thus confer its name. Its Spanish name describes its appearance as viewed from the sea.

21. Pico San Esteban (San Esteban Peak) [5]

This summit overlooks the southwestern part of San Esteban. At 1,804 feet (Anonymous 1976a), it is the highest point on the island.

22. La Fortaleza (The Fortress) [5]

This distinctive but relatively low peak overlooks the south coast and much of the interior of the island. It was named for its sheer rock walls and relative inaccessibility.

23. Pico del Sur (South Peak) [5]

This mountain at the edge of the sea cliffs is the highest point in the southeastern corner of the island.

24. *Icámajoj Zaaj* 'Cook-agaves Cave [or Mountain]' [3]

This high and massive mountain in the center of San Esteban dominates the interior of the island. Its name seems to be comparatively recent. The word *Zaaj* can mean either "cliff" or "cave," and the mountain probably takes its name from the important habitation caves of the same name at its base. The caves in turn were named for the nearby pit ovens which the recent Seris have used for baking agave. Hence the pit ovens provided the name for the caves, which in turn provided the name for the mountain that towers above them.

The Seris say that the name the San Esteban people used for the caves was *Iip Hant Itox Zaaj* "Cave Where the Tails Drag," because scurrying chuckwallas left tracks in the coarse sand outside the cave. It is not clear whether the mountain also bore this name.

Arroyos

25. ARROYO LIMANTOUR (LIMANTOUR ARROYO) [1,2]

The Big Valley [4]

This is the largest drainage on San Esteban, extending across the entire island from the northwestern corner to the eastern shore. Its upper and lower reaches broaden into substantial valleys. All Mexican fishermen use the name "Limantour," but nobody knows its origin. One man assumed that it was the name used on maps of the island (there are no published maps with named features) while another guessed it was a man's surname, probably a North American. The arroyo was likely named around the turn of the century for José Yves Limantour the younger (1854–1935), who served as Secretary of the Treasury under President Porfirio Díaz from 1893 to 1911.

26. ARROYO BONITO (PRETTY ARROYO) [5]

This is the first arroyo north of A. Limantour. It flows southeast, draining the southeast slopes of Pico Rojo. It was named for the beauty of this area.

27. ARROYO DE LAS CUEVITAS (LITTLE CAVES ARROYO) [5]

This arroyo drains southward into A. Limantour from the saddle between Pico Rojo and *Icámajoj Zaaj*. It was named for the many small caves there, though in fact it has no more caves than most other arroyos.

28. ARROYO DEL FARO (LIGHTHOUSE ARROYO) [2]

This arroyo drains northeast from the saddle between Pico Rojo and *Icámajoj Zaaj* toward the island's northeastern corner, where the automated lighthouse is located.

29. ARROYO MUERTE (DEAD ARROYO) [5]

This arroyo drains northward into middle Arroyo Limantour. It was named for the utter absence of animals or animal sounds when our archaeological group first explored it.

Water Sources

30. *Seenel Iitxo* 'Many Butterflies' [3]

This important tinaja is said to be located somewhere near the base of Male or Female Mountain. It is a place where water was available for long periods during the year. Its name derives from the large number of butterflies that would come there to drink.

31. *Haxáacoj* 'Water-Large' [3]

This water source was somewhere near the southwestern corner of the island. It was considered the only permanent water, though even it sometimes failed to provide enough for the San Esteban population. Most Seris say it was a place near the beach where one could dig for water, although some believe it was a tinaja high in an arroyo. The name probably referred to the beach well, but in fact there is a tinaja high in the arroyo behind the beach.

Rock Art

32. Las Pinturas (The Paintings) [1]

Fishermen from Bahía Kino refer to a petroglyph cave (G15) by this term. Very few have actually been there, but everyone knows from hearsay that one of the figures (which recently disappeared) depicted a sailing vessel, called "*El Galeon*." Though this and the other figures are actually petroglyphs rather than paintings, the Seris agree that there are, or were, pictographs in this area. Apparently, they have eroded away.

Notes

Chapter One

1. Herrera says that his great-grandfather Quicilio (Porfirio Díaz's father) was living at Tecomate when the mainland people came over. Though Quicilio was not a San Esteban person, the invaders thought he was. So he went southward with the San Esteban people and lived with them for some time on San Esteban Island. This chance event may explain why Quicilio later decided to take his whole family, including his son Porfirio Díaz, to live with the San Esteban people.

2. The coast of Tiburón that was considered San Esteban territory faces directly southwest, though it has sometimes been referred to as the "south coast" or "southern shore" (Moser 1963: 16; Felger and Moser 1985:98). Moser's notes suggest that the southern portion of Tiburón's west coast may also have been San Esteban territory.

3. *Cöimáxp* was also known by the Spanish name Juan Diego. He was the paternal uncle of Coyote Iguana, the most famous of the San Esteban people (see pp. 25, 237–38).

4. It was thought that other Seris who ate agave would also become pale (Felger and Moser 1985:226) but there seems to be no explanation for this effect.

5. A genetic trait of this kind, pervading the San Esteban population but absent among other Seris, is consistent with the modern Seri belief that these folk were endogamous, rarely intermarrying with other Seris.

6. This would be a prodigious feat of strength. Live California sea lion females average about 250 pounds and males 600 pounds or more (Kasper 1980:3). Even after butchering and discarding the bones and blubber, the load of meat to be carried back to camp would be very heavy.

7. This would be easier that it might appear. A network of arroyos connects most parts of the island. With periodic brush clearing, these arroyos would serve as good paths of gentle gradient that would make running easy. Indeed, from time to time the arroyos are naturally cleared of brush by flash floods, as happened in August 1992 as a result of Hurricane Lester, which transformed several brush-choked arroyos into clear highways.

8. A skillfully thrown rock is a much more lethal weapon than many people realize. Father Francisco Antonio Pimentel, who accompanied the Spanish military campaign against the Seris on Tiburón Island in 1750, noted that Seri defenders broke the legs of attacking soldiers with thrown rocks, and rocks were commonly used as weapons against enemies by Baja California Indians (Venegas [1759] 1966a:424; Clavigero [1789] 1971:161, 167, 228; Crosby 1994:31, 87). Also during the eighteenth century, Father Miguel del Barco ([ca. 1770s] 1980:100) saw peninsular Indians successfully hunting ducks with thrown rocks. During the course of archaeologi-

cal fieldwork on Tiburón Island in the 1970s, our group watched Mexican marines stationed at Tecomate use expertly-aimed rocks to add variety to their dinner menu by picking off ducks swimming well off shore. Seri boys today will frequently throw rocks to bring down seagulls for sport (Mary Beck Moser 1996:pers. comm.). To appreciate the potential of rocks as weapons in the hands of someone who has grown up using them, one has only to consider the force and accuracy with which a baseball can be thrown by a professional baseball pitcher.

9. The place where a man who went over the edge would crash is an area of shallow water over a sea floor of large boulders. At high tide most of the rocks are underwater, and there is a reasonable chance that a person might survive the fall. But at low tide, some of the rocks protrude above the water and many others lie just below the surface. At these times, a trip off the cliff would more likely be deadly.

10. It is inviting to interpret the aggressive and self-destructive behavior attributed to the San Esteban people as a consequence of population pressure. This would be an especially appealing interpretation if the actual population had been anywhere near the figure given by Porfirio Díaz (100 men, implying 400 people or more). Even Roberto Herrera's estimate of 250 people probably would have resulted in a greater population density than was sustained in any nearby and ecologically comparable area.

Estimating sustainable population size for the San Esteban people by any technique is likely to be a rather speculative venture. Yet it may be possible to get at least a rough idea from population figures of adjacent areas, if these figures predate the worst disruptions of European contact. The most obvious place to look is Tiburón Island, though unfortunately the data from there may not be reliable. Only two population figures are known that stand much chance of reflecting aboriginal conditions. The only one that unquestionably predates European disruption is from 1636, when Captain Francisco de Ortega reported about 50 Indians at a single camp. Amazingly, despite three weeks exploring the island, Ortega makes no mention of any other people. Taken at face value, 50 Indians on an island of some 466 square miles gives an implausibly low population density of 0.1 person per square mile. For Orgeta's figure, there must be an additional caveat because his garbled geography leaves the identification of this island as Tiburón open to question (see Note 95 for Chapter 2).

The other figure comes from 1729, when Father Nicolás de Perera persuaded 151 Seris to leave Tiburón for the Sonora missions (see p. 84). At the time, the Indians convinced Perera that this was essentially the entire resident population of the island, though he later discovered that this was not the case. If we assume for the sake of argument that Perera removed only half the resident Seris, Tiburón's population density would still have been less than 0.6 persons per square mile. However, any estimate from the eighteenth century is suspect, for by then European contact had already begun to alter Seri demographics.

Probably the most that can be surmised from Ortega's and Perera's figures is that Tiburón's resident population, and population density, under aboriginal conditions was low. This in turn implies that San Esteban's population, if stable, must also have been quite low. Indeed, using the density figure of 0.6 would give San Esteban Island, at about 16 square miles, an absurdly small population of just under 10 people. However, their territory also included the southwest coast of Tiburón Island, a strip 20 miles long by perhaps 5 deep (100 square miles). At 0.6 persons per square mile, the two areas together imply a sustainable population of around 70 people.

In a much better documented situation, Homer Aschmann found that population densities among the neighboring Cochimí in Baja California at the time of European contact had averaged about one person per square mile (Aschmann 1967:Table 7). Assuming this density, San Esteban and the southwest coast of Tiburón Island together might have supported a population of around 116 people.

Aschmann also figured Cochimí density in relation to linear miles of available coastline. He concluded that the more productive stretches of coast may have supported a maximum of five people per linear mile (Aschmann 1967:180). Based on this figure, James Hills (1973:127-28) calculated that San Esteban Island itself, with about 15 miles of coastline, might have supported around 75 people. Adding the 20 linear miles of Tiburón's southwest coastal strip would bring the total to 175.

This method of figuring, however, may not be appropriate for a small island like San Esteban. It assumes a truly linear coastline, with a wide swath of land behind it that actually provides the bulk of the food supply (Aschmann 1967:180). The coastline of San Esteban is not linear, but wraps around on itself, encompassing a land area of about 16 square miles. In terms of area and terrestrial resources, this is the equivalent of a linear coastline that is 5 miles deep but only 3.2 miles long. Thus with an *effective* linear coastline of only 3.2 miles, at five people per linear mile, San Esteban would have supported about 16 people. Adding to this the 100 people that could have been supported by the 20 miles of Tiburón's southwest coast suggests a total sustainable population of about 116 for the San Esteban people.

Although these are obviously all crude calculations at best, they indicate that the San Esteban population, if stable, must have been quite small, probably not very much larger than 100 people. If this is so, San Esteban and the southwest coast of Tiburón Island together could not have supported the number of people estimated by Díaz or Herrera. And that brings us back to the question of population pressure. Although the estimates of Díaz and Herrera may be exaggerated, it is entirely possible that the San Esteban population at one time *was* too large to be stable.

If, as Herrera maintained, the San Esteban people were the original inhabitants of Tiburón who were pushed southward by other Seris, it could well be that they became severely overcrowded as they were forced into the southwest coastal strip of Tiburón and eventually onto San Esteban itself. Indeed, the displacement is said to have caused so much "trouble and fighting" among themselves that it split the population (see p. 25). One faction apparently headed westward in their balsas, and this may have helped alleviate the immediate pressure. But especially if the remaining people really did try to live en masse on San Esteban whenever the water supply permitted, they may have created for themselves a perpetual state of overcrowding. The reckless and self-destructive behavior for which the San Esteban people were famous, especially their deadly game of "chicken," might have functioned as an unwitting mechanism for continuing to reduce their numbers. It is possible that these measures worked, for there is a hint that the population did eventually reach a more stable size. The one independent account that seems to describe their extinction states that about a hundred people were rounded up and led away (see pp. 244–45).

11. The other Seris may have viewed the San Esteban people in much the way that urban residents of mid-southern states, such as Kentucky and Tennessee, regard rural "mountain people."

12. Very little is known specifically of the San Esteban dialect, which has probably not been spoken since the latter part of the nineteenth century. Edward Moser (1963:18) states that the expressions still remembered are characterized by sharp pitch contours and heavy stress. Only a few words were recalled by Porfirio Díaz that were distinctive to this dialect:

English	San Esteban	Gloss	Modern Seri	Gloss
cow	*hant csii*	'land he-who-smells'	*ziix cooha*	'thing crier'
horse	*hant cataxáacoj*	'land he-whose-steps-are-large'	*caay*	'horse'
jewfish	*lamz*	?	*maasni caacoj*	'jewfish large'
lobster	*ziix hast imócl quiij*	'thing rock under seated'	*ptcamn*	?
parrot	*cölel*	?	*zel*	?
small parrot	*coléelo*	?	—	—
shark (generic)	*tohni*	?	*hacat*	?
shark (one species)	*haac*	?	—	—
hair	*itáai*	?	*ilít*	'his-hair; his-head'

(table continues on next page)

English	San Esteban	Gloss	Modern Seri	Gloss
sandal	*hant ihaquéesjc*	'land to-cause-a-rustling-sound (?)'	—	—
star	*hamác*	'fire'	*azoj*	'star'
thing	*zah*	—	*ziix*	'thing'
firstborn child	*quihs*	—	*hiquetíi*	'my-firstborn-child'
nephew/son	*quitáaxza*	?	—	—
I'm happy	*haplipáhi*	?	*hiisax hant coitiha*	'my-spirit down touches'

In 1990, four more San Esteban words were elicited from elderly Seris by Mary Beck Moser and Stephen Marlett (1990:pers. comms.):

English	San Esteban	Gloss	Modern Seri	Gloss
sea lion	*ziix ccah*	'thing that-makes-sound'	*xapóo*	—
fish	*ziix quipxási*	'thing that-has-flesh'	*zixcám*	—
blood	*xica isxéno caap*	'stuff stomach stand'	*hait*	'blood'
salt	*ziix iqui acáai*	'thing with to-put'	*hantíp*	'land-its-(?)'

13. In describing Father Consag's 1751 exploration of northern Baja California, the Jesuit historian Francisco Clavigero notes that some of the Indians who had not had previous contact with Europeans before were:

> greatly astonished on seeing horses, [and] they begged the captain to permit them to lead the animals to graze near that place where their relatives lived so that they might see them also (Clavigero [1789] 1971:329).

14. This probably means that he did not understand why the stock was set at an angle from the barrel.

15. This is noteworthy not only because the San Esteban people fought so much among themselves but also because the other Seri bands frequently fought with each other (Moser 1963).

16. Seri plant foods are examined in detail by Felger and Moser (1985) while Malkin (1962) discusses animal foods.

17. Originally classified as *Agave dentiens*, this plant has since been reclassified as an endemic subspecies *Agave cerulata* subsp. *dentiens* (Gentry 1978:43–44, 1982:369–71). Three other subspecies of *A. cerulata* occur on the adjacent portions of Baja California and Ángel de la Guarda Island, about 40 miles northwest of San Esteban (Gentry 1978:35–48; Moran 1983:380), though it may be that the latter is also *A. cerulata dentiens* (Gentry 1982:369). There have been unconfirmed sightings by Seris, Mexican fishermen, and North American sport fishermen of small stands of a similar agave on neighboring San Lorenzo Norte (Las Ánimas) Island.

18. It has been reported previously that the San Esteban people dug huge pits and baked as many as a hundred agave hearts at a time, marking each heart to identify the owner (Felger and Moser 1970:164, 1985:222). This is almost certainly incorrect. Although there are a number of large agave baking pits on the island, they were probably constructed not by the San Esteban people but by other Seris who came to the island to collect agave in the late nineteenth and early twentieth centuries. These pits occur only on the portion of the island utilized by these later

visitors, and virtually identical pits can be seen on the southwest coast of Tiburón, at well-known camps where the Seris say these later visitors often brought the raw hearts to be cooked. As Roberto Herrera pointed out, the San Esteban people, with a large supply of plants readily at hand, would have had no reason to cook agave in such quantities and, therefore, would not have dug the huge pits. In fact, archaeological evidence suggests that the San Esteban people did not cook agave hearts in pits at all, but directly on the ground surface, as did the Indians throughout much of Baja California. Moreover, the very largest and most spectacular agave pits on San Esteban are probably not even aboriginal but rather the legacy of a Mexican distilling operation that functioned there briefly in the late 1870s (see pp. 138–40).

19. These are *Pachycereus pringlei* and *Stenocereus gummosus*, respectively. There is also a small stand of organ pipe (*pitahaya dulce*) cactus (*Stenocereus thurberi*) in the northwestern corner of the island, but perhaps not enough to have been nutritionally important.

20. These animals are *Sauromalus varius* and *Ctenosaura hemilopha*, respectively. The iguana was likely introduced on San Esteban by humans at some time in the past (Grismer 1994:28).

21. *Asclepias albicans.*

22. Later Seris who visited San Esteban had a different technique. Threatened chuckwallas typically wedge themselves under rocks by inflating the space under their loose skin with air. It is said that all the person had to do was poke the animal with a sharp stick to puncture and deflate its skin, and then pull the chuckwalla out.

23. The Seris may be referring to the rock clusters and rockpile cairns that dot the island. However, these features are not likely the result of digging out chuckwallas, for they are purposeful constructions and often occur in locations where chuckwallas are least numerous.

24. Several species of octopus are known from this part of the Gulf. The sea snail (*Nerita scabricosta*) can be found in quantity around El Monumento on the eastern shore of San Esteban.

25. *Heterodontus francisci*, a five foot bottom-feeder that eats mollusks, crabs, and other invertebrates.

26. The Seris say that the people on Tiburón Island were not nearly as proficient with the fish spear as the San Esteban men. However, Porfirio Díaz was respected for his skill with this weapon (Felger and Moser 1985:130).

It is said that the idea of the barbed harpoon head came from the San Esteban barbed fish spear. For a long time, the other Seris hunted turtles with only smooth-pointed harpoons. But it was hard to pull a sea turtle over to the balsa when it was held with one of these unbarbed tips. The Seris say that even when metal first began to be used for harpoon heads, they were still just smooth points. Indeed, when Lieut. R. W. H. Hardy visited Tiburón Island in 1826, he saw unbarbed harpoon heads made of iron (Hardy [1829] 1977:296–97).

But long ago a man named Julio saw the San Esteban people using barbed fish spears. He got one and showed the other Seris how it worked. They were greatly surprised by it and copied the idea, adapting it to harpoon heads. According to Roberto Herrera, this all happened before the time of his father, Antonio Herrera (see Figure 10.3), who was born in 1895.

27. *Echinocereus grandis*, a species endemic to San Esteban and San Lorenzo Islands.

28. *Zalophus californianus.* Despite intensive commercial hunting from the latter part of the nineteenth century until well into the twentieth, sea lions continue to inhabit the beaches of San Esteban Island in great numbers.

29. The bones were presumably left on the beach and would have quickly disintegrated or been washed away. This would explain why sea lion bones do not show up on beaches or at archaeological sites on the island.

30. The scarcity of water was probably the critical factor that set limits on the size of the San Esteban population and governed many of their activities (Felger and Moser 1985:98).

31. Apparently, these four bedrock pools are known only from tradition, for nobody claims to have personally seen any of them. On their visits to the island since the late nineteenth century, the Seris have not relied on San Esteban water but rather have brought it with them. There may have been more water available on San Esteban than the present Seris are aware of, for many other possible bedrock pools were noted during the course of archaeological survey of the island.

32. This beach well (*batequi*) is apparently the only water source that any Seris alive today have actually seen. Once during the 1960s, Richard Felger and Alexander Russell dug for water there. They did find water about a foot below the surface, but their hole filled only very slowly (Richard S. Felger 1980:pers. comm.). It is possible that this location produced much more water in the past than it has in recent times, for water sources in arid country often change their output over time and even disappear completely.

33. The concept of *ihízitim* was introduced briefly by Edward Moser in a paper on traditional Seri band structure (Moser 1963:21–22). He characterized them as well-integrated social units based on principles of patrilineal descent, patrilocal residence, and exogamy. Members are said to have worked and fought together and exercised exclusive rights over the resources within their territories.

While there seems to be no question of the former existence of these units, Moser's interpretation of them has been challenged on several counts (Bahre 1980; Sheridan 1982, 1996:196–97, 1999:10–12). Especially subject to criticism have been his identification of the *ihízitim* as a "clan," his omission of specific cultural data in support of his interpretations of its role in Seri social structure, and the seeming incompatibility between these units as he described them and the ecological realities of the Seri environment. On the interpretation of the *ihízitim* as a "clan," Moser was surely mistaken. But many of the other apparent problems can probably be resolved if Moser's characterization is understood as a description of the *ihízitim* in highly idealized form, not as they actually functioned in ordinary life. This is especially clear for San Esteban, which could not possibly have been divided into four truly separate groups with exclusive territories. Thus the Seris articulate ideal culture by claiming that each *ihízitim* "owned" its territory, lived there, and held exclusive rights to the resources within it. But under the circumstances of real life, there is no question that all Seris were highly mobile and that territorial boundaries were highly permeable. This was especially true when resources were scarce or when tragedy struck. At these times, members of one *ihízitim* would readily join those of another and share their resources, as the oral accounts of the San Esteban people explicitly state. And it should be recalled that the deaths of several relatives from snail fever is probably what prompted Porfirio Díaz's family to leave their traditional home on Tiburón Island and move in with the San Esteban people.

Additional data, which Moser recorded but did not cite, suggest that in everyday life the *ihízitim* functioned most strongly to establish social identity. Wherever people actually resided, they identified with their *ihízitim* and were identified by others as members of that group and its territory. Even today, people name their dogs after landmarks in their *ihízitim*.

34. Thus the idea of *ihízitim* seems to integrate a territory, its resources, its major camp, and its people into a single unifying concept. This is something like the concept of "New Yorker," which simultaneously links a major city, its resources, and its special character, with all the people who are "from" there—who identify with New York—even if they are not living there now.

35. Seris visiting the island in more recent times have almost always camped at *Pajíi*. For many decades, it has also been the winter camp of Mexican fishermen. Any archaeological remains that might have been left there by the San Esteban people have long since disappeared.

36. The black skipjack (*Euthynnus lineatus*) is a common fish known locally as *barrilete*.

37. It is the protected cove called San Pedro by Mexican fishermen.

38. There are actually several separate sea caves in this vicinity that fit the Seri description.

39. It is at the beach that Mexican fishermen know as Playa La Freidera.

40. The fact that nearly all of the camps recalled today are on the coast probably reflects the reluctance of recent Seris to venture very far into the island's interior. Whatever they may once have known of the inland camps of the San Esteban people (apart from *Icámajoj Zaaj*) has apparently been forgotten. Archaeological survey shows that there were many camps throughout the interior of the island.

41. The word *zaaj* can mean either 'cave' or 'cliff.' This enables *Icámajoj Zaaj* to refer to two different features. In its meaning of 'cliff' it refers to the massive mountain that dominates the central part of the island. In its other meaning, *Icámajoj Zaaj* is the modern Seri name for the large cave at the base of this mountain said to have been used by the San Esteban people.

A few older men remember seeing this cave during trips to the island many years ago. The nearby agave baking pits, from which the modern name for the cave derives, were almost certainly dug and used by these more recent visitors, not the San Esteban people.

42. This cave, or rather a series of almost connected caves, has been given the prosaic archaeological designation G4. Unfortunately, neither smoke blackening nor pictographs are evident today. This cave complex formed in a highly friable mud flow conglomerate, and it is quite possible that erosion of the cave walls has obliterated smoke blackening and pictographs that might have been plainly visible just a few decades ago.

43. This statement must apply to those times when they traveled to the southwest coast of Tiburón Island, because there are no dunes at all on San Esteban. Other Seri groups preferred to camp on dunes because of the softness of the sand (Bowen 1976:23).

44. This statement is well supported by archaeological observation. The scatter of cultural material below habitation caves is exceedingly thin. Some open sites (camp clearings) have a small scatter of associated artifacts, but others have none at all.

45. Polygyny was formerly practiced among all Seri groups, but not to this extreme. If the San Esteban men gambled with their own lives as often as the Seris today believe, there would have been many more adult women than men. One way of dealing with a seriously imbalanced adult sex ratio would have been to permit polygynous families with several co-wives.

46. Though boiling food in pottery vessels may have been the conventional cooking method of the San Esteban people, the idea that they ate much of their food raw would help explain why comparatively little pottery has been found archaeologically on the island.

47. Carrying water in nonbreakable containers makes good sense on San Esteban's steep and treacherous terrain. On the Sonoran mainland, where there are vast tracts of level ground, Seris carried water from their sources to camp in large pottery ollas.

48. This is consistent with the archaeological record. San Esteban seems to have relatively few artifacts in only a limited range of types.

49. Large scallop shells of the genus *Pecten*, which are sometimes tossed up on San Esteban beaches during storms, would have made excellent knives. Although a few of these shells, both whole and fragmentary, have been found at habitation sites, none show intentional sharpening or other modification of their edges.

50. *Phragmites australis*.

51. Felger and Moser (1985:310) give an excellent description of the manufacture and use of the balsa.

52. This superstructure must have resembled the traditional Seri Quonset-style house (Felger and Moser 1985:114–17).

53. Their orientation toward Baja California, rather than the Sonoran mainland, makes sense in terms of regional geography as perceived from San Esteban. From this vantage point, the southwest coast of Tiburón Island appears prominent and close. But the closest portion of the Sonoran mainland is about 35 miles away, and it is such low-lying terrain that it is virtually invisible from San Esteban. The visual effect is that there is no land east of Tiburón. On the other hand, a few miles to the west lies the long hulk of San Lorenzo Island, and beyond it are the mountains of Baja California, which appear tall, extensive, and not very distant (see Figure 13.13). From San Esteban Island, west is the obvious direction to go.

54. The plant is desert tobacco (*Nicotiana obtusifolia* [=*N. trigonophylla*]). The name *poora* is probably derived from *puro*, the Spanish word for "cigar" (Felger and Moser 1985:369).

Desert tobacco occurs throughout the Seri area, including both San Esteban and San Lorenzo Islands. Visual examination of plant specimens from the two islands shows no obvious botanical differences (Richard S. Felger 1984:pers. comm.). However, there may be some chemical differences, for the Seris say that the San Lorenzo plants have a superior flavor (Felger and Moser 1985:369).

55. For this to have been possible, there must have been fresh water available on San Lorenzo. Today, there are apparently no permanent sources of water there, and even temporary water is

rare. On the south island of San Lorenzo, the only potential waterhole known is a single bed-rock pool that may or may not hold water after a rain. On the north island (Ánimas Island), Daniel W. Anderson has seen several small bedrock pools filled with water immediately after a major summer downpour (Daniel W. Anderson 1984:pers. comm.), though it is doubtful that these pools could have supported very many people for very long.

The archaeological evidence of human activity on the two San Lorenzo Islands is also mea-ger. Twelve days of survey on the south island in 1983 revealed only five localities with any artifacts or features at all. However, even if a group of San Esteban people did spend an entire year on San Lorenzo, there might not be much evidence of their stay. On San Esteban, there is very little nonperishable evidence of Mexican fishermen, though these men have been camping at El Monumento for decades.

One of the few archaeological sites on San Lorenzo, probably a camp, is situated just behind the beach near the south end of the south island. It has some vague clusters of rocks and cleared areas, a few chipped and ground cobbles, and a thin scatter of shell and bone fragments. How-ever, none of these sparse remains has any diagnostic value, so there is no way to determine whether they were produced by San Esteban people, more recent Seris, Indians from Baja Cali-fornia, or the Mexican fishermen who have traditionally camped in this general area.

56. An abbreviated version of this story has been published both in Seri and Spanish by Edward and Mary Beck Moser in a Seri language literacy booklet (Herrera et al. 1976).

57. San Lorenzo Norte, also known as Las Ánimas Island.

58. There are actually two such features. Morales is correct that they are not true estuaries, but rather salt water lagoons. Both are located on the west coast of San Lorenzo, facing Baja California. However, they are both on the south island, not San Lorenzo Norte (see Figure 1.13).

59. Sea lions were abundant on the shores of San Lorenzo during the late nineteenth century, and the island was frequently visited by Mexican sea lion hunters at this time.

60. This animal is actually a chuckwalla (*Sauromalus hispidus*) similar in appearance to the piebald chuckwalla (*S. varius*) of San Esteban Island except for its dark skin. It occurs on Ángel de la Guarda Island as well as the two San Lorenzo Islands, plus Alcatraz and some small islets in Bahía de los Ángeles, where it has probably been introduced (Grismer 1994:35).

61. In other words, because of his power as a shaman, his was the only balsa to survive the shark attack.

Today, the Seris refer to this individual either as *Cmaacoj Ofícj Coil* "Old Blue Shirt Man" or *Ziij Ctam Ofícj Coil* "The Deceased Blue Shirt Man." It is said that he was a young man when the shark attack occurred. On the basis of remembered genealogical relationships, Edward Moser estimated that this event must have occurred sometime between about 1820 and 1835.

62. This would be the camp called *Coftécöl Iifa* 'Chuckwalla-large Peninsula,' which is just east of the prominent spit of the same name at the southwestern corner of the island.

63. These are the 6,500-foot cones of Los Tres Vírgenes volcanoes, about 80 miles due south of San Esteban. Although they are actually on the peninsula of Baja California, from the vantage point of San Esteban they appear to be islands rising directly out of the sea.

64. Other Seris say this creature was like a whale and spouted water.

65. This is Arroyo Limantour.

66. Documentary sources also suggest that the Seris may have raided Baja California during the first quarter of the nineteenth century. One incident, involving a raid on Santa Gertrudis mission in 1802 by five Indians suspected to be Seris, was carefully described by Interim Gov-ernor José Joaquín de Arrillaga. By 1824, Fray Francisco Troncoso claimed that Seris had "of-ten" crossed the Gulf in balsas and attacked the mission of Loreto (see pp. 232–34). These would have been substantial expeditions, for Loreto lies about 200 miles southeast of San Esteban. Both Arrillaga and Troncoso, and later McGee (1898:82), assumed that these Seri raiders must have been from Tiburón Island, but they would have had no way of knowing if they were San Esteban people instead.

67. In a different version of *Cöimáxp*'s death, the shark attack occurred when he and his family were returning from Baja California in two of the huge 15-passenger covered balsas.

68. The town of Mulegé is about 130 miles south-southeast of San Esteban Island.

69. This unquestionably describes Mulegé, the only place in Baja California where a fresh water stream empties into a tree-lined estuary.

70. This statement contradicts the Seris' otherwise firm belief that the San Esteban people did not use the bow and arrow.

71. This part of the narrative, involving the "ghostly form" (*bulto* in Moser's notes), does not seem to make much sense. The problem may stem from confusion with an incident that occurred during a later trip to Baja California, one that was made sometime around the turn of the twentieth century, and by Seris who were not members of the San Esteban group. The story of this trip was told by Jesús Morales, whose father's brother was among the participants. Morales said that when the Seris reached the peninsula, they saw "something" lying on the beach. When they saw it get up and begin to run back and forth, they realized it was a coyote. As they explored ashore, the men came to some huts built of ocotillo, a grave with a carrying yoke lying across it, and various artifacts. They also saw some donkeys, and thinking they were horses, killed some, put the meat in their boats, and left. Morales gave no indication that the Seris who made this trip encountered or attacked any people (Mary Beck Moser 1997:pers. comm.).

72. According to an earlier interpretation (Gerhard and Gulick 1962:144), the name "Cachanilla" (or "Cachanía"), is derived from "Rosalía" and used as a slang term in Baja California to refer to people from the town of Santa Rosalía (not Mulegé). If this is correct, the term must have expanded in both meaning and use, for it is now often used by Sonoran fishermen to refer to anyone from Baja California (Elfego Briseño 1982:pers. comm.). However, it may be that the term derives not from "Rosalía," but is simply the diminutive of "*cachana*," the Spanish name for arrowweed (*Pluchea sericea*), which is common throughout the peninsula (Gary Nabhan 1998: pers. comm.).

As to the Seri belief about these people, Elisa Villalpando, who grew up in Santa Rosalía, notes that the town is a seaport, that some of the residents are fishermen, and that at certain times of the year they do in fact hunt sea turtles. But she has never heard of a special group of fishermen who are especially friendly toward the Seris (Elisa Villalpando 1983:pers. comm.). It may be that when fishermen from Mulegé, Santa Rosalía, or other peninsular towns come to Sonora, they keep to themselves simply because they are strangers. They may also be friendlier toward the Seris because they do not share the prejudices toward them common among Sonorans. Moreover, many of these fishermen may well be of Sonoran Indian ancestry. In the nineteenth century, large numbers of Yaquis were brought to Baja California from Sonora as unskilled labor. These factors, coupled with a real or perceived dark skin and prowess in sea turtle hunting, may be the basis for the Seri belief that the ancestors of the Cachanillas were San Esteban people.

73. This remarkable oral biography by Morales and Herrera was recorded on tape by Edward and Mary Beck Moser and published by Edith Lowell (1970). One portion of it describes the circumstances surrounding the sensational kidnapping of Lola Casanova, which took place on February 23, 1850. Although certain aspects of the incident and its aftermath were recorded on the spot by the Mexican authorities (see pp. 237–39), Lowell (1970:158) concludes that the Seri oral accounts may be more accurate than subsequent Mexican versions.

74. These two spirits are known by the names *Hast Ctam* 'Mountain Male' and *Hast Cmaam* 'Mountain Female,' which are also the names of two prominent peaks near the northwestern corner of San Esteban Island (see Figures 1.3, 1.10, and 13.2). According to the present Seris, these two peaks were once people who were turned into mountains long ago. In Seri belief, mountains and many other natural features and objects have spirits, or power, but there is usually no name for the spirit or power apart from the feature in which it resides (Mary Beck Moser 1997:pers. comm.). Hence the names of these two spirits are simply the names of the mountains they now inhabit.

75. In other words, this incident helped establish the character of women.

76. Perhaps this is something that might be done by an irate person to vent his anger.

77. The normal procedures for the vision quest are described by Felger and Moser (1985:103–4). There seems to be a belief that at least a few San Esteban people, including Coyote Iguana,

did seek visions in the ordinary Seri manner. The Seris today know of three caves along the shoreline of San Esteban that they regard as vision caves. One is a spectacular recess at the northwestern corner of the island (see Appendix D). Another is somewhere near the northeastern corner of the island, and the third is near the southwestern corner. Since the Seris today are quite sure that Seris living on Tiburón and the mainland did not go to San Esteban to seek visions, the only way these could have been vision caves is if they were used by the San Esteban people themselves. More likely, perhaps, the Seris refer to them as vision caves because they *look* like appropriate places to seek visions, not because they are remembered as places that were ever actually used on any specific vision quest.

78. It is not clear whether San Esteban women who became shamans sought visions in the same manner as the men.

79. Roberto Herrera said that the vision seeker drank a mixture of fish blood and fish scales. When the current took him away from the island, he would paddle back to shore, but he would not set foot on land. Griffen (1959:16) reports that Seri vision seekers limited their liquid intake to small amounts of sea water, but he does not specify this as a San Esteban practice.

80. It is not clear what this statement means.

81. If so, the crypts are well hidden, for not a single burial has been found on San Esteban Island.

82. Although the oral accounts maintain that the San Esteban people would defend themselves against intruders, it may be that, like other Seris, they often tried to avoid potentially hostile strangers by hiding. Seris elsewhere earned a well-deserved reputation as formidable fighters, yet they often chose to avoid armed confrontation when they could. During the eighteenth and nineteenth centuries, as conflicts became frequent, the Seris became increasingly adept at not showing themselves. Although there were many episodes of fierce combat, several of the formal military campaigns, especially those that went to Tiburón Island, ended in failure for the Europeans, in large part because the soldiers could find so few Indians. Even ethnologist WJ McGee was unable to make contact with any Seris during his harrowing 1895 visit to Tiburón Island (see pp. 226–28). On an island as rugged as San Esteban, people who knew the terrain probably would have had little difficulty avoiding strangers by hiding if they chose to do so. Perhaps the instances alluded to, when the San Esteban people fought off intruders, were times they were caught by surprise and felt they had no choice but to respond with force.

83. An abbreviated narrative of these events was published by Edward Moser (1963:25–26). His version is a composite, based largely on Roberto Herrera's account, but incorporating some of what other Seris said about the incident and its aftermath. An earlier account that seems to describe the same events was published by Dane and Mary Coolidge, based on information obtained from Jesús Félix (also known as "Buro Alazán") in 1932 (Coolidge and Coolidge 1939: 164–65).

The Seri tradition of how the San Esteban people were exterminated is one of the most bitterly recited episodes in the long and tragic history of their relations with Europeans. The uncharacteristically sketchy nature of the accounts can probably be attributed to the obvious fact that few if any of the people who directly experienced it lived to tell about it.

Nor is there any clear indication of precisely when the extinction might have occurred. No official Mexican report of it has yet come to light, and the Seris are certain only that it took place in the latter part of the nineteenth century. However, it is said that it happened shortly after Porfirio Díaz and his family moved away from San Esteban, and that the family left when Díaz was still a boy. This means that if it is possible to estimate Díaz's birth date, it might also be possible to bracket a relatively narrow span during which the extinction must have occurred.

There are several indirect ways of estimating when Díaz was born. Two of them rely on a single Mexican government document. This document is the first known census of the Seris, taken late in 1890 at the order of Sonoran Governor Ramón Corral. Díaz does not appear in it (at least not under his usual name), but his sister Angelita is clearly listed by name and correctly identified as the wife of Manuel Encinas. The census gives her age as 23 years, which would establish her birth date as 1867 (Monteverde 1891:569).

Unfortunately, there is no way to be certain of the precise birth order of Angelita, Porfirio, and their siblings. In the 1960s, the Seris were quite certain that Angelita was older than Porfirio, but all of the people questioned in 1991 thought that Porfirio was the older of the two (Mary Beck Moser 1991:pers. comm.). There is no sure way to resolve this discrepancy, but the earlier belief, that Angelita was the eldest child, is consistent with other data. According to this view, after Angelita, the next child was Ilario Covilla, followed by Porfirio and his twin sister Margarita, and then three other children. The census indicates that in 1890, the mean interval between siblings age 12 and under was a little less than three years. If we assume a spacing of three years between births in Díaz's family, Porfirio would have been born about six years after Angelita, or around 1873.

Another approach to estimating Porfirio's birth date is by way of his twin sister Margarita. Like Porfirio, she is missing from the census. But her future husband, Ramón Blanco, is listed. His age is given as 13 years, so he must have been born about 1877. According to the census, nearly all of the people who were under age 40 in 1890 had married somebody within six years of their own age. Thus if we assume that Blanco later married a woman within approximately six years of his own age, his future wife Margarita, and her twin Porfirio, would have been born between 1871 and 1883.

One might well question the accuracy of the ages which the Mexicans recorded for Seris who, in 1890, did not keep close track of the calendar date of their births. It is not clear how the Mexicans determined the Seri ages, and the census does contain a number of errors. But some figures are demonstrably accurate. The census gives the age of Juan Tomás (see Figure 10.3) as 32 years. The Seris say that he was born the year the big ship burned off Patos Island. That vessel, the *John Elliot Thayer*, was destroyed by fire in 1858 (see pp. 122–24) which would have made Juan Tomás precisely 32 years old at the time of the census.

When Porfirio Díaz died in 1959, nobody knew just how old he was, but many Seris and non-Indians guessed that he must have been about 90. If this were correct, it would place his date of birth sometime around 1869, slightly earlier than the dates derived from the 1890 census data. However, elderly Seris often seem older than their actual years. Estimates of old peoples' ages have usually erred on the high side in those cases where it has been possible to reliably establish their birth dates (Mary Beck Moser 1995:pers. comm.). If estimates of Díaz's age based on appearance (see Figure I.4) have been subject to this kind of exaggeration, it may be that he was closer to 80 or 85 when he died, which would imply a birth date between about 1874 and 1879.

Díaz's birth date can also be estimated from photographs taken of him over his lifetime. The earliest photograph known positively to be of him was taken in 1930 by A. L. Kroeber, who referred to him even at that time as an "elderly man" (Kroeber 1931:Fig. 3). However, it is likely that he was photographed much earlier. William Dinwiddie, the photographer with McGee's 1894 expedition, photographed a young man who is identified only as a "Seri Runner" in the published report (McGee 1898:Pl. 21). But the original negative identifies the subject as "Louis," which may be a misrecording of "Díaz." Many Seris and non-Seris who knew Díaz have seen the photograph (see Figure I.3), and there is widespread conviction that he is the "Seri Runner." Dinwiddie's photograph appeared again in 1937 in Eduardo Villa's history of Sonora, where it is explicitly identified as a photograph of Porfirio Díaz (Villa 1937:33).

Two forensic anthropologists have compared the Dinwiddie photograph with Kroeber's photograph as well as later photographs of Díaz and have similarly concluded that the young man in the 1894 photograph is probably Díaz (Roger M. LaJuenesse 1986:pers. comm.; Walter H. Birkby 1987:pers. comm.). Though age is difficult to judge precisely from photographs, both anthropologists estimate that the person in the 1894 photograph was between 15 and 25 years of age at the time. If the subject were indeed Díaz and if the estimated age range is correct, it would place his date of birth between about 1869 and 1879. Thus several approaches suggest that Porfirio Díaz was born sometime between about 1869 and 1883, and most likely sometime in the 1870s.

The next step is to estimate when Díaz and his family left San Esteban Island. The Seris believe that they departed shortly before the massacre and when Díaz was still a boy. Moser's notes contain one specific age estimate, that Díaz was between four and six years old when the massacre took place, though it is unclear whether this was a Seri opinion or Moser's inference. Using this figure, the family would have left the island no later than between about 1873 and 1889. However, Díaz's youth at the time of the massacre, like his age when he died, has likely been exaggerated, for it is highly unlikely that the elderly Díaz could have recalled so much detail from a period this early in his life. Moreover, Díaz's parents produced three more children after Díaz himself. If we assume the same three-year birth spacing implied by the Mexican census, Díaz would have been at least nine years old by the time his father died and the remaining family left San Esteban for good. Hence he might still have been a "boy" in the sense of preadolescent, but his age might have been more in the range of nine to twelve years, a period far more likely to be preserved within the memory of an old man. Using a round number, if Díaz were about 10 years old at the time of departure, then he and his family would have left San Esteban between 1879 and 1893.

While it is said that the San Esteban people were wiped out soon after Díaz and his family left the island, we do not know whether that means a few days, months, or even a couple of years. If the massacre took place immediately afterwards, it would have occurred between 1879 and 1893. If two years passed, they would have been wiped out sometime between 1881 and 1895.

Thus while some assumptions are unavoidable, several lines of reasoning give roughly the same result. They all suggest that Díaz was probably born during the 1870s, and that the San Esteban people met their demise sometime between the early 1880s and the early 1890s.

During the interval between 1879 and 1895, three formal military expeditions are known to have been mounted against the Seris (see Chapter 10). The 1880 campaign was apparently a mainland operation which would not likely have encountered the San Esteban people. The well-documented 1894 expedition to Tiburón Island saw no Seris. This leaves the third expedition, which set sail into the Gulf in June 1890. What happened during this campaign has never been made public.

84. The cycle of Seri raids and European reprisals is well documented and extends back to the seventeenth century. From time to time the government launched large-scale military campaigns that had, as their explicit goal, the complete extermination of the Seris. Many of these formal campaigns were unsuccessful, killing and capturing few if any individuals. The military was far more effective when it adopted "search-and-destroy" tactics, scouring the coastal region and killing small groups of Seris caught by surprise in their camps. In the mid-nineteenth century, Mexican cowboys who adopted these tactics are thought to have hunted down and killed half the Seri population in only about a dozen years (McGee 1898:113). Seri raids and reprisals by ranchers or government forces continued sporadically into the early years of the twentieth century.

85. Thus the people camped at *Xnit* may have been the mainland Seris who shifted the blame for their own raids to the unsuspecting San Esteban people and then lured them to their doom.

86. The stone corral at *Pazj Hax*, cited here and also by Herrera in the account which follows, is approximately 65 feet long and 13 feet wide. In late 1980 the structure was still intact, with walls standing more than 4 feet high (see Figure 1.15). It was definitely built prior to 1904, when it was discovered and photographed by Governor Izábal's soldiers (see Figure 1.14). Roberto Herrera, who had seen the corral several times from the air, believed that it was used to imprison Seris during Izábal's 1904 campaign (Herrera Marcos 1988:499–500), but he was equally certain that it had been built earlier to incarcerate the San Esteban people. Roberto Thomson, a Sonoran who was well informed about Seri-Mexican hostilities of the period, had also seen the corral and also believed that this was the structure used to contain the San Esteban people during the military action that exterminated them (Alexander Russell 1980:pers. comm.).

The adults who were executed in the corral may have been buried nearby. In 1904, when Izábal's troops discovered the corral, they also found a "*cementerio Seri*" above it:

> Some [of our group] encountered a Seri cemetery, situated on a small mesa. As one can imagine, the graves of this tribe are exceedingly crude: a moderately deep hole, the corpse wrapped in its rags, [with] dirt and a layer of rocks on top of it. Close to the cemetery there was a small fort [the stone corral] also built of rocks. (García y Alva 1905–1907)

García y Alva's assumption that the cemetery was Seri may be only partially correct. In the past, the Seri did not bury their dead in formal cemeteries but simply somewhere close to the place they died. Those who died in battle were usually left where they fell and not buried at all. A recognizable cemetery area is therefore not likely a feature to have been built by the nineteenth century Seris. If some of the San Esteban people were shot near the corral, the corpses in this cemetery would presumably be Seri, but the graves themselves would probably have been the work of the soldiers, intent on disposing of the bodies in a quick and expedient manner.

87. Yaqui Indians were also dealt with in this manner. According to the Mexican writer Santa de Caborca:

> A colonel in the army, Antonio Rincón, in July, of 1892, took two hundred Yaquis, men, women and children, prisoners, and carried them in the gunboat *El Demócrata* and dropped them in the ocean between the mouth of the Yaqui river and the seaport of Guaymas, all of them perishing. (Turner 1969:31)

88. Pueblo de Seris (or Villa de Seris) is today essentially a suburb of Hermosillo. Its beginnings date from 1704, when an unsuccessful Seri mission named Nuestra Señora de Guadalupe was established on the south bank of the Río Sonora. Across the river, a military garrison called San Pedro de la Conquista de Pitic was established in 1741, but neither settlement amounted to much for the next few decades. In 1771, at the end of 20 years of warfare between Spaniards and Seris, Pueblo de Seris was established on the site of the moribund mission as a place to relocate hostile Indians (Roca 1967:172–73; Kessell 1975:76–77; Radding 1997:212–13). Here, next to the presidio of Pitic, Seris were to be given land, molded into farmers, Christianized, and thereby transformed into productive citizens. However, few Seris stayed there for long. By the early nineteenth century, Pitic (later renamed Hermosillo) had grown into a sizable town, and Mexicans had taken over most of the designated Seri lands. In the aftermath of nineteenth century Mexican military expeditions, Pueblo de Seris often became a sort of prison camp for captured Seris, though nearly all the Indians quickly managed to escape. Except for these times, the Seri population rarely ever exceeded a few families, and much of the time the erstwhile pueblo was deserted. The last time the government forcibly relocated Seris there was in 1880.

89. Moser's notes include another account of this incarceration at Pueblo de Seris. In this version, the men became homesick for the sea. An epidemic struck and killed off most of the captives. One man became quite sick and sliced his thigh with a knife, believing in his delirium that he was cutting a rooster fish. The people who survived the illness escaped and set out for Tiburón Island, but more died along the way. Only a few reached Tiburón, where they joined the other Seris who were living there.

A similar account was related to Dane Coolidge in 1932 by Jesús Félix ("Buro Alazán"). In this variant, the epidemic that killed the Seris is specifically identified as smallpox (Coolidge and Coolidge 1939:156).

90. Herrera said that the governor who ordered this expedition was Rafael Izábal. In this he was mistaken, for Izábal did not assume office until 1903, which is long after the Seris believe the San Esteban people were exterminated. However, Izábal did order and personally lead the 1904 military expedition to Tiburón Island (see Figures 10.7 and 10.8), which also rounded up a large number of Seris (García y Alva 1905–1907). Despite the confusion about who was governor, Herrera knew that the 1904 campaign was not the one that wiped out the San Esteban people, and his description of this later event is very different (see pp. 256–58).

According to Sonoran Roberto Thomson, the warship *Demócrata* (see Figure 7.3) was the vessel that was sent to round up the San Esteban people (Alexander Russell 1980:pers. comm.). Around the end of the nineteenth century, this vessel saw frequent service against rebellious Yaquis as well as Seris. It took soldiers to Tiburón Island in the mysterious 1890 expedition and was the vessel that transported Izábal's troops to Tiburón Island in 1904 (García y Alva 1905–1907).

91. Moser included this part of the story in his published summary of the San Esteban people's demise (Moser 1963:25). Later, however, Herrera told Moser that he (Herrera) had been mistaken in linking the events on Punta Santa Rosa with the extinction of the San Esteban people.

The Santa Rosa affair, he said, was actually part of a different roundup that involved Seris from the Kino Bay region.

In a somewhat different version of the wiring incident, José Manuel stated that the Seris who were rounded up included some San Esteban people as well as Seris from Tiburón Island and the mainland. He said that many of the babies and older people were burned. The pretty young women and young men were led away with wires through their index fingers, though some pulled away and escaped (Mary Beck Moser 1981:pers. comm.). However, in line with Herrera's later assessment, Manuel gave no indication that this incident had anything to do with the final extermination of the San Esteban people.

92. Deportation had been tried previously as a solution to difficulties with Seris and other Indians. In 1750, the Spaniards deported the women of 80 Seri families to Guatemala, an action that helped precipitate 20 years of guerilla warfare (Spicer 1962:108). Another major deportation to the Caribbean was apparently carried out in 1784 (Sheridan 1999:433). By the 1790s, Apache prisoners, including women and children, were routinely being shipped to Cuba because prisoners previously deported to southern Mexico had shown an uncanny ability to escape and return to their homeland (Weber 1992:232). In the late nineteenth century, southern Mexico was again the favored destination, and in 1895, 12 Seris were exiled there (see p. 253). During the first decade of the twentieth century, deportation was employed on a massive scale to deal with Yaqui prisoners of war. By 1908, at least 5,000 had been deported, most of them sold to owners of henequen and sugar cane plantations in southern Mexico (Spicer 1962:82–83; HuDeHart 1984:155–200; Figueroa Valenzuela 1985:160–61; López Soto 1993:400). In 1910, Colonel Francisco B. Cruz, the officer directly in charge of transporting Yaquis to Yucatán, told John Kenneth Turner that in the previous three and a half years, he had made delivery of 15,700 Yaquis, above and beyond the 10 to 20 percent who had died en route (Turner 1969:35).

93. There may be no way to fully reconcile these versions of the extinction, nor to completely match the Seri accounts with documented military expeditions. However, one can come close if the Seri accounts are interpreted as an inadvertent fusion of two separate incidents, as Roberto Herrera eventually concluded (see Note 91). The main elements in one of these incidents would be the roundup at Punta Santa Rosa on the mainland, the burning and wiring together of the captives, leading them away to a forced relocation at Pueblo de Seris, the epidemic, and the eventual escape back to the coast. In fact, these elements probably comprise the Seri version of documented events that took place in 1880 (see pp. 240–42). According to Mexican records, in that year a military campaign to the mainland coast across from Tiburón succeeded in capturing about 150 Seris. The Indians were taken to Pueblo de Seris, given a subsidy, and encouraged to become farmers. A number of people became gravely ill, and several died. Before long the rest revolted, and most of the survivors escaped back to the coast (Corral [1885] 1959:258; Troncoso 1905:18; Spicer 1962:113).

Because the 1880 campaign was apparently strictly a mainland operation, it is difficult to see how any of the reclusive San Esteban people could have been involved. It may be that the idea that they were among the captives wired together and incarcerated at Pueblo de Seris is one of the ways the Seris have unconsciously merged this event with the extinction of the San Esteban people.

Shorn of these elements, the remaining portions of the Seri accounts seem to tell of an altogether different incident, and comprise a credible description of the extinction of the San Esteban people. They include the soldiers going by ship to Tiburón and perhaps also San Esteban Island, luring the San Esteban people to the stone corral, killing some there, loading the rest on the ship, throwing the men overboard, deporting the women, and ending with few or no survivors. In this case, no corresponding military campaign is known from Mexican records, although the circumstances surrounding the enigmatic June 1890 expedition of the gunboat *Demócrata* into the Gulf suggest this as a possibility (see pp. 243–47, 435).

Finally, it is conceivable that Herrera was right in the first place and that the events at Punta Santa Rosa were indeed connected with the extinction of the San Esteban people. Although no Indians were ever relocated at Pueblo de Seris after the 1880 roundup, the soldiers who sailed aboard the *Demócrata* on the mysterious 1890 expedition to Tiburón Island evidently also went ashore somewhere on the mainland (Corral 1891:369). One might speculate that they took the San Esteban people from the Tiburón corral to Punta Santa Rosa with the intent of marching them to Pueblo de Seris. If tensions were running high, it is not hard to imagine that a plan like this might have gone badly awry somewhere along the way, and that the San Esteban people neither arrived at Pueblo de Seris nor were ever seen again. One need only recall what happened just six months later and some 1,200 miles to the north, when a U.S. cavalry unit went berserk at a Sioux encampment in South Dakota, at a place called Wounded Knee Creek.

Chapter Two

94. Converting leagues to miles is a notoriously imprecise task. Not only did the length of the league change by a factor of two between the sixteenth and the end of the nineteenth centuries, but the maritime league frequently differed from the terrestrial league, and the measure meant different things in different circumstances (see Chambers 1975; Ives 1975; Barnes et al. 1981:68-75). Without minimizing these problems, it may be useful to express some distances in more familiar units. The figure adopted here, 2.6 miles to the league, is fairly conventional but it should also be understood as rather arbitrary.

95. There seem to be few doubts that Ortega engaged in some clever manipulation of the authorities, if not outright fraud, when he set out on his voyage. But there has also been some suspicion that his report of the trip was fraudulent as well. Ortega made the mistake of later writing a second, very brief, but somewhat contradictory summary of his voyage (Ortega [1636] 1970). The inconsistencies between the two versions were sufficiently egregious to goad the eminent Colonial historian, Ernest J. Burrus, into flatly declaring that:

> I consider the two reports ... on the third expedition as fictitious, and I deny that he undertook any third voyage of exploration along the coast of the Californias. (Burrus 1972:273)

There is some irony in this accusation, for a few pages later, in his own self-contradiction, Burrus admits that Ortega probably:

> undertook a pearl-fishing voyage along the eastern coast of the peninsula.... Quite likely, although not certainly, he set out on January 11, 1636. (Burrus 1972:280)

Burrus's real contention, it would seem, is not that there was no voyage at all, but that it had been an illegal venture, and Ortega's reports were fraudulent attempts to disguise his pearling activities as legitimate exploration (see also León-Portilla 1973:51–52; Portillo 1982:282–83).

Among the more troublesome aspects of Ortega's reports are the errors in basic geography which, says Burrus, are the result of having fabricated his itinerary from an old and erroneous map (Burrus 1972:281). Indeed, some of his geography is little short of outrageous. Ortega managed to stretch the actual circumference of San Marcos Island from less than 20 miles to a whopping 75. Like nearly all early navigators, his latitude estimates are too high, though Ortega erred far more than most. Had he actually sailed northwest to the claimed 36½° his turn-around point would have been just outside the suburbs of Fresno, California.

For Burrus, Ortega's description of San Sebastián Island is particularly indicative of fraud. Most modern scholars have assumed this island to be San Lorenzo Island (Mosk 1931:148; Cebreiro Blanco 1944:109n26, Map 7; León-Portilla 1973:66), but as Burrus correctly points out, the fit is not a good one (Burrus 1972:278). Ortega describes his island as about 100 miles in circumference, 13 miles from the "mainland," oriented northwest to southeast, with a bay and anchorage on the west side, a large shellmound on this bay and another at the southeastern tip. It has water in wells and in rain-filled tinajas in a ravine on the east side, and three abundant food plants, pitahaya, mescal (agave), and "ciruelo," an unknown plant which Ortega apparently mistook for the plum tree Cyrtocarpa edulis, which is confined to the southern peninsula. And on Ortega's island were Indians who ate maize and were unlike any other people they had seen along the coast of Baja California.

San Lorenzo Island is oriented northwest-southeast, it has *pitahaya agria*, and there is a marginally protected anchorage on its west side. Here, however, the similarity ends. San Lorenzo is far too small, and today, at least, it has little (if any) water or agave. The sparse resources and exceedingly meager archaeological record make it unlikely that 50 people ever congregated there at one time (see also Note 55). But while Burrus is probably correct that San Lorenzo is not Ortega's San Sebastián, it does not necessarily follow that Ortega's island is a fabrication and his report fraudulent, for San Sebastián may simply have been some other island.

A far more likely prospect is Ángel de la Guarda, for despite Burrus's categorical insistence that Ortega never got that far north (Burrus 1972:278), Ángel de la Guarda is a good match in size and orientation, and it has both pitahaya and agave. Unlike Ortega's island, however, it has no harbor and only a marginal anchorage on the west side (Belden 1880:121; Lewis and Ebeling 1971:332–39; Brow 1982:45). The status of fresh water is less certain. Most sources claim that Ángel de la Guarda has no permanent water, but it has long been rumored that temporary pools or flows can sometimes be found in the northern part of the island (Castillo Negrete 1859:357; Fitch 1875:61; Anonymous 1899:34; 1965a:33; Bancroft 1932:354; Murray 1967:63; Lewis and Ebeling 1971:333, 339; Conrad Bahre 1978:pers. comm.; Ruben García 1988:pers. comm.; Raul Espinosa 1989:pers. comm.). Although no Indians are known to have lived there in historic times, temporary water sources would explain the island's substantial archaeological record and might well have enabled 50 people to assemble there from time to time. In addition to artifacts and structures, Indians have left some small shell deposits on the island, though not the great shellmounds of Ortega's narrative (Arnold 1957:Map 7, Pl. 21; Conrad Bahre 1978:pers. comm.).

But this still does not account for the most perplexing aspect of Ortega's description, his reference to maize which, as Ortega's successor Pedro Porter y Casanate noted a few years later (Porter y Casanate [1649] 1970a:858), was unknown to peninsular Indians at that time. It seems highly unlikely that Ortega could have mistaken any other cereal food for maize, and it is unclear why he would have fabricated such an incidental detail in a report about the pearl fisheries.

The island that may best fit Ortega's mysterious San Sebastián is Tiburón. If Ortega found exceptionally promising placers there, he might well have wanted to conceal their location from potential competitors. Indeed, a century later, the adjacent coast was the scene of an intense, if short-lived, pearling boom. One simple way of hiding an excursion to Tiburón in his report would be to falsely position it on the peninsular side of the Gulf, where he clearly spent most of his time. Although the match is not perfect, Ortega's description of San Sebastián gives a realistic picture of Tiburón Island and the Seri Indians.

Tiburón is not, of course, located at 36°, nor is it really oriented northwest to southeast. But this may well have been its *apparent* orientation because Ortega, coming from the peninsula, would almost certainly have made landfall near the south end of the island and then sailed northwest up the long southwest coast. Tiburón is certainly the right size, and the anchorage Ortega describes, which could be Tecomate in Bahía Agua Dulce (see Figure 2.1), is about the right distance from the nearest point on the mainland. Although technically situated on the north coast, Tecomate is just around the corner from the west side of the island, and it is the only anchorage anywhere in the Midriff islands that comes close to fitting other aspects of Ortega's description. The excavated waterholes at Tecomate are the most obvious match for the "wells of brackish water," and this permanent source of water would unquestionably have enabled as many as 50 Indians to be congregated there when the Spaniards arrived. Moreover, Tecomate is the site of what was probably the largest shellmound anywhere among the Midriff islands, and hence the best candidate for the "San Roque" deposit that the Spaniards observed at their anchorage. The shell deposits at the Tecomate site were originally as much as 20 feet deep and extended for nearly a mile along the shoreline (Bowen 1976:32), making Ortega's estimate of more than a league (2.6 miles) for the placer associated with it reasonable, especially if one allows for customary exaggeration.

The identity of Ortega's other shellmound is less certain, but it would presumably have been one of the many deposits that dot the Tiburón shoreline. Similarly, the rain-fed waterholes could be the several large bedrock pools located in canyons on the east coast of the island. Mescal (agave) and pitahaya (both *pitahaya dulce* and *pitahaya agria*) are abundant and were important food sources for the Tiburón people. To Ortega, the resident Seris would certainly have been of "a different nation" from the Indians they had encountered on the peninsula. Most importantly, the Seris at that time knew perfectly well that maize was available "inland" in Sonora, and they regularly traded with Indians of the interior for it, as Father Andrés Pérez de Ribas noted in 1645, a mere nine years after Ortega's visit:

> there are notices of a large population of a different nation, called Heris, who are exceedingly simple, without towns, houses, or fields. They have neither rivers nor streams, and they drink water from ponds and puddles. They sustain themselves by hunting, although at the time of the maize harvest, they go [into the interior of Sonora] with deer hides and salt, which they gather from the sea, to trade with other nations. Those closest to the sea also sustain themselves by fishing. On an island within the same sea, it is said that there live others of the same nation, whose language is considered exceedingly difficult. (Pérez de Ribas [1645] 1944:128)

Whatever other portions of his reports might have been fabricated, Ortega may have merely disguised the identity of Tiburón Island and the resident Seris while giving an otherwise accurate accounting of what he experienced there.

96. By the late seventeenth century, all pearl hunters searched for pearls in much the same manner. There were essentially three ways of going about it (Barco [ca. 1770s] 1980:250–57). One was simply to trade with the peninsular Indians for them; indeed, it was the observation that some of the Indians wore pearl ornaments that first alerted the crew of Cortés's second expedition to the potential wealth of the Gulf. Many of the early expeditions obtained the majority of their pearls by trade, supplying the Indians with metal knives and other items in return. But most of the pearls obtained through trade were flawed. The Indians harvested the pearl oyster for its meat, and they opened the shells by roasting them in fires. Though they sometimes saved the pearls they found in the shell, these pearls were usually burned, which greatly reduced their value to the Spaniards.

Pearl hunters quickly learned that the best guide to the locations of oyster beds was to cruise the shoreline looking for the shellmounds, or *comederos*, of the Indians on the beaches. Since pearls were only of passing interest to the natives, the Spaniards discovered that they could often find pearls by sifting through the shells in these middens. But since midden shells had usually been roasted, the pearls found in this way were generally burned and therefore of reduced value.

The most reliable procedure for finding undamaged, high quality pearls was to dive for them, and here again the coastal shellmounds often served as guides to the location of the oyster beds, called *placeres*. But this proved not to be an infallible road to riches either. For one thing the Indians, in their quest for food, continually harvested the largest oysters most likely to contain large pearls. For another, the pearl hunters themselves, both those operating with and without licenses, collected so many oysters that the beds often played out quickly. A small crew of divers on a good day could bring up several hundred oysters (Bolton 1936:208, 216). Once depleted, many placers never recovered. As a result, most expeditions did not find enough pearls to break even, but as with all gambling ventures, it was the fame of the lucky few that kept the fortune seekers coming.

Despite decreasing odds, diving still offered the best chance of big rewards. The Spaniards, of course, did not do the actual diving themselves. Initially, in compliance with the royal decree that prohibited the use of Indians, some Negroes were imported as divers. But very quickly, the Spaniards began to flagrantly disregard this unenforceable prohibition. Many peninsular natives were already skilled divers because they utilized oysters as a food source. Before long, they were being pressed into service by the Spaniards as pearl divers. In the case of licensed pearlers, relations with the Indians were sometimes good, and mutually satisfactory barter agreements were worked out that entitled an Indian to a knife or other item for a specified number of oysters brought up unopened (Bolton 1936:210; Gerhard 1956:243). However, this was a classic opportunity for exploitation, and it was not long before pearlers, especially those operating without a license, had become notorious for their ruthless abuse of local Indians (Clavigero [1789] 1971: 134, 138, 227; Forbes 1839:66). When the Jesuits arrived at the end of the seventeenth century, an intense fear of Europeans among the peninsular Indians generated by unscrupulous pearlers was one of the obstacles these missionaries would have to overcome (Venegas [1759] 1966b:312; Barco [ca. 1770s] 1980:251).

Chapter Three

97. One contemporary report superficially suggests that Ocio or his successors did indeed find placers on both San Lorenzo and San Esteban Islands. In 1746, three years after Ocio's first expeditions to the northern Gulf, Governor Agustín de Vildósola of Sonora, reporting at length to the Viceroy on the Gulf pearl fisheries, wrote that pearl oysters were known from the waters surrounding both islands (Mosk 1931:216). However, the source of Vildósola's statements was almost certainly William Stratford, the pilot of Father Ugarte's expedition more than two decades earlier. In 1746, both Stratford and Vildósola were living at the Presidio of Pitic (modern Hermosillo), where Stratford had just completed his own comprehensive description of the Gulf. Stratford had continued his sailing career in the Gulf during the 25 years after the Ugarte expedition (Stratford [1746] 1958:65), and although he apparently had never returned to the Midriff region, he would surely have been in a position to know if placers had been discovered on the two islands. In his own report, Stratford noted only his own observations from 1721, that there were shell deposits on San Lorenzo Island and possibly San Esteban, but that neither island had been investigated.

Chapter Six

98. Other visitors, however, not only have written about Rasa's stone structures, but also have praised the precision they perceive in both the form and quality of their construction:

> The stones on Raza Island are not haphazardly heaped in a few random piles but laid up with the great care of practiced stone masons in even, conical piles, each rock carefully fitted beside its neighbor and each course resting in geometric precision on the one beneath. Some of the piles, once precisely stacked have, in the course of time, fallen or been knocked over and lie scattered about the still obvious pattern of their base. The rock walls are laid up of larger boulders in the same careful manner, meeting other courses of rock at true 90° corners. (Lewis and Ebeling 1971:331)

It is so startling to step onto a tiny remote island such as Rasa and find it covered with hundreds of strange structures, that it is no wonder that descriptions have tended toward hyperbole. Nor is there any doubt that some of the cairns and walls on Rasa are strikingly neat, even, and symmetrical. But these are the structures that catch the eye and imprint on the brain, allowing one to ignore the many more structures that are crude, uneven, and ill-proportioned. And the fact is that a considerable number of structures are not cairns, or even fallen cairns, but are simply and literally, haphazard piles of rock. While there is no doubt that the best walls and cairns were competently built, so were the rural stone fences that one can find throughout most of Mexico, New England, and much of the rest of the world. Many of these walls, built by untrained farmers as an expedient means of ridding their fields of unwanted stones, are neat, orderly, and have stood intact for centuries. The competence of the best walls and cairns on Rasa probably reflects neither intensive training nor master craftsmanship, but ordinary skill and proficiency resulting from a little practice. But as one English observer has pointed out, the tidy construction and the orderliness of some of the rows of cairns might also reflect quintessentially English Colonial aesthetic sensibilities and practices. After all, the company that first mined the island on a large scale was British, and it would certainly have installed an Englishman as an on-site administrator and supervisor to direct the labor force (Keith Muscutt 1993:pers. comm.).

Chapter Eleven

99. Most of the specific information in this section, unless otherwise credited, comes from Edward Moser's unpublished notes.

100. Misprinted as "Three."

101. Beginning in the early days of European global maritime exploration, it became common practice to introduce goats on islands in order to provide a food source for mariners and shipwreck victims. In this manner, feral goat populations became established on many islands throughout the world. Their ability to survive on islands with impoverished forage and scant water has astonished nearly all observers. Writing about Hood Island goats in the Galápagos archipelago, one commentator notes that:

> It is miraculous that they can exist at all in this lava desert. They are phenomenal vegetable scavengers, eating the thick, fleshy leaves of the *cryptocarpus* shrub when they can get them, but also turning to a filamentous lichen (*Ushera plicata*), as dry as tinder, seaweed or tough corrugated bark which, I imagine, contains about as much nourishment as steel shavings. Elsewhere I have seen goats persistently eat cardboard. We often saw them drink sea-water and they also lick the stones and twigs wetted by the fine Galapagos mists. (Nelson 1968:239)

There seems to be no question that goats can survive long periods without fresh water. On the Galápagos island of Española, goats are able to withstand a 10 month dry season during which there is no fresh water whatever (Dunson 1974:662). Here, as on many other islands, the animals manage to satisfy their fluid requirements with water derived from plant foods, especially succulents, and by drinking sea water. These strategies will sustain goats for extended periods but not indefinitely; eventually, fresh water is essential (Dunson 1974; Bruce Coblentz 1984:pers. comm.).

Goats were introduced on several of the islands off both coasts of Baja California, where they have continued to play havoc with the native vegetation (Gerhard and Gulick 1962:203–10). There is no indication that mariners ever introduced them on any of the Midriff islands, probably because there was so little maritime traffic that far up the Gulf until the second half of the nineteenth century. However, the hardiness of these animals is so well known that it is quite possible that goats were brought as food to San Esteban, either by Mexicans who came to distill *mescal aguardiente*, or by sea lion hunters. Despite the seasonal scarcity of water, an escaped goat would probably have had no trouble surviving many years on San Esteban.

102. The value of the peso and the dollar were most nearly equal in 1874 and 1875, when the dollar was worth 0.982 pesos and 1.011 pesos, respectively. However, the two currencies were nearly equivalent in value—within ten cents of each other—from 1821 to 1878. After this time, the value of the peso declined rapidly, and by 1897 it had dropped below the half dollar mark (Anonymous 1985f:Cuadro 21.6). Hence the time the fishermen refer to would probably be the 1880s or earlier.

103. Antero Díaz A. (Figure 12.2) was the patriarch of the most prominent family in the town of Bahía de los Ángeles. He was born in 1913 or 1914 and grew up in Zacualpan, Guerrero. In 1935 he came to Bahía de los Ángeles with his wife Cruz. He first worked as a hard rock miner and then took up fishing during the shark liver boom of the late 1930s and early 1940s. Díaz quickly recognized the commercial potential of tourism as North Americans began to filter into the community in increasing numbers, and he soon built the motel-restaurant-general store complex that has become regionally famous as Casa Díaz. He followed this with a number of other business ventures, including a large commercial fishing and turtle hunting operation, real estate, a sport fishing guide service, four-wheel drive vehicle rentals, gasoline concessions, and

a boat charter service which has provided vessels ranging in size from the traditional 20- to 25-foot pangas with outboard motors to the 85-foot diesel yacht *San Agustín II*. At various times Díaz served as port captain, postmaster, and police chief. He died of a stroke on July 2, 1988 (Murray and Poole 1965:120–26; Murray 1967:64–67; Anonymous 1988; Sammy Díaz 1989:pers. comm.).

104. Probably because most of San Esteban's shoreline is narrow and unprotected from storms, no evidence of this activity remains on the island. In contrast, on some of Tiburón Island's protected beaches, shark carcasses lie desiccated or rotting by the hundreds.

Chapter Twelve

105. In the course of archaeological survey, our group climbed the island's six highest peaks and several lesser summits. The only benchmarks we saw were those emplaced in 1958 by Méndez.

106. Pemberton's yacht *Petrel* should not be confused with Bancroft's vessel *Least Petrel* (Bancroft 1932).

Part V.

107. More detailed information about individual features has been deposited in the archives of the Arizona State Museum, University of Arizona, Tucson, and the Centro Regional de Sonora, Instituto Nacional de Antropología e Historia, Hermosillo.

References Cited

Acuña, Rodolfo F.
1974 *Sonoran Strongman: Ignacio Pesqueira and His Times.* University of Arizona Press. Tucson.

Aguilar, F. M.
1890 [Telegram to Sr. Gobnor. R. Corral, June 3, 1890.] Gobernación, Referencia 214.3, *Tribu Seri.* Archivo Histórico del Estado del Sonora, Hermosillo. Microfilm, Hermosillo Film No. 25, Arizona Historical Society. Tucson.

Alarchon, Fernando
[1540] 1904 The Relation of the Navigation and Discovery Which Captaine Fernando Alarchon Made.... In *The Principal Navigations, Voyages, Traffiques & Discoveries of the English Nation,* Vol. 9, by Richard Hakluyt, pp. 279–318. James MacLehose and Sons. Glasgow.

Alden, Farrelly
1859 [Letter to Captain William D. Porter, Commanding, Sloop of War *St. Mary's,* October 25, 1859.] Microfilm, RG 59, General Records of the Department of State, Consular Dispatches, Guaymas, Vol. 1. U.S. National Archives. Washington, D.C.
1861 *Arrivals and Departures of American Vessels at the United States Consulate, Guaymas, from October 1 to December 31, 1861.* Microfilm, RG 59, General Records of the Department of State, Consular Dispatches, Guaymas, Vol. 1. U.S. National Archives. Washington, D.C.
1862 [Letter to William H. Seward, Secretary of State.] Microfilm, RG 59, General Records of the Department of State, Consular Dispatches, Guaymas, Vol. 1. U.S. National Archives. Washington, D.C.
1866 [Report of American vessels at Guaymas for 1865.] In "Report upon the Commercial Relations of the United States with Foreign Countries for the Year 1866," p. 146. *U.S. House of Representatives Executive Document* [unnumbered], 39th Congress, 1st Session, Part 2. Government Printing Office. Washington, D.C.

Alegre, Francisco Javier
[ca. 1780s] *Historia de la Provincia de la Compañía de Jesús de Nueva España,* Tomo 4, Libros 9–
1960 10 (Años 1676–1766). Nueva Edición por Ernest J. Burrus, S.J. y Félix Zubillaga, S.J. Institutum Historicum S.J. Rome.

Alexander, A. B.
1892 Report of A. B. Alexander, Fishery Expert. In "Report upon the Investigations of the U.S. Fish Commission Steamer Albatross for the Year Ending June 30, 1889,"

pp. 450–79. *U.S. House of Representatives Miscellaneous Document* No. 274, 51st Congress, 1st Session. Government Printing Office. Washington, D.C.

Anderson, Charles A.
1950 Geology of Islands and Neighboring Land Areas. In "1940 E. W. Scripps Cruise to the Gulf of California," Pt. 1, pp. 1–53. *Geological Society of America Memoir* 43.

Anderson, Daniel W.
1983 The Seabirds. In *Island Biogeography in the Sea of Cortéz*, edited by Ted J. Case and Martin L. Cody, pp. 246–64. University of California Press. Berkeley.

Anderson, Eric G.
1978 *Plane Safety and Survival.* Aero Publishers. Fallbrook, California.

Andrade, Francisco
1850 *Diario de Operaciones y Novedades Ocurridas en la Marcha Sobre la Isla de Tiburón....* In "Noticias Estadísticas del Estado de Sonora....," by José Francisco Velasco, pp. 175–82. Imprenta de Ignacio Cumplido. México.

Andrade, Guillermo
1882 [Petition to the Ministro de Fomento, Industria y Colonización, April 18, 1882.] *Diario Oficial*, May 27, 1882, pp. 3–4. México.
1883 *Petition to the Superior Court of the City and County of San Francisco, State of California. In the Matter of the Estate of Thomas H. Blythe, Deceased.* November 16, 1883. Andrade Papers Folio 11. Sherman Library. Corona del Mar, California.

Andrade, Guillermo and M. Fernández
1882 [Contract between Guillermo Andrade and the Secretaría de Fomento for colonization of Tiburón and Ángel de la Guarda Islands, January 17, 1882.] Andrade Papers Folio 10. Sherman Library. Corona del Mar, California.

Anonymous
1858 The Burning of the Ship John E. Thayer. *Daily Alta California*, December 16, 1858.
1861 Letter from Guaymas. *Evening* [name incomplete] [newspaper], Wednesday, December 4, 1861. San Francisco, California. Microfilm, RG 59, General Records of the Department of State, Consular Dispatches, Guaymas, Vol. 1. U.S. National Archives. Washington, D.C.
1863 *The Pacific Pearl Company, New York.* William Davison, Printer. Jersey City.
1864 *Proposals for the Organization of the Carmen Island Salt Company.* Office of "El Nuevo Mundo." San Francisco.
1868 *Map of Lower California, from Special Surveys of Coast and Interior, Made for the Lower California Company in 1866–7 by the Company's Engineers Under the Direction of J. Ross Browne.* Papers of Caleb Cushing, Box 336. U.S. Library of Congress. Washington, D.C.
1868[?] The Gulf of California: Special Correspondence of the Telegram, December 20, 1867. *The Telegram* [?] Vol. 1, No. 177. [Probably published in January 1868.] San Francisco[?] Papers of Caleb Cushing, Box 336. U.S. Library of Congress. Washington, D.C.
1873 *Memorandum and Articles of Association of the Gulf of California Phosphate Company Limited.* Microfilm, Z-G1, Reel 110. Bancroft Library, University of California. Berkeley.
1874 *Informe que Rinde la Dirección de la Compañía Mexicana Agrícola, Industrial y Colonizadora de Terrenos del Colorado....* Cosmopolitan Steam Printing Company. San Francisco.
1875a [Plotting sheet for Gulf of California nautical chart.] RG 37, Records of the U.S. Hydrographic Office, 283.16, Portfolio 5. U.S. National Archives, Cartographic and Architectural Branch. Arlington, Virginia.
1875b [Final draft of Gulf of California nautical chart.] RG 37, Records of the U.S. Hydrographic Office, 283.16 Portfolio 1, No. 20. U.S. National Archives, Cartographic and Architectural Branch. Arlington, Virginia.
1875c *Preliminary Chart of the Coasts of Lower California and of the Gulf of California (Sheet*

    II), 1873–1875. [Nautical chart.] RG 37, Records of the U.S. Hydrographic Office, 283.16, Portfolio 2. U.S. National Archives, Cartographic and Architectural Branch. Arlington, Virginia.

1877   *The Coasts of Lower California and of the Gulf of California (Sheet II), 1873–1875. Mexico—Golfo de California, Isla Carmen to Puerto Refugio.* [Nautical chart.] H.O. 620, September, 1877. U.S. Hydrographic Office. Government Printing Office. Washington, D.C.

1878a   Sesión del 1 de Diciembre de 1877. *El Municipio*, Tomo 1, Num. 10, June 24, 1878, p. 4. Guaymas. Microfilm, Roll 5000, Reel 5, Item 20 in "Mexican Newspaper Miscellany, Sonora, 1838–1883." Bancroft Library, University of California. Berkeley.

1878b   Sesión del 8 de Dbre. de 1877. *El Municipio*, Tomo 1, Num. 11, p. 2, July 9, 1878. Guaymas. Microfilm, Roll 5000, Reel 5, Item 20 in "Mexican Newspaper Miscellany, Sonora, 1838–1883." Bancroft Library, University of California. Berkeley.

1878c   Sesión del 22 de Dbre. de 1877. *El Municipio*, Tomo 1, Num. 11, p. 3, July 9, 1878. Guaymas. Microfilm, Roll 5000, Reel 5, Item 20 in "Mexican Newspaper Miscellany, Sonora, 1838–1883." Bancroft Library, University of California. Berkeley.

1878d   Sesión del 29 de Dbre. de 1877. *El Municipio*, Tomo 1, Num. 11, p. 3, July 9, 1878. Guaymas. Microfilm, Roll 5000, Reel 5, Item 20 in "Mexican Newspaper Miscellany, Sonora, 1838–1883." Bancroft Library, University of California. Berkeley.

1878e   Sesión del 29 de Marzo de 1878. *El Municipio*, Tomo 1, Num. 5, p. 1, April 1, 1878. Guaymas. Microfilm, Roll 5000, Reel 5, Item 20 in "Mexican Newspaper Miscellany, Sonora, 1838–1883." Bancroft Library, University of California. Berkeley.

1878f   *Special Resolution of the Gulf of California Phosphate Company, Limited.* September 10, 1878. Microfilm, Z-G1, Reel 110. Bancroft Library, University of California. Berkeley.

1878g   [Untitled article.] *Arizona Sentinel*, Vol. 7, No. 17, p. 3, Saturday, August 3, 1878. Yuma, Arizona.

1881   [Map from U.S.S. *Ranger* cruise in 1881.] Records of the U.S. Hydrographic Office, 181.22, No. 3. U.S. National Archives, Cartographic and Architectural Branch. Arlington, Virginia.

1889   *Memorandum of Association of the Mexican Land and Colonization Company, Limited.* Microfilm, Z-G1, Reel 24. Bancroft Library, University of California. Berkeley.

1890a   Heridos por los Seris. *La Constitución*, Tomo 12, Num. 23, p. 2, June 6, 1890. Hermosillo.

1890b   Los Seris. *La Constitución*, Tomo 12, Num. 27, p. 2, July 4, 1890. Hermosillo.

1890c   Los Indios Seris. *La Constitución*, Tomo 12, Num. 30, p. 1, July 25, 1890. Hermosillo.

1890d   Para la Costa. *La Constitución*, Tomo 12, Num. 33, p. 1, August 15, 1890. Hermosillo.

1891   La Compaña Contra los Seris. *La Constitución*, Tomo 13, Num. 2, pp. 2–3. January 9, 1891. Hermosillo.

1892   [Articles of incorporation of The Gulf of Cortez Fishing Company, January 12, 1892.] State of California Archives. Sacramento.

1893a   Doing the Gulf Coast. *The Yuma Times*, June 21, 1893. Yuma, Arizona. Marston Collection, Huntington Library. San Marino, California.

1893b   From Yuma to the Sea. [Newspaper article] [Name unknown] July 21, 1893. Yuma, Arizona. Microfiche, in Journals of Robinson and Logan of Sloop *Examiner* file. Grand Canyon National Park Museum Collections. Grand Canyon, Arizona.

1894[?]a   Will Be a Perilous Voyage. [Newspaper article] [Name, city, and date unknown.] Microfiche, in Journals of Robinson and Logan of Sloop *Examiner* file. Grand Canyon National Park Museum Collections. Grand Canyon, Arizona.

1894[?]b   Dead or Alive: Speculation as to the Fate of Robinson and Logan. [Newspaper article, ca. June 1894.] [Name and city unknown.] Microfiche, in Journals of Robinson and Logan of Sloop *Examiner* file. Grand Canyon National Park Museum Collections. Grand Canyon, Arizona.

1894[?]c   The Tiburon Mystery: Official Report to the Mexican Government. [Newspaper article] Microfiche, in Journals of Robinson and Flavell of Sloop *Examiner* file. Grand Canyon National Park Museum Collections. Grand Canyon, Arizona.

1894–1897   [Various unknown authors] [Newspaper clippings] Microfiche, in Journals of Robinson and Flavell of Sloop *Examiner*. Grand Canyon National Park Museum Collections. Grand Canyon, Arizona.

1895a   Conquest of Tiburon. *The Capital*, Vol. 2, No. 23, p. 9, December 7, 1895. Los Angeles.

1895b   The Tiburon Expedition. *The Capital*, Vol. 2, No. 24, p. 1, December 14, 1895. Los Angeles.

1895c   Col. John Bradbury. *The Capital*, Vol. 2, No. 26, p. 10, December 28, 1895. Los Angeles.

1895d   Ho! For Tiburon. *Los Angeles Daily Times*, p. 1, November 27, 1895. Los Angeles.

[ca. 1895]   General Andrade's Cannibals. [Newspaper article.] [Name and city unknown.] Microfiche, in Journals of Robinson and Flavell of Sloop *Examiner* file. Grand Canyon National Park Museum Collections. Grand Canyon, Arizona.

1896a   The Tiburon Affair. [Newspaper article] [Publisher and city unknown.] Microfiche, in Journals of Robinson and Logan of Sloop *Examiner* file. Grand Canyon National Park Museum Collections. Grand Canyon, Arizona.

1896b   [Title unknown] *The Times*, Yuma, Arizona[?]. Microfiche, in Journals of Robinson and Logan of Sloop *Examiner* file. Grand Canyon National Park Museum Collections. Grand Canyon, Arizona.

1897a   He Made a Brave Fight for His Life: Details of the Murder of Captain Porter on Tiburon. *The San Diego Chronicle*, p. 1, November 7, 1897. San Diego, California.

1897b   *El Estado de Sonora, México*. J. R. Southworth. Nogales, Arizona.

1897[?]   [Title unknown] [Newspaper article] Dec. 8, 1897[?]. Microfiche, in Journals of Robinson and Logan of Sloop *Examiner* file. Grand Canyon National Park Museum Collections. Grand Canyon, Arizona.

1899   *El Territorio de la Baja California, México*. J. R. Southworth. San Francisco, California.

1900   Exploration of Tiburón. In "Annual Report of the Director of the Bureau of the American Republics for the Year 1899," Part 3. *U.S. House of Representatives Document* No. 175, Part 3, 56th Congress, 1st Session. Government Printing Office. Washington, D.C.

1902   Arizona Charlie to Subdue the Seris. *Dawson Daily News*, August 19, 1902. Dawson City, Yukon Territory, Canada.

193[?]   *Kino Bay: A Hunting and Fishing Preserve in the State of Sonora, Mexico*. [Publisher and city not indicated.]

1956   *How to Survive on Land and Sea: Individual Survival*, revised edition. United States Naval Institute. Annapolis, Maryland.

[1870]   [Newspaper article, title unknown.] March 17, 1870. Number Three in
1965a   "Lower California Frontier: Articles from the San Diego Union, 1870," edited by Florence C. Shipek, pp. 32–37. Dawson's Book Shop. Los Angeles.

[1870]   [Newspaper article, title unknown.] April 7, 1870. Number Four in "Lower Cali-
1965b   fornia Frontier: Articles from the San Diego Union, 1870," edited by Florence C. Shipek, pp. 38–44. Dawson's Book Shop. Los Angeles.

1969   *Search and Rescue: Survival*. Air Force Manual 64–5. Department of the Air Force. U.S. Government Printing Office. Washington, D.C.

1976a   Isla de San Esteban, México [Map.]. Series 1501 Air, Sheet NH 12-10, Edition 1. *Joint Operations Graphic (Air)* 1:250,000. Comisión de Estudios del Territorio Nacional. México. [Reprint of the original map prepared and printed by Aeronautical Chart and Information Center, U.S. Air Force. St. Louis, Missouri.]

1976b Symposium on the Gulf of California. *Natural Resources Journal*, Vol. 16, No. 3, [unnumbered page 449].

1980a Isla de San Esteban H12–10. [Map.] *Carta Topografía 1:250,000*. Dirección General de Geografía del Territorio Nacional, Secretaría de Programación y Presupuesto. México.

1980b Punta Chueca H12-C46. [Map.] *Carta Topografía 1:50,000*. Dirección General de Geografía del Territorio Nacional, Secretaría de Programación y Presupuesto. México.

1980c Bahía Kunkaak H12-C56. [Map.] *Carta Topografía 1:50,000*. Dirección General de Geografía del Territorio Nacional, Secretaría de Programación y Presupuesto. México.

1981a Tijuana. [Map.] *Carta Geológica 1:1,000,000*. Dirección General de Geografía del Territorio Nacional, Secretaría de Programación y Presupuesto. México.

1981b California Academy of Sciences Members' Trips, 1981. *Pacific Discovery*, Vol. 34, No. 4, back cover.

1982 [Letter to María Elisa Villalpando, June 1, 1982, from the Departmento Cartográfico, Secretaría de la Defensa Nacional. Lomas de Sotelo, D.F.]

1984 *Golfo de California—Northern Part*. [Nautical chart.] 61st edition, July 14, 1984. [No. 21008.] U.S. Defense Mapping Agency Hydrographic/Topographic Center. Washington, D.C.

1985a Dancing with Dolphins in Baja California. *Sunset* (October), pp. 126–27.

1985b Naturalists Who Will Take You to Meet Baja's Wildlife. *Sunset* (October), pp. 58–60.

1985c Desert Watch Research Expedition: A 9-Day Expedition to Study the Endangered San Esteban Island Chuckwalla, Sea of Cortez, Mexico. Thursday-Saturday April 18–27. *Sonorensis*, Vol. 6, No. 3, p. 10.

1985d San Esteban Island Expedition: A 10-Day Desert Watch Research Trip to Study Island Chuckwallas in the Sea of Cortez. Saturday-Monday January 11–20, 1986. *Sonorensis*, Vol. 7, No. 1, p. 14.

1985e *Search and Rescue: Survival Training*. AF Regulation 64-4, Volume 1. Department of the Air Force. Headquarters US Air Force. Washington, D.C.

1985f *Estadísticas Históricas de México*, Tomo 2. Instituto Nacional de Estadística, Geografía, e Informática. México.

1988 Antero "Papa" Diaz. *The San Diego Union*, July 6, 1988, Section B, p. 5. San Diego, California.

1989 The Smithsonian Traveler. *Smithsonian*, Vol. 20, No. 9, pp. 190–91.

1992 *The Times Atlas of the World*, ninth comprehensive edition. Times Books. Harper Collins. London.

n.d.a *Prospectus of the Gulf of Cortez Land and Fish Co.* Bancroft Library, University of California. Berkeley.

n.d.b *Arrival and Departure of American Vessels 1859–1872*. Records of the Guaymas Consulate, RG 84, Diplomatic Branch. U.S. National Archives. Washington, D.C.

n.d.c *The Jecker Sonora Contract*. Papers of Caleb Cushing, Box 336. U.S. Library of Congress. Washington, D.C.

Anssa, Juan Bautista de

[1735] 1932 [Statement of Juan Bautista de Anssa.] Translated and annotated by Donald Rowland. In "The Sonora Frontier of New Spain, 1735–1745," by Donald Rowland, pp. 157–62. In *New Spain and the Anglo-American West*, Vol. 1, edited by Charles W. Hackett, George P. Hammond, and J. Lloyd Mecham, pp. 147–64. Privately printed. Los Angeles.

Arnaud, Paul H., Jr.

1970 The Sefton Foundation *Orca* Expedition to the Gulf of California, March-April, 1953. General Account. *Occasional Papers of the California Academy of Sciences* No. 86. San Francisco.

Arnold, Brigham A.
1957   Late Pleistocene and Recent Changes in Land Forms, Climate, and Archaeology
            in Central Baja California. *University of California Publications in Geography*, Vol. 10,
            No. 4, pp. 201–317.
Arrillaga, José Joaquín de
[1796] 1969 *Diary of His Surveys of the Frontier, 1796*, translated by Froy Tiscareno, edited and
            annotated by John W. Robinson. Baja California Travel Series 17. Dawson's Book
            Shop. Los Angeles.
[1802] 1999 Seris in Baja, 1802–3. In *Empire of Sand: The Seri Indians and the Struggle for Span-
            ish Sonora, 1645–1803*, edited by Thomas E. Sheridan, pp. 452–53. University of
            Arizona Press. Tucson.
[1803] 1999 To: Most Excellent Lord Viceroy of New Spain, Félix Berenguer de Marquina. In
            Empire of Sand: The Seri Indians and the Struggle for Spanish Sonora, 1645–1803,
            edited by Thomas E. Sheridan, pp. 353–54. University of Arizona Press. Tucson.
Aschmann, Homer
1967   *The Central Desert of Baja California: Demography and Ecology*. Facsimile of the 1959
            edition reprinted by Manessier Publishing Co. Riverside, California.
Baegert, Johann Jakob
[1772] 1952 *Observations in Lower California*, translated with an introduction and notes by M. M.
            Brandenburg and Carl L. Baumann. University of California Press. Berkeley.
Bahre, Conrad J.
1980   Historic Seri Residence, Range, and Sociopolitical Structure. *The Kiva*, Vol. 45, No.
            3, pp. 197–209.
1983   Human Impact: The Midriff Islands. In *Island Biogeography in the Sea of Cortéz*,
            edited by Ted J. Case and Martin L. Cody, pp. 290–306. University of California
            Press. Berkeley.
Bahre, Conrad J. and David E. Bradbury
1980   Manufacture of Mescal in Sonora, Mexico. *Economic Botany*, Vol. 34, No. 4, pp. 391–400.
Baird, Spencer F.
1861   Appendix to the Report of the Secretary. In *Annual Report of the Board of Regents of
            the Smithsonian Institution ... For the Year 1860*, pp. 55–86. George W. Bowman.
            Washington, D.C.
Bancroft, Griffing
1932   *Lower California: A Cruise. The Flight of the Least Petrel*. G.P. Putnam's Sons. New York.
Bancroft, Hubert Howe
1874   Wild Tribes. Vol. 1 of "The Native Races of the Pacific States of North America."
            Vol. 1 of *The Works of Hubert Howe Bancroft*. D. Appleton and Company. New York.
1884   History of the North Mexican States and Texas, Vol. 1, 1531–1800. Vol. 15 of *The
            Works of Hubert Howe Bancroft*. A. L. Bancroft and Co. San Francisco.
1888   History of Mexico, Vol. 6, 1861–1887. Vol. 14 of *The Works of Hubert Howe Bancroft*.
            The History Company, Publishers. San Francisco.
1889   History of the North Mexican States and Texas, Vol. 2, 1801–1889. Vol. 16 of *The
            Works of Hubert Howe Bancroft*. A. L. Bancroft and Co. San Francisco.
Banks, Richard C.
1969   Relationships of the Avifauna of San Esteban Island, Sonora. *The Condor*, Vol. 71,
            No. 2, pp. 88–93.
Barbastro, Francisco Antonio
[1793] 1991 [Excerpts from an *Informe* of Francisco Antonio Barbastro.] Translated by John
            Higgins. Documentary Relations of the Southwest Project, Arizona State Museum,
            University of Arizona. Tucson.
Barco, Miguel del
[ca. 1770s] *The Natural History of Baja California*, translated by Froylan Tiscareno. Baja Cali-
1980   fornia Travel Series 43. Dawson's Book Shop. Los Angeles.

Barnes, Thomas C., Thomas H. Naylor, and Charles W. Polzer
1981   *Northern New Spain: A Research Guide*. University of Arizona Press. Tucson.

Barrera Bassols, Jacinto
1992   Islas de Baja California. In *Cartografía Histórica de las Islas Mexicanas*, coordinated by Martín Reyes Vayssade, pp. 219–62. Secretaría de Gobernación. México.

Bartlett, John Russell
[1854] 1965 *Personal Narrative of Explorations and Incidents in Texas, New Mexico, California, Sonora, and Chihuahua, Connected with the United States and Mexican Boundary Commission, During the Years 1850, '51, '52, and '53*, Vol. 1. Facsimile of the 1854 edition reprinted by The Rio Grande Press. Chicago.

Bassols Batalla, Ángel
1961   Segunda Exploración Geográfico-Biológica en la Península de Baja California. *Boletín de la Sociedad Mexicana de Geografía y Estadística*, Tomo 92, Nums. 1–3, pp. 7–184. México.

Bauer, K. Jack
1969   *Surfboats and Horse Marines: U.S. Naval Operations in the Mexican War, 1846–48*. United States Naval Institute. Annapolis, Maryland.

Beach, Rex
1927   *Confessions of a Sportsman*. The Star Series. Garden City Publishing Co. Garden City. New York. (Originally published 1921 as *Oh, Shoot! Confessions of an Agitated Sportsman*.)

Beal, Carl H.
1948   Reconnaissance of the Geology and Oil Possibilities of Baja California, Mexico. *Geological Society of America Memoir* 31.

Beck, W., D. J. Donahue, A. J. T. Jull, G. Burr, W. S. Broecker, G. Bonani, I. Hajdas, and E. Malotki
1998   Ambiguities in Direct Dating of Rock Surfaces Using Radiocarbon Measurements. *Science*, Vol. 280, No. 5372, pp. 2132–35.

Belcher, Sir Edward
1843   *Narrative of a Voyage Round the World, Performed in Her Majesty's Ship Sulphur, During the Years 1836–1842* (2 Vols.). Henry Colburn. London.

Belden, Samuel (compiler)
1880   The West Coast of Mexico, from the Boundary Line Between the United States and Mexico to Cape Corrientes, Including the Gulf of California. *U.S. Hydrographic Office, Bureau of Navigation* No. 56. Government Printing Office. Washington, D.C.

Bell, William A.
1870   *New Tracks in North America*, second edition. Chapman and Hall. London.

Bierman, Paul, Alan Gillespie, Charles Harrington, Robert Raymond, Leslie McFadden and Steven Wells
1991   [Letter to the editor.] *American Scientist*, Vol. 79, pp. 111–12.

Blaisdell, Lowell L.
1962   *The Desert Revolution*. University of Wisconsin Press. Madison.

Blinman, Eric, Elizabeth Colson, and Robert Heizer
1977   A Makah Epic Journey: Oral History and Documentary Sources. *Pacific Northwest Quarterly*, Vol. 68, No. 4, pp. 153–63.

Bolton, Herbert Eugene
1919   *Kino's Historical Memoir of Pimería Alta*, Vol. 1. Arthur H. Clark Co. Cleveland.
1936   *Rim of Christendom*. Macmillan Co. New York.
1964   *Coronado: Knight of Pueblo and Plains*. University of New Mexico Press. Albuquerque.

Bombard, Dr. Alain
1953   *The Bombard Story*, translated by Brian Connell. Andre Deutsch. London.

Bourillón Moreno, Luis, Antonio Cantú Díaz Barriga, Fulvio Eccardi Ambrosi,
Enrique Lira Fernández, Jesús Ramírez Ruiz, Enriqueta Velarde González, and
Alfredo Zavala González

1988   *Islas del Golfo de California*. Dirección General de Gobierno de la Secretaría del Gobernación and Instituto de Biología de la Universidad Autónoma Nacional de México. México.

Bourne, Col. [Edward]

1828   Notes on the State of Sonora and Cinaloa. In *Mexico in 1827*, Vol. 1, by H. G. Ward, Appendix C, pp. 559–91. Henry Colburn. London.

Bowen, Thomas

1976   Seri Prehistory: The Archaeology of the Central Coast of Sonora, Mexico. *Anthropological Papers of the University of Arizona*, No. 27. University of Arizona. Tucson.

1983   Seri. In "Southwest," edited by Alfonso Ortiz, pp. 230–49. Vol. 10 of *Handbook of North American Indians*, William C. Sturtevant, general editor. Smithsonian Institution. Washington, D.C.

Bowen, Thomas and Edward Moser

1968   Seri Pottery. *The Kiva*, Vol. 33, No. 3, pp. 89–132.

1970   Material and Functional Aspects of Seri Instrumental Music. *The Kiva*, Vol. 35, No. 4, pp. 178–200.

Bowers, De Moss

1909   An Island of Mystery. *The Wide World Magazine*, Vol. 23, pp. 167–73.

Brow, Dix

1982   *Sea of Cortez Guide*. Western Marine Enterprises. Ventura, California.

Brown Villalba, Cecilia, Lourdes Celis Salgado, and Miguel Messmacher

1982   Los Estados. *El Territorio Mexicano*, Tomo 2. Instituto Mexicano de Seguro Social. México.

Browne, J. Ross

1869a   *Resources of the Pacific Slope: A Statistical and Descriptive Summary....* D. Appleton and Co. New York.

1869b   *Adventures in the Apache Country: A Tour Through Arizona and Sonora with Notes on the Silver Regions of Nevada*. Harper and Brothers. New York.

Browne, Porter Emerson

ca. 1931   *Kino Bay*. Imp. B. Valencia Sucs. Hermosillo.

Bruder, J. Simon

1977   Changing Patterns in Papago Subsistence Strategies: Archaeology and Ethnohistory Compared. *The Kiva*, Vol. 42, Nos. 3–4, pp. 233–56.

Brusca, Richard C.

1980   *Common Intertidal Invertebrates of the Gulf of California*, revised and expanded second edition. University of Arizona Press. Tucson.

Buffum, E. Gould

[1850] 1959 *Six Months in the Gold Mines: From a Journal of Three Years' Residence in Upper and Lower California 1847-8-9*, edited by John W. Caughey. The Ward Ritchie Press. [City not indicated.]

Burrus, Ernest J.

1965   *Kino and the Cartography of Northwestern New Spain*. Arizona Pioneers' Historical Society. Tucson.

1967   *Wenceslaus Linck's Reports and Letters, 1762–1778*, translated, edited, and annotated by Ernest J. Burrus, S.J. Baja California Travel Series 9. Dawson's Book Shop. Los Angeles.

1971   *Juan María de Salvatierra, S.J.: Selected Letters about Lower California*, translated and annotated by Ernest J. Burrus, S.J. Baja California Travel Series 25. Dawson's Book Shop. Los Angeles.

1972   Two Fictitious Accounts of Ortega's "Third Voyage" to California. *Hispanic American Historical Review*, Vol. 52, No. 2, pp. 272–83.

1984   *Jesuit Relations: Baja California 1716–1762*, translated and edited with an introduction by Ernest J. Burrus, S.J. Baja California Travel Series 47. Dawson's Book Shop. Los Angeles.

Burt, William Henry

1932   Descriptions of Heretofore Unknown Mammals from Islands in the Gulf of California, Mexico. *Transactions of the San Diego Society of Natural History*, Vol. 7, No. 16, pp. 161–82.

Busch, Briton Cooper

1985   *The War Against the Seals: A History of the North American Seal Fishery*. McGill-Queen's University Press. Montreal.

Byers, Robert D.

1940   The California Shark Fishery. *California Fish and Game*, Vol. 26, No. 1, pp. 23–38.

Cadieux, Charles L.

1969   Cruising in a Marine Zoo. *Yachting*, Vol. 126, No. 3, pp. 60–61, 100, 102.

Cannon, Ray

1966   *The Sea of Cortez*. Lane Magazine and Book Co. Menlo Park, California.

Carbonel de Valenzuela, Esteban

[1632] 1992 Report of Esteban Carbonel de Valenzuela to Viceroy Marqués de Cerralvo Relative to the Voyage of Francisco de Ortega of 1632..., translated by W. Michael Mathes. In "Ethnology of the Baja California Indians," edited by W. Michael Mathes, pp. 229–33. Vol. 5 of *Spanish Borderlands Sourcebooks*. Garland Publishing. New York.

Cardenas de la Peña, Enrique

1970a   *Semblanza Marítima del México Independiente y Revolucionario*, Volumen 1. Secretaría de Marina. México.

1970b   *Semblanza Marítima del México Independiente y Revolucionario*, Volumen 2. Secretaría de Marina. México.

Cardona, Nicolás de

[1627–   Report of the Exploration of the Kingdom of California by Captain and Comm-
1632]   mander Nicolás de Cardona. In *Geographic and Hydrographic Descriptions of Many*
1974   *Northern and Southern Lands and Seas in the Indies, Specifically of the Discovery of the Kingdom of California (1632), by Nicolás de Cardona*, translated and edited by W. Michael Mathes, pp. 95–106. Baja California Travel Series 35. Dawson's Book Shop. Los Angeles.

Carleton, James H.

1863   [Letter to Lorenzo Thomas, Adjutant General, U.S. Army, February 1, 1863.] *U.S. Senate Executive Document* No. 1, 37th [actually, 38th] Congress, Special Session. Government Printing Office. Washington, D.C.

[Carmony, Neil B. and David E. Brown]

1987   Introduction. In *The Log of the Panthon*, by George F. Flavell, edited by Neil B. Carmony and David E. Brown, pp. 1–15. Pruett Publishing. Boulder, Colorado.

Carron de Fleury, S. E. L.

1869   Notas Geológicas y Estadísticas Sobre Sonora y La Baja-California. *Boletín de la Sociedad de Geografía y Estadística de la República Mexicana*. Segunda Época, Tomo 1, pp. 44–118. Imprenta del Gobierno, En Palacio. México.

Carter, Annetta M.

1979   I. G. Voznesenskii, Early Naturalist in Baja California, Mexico. *Taxon*, Vol. 28, Nos. 1, 2/3, pp. 27–33.

Case, Ted J.

1975   Species Numbers, Density Compensation, and Colonizing Ability of Lizards on Islands in the Gulf of California. *Ecology*, Vol. 56, No. 1, pp. 3–18.

1982   Ecology and Evolution of the Insular Gigantic Chuckwallas, *Sauromalus hispidus* and *Sauromalus varius*. In *Iguanas of the World: Their Behavior, Ecology, and Conservation*, edited by Gordon M. Burghardt and A. Stanley Rand, pp. 184–212. Noyes Publications. Park Ridge. New Jersey.

Case, Ted J. and Martin L. Cody (editors)
1983   *Island Biogeography in the Sea of Cortéz.* University of California Press. Berkeley.

Castetter, Edward F., Willis H. Bell, and Alvin R. Grove
1938   The Early Utilization and the Distribution of Agave in the American Southwest. No. 6 of "Ethnobiological Studies in the American Southwest." *University of New Mexico Bulletin* Whole Number 335, Biological Series, Vol. 5, No. 4. Albuquerque.

Castillo Negrete, Francisco
1859   Geografía y Estadística de la Baja California, 1853. *Boletín de la Sociedad Mexicana de Geografía y Estadística*, Tomo 7, pp. 338–359. Imprenta de A. Boix. México.

Cebreiro Blanco, Luis (editor)
1944   *Colección de Diarios y Relaciones Para la Historia de los Viajes Descubrimientos* 4. Instituto Histórico de Marina. Madrid.

Cerisola, Alejandro
1898   [Report of the voyage of the transport *Oaxaca* to Tiburón Island, to the Secretaría de Guerra y Marina, November 19, 1898.] Gobernación, Referencia 214.3, *Tribu Seri*. Archivo Histórico del Estado de Sonora, Hermosillo. Microfilm, Hermosillo Film No. 26, Arizona Historical Society. Tucson.

Chagnon, Napoleon A.
1983   *Yąnomamö: The Fierce People*, third edition. Holt, Rinehart and Winston. New York.

Chamberlin, Eugene Keith
1949   *United States Interests in Lower California.* Ph.D. dissertation. University of California. Berkeley.
1963   Nicholas Trist and Baja California. *Pacific Historical Review*, Vol. 32, No. 1, pp. 49–63.

Chamberlin, Ralph V.
1924   Expedition of the California Academy of Sciences to the Gulf of California in 1921. The Spider Fauna of the Shores and Islands of the Gulf of California. *Proceedings of the California Academy of Sciences*, Fourth Series, Vol. 12, No. 28, pp. 561–694.

Chambers, George W.
1975   How Long is a Piece of String? *The Journal of Arizona History*, Vol. 16, No. 2, pp. 195–96.

Chapman, Charles E.
1920   The Jesuits in Baja California, 1697–1768. *The Catholic Historical Review*, Vol. 6, No. 1, pp. 46–58.
1939   *A History of California: The Spanish Period.* The Macmillan Co. New York.

Clark, A. Howard
1887a   History and Present Condition of the [Whale] Fishery. In Part 15: The Whale-Fishery, Section 5: History and Methods of the Fisheries, Vol. II-1 of "The Fisheries and Fishery Industries of the United States," prepared by George Brown Goode. *U.S. Senate Miscellaneous Document* 124, Part 6, 47th Congress, 1st Session. Government Printing Office. Washington, D.C.
1887b   Map of the World on Mercator's Projection Showing the Extent and Distribution of the Present and Abandoned Whaling Grounds. Plates Accompanying Section 5: History and Methods of the Fisheries, in "The Fisheries and Fishery Industry of the United States," prepared by George Brown Goode. *U.S. Senate Miscellaneous Document* 124, Part 7, 47th Congress, 1st Session. Government Printing Office. Washington, D.C.

Clavigero, Francisco Javier
[1789] 1971 *The History of [Lower] California*, translated by Sara E. Lake, edited by A. A. Gray. Facsimile of the 1937 Stanford University Press edition reprinted by Manessier Publishing Co. Bryn Mawr, California.

Clayton, J. Bulwer
1895   Men for Tiburon. *The Capital*, Vol. 2, No. 24, p. 8, December 14, 1895. Los Angeles.
Cliff, Frank S.
1954   Snakes of the Islands in the Gulf of California, Mexico. *Transactions of the San Diego Society of Natural History*, Vol. 12, No. 5, pp. 67–98.
Cockerell, T. D. A.
1923   Expedition of the California Academy of Sciences to the Gulf of California in 1921. The Bees (I). *Proceedings of the California Academy of Sciences*, Fourth Series, Vol. 12, No. 7, pp. 73–103.
1924   Expedition of the California Academy of Sciences to the Gulf of California in 1921. The Bees (II). *Proceedings of the California Academy of Sciences*, Fourth Series, Vol. 12, No. 27, pp. 529–60.
Cody, Martin L.
1983   The Land Birds. In *Island Biogeography in the Sea Of Cortéz*, edited by Ted J. Case and Martin L. Cody, pp. 210–45. University of California Press. Berkeley.
Cody, Martin L., Reid Moran, and Henry Thompson
1983   The Plants. In *Island Biogeography in the Sea of Cortéz*, edited by Ted J. Case and Martin L. Cody, pp. 49–97. University of California Press. Berkeley.
Coerver, Don M.
1977   The Perils of Progress: The Mexican Department of Fomento During the Boom Years 1880–1884. *Inter-American Economic Affairs*, Vol. 31, No. 2, pp. 41–62.
1979   The Porfirian Interregnum: The Presidency of Manuel González of Mexico, 1880–1884. *Texas Christian University Monographs in History and Culture*, No. 14. Fort Worth, Texas.
Conn, Charles Gerard
ca. 1909   *The Cruise of the Comfort: An Enjoyable Cruise Down the West Coast of Lower California and into the Gulf of California.* [Privately printed, city not indicated.]
Conner, Edward
1866a   [Letter to Secretary of State William H. Seward, September 11, 1866] Microfilm, RG 59, General Records of the Department of State, Consular Dispatches, Guaymas, Vol. 1. U.S. National Archives. Washington, D.C.
1866b   [Letter to Secretary of State William H. Seward, September 19, 1866] Microfilm, RG 59, General Records of the Department of State, Consular Dispatches, Guaymas, Vol. 1. U.S. National Archives. Washington, D.C.
Conner, Seymour V. and Odie B. Faulk
1971   *North America Divided: The Mexican War 1846–1848.* Oxford University Press. New York.
Consag, Fernando
[1759] 1966 Account of the Voyage of Father Fernando Consag, Missionary of California, Performed ... in the Year 1746. In *A Natural and Civil History of California*, Vol. 2, by Miguel Venegas, Appendix 3. Facsimile of the 1759 edition reprinted by Readex Microprint. [City not indicated.]
Cook de Leonard, Carmen
1953   Los Seris, Antes y Hoy. *Yan*, Vol. 1, pp. 18–28.
Coolidge, Dane and Mary Roberts Coolidge
1939   *The Last of the Seris.* E.P. Dutton and Company. New York.
Cooper, J. G.
1895   Catalogue of Marine Shells, Collected Chiefly on the Eastern Shore of Lower California for the California Academy of Sciences During 1891–2. *Proceedings of the California Academy of Sciences*, Second Series, Vol. 5, pp. 34–48.
Corral, Ramón
1891   *Memoria de la Administración Pública del Estado de Sonora, Presentada a la Legislatura del Mismo*, Tomo 1. E. Gaxiola y Ca. Guaymas.

1898   [Letter to the Secretario de Guerra y Marina, December 30, 1898.] Gobernación,
            Referencia 214.3, *Tribu Seri*. Archivo Histórico del Estado de Sonora, Hermosillo.
            Microfilm, Hermosillo Film No. 26, Arizona Historical Society. Tucson.
[1885] 1959 Las Razas Indígenas de Sonora. In *Obras Históricas*, by Ramón Corral. Biblioteca
            Sonorense de Geografía e Historia. Hermosillo. [Reprinted in abridged form in
            Troncoso (1905).]

Correa, Manuel
[1750] 1946 Descripción de la Isla del Tiburón. In "Diario de lo Acaecido y Practicado en la
            Entrada que se Hizo a la Isla del Tiburón éste Año 1750," by Francisco Antonio
            Pimentel, pp. 552–58. *Boletín del Archivo General de la Nación*, Tomo 17, Número
            4, pp. 503–74. Secretaría de Gobernación. México.

Craighead, Frank C., Jr. and John J. Craighead
1984   *How to Survive on Land and Sea*, fourth edition, revised by Ray E. Smith and D.
            Shiras Jarvis. Naval Institute Press. Annapolis, Maryland.

Craven, Tunis Augustus Macdonough
1973   *A Naval Campaign in the Californias—1846–1849. The Journal of Lieutenant Tunis
            Augustus Macdonough Craven, U.S.N. United States Sloop of War, Dale*, edited by John
            Haskell Kemble. The Book Club of California 144. The Ward Ritchie Press. Los
            Angeles.

Crosby, Harry W.
1984   *The Cave Paintings of Baja California*, revised edition. The Copley Press. La Jolla,
            California.
1994   *Antigua California: Mission and Colony on the Peninsular Frontier, 1697–1768*. Uni-
            versity of New Mexico Press. Albuquerque.

Cserna, Zoltan de
1961   *Tectonic Map of Mexico 1:2,500,000*. Geological Society of America.

Cunningham, Capt. William H.
1958   *Log of the Courier 1826–1827–1828*, edited by Glen Dawson. Early California Travel
            Series 44. Glen Dawson. Los Angeles.

Davis, Edward H.
1929   [Field Notes.] Typescript in the National Museum of the American Indian, Smith-
            sonian Institution. New York. [Formerly Heye Foundation.]
1965   Unfinished Book Manuscript. In *Edward H. Davis and the Indians of the Southwest
            United States and Northwest Mexico*, arranged and edited by Charles Russell Quinn
            and Elena Quinn, pp. 140–209. Elena Quinn, Downey, California.

Davis, Emma Lou
1978   The Non-Destructive Archaeologist: or How to Collect Without Collecting. *Pa-
            cific Coast Archaeological Society Quarterly*, Vol. 14, No. 1, pp. 43–55.

Day, Gordon M.
1972   Oral Tradition as Complement. *Ethnohistory*, Vol. 19, No. 2, pp. 99–108.

Deasy, George F. and Peter Gerhard
1944   Settlements in Baja California: 1768–1930. *The Geographical Review*, Vol. 34, No.
            4, pp. 574–86.

Densmore, Llewellyn D., III, Erika D. Pliler, and Howard E. Lawler
1994   A Molecular Approach for Determining Genetic Variation in Captive and Natural
            Populations of the Piebald Chuckwalla (*Sauromalus varius*). In "Captive Manage-
            ment and Conservation of Amphibians and Reptiles," edited by James B. Murphy,
            Kraig Adler, and Joseph T. Collins, pp. 343–51. *Contributions to Herpetology*, Vol. 11.
            Society for the Study of Amphibians and Reptiles. Ithaca, New York.

Derby, George H.
1852   Report of the Expedition of the United States Transport "Invincible" ... to the Gulf
            of California and River Colorado.... In "Report of the Secretary of War....," pp. 2–
            28. *U.S. Senate Executive Document* No. 81, 32nd Congress, 1st Session. Govern-
            ment Printing Office. Washington, D.C.

Desonie, Dana L.
1985   *Geology and Petrology of Isla San Esteban, Gulf of California, Mexico.* Master's thesis.
            University of Oregon. Eugene.
1992   Geologic and Geochemical Reconnaissance of Isla San Esteban: Post-Subduction
            Orogenic Volcanism in the Gulf of California. *Journal of Volcanology and Geother-
            mal Research*, Vol. 52, pp. 123–40.
Dewey, George
1916   *Autobiography of George Dewey.* Charles Scribner's Sons. New York.
Dickerson, M. C.
1919   Diagnoses of Twenty-three New Species and a New Genus of Lizards from Lower
            California. *Bulletin of the American Museum of Natural History*, Vol. 41, Art. 10, pp.
            461–77.
Dios Bonilla, Juan de
1962   *Historia Marítima de México.* Editorial Litorales. México.
Dixon, James R.
1966   Speciation and Systematics of the Gekkonid Lizard Genus *Phillodactylus* of the Is-
            lands of the Gulf of California. *Proceedings of the California Academy of Sciences*,
            Fourth Series, Vol. 33, No. 13, pp. 415–52.
Dolzani, Michael
1988   A Bridge Over Time. *Mammoth Trumpet*, Vol. 4, No. 4, pp. 1, 4–6.
Dorn, Ronald I.
1991   Rock Varnish. *American Scientist*, Vol. 79, pp. 542–53.
1994   Surface Exposure Dating with Rock Varnish. In *Dating in Exposed and Surface Con-
            texts*, edited by Charlotte Beck, pp. 77–113. University of New Mexico Press. Al-
            buquerque.
1998   Response. *Science*, Vol. 280, No. 5372, pp. 2135–39.
Duflot de Mofras, Eugen
[1844] 1937 *Duflot de Mofras' Travels on the Pacific Coast*, Vol. 1, translated, edited, and annotated
            by Marguerite Eyer Wilbur. The Fine Arts Press. Santa Ana, California.
Dunne, Peter Masten
1968   *Black Robes in Lower California.* Second Printing. University of California Press. Ber-
            keley. (Originally published 1952.)
Dunson, William A.
1974   Some Aspects of Salt and Water Balance of Feral Goats from Arid Islands. *Ameri-
            can Journal of Physiology*, Vol. 226, No. 3, pp. 662–69.
Dupont, Samuel F.
1882   The War with Mexico: The Cruise of the U.S. Ship Cyane During the Years 1845–48.
            From the Papers of Her Commander, the Late Rear-Admiral S. F. Dupont. *Proceedings
            of the United States Naval Institute*, Vol. 8, No. 3, Whole No. 21, pp. 419–37.
DuShane, Helen
1971   Introduction. In *The Baja California Travels of Charles Russell Orcutt*. Baja Califor-
            nia Travel Series 23. Dawson's Book Shop. Los Angeles.
[Elizondo, Domingo]
[1771] 1999 Relación of the Expedition of the Provinces of Sinaloa, Ostimuri, and Sonora in the
            Kingdom of Nueva España. In *Empire of Sand: The Seri Indians and the Struggle for
            Spanish Sonora, 1645–1803*, edited by Thomas E. Sheridan, pp. 275–344. Univer-
            sity of Arizona Press. Tucson.
Elliott, Henry W.
1887   The Sea-Lion Hunt. In Part 18: The Seal and Sea-Otter Industries, Section 5:
            History and Methods of the Fisheries, Vol. II-4 of "The Fisheries and Fishery In-
            dustries of the United States," prepared by George Brown Goode. *U.S. Senate Mis-
            cellaneous Document* 124, Part 6, 47th Congress, 1st Session. Government Printing
            Office. Washington, D.C.

Ellis, Richard
1991   *Men and Whales*. Alfred A. Knopf. New York.
Elmer, F. B.
1865   [Report of American vessels at La Paz for 1863.] In "Report upon the Commercial
            Relations of the United States with Foreign Countries for the Year 1963," p. 146.
            U.S. House of Representatives Executive Document 60, Part 2, 38th Congress, 2nd
            Session. Government Printing Office. Washington, D.C.
1867   [Report of American vessels at La Paz for 1865.] In "Report upon the Commercial
            Relations of the United States with Foreign Countries for the Year 1865," pp. 776–
            77. *U.S. House of Representatives Executive Document 81*, Part 2, 39th Congress, 2nd
            Session. Government Printing Office. Washington, D.C.
Emerson, William K.
1958   Results of the Puritan-American Museum of Natural History Expedition to West-
            ern Mexico: 1. General Account. *American Museum Novitates* No. 1894, pp. 1–25.
Emerson, William K. and Leo George Hertlein
1964   Invertebrate Megafossils of the Belvedere Expedition to the Gulf of California.
            Transactions of the San Diego Society of Natural History, Vol. 13, No. 17, pp. 333–368.
Emerson, William K. and Morris K. Jacobson
1964   Terrestrial Mollusks of the Belvedere Expedition to the Gulf of California. *Trans-
            actions of the San Diego Society of Natural History*, Vol. 13, No. 16, pp. 313–32.
Emory, William H.
1857   Report on the United States and Mexican Boundary Survey, Made Under the Direc-
            tion of the Secretary of the Interior. *U.S. House of Representatives Executive Document* 135,
            34th Congress, 1st Session. 2 Volumes [Volume 2 is dated 1859.] Government Print-
            ing Office. Washington, D.C.
Escalante, Juan Bautista de
[1700] 1999 Diary of Alférez Juan Bautista de Escalante, 1700. In *Empire of Sand: The Seri Indi-
            ans and the Struggle for Spanish Sonora, 1645–1803*, edited by Thomas E. Sheridan,
            pp. 36–70. University of Arizona Press. Tucson.
Espinosa, Rafael
1854   Reseña Estadística Sobre La Antigua o Baja California. *Boletín de la Sociedad Mexicana
            de Geografía y Estadística*, Tomo 4, pp. 16–127. Imprenta de I. Cumplido. México.
Esteva, José
1865   *Memoria Sobre la Pesca de la Perla en la Baja California*. A. Boix. México.
Evermann, Barton W. and Oliver P. Jenkins
1892   Report upon a Collection of Fishes Made at Guaymas, Sonora, Mexico, with De-
            scriptions of New Species. *Proceedings of the United States National Museum*, Vol. 14,
            1891. Smithsonian Institution. Washington, D.C.
Evers, Edward
1873   [Letter to Commander George Dewey, U.S.N., October 1873.] RG 52, No. 283.6.
            Records of the Bureau of Medicine and Surgery. U.S. National Archives. Washing-
            ton, D.C.
1874   [Letter to Commander George Dewey, U.S.N., April 7, 1874.] RG 52, No. 283.6.
            Records of the Bureau of Medicine and Surgery. U.S. National Archives. Washing-
            ton, D.C.
Ewald, Ursula
1985   *The Mexican Salt Industry 1560–1980: A Study in Change*. Gustav Fischer Verlag.
            New York.
Faulk, Odie B.
1969   Introduction. In "Derby's Report on Opening the Colorado 1850–1851," pp. 7–16.
            Spanish Borderlands Document No. 1. University of New Mexico Press. Albuquerque.
Felger, Richard S.
1966   *Ecology of the Gulf Coast and Islands of Sonora, Mexico*. Ph.D. dissertation. University
            of Arizona. Tucson.

1976   Investigación Ecológica en Sonora y Localidades Adyacentes en Sinaloa: Una Per-
            spectiva. In "Sonora: Antropología del Desierto," coordinated by Beatriz Braniff C.
            and Richard S. Felger, pp. 21–62. *Colección Scientífica Diversa* 27. Instituto Nacional
            de Antropología e Historia. México.

Felger, Richard S., Kim Cliffton, and Phillip J. Regal
1976   Winter Dormancy in Sea Turtles: Independent Discovery and Exploitation in the
            Gulf of California by Two Local Cultures. *Science*, Vol. 191, No. 4224, pp. 283–85.

Felger, Richard S. and Charles H. Lowe
1976   The Island and Coastal Vegetation and Flora of the Northern Part of the Gulf of
            California. *Natural History Museum of Los Angeles County Contributions in Science* No.
            285. Los Angeles.

Felger, Richard S. and Mary Beck Moser
1970   Seri Use of Agave (Century Plant). *The Kiva*, Vol. 35, No. 4, pp. 159–67.
1974   Columnar Cacti in Seri Indian Culture. *The Kiva*, Vol. 39, Nos. 3–4, pp. 257–75.
1976   Seri Indian Food Plants: Desert Subsistence Without Agriculture. *Ecology of Food
            and Nutrition*, Vol. 5, pp. 13–27.
1985   *People of the Desert and Sea: Ethnobotany of the Seri Indians*. University of Arizona
            Press. Tucson.

Fenochio, A.
1873   Noticia Sobre la Manera de Preparar el Veneno que Usan los Indios "Ceris" en sus
            Flechas. In *Boletín de la Sociedad de Geografía y Estadística de la Republica Mexicana*,
            pp. 157–58. Tercera Epoca, Tomo 1. Imprenta de Díaz de León y White. México.

Fergusson, David
1863   [Report of Major D. Fergusson on the country, its resources, and the route between
            Tucson and Lobos Bay.] *U.S. Senate Executive Document* No. 1, 37th [actually, 38th]
            Congress, Special Session. Government Printing Office. Washington, D.C.

Fernández, M.
1882   [Letter to Guillermo Andrade, May 22, 1882.] *Diario Oficial*, May 27, 1882, p. 4.
            México.

Fernández Leal, Manuel
1897   [Revised contract between Guillermo Andrade and the Secretaría de Estado y del
            Despacho de Fomento, April 10, 1897.] Andrade Papers Folio 10. Sherman Library.
            Corona del Mar, California.

Figueroa Valenzuela, Alejandro
1985   Los Indios de Sonora Ante la Modernización Porfirista. In *História General de So-
            nora*, Tomo 4, coordinated by Cynthia Radding de Murrieta, pp. 139–163. Go-
            bierno del Estado de Sonora. Hermosillo.

Findlay, Alexander Geo.
1870   *A Directory for the Navigation of the North Pacific Ocean….*, second edition. Richard
            Holmes Laurie. London.

Fisher, Richard D.
1985   *A Travellers' Guide to the National Parks and Natural Areas of Northwestern Mexico*.
            Sunracer Publications. Tucson.
1988   *National Parks of Northwest Mexico II*. Sunracer Publications. Tucson.

Fitch, Frederick G.
1875   [Letter to Albert K. Owen, August 21, 1872.] In *The Austin-Topolovampo Pacific
            Railroad Route*, pp. 60–66. A. K. Owen Papers. Woodward Library, California State
            University, Fresno. Fresno, California.
1886   [Letter to Albert K. Owen, April 17, 1886.] A. K. Owen Papers. Woodward Library,
            California State University, Fresno. Fresno, California.

Flavell, George F.
1893   In an Open Sailboat: George Clark's Trip Down the Colorado and Gulf of Mexico.
            Arizona Enterprise, May 11, 1893. Marston Collection, Huntington Library. San
            Marino, California.

1894a   [Journals of Robinson and Flavell of the Sloop *Examiner*.] Microfiche, Grand Canyon National Park Museum Collections. Grand Canyon, Arizona.

1894b   [Letter to Vice-Consul Charles E. Hale, August 22, 1894.] Microfilm, RG 59, Microcopy 284, Roll 5, U.S. National Archives Diplomatic Branch, Consular Reports. Washington, D.C.

[1894?]   The Truth at Last: The Famous Expedition to Tiburon Island. *The Times* [?] [Newspaper article] Microfiche, in Journals of Robinson and Flavell of Sloop *Examiner*. Grand Canyon National Park Museum Collections. Grand Canyon, Arizona.

Fogelson, Raymond D.

1989   The Ethnohistory of Events and Nonevents. *Ethnohistory*, Vol. 36, No. 2, pp. 133–47.

Fontana, Bernard L.

1969   American Indian Oral History: An Anthropologist's Note. *History and Theory*, Vol. 8, No. 3, pp. 366–70.

1971   *The Seri Indians* in Perspective. Unpaginated introduction to the 1971 facsimile edition of "The Seri Indians," by WJ McGee (McGee 1898). The Rio Grande Press. Glorieta, New Mexico.

Fontana, Bernard L. and Hazel M. Fontana

1983   [Introduction to "A Search for the Seris."] In *Tales from Tiburon*, edited by Neil B. Carmony and David E. Brown, pp. 23–26. The Southwest Natural History Association. Phoenix.

Forbes, Alexander

1839   *California: A History of Upper and Lower California*. Smith, Elder and Co. Cornhill. London.

Forbes, J. Alexander

[1893]   *Consular Report for the District of Guaymas, Mexico*. [Submitted to W. Q. Gresham, Secretary of State, ca. April 1893.] Microfilm, RG 59, Microcopy 284, General Records of the Department of State, Consular Dispatches, Guaymas, Vol. 9. U.S. National Archives. Washington, D.C.

Forbes, Jack D.

1957   Historical Survey of the Indians of Sonora, 1821–1910. *Ethnohistory*, Vol. 4, No. 4, pp. 335–68.

Forbes, Robert A.

1952   *Crabb's Filibustering Expedition into Sonora, 1857*. Arizona Silhouettes. Tucson.

Foster, John W.

1984   A Late Period Seri Site from Bahía de Los Angeles, Baja California. *Pacific Coast Archaeological Society Quarterly*, Vol. 20, No. 1, pp. 61–68.

Fraser, C. McLean

1943a   General Account of the Scientific Work of the *Velero III* in the Eastern Pacific, 1931–41. Part 1: Historical Introduction, *Velero III*, Personnel. *Allan Hancock Foundation Publications of the University of Southern California*, First Series, Vol. 1, Parts 1, 2, 3, 1943. University of Southern California Press. Los Angeles.

1943b   General Account of the Scientific Work of the *Velero III* in the Eastern Pacific, 1931–41. Part 3: A Ten-Year List of the *Velero III* Collecting Stations (Charts 1–115). *Allan Hancock Foundation Publications of the University of Southern California*, First Series, Vol. 1, Parts 1, 2, 3, 1943. University of Southern California Press. Los Angeles.

Gárces, Francisco

[1775–   *On the Trail of a Spanish Pioneer: The Diary and Itinerary of Francisco Gárces in his*
1776]   *Travels Through Sonora, Arizona, and California 1775–1776*, Vol. 1, translated and
1900   edited by Elliott Coues. Francis P. Harper. New York.

García, C. Trinidad

1878   [Decree regulating the Línea Acelerada del Golfo de Cortés, December 13, 1877.] *Diario Oficial*, April 13, 1878. México.

García, C. Trinidad and Guillermo Andrade
1877   [Contract to establish the Línea Acelerada del Golfo de Cortés, November 19,
            1877.] *Diario Oficial*, November 22, 1877. México.
García y Alva, Federico (director and editor)
1905–1907   *México y sus Progresos: Album-Directorio del Estado de Sonora. Obra Hecha con Apoyo del
            Gobierno del Estado.* Imprenta Oficial Dirigida por Antonio B. Monteverde. Her-
            mosillo, Sonora. [Unpaginated]
1988   The Seri Race: Governor Rafael Izábal's Expedition to Tiburón Island in 1904.
            [Excerpt of *Album-Directorio del Estado de Sonora*, translated by Mary Beck Moser.]
            In "Seri History (1904): Two Documents," by Mary Beck Moser, pp. 471–93. *Jour-
            nal of the Southwest*, Vol. 30, No. 4, pp. 469–501.
Garrison, A. F.
1873   [Report of the U.S. Vice-Consul in Guaymas for 1872.] In "Report upon the Com-
            mercial Relations of the United States with Foreign Countries for the Year 1873,"
            pp. 684–95. *U.S. House of Representatives Executive Document* No. 160, 42nd Con-
            gress, 3rd Session. Government Printing Office. Washington, D.C.
1877   [Report of the U.S. Vice-Consul in Guaymas for 1876.] In "Report upon the Com-
            mercial Relations of the United States with Foreign Countries for the Year 1877,"
            pp. 755–59. *U.S. House of Representatives Executive Document* No. 45, 44th Congress,
            2nd Session. Government Printing Office. Washington, D.C.
Gasser, Robert E.
1982   Are Roasting Pits Always Roasting Pits? *The Kiva*, Vol. 47, No. 3, pp. 171–76.
Gastil, R. Gordon and Daniel Krummenacher
1977   Reconnaissance Geology of Coastal Sonora Between Puerto Lobos and Bahía Kino.
            Geological Society of America Bulletin, Vol. 88, pp. 189–98.
Gastil, Gordon, John Minch, and Richard P. Phillips
1983   The Geology and Ages of the Islands. In *Island Biogeography in the Sea Of Cortéz*,
            edited by Ted J. Case and Martin L. Cody, pp. 13–25. University of California
            Press. Berkeley.
Gentry, Howard Scott
1949   Land Plants Collected by the *Velero III*, Allan Hancock Pacific Expeditions 1937–
            1941. *Allan Hancock Pacific Expeditions*, Vol. 13, No. 2. University of Southern Cali-
            fornia Press. Los Angeles.
1972   The Agave Family in Sonora. *Agriculture Handbook* No. 399. Agricultural Research
            Service, U.S. Department of Agriculture. Government Printing Office. Washing-
            ton, D.C.
1978   The Agaves of Baja California. *Occasional Papers of the California Academy of Sciences*,
            No. 130. San Francisco.
1982   *Agaves of Continental North America.* University of Arizona Press. Tucson.
Gerhard, Peter
1945   Baja California in the Mexican War, 1846–1848. *The Pacific Historical Review*, Vol.
            14, No. 4, pp. 418–24.
1956   Pearl Diving in Lower California, 1533–1830. *The Pacific Historical Review*, Vol. 25,
            No. 3, pp. 239–50.
1958   The Tres Marías Pirates. *The Pacific Historical Review*, Vol. 27, No. 3, pp. 239–44.
1960   *Pirates on the West Coast of New Spain 1575–1742.* Arthur H. Clark Company. Glen-
            dale, California.
1963   *Pirates in Baja California.* Editorial Tlilan. Tlapalan. México.
1982   *The North Frontier of New Spain.* Princeton University Press. Princeton, New Jersey.
Gerhard, Peter and Howard E. Gulick
1962   *Lower California Guidebook*, third edition. Arthur H. Clark Co. Glendale, California.
Gibbons, Euell
1964   *Stalking the Blue-Eyed Scallop.* David McKay Co. New York.

1973   *Stalking the Faraway Places.* David McKay Co. New York.

Gil de Bernabé, Juan Chrisóstomo

[1772] 1999 Gil to Sastre, September 16, 1772. In *Empire of Sand: The Seri Indians and the Struggle for Spanish Sonora, 1645–1803*, edited by Thomas E. Sheridan, pp. 406–8. University of Arizona Press. Tucson.

Gilbert, Benjamin Franklin

1955   French Warships on the Mexican West Coast, 1861–1866. *The Pacific Historical Review*, Vol. 29, No. 1, pp. 25–37.

Gilg, Adamo

[1692] 1965 [Letter to the Reverend Father Rector of the College of the Society of Jesus, Brunn, Moravia.] In "The Seri Indians in 1692 as Described by Adamo Gilg, S.J.," translated and edited by Charles C. Di Peso and Daniel S. Matson, pp. 40–56. *Arizona and the West*, Vol. 7, No. 1, pp. 33–56.

Gilmore, Raymond M.

1957   Whales Aground in Cortés' Sea. *Pacific Discovery*, Vol. 10, No. 1, pp. 22–27.

Gilmore, Raymond M. and Gifford Ewing

1954   Calving of the California Grays. *Pacific Discovery*, Vol. 8, No. 3, pp. 13–15, 30.

Gilmore, Raymond M. and James G. Mills

1962   Counting Gray Whales in the Gulf of California. *Pacific Discovery*, Vol. 15, No. 2, pp. 26–27.

Goldberg, Mitchell S.

1973   Naval Operations of the United States Pacific Squadron in 1861. *The American Neptune*, Vol. 33, No. 1, pp. 41–51.

González, Manuel and Carlos Pacheco

1882   [Title to 32,015 hectares of land on Tiburón Island, issued to Guillermo Andrade, December 4, 1882.] Andrade Papers Folio 11. Sherman Library. Corona del Mar, California.

1884   [Title document for San Esteban Island, February 25, 1884.] Andrade Papers Folio 10. Sherman Library. Corona del Mar, California.

González Cabrera Bueno, José

[1734] 1970 *Navegación Especulativa y Práctica.* Colección Chimalistac de Libros y Documentos Acerca de la Nueva España 31. Ediciones José Porrua Turanzas. Madrid. [Facsimile of the 1734 edition.]

González Reyna, Jenaro

1956   [Map accompanying] *Riqueza Minera y Yacimientos Minerales de México.* Tercera edición. Congreso Geológico Internacional, sesión 20. Departamento de Investigaciones Industriales, Banco de México. México.

Goss, N. S.

1888   New and Rare Birds Found Breeding on the San Pedro Martir Isle. *The Auk*, Vol. 5, No. 3, pp. 240–44.

Gracida Romo, Juan José

1985   Genesis y Consolidación del Porfiriato en Sonora (1883–1895). In *Historia General de Sonora*, Tomo 4, coordinated by Cynthia Radding de Murrieta, pp. 17–74. Gobierno del Estado de Sonora. Hermosillo.

Gray, A. B.

1856   *Survey of a Route for the Southern Pacific R.R., on the 32nd Parallel, by A. B. Gray, for the Texas Western R.R. Company.* Wrightson and Co.'s ("Railroad Record") Print. Cincinnati, Ohio. [Reprinted as *The A. B. Gray Report*, edited by L. R. Bailey. Westernlore Press. Los Angeles (1963).]

Greenhouse, Ruth, Robert E. Gasser, and Jannifer W. Gish

1981   Cholla Bud Roasting Pits: An Ethnoarchaeological Example. *The Kiva*, Vol. 46, No. 4, pp. 227–42.

Griffen, William B.

1959   Notes on Seri Indian Culture, Sonora, Mexico. *Latin American Monograph Series* 10. University of Florida Press. Gainesville.

Grindell, Edward P.

1907   The Lost Explorers: The Mystery of a Vanished Expedition. *The Wide World Magazine*, Vol. 19, No. 112, pp. 376–89. [Reprinted in abridged form in *Tales from Tiburon*, edited by Neil B. Carmony and David E. Brown, pp. 58–69 (1983). The Southwest Natural History Association. Phoenix.]

Grismer, L. Lee

1994   Geographic Origins for the Reptiles on Islands in the Gulf of California, México. *Herpetological Natural History*, Vol. 2, No. 2, pp. 17–40.

Guillemin Tarayre, Edmond

1869   *Exploration Minéralogique des Régions Mexicaines Suivie de Notes Archéologiques et Ethnographiques*. Imprimerie Impériale. Paris.

Guzmán, Blas de

1685   *Descripción de la Nueva Situación del Golfo de California que Hizo el Cap.ⁿ Dⁿ Blas de Guzmán en su Descubrimiento*. [Map, copy.] Bancroft Library, University of California. Berkeley.

Hager, Anna Marie

1968   *The Filibusters of 1890*. Baja California Travel Series 14. Dawson's Book Shop. Los Angeles.

Hale, Charles A.

1989   *The Transformation of Liberalism in Late Nineteenth-Century Mexico*. Princeton University Press. Princeton, New Jersey.

Hale, Charles E.

1894a   [Letter to Edwin F. Uhl, Assistant Secretary of State, September 4, 1894.] Microfilm, RG 59, Microcopy 284, General Records of the Department of State, Consular Dispatches, Guaymas, Vol. 9. U.S. National Archives. Washington, D.C.

1894b   [Letter to Edwin F. Uhl, Assistant Secretary of State, December 23, 1894.] Microfilm, RG 59, Microcopy 284, General Records of the Department of State, Consular Dispatches, Guaymas, Vol. 9. U.S. National Archives. Washington, D.C.

1895a   [Letter to Edwin F. Uhl, Assistant Secretary of State, January 21, 1895.] Microfilm, RG 59, Microcopy 284, General Records of the Department of State, Consular Dispatches, Guaymas, Vol. 9. U.S. National Archives. Washington, D.C.

1895b   [Letter to Edwin F. Uhl, Assistant Secretary of State, October 16, 1895.] Microfilm, RG 59, Microcopy 284, General Records of the Department of State, Consular Dispatches, Guaymas, Vol. 9. U.S. National Archives. Washington, D.C.

Halleck, H. Wager

1850   [Letter to Colonel R. B. Mason, April 12, 1848.] In *U.S. House of Representatives Executive Document* No. 17, 31st Congress, 1st Session, pp. 606–12. Government Printing Office. Washington, D.C.

Hamilton, Leonidas Le Cenci

1883   *Hamilton's Mexican Handbook; A Complete Description of the Republic of Mexico....* D. Lothrop and Co. Boston.

Hammond, George P.

1967   Introduction. In *Informe on the New Provence of California 1702* by Francisco María Piccolo, S.J., translated and edited by George P. Hammond, pp. 3–25. Baja California Travel Series 10. Dawson's Book Shop. Los Angeles.

Hardy, Lieut. R. W. H.

[1829] 1977 *Travels in the Interior of Mexico in 1825, 1826, 1827, & 1828*. Facsimile of the 1829 edition reprinted by The Rio Grande Press. Glorieta, New Mexico.

[*Hassler* Deck Logs]

1880–1881 [Deck Logs of the U.S.S. *Hassler*.] RG 23, Records of the Bureau of Naval Personnel. U.S. National Archives. Washington, D.C.

Hayden, Julian D.

1967 A Summary Prehistory and History of the Sierra Pinacate, Sonora. *American Antiquity*, Vol. 32, No. 3, pp. 335–44.

1976 Pre-Altithermal Archaeology in the Sierra Pinacate, Sonora, Mexico. *American Antiquity*, Vol. 41, No. 3, pp. 274–89.

1982 Ground Figures of the Sierra Pinacate, Sonora, Mexico. In *Hohokam and Patayan: Prehistory of Southwestern Arizona*, edited by Randall H. McGuire and Michael B. Schiffer, Appendix 1, pp. 581–88. Academic Press. New York.

1998 *The Sierra Pinacate*. University of Arizona Press. Tucson.

Henderson, David A.

1972 *Men and Whales at Scammon's Lagoon*. Baja California Travel Series 29. Dawson's Book Shop. Los Angeles.

1984 Nineteenth Century Gray Whaling: Grounds, Catches and Kills, Practices and Depletion of the Whale Population. In *The Gray Whale* Eschrichtius robustus, edited by Mary Lou Jones, Steven L. Swartz, and Stephen Leatherwood, pp. 159–86. Academic Press. New York.

Hendricks, William O.

1967 *Guillermo Andrade and Land Development on the Mexican Colorado River Delta, 1874–1905*. Ph.D. dissertation. University of Southern California. Los Angeles.

1976 The Lost Cucapa Reservation. *Pacific Coast Archaeological Society Quarterly*, Vol. 12, No. 1, pp. 47–53.

1978 Rewards of Road Building in the 1870s. In *Brand Book Number Five*, edited by Alex Summers, pp. 140–49. San Diego Corral of the Westerners. San Diego, California.

Herbert, Chas. E.

1885 *Mapa Oficial del Estado de Sonora, Republica de Mexico*. [Map.] Bancroft Library, University of California. Berkeley.

Hernández, Fortunato

1902 *Las Razas Indígenas de Sonora y la Guerra del Yaqui*. Talleres de la Casa Editorial "J. de Elizalde." México.

Hernandez, Ruben

1989 Mexican Tied to 20-Ton Drug Haul Found Living in Tent on Empty Isle. *The Tucson Citizen*, October 12, 1989, Section A, pp. 1–2. Tucson.

Hernández García, Miguel Ángel

1979 La Importancia de Declarar Zonas de Reserva Faunística. Algunas Islas del Golfo de California y Otras Areas Adyacentes. In "III Simposio Binacional Sobre el Medio Ambiente del Golfo de California," pp. 78–81. *Memoria Proceedings*, Publicación Especial No. 14, Instituto Nacional de Investigaciones Forestales, Secretaría de Agricultura y Recursos Hidráulicos. [City not indicated.]

Hernández Sánchez-Barba, Mario

1957 *La Última Expansión Española en América*. Instituto de Estudios Polílticos. Madrid.

Herrera Marcos, Roberto

1988 Yaqui Hands, translated by Mary Beck Moser. In "Seri History (1904): Two Documents," by Mary Beck Moser, pp. 493–501. *Journal of the Southwest*, Vol. 30, No. 4, pp. 469–501.

Herrera T., Roberto, Jesús Morales, and Juan Topete

1976 *Zíx Anxö Cóohhiit Hapáh Quih Czáxö Zíx Quihmáa Táax Mos Czáxöiha*. Instituto Lingüístico de Verano. México.

Heyerdahl, Thor

1968 *Kon-Tiki*, translated by F. H. Lyon. Pocket Books. New York. (Originally published 1950.)

Hills, R. James
1973   *An Ecological Interpretation of Prehistoric Seri Settlement Patterns in Sonora, Mexico.*
            Master's thesis. Arizona State University. Tempe.
1989   In Search of the Seris. *Arizona Highways*, Vol. 65, No. 1, pp. 38–45.
Hinsley, Curtis M., Jr.
1981   *Savages and Scientists: The Smithsonian Institution and the Development of American An-
            thropology 1846–1910.* Smithsonian Institution Press. Washington, D.C.
Hoffman, Jack
1983   The Grindell Prospecting Party. In *Tales from Tiburon*, edited by Neil B. Carmony and
            David E. Brown, pp. 70–84. The Southwest Natural History Association. Phoenix.
Holden, Robert H.
1990   Priorities of the State in the Survey of the Public Land in Mexico, 1876–1911. *His-
            panic American Historical Review*, Vol. 70, No. 4, pp. 579–608.
Hovens, Pieter
1991   The Origins of Anthropology in Baja California: The Fieldwork and Excavations
            of Herman Ten Kate. *Pacific Coast Archaeological Society Quarterly*, Vol. 27, No. 4,
            pp. 15–22.
Hu-DeHart, Evelyn
1984   *Yaqui Resistance and Survival: The Struggle for Land and Autonomy 1821–1910.* Uni-
            versity of Wisconsin Press. Madison.
Hudson, Charles
1966   Folk History and Ethnohistory. *Ethnohistory*, Vol. 13, Nos. 1–2, pp. 52–70.
Huey, Laurence M.
1953   Fisher Folk of the Sea of Cortéz. *Pacific Discovery*, Vol. 6, No. 1, pp. 8–13.
Hussey, Andrew S.
1859   [Journal of Andrew S. Hussey, Master of the Brig *Floyd*, January-October 1859.] Mi-
            crofilm, International Marine Archives, Reel 226. Whaling Museum, Old Dart-
            mouth Historical Society. New Bedford, Massachusetts.
Hutchinson, George Evelyn
1950   The Biogeochemistry of Vertebrate Excretion. No. 3 of "Survey of Existing Knowl-
            edge of Biogeochemistry." *Bulletin of the American Museum of Natural History*, Vol.
            96 [whole volume]. New York.
Huycke, Harold D., Jr.
1970   *To Santa Rosalia, Further and Back.* The Mariners Museum. Newport News, Virginia.
Imray, James
1849   *Chart of the Coast of California from San Blas to San Francisco.* [Nautical Chart.] James
            Imray. London.
1853   *Sailing Directions for the West Coast of North America.* James Imray. London.
Irigoyen, Ulises
1943a   *Carretera Transpeninsular de la Baja California*, Libro 1. Editorial América. México.
1943b   *Carretera Transpeninsular de la Baja California*, Libro 2. Editorial América. México.
Ives, Joseph C.
1861   Report upon the Colorado River of the West, Explored in 1857 and 1858 by Lieu-
            tenant Joseph C. Ives.... *U.S. House of Representatives Executive Document* No. 90,
            36th Congress, 1st Session. Government Printing Office. Washington, D.C.
Ives, Ronald L.
1975   How Tall is a Man? *The Journal of Arizona History*, Vol. 16, No. 2, pp. 197–98.
Johnson, E. J.
1894   From Zone to Zone on Horseback. Colonel E. J. Johnson Continues His Interest-
            ing Wanderings. Singular Disappearance of R. E. L. Robinson, a Philadelphian, on
            the Island of Tiburon—General Torres' Statement. *The Inquirer*. [Newspaper ar-
            ticle] Microfiche, in Journals of Robinson and Flavell of Sloop *Examiner* file. Grand
            Canyon National Park Museum Collections. Grand Canyon, Arizona.

Johnson, Robert Erwin
1963   *Thence Round Cape Horn.* United States Naval Institute. Annapolis, Maryland.
Johnston, Ivan Murray
1924   Expedition of the California Academy of Sciences to the Gulf of California in 1921.
            The Botany (The Vascular Plants). *Proceedings of the California Academy of Sciences,*
            Fourth Series, Vol. 12, No. 30, pp. 951–1218.
Jones, Fayette A.
1910   The Jones Expedition to Tiburon Island, Mex. *The Mining World,* Vol. 32, No. 5,
            pp. 269–70.
Jones-Gates, Kathy
1980   History of Elusive "Arizona Charlie." *The Whitehorse Star,* July 18, 1980, p. 3.
            Whitehorse, Yukon Territory, Canada.
Jordan, David S. and Charles H. Gilbert
1882   List of Fishes Collected by Lieut. Henry E. Nichols, U.S.N., in the Gulf of Cali-
            fornia and on the West Coast of Lower California, with Descriptions of Four New
            Species. *Proceedings of the United States National Museum,* Vol. 4, 1881, pp. 273–79.
            Department of the Interior: U.S. National Museum 27. Washington, D.C.
Kasper, Jan C.
1980   Skeletal Identification of California Sea Lions and Harbor Seals for Archaeologists. *Eth-*
            nic Technology Notes, No. 17. San Diego Museum of Man. San Diego, California.
Kemble, John Haskell
1963   To Arizona by Sea 1850–1877. In *The Westerners Brand Book,* Book 10, pp. 137–52.
            Los Angeles Corral. [Publisher and city not indicated.]
Kessell, John L.
1975   Friars, Bureaucrats, and the Seris of Sonora. *New Mexico Historical Review,* Vol. 50,
            No. 1, pp. 73–95.
King, Jean Beach
1989   *Arizona Charlie: A Legendary Cowboy, Klondike Stampeder and Wild West Showman.*
            Heritage Publishers. Phoenix.
Kinnaird, Lawrence
1958   *The Frontiers of New Spain: Nicolás de Lafora's Description 1766–1768.* Quivera So-
            ciety Publications 13. The Quivera Society. Berkeley, California.
Kirchner, John A.
1983   Gypsum and Manganese in Baja California Sur: Isla San Marcos and Mina Lucifer.
            In *XXI Simposio de la Asociación Cultural de las Californias,* pp. 39–44. La Paz, Baja
            California Sur.
Klauber, Laurence M.
1949   Some New and Revived Subspecies of Rattlesnakes. *Transactions of the San Diego*
            Society of Natural History, Vol. 11, No. 6, pp. 61–116.
Krause, Chester L. and Clifford Mishler
1994   *1994 Standard Catalog of World Coins,* 21st edition. Krause Publications. Iola, Wis-
            consin.
Kroeber, Alfred L.
1931   The Seri. *Southwest Museum Papers,* No. 6. Los Angeles.
Kroeber, Theodora
1961   *Ishi in Two Worlds.* University of California Press. Berkeley.
Krull, Dr. Guillermo
1894   Estudio Sobre Dos Guaneras i la Descomposición del Guano (Conclusion). *Boletín*
            de la Sociedad Nacional de Minería: Revista Minera, Publicación Mensual, Año 11, Vol.
            6, Serie 2, pp. 306–14. Santiago de Chile.
Kunz, George F.
1905   Gems, Jewelers' Materials, and Ornamental Stones of California. *California State*
            Mining Bureau Bulletin No. 37. San Francisco.

Kunz, George Frederick and Charles Hugh Stevenson
1908   *The Book of the Pearl*. Macmillan and Co. London.
Kutsche, Paul
1963   The Tsali Legend: Culture Heroes and Historiography. *Ethnohistory*, Vol. 10, No. 4, pp. 329–57.
Lara-Gongora, Guillermo, Kent R. Beaman, L. Lee Grismer, and Howard E. Lawler
1993   *Lampropeltis Getula Californiae (California Kingsnake)*. *Herpetological Review*, Vol. 24, No. 2, pp. 67–68.
Lassépas, Ulises Urbano
1859   *De la Colonización de la Baja California y Decreto de 10 de Marzo de 1857*. Primer Memorial. Imprenta de Vicente García Torres. México.
Lassépas, Ulises and Roberto L. D. Aumaile
1863   *New Map of the North-Western States of Mexico*. Henry Payot. San Francisco.
[Lawler, Howard E.]
1990   Adventures on a Desert Island. *Employee/Volunteer Newsletter* [of the Arizona-Sonora Desert Museum], Vol. 14, No. 12, pp. 3–4.
Lawler, Howard E.
1992   The Biota of Isla San Esteban in the Gulf of California, Part 1. *Sonoran Herpetologist*, Vol. 5, No. 3, pp. 24–27.
Lawler, Howard E., Thomas R. Van Devender, and James L. Jarchow
1994   Ecological and Nutritional Management of the Endangered Piebald Chuckwalla (*Sauromalus varius*) in Captivity. In "Captive Management and Conservation of Amphibians and Reptiles," edited by James B. Murphy, Kraig Adler, and Joseph T. Collins, pp. 333–41. *Contributions to Herpetology*, Vol. 11. Society for the Study of Amphibians and Reptiles. Ithaca, New York.
Lawlor, Timothy E.
1969   *Evolution of* Peromyscus *on Northern Islands in the Gulf of California, Mexico*. Ph.D. dissertation. University of Michigan. Ann Arbor.
1971   Evolution of *Peromyscus* on Northern Islands in the Gulf of California, Mexico. *Transactions of the San Diego Society of Natural History*, Vol. 16, No. 5, pp. 91–124.
Leavitt, Francis Hale
1943a   Steam Navigation on the Colorado River. [Beginning] *California Historical Society Quarterly*, Vol. 22, No. 1, pp. 1–25.
1943b   Steam Navigation on the Colorado River. [Concluded] *California Historical Society Quarterly*, Vol. 22, No. 2, pp. 151–74.
Le Boeuf, Burney J., David Aurioles, Richard Condit, Claudio Fox, Robert Gisiner, Rigoberto Romero, and Francisco Sinsel
1983   Size and Distribution of the California Sea Lion Population in México. *Proceedings of the California Academy of Sciences*, Vol. 43, No. 7, pp. 77–85.
Lee, E. C. B. and Kenneth Lee
1980   *Safety and Survival at Sea*, revised and expanded edition. A Ginger Book. W.W. Norton and Company. New York.
Legrand, Rafael
1897   [Report of Martín Méndez to Rafael Legrand, Bahía de los Ángeles, October 24, 1897.] RG 84, Diplomatic Branch. Miscellaneous Correspondence, Guaymas Post, 1883–1904. U.S. National Archives. Washington, D.C.
Leighly, John
1972   *California as an Island*. The Book Club of California. San Francisco.
León-Portilla, Miguel
1973   *Voyages of Francisco de Ortega, California 1632–1636*. Baja California Travel Series 30. Dawson's Book Shop. Los Angeles.
Lerdo de Tejada, Sebastián
1873   [Decree of President Lerdo de Tejada.] *Diario Oficial*, Número 115, April 25, 1873. México.

1874 [Decree of President Lerdo de Tejada.] *Diario Oficial*, Número 202, July 21, 1874. México.

Lewis, Leland R. and Peter E. Ebeling

1971 *Baja Sea Guide*, Vol. 2. Miller Freeman Publications. San Francisco.

Lindblad, Sven-Olof, Andrew Jaffe, George Lindsay, Robert K. Johnson, Peter Butz, James C. Simmons, Linda Leigh, Dennis Cornejo, Ian McTaggart-Cowan, Dotte Larsen, Geraldine Lindsay, and Keith Shackleton

1985 *Baja California Circumnavigated*. Special Expeditions. New York.

Lindsay, George E.

1947 A Cruise in the Gulf of California. [Part 1.] *Cactus and Succulent Journal*, Vol. 19, No. 12, pp. 182–86.

1948a A Cruise in the Gulf of California. [Part 2.] *Cactus and Succulent Journal*, Vol. 20, No. 1, pp. 7–9.

1948b A Cruise in the Gulf of California. [Part 4.] *Cactus and Succulent Journal*, Vol. 20, No. 3, pp. 31–35.

[ca. 1961] *Expedition to the Gulf of California 1952*. The Sefton Foundation, Stanford University. Reprinted by Belvedere Scientific Fund. San Francisco, California.

1962 The Belvedere Expedition to the Gulf of California. *Transactions of the San Diego Society of Natural History*, Vol. 13, No. 1, pp. 1–44.

1964 Sea of Cortéz Expedition of the California Academy of Sciences June 20-July 4, 1964. *Proceedings of the California Academy of Sciences*, Fourth Series, Vol. 30, No. 11, pp. 211–42.

1966a The Gulf Island Expedition of 1966. *Pacific Discovery*, Vol. 19, No. 5, pp. 2–11.

1966b The Gulf Islands Expedition of 1966. *Proceedings of the California Academy of Sciences*, Fourth Series, Vol. 30, No. 16, pp. 309–55.

1983 History of Scientific Exploration in the Sea of Cortéz. In *Island Biogeography in the Sea of Cortéz*, edited by Ted J. Case and Martin L. Cody, pp. 3–12. University of California Press. Berkeley.

Lindsay, Geraldine and George Lindsay

1981 Baja California Circumnavigated. *Pacific Discovery*, Vol. 34, No. 6, pp. 1–13.

Lingenfelter, Richard E.

1978 *Steamboats on the Colorado River 1852–1916*. University of Arizona Press. Tucson.

Lluch Belda, Daniel

1969 El Lobo Marino de California *Zalophus californianus californianus* (Lesson 1828) Allen, 1880: Observaciones Sobre Su Ecología y Explotación. In *Dos Mamíferos Marinos de Baja California*, edited by Daniel Lluch Belda, Lowell Adams, and S. G. Losocki. Instituto Mexicano de Recursos Naturales Renovables, A.C. México.

Lockington, W. N.

1882 List of Fishes Collected by Mr. W. J. Fisher, upon the Coasts of Lower California, 1876–1877, with Descriptions of New Species. In *Proceedings of the Academy of Natural Sciences of Philadelphia, 1881*, pp. 113–20.

López, Luis

1894 [Report to General Luis E. Torres, recorded July 3, 1894.] Gobernación, Referencia 214.3, *Tribu Seri*. Archivo Histórico de Estado de Sonora, Hermosillo. Microfilm, Hermosillo Film No. 26, Arizona Historical Society. Tucson.

López Rámos, Ernesto

1976 *Carta Geológica de la República Mexicana*, 4ª Edición. 1:2,000,000. [Map.] Comite de la Carta Geológica de México. México.

López Soto, Virgilio

1993 En Torno a la Deportación de los Yaquis. In *Memoria: XVI Simposio de Historia y Antropología de Sonora*, pp. 379–402. Instituto de Investigaciones Históricas. Universidad de Sonora. Hermosillo.

Love, Frank
1978   Poston and the Birth of Yuma. *The Journal of Arizona History*, Vol. 19, No. 4, pp.
            403–16.
Lowe, Charles H., Jr.
1955   An Evolutionary Study of Island Faunas in the Gulf of California, Mexico, with a
            Method for Comparative Analysis. *Evolution*, Vol. 9, No. 3, pp. 339–44.
Lowe, Charles H., Jr. and Kenneth S. Norris
1955   Analysis of the Herpetofauna of Baja California, Mexico. III. New and Revived Rep-
            tilian Subspecies of Isla de San Esteban, Gulf of California, Sonora, Mexico, with
            Notes on Other Satellite Islands of Isla Tiburón. *Herpetologica*, Vol. 11, Pt. 1, pp.
            89–96.
Lowe, Herbert N.
1933a   The Cruise of the "Petrel" [Part 1.] *The Nautilus*, Vol. 46, No. 3, pp. 73–76.
1933b   The Cruise of the "Petrel" [Part 2.] *The Nautilus*, Vol. 46, No. 4, pp. 108–15.
Lowell, Edith S.
1970   A Comparison of Mexican and Seri Indian Versions of the Legend of Lola Casa-
            nova. *The Kiva*, Vol. 35, No. 4, pp. 144–58.
[Lower California Company]
1870   *Title Papers of the Lower California Company to Lands, etc., in the Territory of Lower
            California, and in the States of Sonora and Sinaloa, of the Republic of Mexico.* Evening
            Post Steam Presses. New York.
Luna, Jesús
1973   *The Public Career of Don Ramón Corral.* Ph.D. dissertation. North Texas State Uni-
            versity. Denton, Texas.
MacMullen, Jerry
1964   Seals, Rheumatic Indians Helped S.D. Guano Trade. *The San Diego Union*, Section
            G, p. 2, April 19, 1964. San Diego, California.
1968   Tiburon's Double Murder Still Puzzles Historians. *The San Diego Union*, Section
            G, p. 2, January 7, 1968. San Diego, California.
Madden, Henry Miller
1949   *Xantus, Hungarian Naturalist in the Pioneer West.* Books of the West. Palo Alto, Cali-
            fornia.
Madsen, John H.
1993   Rock Cairn and Talus Pit Features in the Los Robles Community. In "Between
            Desert and River: Hohokam Settlement and Land Use in the Los Robles Commu-
            nity," edited by Christian E. Downum, pp. 96–106. *Anthropological Papers of the Uni-
            versity of Arizona* No. 57. Tucson.
Malakoff, David
1998   Rock Dates Thrown into Doubt, Researcher Under Fire. *Science*, Vol. 280, No.
            5372, pp. 2041–42.
Malkin, Borys
1962   Seri Ethnozoology. *Occasional Papers of the Idaho State College Museum*, Number 7.
            Pocatello, Idaho.
Mange, Juan Mateo
1954   *Unknown Arizona and Sonora 1693–1721*, Part 2, translated by Harry J. Karns and
            Associates. Arizona Silhouettes. Tucson.
Martínez, Pablo L.
1960   *A History of Lower California*, translated by Ethel Duffy Turner. Editorial Baja Cali-
            fornia. México.
Massey, William C.
1966   Archaeology and Ethnohistory of Lower California. In "Archaeological Frontiers
            and External Connections," edited by Gordon F. Ekholm and Gordon R. Willey,

pp. 38–58. Vol. 4 of *Handbook of Middle American Indians*, Robert Wauchope, general editor. University of Texas Press. Austin.

Massey, William C. and Carolyn M. Osborne

1961   A Burial Cave in Baja California: The Palmer Collection, 1887. *Anthropological Records* 16:8. University of California Press. Berkeley.

Mathes, W. Michael

1966   General Introduction. *The Pearl Hunters in the Gulf of California 1668. Summary Report of the Voyage Made to the Californias by Captain Francisco de Lucenilla. Written by Father Juan Cavallero Carranco*. Transcribed, translated, and annotated by W. Michael Mathes. Baja California Travel Series 4. Dawson's Book Shop. Los Angeles.

1969   *The Capture of the Santa Ana, Cabo San Lucas, November, 1587. The Accounts of Francis Pretty, Antonio de Sierra, and Tomás de Alzola*, transcribed, translated, and annotated by W. Michael Mathes. Baja California Travel Series 18. Dawson's Book Shop. Los Angeles.

1970   Introducción General. In *Californiana II: Documentos Para la Historia de la Explotación Comercial de California 1611–1679*, 2, edited with notes by W. Michael Mathes, pp. xxxil-xlix. Colección Chimalistac de Libros y Documentos Acerca de la Nueva España 30. Ediciones José Porrua Turanzas. Madrid.

1974   *Geographic and Hydrographic Descriptions of Many Northern and Southern Lands and Seas in the Indies, Specifically of the Discovery of the Kingdom of California (1632), by Nicolás de Cardona*, translated and edited by W. Michael Mathes. Baja California Travel Series 35. Dawson's Book Shop. Los Angeles.

1981   California's First Explorer: *Sebastián Vizcaíno. The Pacific Historian*, Vol. 25, No. 3, pp. 8–14.

1992a   A Spanish Voyage to California in 1644: The Report of Pedro Porter y Casanate. In "Ethnology of the Baja California Indians," edited by W. Michael Mathes, pp. 245–53. Vol. 5 of *Spanish Borderlands Sourcebooks*, David Hurst Thomas, general editor. Garland Publications. New York.

1992b   Introduction. In "Ethnology of the Baja California Indians," edited by W. Michael Mathes, pp. xiii–xvi. Vol. 5 of *Spanish Borderlands Sourcebooks*, David Hurst Thomas, general editor. Garland Publications. New York.

Mathiessen, Peter

1984   The Desert Sea. *Geo*, Vol. 6, (September), pp. 116–25, 128–31.

Matthews, John A.

1994   Lichenometric Dating: A Review with Particular Reference to "Little Ice Age" Moraines in Southern Norway. In *Dating in Exposed and Surface Contexts*, edited by Charlotte Beck, pp. 185–212. University of New Mexico Press. Albuquerque.

Maury, M. F.

1851   Whale Chart (Preliminary Sketch). *H. O. Miscel.* No. 8514. U.S. Hydrographic Office. Washington, D.C.

Maya, Armando

1968   *The Natural History of the Fish-Eating Bat*, Pizonyx vivesi. Ph.D. dissertation. University of Arizona. Tucson.

Maza, Francisco F. de la (compiler)

1893   *Código de Colonización y Terrenos Baldíos de la República Mexicana*. Oficina Tip. de la Secretaría de Fomento. México.

McCormick, Richard C.

1865   Arizona. In *State, Territorial and Ocean Guide Book of the Pacific....* Sterling M. Holdredge. San Francisco. Microfilm, No. 2623 in "Western Americana, Frontier History of the Trans-Mississippi West, 1550–1900." University of Oregon Library. Eugene.

McGee, WJ

1894   *Papago Trip, 1894.* [Notebooks of a trip through Papago country in 1894 and a second expedition in Papago-Seri country, 1895.] Microfilm, Film 119. University of Arizona Library. Tucson.

1898   The Seri Indians. *Seventeenth Annual Report of the Bureau of American Ethnology*, Part 1. Government Printing Office. Washington, D.C. [Reprinted 1971 in facsimile edition by The Rio Grande Press. Glorieta, New Mexico.]

1901   The Wildest Tribe in North America: Seriland and the Seri. [Part 1.] *The Land of Sunshine*, Vol. 14, No. 5, pp. 364–76.

[1895] 1983 The Journal of WJ McGee, transcribed by Bernard L. Fontana and Hazel Fontana. In *Tales from Tiburon*, edited by Neil B. Carmony and David E. Brown, pp. 29–55. The Southwest Natural History Association. Phoenix.

McGee, WJ and Willard D. Johnson
1896   Seriland. *National Geographic Magazine*, Vol. 7, No. 4, pp. 125–33.

McGuire, Randall H.
1982   Problems in Culture History. In *Hohokam and Patayan: Prehistory of Southwestern Arizona*, edited by Randall H. McGuire and Michael B. Schiffer, pp. 153–222. Academic Press. New York.

McVaugh, Rogers
1956   *Edward Palmer: Plant Explorer of the American West*. University of Oklahoma Press. Norman.

Meadows, C.
1902   Charlie Meadows Is Preparing for His Expedition. *Daily Klondike Nugget*, August 23, 1902. Dawson City, Yukon Territory, Canada.

Meko, David M., Charles W. Stockton, and William R. Boggess
1980   A Tree-Ring Reconstruction of Drought in Southern California. *Water Resources Bulletin*, Vol. 16, No. 4, pp. 594–600.

Meko, David and Donald A. Graybill
1995   Tree-Ring Reconstruction of Upper Gila River Discharge. *Water Resources Bulletin*, Vol. 31, No. 4, pp. 605–16.

Méndez G., Cleofas
1958   [Field notes for "Esteban" station, March 1958.] Copy in Bowen's possession.

Miller, Joseph, (editor)
1972   *The Arizona Rangers*. Hastings House, Publishers. New York.

Miller, Robert Ryal
1974   Cortés and the First Attempt to Colonize California. *California Historical Quarterly*, Vol. 53, No. 1, pp. 4–16.

Mills, Hazel Emery
1941   The Arizona Fleet. *The American Neptune*, Vol. 1, No. 3, pp. 255–74.

Monteverde, Enrique
1891   Padrón de la Tribu Seris Sometidos a la Paz, Con Expresión de Sus Nombres, Sexo, Edad y Lugar de Su Nacimiento. In *Memoria de la Administración Pública del Estado de Sonora, Presentada a la Legislatura del Mismo*, Tomo 1, by Ramón Corral, pp. 567–73. E. Gaxiola y Ca. Guaymas.

Moran, Reid
1966   Plant Collections from the Northern Gulf Islands, April, 1966. In "The Gulf Islands Expedition of 1966," by George E. Lindsay, pp. 339–40. *Proceedings of the California Academy of Sciences*, Fourth Series, Vol. 30, No. 16, pp. 309–55.

1968   Cardón. *Pacific Discovery*, Vol. 21, No. 2, pp. 2–9.

1980a   *Monthly Report of the Botany Department, March 1980*. San Diego Natural History Museum. San Diego.

1980b   *Monthly Report of the Botany Department, April 1980*. San Diego Natural History Museum. San Diego.

1983   Vascular Plants of the Gulf Islands. In *Island Biogeography in the Sea of Cortéz*, edited by Ted J. Case and Martin L. Cody, Appendix 4.1, pp. 348–81. University of California Press. Berkeley.

Morley, W. R.
1882   *Map of the State of Sonora, Mexico, Showing Railway Surveys and Reconnoissances.* [Map attached to a letter from A. Willard to W. Hunter, Second Assistant Secretary of State, November 9, 1883.] Microfilm, RG 59, General Records of the Department of State, Consular Dispatches, Guaymas, Vol. 5. U.S. National Archives. Washington, D.C.

Moser, Edward
1963   Seri Bands. *The Kiva*, Vol. 28, No. 3, pp. 14–27.

Moser, Edward and Richard S. White
1968   Seri Clay Figurines. *The Kiva*, Vol. 33, No. 3, pp. 133–54.

Moser, Mary Beck
1970   Seri Elevated Burials. *The Kiva*, Vol. 35, No. 4, pp. 211–16.
1988   Seri History (1904): Two Documents. *Journal of the Southwest*, Vol. 30, No. 4, pp. 469–501.

Mosk, Sanford A.
1931   *Spanish Voyages and Pearl Fisheries in the Gulf of California: A Study in Economic History.* Ph.D. dissertation. University of California. Berkeley.
1934   The Cardona Company and the Pearl Fisheries of Lower California. *The Pacific Historical Review*, Vol. 3, No. 1, pp. 50–61.
1941   Capitalistic Development in the Lower California Pearl Fisheries. *The Pacific Historical Review*, Vol. 10, No. 4, pp. 461–68.

Mowry, Sylvester
[1864] 1973 *Arizona and Sonora: The Geography, History, and Resources of the Silver Region of North America*, third edition. Facsimile edition reprinted by Arno Press. New York.

Muñoz Lumbier, Manuel
1919   Algunos Datos Sobre las Islas Mexicanas Para Contribuir al Estudio de Sus Recursos Naturales. *Anales del Instituto Geológico de México*, Número 7. Secretaría de Industria, Comercio y Trabajo, Departamento de Exploraciones y Estudios Geológicos. México.

Murillo, Luis B.
1877   Noticia de la Entrada y Salida de Pasajeros, en éste Puerto del 1 al 18 de Mayo. *El Triunfo de Sonora*, Año 1, Num. 1, p. 4, May 23, 1877. Guaymas. Microfilm, Roll 5000, Reel 5, Item 28 in "Mexican Newspaper Miscellany, Sonora, 1838–1883." Bancroft Library, University of California. Berkeley.

Murray, Spencer
1967   *Cruising the Sea of Cortez.* Revised second printing by Best-West Publications. Desert Printers. Palm Desert, California.

Murray, Spencer and Ralph Poole
1965   *PowerBoating the West Coast of Mexico.* Desert-Southwest. Palm Desert, California.

[*Narragansett* Deck Logs]
1873–1875 [Deck Logs of the U.S.S. *Narragansett*.] RG 24, Records of the Bureau of Naval Personnel. U.S. National Archives. Washington, D.C.

Nava, Diego de la
[1632] 1992 Opinion Given by Licentiate Diego de la Nava … on 19 November 1632 … with a Statement of What He Saw and Understood on the Voyage He Made … with Captain Francisco de Ortega in the Same Year, translated by W. Michael Mathes. In "Ethnology of the Baja California Indians," edited by W. Michael Mathes, pp. 221–27. Vol. 5 of *Spanish Borderlands Sourcebooks*, David Hurst Thomas, general editor. Garland Publishing. New York.

Nava, Pedro de
[1798] 1999 Another Proposed Expedition to Tiburón Island, 1798. In *Empire of Sand: The Seri Indians and the Struggle for Spanish Sonora, 1645–1803*, edited by Thomas E. Sheridan, pp. 448–51. University of Arizona Press. Tucson.

Navarro, Cayetano
1850a   Apuntes p.ª el Diario de Campaña contra los Seris Copiada desde el Día 27 de Marzo—1850. Gobernación, Referencia 214.3, *Tribu Seri*. Archivo Histórico del Estado de Sonora, Hermosillo. Microfilm, Hermosillo Film No. 25, Arizona Historical Society. Tucson.
1850b   [Dispatch to Governor José de Aguilar, April 22, 1850.] Gobernación, Referencia 214.3, *Tribu Seri*. Archivo Histórico del Estado de Sonora, Hermosillo. Microfilm, Hermosillo Film No. 25, Arizona Historical Society. Tucson.
1850c   [Report to Governor José de Aguilar, April 24, 1850.] Gobernación, Referencia 214.3, *Tribu Seri*. Archivo Histórico del Estado de Sonora, Hermosillo. Microfilm, Hermosillo Film No. 25, Arizona Historical Society. Tucson.
1851   [Letter to Governor José de Aguilar, February 24, 1851.] Gobernación, Referencia 214.3, *Tribu Seri*. Archivo Histórico del Estado de Sonora, Hermosillo. Microfilm, Hermosillo Film No. 25, Arizona Historical Society. Tucson.

Nelson, Bryan
1968   *Galapagos: Islands of Birds*. Longmans, Green and Co. London.

Nelson, Edward W.
1922   Lower California and Its Natural Resources. National Academy of Sciences, Vol. 16, *First Memoir*. Government Printing Office. Washington, D.C.

Nelson, Stewart B.
1971   *Oceanographic Ships Fore and Aft*. Office of the Oceanographer of the Navy. Government Printing Office. Washington, D.C.

Nentvig, Juan
[1764] 1980 *Rudo Ensayo*, translated, clarified, and annotated by Alberto Francisco Pradeau and Robert R. Rasmussen. University of Arizona Press. Tucson.

Nichols, Henry E.
1881   [Cruise report for September 1880 to April 1881, addressed to C. P. Patterson, Superintendent, Coast and Geodetic Survey, May 8, 1881.] RG 23, Coast and Geodetic Survey, Assistants I-N (1881). U.S. National Archives. Washington, D.C.

Nieto, R. F.
1897   [Letter to the U.S. Consular Agent in Guaymas, November 18, 1897.] RG 84, Diplomatic Branch. Miscellaneous Correspondence, Guaymas Post, 1883–1904. U.S. National Archives. Washington, D.C.

Norris, Kenneth S. and William R. Dawson
1964   Observations on the Water Economy and Electrolyte Excretion of Chuckwallas (Lacertilia, *Sauromalus*). *Copeia*, No. 4, pp. 638–46.

North, Arthur Walbridge
1908   *The Mother of California*. Paul Elder and Company. New York.

Nunis, Doyce B., Jr.
1977   *The Mexican War in Baja California*. Baja California Travel Series 39. Dawson's Book Shop. Los Angeles.

Ober, Frederick A.
1884   *Travels in Mexico and Life Among the Mexicans*. Estes and Lauriat. Boston.

O'Donnell, Dennis Joseph
1974   *Green Turtle Fishery in Baja California Waters: History and Prospect*. Master's thesis. California State University, Northridge. Northridge, California.

Ogden, Adele
1941   *The California Sea Otter Trade 1784–1848*. University of California Press. Berkeley.

Orozco y Berra, Manuel
1864   *Carta Etnográfica de México*. [Map.] Bancroft Library, University of California. Berkeley.
1880   *Historia Antigua y de las Culturas Aborígenes de México*. Tomo Primero. Edición segundo. Ediciones Fuente Cultural. México.

Ortega, Francisco de

[1636] 1944 Tercera Demarcación, que Yo, el Capitán y Cabo, Francisco de Ortega, Salgo a Hacer desde éste Puerto de Santa Catalina (23), Provincia de Sinaloa, a las Islas Californias.... In *Colección de Diarios y Relaciones Para la Historia de los Viajes Descubrimientos* 4, edited by Luis Cebreiro Blanco, pp. 102–10. Instituto Histórico de Marina. Madrid.

[1636] 1970 Relación Circunstanciada de los Tres Viages que el Capitán Francisco de Ortega Hizo al Descubrimiento de las Islas Californias y Tierra Firme de Ellas desde el Año de 1631 hasta el de 1636.... In *Californiana II: Documentos Para la Historia de la Explotación Comercial de California 1611–1679*, 1, edited with notes by W. Michael Mathes, pp. 480–86. Colección Chimalistac de Libros y Documentos Acerca de la Nueva España 29. Ediciones José Porrua Turanzas. Madrid.

[1634] 1992 Deposition of Francisco de Ortega Relative to His Voyage to La Paz and Relations with the Pericu, Remitted to Viceroy Marques de Cerralvo from Sinaloa, 8 April 1634, translated by W. Michael Mathes. In "Ethnology of the Baja California Indians," edited by W. Michael Mathes, pp. 233–44. Vol. 5 of *Spanish Borderlands Sourcebooks*, David Hurst Thomas, general editor. Garland Publishing. New York.

Osburn, Raymond C. and John Treadwell Nichols

1916 Shore Fishes Collected by the "Albatross" Expedition in Lower California with Descriptions of New Species. *Bulletin of the American Museum of Natural History*, Vol. 35, Art. 16, pp. 139–81.

Osorio Tafall, B. F.

1944 La Expedición del M. N. "Gracioso" Por Aguas del Extremo Noroeste Mexicano. I.—Resumen General. *Anales de la Escuela Nacional de Ciencias Biológicas*, Vol. 3, Nums. 3–4, pp. 331–60. Secretaría de Educación Pública, Instituto Politécnico Nacional. México.

1946 Contribución al Conocimiento del Mar de Cortés. *Boletín de la Sociedad Mexicana de Geografía y Estadística*, Tomo 62, Num. 1, pp. 89–130.

Pacheco, Carlos and Guillermo Andrade

1884 *Contrato Celebrado Entre el Secretario de Fomento, General Carlos Pacheco, a Nombre del Ejecutivo de la Unión, y los Sres. Guillermo Andrade y Socios de la Compañía Mexicana Colonizadora e Industrial, Para el Arrendamiento de la Tercera Parte de las Islas Tiburón y San Esteban*. Feb 20, 1884. Andrade Papers Folio 10. Sherman Library. Corona del Mar, California.

1885 [Revised contract for Ángel de la Guarda, Tiburón, and San Esteban Islands, August 10, 1885.] *Diario Oficial*, August 18, 1885, pp. 1–2. México.

Pacheco, Carlos, Carlos Quaglia, and Luis García Teruel

1893 [Contract of December 18, 1885.] In *Código de Colonización y Terrenos Baldíos de la República Mexicana*, by Francisco F. de la Maza, pp. 999–1011. Oficina Tip. de la Secretaría de Fomento. México.

Palóu, Fray Francisco

[1783] 1966 *Historical Memoirs of New California by Fray Francisco Palóu, O.F.M.*, Vol. 1, translated and edited by Herbert Eugene Bolton. Russell and Russell. New York.

Parra and Astiasaran [given names unknown]

1850 [Decret.º N.º 126.], March 11, 1850. Gobernación, Referencia 214.3, *Tribu Seri*. Archivo Histórico del Estado de Sonora, Hermosillo. Microfilm, Hermosillo Film No. 25, Arizona Historical Society. Tucson.

Perera, Nicolás de

[1729] 1999 Father Nicolás de Perera to Nicolás de Oro Regarding Bernal de Huidobro's Expedition to Seri Territory, 1729. In *Empire of Sand: The Seri Indians and the Struggle for Spanish Sonora, 1645–1803*, edited by Thomas E. Sheridan, pp. 127–30. University of Arizona Press. Tucson.

[1740] 1999 Father Nicolás de Perera to the Father Provincial, 1740. In *Empire of Sand: The Seri*

Indians and the Struggle for Spanish Sonora, 1645–1803, edited by Thomas E. Sheridan, pp. 131–33. University of Arizona Press. Tucson.

Pérez Hernández, José María

1872a   *Compendio de la Geografía del Estado de Sonora*. Tip. del Comercio, a Cargo de Mariano Lara (Hijo). México.

1872b   *Compendio de la Geografía del Territorio de la Baja California*. Tip. del Comercio, a Cargo de Mariano Lara (Hijo). México.

Pérez de Ribas, Andrés

[1645] 1944 *Historia de los Triunfos de Nuestra Santa Fé Entre Gentes las Más Bárbaras y Fieras del Nuevo Orbe....*, Vol. 1. Editorial Layac. México.

Peterson, Walt

1992   *The Baja Adventure Book*, second edition. Wilderness Press. Berkeley, California.

Petit-Thouars, Abel du

[1841] 1956 *Voyage of the Venus: Sojourn in California*, translated by Charles N. Rudkin. Early California Travel Series 35. Dawson's Book Shop. Los Angeles.

Pfefferkorn, Ignaz

[1794] 1989 *Sonora: A Description of the Province*, translated and annotated by Theodore E. Treutlein. University of Arizona Press. Tucson.

Phillips, Richard P.

1968   Reconnaissance Geology of Some of the Northwestern Islands in the Gulf of California. In "Abstracts for 1966: Abstracts of Papers Submitted for Six Meetings with Which the Society Was Associated," p. 327. *Geological Society of America Special Papers* No. 101. New York.

Pimentel, Francisco Antonio

[1750] 1946 Diario de lo Acaecido y Practicado en la Entrada que se Hizo a la Isla del Tiburón éste Año 1750. *Boletín del Archivo General de la Nación*, Tomo 17, Número 4, pp. 503–74. Secretaría de Gobernación. México.

[1750] 1999 Diary of What Came to Pass and Was Executed in the Expedition That Was Made to the Island of Tiburón in This Year, 1750. In *Empire of Sand: The Seri Indians and the Struggle for Spanish Sonora, 1645–1803*, edited by Thomas E. Sheridan, pp. 178–207. University of Arizona Press. Tucson.

Porter y Casanate, Pedro

[1649]   Relación Para Su Magestad de lo Subcedido al Almirante Don Pedro Porter Cassanate en el Descubrimiento del Golfo de California: 13 de Abril 1649. In *Californiana II: Documentos Para la Historia de la Explotación Comercial de California 1611–1679*, 2, edited with notes by W. Michael Mathes, pp. 852–59. Colección Chimalistac de Libros y Documentos Acerca de la Nueva España 30. Ediciones José Porrua Turanzas. Madrid. [Also reproduced in full in Portillo (1982:475–79).]

1970a

[1651]   Carta de Pedro Porter al Virrey Conde de Alva, Con Informe Adjunto: 8 de Agosto 1651. In *Californiana II: Documentos Para la Historia de la Explotación Comercial de California 1611–1679*, 2, edited with notes by W. Michael Mathes, pp. 887–901. Colección Chimalistac de Libros y Documentos Acerca de la Nueva España 30. Ediciones José Porrua Turanzas. Madrid. [Also reproduced in full in Portillo (1982: 480–88).]

1970b

[1645] 1992 Report of the Activities of Admiral Don Pedro Porter y Casanate, Knight of the Order of Santiago, from the Time He Left Spain for the Exploration of the Gulf of California in 1643 to the End of 1644. In "A Spanish Voyage to California in 1644: The Report of Pedro Porter y Casanate," by W. Michael Mathes. In "Ethnology of the Baja California Indians," edited by W. Michael Mathes, pp. 245–53. Vol. 5 of *Spanish Borderlands Sourcebooks*, David Hurst Thomas, general editor. Garland Publishing. New York.

Portillo, Álvaro del

1982   *Descubrimientos y Exploraciones en las Costas de California 1532–1650*. Ediciones Rialp, S.A. Madrid.

Poston, Charles D.
1854   *Reconnaissance in Sonora*. [Report sent to Major Samuel P. Heintzelman, Cincinnati, Ohio, September 15, 1854.] Typescript, Sherman Library. Corona del Mar, California.

Powell, T. G.
1968   Mexican Intellectuals and the Indian Question, 1876–1911. *Hispanic American Historical Review*, Vol. 48, No. 1, pp. 19–36.

Preciado, Francisco de
[1540] 1904 A Relation of the Discovery [of the Gulf of California] … Made with Three Ships … Of Which Fleet Was Captaine the Right Worshipful Knight Francis de Ulloa.… In *The Principal Navigations, Voyages, Traffiques & Discoveries of the English Nation*, Vol. 9, by Richard Hakluyt, pp. 206–78. James MacLehose and Sons. Glasgow.

Radding, Cynthia
1997   *Wandering People*. Duke University Press. Durham, North Carolina.

Ramírez, Santiago
1884   *Noticia Histórica de la Riqueza Minera de México*. Oficina Tipográfica de la Secretaría de Fomento. México.

Ramos, Joaquín M.
1887   Informe Relativo a Los Trabajos Ejecutados Por la Comisión Exploradora de la Baja California, el Año de 1884. *Anales del Ministerio de Fomento*, Tomo 8. México.

[*Ranger* Deck Logs]
1881   [Deck Logs of the U.S.S. *Ranger*.] RG 24, Records of the Bureau of Naval Personnel. U.S. National Archives. Washington, D.C.

Rathbun, Richard
1894   Summary of the Fishery Investigations Conducted in the North Pacific Ocean and Bering Sea from July 1, 1888, to July 1, 1892, by the U.S. Fish Commission Steamer Albatross. In "Bulletin of the United States Fish Commission, Vol. 12 for 1892," pp. 127–99. *U.S. House of Representatives Miscellaneous Document* No. 122, 53rd Congress, 2nd Session. Government Printing Office. Washington, D.C.

Redondo, José María
1862   [Letter to the Governor of Sonora, September 26, 1862.] Gobernación, Referencia 214.3, *Tribu Seri*. Archivo Histórico del Estado de Sonora, Hermosillo. Microfilm, Hermosillo Film No. 25, Arizona Historical Society. Tucson.

Reeder, William G. and Kenneth S. Norris
1954   Distribution, Type Locality, and Habits of the Fish-Eating Bat, *Pizonyx vivesi*. *Journal of Mammalogy*, Vol. 35, No. 1, pp. 81–87.

Reid, J. Jefferson and Stephanie Whittlesey
1997   *The Archaeology of Ancient Arizona*. University of Arizona Press. Tucson.

Revere, Joseph Warren
[1849] 1947 *Naval Duty in California*. Biobooks. Oakland, California.

Richards, H. M. M.
1913   A Lebanonian Amongst a Strange People. *Papers and Addresses of the Lebanon County* [Pennsylvania] *Historical Society*, Vol. 6, No. 4, pp. 77–92.

Riley, Carroll L.
1997   Introduction. In *The Coronado Expedition to Tierra Nueva*, edited by Richard Flint and Shirley Cushing Flint, pp. 1–28. University Press of Colorado. Niwot, Colorado.

Rittenhouse, Jack D.
1965   *Disturnell's Treaty Map*. Stagecoach Press. Santa Fe, New Mexico.

Ritter, Eric W.
1977   Talus Depression Hunting Blinds in the Bahía Concepción Region of Baja California. *Pacific Coast Archaeological Society Quarterly*, Vol. 13, No. 1, pp. 1–10.
1981   The Description and Significance of Some Prehistoric Stone Features, South-Central Baja California, Mexico. *Pacific Coast Archaeological Society Quarterly*, Vol. 17, No. 1, pp. 25–42.

Ritter, E. W., L. A. Payen, and C. H. Rector
1984   An Archaeological Survey of Laguna La Guija, Baja California. *Pacific Coast Archaeological Society Quarterly*, Vol. 20, No. 1, pp. 17–26.

Riva Palacio, Vicente
1877   *Memoria Presentada al Congreso de la Unión por el Secretario de Estado y del Despacho de Fomento, Colonización, Industria y Comercio de la República Mexicana*. Imprenta de Francisco Díaz de León. México.

Robeson, George M.
1874   Report of the Secretary of the Navy [for 1874]. *U.S. House of Representatives Executive Document* No. 1, Part 3, 43rd Congress, 2nd Session. Government Printing Office. Washington, D.C.
1875   Report of the Secretary of the Navy [for 1875]. *U.S. House of Representatives Executive Document* No. 1, Part 3, 44th Congress, 1st Session. Government Printing Office. Washington, D.C.

Robinson, Michael David
1972   *Chromosomes, Protein Polymorphism, and Systematics of Insular Chuckwalla Lizards* (*Genus* Sauromalus) *in the Gulf of California, Mexico*. Ph.D. dissertation. University of Arizona. Tucson.

Robinson, R. E. L.
1894   [Journals of Robinson and Flavell of the Sloop *Examiner*.] Microfiche, Grand Canyon National Park Museum Collections. Grand Canyon, Arizona.

Robinson, Tomás
1863   Informe del Gefe de la Comisión Científica Nombrada para la Localización del Puerto de la Libertad, en el Distrito del Altar. *Boletín de la Sociedad Mexicana de Geografía y Estadística*, 1ª Época, Tomo 10. Imprenta de Vicente García Torres. México. [English translation published as *Report of the Scientific Commission ... for the Survey of the Port of La Libertad, in the District of Altar, (Sonora, Mexico)....* Henry Payot, Bookseller and Publisher. San Francisco.] [No date.]

Roca, Paul M.
1967   *Paths of the Padres Through Sonora: An Illustrated History and Guide to its Spanish Churches*. Arizona Pioneers' Historical Society. Tucson.

Rogers, Frederick S.
1930   [Field notes.] San Diego Museum of Man. San Diego, California.

Rogers, Malcolm J.
1939   Early Lithic Industries of the Lower Basin of the Colorado River and Adjacent Desert Areas. *San Diego Museum Papers*, No. 3. San Diego, California.
1966   *Ancient Hunters of the Far West*, edited by Richard F. Pourade. Union-Tribune Publishing Co. San Diego, California.

Rogers, Captain Woodes
1712   *A Cruising Voyage Round the World....* Printed for A. Bell and B. Lintot. London.

Rose, Robert
1859   [Letter to His Excellency Ignacio Pesqueira, Governor of the States of Sonora and Sinaloa, May 27, 1859.] Microfilm, RG 59, General Records of the Department of State, Consular Dispatches, Guaymas, Vol. 1. U.S. National Archives. Washington, D.C.

Ruibal Corella, Juan Antonio
1985   La Época de la Reforma. In *Historia General de Sonora*, Tomo 3, edited by Armando Quijada Hernández and Juan Antonio Ruibal Corella, pp. 151–69. Gobierno del Estado de Sonora. Hermosillo.

Ruiz, Ramón Eduardo
1988   *The People of Sonora and Yankee Capitalists*. University of Arizona Press. Tucson.

Ruiz Naufal, Victor M., Ernesto Lemoine, and Antonio Gálvez Medrano
1982   La Nación. *El Territorio Mexicano*, Tomo 1. Instituto Mexicano del Seguro Social. México.

Sales, Luis
[1794] 1956 *Observations on California 1772–1790*, translated and edited by Charles N. Rudkin. Early California Travel Series 37. Glen Dawson. Los Angeles.

Salvatierra, Juan María de
1710 Copia de una Carta del P. Juan María de Salvatierra para el P. Provincial Antonio Xardon: en que le Da Cuenta de su Ida a la Costa de los Seris, para Remedias la Lancha Varada, y Sucessas de éste Visage. Dada en California a 3 de Abril del Año de 1710. Microfilm, Archivo General de la Nación *Historia*, Tomo 308, ff. 389–404. Bancroft Library, University of California. Berkeley.

Sánchez Facio, M.
1889 *The Truth About Lower California*. [Publisher not indicated.] San Francisco, California.

Scammon, Charles M.
1869 Report of Captain C. M. Scammon, of the U.S. Revenue Service, on the West Coast of Lower California. In *Resources of the Pacific Slope….*, by J. Ross Browne, pp. 123–31. D. Appleton and Co. New York.
1874 *The Marine Mammals of the North-Western Coast of North America*. John H. Carmany and Co. San Francisco.

Scheina, Robert L.
1970 The Forgotten Fleet: The Mexican Navy on the Eve of War, 1845. *The American Neptune*, Vol. 30, No. 1, pp. 46–55.

Schiffer, Michael B. and Susan J. Wells
1982 Archaeological Surveys: Past and Future. In *Hohokam and Patayan: Prehistory of Southwestern Arizona*, edited by Randall H. McGuire and Michael B. Schiffer, pp. 345–83. Academic Press. New York.

Schmidt, Karl Patterson
1922 The Amphibians and Reptiles of Lower California and the Neighboring Islands. *Bulletin of the American Museum of Natural History*, Vol. 46, Art. 11, pp. 607–707.

Schwartzlose, Richard A. and John R. Hendrickson
1983 Bibliography of the Gulf of California: Marine Sciences. *Instituto de Ciencias del Mar y Limnología, Universidad Autónoma de México Publicación Especial* 7. México.

Seamann, Berthold
1853 *Narrative of the Voyage of H.M.S. Herald During the Years 1845–1851*, Vol. 2. Reeve and Company. London.

Shaler, William
1808 *Journal of a Voyage Between China and the Northwestern Coast of America, Made in 1804*. [An excerpt from the American Register, or General Repository of History, Vol. 3. Philadelphia.] Microfilm, No. 4856 in "Western Americana, Frontier History of the Trans-Mississippi West, 1550–1900." University of Oregon Library. Eugene.

Sheldon, Charles
1979 *The Wilderness of Desert Bighorns and Seri Indians*, edited by David E. Brown, Paul M. Webb, and Neil B. Carmony. The Arizona Desert Bighorn Sheep Society. Phoenix. [The account of Sheldon's 1921–1922 Seri trip is also reproduced in *Tales from Tiburon*, edited by Neil B. Carmony and David E. Brown, pp. 85–145 (1983). The Southwest Natural History Association. Phoenix.]

Shelvocke, George
[1726] 1928 *A Voyage Round the World*. Cassell and Company. London.

Sheridan, Thomas E.
1979 Cross or Arrow? The Breakdown in Spanish-Seri Relations 1729–1750. *Arizona and the West*, Vol. 21, No. 4, pp. 317–34.
1982 Seri Bands in Cross-Cultural Perspective. *The Kiva*, Vol. 47, No. 4, pp. 185–213.
1996 The Comcáac (Seris): People of the Desert and Sea. In *Paths of Life*, edited by Thomas E. Sheridan and Nancy J. Parezo, pp. 187–211. University of Arizona Press. Tucson.

Sheridan, Thomas E. (editor)
1999   *Empire of Sand: The Seri Indians and the Struggle for Spanish Sonora, 1645–1803.* University of Arizona Press. Tucson.
Shreve, Forrest and Ira L. Wiggins
1964   *Vegetation and Flora of the Sonoran Desert* (2 Vols.). Stanford University Press. Stanford, California.
Simpson, Lesley Byrd
1938   Preface. In *California in 1792: The Expedition of José Longinos Martínez*, translated by Lesley Byrd Simpson. Huntington Library Publications. San Marino, California.
Sisson, George H.
1886   [Letter to Company President Edgar T. Welles, March 8, 1886.] In *The International Company of Mexico*, p. 10. [Publisher and city not indicated.]
Slevin, Joseph R.
1923   Expedition of the California Academy of Sciences to the Gulf of California in 1921: General Account. *Proceedings of the California Academy of Sciences*, Fourth Series, Vol. 12, No. 6, pp. 55–72.
Smith, Charles B.
1860   [Report of the U.S. Consul in La Paz for 1858.] In "Annual Report of the Commercial Relations Between the United States and Foreign Nations," pp. 418–21. *U.S. House of Representatives Executive Document* No. 4, Part 1, 36th Congress, 1st Session. Government Printing Office. Washington, D.C.
Smith, Persifor F.
1850   [Letter to Brigadier General R. Jones, Adjutant General, April 5, 1849.] *U.S. House of Representatives Executive Document* No. 17, 31st Congress, 1st Session, pp. 716–19. Government Printing Office. Washington, D.C.
Smith, William Neil
1974   The Seri Indians and the Sea Turtles. *The Journal of Arizona History*, Vol. 15, No. 2, pp. 139–58.
Soulé, Michael
1967   Phenetics of Natural Populations I. Phenetic Relationships of Insular Populations of the Side-Blotched Lizard. *Evolution*, Vol. 21, No. 3, pp. 584–91.
Soulé, Michael and Allan J. Sloan
1966   Biogeography and Distribution of the Reptiles and Amphibians on Islands in the Gulf of California, Mexico. *Transactions of the San Diego Society of Natural History*, Vol. 14, No. 11, pp. 137–56.
Soulié, Maurice
1927   *The Wolf Cub: The Great Adventure of Count Gaston de Raousset-Boulbon in California and Sonora*, translated by Farrell Symons. The Bobbs-Merrill Co. Indianapolis, Indiana.
Spence, Tomás
1850   Carta y Oficio de don Tomás Spence, que se Cita en la Página Respectiva. In *Noticias Estadísticas del Estado de Sonora...*, by José Francisco Velasco, pp. 163–74. Imprenta de Ignacio Cumplido. México.
Spicer, Edward H.
1962   *Cycles of Conquest: The Impact of Spain, Mexico, and the United States on the Indians of the Southwest, 1533–1960.* University of Arizona Press. Tucson.
1980   *The Yaquis: A Cultural History.* University of Arizona Press. Tucson.
Stanly, Fabius
1848   [Report to Lieut. Commanding Edward M. Yard, February 22, 1848.] Microfilm, RG 45, Records of the Office of Naval Records and Library, Area files A-9, Microcopy 625, Roll 285, No. 301. U.S. National Archives. Washington, D.C.
Starbuck, Alexander
[1878] 1964 *History of the American Whale Fishery from its Earliest Inception to the Year 1876* (2

Vols.). Argosy-Antiquarian Ltd. Sentry Press. New York. [Reprint of the 1878 "Report of the U.S. Commission on Fish and Fisheries" Part 4. Government Printing Office. Washington, D.C.]

Stearns, Robert E. C.

1879   Description of a New Species of Dolobella, from the Gulf of California, with Remarks on Other Rare or Little-known Species from the Same Region. In *Proceedings of the Academy of Natural Sciences of Philadelphia, 1878*, pp. 395–401.

1895   The Shells of the Tres Marias and Other Localities Along the Shores of Lower California and the Gulf of California. *Proceedings of the United States National Museum*, Vol. 17, 1894, pp. 139–204. Smithsonian Institution. Washington, D.C.

Steinbeck, John

1975   *The Log from the Sea of Cortez*. Viking Press. New York.

Stevens, Robert Conway

1963   *Mexico's Forgotten Frontier: A History of Sonora, 1821–1846*. Ph.D. dissertation. University of California. Berkeley.

Stone, Charles P.

1858   [Letter to Lewis Cass, Secretary of State, December 23, 1858.] Microfilm, RG 59, General Records of the Department of State, Consular Dispatches, Guaymas, Vol. 1. U.S. National Archives. Washington, D.C.

Stratford, Guillermo

[1746] 1958 Descripción de las Californias Desde el Cabo de San Lucas. Sus Misiones, Puertos, Bahías, Placeres, Naciones Reducidas y Gentiles, que se Tiene Noticia la Habitan y de la Contracosta en la Parte del Norte, por Guillermo Stratford. Documento Número 3 in "Tres Documentos Sobre el Descubrimiento y Exploración de Baja California por Francisco María Piccolo, Juan de Ugarte y Guillermo Stratford," edited by Roberto Ramos. *Documentos Para la Historia de Baja California*, Número 1. Editorial Jus. México.

Streets, Thomas H.

1877   Contributions to the Natural History of the Hawaiian and Fanning Islands and Lower California.... *Bulletin of the United States National Museum* No. 7. Department of the Interior: U.S. National Museum 7. Washington, D.C.

Stuiver, Minze and Gordon W. Pearson

1986   High-Precision Calibration of the Radiocarbon Time Scale, A.D. 1950–500 B.C. *Radiocarbon*, Vol. 28, No. 2B, pp. 805–38.

Sturtevant, William C.

1966   Anthropology, History, and Ethnohistory. *Ethnohistory*, Vol. 13, Nos. 1–2, pp. 1–51.

Sykes, Glenton G.

1976   Five Walked Out! The Search for Port Isabel. *The Journal of Arizona History*, Vol. 17, No. 2, pp. 127–36.

Sykes, Godfrey

1915   The Isles of California. *Bulletin of the American Geographical Society*, Vol. 47, No. 10, pp. 745–61.

1937   *The Colorado Delta*. Carnegie Institution of Washington and The American Geographical Society of New York. Washington, D.C.

Sylber, Charles K.

1988   Feeding Habits of the Lizards *Sauromalus varius* and *S. hispidus* in the Gulf of California. *Journal of Herpetology*, Vol. 22, No. 4, pp. 413–24.

Tannenbaum, Frank

1933   *Peace by Revolution: An Interpretation of Mexico*. Columbia University Press. New York.

Tanner, Z. L.

1892   Report upon the Investigations of the U.S. Fish Commission Steamer Albatross for the Year Ending June 30, 1889. In "United States Commission of Fish and Fisheries Part 16: Report of the Commissioner for the Fiscal Year Ending June 30,

1889," Appendix 4. *U.S. House of Representatives Miscellaneous Documents* No. 274, 51st Congress, 1st Session. Government Printing Office. Washington, D.C.

1895   The U.S. Commission of Fish and Fisheries and Its Relations with the United States Navy. *Proceedings of the United States Naval Institute*, Vol. 21, No. 1, Whole No. 73, pp. 107–24.

Taylor, Alexander S.

[1869] 1971 *A Historical Summary of Baja California*, edited with an introduction by Walt Wheelock. Socio-Technical Books. Pasadena, California. [Originally published as an Appendix to *Resources of the Pacific Slope....* by J. Ross Browne (1869).]

Thomas, David Hurst

1983   The Archaeology of Monitor Valley. 2. Gatecliff Shelter. *Anthropological Papers of the American Museum of Natural History*, Vol. 59, Part 1. New York.

1990   *Archaeology*, second edition. Holt, Rinehart and Winston. New York.

Thomson, Roberto

1931   Beads Tame Last Cannibal Tribe. *Popular Science Monthly*, Vol. 118, No. 1, pp. 59, 137–38.

1969   [Transcript of a taped interview with Roberto Thomson by Scott Ryerson.] In Ryerson's possession.

1989   La Hacienda de Costa Rica. In *Pioneros de la Costa de Hermosillo*, by Roberto Thomson, pp. 27–39. Artes Gráficas y Editoriales Yescas. Hermosillo, Sonora.

n.d.   El Monte de las Sombras. [Independently paginated chapter in *Apuntes Para la História de la Tribu Seri.*] Manuscript in the possession of Scott Ryerson.

Tout, Otis B.

[1931]   *The First Thirty Years, Being an Account of the Principal Events in the History of Imperial Valley....* Otis B. Tout, Publisher. San Diego, California.

Townsend, Charles Haskins

1891   Report upon the Pearl Fishery of the Gulf of California. *Bulletin of the United States Fish Commission*, Vol. 9 for 1889.

1912   Mammals Collected in Lower California, with Descriptions of New Species. *Bulletin of the American Museum of Natural History*, Vol. 31, Art. 13, pp. 117–30.

1916   Voyage of the "Albatross" to the Gulf of California in 1911. *Bulletin of the American Museum of Natural History*, Vol. 35, Art. 24, pp. 399–476.

1935   The Distribution of Certain Whales as Shown by Logbook Records of American Whaleships. *Zoologica* (Scientific Contributions of the New York Zoological Society), Vol. 19, No. 1.

Trelease, William

1912   The Agaves of Lower California. *Missouri Botanical Garden Twenty-second Annual Report*, pp. 37–65. St. Louis, Missouri.

Troncoso, Francisco

1849   [Report of Fr. Francisco Troncoso.] In *Noticias Estadísticas de Sonora y Sinaloa, Compiladas y Amplificadas Para la Comisión de Estadística Militar*, by José Agustín de Escudero, pp. 13–23. Tipografía de R. Rafael. México.

Troncoso, Francisco P.

1905   *Las Guerras Con Las Tribus Yaqui y Mayo del Estado de Sonora*. Tipografía del Departamento de Estado Mayor. México.

Trujillo G., P.

1967   *Bibliografía de Baja California*. Primer Tomo. Editoriál Californidad, Asociación de Escritores de Baja California. Tijuana, Baja California.

Trumbull, Robert

1943   *The Raft*. Garden City Publishing Co. Garden City, New York.

Tuohy, Donald R.

1984   On Sleeping Circles in Baja California ... and Elsewhere. *Pacific Coast Archaeological Society Quarterly*, Vol. 20, No. 1, pp. 37–49.

Turner, David
1871   [Report of the U.S. Consul in La Paz for 1870.] In "Report upon the Commercial
            Relations of the United States with Foreign Countries for the Year 1870," pp. 302–
            4. *U.S. House of Representatives Executive Document* No. 93, 41st Congress, 3rd Ses-
            sion. Government Printing Office. Washington, D.C.

Turner, John Kenneth
1969   *Barbarous Mexico*. University of Texas Press. Austin. (Originally published 1910.)

Turner, Raymond M.
1990   Long-Term Vegetation Change at a Fully Protected Sonoran Desert Site. *Ecology*,
            Vol. 71, No. 2, pp. 464–77.

Tweed, William
1973   *The Seri Indian Frontier of New Spain: 1617–1762*. Master's thesis. Texas Christian
            University Fort Worth.

Ugarte, Juan de
[1722] 1958 Relación del Descubrimiento del Golfo de California o Mar Lauretano, por el Padre
            Juan de Ugarte en el Año de 1722. Documento Número 2 in "Tres Documentos
            Sobre el Descubrimiento y Exploración de Baja California por Francisco María
            Piccolo, Juan de Ugarte y Guillermo Stratford." Edited by Roberto Ramos. *Docu-
            mentos Para la Historia de Baja California*, Número 1. Editorial Jus. México.

Ulloa, Francisco de
[1540] 1924 The Narrative of Ulloa. In "The Voyage of Francisco de Ulloa," by Henry R. Wag-
            ner, pp. 315–67. *California Historical Society Quarterly*, Vol. 3, No. 4, pp. 307–83.

Urgell, J.
1890   [Telegram to Sr. Gobnor. R. Corral, June 3, 1890.] Gobernación, Referencia 214.3,
            Tribu Seri. Archivo Histórico del Estado de Sonora, Hermosillo. Microfilm, Her-
            mosillo Film No. 25, Arizona Historical Society. Tucson.

Valencia, Leopoldo
1878   Sesión del día 22 de Febrero de 1878. *El Municipio*, Tomo 1, Num. 4, Marzo 15 de
            1878. Guaymas. Microfilm, Roll 5000, Reel 5, Item 20 in "Mexican Newspaper
            Miscellany, Sonora, 1838–1883." Bancroft Library, University of California. Ber-
            keley.

Van Duzee, Edward P.
1923   Expedition of the California Academy of Sciences to the Gulf of California in 1921.
            The Hemiptera (True Bugs, etc.). *Proceedings of the California Academy of Sciences*,
            Fourth Series, Vol. 12, No. 11, pp. 123–200.

van Rossem, A. J.
1930a   New Sonora Races of *Toxostoma* and *Pheugopedius*. *Transactions of the San Diego Society
            of Natural History*, Vol. 6, No. 11, pp. 207–8.

1930b   Four New Birds from Northwestern Mexico. *Transactions of the San Diego Society of
            Natural History*, Vol. 6, No. 14, pp. 213–26.

1931   Report on a Collection of Land Birds from Sonora, Mexico. *Transactions of the San
            Diego Society of Natural History*, Vol. 6, No. 19, pp. 237–304.

1932   The Avifauna of Tiburón Island, Sonora, Mexico, with Descriptions of Four New Races.
            Transactions of the San Diego Society of Natural History, Vol. 7, No. 12, pp. 119–50.

1945   A Distributional Survey of the Birds of Sonora, Mexico. *Occasional Papers, Museum of
            Zoology, Louisiana State University* No. 21. Louisiana State University. Baton Rouge.

van Rossem, A. J., and The Marquess Hachisuka
1937   A Further Report on Birds from Sonora, Mexico, with Descriptions of Two New Races.
            Transactions of the San Diego Society of Natural History, Vol. 8, No. 23, pp. 321–36.

Vansina, Jan
1985   *Oral Tradition as History*. University of Wisconsin Press. Madison.

Vasey, George and J. N. Rose
1890   List of Plants Collected by Dr. Edward Palmer in Lower California and Western

Mexico in 1890. *Contributions from the U.S. National Herbarium*, Vol. 1, No. 3, pp. 63–90. U.S. Department of Agriculture, Division of Botany. Washington, D.C.

Velarde G., María Enriqueta

1989   *Conducta y Ecología de la Reproducción de la Gaviota Parda* (Larus heermanni) *en Isla Rasa, Baja California*. Ph.D. dissertation. Universidad Nacional Autónoma de México. México.

1992   Predation of Heermann's Gull (*Larus heermanni*) Chicks by Yellow-footed Gulls (*Larus livens*) in Dense and Scattered Nesting Sites. *Colonial Waterbirds*, Vol. 15, No. 1, pp. 8–13.

Velasco, José Francisco

1850   *Noticias Estadísticas del Estado de Sonora….* Imprenta de Ignacio Cumplido. México.

Velázquez, José M.

1882   *Copia de la Escritura de Sociedad Anónima Fundadora de la "Compañía Mejicana Colonizadora e Industrial," Formada por los Señores Lic. Manuel Romero Rubio, Agustín R. González y Guillermo Andrade.* Instrumento Num. 3, Notaria Pública de José M. Velázquez. January 5, 1882. México. Andrade Papers Folio 10. Sherman Library. Corona del Mar, California.

Venegas, Miguel

[1754] 1929 *Juan María de Salvatierra*, translated, edited, and annotated by Marguerite Eyer Wilbur. Arthur H. Clark Co. Cleveland, Ohio.

[1759]   *A Natural and Civil History of California*, Vol. 1. Facsimile of the 1759 edition re-
1966a   printed by Readex Microprint Corp. [City not indicated.]

[1759]   *A Natural and Civil History of California*, Vol. 2. Facsimile of the 1759 edition re-
1966b   printed by Readex Microprint Corp. [City not indicated.]

Vildósola, Agustín de

[1735] 1932 [Statement of Don Agustín de Vildósola.] Translated and annotated by Donald Rowland. In "The Sonora Frontier of New Spain, 1735–1745," by Donald Rowland, pp. 151–57. In *New Spain and the Anglo-American West*, Vol. 1, edited by Charles W. Hackett, George P. Hammond, and J. Lloyd Mecham, pp. 147–64. Privately printed. Los Angeles.

Villa, Eduardo W.

1937   *Compendio de Historia del Estado de Sonora*. Editorial "Patria Nueva." México.

Villa Ramírez, Bernardo

1976   Isla Raza, Baja California, Enigma y Paradigma. *Supervivencia*, Vol. 2, pp. 17–29.

Villa Salas, Avelino B.

1979   Semblenza Histórica de Los Simposios Sobre el Medio Ambiente del Golfo de California. In "IV Simposio Sobre el Medio Ambiente del Golfo de California — La Producción Sostenida de Alimentos, Materias Primas y Empleos," pp. 21–24. *Memoria*, Publicación Especial No. 17. Instituto Nacional de Investigaciones Forestales, Secretaría de Agricultura y Recursos Hidráulicos. Mazatlán, Sinaloa.

Villalpando C., María Elisa

1984   *Correlación Arqueológico-Etnográfica en Isla San Esteban, Sonora, México*. Tesis que para Optar por el Título de Licenciado en Arqueología, Escuela Nacional de Antropología e Historia. México.

1989   Los que Viven en las Montañas: Correlación Arqueológico-Etnográfica en Isla San Esteban, Sonora, México. *Noroeste de México*, No. 8. Centro Regional de Sonora, Instituto Nacional de Antropología e Historia. Hermosillo.

Vizcaíno, Sebastián

[1596] 1930 Vizcaíno's Narrative. In "Pearl Fishing Enterprises in the Gulf of California," by Henry R. Wagner, pp. 204–18. *Hispanic American Historical Review*, Vol. 10, No. 2, pp. 188–220. [See also: Relation of Sebastián Vizcaíno: August-November 1596, translated by W. Michael Mathes. In "Ethnology of the Baja California Indians," edited by W. Michael Mathes, pp. 135–43, 1992. Vol. 5 of *Spanish Borderlands Sourcebooks*, David Hurst Thomas, general editor. Garland Publishing. New York.]

Vogt, William
1946   Report of an Airplane Inspection Trip Made over the Islands in the Gulf of California and off the Pacific Coast of Lower California. In *Report on Activities of the Conservation Section, Division of Agricultural Cooperation, Pan American Union (1943–1946)*, Appendix 4, pp. 110–16. Pan American Union. Washington, D.C.

Voss, Stuart F.
1982   *On the Periphery of Nineteenth-Century Mexico: Sonora and Sinaloa 1810–1877.* University of Arizona Press. Tucson.

Wagner, Henry R.
1924   The Voyage of Francisco de Ulloa. *California Historical Society Quarterly*, Vol. 3, No. 4, pp. 307–83.

1930   Pearl Fishing Enterprises in the Gulf of California. *Hispanic American Historical Review*, Vol. 10, No. 2, pp. 188–220.

1937   *The Cartography of the Northwest Coast of America to the Year 1800* (2 Vols.). University of California Press. Berkeley.

Walford, Lionel A.
1945   Observations on the Shark Fishery in the Central Part of the Gulf of California.... *Fishery Leaflet* 121. U.S. Department of the Interior, Fish and Wildlife Service. Washington, D.C.

Walker, Henry P. and Don Bufkin
1979   *Historical Atlas of Arizona.* University of Oklahoma Press. Norman.

Walker, Lewis Wayne
1965   Baja's Island of Birds. *Pacific Discovery*, Vol. 18, No. 3, pp. 27–31.

Ward, H. G.
1828   *Mexico in 1827*, Vol. 1. Henry Colburn. London.

Watson, Sereno
1889   Upon a Collection of Plants Made by Dr. E. Palmer, in 1887, About Guaymas, Mexico, at Muleje and Los Angeles Bay in Lower California, and on the Island of San Pedro Martin [Mártir] in the Gulf of California. No. 1 of "VI. Contributions to American Botany." *Proceedings of the American Academy of Arts and Sciences*, New Series, Vol. 16, Whole Series, Vol. 24, pp. 36–87. University Press: John Wilson and Son. Boston.

Weber, David J.
1992   *The Spanish Frontier in North America.* Yale University Press. New Haven.

West, Carolyn
1963   Cortez Came Later. *Yachting*, Vol. 113, No. 1, pp. 62–64, 372, 374–77.

West, Carolyn and Jack West
1984   *Cruising the Pacific Coast, Acapulco to Skagway*, fourth edition, revised. Pacific Search Press. Seattle.

West, Robert C.
1993   *Sonora: Its Geographical Personality.* University of Texas Press. Austin.

Wiget, Andrew O.
1982   Truth and the Hopi: An Historiographic Study of Documented Oral Tradition Concerning the Coming of the Spanish. *Ethnohistory*, Vol. 29, No. 3, pp. 181–99.

Wilkes, Charles
1845   *Narrative of the United States Exploring Expedition During the Years 1838, 1839, 1840, 1841, 1842*, Vol. 5. Lea and Blanchard. Philadelphia.

Wilkins, Harold T.
1939   *Treasure Hunting.* Bruce Humphries. Boston.

Willard, Alexander
1869   [Report of the U.S. Consul in Guaymas for 1868.] In "Report upon the Commercial Relations of the United States with Foreign Countries for the Year 1868," pp. 643–47. *U.S. House of Representatives Executive Document* No. 87, Part 1, 40th Congress, 3rd Session. Government Printing Office. Washington, D.C.

1870   [Letter to Assistant Secretary of State J.C.B. Davis, June 3, 1870.] Microfilm, RG 59, General Records of the Department of State, Consular Dispatches, Guaymas, Vol. 2. U.S. National Archives. Washington, D.C.

1871   [Report of the U.S. Consul in Guaymas for 1870.] In "Report upon the Commercial Relations of the United States with Foreign Countries for the Year 1870," pp. 296–302. *U.S. House of Representatives Executive Document* No. 93, 41st Congress, 3rd Session. Government Printing Office. Washington, D.C.

1872   [Report of the U.S. Consul in Guaymas for 1871.] In "Report upon the Commercial Relations of the United States with Foreign Countries for the Year 1871," pp. 899–906. *U.S. House of Representatives Executive Document* No. 220, 42nd Congress, 2nd Session. Government Printing Office. Washington, D.C.

1874a   [Report of the U.S. Consul in Guaymas for 1873.] In "Report upon the Commercial Relations of the United States with Foreign Countries for the Year 1872," pp. 826–34. *U.S. House of Representatives Executive Document* No. 143, 43rd Congress, 1st Session. Government Printing Office. Washington, D.C.

1874b   [Letter to W. Hunter, Second Assistant Secretary of State, October 12, 1874.] Microfilm, RG 59, General Records of the Department of State, Consular Dispatches, Guaymas, Vol. 2. U.S. National Archives. Washington, D.C.

1875a   [Report of the U.S. Consul in Guaymas for 1874.] In "Report upon the Commercial Relations of the United States with Foreign Countries for the Year 1874," pp. 843–50. *U.S. House of Representatives Executive Document* No. 157, 43rd Congress, 2nd Session. Government Printing Office. Washington, D.C.

1875b   [Report of the U.S. Consul in Guaymas for 1875, September 30, 1875.] Microfilm, RG 59, General Records of the Department of State, Consular Dispatches, Guaymas, Vol. 3. U.S. National Archives. Washington, D.C.

1876a   [Letter to W. Hunter, Second Assistant Secretary of State, March 8, 1876.] Microfilm, RG 59, General Records of the Department of State, Consular Dispatches, Guaymas, Vol. 4. U.S. National Archives. Washington, D.C.

1876b   [Letter to W. Hunter, Second Assistant Secretary of State, February 28, 1876.] Microfilm, RG 59, General Records of the Department of State, Consular Dispatches, Guaymas, Vol. 4. U.S. National Archives. Washington, D.C.

1878   [Report of the U.S. Consul in Guaymas for 1877.] In "Report upon the Commercial Relations of the United States with Foreign Countries for the Year 1877," pp. 726–31. *U.S. House of Representatives Executive Document* No. 102, 45th Congress, 2nd Session. Government Printing Office. Washington, D.C.

1879   [Report of the U.S. Consul in Guaymas for 1878.] In "Report upon the Commercial Relations of the United States with Foreign Countries for the Year 1878," pp. 949–55. *U.S. House of Representatives Executive Document* No. 108, 45th Congress, 3rd Session. Government Printing Office. Washington, D.C.

1880   [Report of the U.S. Consul in Guaymas for 1879.] In "Report upon the Commercial Relations of the United States with Foreign Countries for the Year 1879," pp. 430–38. *U.S. House of Representatives Executive Document* No. 90, Part 1, 46th Congress, 2nd Session. Government Printing Office. Washington, D.C.

1884a   [Report of the U.S. Consul in Guaymas for 1883.] In "Report upon the Commercial Relations of the United States with Foreign Countries for the Year 1883," pp. 226–33. *U.S. House of Representatives Executive Document* No. 176, Part 2, 48th Congress, 1st Session. Government Printing Office. Washington, D.C.

1884b   [Report of the U.S. Consul in Guaymas for 1884, December 31, 1884.] Microfilm, RG 59, General Records of the Department of State, Consular Dispatches, Guaymas, Vol. 6. U.S. National Archives. Washington, D.C.

1885a   Marine extended protest of Ship *Ellen Goodspeed*, Redford Kelley, Master, August, 1885. RG 84, Diplomatic Branch. Miscellaneous Correspondence, Guaymas Post, 1883–1904. U.S. National Archives. Washington, D.C.

1885b   [Report of the U.S. Consul in Guaymas for 1885, December 31, 1885.] Microfilm, RG 59, General Records of the Department of State, Consular Dispatches, Guaymas, Vol. 6. U.S. National Archives. Washington, D.C.

1887a   [Report of the U.S. Consul in Guaymas for 1886.] In "Report upon the Commercial Relations of the United States with Foreign Countries for the Year 1886," pp. 875–81. *U.S. House of Representatives Executive Document* No. 171, 49th Congress, 2nd Session. Government Printing Office. Washington, D.C.

1887b   [Letter to James D. Porter, Assistant Secretary of State, April 22, 1887.] Microfilm, RG 59, General Records of the Department of State, Consular Dispatches, Guaymas, Vol. 7. U.S. National Archives. Washington, D.C.

1888   [Report of the U.S. Consul in Guaymas for 1887.] In "Report upon the Commercial Relations of the United States with Foreign Countries for the Year 1887," pp. 588–94. *U.S. House of Representatives Executive Document* No. 402, 50th Congress, 1st Session. Government Printing Office. Washington, D.C.

1889   [Report of the U.S. Consul in Guaymas for 1888.] In "Report upon the Commercial Relations of the United States with Foreign Countries for the Year 1888," pp. 33–38. *U.S. House of Representatives Executive Document* No. 437, 51st Congress, 1st Session. Government Printing Office. Washington, D.C.

1890   [Annual Report 1890. Addressed to Hon. W. F. Wharton, Assistant Secretary of State, December 31, 1890.] Microfilm, RG 59, General Records of the Department of State, Consular Dispatches, Guaymas, Vol. 8. U.S. National Archives. Washington, D.C.

1891   [Annual Report 1891. Addressed to Hon. W. F. Wharton, Assistant Secretary of State, December 31, 1891.] Microfilm, RG 59, General Records of the Department of State, Consular Dispatches, Guaymas, Vol. 8. U.S. National Archives. Washington, D.C.

Williams, Michael
1911   Tenderfeet on Tiburon. *The Outing Magazine*, Vol. 59 (October), pp. 97–110.

Wilson, Thomas
1890   Report on the Department of Prehistoric Anthropology in the U.S. National Museum. In *Report of the U.S. National Museum for the Year Ending 1888*. Government Printing Office. Washington, D.C.

Wise, Henry Augustus
1849   *Los Gringos: Or, an Inside View of Mexico and California, with Wanderings in Peru, Chili, and Polynesia*. Baker and Scribner. New York.

Woodward, Arthur
1955   *Feud on the Colorado*. Great West and Indian Series 4. Westernlore Press. Los Angeles.

Woodward, Arthur (editor)
1966   *The Republic of Lower California 1853–1854*. Baja California Travel Series 6. Dawson's Book Shop. Los Angeles.

Wyllys, Rufus Kay
1932   The French in Sonora (1850–1854). *University of California Publications in History*, Vol. 21. University of California Press. Berkeley.

Yard, Edward M.
1848a   [Report to Commodore W. Branford Shubrick, Commanding Pacific Squadron, February 13, 1848.] Microfilm, RG 45, Records of the Office of Naval Records and Library, Area files A-9, Microcopy 625, Roll 285, No. 244. U.S. National Archives. Washington, D.C.

1848b   [Report to Commodore W. Branford Shubrick, Commanding Pacific Squadron, April 4, 1848.] Microfilm, RG 45, Records of the Office of Naval Records and Library, Area files A-9, Microcopy 625, Roll 286, No. 303. U.S. National Archives. Washington, D.C.

REFERENCES CITED

Yates, John D.
1975   Insurgents on the Baja Peninsula: Henry Halleck's Journal of the War in Lower California, 1847–1848. *California Historical Quarterly*, Vol. 54, No. 3, pp. 221–44.
Yetman, David
1988   *Where the Desert Meets the Sea: A Trader in the Land of the Seri Indians.* Pepper Publishing. Tucson.
Zárate, José C.
1920   Expedición a las Islas Medio, San Pedro Mártir, San Esteban, Tiburón y Patos en el Golfo de California. *Boletín de Industria, Comercio y Trabajo*, Tomo 4, Nums. 4, 5, y 6, pp. 74–89. México.
Zavala C., Palemón
1984   *Perfiles de Sonora.* Gobierno del Estado de Sonora. Hermosillo.

Index

Note: Names of ships and boats are marked with an asterisk (*). Numbers in bold refer to figures.